LAN Technologies Explained

LAN Technologies Explained

PHILIP MILLER AND MICHAEL CUMMINS

DIGITAL PRESS
Boston, Oxford, Auckland, Johannesburg, Melbourne, New Delhi

Library of Congress Cataloging-in-Publication Data
Miller, Philip, 1956-
   LAN technologies explained / Philip Miller and Michael Cummins.
      p. cm.
   Includes bibliographical references and index.
   ISBN 1-55558-234-6 (pbk. : alk. paper)
      1. Local area networks (Computer networks) I. Cummins, Michael. II. Title.

TK5105.7 .M555 2000
004.6'8—dc21

99-055965

British Library Cataloguing-in-Publication Data
A catalogue record for this book is available from the British Library.

The publisher offers special discounts on bulk orders of this book.
For information, please contact:
Manager of Special Sales
Butterworth–Heinemann
225 Wildwood Avenue
Woburn, MA 01801-2041
Tel: 781-904-2500
Fax: 781-904-2620

For information on all Digital Press publications available, contact our World Wide Web home page at: http://www.bh.com/digitalpress

10 9 8 7 6 5 4 3 2 1

Printed in the United States of America

To my children, Stuart and
Nicole, my wife Karen, and my
parents Audrey and Mervyn.

Philip Miller

To Joanne, Andrew, and Victoria
whose patience and love make
everything possible.

Michael Cummins

Table of Contents

Preface xxiii

Section A   An Introduction to LANs and Networking 1

Chapter 1   Introduction 3
1.1   LANs and Other Networks 4
    1.1.1   Metropolitan Area Networks (MANs) 4
    1.1.2   Wide Area Networks (WANs) 5
    1.1.3   So What Is a LAN? 5
1.2   LAN Topologies 6
    1.2.1   Star Topology 6
    1.2.2   Bus Topology 7
    1.2.3   Ring Topology 8
    1.2.4   Tree Topology 9
1.3   Standardization and Architectures 10
    1.3.1   The OSI Reference Model 11
    1.3.2   IEEE Standards 14
1.4   Summary 17

Section B   Ethernet/IEEE 802.3 (ISO/IEC 8802-3) 19

Chapter 2   An Introduction to Ethernet and IEEE 802.3 21
2.1   What Is Ethernet? 21
2.2   A Brief History of Ethernet 22
2.3   Ethernet Standards 24
    2.3.1   Ethernet/802.3 Standards 25
    2.3.2   The Next Generations 26
2.4   The Problems Associated with Ethernet 27
2.5   The Differences Between Ethernet and IEEE 802.3 29
2.6   Summary 29

Chapter 3   Basic Overview 31
3.1   The Ethernet/802.3 Cable Plant 31
    3.1.1   Coaxial Cable 32
    3.1.2   Twisted Pair Cable 34
    3.1.3   Fiber Optic Cable 35
    3.1.4   A Summary of Ethernet/802.3 Media 38
3.2   Mixing Media and Interconnection 38
    3.2.1   Repeaters 39
    3.2.2   Bridges/Switches 39
    3.2.3   Routers 39
    3.2.4   Media Converters 39
3.3   Ethernet/802.3 Topology 39

	3.3.1	Bus Topology	40
	3.3.2	Star Topology	40
	3.3.3	Tree Topology	41
3.4	Basic Ethernet/802.3 Requirements		41
3.5	Summary		43

Chapter 4   Media Access Control 45

4.1	MAC/Upper Layer Interaction		46
4.2	MAC Frame Structure		47
	4.2.1	Destination Address	48
	4.2.2	Source Address	50
	4.2.3	Length/Type	50
	4.2.4	Information and Padding	52
	4.2.5	Frame Check Sequence	53
4.3	Invalid MAC Frames		54
4.4	CSMA/CD Operation		54
	4.4.1	Frame Transmission and Reception with No Collision	55
	4.4.2	Frame Transmission and Reception with Collisions	56
	4.4.3	Truncated Binary Exponential Back-off	60
	4.4.4	Medium Access Time and Overall Performance	61
4.5	The Need for Minimum and Maximum Sized Frames		62
	4.5.1	Out-of-Window Collisions	64
4.6	Summary		64

Chapter 5   PLS and AUI 65

5.1	Modes of Operation		66
5.2	DTE to MAU Interchange Circuits		67
	5.2.1	DTE to MAU Connection	68
5.3	Signal Encoding		69
5.4	PLS/AUI Functionality		70
	5.4.1	PLS to PMA (DTE to MAU) Signaling	70
	5.4.2	PLS to PMA (DTE to MAU) Protocol	72
	5.4.3	PMA to PLS (MAU to DTE) Protocol	73
	5.4.4	PLS to MAC Interface Signaling	74
5.5	Frame Structure		75
5.6	Summary		76

Chapter 6   10Mbps MAUs 77

6.1	MAU Modes of Operation		78
6.2	MAU/Medium Dependent Interface		78
6.3	Transmission and Reception		80
	6.3.1	Medium Signaling Levels	81
6.4	Collision Detection		84
	6.4.1	Coaxial Cable Types (10Base5 and 10Base2)	84
	6.4.2	Twisted Pair Media (10Base-T)	85
	6.4.3	Fiber Media (10Base-F)	85
6.5	Jabber Protection		85
6.6	Signal Quality Error Test - SQE(T)		86
6.7	Other MAU Features		87

	6.7.1	Link Integrity Test	87
	6.7.2	Reverse Polarity Detection and Correction	87
	6.7.3	Extended Distance Working	88
	6.7.4	Redundant MAUs	88
6.8		Multi-Port MAUs	89
	6.8.1	Limitations on Multi-Port MAU Usage	90
6.9		MAU Management	91
	6.9.1	Managed Objects	91
6.10		Summary	92

Chapter 7   10Base-F 93

7.1		Advantages of Optical Fiber	93
7.2		Optical Characteristics	94
7.3		10Base-FL	95
	7.3.1	10Base-FL Signaling	96
7.4		10Base-FB	97
	7.4.1	10Base-FB Signaling	98
7.5		10Base-FP	99
7.6		Summary	100

Chapter 8   10Mbps Repeaters 101

8.1		Repeater Usage	102
	8.1.1	Signal Attenuation	102
	8.1.2	Jitter	102
	8.1.3	Typical Repeater Installations	103
8.2		Repeater Functionality	106
	8.2.1	Signal Regeneration, Symmetry, and Re-timing	107
	8.2.2	Preamble Generation	107
	8.2.3	Collision Detection and Forwarding	108
	8.2.4	Jabber Lockup Protection	110
	8.2.5	Partitioning	110
8.3		Repeater Limitations	111
	8.3.1	Transmission System Model 1	112
	8.3.2	Transmission System Model 2	114
8.4		Resilient Links	117
8.5		Security	118
	8.5.1	Access Lists	119
	8.5.2	Data Security	120
8.6		Repeater Management	121
	8.6.1	Managed Objects	122
8.7		Summary	124

Chapter 9   100Base-TX and -FX 125

9.1		Reconciliation Sublayer (RS) and Media Independent Interface (MII)	126
	9.1.1	Service Primitive to MII Mapping	127
	9.1.2	Transmit and Receive Data Encoding	129
	9.1.3	Management Functions	129
	9.1.4	MII Frame Formats	133
	9.1.5	Contact Assignments	134

9.2   Physical Coding Sublayer (PCS) and Physical Medium Attachment (PMA) for 100Base-X 135
      9.2.1   PCS/PMA Functions 135
      9.2.2   Data Encoding 136
      9.2.3   Encapsulation 139
      9.2.4   Mapping the MII to the PMA 139
      9.2.5   Comparison to Other PMAs 140
9.3   PMD Sublayer and MDI for 100Base-Tx and 100Base-Fx 140
      9.3.1   100Base-Tx PMD and MDI 140
      9.3.2   100Base-Fx PMD and MDI 141
9.4   Repeaters for 100Mbps Baseband Networks 141
      9.4.1   Classes of 100Base-X Repeaters 142
      9.4.2   Repeater Functionality 143
9.5   Designing 100Mbps Networks Using Repeaters 144
      9.5.1   Multi-Segment Networks Within a Single Collision Domain 144
      9.5.2   Transmission System Model I 145
      9.5.3   Transmission System Model II 146
9.6   Summary 148

Chapter 10   Gigabit Ethernet 149
10.1   MAC Extension 150
      10.1.1   Carrier Extension 152
      10.1.2   Frame Bursting 152
      10.1.3   A Comparison of Ethernet/802.3 Parameters 153
10.2   Reconciliation Sublayer and Gigabit Media Independent Interface 154
      10.2.1   PLS Service Primitive to GMII Mapping 154
      10.2.2   Transmit and Receive Data Encoding 156
      10.2.3   Management Functions 157
      10.2.4   GMII Frame Format 159
10.3   Physical Coding Sublayer and Physical Medium Attachment for 1000Base-X. 161
      10.3.1   Data Encoding 162
      10.3.2   GMII to PMA Mapping 171
10.4   PMD and MDI for 1000Base-LX and 1000Base-SX 171
      10.4.1   General Fiber Requirements for 1000Base-SX and 1000Base-LX 171
      10.4.2   MDI Requirements for 1000Base-SX and 1000Base-LX 173
      10.4.3   1000Base-SX 173
      10.4.4   1000Base-LX 173
10.5   PMD and MDI for 1000Base-CX and 1000Base-T 173
      10.5.1   1000Base-CX 174
      10.5.2   1000Base-T 174
10.6   Repeaters for 1000Mbps Baseband Networks 176
      10.6.1   1000Base-X Repeater Functionality 177
      10.6.2   1000Base-X Repeater Configuration Limitations 177
      10.6.3   Transmission System Model I 178
      10.6.4   Transmission System Model II 179
10.7   Summary 180

Chapter 11   Auto-Negotiation 183
11.1   Auto-Negotiation Principles 184

	11.1.1	Device Operation	185
11.2	Basic Auto-Negotiation Operation		186
	11.2.1	Technology Priorities	188
	11.2.2	Timing	188
	11.2.3	Parallel Detection	189
11.3	The Next Page Function		190
11.4	The Complete Auto-Negotiation Process		191
11.5	Summary		192

Chapter 12   Full Duplex Operation **193**

12.1	Basic Full Duplex Operation		193
	12.1.1	Uses of Full Duplex Operation	194
12.2	Architectural Changes		196
	12.2.1	Service Primitive Changes	197
12.3	MAC Control		198
	12.3.1	MAC Control Frames	198
	12.3.2	MAC Control Pause Operation	199
12.4	Flow Control		199
12.5	Summary		200

Chapter 13   802.3 Variants **201**

13.1	1Base5		201
	13.1.1	1Base5 Architecture	202
	13.1.2	1Base5 Operation	204
13.2	10Broad36		205
	13.2.1	10Broad36 Operation	206
	13.2.2	Transmission and Reception	208
	13.2.3	MAU Frequency Allocations	208
	13.2.4	Cabling (Electrical) Requirements	209
13.3	100Base-T2		209
	13.3.1	100Base-T2 PCS, PMA, and MDI	210
	13.3.2	100Base-T2 Auto-Negotiation	211
13.4	100Base-T4		214
	13.4.1	100Base-T4 PCS and PMA	215
	13.4.2	100Base-T4 Medium Dependent Interface (MDI)	216
13.5	Summary		217

Chapter 14   100VG-AnyLAN **219**

14.1	100VG-AnyLAN Architecture		219
	14.1.1	100VG-AnyLAN Operation	220
	14.1.2	Cable Plant and Limitations	223
14.2	Media Access Control (MAC)		223
	14.2.1	End Node Polling and Demand Priority	224
	14.2.2	End Node Training	227
14.3	Physical Medium Independent Sub-Layer (PMI)		230
	14.3.1	Quartet Channeling	231
	14.3.2	Data Scrambling	231
	14.3.3	5B6B Encoding	231
14.4	Medium Independent Interface Sub-Layer (MII)		232

14.5   Physical Medium Dependent Sub-Layer (PMD).................................... 232
        14.5.1   Multiplexing.. 232
        14.5.2   NRZ Encoding.. 233
        14.5.3   Link Status Control... 233
        14.5.4   Full/Half Duplex Cable Operation 234
14.6   Medium Dependent Interface (MDI) 235
14.7   Security.. 235
14.8   Future Enhancements to 802.12.. 236
        14.8.1   Full Duplex Demand Priority... 236
        14.8.2   High Speed Demand Priority.. 236
        14.8.3   Redundant Link Support 236
        14.8.4   2-Pair Category 5 UTP PMD 237
14.9   An Example of 100VG-AnyLAN Data Flow.. 237
14.10   Summary 238

Chapter 15   Bridges and Switches 239
15.1   Why Bridge or Switch?.. 239
        15.1.1   Bridges Vs Switches.. 241
15.2   Bridge/Switch Applications.. 243
        15.2.1   Isolating Areas of High Utilization...................................... 243
        15.2.2   Linking Geographically Distant LANs 244
        15.2.3   Creating Secure Environments 245
        15.2.4   Constructing Resilient Networks.. 246
        15.2.5   Bridge/Switch Limitations 249
15.3   Bridge/Switch Method of Operation.. 249
        15.3.1   The Filter Table.. 250
        15.3.2   Bridge/Switch Address Learning 254
        15.3.3   Protocol Prioritization 254
        15.3.4   Frame Ordering.. 255
        15.3.5   Transit Delays... 255
        15.3.6   Bridge Model of Operation 256
15.4   IEEE 802.1D Spanning Tree Protocol and Algorithm....................... 257
        15.4.1   Bridge/Switch Port States 258
        15.4.2   Spanning Tree Operation 259
        15.4.3   Spanning Tree Parameter Values 262
        15.4.4   Loop Detection and Topology Changes 263
        15.4.5   Spanning Tree Domains 264
15.5   Switch Types.. 265
        15.5.1   Store and Forward Switching.. 265
        15.5.2   Cut Through Switching 266
        15.5.3   Fragment Free Switching.. 266
        15.5.4   Adaptive Switching 266
15.6   Virtual LANs (VLANs)... 267
        15.6.1   VLAN Types.. 268
        15.6.2   Inter-Switch VLANs.. 268
15.7   Embedded Routing Information Field (E-RIF) Format 271
15.8   The Generic Attribute Registration Protocol (GARP)....................... 274
        15.8.1   GARP Protocol Operation... 274

15.8.2   GARP Multicast Registration Protocol (GMRP) 276
15.8.3   GARP VLAN Registration Protocol (GVRP) 277
15.9   Port Trunking...278
15.10 Layer 3 Switches...278
15.11 Layer 4 Switches and Beyond...279
15.12 Problems Associated with Bridges/Switches.................................279
15.13 Summary..280

Section C   Token Ring/IEEE 802.5 (ISO 8802-5) 281

Chapter 16   Token Ring Introduction 283
16.1   A Brief History of Token Ring...283
16.2   Basic Method of Operation 284
16.3   4Mbps and 16Mbps Operation..287
16.4   Early Token Release 287
16.5   Summary..288

Chapter 17   The Physical Layer...289
17.1   Physical Signalling Path...289
17.2   Encoding Techniques 291
       17.2.1   Differential Manchester Encoding 292
17.3   Ring Latency 293
       17.3.1   Fixed Latency Buffer 293
       17.3.2   Elasticity Buffer 294
17.4   Physical Error Detection...294
       17.4.1   Burst Errors 295
       17.4.2   Frequency Errors 295
17.5   Media Types 295
       17.5.1   IBM Shielded Twisted Pair (STP).......................................296
       17.5.2   Unshielded Twisted Pair (UTP) 297
       17.5.3   Foil Screened Twisted Pair (FTP).......................................298
       17.5.4   Media Filters...298
       17.5.5   Fiber Optic Cable 299
17.6   Physical Topology 300
       17.6.1   Multi-Station Access Units (MSAUs or MAUs)...................300
       17.6.2   Phantom Current 302
       17.6.3   Trunk Ports 303
       17.6.4   Ring Wrap 304
       17.6.5   Drive Distances 305
       17.6.6   Adjusted Ring Length (ARL) 306
       17.6.7   Station Counts 307
       17.6.8   Active vs Passive 307
       17.6.9   Fiber Optic MAUs 308
17.7   Network Design 309
17.8   Summary..312

Chapter 18   The Media Access Control (MAC) Layer..............................313
18.1   The Token 313

18.1.1   Token Format 314
18.1.2   Starting Delimiter... 314
18.1.3   Access Control Field... 314
18.1.4   The Ending Delimiter 315
18.1.5   Token Validity 315
18.1.6   Token Holding Time... 316
18.2   Abort Sequence 316
18.3   Frame Formats... 317
18.3.1   Starting Delimiter (SD) 317
18.3.2   Access Control Field (AC) 317
18.3.3   Frame Control Field (FC) 318
18.3.4   Destination Address (DA) 318
18.3.5   Source Address (SA) 318
18.3.6   Routing Information Field (RIF)... 319
18.3.7   Data Field 319
18.3.8   Frame Check Sequence (FCS)... 319
18.3.9   Ending Delimiter (ED)... 320
18.3.10   Frame Status Field (FS) 320
18.3.11   Inter-Frame Gap (IFG)... 320
18.3.12   Frame Validity 320
18.4   MAC Addressing.. 321
18.4.1   Unicast Addresses... 321
18.4.2   Multicast Addresses.. 321
18.4.3   Broadcast Addresses 322
18.4.4   Functional Addresses.. 322
18.4.5   Null Address 323
18.4.6   Administering Addresses 323
18.5   MAC Frames.. 324
18.6   Station Operation 333
18.6.1   Transmitting... 333
18.6.2   Token Transmission 334
18.6.3   Fill Pattern... 334
18.6.4   Repeating 335
18.6.5   Frame Reception 335
18.6.6   Frame Stripping 336
18.6.7   Station Counters... 337
18.6.8   Station Flags 338
18.6.9   Station Timers 343
18.7   Station Insertion.. 345
18.7.1   Lobe Test 346
18.7.2   Phantom Current.. 346
18.7.3   Ring Speed Test.. 346
18.7.4   Active Monitor Test 347
18.7.5   Duplicate Address Detection... 347
18.7.6   Neighbor Notification 348
18.7.7   Request Initialization 348
18.8   Access Priority 349
18.9   Summary 351

Chapter 19   Ring Management..**353**

19.1   Token Ring Errors...353

       19.1.1   Fault Domain 353

       19.1.2   Fault Reporting 354

       19.1.3   Error Counters..355

19.2   Active Monitor Functions 356

       19.2.1   Ring Recovery 356

       19.2.2   Ring Purge 356

19.3   Claim Token...357

19.4   The Beacon Process 360

19.5   Automatic Beacon Resolution..362

19.6   Standby Monitor Functions 363

19.7   Additional Server Functions...363

       19.7.1   The Ring Parameter Server (RPS) 364

       19.7.2   The Configuration Report Server (CRS) 364

       19.7.3   The Ring Error Monitor (REM) 364

19.8   Summary..364

Chapter 20   Source Route Bridging **365**

20.1   What Is Source Route Bridging (SRB)?..365

20.2   Routing Information Field (RIF) 367

       20.2.1   Routing Control Field 367

       20.2.2   Route Designators 370

20.3   Route Discovery...370

20.4   Multiple Path Networks 374

20.5   Spanning Tree in Source Route Bridged Networks 375

20.6   Source Route Bridging vs Transparent Bridging...............................376

20.7   Source Route Transparent Bridges 377

20.8   Summary..377

Chapter 21   Dedicated Token Ring **379**

21.1   Structure of a DTR Network...380

21.2   Operating Modes 382

       21.2.1   Classic Token Ring Station 382

       21.2.2   DTR Station..382

       21.2.3   C-Port Operation in Port Mode 382

       21.2.4   C-Port Operation in Station Emulation Mode....................383

21.3   DTR Access Protocol Support 383

       21.3.1   DTR Timers..384

       21.3.2   Policy Flags and Variables 387

21.4   TXI Join Process...390

       21.4.1   Bypass State 390

       21.4.2   DTR Registration...390

       21.4.3   Lobe Media Test (LMT) 393

       21.4.4   Duplicate Address Check (DAC)..394

21.5   TXI Transmit Operation 395

       21.5.1   Transmit Functional Model 396

       21.5.2   TXI Heart Beat 398

       21.5.3   TXI Hard Error Recovery..399

21.6   DTR Frame Format...401
            21.6.1   DTR Frame Fields 401
21.7   DTR MAC Frames 403
            21.7.1   Management Routing Interface (MRI) 406
21.8   Summary 406

Chapter 22   High Speed Token Ring..**409**
22.1   Summary 413

Section D   Fiber Distributed Data Interface (FDDI) 415

Chapter 23   FDDI Introduction...**417**
23.1   What Is FDDI?...417
            23.1.1   FDDI and the OSI Model 418
            23.1.2   FDDI Network Environments 419
23.2   FDDI Topology 420
23.3   Basic Method of Operation 421
            23.3.1   Wrap Mode 424
23.4   Summary 425

Chapter 24   Physical Medium Dependent (PMD)...........................**427**
24.1   Multimode Fiber PMD (MMF-PMD) 428
24.2   Singlemode Fiber PMD (SMF-PMD) 429
24.3   Twisted Pair PMD (TP-PMD)...430
            24.3.1   MLT-3 Coding 431
            24.3.2   Cables and Connectors..432
24.4   FDDI Node Types 432
            24.4.1   Dual Attached Station (DAS) 433
            24.4.2   Single Attached Station (SAS) 433
            24.4.3   Dual Attached Concentrator (DAC)..................................433
            24.4.4   Single Attached Concentrator (SAC)................................434
            24.4.5   Null Attached Concentrator (NAC) 434
24.5   Port Types and Connections..435
            24.5.1   A Port..435
            24.5.2   B Port 436
            24.5.3   M Port...436
            24.5.4   S Port..436
            24.5.5   Valid Connections..437
24.6   Dual Homing 437
24.7   Optical Bypass Relay (OBR) 439
24.8   Summary 440

Chapter 25   Physical Layer Protocol (PHY)....................................**441**
25.1   Encoding/Decoding...441
            25.1.1   Non-Return to Zero Inverting (NRZI)..............................442
            25.1.2   4 Bit/5 Bit Encoding..442
25.2   Symbol Types 443
25.3   Line States 444
            25.3.1   Quiet Line State (QLS)..444

	25.3.2 Idle Line State (ILS)	444
	25.3.3 Halt Line State (HLS)	444
	25.3.4 Master Line State (MLS)	444
	25.3.5 Active Line State (ALS)	445
	25.3.6 Noise Line State (NLS)	445
25.4	Elasticity Buffer	445
25.5	Summary	446

Chapter 26   Media Access Control (MAC) **447**
26.1	The Token	448
	26.1.1 Start Delimiter (SD)	448
	26.1.2 Frame Control (FC) Field	449
	26.1.3 End Delimiter (ED)	449
26.2	Frame Format	449
	26.2.1 Preamble	450
	26.2.2 Start Delimiter (SD)	450
	26.2.3 Frame Control (FC)	450
	26.2.4 Destination Address (DA)	450
	26.2.5 Source Address (SA)	451
	26.2.6 Routing Information (RI)	451
	26.2.7 Data	451
	26.2.8 Frame Check Sequence (FCS)	451
	26.2.9 Ending Delimiter (ED)	451
	26.2.10 Frame Status (FS)	451
26.3	FDDI Addressing	452
	26.3.1 Unicast Addresses	452
	26.3.2 Multicast Addresses	452
	26.3.3 Broadcast Addresses	452
26.4	MAC Receiver/Transmitter States	452
	26.4.1 MAC Receiver	453
	26.4.2 MAC Transmitter	454
	26.4.3 Runts and Other Spurious Symbols	455
26.5	Summary	455

Chapter 27   FDDI Ring Operation **457**
27.1	Service Classes	457
	27.1.1 Asynchronous Service	457
	27.1.2 Synchronous Service	457
27.2	Ring Scheduling Algorithm	458
	27.2.1 Asynchronous Data Priority Mechanism	459
27.3	Token Types	460
	27.3.1 Restricted Tokens	460
	27.3.2 Non-restricted Tokens	461
27.4	Claim Token Process	461
	27.4.1 Ring Initialization	462
27.5	Error Recovery	463
	27.5.1 The Beacon Process	463
	27.5.2 Trace Function	464
27.6	Summary	466

Chapter 28   Station Management (SMT)..**467**
28.1   SMT Architecture...467
28.2   Frame Based Management..468
       28.2.1   Neighbor Notification Protocol 470
       28.2.2   Status Report Protocol 471
       28.2.3   Status Information Protocol...472
       28.2.4   Parameter Management Protocol.....................................473
       28.2.5   Echo Protocol 474
       28.2.6   Resource Allocation Protocol 474
       28.2.7   Extended Frame Services Protocol..................................475
28.3   Connection Management 476
       28.3.1   Entity Co-ordination Management (ECM)........................476
       28.3.2   Physical Connection Management (PCM)..........................477
       28.3.3   Configuration Management (CFM)....................................479
28.4   Ring Management...480
       28.4.1   Duplicate Address Detection...480
       28.4.2   Stuck Beacon Recovery (Trace Initiation).......................480
28.5   Summary 481

Chapter 29   Bridging In FDDI Networks..**483**
29.1   Encapsulation Bridging..484
29.2   Translational Bridging 486
       29.2.1   Bit Transmission Ordering 487
29.3   Ethernet - FDDI Bridging 488
       29.3.1   Ethernet to FDDI Translation 490
       29.3.2   FDDI to Ethernet Translation 494
       29.3.3   Possible Complications..497
29.4   Token Ring - FDDI Bridging 498
29.5   FDDI Switching...499
29.6   Summary 499

**Section E   Logical Link Control ANSI/IEEE 802.2 (ISO 8802-2)
                The SubNetwork Access Protocol (SNAP)..........501**

Chapter 30   Logical Link Control..**503**
30.1   LLC PDU Structure..504
       30.1.1   LLC Addressing..505
       30.1.2   LLC Control 506
30.2   Types and Classes of LLC 507
       30.2.1   Type 1 LLC 508
       30.2.2   Type 2 LLC 510
       30.2.3   Type 3 LLC 514
30.3   Route Determination and LLC Route Determination Entity 516
       30.3.1   LLC Support in Route Determination 516
       30.3.2   RDE PDU Encoding...518
30.4   The Sub Network Access Protocol (SNAP)...519
       30.4.1   SNAP Support for the Route Determination Entity (RDE)...........520
       30.4.2   Examples of LLC/SNAP Usage 521

| 30.5 | Common Implementations | 521 |
| 30.6 | Summary | 523 |

Section F An Introduction to Internetworking 525

Chapter 31 Internetworking Introduction 527
31.1	TCP/IP	528
	31.1.1	A Brief History of TCP/IP	530
	31.1.2	TCP/IP Related Protocols	530
	31.1.3	Routing Protocols	534
	31.1.4	Supporting Services	535
	31.1.5	Standardization	536
31.2	Other Protocols	537
	31.2.1	Non-Routable Protocols	538
31.3	Summary	538

Chapter 32 IP Addressing 541
32.1	IP Address Structure	542
	32.1.1	Dotted Decimal Notation	543
	32.1.2	User Address Classes	544
	32.1.3	"Special" Address Classes	546
32.2	Subnetting	548
	32.2.1	Subnet Mask Operation	549
	32.2.2	Guidelines for Implementing Subnets	552
32.3	Routing Fundamentals	552
32.4	Address Resolution	554
	32.4.1 Address Resolution Protocol (ARP)	555
	32.4.2 ARP Frame Format	555
	32.4.3 The Reverse Address Resolution Protocol (RARP)	557
32.5	The Dynamic Host Configuration Protocol (DHCP)	558
32.6	IP Version 6 Addressing	559
32.7	Summary	561

Chapter 33 The Internet Protocol 563
33.1	IP Datagram Encapsulation	563
33.2	The IP Datagram Header	564
	33.2.1	IP Datagram Options	567
	33.2.2	Datagram Fragmentation	568
33.3	The Internet Control Message Protocol (ICMP)	569
	33.3.1	Echo Request/Reply	571
	33.3.2	Destination Unreachable	571
	33.3.3	Source Quench	572
	33.3.4	Redirect	572
	33.3.5	Router Advertisement and Solicitation	573
	33.3.6	Time Exceeded	573
	33.3.7	Parameter Problem	574
	33.3.8	Timestamp Request/Reply	574
	33.3.9	Information Request/Reply	574

      33.3.10 Address Mask Request/Reply 575
33.4   Summary 575

Chapter 34   Routing Principles 577
34.1   Routers.. 577
      34.1.1   Router Specifications 579
      34.1.2   Basic Router Operation 580
34.2   The Routing Table.. 581
      34.2.1   Route Quality 582
      34.2.2   Other Routing Table Information 584
34.3   Packet Processing... 585
34.4   Static Routes.. 586
      34.4.1   The Default Route 586
34.5   Broadcast and Multicast Forwarding 586
34.6   Summary 588

Chapter 35   IP Routing Protocols 589
35.1   Routing Information Protocol (RIP)... 590
      35.1.1   RIP Metrics 590
      35.1.2   Protocol Format... 591
      35.1.3   Protocol Operation 593
      35.1.4   RIP Updates and Timers 594
      35.1.5   Split Horizon, Poison Reverse, and Infinity 595
      35.1.6   RIP Version II 596
35.2   Open Shortest Path First (OSPF)... 597
      35.2.1   OSPF Metrics... 597
      35.2.2   Type-of-Service Routing 598
      35.2.3   Equal Cost Multi-Path Routing 599
      35.2.4   Areas 599
      35.2.5   OSPF Operation and Protocol Format 601
      35.2.6   Creating the Routing Table 604
      35.2.7   Maintaining Adjacency.. 604
35.3   Exterior Gateway Protocols 604
      35.3.1   Exterior Gateway Protocol (EGP)... 605
      35.3.2   Border Gateway Protocol (BGP) 606
35.4   Route Aggregation 607
35.5   Summary 608

Chapter 36   IPX... 609
36.1   IPX Architecture... 609
36.2   IPX Addressing... 610
36.3   IPX Datagram Format.. 612
36.4   Routing Information Protocol (RIP)... 614
36.5   Service Advertisement Protocol (SAP) 615
36.6   NetWare Link Services Protocol (NLSP).. 616
36.7   NetWare Core Protocol (NCP)... 617
36.8   Summary 617

Chapter 37   Layer 3 Switching 619
37.1   Classical IP Over ATM (IPOA) and Multi-Protocol Over ATM (MPOA) 621

37.2   IP Switching 621
37.3   Tag Switching 621
37.4   Cell-Switched Router (CSR) 622
37.5   Aggregate-Route Based IP Switching (ARIS) 622
37.6   Multi-Protocol Label Switching (MPLS) 623
37.7   Summary 623

Section G   Cabling Infrastructure 625

Chapter 38   Original LAN Cabling Implementations 627
38.1   Ethernet 10Base5 627
     38.1.1   Ethernet 10Base5 Cable 627
     38.1.2   10Base5 Connectivity 630
     38.1.3   10Base5 Design Summary 632
38.2   Ethernet 10Base2 633
     38.2.1   10Base2 Connectivity 634
38.3   Token Ring 635
     38.3.1   IBM Cabling System (ICS) 635
     38.3.2   STP Connectivity 638
38.4   Summary 639

Chapter 39   Structured Cabling Systems 641
39.1   Basic Principles 642
     39.1.1   SCS Objectives 642
     39.1.2   Topology 643
     39.1.3   SCS Components 645
39.2   Structured Cabling Standards 646
     39.2.1   U.S. Standards 647
     39.2.2   Technical Service Bulletins (TSBs) 647
     39.2.3   Additional US Standards 648
     39.2.4   International Standards 649
39.3   Areas within an SCS System 650
     39.3.1   Transition Points 652
     39.3.2   Distance Limits 653
39.4   Twisted Pair Media Options 654
     39.4.1   Cable Construction 654
     39.4.2   Transmission Characteristics 655
     39.4.3   UTP Categories 657
     39.4.4   UTP Connector 659
39.5   Fiber Optic Media 660
     39.5.1   Fiber Optic Cable Construction 661
     39.5.2   Principles of Fiber Optic Transmission 662
     39.5.3   Fiber Optic Connectors 664
     39.5.4   Fiber Optic Performance Criteria 664
39.6   Application Classes 666
39.7   SCS Patching Options 667
     39.7.1   Inter-Connect Patching 667
     39.7.2   Cross-Connect Patching 668

39.8   SCS and LAN Applications 669
        39.8.1   Mapping Ethernet onto SCS 669
        39.8.2   Mapping Token Ring onto SCS 670
        39.8.3   Mapping FDDI onto SCS... 671
39.9   Electro-Magnetic Compatibility 672
39.10 Design Guidelines 674
        39.10.1 The Design Process 674
        39.10.2 The Work Area 674
        39.10.3 Distributor Layout... 676
        39.10.4 The Backbone 677
39.11 Testing and Certification 679
        39.11.1 TSB 67 679
        39.11.2 TSB 95 684
39.12 Future Trends 686
39.13 Summary 686

Appendices 687

Appendix A   Vendor Identification and Addressing 689
A.1   Vendor Identification... 689
A.2   Multicast Addresses 691
A.3   Broadcast Addresses 693

Appendix B   Ethernet Type Codes 695

Appendix C   A Glossary of Networking Terms 699
C.1   Networking Terms... 699

Appendix D   Bibliography 731
D.1   ISO/IEC, and ANSI/IEEE Standards 731
D.2   RFCs 732
D.3   Other References 733

Index 735

Preface

Welcome to the world of networking, or more specifically, the world of the high-speed Local Area Network (or LAN). The technologies here are significant, since this is one of the fastest growing areas of networking today, and will no doubt stay that way for many years to come. In fact, this all-important aspect of computer communications is often overlooked, and is certainly frequently confused with the applications that are run on the LAN infrastructure itself. One of the things that we hope to achieve through this book then, is to explain how our networks are constructed. Once we have an understanding of this, we can then build on that knowledge to explain a little more about how this fits with the other elements (devices and protocols) that are required to achieve meaningful communication between machines.

We must be clear what we really mean. In our homes, most of us now have a computer, and this in turn is often connected to the Internet via a modem of some description. In essence, the connection then becomes the portal of a Wide Area Network (WAN) that spans our globe and, in effect, invades every one of our lives today. Speed is a key factor here, yet no WAN connection can match the speeds available locally. Information flow cannot be stemmed, and our thirst for knowledge is driving the pace at which the Internet has evolved. Bandwidth is the key to moving this data, and high bandwidth connections are just not possible over wide area links. But while all of this may be true, this is not the focus of this volume. Through these pages, we shall look specifically at the LAN, where most bulk data is moved and stored. Here is where we see vast developments as we move data at thousands of Megabits per second, and most importantly, where we see competing technologies that have no overlap, and little or no inter-operability. Here we must be aware of the physical cable plant, and apply best installation practices if we are to ensure trouble-free operation. Finally, we must know the requirements of our installation so that we know not to exceed the design limitations. Hence it is in these areas that we shall devote our time.

Our Internet Service Providers (those companies offering Internet access and services) have many systems at their Points-of-Presence (POPs), and indeed at their main sites. It goes without saying then, that these systems need to be connected together, so that the remote access devices that we have used to connect us can communicate with the mail server that will eventually deliver our mail. Our workplaces today are wired so that we can share information with our fellow workers, and share expensive peripherals such as high-speed printers, network faxes, and maybe even the company's Internet connection. To do this, we require an infrastructure over which our data will flow, and therefore allow data transfer between devices. Just as important though, all of the devices need to understand the access methodologies that are in use for the technology employed, and then of course adhere to them religiously. Now our simple cable system becomes a real Local Area Network, and the process of moving data becomes a reality, no matter how we choose to do it.

This volume really has only one goal then - to present the ultimate introduction to the LAN technologies that are in everyday use, yet which we take for granted. We go to work, and we connect our laptop to its docking station, and in so doing connect it to the network. Yet do we really think of what is happening when we do? Indeed, should we care? The simple answer is that we should if we are responsible for the network infrastructure itself, since as we have said, we must know the design limitations of the infrastructures that we are supporting. Equally, by understanding a little of what is actually happening on the cable itself, we can better understand some of the intricacies of networking generally and shatter many of the myths that can surround what many see as a black art.

The volume itself is split into seven sections (A through G). Through these we examine and discover the basic elements of the three major LAN technologies (Ethernet, Token Ring, and FDDI), and then introduce the cable plant at the Physical level, and also introduce Routing at the higher level. Indeed, it is our belief that in order to fully understand the technologies, you will need to have an understanding of both the physical and logical attributes that comprise the network that you connect to. Taking each of these in slightly more detail, section A provides a basic overview of networking, the standards-making bodies, and the architectures involved. Section B represents possibly the fastest moving sector of Local Area Networks covering all of the entire Ethernet, and IEEE 802.3 technologies. This section tracks the entire history of Etherent/802.3 technologies from legacy 10Mbps coaxial cable based systems, through twisted pair and fiber 10Mbps and 100Mbps solutions, to present day Gigabit solutions. It examines the access methods, media requirements, and design limitations of each technology, and compares and contrasts these. Sections C and D cover Token Ring/IEEE 802.5 and the Fiber Distributed Data Interface (FDDI) respectively, and again look at the historical development of both from their early introduction to present day developments such as Dedicated Token Ring, etc.

Section E provides a discussion of the Logical Link Control (LLC)/IEEE 802.2 standard as used by IEEE 802.3, IEEE 802.5, and FDDI, and also introduces the Sub-Network Access Protocol (SNAP). Section F covers Internetworking, or Routing by any other name. Although section F is an introduction, it provides more than a broad overview, and therefore covers the major protocols used such as the Internet Protocol (IP), and Novell's Internetwork Packet Exchange (IPX). In addition, we examine routing protocols such as the Routing Information Protocol (RIP) and the Open Shortest Path First (OSPF) protocol used in IP, and RIP and the Service Advertisement Protocol (SAP) used in IPX. Finally, in section G we examine the very core of any network - the cable plant that provides the infrastructure over which our data can flow. In this section we look at the evolution of cabling, best installation practices, and some of the more intricate and technical aspects of what, at first, may seem simple and benign.

Any book on a subject that is diverse and incorporates technologies that are moving at such a rapid pace can rarely be considered little more than a snapshot of a given moment in time. What we hope we have achieved though, is to ensure that the information included here is as up to date as possible at the time of publication, and in essence, we hope that we have achieved this goal. Certainly technology advances will continue to be made, and we shall address these as they become available, hopefully in future editions and/or volumes. In any event, the one constant within the networking world is change, and it is this that both opens information to the masses, and in turn, enriches our lives in so many ways. The pace may be faster than ever before, yet we continue to rise to the challenges that this brings.

Finally, we must not forget that a work like this is a combination of many efforts. True, it is the authors who receive the publicity and earn the right to present their names on the front cover and the spine. In truth though, things in life are rarely that simple. As a result, we have relied on a number of people who have assisted in many ways. Firstly, we would like to thank our employers for the support that they have given. Greg Shortell and Tony Kenyon of Nokia Internet Communications in particular, and especially Tony for allowing us to use his μscope package once more. In addition, we must mention Jim Neenan of Logical (UK), and of course Pam Chester of Digital Press. Pam deserves special mention because it is she who has provided constant encouragement, and also ensured that we did not stray too far from the agreed content and timescales that we set so long ago. Finally though, our hats come off to a mutual friend, Brian Hill, for his ideas, presentation flair, technical knowledge, and general willingness to debate areas of the text upon which we could not agree. Brian single-handedly proofread the entire volume at least once, and many parts repeatedly. In truth, we have to remove our combined hats to anyone who could do that, since this takes friendship to a completely different level!

Section A

An Introduction to LANs and Networking

Introduction

In order to introduce Local Area Networks (LANs), or indeed networks of any type at all, we need to understand just a little of the history of computing. Computing itself is possibly the biggest success story of the 20th century, and has, and indeed is, evolving at such a rate that even the professionals of the industry find it hard to keep up.

Looking back into the distant past of the 1960s, and early 1970s, computing revolved around the *mainframe* - the large dinosaurs of the past. Terminals, or workstations - there were none. These machines were *batch processors* that were programmed by punched cards, punched paper tape, or similar, and their output was to printers only. As we move forward, we see interactive computing starting to appear, and then we find firstly *teletype*, and then screen based terminals as in figure 1-1. The revolution had started.

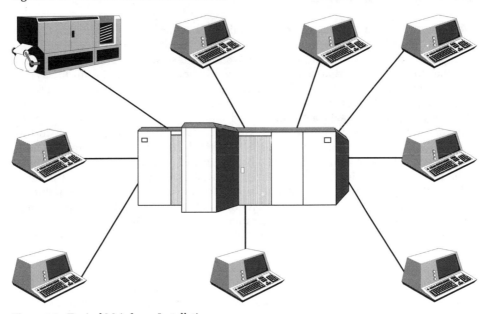

Figure 1-1: Typical Mainframe Installation

Yet it is not really the terminals that we should look to initially. Certainly, the low cost terminal, and more especially the Personal Computer (PC), have each played their part in *opening* the world of computing to the masses. But it is the processor that we shall look to first. Mainframe computing comes at a price, and one that could not be met by most smaller companies. These monoliths would cost hundreds of thousands of dollars, or even millions, yet the processors were based on a *timesharing* architecture. This meant that each task, or user, would get a small amount of processing time, and the processor would *poll* the tasks in a *round-robin* fashion. Typically, background tasks, depending upon their priority, would receive a slightly longer *time-slice* than foreground tasks, but they would be polled less frequently. A foreground task that had no data to process would also give up its time-slice when its turn came around. Nonetheless, the net effect of all this was that the processor would become overloaded as more and more terminals or workstations were added. The solution - add another processor, or replace the processor with one that was faster, or generally more powerful. In either case, we were looking at an expensive, or so-called, *forklift* upgrade.

The solution was simple, but we had to wait ten to fifteen years for it - *distributed processing*! In other words, let the high powered, low cost Personal Computers (PCs) that were being introduced do the processing at the desktop, and let the centralized processors do the data storage, and sharing of more expensive resources. All we needed now, was to find a cheap, effective, method to connect all the resources and processors, because for the first time they were not all housed in the same system. The answer, is the *Local Area Network*, or LAN.

1.1   LANs and Other Networks

One definition of a Local Area Network might be *"a collection of devices that are inter-connected via a common transportation medium, for the purposes of transferring data."* Although this is true, we might also wish to expand on this and say that the maximum diameter[1] of the network would typically be up to say 5 to 10km - hence the name *local*. But beware. Our definitions are becoming clouded from the perspective of the end-user. Do these people know where the resources that they are using are located, or indeed should they need to? Obviously the answer is that there is no need to know, but the point is that LAN-to-LAN connectivity is now so seamless, that it is difficult to tell. For example, vendors today can claim that with *long haul* fiber optics, they can take Ethernet LANs to over 100km, and at gigabit speeds! From our first definition above, we still have a LAN, although now it is anything but local. To understand what a LAN is then, it might actually be better to examine what other network types there are, and attempt to define them. What we have left may then suffice for our arguments as to what a LAN really is.

1.1.1   Metropolitan Area Networks (MANs)

The traditional definition of a Metropolitan Area Network (MAN) is one that would typically cover areas such as campuses, or small communities. Examples of these

---

[1] The diameter of the network is the maximum distance between two end stations.

networks may use the Fiber Distributed Data Interface (FDDI), where we can cover geographic distances of up to several hundreds of kilometers, and transfer data at 100Mbps. Traditionally, network technologies such as Ethernet/802.3, and Token Ring/802.5 could not match FDDI in terms of either speed or distance. Hence, for many years, FDDI held dominance in this market segment with a 100Mbps transfer rate, and the distances that would be available only with fiber as the backbone. Many large organizations implemented FDDI backbones, that then connected to 10Mbps Ethernet LANs. At that time, there was no 100Mbps Ethernet/802.3 standards, so our backbone was now 10 times faster than the LANs that it interconnected.

The same was not true of Token Ring though. For some reason, few companies ever implemented mixed FDDI/Token Ring environments. This was possibly because of the higher speed that Token Ring offered, since this was 16Mbps. However there is no real proof that this is the case, it almost seemed that vendors just did not want to champion this particular cause.

1.1.2 Wide Area Networks (WANs)

Wide Area Networks know no geographic bound. They rely upon the infrastructures that the telephone carriers have already installed, and therefore provide for world-wide coverage. Organizations do not therefore own their links, but instead either *lease* them, or pay a *per-call* charge to the telecommunications operator when data is transferred.

One major problem with WAN links is that they cannot provide the high speeds that are available with LANs. Typical link speeds would be anything from 56/64kbps to 1.54/2Mbps, although with satellite links speeds of up to 45Mbps are possible - but at a price. Our WAN then, is there, to link our LANs (or MANs) together over any geographic distance.

1.1.3 So What Is a LAN?

So, having looked at these other network types, we know that WANs are used to link LANs and MANs together, but today one could be forgiven in thinking that there is little to choose between a LAN and a MAN. Certainly, the distinction is fuzzy, and it is becoming more so with increased LAN speeds, increased distances, and lower costs of ownership. Add to this, the fact that WAN speeds are also increasing, prices are falling, and that these services are becoming more accessible, and we see the worlds of networking merge more and more into one.

If we must have a definition of a LAN, then we can revert to our original statement at the start of this section - a LAN is *"a collection of devices that are interconnected via a common transportation medium, for the purposes of transferring data."* Typically this will be over a small geographic distance, normally a single building, or at most a campus. It will be privately owned (as opposed to being leased from a carrier), and it will normally have a data rate of somewhere between 10Mbps, and 1000Mbps (1Gbps). Today, it will almost certainly be an Ethernet/802.3 network, although we must not forget that there are a large number of other network types. For example, many institutions still use Token Ring networks, particularly those that demand high reliability. In addition, there are a large number of *legacy* FDDI networks that are used as building backbones, typically with Ethernets used for *horizontal* networks. Finally, we must not forget that there are further network types such as Asynchronous Transfer Mode (ATM), and many organizations are using this for their backbones today. In particular ATM couples the ability to transport time critical data such as that demanded by multimedia applications, over relatively large distances and at speeds that range from 25Mbps, through 155Mbps to 625Mbps.

1.2   LAN Topologies

The *topology* of a network is the manner in which each element of it connects to its partner both *physically*, and *logically*. Over the years, several different methods of physical interconnection have evolved, and while each has its own particular merits and shortcomings, none can really be said to be vastly superior to any other. In this section, we will introduce the four most popular topologies, and briefly describe the advantages and disadvantages of each.

1.2.1   Star Topology

This is possibly the oldest of all topologies, with its roots firmly in the mainframe environment. As figure 1-2 shows, we have a central hub through which all traffic flows. The obvious disadvantage of this system is that the hub itself is a single point of failure. If the hub should fail, then all stations connected to it will lose connectivity with the rest of the network.

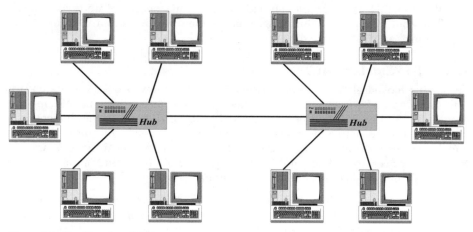

Figure 1-2: Star Topology LAN

The advantages of this system are that it is simple to implement, and since all devices connect to a central point, we can monitor the network easily and efficiently. That is not to say that we cannot expand the network though. Where we need to add more devices, we simply interconnect further hubs as shown in figure 1-2.

We see this type of topology in just about all LAN types, but do not be fooled. Ethernet/802.3 may use a *physical* Star topology for interconnection, but logically the topology is a Bus. Equally, Token Ring and FDDI may use a *physical* Star topology to connect devices such as *concentrators*, and *Multi-Station Attachment Units* (MAUs), but logically they operate as a Ring.

1.2.2   Bus Topology

The Bus Topology is most commonly found in Ethernet/802.3 (ISO/IEC 8802-3) environments, although it can also be found in other LANs such as *ArcNet* that uses the *Token Passing Bus* standard of IEEE 802.4 (ISO/IEC 8802-4). Typically implemented in coaxial cable, and terminated at each end, this topology is simple and inexpensive to install, and equally simple and inexpensive to expand. These advantages then also become some of its major disadvantages as well, since bus topology networks are often expanded without thought or planning, and they grow beyond their design limitations. In addition, any break in the cable renders the entire network inoperable, and speeds are limited to just 10Mbps at best. Figure 1-3 shows a simple example of a Bus Topology LAN which could conform to either Ethernet/802.3, or IEEE 802.4.

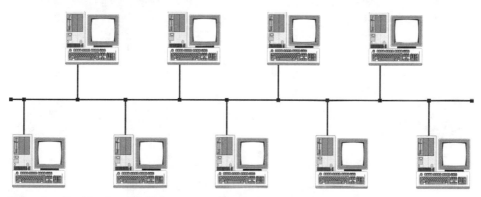

Figure 1-3: Bus Topology LAN

In operation, IEEE 802.3 (ISO/IEC 8802-3) LANs operate what is known as a *Carrier Sense, Multiple Access with Collision Detection* (CSMA/CD) access method. Stations that have data to transmit, will first *listen* on the medium to ensure that it is free, and only when it is will they commence transmission. These transmissions will then be received by *all* attached stations, but will be discarded by any station to which they were not addressed. In essence, this is a classic definition of a *broadcast* LAN topology.

The access method described, also has a down side since it is possible for multiple stations to transmit at the same time. Where this occurs, we experience what is known as a *collision*, and those stations involved must cease transmission for a random amount of time before re-transmitting their data. This ensures that the collision has cleared, and being a random timer, also attempts to ensure that frames from the same stations do not collide again.

Unlike IEEE 802.3 LANs where any station can transmit provided that the medium is free, IEEE 802.4 LANs use a *Token Passing Bus* access protocol. In this case, stations may only transmit when they are in possession of a special frame called a *Token*, and therefore station access is strictly controlled. As a result collisions do not occur, but all stations will receive the transmissions of any other. The environment is therefore still based upon broadcast principles as with Ethernet/802.3 LANs.

1.2.3 Ring Topology

Figure 1-4 shows a LAN using a Ring topology. This is normally associated with Token Ring and FDDI environments although, as we have said before, these LANs are often presented as Star Topology networks *physically*.

Certainly, when we talk of Token Ring and FDDI environments, we have a relatively complex access protocol, and an ordered method of station access. That said, with Ring Topologies, we have an extremely resilient LAN. One of the reason for this is that these environments can use *dual*, *counter-rotating* rings that can

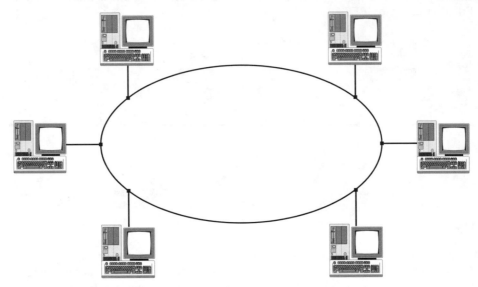

Figure 1-4: Ring Topology LAN

tolerate single cable breaks. The LAN access devices simply detect the break and re-route the data over a backup path. The LAN then becomes *self-healing*. In addition, since station access is strictly controlled, we can easily predict the latency of the LAN. Thus, stations take turns in accessing the LAN, and therefore networks employing this topology are generally said to be *deterministic* since we can predict performance relatively accurately based upon the number of stations involved.

The disadvantages associated with Ring Topologies are that the technologies that use them tend to be expensive to implement. This is due, in part, to the fact that the access protocols are more complex, and the devices are correspondingly more intelligent. Also, Token Ring and FDDI LANs have never achieved the same level of popularity that Ethernet/802.3 enjoys. This means that access devices are not produced in the same quantities, and the prices remain considerably higher.

In terms of operation, a station that has data to transmit will wait for an invitation in the form of a special frame called a *Token*. Once acquired, this special frame allows the station to transmit for a limited amount of time. As such, the station will now transmit its data to its downstream neighbor who will examine the frame, determine if it is addressed to it, and then pass it to its downstream neighbor. Where, on examination of the frame, a station finds that it is destined for itself, that station will copy the frame to memory, mark the frame that it has received the data, and pass the frame to its downstream neighbor anyway. The reasons for this are two-fold. Firstly, the frame may be destined for more than one station. Secondly, by passing the frame from station to station, it will eventually arrive back at the station that sent it. The transmitting station can then check to see whether the data was received, and also remove the frame from the LAN. In effect, this too, describes a *broadcast* LAN.

1.2.4 Tree Topology

This topology is little used today, but is employed in the IEEE 802.3 10Broad36 specifications that use a *broadband* signaling system. As such, any discussion on topologies can never be complete without at least mentioning this topology.

As we have said, the 10Broad36 specification uses a broadband signaling system meaning that *multiple* signals can exist on the physical medium at any one time.

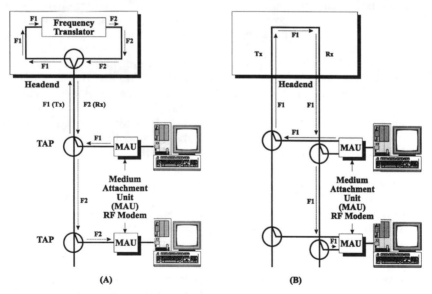

Figure 1-5: Tree Topology - Basic Operation

Each of the signals are then *frequency division* multiplexed so that they do not interfere with each other, and can therefore co-exist. Also, the topology is based on a single cable segment that passes via a device known as a *Headend*. Two variants exist namely those that utilize a single cable system, and those that use a dual cable system. In the case of the single cable system, the Headend is responsible for translating the *Transmit Frequency* to the *Receive Frequency*. In the second variant, only one frequency is used, and the Headend is responsible for *turning the signal around*, such that the data transmitted via the *transmit* (Tx) cable, is received over the *receive* (Rx) cable. In both cases, a device can monitor its own transmissions since we really have a *broadcast* medium, in a similar fashion to all of the other topologies that we have discussed. Figure 1-5 shows a typical example of how this system is implemented in both single and dual cable environments.

1.3   Standardization and Architectures

One of the overriding problems facing the developers of our modern-day networks, was how to make the technology *open*, and freely available. The Mainframe environments of the past were based on proprietary solutions. The newly developing LANs however, had to be based on open standards to provide full vendor interoperability, and therefore instill user confidence. The days of end-users being locked into a single vendor were now numbered as the standards would define everything from cables and connectors, through to user access methods. Five main standards making bodies exist within computer networking, and these are each briefly introduced below:

- **The International Standards Organization (ISO)**
  The International Standards Organization (ISO) is *the* authoritative body responsible for the creation and ratification of internationally accepted standards. This body is comprised of many separate standards groups from different countries and vendors, and produce standards that relate to items that are as diverse as the sizing of an air vent such that a finger cannot become caught in it, through to computer communications. The ISO was also responsible for the introduction of the OSI Reference Model that conceptualizes computer communications through a seven layer architectural model. This will be discussed further in section 1.3.1 however. In short, do not underestimate the work of the ISO. It produces a large number of standards that, if followed by all, ensure the smooth operation of so many things that we all take for granted in everyday life.

- **The Institute of Electrical and Electronic Engineers (IEEE)**
  It is possibly the IEEE that we should thank for the introduction of LAN standards in the first instance. The IEEE are most actively involved with data communications today, and are best known for their IEEE 802.x[2] series of standards. These standards include most popular LAN technologies such as

---

[2] It is interesting to note that the IEEE 802.x standards are so named since work commenced in February (2) 1980 (80). The final number, i.e. 3 (as in 802.3) then relates to the committee responsible for this standard.

Ethernet (or IEEE 802.3), and Token Ring (or IEEE 802.5). It is interesting to note that many of these standards have now been adopted by the ISO, and have been ratified as *International Standards*. A further discussion of IEEE standards can be found in section 1.3.2.

- **The American National Standards Institute (ANSI)**
  ANSI is the American Standards making body and has been involved in furthering computer related standards for many years. In terms of LAN standards, ANSI was responsible for the introduction and ratification of the X3T9.5 *Fiber Distributed Data Interface* (FDDI) standards.

- **The Electrical Industries Association (EIA)**
  The Electrical Industries Association is responsible for several standards in the world of data communications, most notably those surrounding *serial* data communications. The EIA is possibly best known for the work it did to define and ratify the RS-232 series of standards, which are now recognized world-wide.

- **The Telecommunications Industries Association (TIA)**
  The TIA, in concert with the EIA, were jointly responsible for the introduction of the initial *Structured Cabling* standards under the guise of EIA/TIA 568. This was later adopted by the ISO as the basis for their ISO/IEC 11801 standard, which has been ratified as an International Standard through them.

1.3.1 The OSI Reference Model

As we have already said, it was the International Standards Organization that introduced what has possibly become the most widely accepted communications framework, or *architecture*. Few people involved in networking and data communications will have not heard of this, but still many do not fully understand its significance. The architecture itself is conceptual, but breaks the role of communications into seven distinct tasks. Developers and vendors can then each produce component parts of the whole, yet provided that the *interface*[3] between layers remains constant, we will have assured interoperability. Figure 1-6 shows the OSI Reference Model, and the layers to which many of the standards that we shall discuss further in this volume relate. Also, each of the seven layers is introduced and briefly described.

The definition of this model was not a simple task, and our discussions in this section merely touch on the true complexity of communications generally. The ISO started work on the definition of the Reference Model back in 1978, yet we had to wait until 1984 before it was formally introduced. As you might imagine then, communications of this kind are not for the faint hearted. That said, in LAN terms we deal only with the lower layers as our figure shows. Thus, as far as this volume is concerned, we are broadly shielded from many of the more complex upper layers.

---

[3] An interface between layers of the OSI Model is referenced by a number of Primitives that define the commands, responses, and data passed between neighboring layers.

We will examine the *Network* Layer in some detail when we discuss *Internetworking*, and we shall briefly touch on some applications in that same section. Broadly though, this volume will concentrate on the *Physical*, and *Data Link*, or *Technology Dependent* Layers.

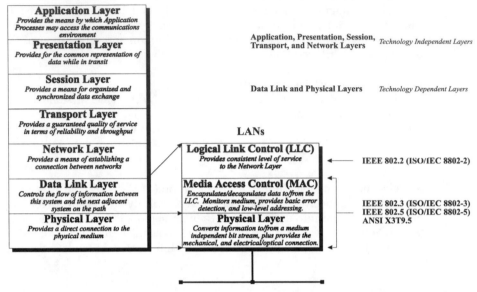

Figure 1-6: The ISO Reference Model

- **Physical Layer**
  The Physical Layer specifies the electrical (and/or optical, or even radio) signaling, and the mechanical/physical connections applicable to the medium type in use. We shall look at media (cabling) and connectors in some depth later in this volume. In addition, we shall also discuss the relevant media requirements, and connection methods that are employed for each technology as it is discussed.

- **Data Link Layer**
  The Data Link Layer is used to mask the vagaries of the physical layer (and with that, the medium) from the upper layers (i.e. the Network Layer). For LAN implementations, the Data Link Layer is further divided into two *sub-layers* namely the Media Access Control (MAC), and the Logical Link Control (LLC).

  - **Media Access Control (MAC)**
    The MAC is peculiar to the particular access method employed on the LAN. The MAC itself performs many functions such as the reception of

data from the upper layers (LLC),[4] and the encapsulation of this into *frames* according to the requirements of the LAN access method employed. In addition, the MAC monitors the communications channel to determine when the channel is clear, and then passes the frame to the Physical Layer for transmission. Equally, in terms of reception, the MAC accepts incoming data frames from the Physical Layer. It then decapsulates the data and checks its integrity by using a simple CRC. Finally, in the case of Ethernet/802.3 LANs, the MAC is responsible for *collision detection*, and the recovery from these conditions.

- **Logical Link Control (LLC)**
  The LLC sub-layer itself is designed to provide a consistent level of service to the Network Layer, regardless of the MAC (i.e. LAN access method) in use. In actual fact, the Logical Link Control sub-layer is not present in *Ethernet* networks, but is used in all other LANs including IEEE 802.3[5] (ISO/IEC 8802-3) networks.

- **Network Layer**
  The Network Layer is beyond the scope of any LAN standard, but provides us with a means to communicate between logical *networks* (as opposed to LANs). It therefore includes facilities such as network *routing*, *addressing*, and in some cases, *flow control*.

- **Transport Layer**
  This layer provides the basic interface between the *Session Layer*, and the underlying network-dependent protocols. It is this layer that will typically provide for *connection-oriented* sessions, that demand the exchange of data in an orderly and reliable manner. This reliability, which is not generally available at the *Network Layer*, is normally implemented as a *Sequence Number/Acknowledgment* system. This then ensures that all data is received, and in an ordered manner.

- **Session Layer**
  The Session Layer provides a method by which two systems may organize and synchronize their dialogue, and therefore manage the exchange of data between themselves. The Session Layer itself is possibly the most complex of them all and optionally provides for both *Full*, and *Half Duplex* operation.

- **Presentation Layer**
  The Presentation Layer is concerned solely with the presentation of data while in transit. Systems in heterogeneous networks are liable to represent their data in a multitude of ways. Thus, where we wish to transfer data between disparate systems, we must choose a representation that is acceptable to *all* systems involved in the transfer. This layer is not concerned

---

[4] The LLC sub-layer is not used in Ethernet (as opposed to 802.3) environments. In this case, data is passed directly between the Ethernet Data Link Layer (MAC sub-layer), and the Network Layer.
[5] This distinction between Ethernet and IEEE 802.3 is significant, and will be discussed later.

with the eventual representation of data when it arrives at its destination, since the application should perform any eventual translation required before the data is stored. It is however the task of this Layer to negotiate, and use, a common representation for data while it is in transit.

- **Application Layer**
  Contrary to many beliefs, this layer does not represent the actual application, but instead is the *Application Protocol*. As such, the Application Layer provides the application itself with a *gateway* to the communications environment. Certainly, many *Application Protocols* do have applications of the same name, i.e., Telnet, FTP, etc., but this is not always the case. For example, mail applications would use the *Simple Mail Transfer Protocol* (SMTP), and the *Post Office Protocol* (POP), but these programs have names that tend to be far more exotic such as *Outlook*, or *Eudora*. Equally, web browsers use the *Hyper-Text Transfer Protocol* (HTTP), yet these often have names that are far more akin to the tasks that they perform, such as Microsoft's *Internet Explorer* for example.

1.3.2 IEEE Standards

There are many standards that exist within LAN technologies and Ethernet/802.3, and Token Ring/802.5 are but examples of just two such families. Figure 1-7 shows some of these standards families aligned to International standards that, while not necessarily 100% applicable to this particular discussion, do demonstrate the breadth of work that is taking place in LANs, and indeed MANs generally.

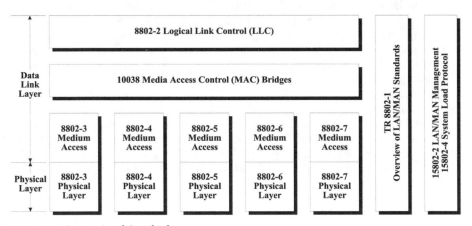

Figure 1-7: International Standards

At this point we should note that figure 1-7 shows only a sample of standards that have been adopted by the International Standards Organization (ISO). Because this relates to the ISO however, Ethernet (in broad terms) is referred to as 8802-3. In actual fact, Ethernet-type networks are sometimes referred to as being 802.3, networks and devices are described as being IEEE 802.3 compliant. This is because it was the IEEE that initially developed the standards, although IEEE and ISO/IEC standards do differ. As a result, it is worth outlining where these differences exist through a comparison of figures 1-7 and 1-8. The discussion that then follows, further describes some of the work undertaken by the various standards committees, and briefly introduces a broad cross-section of IEEE and ISO/IEC standards. When we view this list, it then becomes clear just how many different LAN/MAN types actually exist, and how many related standards there actually are.

Equally, development continues in the area of LANs and MANs, and it is the IEEE that has become the driving force. Hence, as new specifications are ratified by the IEEE, we find the ISO/IEC documents lagging significantly behind. In figure 1-8 we see the standards associated purely with the IEEE, and then briefly describe these and other IEEE standards, that are applicable to discussions on LAN Technologies.

- **802** Overview and Architecture - provides a general overview of all standards documents within the 802 family.

- **802.1** Provides for an entire subsection of documents related to management and bridging:

  - **802.1B** and **802.1k** LAN/MAN Management - also known as ISO/IEC 15802-2.

  - **802.1D** (MAC) Bridges - also known as ISO/IEC 10038 - Specifically, this standard defines how IEEE 802.x LANs may be interconnected and also provides for resilient links - chapter 15 describes *Bridging* in an Ethernet/802.3 environment.

  - **802.1E** System Load Protocol - also known as ISO/IEC 15802-4 - defines a set of services for the loading of systems on IEEE 802.x LANs.

- **802.2** Logical Link Control (LLC) - also known as ISO/IEC 8802-2 - used in conjunction with the Medium Access standards (802.3/802.5 etc.), this standard defines Data Link Layer services to the Network Layer.

- **802.3** CSMA/CD Access Method and Physical Layer Specifications - also known as ISO/IEC 8802-3 - this standard is discussed in detail in this volume together with that of IEEE 802.5 (ISO/IEC 8802-5), and ANSI X3T9.5 *FDDI*. The 802.3 standard has been through many changes and additions since it was first introduced and is possibly one of the most widely implemented network types. The 802.3 standards and revisions are discussed in greater detail in the chapters immediately following.

- **802.4** Token Passing Bus Access Method and Physical Layer Specifications - also known as ISO/IEC 8802-4 - This standard defines a method, over *bus topologies*, by which medium Access is granted through the use of a token.

- **802.5** Token Passing Ring Access Method and Physical Layer Specifications - also known as ISO/IEC 8802-5 - Defines a method, over *ring topologies*, by which medium Access is granted through the use of a token. This access method is discussed in detail in chapters 16 to 22 of this volume.

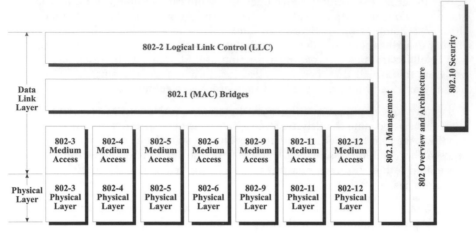

Figure 1-8: IEEE Standards

- **802.6**   Distributed-Queue, Dual-Bus Access Method and Physical Layer Specifications - also known as ISO/IEC 8802-6.

- **802.7**   IEEE Recommended Practice for Broadband Local Area Networks - This is a recommendation only and has not been adopted by the ISO. Hence, there is no ISO reference associated.

- **802.9**   Integrated Services (IS) LAN Interface at the Medium Access Control (MAC) and Physical (PHY) Layers - also known as ISO/IEC DIS 8802-9 - defines a unified access method that offers integrated services (IS) to the desktop for a variety of publicly and privately administered backbone networks (e.g., ANSI FDDI, IEEE 802.x, and ISDN). In addition, the interface at the MAC sublayer and the PHY Layer is specified.

- **802.10**   Interoperable LAN/MAN Security - As with 802.7, there is no ISO standard associated with this standard - defines a security protocol that can be used to protect IEEE 802 Local Area Networks (LANs) and Metropolitan Area Networks (MANs), through the use of an Open Systems Interconnection (OSI) Layer 2 security protocol. Security services of confidentiality and connectionless integrity can be provided. In conjunction with key management or system management, the security services of data origin authentication and access control may also be used.

- **802.11**   Wireless LAN Medium Access Control (MAC) Sublayer and Physical Layer Specifications - the Wireless LAN is an area where there is a great deal of work proceeding at this time. As yet though, this standard has not been adopted by the ISO.

- **802.12**   Demand Priority Access Method, Physical Layer and Repeater Specifications - Although not adopted by the ISO, 802.12 is applied to the 100VG-AnyLAN system. This is discussed in chapter 14.

Introduction

- **802.14** Standard Protocol for Cable-TV-Based Broadband Communication Networks - To provide for digital communication services over a branching bus system constructed from fiber and/or coaxial cable, as used in cable TV distribution networks. By specifying a MAC and PHY(s), the standard is architecturally consistent with 802-compatible LANs with distances of approximately 160 kilometers round trip accommodated.

1.4 Summary

Having examined a little of the history of networks generally, and LANs in particular, maybe we can now appreciate the need for these standards, so that interoperability can be assured. The ideas about LANs are not particularly new. They have been around for many years, and although they have possibly evolved faster than any other area of computing, much has been out of necessity rather than through any other desire. Historically, we moved away from the dinosaur of the mainframe, to cheaper, distributed processing, platforms. With this, came the need for interconnection, and the LAN was born. Standardization became the order of the day, since users were moving away from the one-stop shop approach that was engendered by mainframe vendors. Proprietary systems were out, and standards based solutions were called for.

The thirst for bandwidth came with the applications that were being distributed, and the sheer volumes of data that needed to be moved. Looking back, our humble 10Mbps Ethernet/802.3 LAN, or even our 4Mbps Token Ring was more than sufficient for the needs of the past. Today, faster processors mean that we can now handle graphical applications, and with that comes the requirement to move the data that these applications demand. Enter the world of high speed networking!

Section B

Ethernet/IEEE 802.3
(ISO/IEC 8802-3)

An Introduction to
Ethernet and
IEEE 802.3

In this section we will discuss what has become the single most significant technology in networking. Today, Ethernet-type ports account for well in excess of 70% of the total installed worldwide, and that number will continue to grow almost exponentially. The reason? Many would argue that it is simply because it is the *best* technology available. Some, that it is the single technology that is keeping pace with users demands. Others, that it is most cost effective in terms of installation.

That its the *best* technology is questionable, to say the least. In a similar vein, although it has undergone significant improvements in recent years, and although it is constantly being developed, that is not necessarily what has made it so popular. Cost effective it is, though, and that cannot be ignored when discussing popularity. The biggest driving force behind Ethernet however, has to be that the technology was made available to vendors at an early stage. While proprietary elements do exist, none provide extensions to the access protocol itself, and therefore interoperability between vendors is assured. Where such proprietary extensions do exist, these are generally related to cable lengths and connector types - the infrastructure, so to speak. Generally though, users can find good quality components available from all major manufacturers, and with that inherent competition, extremely competitive pricing.

So, is Ethernet the panacea for our network headaches and does it really provide a future-proofed infrastcture? The simple answer here is no - Ethernet, like the other technologies presented in this volume, has problems that vendors are striving to address. True, many of the problems are not the fault of the network itself but are associated with applications instead. Modern, graphical-based, applications consume huge amounts of bandwidth to transport data from server to client or vice versa. High power computers on the desktop are commonplace, and users today are becoming increasingly impatient. High speed links are therefore a prerequisite in order to give the illusion that all data is held locally rather than on large *super servers*. With that, comes the need for raw data movement, and that in turn leads to the need for higher and higher-speed links, something that Ethernet is at least addressing.

2.1   What Is Ethernet?

Put in the simplest of terms, Ethernet can be described as a *standard* that defines a communications system for carrying digital data between locally connected computer systems. In real terms, we have multiple computer systems that share a common communications channel (referred to as the *Ether*) which is a passive broadcast medium. It is a multi-access technology and there is no central control of stations. This means that multiple stations may access the communications channel (or transmission media), without the need for *polling* or ordered access. Where stations have data to transmit, and the communications channel is free - they simply transmit. At all other times, stations merely *listen* to see if the communications channel is carrying data destined for them. Finally, Ethernet is *frame-oriented*, meaning that data is split into variable-length *frames* for transmission. Provided that certain rules governing the minimum and maximum sizes of these frames are adhered to, stations may then transmit any amount of data within these bounds.

In actual fact, the real definition is that *Ethernet* specifies the arbitration method for media access known as *Carrier Sense Multiple Access with Collision Detection* or CSMA/CD, the allowable media types, and the devices used to connect stations to the media itself. Although this may all seem very simple, because of the variety of media supported and the multitude of devices that are used in modern networks, Ethernet networking has actually become quite complex.

2.2 A Brief History of Ethernet

It was actually only very recently (in relative terms) that Ethernet was born. It's place of birth was the Xerox Palo Alto Research Center (PARC) in California, its date of birth was 1972, and its father a gentleman by the name of Bob Metcalfe.

Ethernet was not the first network of its kind, and Metcalfe was not the first network designer. In the early 1970s Norman Abramson and his colleagues at the university of Hawaii created a ground-based radio network (called "Aloha") where users, without coordination, competed for the use of a shared *channel*. It took Metcalfe, however, to refine this idea and give us the LAN (figure 2-1), which is broadly based upon the same principles.

In 1972 Metcalfe and his colleagues had developed an experimental network to interconnect Xerox Alto computers. Broadly based on the Aloha system, Metcalfe devised an improved arbitration system that included being able to detect when *collisions* occurred. Ethernet was born, albeit slower and far less refined than what we have today.

The original experimental Ethernet had a transmission rate of just 2.94Mbps. Its medium was 75Ω coaxial cable (common at the time due to the explosion of cable television in the US that also used this cable), supported 256 stations, and the maximum end-to-end length was just 1km. Compared with today's high speeds, long distances, and plethora of media types, this all seems extremely limited. Nevertheless, this was a major step forward, and a firm foundation on which they could build. Xerox were indeed visionaries if we consider that at the time all this was going on, nobody had heard of high power *Personal Computers*, *Client-Server* architectures, or even *networks*. Those machines that did exist were the huge dinosaurs of the past that communicated with users through locally-attached *dumb* terminals, and communicated with each other using proprietary protocols over slow-speed serial links. Nonetheless, the network was alive and was about to transform the way in which we viewed computer communications.

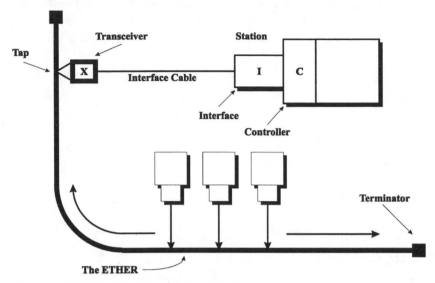

Figure 2-1: Bob Metcalfe's Original Ethernet Design

In 1976, Bob Metcalfe and David Boggs published a paper entitled "Ethernet Distributed Packet Switching for Local Computer Networks," and in 1977 a patent was granted to which Xerox owned all rights. Had this remained so, then it is highly likely that we would have seen far less development in this field, and Ethernet would certainly not be enjoying the market share that it does today. Instead, Xerox formed a consortium together with Digital Equipment Corporation (DEC) and Intel in 1979, to create an open standard that anyone could use. In 1980, the consortium announced a standard for a 10Mbps version of Ethernet - Ethernet version I. This standard, taking the first letters of each of the companies concerned, then became known simply as *DIX Ethernet*.

Two versions of Ethernet have been released to date. The first, Version 1, in September 1980 quickly became a *defacto* LAN standard. The year 1980 however is also significant in that it was at this time that the Institute of Electrical and Electronic Engineers (IEEE) adopted this technology as the starting point for their 802.3 standard. Ethernet version 2, released in November 1982, was based on a draft of the soon to be released 802.3 standard that was then formally adopted in June 1983. Table 2-1 summarizes the differences between the original *experimental* Ethernet and Ethernet version II. The terms used here, will be discussed in later chapters, but it does serve to show where similarities between the two systems exist.

From then, we could say, the rest is history. Ethernet/802.3 has gone from strength to strength. It was the first technology to be introduced by the IEEE as a standard from any of their "802" working groups, and development continues at a wild pace. Certainly it has its opponents, but none seems to have sufficient voice to stem the demand let alone the development of the technology. In fact, Ethernet/802.3 could be said to be a household name (if that were possible) and there is not a serious vendor today that could refuse to recognize its significance.

Table 2-1: Experimental Ethernet Comparison

Parameter	Experimental Ethernet	Ethernet Version II
Data Rate	2.94Mbps	10Mbps
Maximum end-to-end Length	1km	2.5km
Maximum Segment Length	1km	500m
Maximum Number of Stations	256	1024
Encoding Technique	Manchester	Manchester
Coaxial Cable Impedance	75W	50W
Coaxial Cable Signal Levels	0 to +3V	0 to -2V
Transceiver Cable Connections	15 and 25 pin "D" Type	15 pin "D" Type
Length of Preamble	1 bit	64 bits[1]
Length of CRC	16 bits	32 bits
Length of Address Fields	8 bits	48 bits

2.3 Ethernet Standards

We should not really talk of *Ethernet* "Standards" since these do not actually exist. A patent - yes; a *de facto* standard - yes; but not a standard in the truest sense of the word as it is internationally accepted. Instead, maybe it is better to talk in terms of Ethernet-*like* standards, the *CSMA/CD* access method, or those standards from the IEEE and ISO, namely IEEE 802.3 or ISO/IEC 8802-3.

In our *Brief History* of the previous section, we said that Ethernet was adopted very early by the Institute of Electrical and Electronic Engineers (IEEE). Although this is a *bona-fide* standards body, it required International recognition by the ISO before it could claim to be an International standard. Hence, when talking of *Ethernet-type* networks, we really have to talk in terms of Ethernet, IEEE 802.3 and/or ISO/IEC 8802-3.

We should also note that although many people will claim to be running Ethernet networks, they are in fact running 802.3 networks. The problem, and indeed the confusion, revolves around the fact that they are similar in operation, and both share common media types. If we were to avoid the real technicalities, we see the similarities and can forgive the chaos that this can create. To avoid further confusion relating to all of these standards here, we shall use the terminology Ethernet/802.3 to describe this network technology, except where we really do need to be specific and talk only of one or the other.

Finally, before leaving this section, we should spend a little time describing the scope of these standards. As we said in the previous chapter, only the *Physical* and *Data Link* layers of the OSI model are referenced. This is normal since all such

---

[1] Ethernet uses a Preamble of 64 bits (8 octets) that end with the 802.3 Start Frame Delimiter (SFD) pattern of 10101011.

standards relate only to this area of the OSI Model, and LAN technologies are transparent to upper layer protocols. As such, upper layer protocols may be encapsulated within any LAN frame structure and transported across the network. Hence, each of these standards, and indeed the remainder of this text, will concentrate on these lower two layers only. Layer 3 (Network Layer) protocols are specific to the protocol suite to which they relate, and are therefore beyond the scope of this discussion. For information on *upper* layer protocols, please refer to related materials on a per-protocol basis.

2.3.1 Ethernet/802.3 Standards

In reality, while we can talk of Ethernet and IEEE 802.3 standards there is really no single document that defines them. Even the IEEE 802.3 standard, due to the way in which it has been developed and evolved, comprises multiple documents that have come together to form one master volume. IEEE 802.3 therefore describes a whole family of specifications. Table 2-2 lists those that are applicable at the time of writing, but these will no doubt be supplemented within a short space of time, and the reader is therefore urged to regularly visit the IEEE web site (URL: http://www.ieee.org) in order to remain abreast of current developments in this area.

Table 2-2: IEEE 802.3 Development

IEEE Standard	*Date Approved*	*Description*
802.3-1985	IEEE - 23 June 1983 ANSI - 31 December 1984	Original 10Mbps Standard including MAC, PLS, AUI, 10Base5
802.3a-1988	IEEE - 15 November 1985 ANSI - 28 December 1987	10Mbps MAU for 10Base2 Clause 10 of 8802-3 Standard
802.3b-1985	IEEE - 19 September 1985 ANSI - 28 February 1986	10Mbps Broadband MAU - 10Broad36 Clause 11of 8802-3 Standard
802.3c-1985	IEEE - 12 December 1985 ANSI - 4 June 1986	10Mbps Baseband Repeater Clause 9.1-9.8 of 8802-3 Standard
802.3d-1987	IEEE - 10 December 1987 ANSI - 9 February 1989	10Mbps Fiber MAU for FOIRL Clause 9.9 of 8802-3 Standard
802.3e-1987	IEEE - 11 June 1987 ANSI - 15 December 1989	1Mbps MAU and Hub - 1Base5 Clause 12 of 8802-3 Standard
802.3F	Withdrawn	MAU & Baseband Medium Spec./Type 1BASE5 Multi-point Extension
802.3h-1990	IEEE - 28 September 1990 ANSI - 11 March 1991	10Mbps Layer Management for DTEs Clause 5 of 8802-3 Standard
802.3i-1990	IEEE - 28 September 1990 ANSI - 11 March 1991	10Mbps MAU for UTP 10Base-T Clauses 13 and 14 of 8802-3 Standard
802.3j-1993	IEEE - 15 September 1993 ANSI - 15 March 1994	10Mbps Fiber MAU 10Base-FP/FB/FL Clauses 15 to 18 of 8802-3 Standard
802.3k-1993	IEEE - 17 September 1992 ANSI - 8 March 1993	10Mbps Layer Management, Repeaters Clause 19 of Standard
802.3l-1992	IEEE - 17 September 1992 ANSI - 23 February 1993	10Mbps PICS Proforma 10Base-T MAU Clause 14.10 of 8802-3 Standard

Table 2-2: IEEE 802.3 Development (Continued)

IEEE Standard	Date Approved	Description
802.3m-1995	IEEE - 21 September 1995 ANSI - 8 August 1996	Maintenance 2
802.3n-1995	IEEE - 21 September 1995 ANSI - 8 April 1996	Maintenance 3
802.3p-1993	IEEE - 17 June 1993 ANSI - 4 January 1994	Management 10Mbps Integrated MAUs Clause 20 of 8802-3 Standard
802.3q-1993	IEEE - 17 June 1993 ANSI - 4 January 1994	10Mbps Layer Management GDMO Clause 5 of 8802-3 Standard
802.3r-1995	IEEE - 29 July 1996 ANSI - 6 January 1997	Protocol Implementation Conformance Statement (PICS) Proforma for 10Base5
802.3s-1995	IEEE - 21 September 1995 ANSI - 8 April 1996	Maintenance 4
802.3t-1995	IEEE - 14 June 1995 ANSI - 12 January 1996	120Ω Informative Annex to 10Base-T
802.3u-1995	IEEE - 14 June 1995 ANSI - 4 April 1996	100Mbps MAC, PLS, MAU & Repeaters 100Base-X Clauses 21 - 30 of Standard
802.3v-1995	IEEE - 12 December 1995 ANSI - 16 July 1996	150Ω Informative Annex to 10Base-T
802.3w	Withdrawn	Standard for Enhanced Media Access Control Algorithm
802.3x-1997	IEEE - 20 March 1997 ANSI - 5 September 1997	Specification for 802.3 Full Duplex Operation
802.3y-1997	IEEE - 20 March 1997 ANSI - 5 September 1997	Physical Layer Specification for 100 Mb/s System 100BASE-T2
P802.3z	IEEE - 25 June 1998	PHY, MAC, PMD, Repeater & Mgmt Parameters for 1,000 Mb/s Operation
P802.3aa	IEEE - 25 June 1998	Maintenance 5 (100 BASE-T) Corrects inaccuracies
P802.3ab	IEEE - 26 June 1999	PHY for 1000 Mb/s Operation over 4 pairs of Cat 5 Cable, Type 1000BASE-T
P802.3ac	IEEE - 16 September 1998	Frame extensions for VLAN tagging on 802.3 networks
P802.3ad	IEEE - 25 June 1998 New Standards Project	Aggregation of Multiple Link Segments

2.3.2 The Next Generations

So far, we have described a brief timeline of Ethernet/802.3 standards, from which clearly work will continue for a long time. Many of these improvements will be the provision of greater bandwidths with greater controls. But what other developments can we expect?

In truth, that is almost anybody's guess. It is however fair to say that work is currently centered on Gigabit technologies (and of course even higher speeds), and in particular enabling these technologies over copper media. By allowing the use of copper in this way, we of course preserve investment in existing cable plant, and reduce the cost of new installations. In addition, flow control (ensuring no data loss) and bandwidth reservation (for real time applications) are high on the agendas of many vendors. Also, and although this could be argued to be on the very fringes of Ethernet/IEEE 802.3 technology, vendors are now developing products that extend fiber installations. This results in large cost savings in the installation of fiber plant that, although it must be said is falling in price, still remains expensive compared to other media types. Removing many of the limitations imposed by this medium is therefore a very attractive proposition to many users.

Most significant are the lasers that are used. Advances in laser technology now provides the capability to run Gigabit speeds at distances in excess of 100km. It does not stop there, however. Other areas of development specifically aimed at fiber installations include *splitter/combiners* that enable 10Mbps, 100Mbps, and even Gigabit technologies to run over a single fiber strand instead of the traditional two strands (one for transmit and one for receive) thereby doubling the capacity of installed fiber plant. Finally, through the use of *Wave Division Multiplexing* (WDM), it is now also possible to run multiple, concurrent Gigabit links over a single fiber optic pair, thereby multiplying the capacities of the installation.

Much of this is very close to market, and indeed some vendors have already announced availability. Quite how these enhancements will affect the grip that Ethernet/IEEE 802.3 has on the market, however, will depend very much on the costs involved, and timescales required to gain complete acceptance. Certainly, major vendors will not wish to be last to offer such products, and this will only fuel the race to provide the products.

2.4 The Problems Associated with Ethernet

Many people talk of Ethernet/802.3 networks and give glowing reports as to performance and ease of implementation. The casual observer then, might be forgiven for believing that everything here is marvelous and that problems rarely exist. In actual fact, this is not the case, and networks of this kind can suffer from some extremely ugly problems. In defense of Ethernet/802.3 networks, however, we must make it clear that it is not really the technology that is always to blame. For instance, many Ethernet/802.3 networks often tend to evolve rather than follow any structured plan. These networks could therefore be said to be victims of their own success since Ethernet/802.3 is so easy to extend. At this point though, beware! Networks that evolve without structure tend to consume large quantities of financing as managers and users throw money at resolving the bottlenecks that they create. Even worse, these networks today are the time bombs that create the disasters of tomorrow. To illustrate this point, consider the problems that are associated with the following cable types.[2]

- **Coaxial Cable**
  Although rarely installed today, coaxial cable was the mainstay of original Ethernet/802.3 installations and much remains in use. 10Base5 (or *Thick*

---

[2] Physical media are discussed in detail in section G.

Ethernet) used coaxial cable known as RG8 and 10Base2 (or *Thin Ethernet*) used RG58 cable plant that *must* be terminated at each end. That means if a break occurred, the entire segment was down. In Ethernet/802.3 networks there is no *self healing* as there is with ring topologies, so total outage occurs.

Additionally, all too often the cable was merely extended when new parts of a building required connection. This led to out-of-specification cable lengths being installed, and therefore network errors that were extremely hard to locate.

Then of course we have the problems of station placement and reflected signals. Coaxial cable installations have a requirement whereby minimum station separation and cable bend radii must be maintained. Failure to adhere to these requirements results in signal reflections that can cause spurious errors on station transmissions, which again are difficult to place.

- **Twisted Pair Cables**
  The biggest problems here are poor cable installation, and poorly fitted connectors. Many installers were, traditionally, unaware that it is not sufficient to use simple *straight through* cables for 10BaseT/100BaseTx installations. Instead, pins 3 and 6 of the RJ45 connector *must* form a pair. Equally, installation of Category 5 cable is not adequate. All connectors, patch panels and patch leads must also conform in this regard if the installation is to successfully run at speeds in excess of 10Mbps.

- **Fiber Optic Cables**
  Fiber optic cable plant must be of the correct type if we are to successfully run data over it. Specifying distance is not enough; we must specify the *link budget* (or amount of loss) that we can tolerate. Equally, strange as it may seem, fiber cables can be too short. If this happens, then we saturate the fiber and signals will fail to pass without error.

Ethernet/802.3 networks are also non-deterministic. This means it is very difficult to predict performance based upon the number of users or stations attached. Hence, with poorly configured networks, we can end up throwing money at them to resolve perceived bottlenecks. Well, today the word is switching.[3] Need more bandwidth? Put in a switch! At least that seems to be the philosophy of many.

True, switches can assist in the battle for bandwidth, and yes, networks can run better where they are installed correctly. But let us consider the example of a company that purchases, say, a 20 port, 10Mbps/100Mbps switch to replace an existing repeater.[4] Let us assume that, at the time of installation, all of the devices that are connected are using 10Mbps interface cards; an improvement in throughput will almost certainly be seen, and a simple calculation tells us that the maximum bandwidth requirement of our switch will be 20 × 10Mbps or 200Mbps (based upon 20 users each using 10Mbps devices).

[3] Switching and Switched Ethernet/802.3 Networks are discussed in detail in chapter 15.
[4] Repeaters provide a shared, contention based network and are discussed in chapter 8.

An Introduction to Ethernet and IEEE 802.3

What if our aspiring network manager now realizes that each port can run at 100Mbps and can utilize *Full Duplex*[5] communications as well? If he now converts the interface cards of all attached stations to run in this mode (Full Duplex at 100Mbps), the maximum required bandwidth of the switch increases to 20 × 200Mbps or 4Gbps! If the switch cannot handle this, it starts to drop packets, and suddenly performance can be worse than when we started out!

So, the moral of the story is that planning is crucial and analysis of network needs is a requirement before changes are made. Determine where any changes will have maximum effect, and then analyze if they have actually achieved the required result. If the skills are not available in-house, consider hiring them in. Throwing good money after bad is certainly not the preferred method of creating better networks.

2.5   The Differences Between Ethernet and IEEE 802.3

Not least of all of the problems that we have with Ethernet and *Ethernet-like* networks is that Ethernet and IEEE 802.3 networks are definitely *not* the same. As we shall see later, differences do exist, and many might argue that back in 1982/83 a golden opportunity was missed when Ethernet version 2 and IEEE 802.3 diverged. Whether this is right or wrong is immaterial and today we must work with what we have. Co-existence is definitely not a problem. Each uses the same access protocol and arbitration techniqs. They both have identical minimum and maximum frame sizes, and use the same formula for calculating the frame check sequence. The problem is simply the interpretation of one field within the frame, and it is this that prevents Ethernet and IEEE 802.3 stations from communicating with one another. Thus, stations using Ethernet II cannot talk to those using 802.3, or vice versa.

So which is better - Ethernet or IEEE 802.3? The answer is that there is no real difference in terms of performance, or any other criteria that you wish to apply. No winners, and no losers. Each has its own following and will continue to do so. For example, Novell now favors the use of IEEE 802.3 with IEEE 802.2 (LLC) encapsulation,[6] as does Windows with its use of NetBIOS. Most TCP/IP[7] implementations on the other hand favor Ethernet II. To say that Ethernet was superior to IEEE 802.3 (or indeed that IEEE 802.3 was superior to Ethernet II) based on implementations would be foolish, and would certainly serve no practical purpose at all.

2.6   Summary

We have used this chapter to introduce the very basis upon which Ethernet/802.3 has been founded, its pedigree, and some of the many developments that are taking place in this fast-expanding area of networking. Perfect it is not - but then in our

---

[5] Full Duplex means simultaneous transmission and reception and is discussed in chapter 12.
[6] See section E for a complete discussion of IEEE 802.2 - Logical Link Control (LLC).
[7] A full discussion of TCP/IP and its associated application protocols is beyond the scope of this book. However refer to section F for a brief overview of the protocol suite and discussion of routing (Internetworking) in an IP environment.

imperfect world, what is? In command of the networking market - it would most certainly appear to be. With development driven by user demands for higher bandwidths, greater distances, and lower costs, Ethernet/802.3 technology is rising to the task possibly faster than any other single technology.

Fighting off the challenge for dominance by Token Ring, FDDI, and ATM in the LAN market place, this technology appears ideally placed; but do not be fooled. Ethernet/802.3, being *frame-based* cannot compete in multimedia applications that require real time data transfer. For this, *cell-based* technologies must be used, and that leaves only ATM as the technology of choice. Until such time as we have true bandwidth reservation and proper flow controls in place, this situation will certainly not change.

Through the next chapters we shall see just how Ethernet/802.3 works, the components and signaling techniques used, and of course its limitations. Taking a logical look at each layer in turn, we shall examine the options available and how the technology itself has evolved. In short, we will take it apart and examine each element individually.

Basic Overview

Ethernet and IEEE 802.3 (ISO/IEC8802-3) networks are termed *Local Area Networks* (LANs) since, by their conventional definition, they can span only relatively local geographic areas. Traditionally, LANs would span no more than say 10kms, and ran at speeds that did not exceed 100Mbps. Wide Area Networks (WANs) on the other hand, would potentially enjoy worldwide coverage but would be limited to speeds of only say 2Mbps. Today, our definitions are changing in line with advances in technology. The differentiation between LANs and WANs is fast becoming a gray area and the term "Metropolitan Area Network" (MAN) of the early 1990s is used far less today. For example, in this volume we see examples of technologies such as the Fiber Distributed Data Interface (FDDI) that broke the bounds of the more traditional view of a LAN, and introduced the *MAN* to our glossary of terms. Also, since the move is to now join these LANs by faster and faster WAN links, we are now actively burying the LAN/WAN distinction as we move to seamless LAN-to-LAN communications.

Faster, larger, FDDI networks were heralded as being a panacea that would cure the bandwidth ills imposed by the early Ethernet/802.3 and Token Ring technologies. Today, our humble Ethernet network can run at Gigabit speeds (1000Mbps) - ten times faster than FDDI, and at a fraction of the cost. Likewise, the 155Mbps Asynchronous Transfer Mode (ATM) network is complex and expensive, and therefore severely threatened by anything that is relatively simple, cost effective, and most importantly can run at Gigabit speeds. But do not let pure speed cloud the real issues of networking. True, speed is important to a network, but so too are the applications that must use it. Simple bulk transfers consume huge amounts of bandwidth but have little regard of timing. On the other hand, real-time applications may require only modest bandwidth allocation yet are time-critical. It is therefore these latter applications that will find it difficult to use the bandwidths available to Ethernet. As we can see then, the choice of technology is wide, and given the applications that must be supported we must decide which technology or indeed technologies to apply. Whatever choice(s) we make however, all networking technologies have individual fundamental requirements regarding supported hardware and media, and it is these that we will discuss here.

3.1   The Ethernet/802.3 Cable Plant

Ethernet/802.3 can run over several different cable types. Although originally developed using a common coaxial cable to which all computers were attached, developments, fueled by user demands, now enable this technology to use different cable types depending on local office requirements. In this section we shall examine some of the common cabling types used with this technology, in order to better understand the principles and practices involved with Ethernet/802.3 networks.

3.1.1 Coaxial Cable

Early Ethernet (and indeed 802.3) networks used coaxial cable as their medium. Although rarely installed in today's networks, much still exists and is perfectly adequate for many applications. Sometimes referred to as *Thick Ethernet* (or from the IEEE world, 10Base5), this uses RG8 (Belden 9880), 50Ω, cable which is either 10.28mm (0.405 inches) or 9.53mm (0.375 inches) in diameter. The cable generally has a yellow PVC or orange Teflon jacket, and must be terminated using a 50Ω resistive load at each end. Termination resistors are encased in "*N*" *Type* screw fit connectors, and the cable must be grounded at one point along its length.

This type of media is restricted to segment (cable) lengths of 500m (1641.67 ft), and the number of station attachments (or *Taps*) that may be made to each segment is 100. In addition, taps must be separated by at least 2.5m (8.21 ft); as an aid, the cable is marked with black bands 2.5m apart. This is not to say that stations may *only* be placed on these bands. Since the cable is normally placed in generally inaccessible locations such as floor or ceiling trays, it is easy to see where a station can be placed without revealing the entire cable run. Where greater cable length is required, or where station numbers need to be increased, repeaters, bridges, switches, or routers must be installed.

Also, installers try to minimize the number of joins and bends, since these can create signal *reflections* that can disrupt network traffic. Because 500m of this type of cable is virtually impossible to handle, it is recommended that segments are installed using what are known as *lambda* lengths of 23.4m (76.83 ft), or odd multiples thereof, and joints are made using in-line "N" Type barrel connectors. Since the velocity of propagation in this type of cable is 0.77c,[1] 23.4m broadly equates to a single wavelength at 10MHz given the formula:

$$\lambda = (\text{speed of light/Frequency in Hertz}) \times \text{Velocity of propagation}$$

or

$$\lambda = (300,000,000/10,000,000) \times 0.77 = 23.1\text{m}$$

Where there is no alternative but to bend the cable, it is recommended that a minimum bend radius of 203mm (8 inches) or preferably 254mm (10 inches) is used. In addition, it is recommended that to reduce the effects of Electromagnetic

---

[1] "c" is the symbol for the speed of light in a vacuum (300,000,000m/s).

Interference (EMI), the cable is not installed within 1m of fluorescent lighting, or parallel to power cables.

Finally, station attachment is always through a *Transceiver* or MAU[2] that is never integrated into the Network Interface Card (NIC) of the attached device. These relatively simple devices are coupled directly to the cable, and each allows the connection of one or more stations. Figure 3-1 shows a simple example of these configuration rules, which you will notice is almost identical to Bob Metcalfe's original diagram that we saw in figure 2-1.

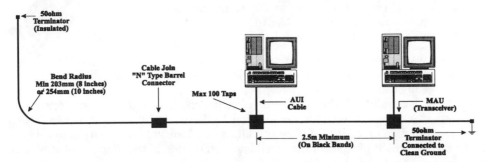

Figure 3-1: *Thick Ethernet* (10Base5) Installation

Cable joints are always made using screw fitting, "N" Type *Barrel* connections that simply join two male "N" Type plugs. Transceivers are then added using either *intrusive* "N" Type screw connections where the cable must be broken for installation, or alternatively by using what is known as a non-intrusive, *Vampire Tap* or *Bee-Sting Connector* that can be installed with the cable *live*. Figure 3-2 shows a sample of these connector types.

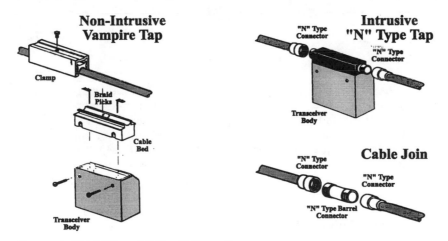

Figure 3-2: Thick Ethernet (10Base5) Connections

---

[2] MAUs or Transceivers are discussed in chapter 6.

Another type of coaxial media, again rarely installed today, is what is known as either *Thin Ethernet*, *Thin-wire Ethernet*, *Cheapernet*, or more correctly, 10Base2. This uses the thinner, less expensive RG58 cable which, due to its lower velocity of propagation (0.65c minimum) and higher attenuation, has a maximum segment length of 185m (607.42 ft), and a maximum station count of 30 stations per segment. Apart from this, the cable has a minimum bend radius of 50.8mm (2 inches), minimum station separation is 0.5m (19.7 inches), and connections are made using either solder-on or crimp-fit Bayonet Neill Concelman (or BNC) connectors as shown in figure 3-3.

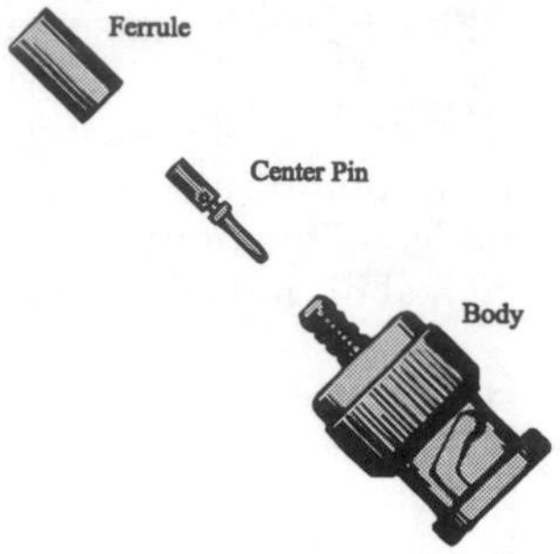

This was a popular choice for small LANs in the earlier days of Ethernet/802.3 since it was easy to install, and most importantly, cheap. Most specifically, and certainly one of the overriding factors, was that new stations could simply be daisy-chained from existing cables. Also, many station NICs incorporated an *on-board* MAU, which allowed stations to be directly connected to the media, which of course further reduced installation costs. Figure 3-4 shows an example of the rules concerning 10Base2 installations.

Figure 3-3: BNC Connector

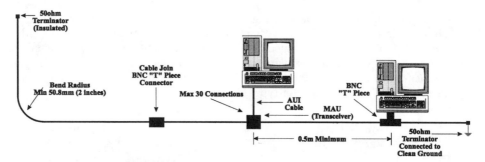

Figure 3-4:   10Base2 Installation and Configuration Rules

A final type of coaxial installation is that of 10Broad36,[3] although it is true to say that this is extremely rare and used only in very specialized installations. For this media type, a Broadband, 75Ω cable of up to 3.6km is used, which is similar to that found in Cable TV systems. The bandwidth available is then split into a number of channels using Frequency Division Multiplexing (FDM) techniques, and Ethernet/802.3 is run over each channel. The velocity of propagation over this media is 0.65c, and connections to the media are made via Ethernet modems that translate the signal to/from the desired frequency.

3.1.2   Twisted Pair Cable

Broadly speaking two types of Twisted Pair media exist within Ethernet/802.3 environments. These media types are Shielded and Unshielded Twisted Pair, and

---

[3] 10Broad36, is discussed in chapter 13.

Basic Overview

are always used in a point-to-point configuration, requiring the use of a hub for station interconnection as shown in figure 3-5. 10Base-T, as the early implementations using this medium were known, defined transmission over two pairs of Category[4] 3 (or higher grade) 100Ω copper twisted pair cable. Using Category 5 cable however also allows the medium to be used at 100Mbps speeds (100Base-Tx). In all cases, the standard connector type is the RJ45 connector (figure 3-6), and in order to achieve best performance, no more than 100m (328.33 ft) is supported.

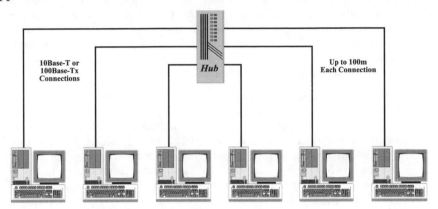

10Base-T or 100Base-Tx Connections

Hub

Up to 100m Each Connection

Figure 3-5: 10Base-T/100Base-Tx Installation

As you will notice, there are far fewer restrictions placed on this media type than with coaxial cables. For example, twisted-pair cables do not have the same constraints with regard to bend radii, although standard practices relating to installation in electrically noisy environments are still applicable. Also, some care must be taken if an installation originally specified for use at 10Mbps is to be used at higher data rates, since connectors, like cables, are categorized in a similar way. Thus, Category 5 cable terminated with Category 3 connectors renders the whole installation suitable only for use at 10Mbps. Connections, including all patch panel connections, must be of high quality if high data

Figure 3-6: The RJ45 Connector

rates are to be used, and the use of flat cable (known as *Silver Satins*) for patch leads must be avoided at all costs. In short, twisted pair cable must be used throughout, and all cables and connectors must be professionally installed.

3.1.3   Fiber Optic Cable

The final media type supported in Ethernet/802.3 installations is fiber optic cable. Although traditionally considered extremely expensive, installation costs have now

---

[4] The Category of cable is defined by the EIA/TIA-568 and ISO/IEC 11801 standards. Three categories are defined (3 though 5) which effectively grade the cable in terms of, among other things, Common Mode Rejection, Insertion Loss, and Near End Crosstalk (NEXT).

fallen dramatically thus opening the advantages of this versatile and secure media type to a far wider user base. Benefits include longer distances, the ability to install the media in otherwise electrically hostile environments, and of course security, since it does not radiate any signal. Equally - when discussing security - it is worth noting that since it is a point-to-point topology, additional connections cannot be made without breaking the cable. In addition, the new gigabit standards today support this important media type, providing fiber with a new lease of life.

Two major types of fiber exist, namely Multimode and Single Mode. Thus, whenever we talk of fiber, it is important that we know which variant we are referring to. Multimode fibers tend to have a larger diameter *core* than their Single mode counterparts, and are used for shorter distances. Typically, however, most installations use Multimode fibers since these tend to be less expensive, and distance is not normally a major issue in most LANs.

Fiber is categorized by the dimensions of the core and its cladding.[5] The standards recommend the use of 62.5/125 cable, meaning that the core is 62.5 microns[6] in diameter and the cladding is 125 microns. That said, the standards also recognize other fiber types such as 50/125 and 100/140. Connections are normally made through one of three standard connectors, known as the *Straight Tip* (ST) connector, the *Subscriber Connector* (SC) connector (both shown in figure 3-7), or through the less popular *Sub-Miniature Assembly* (SMA) connector. Also, being a point-to-point topology, like twisted pair technologies, only one device may be connected per fiber pair.

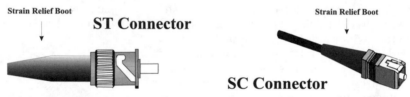

Figure 3-7: Fiber Optic Connectors

As you might imagine, the world of fiber is complex and no more so than when used in Ethernet/802.3 networks. The reason is that there are now several standards and specifications for fiber implementations in the Ethernet/802.3 world. Thus, we must take care in knowing to which specification our equipment adheres, and plan our network accordingly.

- **FOIRL**
  The Fiber Optic Inter-Repeater Link (FOIRL) specification was introduced with the original IEEE 802.3 standard. It allowed up to 1km of fiber, and was designed for 10Mbps operation. As its name suggests, its primary use was to link repeaters. Since then however, many vendors have introduced equipment that allowed the connection of DTEs, and this tended to fuel its popularity for secure or hostile environments.

---

[5] See section G for a discussion of fiber optic cable construction.
[6] One micron is one thousandth of a millimeter.

Basic Overview

- **10Base-FL**

  10Base-FL was the standardization of FOIRL for use in any 10Mbps implementation. It supports 2km of fiber, and is backwards compatible with its predecessor (FOIRL), however there the segment length is limited to 1km.

- **10Base-FP**

  This is a little-used variant of the 10Base-F standards, and is based on a totally passive star system to link repeaters and DTEs together over segments of up to 1km in length. 10Base-FP is totally stand-alone in that there is no compatibility with other 10Base-F devices. So, while these devices are ideal for environments that have no power or are electrically hostile, this standard has little application in most LANs today. As a direct result, few vendors manufacture compliant devices.

- **10Base-FB**

  10Base-FB is a standard specifically designed for backbone installations. Based upon *Synchronous* transmission between repeaters (there is no support for DTEs), this allows up to 2km per segment, with up to 30 repeaters. Popularity for this standard was never really high, since soon after its introduction, switching became commonplace in Ethernet/802.3 networks, and 100Base-Fx was ratified. This then started the demise of the 10Mbps backbone that continues today.

- **100Base-Fx**

  This 100Mbps Baseband system can be used for interconnection of both repeaters and DTEs. Unlike its 10Mbps counterparts, this is the only 100Mbps standard that exists over fiber and can be implemented in both shared and switched environments. For example, stations can be attached directly using this technology, and 100Mbps fiber can also be used as an uplink for hubs and switches that provide lower speed (say, 10Mbps) services.

- **1000Base-Lx and 1000Base-Sx**

  The 1000Base standards relate to Gigabit Ethernet, the latest in this long line of fiber-based technology. Two specifications exist, namely Lx and Sx, each defining a different maximum segment length. In the case of Sx (or short haul), segments may be up to 275m and in the case of Lx (or long haul), 550m for Multimode fiber and 5000m for Single Mode fiber. Once again, although primarily used as an uplink technology to link hubs and switches, DTEs can, if required, be attached directly if using devices that comply with this standard.

Although we have said that fiber prices have fallen dramatically over the years, users have invested huge sums in creating networks that are based on a *copper* infrastructure. As such, we find few installations based solely on fiber. Instead, typically we find 10Base-T/100Base-Tx mixed with 10Base-FL and/or 100Base-Fx or indeed 1000Base-Sx/Lx.

Figure 3-8 shows how a typical installation might look where these technologies are mixed.

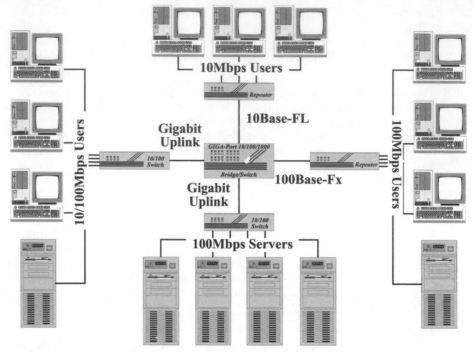

Figure 3-8: Typical Mixed Media Installation

3.1.4 A Summary of Ethernet/802.3 Media

As we have seen, Ethernet/802.3 networks can (and do) use a wide variety of network media. Table 3-1 summarizes and compares the characteristics of each.

Table 3-1: Ethernet/802.3 Media Types

| | | Coaxial Cable | | UTP | Fiber |
	10Base5	10Base2	10Broad36	10/100	To 1000
Min Vel. of Prop.	0.77c	0.65c	0.65c	0.59c	0.62c
Impedance	50Ω	50Ω	75Ω	100Ω	-
Max Seg. Length	500m	185m	3600m	100m	5km max.
Stations per Seg.	100	30	-	2	2

3.2 Mixing Media and Interconnection

From our discussions above, it is clear that networks of any size or complexity normally are comprised of a number of different media types. Obviously it is physically impossible to join certain of these media together without some sort of active connection device, but what exactly can we use? For example, we cannot directly connect a fiber cable to a piece of twisted pair, nor can we connect a device that runs at 1000Mbps to one that runs at 10Mbps. So what devices are available, and in the broadest of terms, what do they do?

3.2.1   Repeaters

Sometimes referred to as *Hubs*, these are possibly the simplest of all devices. They allow the interconnection of devices over different media types but use only a single, fixed, speed. In operation, any data that arrives at one port is *repeated* to all other ports simultaneously, and exactly as it arrived. This then means that the media are being *shared*, and that these devices do nothing to improve network performance. These devices are discussed in detail in chapter 8.

3.2.2   Bridges/Switches

Both of these units perform a broadly similar function. Both will receive a data frame on one port, and then forward that frame to only those ports that need it. So the difference between Bridges and Switches? Switches are faster and operate at what is termed *wire speed* (or in other words - with no delay). Like repeaters, Bridge and Switch ports can be of any type, thereby allowing media to be mixed. In addition, these devices have a degree of buffering internally, and are therefore able to perform speed translation (that is 10/100/1000Mbps). Finally, due to their *selective forwarding* capabilities, when they are correctly placed within the network these devices can be used to improve overall network throughput. Bridges and Switches are discussed in chapter 15.

3.2.3   Routers

Routers operate at the Network Layer (layer 3) of the OSI model, and are therefore protocol-dependent devices. Nonetheless, these devices, like bridges and switches, selectively forward data to only those destinations that should receive it, although port densities are normally very much reduced compared with their bridge/switch counterparts. A full discussion on routers is beyond the scope of this volume although routing (Internetworking) is introduced in section F.

3.2.4   Media Converters

Media converters, as developed by several vendors, are totally non-standard devices. Generally, these units take, say, UTP and convert it to fiber or vice versa. The result however is a compromise, since either the fiber or the UTP (or of course both) segment lengths can be greatly reduced.

3.3   Ethernet/802.3 Topology

The original Ethernet/802.3 specification called for a Bus topology where each co-operating computer was attached to a common coaxial cable, the *"Ether."* As we have seen from the previous section though, more modern applications allow point-to-point operation over simple twisted-pair cables or fiber optics. So, what is the *real* topology of Ethernet/802.3 networks? For example, are these networks simple buses, stars, or trees? How do these topologies relate to the technologies that we have already discussed, and how do they relate to each other?

3.3.1 Bus Topology

The Bus topology comes from the earliest manifestation of Ethernet, is based on coaxial cable, and as can be seen from figure 3-9, the topology is undeniably that of a bus. Operation is simple, and due to the common transmission path all stations receive all transmissions regardless of the intended recipient(s). Stations at which the transmissions are not directed then merely discard the data as irrelevant. As a result, the medium is *shared* by all stations. Of potentially more concern however, is the fact that there can be no privacy with this topology, the network is open to eavesdropping, and potentially malicious attack.

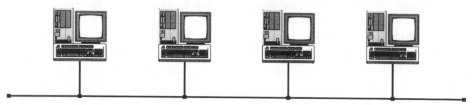

Figure 3-9: Bus Topology Network

3.3.2 Star Topology

This form of Ethernet/802.3 is possibly the most commonplace today, with companies tending to move towards *Standards-based* cabling systems that accommodate today's needs with ease of reconfiguration, and additionally provide us with a means of adapting to tomorrow's technologies. With this type of topology we must make a distinction between the physical and logical topologies, but to do this we must first understand the interconnection of devices. Figure 3-10 shows a typical Ethernet/802.3 configuration, using unshielded twisted pair cable. In this diagram, a single key element, the *Hub*, is crucial to the topology, since it is through this that communication is possible.

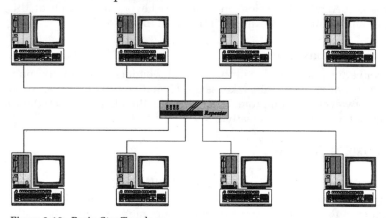

Figure 3-10: Basic *Star* Topology

Physically, the topology of our network now forms a Star with the vertices connected back to the Hub. However, Ethernet/802.3 networks were originally designed to work with *shared* media, forming what are called *Collision Domains*.

Basic Overview

Hence, the basic technology remains broadcast-based, and therefore the transmissions of any station will be received by all others. In actual fact our Hub is a simple repeater, faithfully reproducing any data received on one port at each of the others. Although we have a physical star topology then, we can say that the *logical topology* remains that of a Bus.

Before leaving this topology type, it is important that we mention the migration path that many networks tend to be taking. Today, many networks are moving away from shared media and changing to newer *switched* Ethernet/802.3 technologies. In this case, the hub at the center is now replaced with a switch, thereby subtly changing the description we have just given above. Switches (and indeed bridges) are used to link collision domains, and therefore split the network into a number of *logical* shared-media *bus topology* LANs. So, replacing our hub in figure 3-10 with a switch will result in eight *logical* bus topology LANs, all interconnected. Communications paths are enhanced, the physical topology remains constant, and the logical topology is expanded to become multiple shared-media networks, each with only one station attached. The overriding point though, is that the basic principle of operation of Ethernet/802.3 networks has not changed since its first inception - it is, and always will be, a *Bus Topology* (at least logically).

3.3.3 Tree Topology

It is true to say that this topology is little seen today, although no discussion of Ethernet/802.3 can be considered complete without its mention. The little used specification defining this topology is known simply as 10Broad36, which as its name suggests, is Broadband-based and supports segment lengths of 3.6km. Being broadband, networks of this type can carry multiple Ethernet/802.3 channels within pre-defined frequency bands. Figure 3-11 shows an example of this topology type that is then discussed in detail in chapter 13.

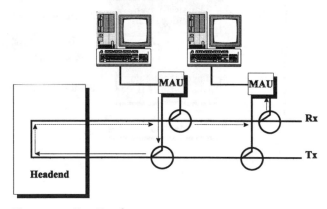

Figure 3-11: Tree Topology

3.4 Basic Ethernet/802.3 Requirements

The basic requirements for Ethernet/802.3 networks are shown in figure 3-12. Here we see the relationship between the OSI Reference Model, those layers that relate to the Ethernet/802.3 standard, and how these apply to the physical hardware and software of the connected device.

Typically, the Network Interface Card (NIC) implements the Media Access Control (MAC) and Physical Layer Signaling (PLS) sublayers. The Attachment Unit Interface (AUI) is then used to connect the Station (Host) to the Medium Attachment Unit (MAU) by means of a cable commonly known as the Attachment Unit Interface cable, or simply as the *AUI* or *Drop* Cable. The connection of this cable is then through a 15 pin "D" Type connector, normally fitted with a slide lock to prevent the cable from becoming disconnected. Certainly this was true of many older implementations, although today it is unusual to see stations connected in this way. In the earlier days of 10Base5 coaxial installations, stations were connected to the cable (the *Ether*) through a Transceiver (the more common name for the MAU). Today, the functionality supplied by this device is incorporated on many Interface cards, thereby relieving the need for the AUI cable and MAU. Many interface cards however still retain an AUI or "DIX[7] Ethernet" connector that allows connection to the media of your choice. Thus, a NIC that has both 10BaseT (RJ45) and AUI connectors can still be connected via 10BaseFL provided that the correct MAU (transceiver) is used.

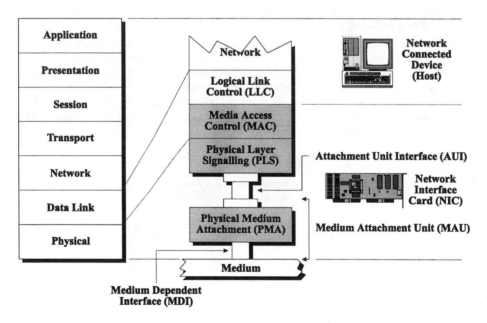

Figure 3-12: Ethernet/802.3 System Requirements

Whether the NIC supports the MAU functionality or not, the Medium Dependent Interface (MDI) differs depending upon the type of media used for connection to the network. Standard connector types that are used on both NICs and MAUs were

---

[7] DIX is the common name given to the amalgamation of Digital, Intel, and Xerox - the original developers of the Ethernet standard.

discussed in section 3.1 together with the media types that they represent. These connectors and their specific requirements are then further examined in the chapters that follow.

The Logical Link Control[8] (LLC) and all other, *higher*, layers are typically implemented as part of the station software, and will therefore vary dramatically from implementation to implementation. While it is important to consider which software package(s) will be required to run on selected cards, it is true to say that for the purposes of discussing the Ethernet/802.3 standard these can generally be ignored. When selecting Network Interface Cards (NICs) for small (PC) systems, they will normally be supplied with the driver software for the relevant operating system. Those that work with MS-DOS normally provide a Data Link Library (DLL) driver and/or generic drivers that adhere to the Network Driver Interface Specification (NDIS) from Microsoft, or Novell's Open Datalink Interface (ODI). Conversely, those NICs that are designed to operate with larger systems may not be supplied with any additional software since the operating system has built-in support for network cards. The UNIX operating system, for example, was the original platform for TCP/IP. As such, these systems offer networking as part of the kernel installation process, although it has to be said that the number of vendors manufacturing NICs is more limited than for PCs.

Finally, before leaving this section, it is important to note that so far we have made little distinction between Ethernet and 802.3 type networks. In talking of the LLC however, one distinction has to be drawn, and that is that Ethernet does not use the LLC at all. Instead, higher layer protocol identification is achieved directly through the MAC header rather than through IEEE 802.2/ISO 8802-2 information. This difference will be discussed in more detail in chapter 4.

3.5   Summary

Throughout this chapter we have concentrated on the Physical layer characteristics of Ethernet/802.3 networks and how stations communicate at the most basic of levels. This is not the last time that we shall discuss media. This important topic is discussed in further detail within relevant chapters, along with signaling. 10Base-F, since it has so many specifications is also discussed further in chapter 7. In addition, further information relating purely to media characteristics can be found in section G.

Ethernet/802.3 networks are simple to implement and use readily available, inexpensive components. In part, this is one of the reasons why we see many of the problems that we do, and why we must take extra care when extending the network. Ease of installation has little regard for configuration guidelines, and is certainly no excuse to cut corners. On a more positive note, a well-installed network using components from reputable vendors will provide good service, and present few problems during its lifetime.

Finally, Ethernet and 802.3 are not the same, although this is a common misconception among many of the millions of users who have implemented this

---

[8] See section E for a complete discussion of the Logical Link Control layer.

type of network.   True, both technologies can co-exist, and we shall see further evidence of this in the coming chapters.   Sharing media and other physical layer attributes however does not constitute absolute interoperability as some would have you believe.

Media Access Control

In this chapter we shall discuss the services provided by the MAC layer, the actual MAC frame format, and exactly how the medium is accessed. When we talk of the services provided by the MAC layer however, we must define to whom these services apply. When talking of an IEEE 802.3 environment, then these services are provided to the Logical Link Control (LLC) layer. In Ethernet however, the LLC is not used and therefore our services are provided directly to the Network layer instead. In any event, the MAC layer provides a set of clearly defined services to the layer above, and it is these that we shall examine here.

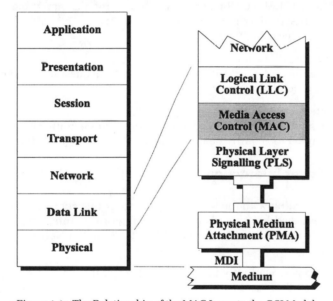

Figure 4-1: The Relationship of the MAC Layer to the OSI Model

In the most general of terms, the standards define the MAC layer as being a medium-independent facility built upon the medium-dependent Physical Layer. More specifically however, we can break this functionality down and say that this layer provides two major functions namely data encapsulation, and media access management. While these may appear simple when compared to technologies such as Token Ring and FDDI, they are relatively complex in their own right. This complexity is born of the fact that Ethernet/802.3 networks place greater constraints upon the actual allowable payload size, and access to the medium is not controlled by any *ordering* mechanism.

- **Data Encapsulation/Decapsulation**
  Our MAC layer is responsible for the encapsulation of data at transmission, and subsequent decapsulation by receiving stations. Furthermore, we can define those specific functions of encapsulation/decapsulation as follows:

  - Data Framing
    The provision of Frame Boundary delimitation and synchronization information.

  - Addressing
    The provision of such information so as to determine the identities of the frame's source and potential destination(s).

  - Error Detection
    The ability to detect, with reasonable accuracy, errors that have occurred as a result of transmission.

- **Medium Access Management**
  Since Ethernet/IEEE 802.3 networks are based upon a shared medium that is contention based, it is important that our MAC layer is able to access the medium with regard to the following:

  - Medium Allocation
    The ability of the MAC layer to defer transmission in favor of other stations (collision avoidance).

  - Contention Resolution
    The ability to recover from situations where multiple stations have attempted to acquire the medium simultaneously (collision handling).

4.1   MAC/Upper Layer Interaction

In essence, when dealing with the MAC layer, we are primarily interested in just the two functions described below. Also, when talking of this interaction with Upper Layers, we refer to the LLC in the case of IEEE 802.3, or the Network Layer in the case of Ethernet.

As figure 4-2 shows, we firstly have a *Data_Request* that the upper layer uses to signal the MAC that there is data to be transmitted to one or more (in the case of a broadcast[1] or multicast) network station(s). Unlike some other access methods however, the MAC used by Ethernet/IEEE 802.3 provides only a single *Quality of Service* (QOS), regardless of that requested by the upper layer.

---

[1] Broadcasts and Multicasts allow a single source station to simultaneously transmit data to multiple recipients. These Broadcast and Multicast addresses are discussed in section 4.2.1.

Media Access Control

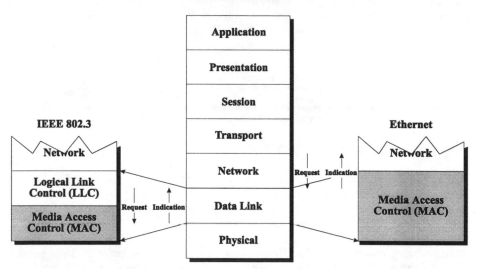

Figure 4-2: MAC/Upper Layer Interaction

Secondly, there is the *Data_Indication*, that the MAC uses to signal to the upper layer that data is present and needs to be passed. This data will have arrived from another network host, but will only be passed up (and will therefore only generate an Indication) if the following criteria are met:

- It was validly formed in that it comprises the correct number of fields, each of which is correctly formatted.

- The frame was received without error, that is the frame has no errors and the Frame Check Sequence[2] field re-computes correctly.

- It is addressed to the local MAC address or the broadcast address. Alternatively, the frame may be addressed to a multicast (group) address, in which case it will be passed up to the upper layer provided that the station is a member of that group.

4.2   MAC Frame Structure

The MAC layer frame structure of both Ethernet and IEEE 802.3 comprises eight fields, each of which are of fixed length, except for the actual data Payload. Frames of this type have pre-defined minimum and maximum lengths[3] that relate to the total number of octets between the start of the Destination Address (DA) and the end of the Frame Check Sequence (FCS), inclusive. The actual frame format is shown in figure 4-3 and is transmitted from left-to-right, with each field (except the Frame Check Sequence) transmitted *Least Significant Bit* (LSB) first.   This

---

[2] The Frame Check Sequence (FCS) is discussed in section 4.2.5.
[3] The need for minimum size frames is discussed in section 4.5.

transmission of the Least Significant Bit first (or *canonical* form as it is known) is peculiar to Ethernet/802.3 technologies and, as we shall see in other sections, is opposite to the transmission order for Token Ring and FDDI.

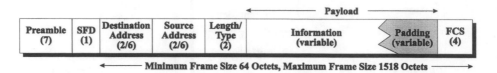

Figure 4-3:   MAC Frame Structure for Ethernet/IEEE 802.3 Frames

The *Preamble* field is 7 octets in length and comprises a bit pattern of alternating ones and zeroes (i.e., **10101010 10101010 1010......** etc.). The purpose of this field is to ensure that, on data reception, the Physical Layer Signaling (PLS) circuits become synchronized with the incoming data stream. Failure to supply sufficient octets in this field may result in misread data, caused by the transmitting and receiving stations being out-of-sync. The single octet *Start Frame Delimiter* (SFD) is used to indicate the actual start of the frame and hence the beginning of valid data. The pattern of this field is similar to the Preamble, with the exception that this field ends with two consecutive bits set to 1 (i.e., **10101011**$_2$).

4.2.1   Destination Address

The *Destination Address* field contains the address of the station(s) to which the frame is directed, and is transmitted Least Significant Bit (LSB) first.[4] This field can be of either 2 or 6 octets (16 or 48 bits) in length, although it is true to say that very few implementations are now found using the two octet addressing scheme. Where this smaller scheme is used however, it is a requirement that the Source and Destination address size is the same for *all* stations on the LAN. This field is then of the form shown in figure 4-4.

In both forms, the Least Significant Bit is referred to as the *Individual or Group Address* (I/G) bit. When a Destination Address has this bit set (i.e., equals 1), it indicates that the frame is potentially addressed to multiple destination stations (a group of none, one, or more). When the bit is set to zero, it indicates that the frame is destined for a single recipient. Addresses formed in this way are then designated as follows:

- **Unicast Addresses**
  Here, the I/G bit is set to zero, indicating that the frame is destined for a single station. At first, this may seem at variance to the fundamental premise on which Ethernet/IEEE 802.3 is built, since this is a broadcast technology - all stations connected to the local LAN segment receive all traffic. In actual fact, this type of address is used to inform *all* receiving MACs that we are addressing only one station. It is the MAC layer that then determines,

[4] Although this field is always transmitted Least Significant Bit first, when writing it is normal to represent this field Most Significant Bit first. This can lead to considerable confusion.

through examination of the Destination Address field of the incoming frame, whether the data is directed at it, and therefore whether the data should be passed up.

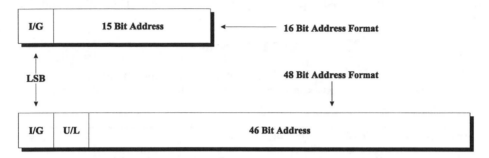

Figure 4-4:   Ethernet/IEEE 802.3 Address Formats

- **Multicast Addresses**
  With these addresses, the I/G bit is set to indicate that the frame is intended for all members of a specific *Multicast Group*. For example, the address 01-80-C2-00-00-00 (expressed in hexadecimal and Most Significant Bit first) is used by all IEEE 802.1D[5] (Spanning Tree) compliant bridges, in order for them to determine where loops exist and to identify least desirable paths. In this way, they are able to block these paths and therefore form a loop-free topology. Similarly, any station that receives a multicast frame but is not part of the relevant group (as indicated by the Destination Address field) will discard the frame as irrelevant, without further processing.

  There is no requirement that stations must be capable of generating multicasts, however it is a requirement that these addresses are recognized and that appropriate actions are taken.

- **The Broadcast Address**
  The Broadcast Address is a special type of Group Address used where a frame is directed to *all* stations connected to the LAN. In this instance, the address used is FF-FF-FF-FF-FF-FF$_{16}$ (all bits set to 1). While stations do not need to be able to generate broadcast frames (and therefore do not need to form frames with the Broadcast Address as the destination), it is a requirement that all stations must be able to recognize frames sent to this address and act on them accordingly.

For the 48 bit addressing scheme, the second bit is referred to as the *Universal or Local* (U/L) address bit. This bit is used to indicate whether the address is *globally* (Universally) administered and, hence, provides a globally unique address, or is *locally* administered and is therefore unique only within the specific LAN. While it could be argued that locally administered addresses have certain advantages from the point of view of inventory control, within an Ethernet/IEEE 802.3 environment

---

[5] The IEEE 802.1D, Spanning Tree Protocol is discussed in detail in chapter 15.

it is rare to find *Locally Administered* addressing of any type.[6] Instead, addresses usually follow the Universally Administered scheme, whereby the address space is divided into two equal parts, namely the *Organizationally Unique Identifier* (OUI) and a unique identifier assigned at the time of manufacture. The address then has the form:

XX-YY-ZZ-ab-cd-ef

Where XX-YY-ZZ is the OUI, and ab-cd-ef is the unique identifier assigned at manufacture. Table 4-1 lists some common vendor IDs, a full list of which can be found in Appendix A.

Table 4-1: Ethernet/IEEE 802.3 Vendor Ids

OUI (in Hex)	Vendor	OUI (in Hex)	Vendor
00-00-0C	Cisco Systems	02-60-8C	3Com
00-00-1D	Cabletron Systems	08-00-20	Sun Microsystems
00-00-A2	Bay (formerly Wellfleet)	08-00-69	Silicon Graphics
00-00-C0	Western Digital	08-00-87	Xyplex Networks

OUIs are never assigned with either of the two least significant bits set in the first octet. This then allows proprietary multicast addresses to be formed where required, and additionally implies a global address administration. Hence, the range for octet XX must always be in the range 00_{16} to FC_{16} (expressed most significant bit first). In the case of 16 bit addressing, there is no Universal or Locally Administered bit. Thus, all stations must adhere to the same scheme.

As the name suggests, the allocation of Organizationally Unique Identifiers is controlled by a central body, in this case the IEEE. Applications for OUIs should be addressed to: The Registration Authority, IEEE Standards Department, P.O. Box 1331, 445 Hoes Lane, Piscataway, NJ 08855-1331, USA.

4.2.2   Source Address

This field is used to identify the station responsible for the transmission of the frame, and therefore the address of the station to which replies should be directed (if required). As with the Destination Address field, this field may be either 2 or 6 octets in length, subject to the same constraint that *all* stations on the LAN must conform to the same addressing scheme. In addition, since it would be illogical to assume that a single frame could emanate from multiple source stations, the Individual or Group address bit is always set to zero. Hence, the Source Address field could be said to always contain a Unicast Address.

4.2.3   Length/Type

This two-octet field is interpreted differently, depending upon whether the frame is an IEEE 802.3 frame, or Ethernet II. In the case of the IEEE 802.3 frame, this field is

---

[6] This is in direct contrast to IBM Token Ring environments where Local Address administration is commonplace. See section C (Token Ring/IEEE 802.5) for further information.

used to indicate the length of the Information field. Hence, since the maximum payload for this LAN technology is 1500_{10} octets, the value of this field will be between 0000_{16} and $05DC_{16}$. In the case of Ethernet II frames, the field is referred to as the EtherType, and is used to indicate the Type (or protocol) of the Information. Sample EtherTypes are shown in table 4-2, and a full listing can be found in appendix B.

Table 4-2: EtherType Codes

EtherType	Protocol	EtherType	Protocol
0600	Xerox NS IDP	8035	Reverse ARP
0800	Internet Protocol (IP)	809B	AppleTalk
0806	ARP	8137	Novell IPX
6004	DEC Local Area Transport	8138	Novell IPX

You will notice from the table that the values of EtherType start from 0600_{16}. This is no accident. The interpretation of this field is the *only* difference between the two frame formats (Ethernet II and IEEE 802.3). Thus, it follows that in order for the two architectures to co-exist on the same LAN at the same time, there must be no overlap in the values assigned here. Hence, with just a handful of proprietary exceptions, the largest possible 802.3 frame size produces a *Length* field of $05DC_{16}$ that is equal to 1500_{10}, and is smaller than the smallest *legal* Ethernet Protocol Identifier (0600_{16}). It is possible for stations using either access protocol to exist on the same LAN, although Ethernet II stations will be unable to communicate with IEEE 802.3 stations or vice versa.

From the discussion above, it is clear that a prime opportunity to merge the two standards was sadly missed. So, given that 802.3 is an Internationally agreed standard, why did the architects of the Ethernet system feel that is was so important that we know the protocol being carried in the frame? Obviously it was not felt important in IEEE 802.3, so why the difference? The answer of course lies in the fact that both systems require protocol identification, and it is just that each uses a different method through which this is actually achieved. To explain this more fully though, we need to understand that many hosts run multiple protocols, and therefore that they need to be able to distinguish between them.

For example, if we consider figure 4-5, we may have a device (such as a PC) that has the capability to run TCP/IP, NetBIOS/NetBEUI, and Novell NetWare. When a frame arrives at the PC, we will then need to determine its protocol type so that we can pass the information that it is carrying to the relevant upper layer for processing. TCP/IP commonly runs over Ethernet II, so we can determine the protocol from the EtherType field. NetBIOS/NetBEUI runs over IEEE 802.3 which of course has no identifier, so now we have a problem. Most commonly, we find that those protocols using 802.3 actually use the 802.3 MAC, followed by the 802.2 Logical Link Control[7] (LLC) which has an in-built method for protocol identification. Indeed, returning to TCP/IP, we find that this can also run over this hybrid 802.3/802.2 method as well. Novell NetWare can run over a multitude of

---

[7]   IEEE 802.2 LLC is described in detail in section E.

technologies such as 802.3/802.2 as previously described, 802.3/802.2/SNAP[8] (which is a derivation of 802.3/802.2), Ethernet II, or alternatively what is commonly called *Raw 802.3*. In Raw 802.3, the Novell *Internetwork Packet eXchange* (IPX) protocol directly follows the *Length* field of the 802.3 frame. Thus, although we know the length of the information, we have no Protocol ID to identify it as IPX. In this case we *guess* the protocol, since the first field of the IPX header is the unused Checksum field which is always set to $FFFF_{16}$. Although this last method does not have the capability to be totally foolproof, it works extremely well and is the method adopted by all vendors today.

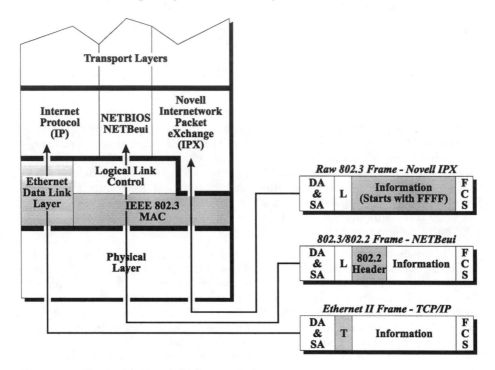

Figure 4-5:   The Need for Protocol Determination

4.2.4   Information and Padding

The *Information* field is transmitted Least Significant Bit (LSB) first. This field contains the actual data being transported, and since there are no restrictions as such, can contain any data pattern. The actual length of the data must not exceed 1500 octets, and in the case of the 802.3 frame, will be indicated by the Length field. In the case of Ethernet frames there is no length indication, so the size of this field must then be determined by other means at the higher layers.

In order that the *Carrier Sense, Multiple Access with Collision Detection* (CSMA/CD) system used in these networks operates correctly, there is a

---

[8]   The Sub Network Access Protocol (SNAP) is described in detail along with the Logical Link Control (LLC) in section E.

requirement that all frames must be a minimum of 64 octets in length.[9] When talking of the length of a frame, we calculate this as being the number of octets from the start of the Destination Address to the end of the Frame Check Sequence fields - in short, all fields with the exception of the Preamble and Start Frame Delimiter. Since most fields are of a fixed length, we have an overhead of some 18 octets (assuming 6 octet addressing), therefore requiring a minimum Information field of 46 octets. Where we wish to transport less data than this, a *Pad* field is added to make the Information field up to our 46 octet minimum. The actual content of the padding is undefined, but would possibly be made up of null octets (00_{16}), or whatever remained in the buffer from a previous operation.

4.2.5 Frame Check Sequence

The *Frame Check Sequence* (FCS) field is used by receiving stations to ensure that the frame has been received intact. The 32 bit (4 octet) field is actually a Cyclic Redundancy Check (CRC), computed over the entire frame, but excluding the *Preamble*, *Start Frame Delimiter*, and *Frame Check Sequence*, as shown in figure 4-6. This value is then calculated and encoded using the following generating polynomial:

$$G(x)=x^{32}+x^{26}+x^{23}+x^{22}+x^{16}+x^{12}+x^{11}+x^{10}+x^{8}+x^{7}+x^{5}+x^{4}+x^{2}+x+1$$

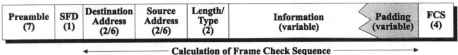

Figure 4-6:   Calculation of FCS

Mathematically, this is then calculated using the following procedure:

- The first 32 bits of the frame are complemented.

- The *n* bits of the frame are then considered to be the coefficients of a polynomial M(x) of degree n-1. (The first bit of the Destination Address field corresponds to the $x^{(n-1)}$ term and the last bit of the Information/Pad field corresponds to the x^0 term.)

- M(x) is multiplied by x^{32} and divided by G(x), producing a remainder R(x) of degree <31.

- The coefficients of R(x) are then considered to be a 32 bit sequence.

- The bit sequence is complemented, and the result is the CRC which is placed in the Frame Check Sequence field such that the x^{31} term is the left most bit of the first octet, and the x^0 term is the right most bit of the last octet.

Stations transmitting frames calculate the Frame Check Sequence in this way, and place the CRC value calculated in the FCS field of the frame. This field is then

---

[9] For a complete discussion of the CSMA/CD access method see Section 4.4.

transmitted *Most Significant Bit* (MSB) first. On reception, stations receiving the frame perform a similar calculation as the frame arrives, and then compare the newly computed value with that of the FCS received. By using a 32 bit CRC in this way, it has then been calculated that the chances of not detecting bad data as it is received are reduced to 2^{32-1} (or 4.3 billion) to 1.

4.3 Invalid MAC Frames

There are several conditions that constitute frame errors in Ethernet II and IEEE 802.3 environments. In all cases, detection of an error will cause the frame to be discarded without sending any indication to the transmitting station. It is then the task of the upper layers to recover from such conditions as they occur. Stations, and other network devices receiving frames in error, may log errors as they occur, thereby providing statistical information to management stations. However, there is no requirement that they do so, and any reporting of such errors is purely implementation specific. Typical error conditions are where:

- The length of the frame is inconsistent with the length indicated by the Length field. This occurs only with IEEE 802.3 frames since Ethernet II frames have no inherent length indicator.

- The frame is too short, i.e., the frame is less than 64 octets in length (excluding the Preamble and Start Frame Delimiter). These errors are often referred to as *Runt* frames.

- The frame is too long, i.e., the frame exceeds 1518 octets (excluding the Preamble and Start Frame Delimiter). These errors are often referred to as *Giant* frames.

- The frame is not an integral number of octets in length. This is most likely caused by one (or more) bits being dropped, and is often referred to as being an *Alignment* error.

- The received Frame Check Sequence does not match the FCS as calculated over the incoming frame. These conditions are referred to simply as CRC errors or FCS errors.

4.4 CSMA/CD Operation

Ethernet and IEEE 802.3 operate an access method that is called *Carrier Sense, Multiple Access, with Collision Detection* (or more commonly, CSMA/CD). Remember that Ethernet/802.3 networks are broadcast in nature, and are contention based, meaning that all stations must acquire the medium when they have data to transmit. This medium access method then, as its name suggests, requires all stations to have the ability to sense the carriers of other stations on the network, and to defer their own transmissions if any other station has already acquired the medium.

The *Multiple Access* section of the name can be misleading, since it does not mean that multiple stations may access the medium simultaneously. Instead,

Multiple Access implies that there are no priority mechanisms, and that all stations have equal rights to use the medium - provided of course that it is available. Finally, *Collision Detection* has to be employed because it is possible that two or more stations may sense that the medium is free, and commence transmission at the same time. This results in corrupted data (a *collision*) that will require re-transmission.

4.4.1 Frame Transmission and Reception with No Collision

When a station has data to transmit, the MAC layer constructs the frame from the data provided by the upper layer (LLC or Network). To do this, it prepends the Destination and Source Addresses, the Length or Type field, and appends any Padding that may be required to conform with the specification requirements regarding the minimum size of frame.[10] Finally, it calculates the Frame Check Sequence (FCS), and places this into the relevant portion of the frame.

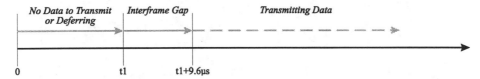

Figure 4-7: Transmission Without Collision

The MAC layer next monitors the *Carrier Sense* signal from the *Physical Layer Signaling* (PLS) sublayer in an attempt to avoid contention. When this signal is false, it indicates that there are no other stations accessing the medium, and it is therefore free. When true, it means that a carrier is already present on the medium, and therefore the station must *defer* sending any data of its own. Failure to defer sending at this time would result in unnecessary collisions, and therefore would increase medium access time for all stations. Figure 4-7 shows a LAN where station B has data to transmit. This figure shows our LAN based upon coaxial cable, although the same scenario is valid for media of any type within a single collision domain.

---

[10] For a complete discussion on Minimum Frame Size see section 4.5.

Once the station has determined that the medium is free, it then continues to defer for a further time known as the *Inter-frame Gap*. This delay is a mandatory *quiet period* on the medium between frames, to ensure that the physical medium and other CSMA/CD MAC layers recover before the next frame is transmitted. This delay is of a fixed 9.6µs duration for 10Mbps systems, as shown in the timeline portion of the figure. Assuming that the medium is not in use, at the end of the Inter-frame Gap the station now commences transmission via the Physical Layer Signaling sublayer.

All other stations on the LAN will now detect the presence of the frame, and they will synchronize with the incoming preamble. The MAC layers of these stations will then be alerted to the arrival of the frame by receiving a *Carrier Sense* signal from their Physical Layer Signaling sublayers. The MAC then decapsulates the frame, and checks the Frame Check Sequence. Assuming that the Destination Address of the frame is the same as the MAC address of the receiving station, and assuming that the frame has been received without error, the MAC layer will now pass the data to the upper layers. The same scenario also applies where the Destination Address is the Broadcast address, or indeed a Multicast (group) address to which this station belongs, provided that the frame is received error-free. Should this frame *not* be destined for this station in any way, the data will be discarded.

4.4.2   Frame Transmission and Reception with Collisions

In the previous section we examined the mechanics of simple frame transmission and reception. In Ethernet/IEEE 802.3 environments, however, operation is rarely that simple. Because of the manner in which this contention-based network technology operates, it is possible that two (or indeed more) stations may decide that the medium is free, and then attempt to transmit simultaneously. Where this

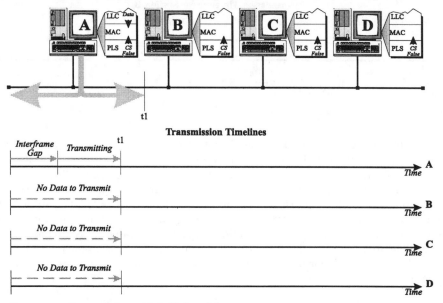

Figure 4-8:   Transmission with Collisions (1)

occurs, the two (or more) signals will interfere with each other, causing what is commonly called a *collision*. Consider the scenario of figure 4-8, where we revisit our LAN discussed in the previous section, only this time it is station A that has data to transmit, and we shall play the transmission in *slow motion*.

If we make the assumption that the medium is free (and has been so for some time) we can ignore the fact that station A would need to defer as would be the case if the *Carrier Sense* (CS) signal from the *Physical Layer Signaling* layer were to be true. Hence, as our figure shows, Station A merely has to wait for the Inter-frame Gap time to expire before commencing transmission.

We now freeze the transmission at time t1 so that we can examine the transmission timelines and the statuses of each of the stations' Physical Layer Signaling layers. From this, we can see that stations B, C, and D have no data to transmit and that, as yet, these stations have not seen the signal from Station A. This is apparent since the Carrier Sense signal for each of these stations is false. At Station A however, the CS signal will now be true, since it is a requirement that all stations monitor the medium at all times. Station A would therefore detect its own signal, and of course it will also know that it is actually transmitting anyway. As far as station A is concerned then, the medium is now busy. As for the other stations, they still consider it to be free.

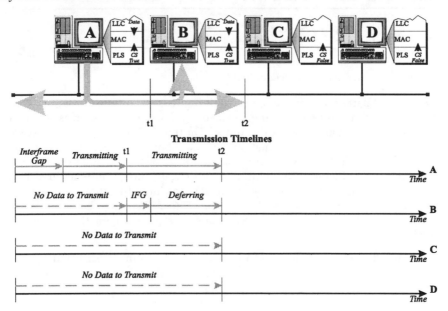

Figure 4-9:   Transmission with Collisions (2)

Restarting our timer, we now see in figure 4-9 that Station A continues its transmission. However, here, we also see that Station B now has data to transmit, and thus starts to time the *Inter-frame Gap* (IFG). Note that in this case however, the IFG timer does not expire because Station B senses the signal from Station A. Hence, Station B stops the IFG timer, and instead defers transmission in an attempt to avoid needless collisions. At time t2 when we stop our clock once more, Station A is still transmitting its data, Station B is deferring its own transmission, and Stations C and D still believe the medium to be available as indicated by their CS signals.

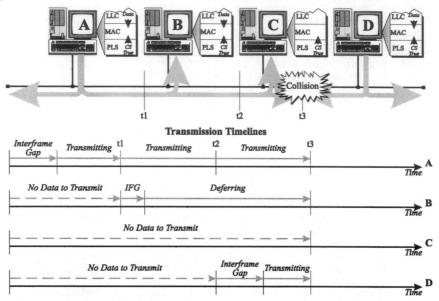

Figure 4-10:   Transmission with Collisions (3)

In the third part of our example, shown in figure 4-10, at time t2 Station D wishes to commence transmission. Having checked the CS signal, it believes the medium to be free and therefore starts its IFG timer. On the expiration of the IFG, since the station has received no information to the contrary, Station D commences transmission which then results in a collision at time t3. Although not shown by the figure, the collision itself will now propagate along the medium in both directions, and will therefore be seen by all stations including those whose data was involved (in this case Stations A and D). Thus, knowing that their data has potentially been compromised, these stations must now take action to ensure the following:

- Since the data was involved in a collision, it cannot be trusted to be error free. Hence if a station had received any or all of the transmission up to that point, it must discard it. It is possible (however unlikely) that the data received up to the point of the collision could represent seemingly valid data complete with a valid CRC.

- Just because the data was involved in a collision, it does not mean that it will no longer be required. Hence, the stations involved in the collision will need to re-send their data, and also attempt to avoid any further collisions.

Figure 4-11 shows the last part of our example, and indeed the first part of our collision recovery mechanism (that of informing all stations that a collision has occurred). Stations are alerted to the fact that a collision has occurred by monitoring the Collision Detect (CD) signal. When this is true, a collision has been detected, and all stations involved in the collision cease transmission of their regular data. Those stations involved however now send what is called a *Jam* signal. This signal is of 32 bit times duration, and is used to enforce the collision by ensuring that all other stations involved in the collision receive the signal. The actual content of the Jam is undefined, however it is mandatory that the bit pattern should not equate to the true CRC value of the data transmitted to the point of the collision. In other words, we attempt to ensure that no station could erroneously believe that what it has received to that point is valid data. In many implementations, the Jam signal transmitted is therefore simply an alternating pattern of ones and zeroes (101010101...... etc.).

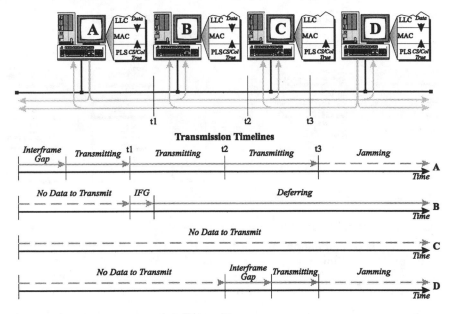

Figure 4-11: Transmission with Collisions (4)

The bits resulting from a collision are decoded by the PLS in the same way as those from any valid frame. However, these *Collision Fragments*, as they are known, must be distinguished from valid data and discarded. Once those stations involved in the collision have completed their Jam signal, the medium can be returned to normal operation, and stations may once again commence transmission. Those stations involved in the collision will need to re-transmit their data, and a method to avoid continual collisions must be sought. Obviously if they were to immediately start transmission after an Inter-frame Gap period, the data would once again collide and very soon a stalemate situation would arise. In order to alleviate this, a system known as *Truncated Binary Exponential Back-off* is used that randomly delays retransmission attempts. This system, described in the next section, provides us with a high probability that the same data will not re-collide, although it provides no guarantees to this effect. Frame transmission and reception is described by the flow diagram of figure 4-12.

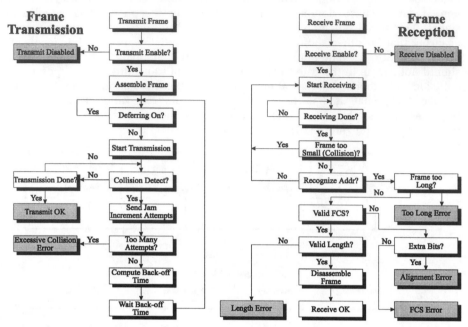

Figure 4-12: Model of Frame Transmission and Reception

4.4.3 Truncated Binary Exponential Back-off

Where a transmission attempt fails due to a collision, it is retried by the CSMA/CD function until such time that it is either successful, or until a maximum number of attempts have failed, all due to collisions. In Ethernet/IEEE 802.3, this maximum number of attempts is a fixed value of 16.

The dynamics of Truncated Binary Exponential Back-off are governed by a parameter known as the *Slot Time* which, from the standard, describes an upper bound on the acquisition time of the medium, and an upper bound on the length of a frame fragment generated by a collision. The standard then goes on to state that the slot time should be larger than the sum of the Physical Layer round-trip propagation time and the Media Access Layer maximum jam time. Put more simply, we can calculate the slot time as being the time to transmit the minimum size frame. Since this is fixed, it can therefore be calculated as follows: the minimum size of frame (excluding Preamble and Start Frame Delimiter) is 64 octets, equating to 512 bits (since an octet is 8 bits). Assuming a transmission speed of 10Mbps, we can conclude that the time taken to transmit the minimum size frame would be 51.2µs for a 10Mbps system.

Once a transmission attempt has ended in a collision, our station will delay re-transmission of the frame for an integer number of slot times. The actual number of slot times to delay before the nth retransmission attempt is then chosen as a random

Media Access Control

integer r in the range of $0 \leq r \leq 2^k$ where k is in the range of 0 to 10. Table 4-3 illustrates these values for successive attempts. Where a station fails after 16 consecutive attempts, the frame is aborted and an error is reported to the upper layers. How this is then handled is implementation specific.

Table 4-3: Back Off Parameters

Retransmission Attempt (Consecutive Collisions)	Max. Number of Slot Times	Retransmission Attempt (Consecutive Collisions)	Max. Number of Slot Times
1	2	9	512
2	4	10	1024
3	8	11	1024
4	16	12	1024
5	32	13	1024
6	64	14	1024
7	128	15	1024
8	256	16	Abort

4.4.4   Medium Access Time and Overall Performance

Clearly, from the discussions above, it can be seen that the length of time it takes a station to transmit a frame is directly related to the number of collisions it experiences. In addition, a station must complete *all* attempts to transmit a frame before any subsequent frames are transmitted. Also, it is clear that the more heavily loaded the medium becomes, the more transmission attempts will potentially be needed. Indeed it is this "collision/back-off" behavior that makes this type of network non-deterministic, since it is impossible to calculate access times based on the number of stations that are connected to the LAN.

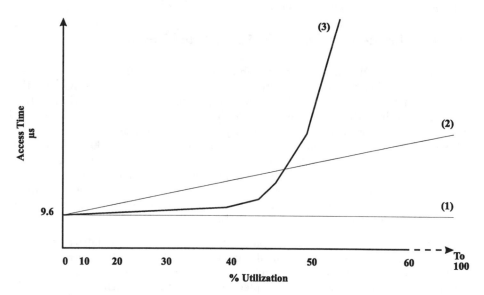

Figure 4-13:   Medium Access Time Versus Percentage Utilization

If we were to plot the access time of a station against the percentage utilization on the medium, we may well see a graph similar to one of the traces shown in figure 4-13. Here, based on a 10Mbps system, we see that for even zero percent utilization we experience a minimum access time of 9.6μs, representing the Inter-frame Gap period. Of the traces, the first shows a steady, equal access time of the Inter-frame Gap period regardless of utilization. In actual fact this is extremely unlikely to ever occur, and would only be achieved where we had just two stations in a constant exchange of data, and all other stations on the LAN were idle. Even then, this trace assumes that both stations take strict turns concerning their transmissions, and that each transmits (on its turn) immediately the Inter-frame Gap period expires.

The second trace shows a seemingly more plausible graph where we see an increase in access time, in line with utilization. This trace would however also be unlikely since back-off periods are multiples of slot times, and these increase exponentially where collisions occur. Once again though, all stations will experience a minimum Inter-fame Gap period when attempting transmission, and therefore we will still maintain a minimum 9.6μs access time for 10Mbps systems.

Our third trace shows the exponential rise in access time as the utilization increases, and is what would most likely be seen on a normal network. Here, access times rise with the inevitable increase in the number of collisions, and in this case, the access time increases dramatically as the utilization reaches around 40%. By the time the utilization reaches a little over 50%, the access time has increased to such an extent that the LAN becomes almost unusable. Of course, the point at which the network becomes unusable may well vary, and the figure of 50% could be regarded as a generalization. Indeed, many network managers would argue that utilization on their network peaks at 80% or even higher. The point however remains, that an exponential rise in access time is normal for this type of network, and that saturation can and does occur.

4.5   The Need for Minimum and Maximum Sized Frames

In order to understand the need for minimum and maximum frame sizes we have to understand a little more about the nature of Ethernet/IEEE 802.3. We have seen that the access method is that of Multiple Access, meaning that there is no prioritization. Also we use a broadcast medium, and in order to guarantee our transmission only one signal can exist on the medium at any time. In addition, in order to avoid collisions, stations listen to the medium for a carrier and defer their own transmissions until they believe it to be free. Thus, if we were to allow one station to transmit a frame of infinite size, we would effectively block all other stations from accessing the medium. Equally, if we were to allow a frame that held up to say 4095 octets or even larger, we could seriously degrade network performance as stations would need to defer their transmissions for longer.

The 1500 octet limit on the frame payload was chosen to allow fair access to the medium while permitting a reasonable amount of data to be transferred. When dealing with complex protocols such as the File Transfer Protocol (FTP) for example, it is not sufficient to just place the data to be transferred within the Information field of the frame. Instead, we must encapsulate our data within

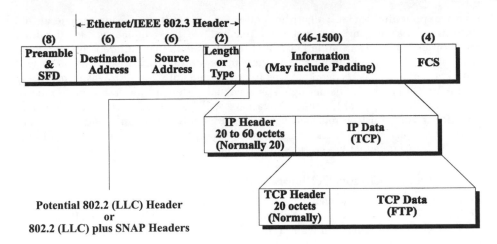

Figure 4-14:   Data Encapsulation

control information, just as the raw Ethernet/IEEE 802.3 information is
encapsulated in the physical frame. Consider figure 4-14 that examines the
encapsulation of data from an FTP session. Our frame carries, as a minimum, an IP
Datagram header of between 20 and 60 octets,[11] and a TCP header of 20 octets[12] as an
overhead to the actual user data. It is also possible that we may be using 802.2
LLC[13] or even 802.2/SNAP. If this were to be the case, then the IP Header would
follow the 3 octet LLC header or the 8 octet LLC/SNAP headers respectively. Even
with this overhead though, each frame can still potentially carry in excess of 1024
octets (1kb) of real user data, so our upper bound of 1500 octets does not really
become a major limitation.

To examine the need for a minimum size frame we need to appreciate the
method of Collision Detection. With the CSMA/CD access method, the station
attempts to acquire the medium once it is sure that it is free. As we have seen
though, there could be (as yet) undetected traffic. When this occurs, a collision
results that will be seen by all stations. Three questions now require answers.
Firstly, which stations actually need to take any action? Secondly, if we are to take
action, what action(s) should we take? And finally, how do these stations know it is
they that must take action?

We have already answered some of these questions in previous sections,
although it is worth now bringing the whole scenario together. In answer to the first
two questions, any station that was receiving data that it believed to be destined for
itself must, on receipt of the collision, discard that data since it must consider it as
being invalid. Also, if the station was transmitting, it must perform the truncated

---

[11] IP Datagram headers are normally sent without options and are therefore only 20 octets in length.
Certain implementations, however, require options to be set in the header, thereby increasing its
size.

[12] TCP Headers will normally only carry options during connection establishment. Once the
connection has been established, the TCP header is normally only 20 octets in length.

[13]   Logical Link Control (LLC) & the Sub Network Access Protocol (SNAP) are discussed in section E.

binary exponential back-off algorithm and schedule a retransmission, provided that the retransmission limit has not been reached. This then leaves just the final question of how does a station know that it was *its* data that collided, and it is here that the need for a minimum size frame can be simply explained. A station will only know that it was *its* data that was involved in a collision, if *it* was transmitting at the time that the collision signal is received. Hence, our frame has to be of sufficient size to guarantee that all stations will have seen our carrier, and any collision signal must be returned before our transmission is terminated. In other words, we must still be transmitting when the collision is received for us to know that it was our data that has collided and therefore requires retransmission.

4.5.1   Out-of-Window Collisions

From our discussions above, we are now left with one more error condition to define, that of a *Late* or *Out-of-Window Collision*. Many Ethernet/IEEE 802.3 devices report this condition when it occurs and therefore some explanation would be of use.

This situation arises when a station receives a collision signal after what is known as the *Collision Window* has expired. The Collision Window is in actual fact the Slot time of 51.2µs (in 10Mbps systems) since if a collision is going to occur, then it should do so within the time it takes to transmit the minimum size frame of 64 octets. If a collision occurs *after* this time it generally implies that either a station is attempting to acquire the medium late, or alternatively it could be due to an out of specification cable such as one that is too long.

4.6   Summary

The MAC layer presented here is possibly the most complex part of the Ethernet/802.3 specification. Totally scaleable, the MAC that we have described is used in 10Mbps, 100Mbps, and even Gigabit systems - fundamentally, operation remains constant with only timing changing in proportion to the higher bit rates.

Collisions are a normal part of Ethernet/802.3 networks and should only become a cause for concern when their rate is excessive. Defining excessive is difficult. Certainly from the point of view of station access, we are dealing with a non-deterministic system and that will never change. We can raise the speed, but the fundamental operation remains constant and therefore backward compatible. Whether this is the right way forward, who can tell? Networks of this type though remain the most popular, so Ethernet/802.3 must be doing something right.

PLS and AUI

The Physical Layer Signaling (PLS) and the Attachment Unit Interface (AUI) together define the electrical and mechanical characteristics of the interface between the Data Terminal Equipment (DTE)[1] and the Medium Attachment Unit (MAU).[2] As you will recall from previous chapters however, depending upon the characteristics and/or architecture of the attached device, the MAU (and therefore the AUI) may indeed be part of the physical Network Interface Card in use (within the DTE). Thus, when discussing these elements of the Ethernet/IEEE 802.3 standard, we must be aware that the AUI may actually be internal to the device.

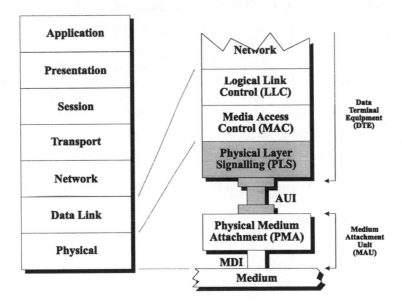

Figure 5-1: PLS/AUI Relationship to the OSI Model

The original design purpose of the interface was to provide an interconnection method that was both simple and inexpensive. In turn, this permitted the development of simple and inexpensive MAUs. With the price of networking

---

[1] The Data Terminal Equipment (DTE) in this case is the station attached to the LAN medium.
[2] A Medium Attachment Unit (MAU) is more commonly referred to as a Transceiver.

devices falling, brought about both by user demand and mass production, it is fair to say that this basic design criteria has been met. In general then, the interface has the following characteristics:

- It is capable of supporting one or more data rates.

  Many network interfaces today are designed to automatically detect, and run at, either 10Mbps or 100Mbps. When the standard was first written however, these devices typically ran at 10Mbps only.

- Where the AUI is external, the device must be capable of driving a signal up to 50m between the Network Interface of the DTE and the MAU.

  Where the AUI is internal, it effectively does not exist. Instead, the MAU is connected to the PLS as part of the internal circuitry of the interface card.

- Support for duplex data transmission.

  While it is true to say that Ethernet/IEEE 802.3 appears to operate in a half duplex mode, with only one station acquiring the medium at any time, the MAU must have the ability to detect other traffic and therefore collisions. This facility should not be confused with a newer system known as *Full Duplex Switched Ethernet* (FDSE),[3] popular with many switch vendors.

- It permits the DTE to test the AUI, MAU, and the Medium to which the device is ultimately attached.

  The testing performed at this level has to remain simple due to the nature and simplicity of the MAU itself. As we shall see in subsequent sections, this testing provides only a basic-level confidence test, allowing the Station (PLS function) to determine transmission has occurred and was successful.

- Support for MAUs catering for differing media types.

  The PLS and AUI are designed to ensure that the DTE remains media independent. As such, the media type to which the station will attach (Coaxial cable, Twisted Pair, or Fiber Optic) is a function of the MAU.

5.1   Modes of Operation

The AUI is designed to operate in two different modes. All interfaces must support the *Normal* mode of operation where the AUI is logically connected to the Medium Dependent Interface (MDI), and where the DTE uses the standard methods for media access as previously described. In this mode, the MAU will also send whatever data it receives from the MDI, back to the DTE (data reception).

The second mode is known as the *Monitor* mode, and is optional. In this mode, the transmission side of the MAU is logically disconnected from the medium, and the MAU merely listens to all data and passes this back to the DTE. This function is useful where we wish to monitor network traffic, although it must be stated that as most data is sent unencrypted, this can lead to serious security breaches on our

[3] See chapters 12 and 15 for full discussions on Full Duplex operation, Ethernet Switching.

networks. Since this mode is optional, only a small percentage of devices are capable of fully supporting operation in this way. When this mode is selected however, the *Signal Quality Error* (SQE)[4] function should remain enabled. Figure 5-2 then shows how these modes of operation are controlled in the broadest terms through a generalized view of the MAU.

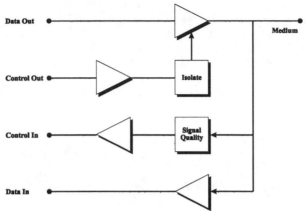

Figure 5-2: Simplified MAU Model

5.2   DTE to MAU Interchange Circuits

The AUI provides differential circuits over which control signals and data are exchanged. In all, the AUI uses four such signaling circuits, it also carries power from the DTE to the MAU, and provides a means by which the MAU may be grounded. These circuits, typically referred to by name, are described in Table 5-1, which also indicates the origin of each.

Data and Control circuits are independently self-clocked. This then eliminates the need for separate timing circuits, and is simply achieved by ensuring that all signals used are encoded as described in section 5.3. Finally, circuit usage is strictly controlled such that the Data circuits carry no control information, and the Control circuits never carry data.

Table 5-1: DTE to MAU Interchange Circuits

		Direction		
Circuit	Name	To MAU	From MAU	Remarks
DO	Data Out	X		Encoded Data from DTE to MAU
DI	Data In		X	Encoded Data from MAU to DTE
CO	Control Out	X		Encoded Control from DTE to MAU
CI	Control In		X	Encoded Control from MAU to DTE
VP	Voltage Plus	X		12V Supplied by DTE
VC	Voltage Common	X		12V Return for VP
PG	Protective Ground	X		Shield

[4] Signal Quality Error (SQE) is the more correct term for a Collision.

5.2.1 DTE to MAU Connection

Physically, the AUI is a cable that comprises individually-shielded twisted-pair wires. The entire cable is then overall screened, and this outer shield is connected to both the MAU and DTE. Each individual screen is electrically isolated from the outer screen, and is by necessity connected to logic ground in the DTE. The standard connector used is the 15 pin "D" connector, typically incorporating Slide Locks. This simple connection then allows easy installation and removal without the need for tools of any kind. By convention, DTEs are always equipped with Female connections that incorporate the lock mechanism. MAUs then use Male connections with locking posts as shown in figure 5-3. This method of connection also allows the direct connection of a MAU to a DTE where physical space permits, and therefore potentially removes the need for the AUI cable at all.

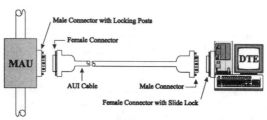

Figure 5-3: DTE to MAU Connection

Table 5-2 shows the pin assignments for the connectors, together with their individual usage. You will recall that the AUI provides differential circuits, and that each cable pair is individually screened. Hence, as the table indicates, each circuit has three individual pins assigned to adhere to this requirement. Two pins for the differential circuit connection, and one for the screen or *shield*.

Table 5-2: AUI Cable Contact Assignments

Contact	Circuit	Usage
1	CI-S	Control In Shield
2	CI-A	Control In Circuit A
3	DO-A	Data Out Circuit A
4	DI-S	Data In Shield
5	DI-A	Data In Circuit A
6	VC	Voltage Common
7	CO-A	Control Out Circuit A
8	CO-S	Control Out Shield
9	CI-B	Control In Circuit B
10	DO-B	Data Out Circuit B
11	DO-S	Data Out Shield
12	DI-B	Data In Circuit B
13	VP	Voltage Plus
14	VS	Voltage Shield
15	CO-B	Control Out Circuit B
Shell	PG	Protective Ground (Conductive Shell of Connector)

Note: In common with other circuits, the Voltage Plus and Voltage Common use a single pair within the sheath. Also, the "A" element of a circuit is always positive relative to the "B" element for a *HI* signal, and negative for a *LO*.

5.3 Signal Encoding

If raw data was to be transferred between the DTE and MAU, it is possible that where a constant bit pattern is to be conveyed, the DTE and MAU would lose synchronization. Consider figure 5-4 where we see three distinct data patterns. In the first, our DTE is transferring an alternating stream of 1s and 0s that, since there are transitions in the data, would maintain synchronization between our two devices. In the other two cases where we are sending a constant stream of either 1s or 0s though, no transitions occur. This makes it unlikely that, in the absence of clocks, the MAU would be able to recover the data from the DTE or vice versa.

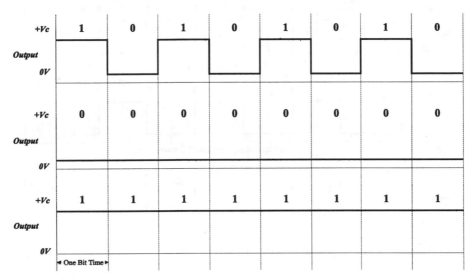

Figure 5-4: Raw Data Streams

Ethernet/802.3 DTEs both transmit and receive data asynchronously, and as we saw in the previous section, the AUI has no provision for separate clocks to which the data may be referenced. Hence, if we are to avoid synchronization problems, we must encode our data such that clocking information and data are combined. A scheme known as *Manchester Encoding* is therefore used in 10Mbps systems to provide this. Other speeds (100Mbps and 1000Mbps) use different schemes, although the basic requirement of encoding remains constant. These other schemes will be discussed later, together with the faster technologies which use them.

With Manchester Encoding, data and clocking are combined into *bit symbols*. Here, each symbol is split into two halves, with the second half containing the binary inverse of the first. Put simply, the first half of the bit cell or symbol is always the logical complement of the data being transmitted, while the second half of the symbol is an un-complemented value of the bit.

Figure 5-5 shows the Manchester Encoding system when applied to a stream of constant 1s, 0s, an alternating bit stream, and random data. As can be seen in the figure, a transition is guaranteed to always occur at the center of the symbol or bit cell time. In addition, where two bits of identical value are presented together, the signal is inverted at the end of the cell thus ensuring compliance with the encoding scheme.

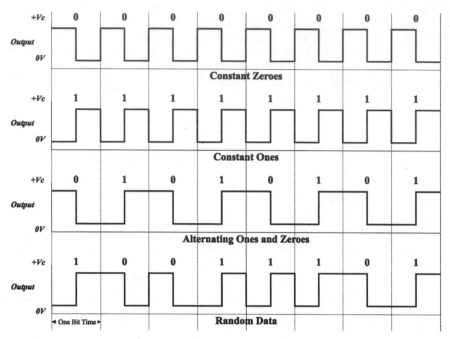

Figure 5-5: Manchester Encoded Data

5.4 PLS/AUI Functionality

When examining the functionality of the DTE and MAU, we see that most of the functionality required by the interface is provided by the DTE. The reasoning behind this is simply that when the standard was first written, 10Base5 was the medium in use. As always, the MAU is located close to the physical medium which, in the case of coaxial cable, was often in an inaccessible location. Hence, should the need to service the MAU arise, it was often difficult and therefore expensive to maintain.

5.4.1 PLS to PMA (DTE to MAU) Signaling

Actual data interchange between the DTE and MAU is defined in terms of both Clocked Data one bits (CD1s), and Clocked Data zero bits (CD0s). In addition, certain *control* signals are defined by the standard as follows:

- **Clocked Data One (CD1)**
  This is a Manchester Encoded data 1 bit which is used on the *Data In* (DI) and *Data Out* (DO) circuits. This is encoded as a *LO* for the first half of the bit cell, and a *HI* for the second half of the bit cell.

- **Clocked Data Zero (CD0)**

  This is a Manchester Encoded data 0 bit which, like the CD1, is used on the *Data In* (DI) and *Data Out* (DO) circuits. This is encoded as a *HI* for the first half of the bit cell, and an *LO* for the second half of the bit cell.

- **Control Signal 1 (CS1)**

  An encoded signal used on the *Control In* (CI) and *Control Out* (CO) circuits. Encoding here takes the form of being a signal at half the standard bit rate (or 5Mbps for 10Mbps systems).

- **Control Signal Zero (CS0)**

  An encoded signal used on the *Control In* (CI) and *Control Out* (CO) circuits. Encoding here takes the form of being a signal at the standard bit rate (10Mbps for 10Mbps systems).

- **Idle (IDL)**

  This is a signal where no transitions on the transmission line exist. IDL signals are used to define the end of a frame and cease to exist after the next LO to HI transition on the circuit.

  The IDL signal always starts with a HI signal level. Thus, an additional transition is added to the bit stream if the last *true* bit sent was a zero. There should be no confusion with CD1s or CD0s since the transition in this case will always occur at the start of the bit cell, and there will be no transition in the middle of the cell. The IDL condition must last for at least 2 bit times and detected within 1.6 bit times at the receiving device for 10Mbps systems.

When examining the signals on the Control In (CI) and Control Out (CO) circuits, these have different meanings depending upon the circuit and signal present. Table 5-3 describes these meanings:

Table 5-3: DTE to MAU/MAU to DTE Control Signaling

Control In Circuit (CI) - MAU to DTE

Signal	Message	Description
IDL	mau_available	MAU is ready to output data
CS1	mau_not_available	MAU is not ready to output data
CS0	signal_quality_error	MAU has detected an error on output data

Control Out Circuit (CO) - DTE to MAU

Signal	Message	Description
IDL	normal	MAU should enter (or remain in) Normal mode
CS1	mau_request[5]	MAU should be made available
CS0	isolate[5]	MAU should enter (or remain in) Monitor mode

In addition, it is important that the signal characteristics are closely adhered to. For example, the frequency tolerance on the CS1 and CS0 signals over the Control Out (CO) circuit is +/-5%, while the CS1 signal on the Control In (CI) circuit it is +/-

---

[5] The mau_request and isolate signals are optional since the use of monitor mode (and therefore switching to it) is optional within the 802.3 standard.

15%. Equally, the tolerance of the CS0 signal when used on the Control In (CI) circuit should not exceed +25% to 15%, with the pulse widths between 35ns and 70ns at the zero crossing point. Finally, the duty cycle for the signals (which would nominally be 50%/50%) should be no worse than 60% to 40%.

5.4.2   PLS to PMA (DTE to MAU) Protocol

The actual protocol between the DTE and the MAU is unidirectional, and is relatively simple in nature. In all, just 5 messages are used, of which only 3 are mandatory. Table 5-4 outlines these message types which are then described in detail below:

Table 5-4: PLS to PMA Messaging

Message	Description
Message	*Description*
output	Output information
output_idle	No data to be output
normal	Cease to isolate MAU
(Optional)	
isolate	Isolate MAU
mau_request	Request that the MAU be made available

output
Whenever the MAC sublayer has data bits to be transmitted onto the medium, it sends these bits (referred to as OUTPUT_UNITs) to the PLS. This then results in the PLS sending data to the PMA as a series of CD0s and/or CD1s on the Data Out circuit. The actual data sent will of course depend upon the composition of the data stream. However, where the data unit (OUTPUT_UNIT) to be transmitted is a binary 1, a CD1 is sent. Where the data unit is a binary 0, the PLS sends a CD0.

output_idle
An output_idle is sent to the PMA whenever the MAC sublayer is not sending data to the PLS. Once the MAC sublayer sends OUTPUT_UNITs to the PLS, the output_idle message is terminated, but is re-established immediately on the completion of data transmission. The actual message itself is an IDL sent from the DTE to the MAU over the Data Out circuit.

normal
The PLS sends a normal message to the PMA whenever it wishes the MAU to revert to normal operation (i.e., after the MAU has been isolated with the isolate message), or when the PLS is reset. The message itself is an IDL sent from the DTE to the MAU on the Control Out circuit.

isolate (optional)
The PLS sends an isolate message to the PMA whenever it requires that the MAU is to be isolated from the physical medium. Isolation in this sense means that the MAU will be prevented from sending any data onto the medium, and will not interfere with the transmissions of other stations. The message here is a CS0 signal transmitted over the Control Out circuit.

mau_request (optional)
This message is only ever sent in two cases. In the first, it is sent when the PLS is receiving a mau_not_available message from the PMA, but it has received the first OUTPUT_UNIT from the MAC sublayer. In this instance, the PLS has data to be transmitted and is indicating the same to the PMA. At the same time, of course, the message requests that the MAU be made available so that the data may be passed. The second situation where this message is used is where the PLS is attempting to determine whether the isolate function is supported. The actual message used is simply an CS1 on the Control Out circuit.

5.4.3 PMA to PLS (MAU to DTE) Protocol

Like the PLS to PMA protocol, communications in the reverse direction (PMA to PLS) are also unidirectional. For the PMA to PLS direction of communication, five message types are again used, although here only one is optional. Table 5-5 outlines the message types used, and again are discussed in detail below:

Table 5-5: PMA to PLS Messaging

Message	Description
input	Input information
input_idle	No input information
signal_quality_error	Error detected by MAU
mau_available	MAU is available for output
(Optional Messages)	
mau_not_available	MAU is not available for output

input
An input message is sent to the PLS whenever the MAU has received a bit from the medium and wishes to transfer it to the DTE. The actual message will be either a CD0 or CD1 sent over the Data In circuit, although if the signal_quality_error[6] message is being received by the PLS, the actual data is unpredictable.

input_idle
The PMA will send an IDL to the PLS whenever the MAU does not have any data to send (i.e., the medium is idle). This signal is always sent over the Data In circuit, and ceases immediately when data is recovered by the MAU and needs to be sent to the DTE. Equally, once data reception halts, the input_idle signal resumes.

signal_quality_error
The signal_quality_error signal takes the form of a CS0 sent by the MAU to the DTE over the Control In circuit. Three distinct conditions will cause the signal_quality_error signal to exist, as follows:

- Improper signals on the medium
  This may take any one of a number of forms, and is generally dependent on the medium in use. Typically, however, this might be caused by a

---

[6] A Signal Quality Error is sent, among other times, whenever a collision is detected. Signal Quality Error (SQE) is in fact the correct term that should be used to define a collision condition.

malfunctioning MAU somewhere on the LAN, or a break or short-circuit in the medium itself.

- Collisions
  These occur when two or more MAUs attempt to acquire the medium at the same time. Whenever the MAU determines that this is the case, a signal_quality_error signal is sent.

- signal_quality_error Message Test
  Where this feature (commonly known as the SQE(T) or *Heart-Beat*) is enabled on the MAU,[7] it will send a signal_quality_error signal to the PLS once each transmission is completed. Care must be taken here, since if the MAU supports SQE(T) then the standard recommends that the unit is shipped (when new) with this feature enabled. This feature *must* be disabled when connecting the MAU to a Repeater, since repeaters interpret this signal as a *real* collision and will disable the port temporarily on excess collisions.

mau_available
The mau_available signal is an IDL sent to the PLS over the Control In circuit. The signal itself is sent whenever the MAU is prepared to accept data for transmission onto the medium.

mau_not_available (optional)
The PMA sends this signal, which comprises a CS1 on the Control In circuit, whenever the MAU is not available to accept data for transmission.

5.4.4   PLS to MAC Interface Signaling

Before leaving the PLS/PMA interface, it is useful to consider the interface between the PLS and MAC. In this interface, the PLS and MAC sublayers communicate via a number of signals as shown in table 5-6. As with the PLS-PMA protocol, this interface defines a means of transferring status and data without undue complication, and is glamorous in its simplicity.

Table 5-6: PLS to MAC Interface Messages

Message	Description
OUTPUT_UNIT	Data sent to the MAU
OUTPUT_STATUS	Response to OUTPUT_UNIT
INPUT_UNIT	Data received from the MAU
CARRIER_STATUS	Indication of Input activity
SIGNAL_STATUS	Indication of error/no error condition

OUTPUT_UNIT
The MAC sublayer sends data (bits) as OUTPUT_UNITs. Each time that the MAC has a bit to send (0 or 1) the MAC sends an OUTPUT_UNIT, and will not send another until it has received an OUTPUT_STATUS as an acknowledgment. Where

---

[7] See chapter 6, 10Mbps Medium Attachment Units (MAUs) for further information on the SQE Test function.

the MAC wishes a CD1 to be transmitted by the PLS, the OUTPUT_UNIT is a 1. Where a CD0 is to be transmitted, the OUTPUT_UNIT is a 0.

OUTPUT_STATUS
The PLS sends OUTPUT_STATUS messages to the MAC in response to an OUTPUT_UNIT. In essence, OUTPUT_STATUS can be considered to be both an acknowledgment (either positive or negative) of OUTPUT_UNITs from the MAC, and a method of synchronizing the output of the MAC sublayer with the data rate of the medium. Two types of OUTPUT_STATUS exist, one known as OUTPUT_NEXT, where the PLS is prepared to accept the next OUTPUT_UNIT, and the other known as OUTPUT_ABORT, where the PLS was not able to process the previous OUTPUT_UNIT.

INPUT_UNIT
INPUT_UNIT messages are sent from the PLS to the MAC each time the PLS receives an *input* signal from the PMA. As with the OUTPUT_UNIT, the INPUT_UNIT will be a 1 if the received data bit was a CD1, and a 0 if the received bit was a CD0.

CARRIER_STATUS
A CARRIER_STATUS message is sent to the MAC each time that the PLS detects a change in the carrier status. CARRIER_ON is sent whenever an *input* or *signal_quality_error* message is received from the PMA if the previous carrier message was CARRIER_OFF. Equally, the PLS will send a CARRIER_OFF message to the MAC if it receives an *input_idle*, no *signal_quality_error*, and the previous status was CARRIER_ON.

SIGNAL_STATUS
The SIGNAL_STATUS signal is sent to the MAC whenever the PLS detects a change in the signal quality. When the PLS receives a *signal_quality_error* from the PMA, and the previously reported status was NO_SIGNAL_ERROR, it sends a SIGNAL_ERROR signal. A NO_SIGNAL_ERROR signal is then sent when it receives no *signal_quality_error*, provided that the previous SIGNAL_STATUS sent was SIGNAL_ERROR.

5.5 Frame Structure

All frames transmitted on the AUI have a defined structure as shown in figure 5-6. In this structure, *Silence* means that there are no transitions. *Preamble* is a pattern of 56 bit times of alternating CD1s and CD0s that ends in a single CD0. The *SFD*, or the Start Frame Delimiter is a single 8-bit pattern of alternating CD1s and CD0s that starts with a single CD1, and ends with two CD1s. *Data* is a number of instances of 8-bit patterns that comprises CD0s and CD1s in any order. The *ETD*, or the End of Transmission Delimiter, is then an IDL signal.

Figure 5-6: AUI Frame Format

5.6 Summary

The PLS and AUI interfaces are relatively simple, and serve to allow the MAC to operate with a number of different PMAs in an independent manner. The MAC, as we have already seen, is totally scaleable to work with any reasonable data rate. The PLS/AUI on the other hand, changes in both functionality and naming once we go to higher rates of data interchange.

Complex it is not, but our Physical Layer Signaling is crucial if we are to achieve an error-free, or at least low error rate transmission. Basically, we must encode data or supply a clock. Failing to do so would mean that we risk synchronization problems, which would present us with a number of problems at any data rate. Manchester Encoding is the method used at 10Mbps, but it is not used at the higher rates. Instead, at 100Mbps[8] our data is first encoded using a scheme know as 4B/5B. When we then run this over copper (twisted-pair) media, we then further encode into MLT-3 or in the case of fiber NRZI.

As for the AUI, apart from the fact that it is rarely used today as an *exposed* cable, it is applicable only to 10Mbps systems. Once again at 100Mbps and above, our terminology changes, as do the technologies applied. In all, the PLS/AUI form what has become a firm foundation on which our later technologies were built, yet are still very much required for maintaining the old.

---

[8] 100Mbps systems are discussed in chapter 9.

10Mbps MAUs

The Medium Attachment Unit (MAU), or *Transceiver* as it is more commonly known, allows the connection of the DTE to the physical network medium. MAUs are designed to be simple and inexpensive, yet should also provide a flexible means of station attachment. As an example of the inherent flexibility, consider that several media standards exist. These standards include coaxial cable, twisted-pair, and fiber, yet the basic functionality of the transceiver remains constant. Indeed, only the Medium Dependent Interface (MDI), and with it the driver circuitry, needs to change to accommodate each of these different media types.

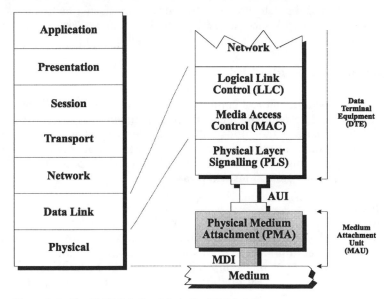

Figure 6-1: The MAU Relationship to the OSI Model

In general then, we can define the major MAU functions as follows:

- Enables the PLS layer to access the medium.

- Provides a mechanism by which the DTE can transmit data onto the medium. In this, the MAU must be capable of driving signals over the entire distance of the physical medium that, in the case of fiber optics, could be up to 2km.

- Allows the reception and recovery of a signal from any other station.

- Detects the presence of collisions on the medium and signals the PLS layer accordingly. In this way, the DTE is able to take appropriate action and re-transmit data if required.

- Ensures that an attached station releases the medium in a timely fashion, and therefore prohibits the station from a situation known simply as *Jabbering*.

- Allows the DTE to test both the medium and the MAU itself.

6.1 MAU Modes of Operation

As we saw in the previous chapter, The Physical Layer Signaling (PLS) sub-layer is able to select two modes of MAU operation. In the first, the so called *Normal Mode*, the MAU is connected to the medium, and all data output from the DTE is transmitted onto it. Equally, in this mode, all data on the medium is passed to the DTE for processing.

In the second mode, known as *Monitor Mode*, the MAU transmit function is disabled, thereby preventing the DTE from transmitting data onto the medium. The reception of data and the detection of collisions are unaffected by this mode, hence monitoring of the network medium is allowed. This second mode is considered optional however, and may not be implemented by all vendors.

6.2 MAU/Medium Dependent Interface

The actual connection method employed at the MAU is dependent upon the medium in use,[1] and therefore on the Medium Dependent Interface (MDI). We have already briefly discussed the configuration rules associated with different media types, and indeed the connectors that are used. At the risk of repetition however, it is worthwhile reiterating and expanding on these for the purpose of explaining the MDI. Typically, these connections will be as follows:

- **10Base5**
  Two connection types exist for this specification. In the first instance, the cable is broken (intrusive connection) and the MAU introduced thereby re-joining the medium. MAUs of this type are equipped with high quality "N" type connectors of 50 ohms impedance to make the connection and to ensure a high reliability. The MDI in this case is two "N" type connectors to join the MAU to the media.

  Alternatively, 10Base5 offers what is known as either a Coaxial "Tap," *Vampire*, or *Beesting* MAU connection. In this *non-intrusive* MAU type, the outer sheath or jacket is pierced to make connection with the shield of the cable. In all there are 4 layers to the shield (2 braids and 2 foil screens). The dielectric is then drilled to within around 0.5mm of the center conductor such that the *vampire* (center pin) pierces through and makes contact with

---

[1] For a complete discussion of media and connector type specifications, please refer to Section G.

the solid center core. Figure 6-2 shows schematically how this system is achieved.

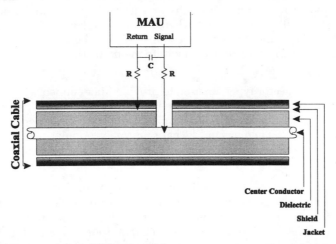

Figure 6-2: Coaxial Tap Connection

- **10Base2**

  10Base2 has only one standardized connector type - The Bayonet Neill Concelman (BNC) connector. For this specification, the cable must be severed to install new connection points, although once the BNC connector has been installed, the MAU may be added at any time without further network disruption. In essence, the cable is broken, new BNC connectors are added to the severed ends of the cable and a BNC "T" piece is used to re-join the cable. The MAU, equipped with a BNC as the MDI, can then be connected as required.

- **10Base-T**

  Like 10Base2, 10BaseT (and indeed 100Base-Tx) has just a single standard connector, the ISO 8877, or RJ45. With this connector, although 8 contacts are available, only 4 are used as shown in figure 6-3 below. Note that for

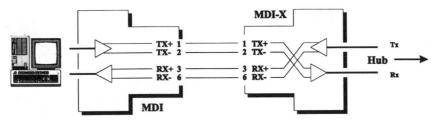

Figure 6-3: 10BaseT Connection (MDI to MDI-X)

Station to Hub (DTE to Repeater) connection, pin assignments are internally crossed. This type of connection, known as a MDI-X, then allows for inexpensive straight through cables to be employed rather than less standard "cross-over" cables. Where Hub-to-Hub (inter-repeater or MDI-X to MDI-X)

links are required, or should two DTEs need to be connected in a back-to-back configuration (MDI to MDI), then a cross-over cable will of course be required. To this end, many hubs are equipped with a single, *switchable* port that allows the user to select whether it will be used as a standard MDI or a MDI-X. Thus, hub-to-hub connections can then be made without the need to use cross-over cables anywhere within the network.

- **10Base-F**

  Several connector types are used to provide fiber connectivity for the 10Base-Fx (10Base-FP, 10Base-FB, 10Base-FL, and FOIRL) specifications. The IEEE 802.3 standard makes specific mention of only one however, the BFOC/2.5 or *Straight Tip* (ST) connector. That said, other popular fiber connector types available are the *Subscriber Connector* (SC) and the *Sub Miniature Assembly* (SMA).

  In contrast to this, 100Base-Fx and indeed 1000Base-Lx/Sx systems, tend to use mainly the SC connector, although it is true to say that the ST connector remains popular with some vendors. This move away from the SMA connector is possibly due to the fact that 100Mbps and 1000Mbps are far newer technologies and therefore tend to use the later connector types only. In addition, the ST and SC connectors are now recognized as being far better optically.

  Due to the nature of fiber, this topology is always point-to-point. Thus, all connections are intrusive, but disrupt only a single station's connection. Equally, since connections rely on one fiber strand for the transmission of data, and one for reception, the individual fibers must be crossed between the two devices (DTE/Hub, etc.) as shown in figure 6-4.

Figure 6-4: Fiber Optic Connections

6.3 Transmission and Reception

The overall functionality of the MAU is relatively simple in terms of data transmission and reception. In essence, where data is received from the DTE on the Data Output (DO) circuit, this data must be transmitted onto the medium within 2 bit times. When data is detected on the medium, it must be passed to the DTE over the Data In (DI) circuit within 5 bit times. Of course no interpretation of data is allowed within the MAU itself during either transmission or reception, and indeed only rudimentary checks are carried out on the transmission system. In short, the MAU takes whatever data is sent from the DTE, and faithfully transmits it in whatever form the medium requires. Reception of data then follows a similar, albeit reverse, path with data recovered from the medium being sent to the DTE.

Two exceptions to this rule exist, and indeed these are the only checks that are made. In the first case, if the *signal_quality_error* Test SQE(T) function is enabled, a basic confidence test is performed at the end of transmission. This function broadly indicates to the attached DTE that the transmission was successful and that the MAU is still working. SQE(T) is discussed in detail in section 6.6. The second, and final, check is that of Jabbering, which prevents stations from holding the medium for excessive periods of time. In this case, if a station has been transmitting for too long, and is therefore preventing other stations from accessing the medium, the MAU will disable the output from the station. This function is discussed in section 6.5.

6.3.1   Medium Signaling Levels

Due to the diversity of media types available for Ethernet/IEEE 802.3 transmission, it is not possible to define the actual signaling characteristics within a single statement. Instead, since each has its own particular attributes, they must be discussed separately.

- **Coaxial Media 10Base5**
  The signal on the coaxial cable due to a single MAU (as measured at the MAU transmitter output) is composed of an AC component and an offset. This signal is then expressed in terms of current immediately adjacent to the MAU connection, and has an offset component of -37mA to -45mA, and an AC component from +28mA up to the offset value. In addition, a MAU must be able to maintain an average DC level of at least 2.2V on the coaxial cable in

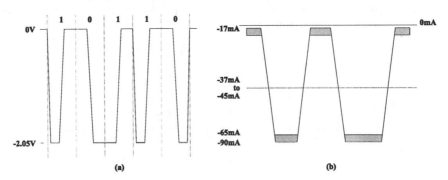

Figure 6-5: Typical Coaxial Cable Waveforms and Recommended Driver Signal Levels

the presence of two or more other MAUs transmitting concurrently. Typical waveforms present on the cable and recommended driver current signal levels are shown in figure 6-5 (a) and (b), respectively.

The actual current at any point on the cable is a function of the transmitted current and the loss to the point of measurement, with negative current defined as being the current out of the center conductor into the MAU. The rise/fall times (10-90%) should be within 25+/-5ns for 10Mbps systems and should match within 2ns. Harmonic content from the bit rate is quoted as per table 6-1.

In terms of Jitter, no more than 2.5ns of edge jitter is acceptable when a pseudo-random Manchester encoded signal is injected into the cable. When determining acceptability of this, it is assumed that the data is sent over the Data Out (DO) circuit through a zero length AUI cable, and when a 25ohm +/-1% resistor is substituted for the coaxial cable connection.

Table 6-1: Harmonic Content of Coaxial Signals

Harmonic	Level Below Fundamental
2nd and 3rd Harmonics	20dB
4th and 5th Harmonics	30dB
6th and 7th Harmonics	40dB
All higher Harmonics	50dB

- **Coaxial Media 10Base-2**

  Except for *Edge Jitter*, the signaling requirements for 10Base-2 media are identical to those of 10Base-5. Edge jitter in this case can be up to 8ns when a pseudo-random, Manchester encoded signal that exhibits no more than 1ns of jitter is injected into the cable at one end.

- **Twisted Pair Media (10Base-T)**

  The characteristics of twisted-pair media generally differ significantly from those of coaxial cable in that we now have distinct transmit and receive paths. In addition, transmission over twisted-pair media is via what is known as *Balanced Differential* signaling. This scheme affords additional protection against data corruption due to Electromagnetic Interference (EMI) as shown in figure 6-6.

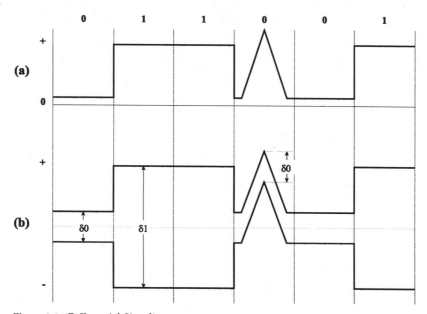

Figure 6-6: Differential Signaling

In the first example (a), we have a simple (non-differential) scheme that signals against a common reference point (ground). In the event of interference, a *spike* can cause a 0 bit to be read as a 1 thereby corrupting our data.

In the second example (b) where a differential signal is used, we utilize a pair of wires for our signal, without a common ground. Thus, a binary 1 would be represented as a *high* positive value on one conductor, and a *high* negative value on the other. Similarly, a binary 0 is represented by a *low* positive value on one conductor and a *low* negative value on the other. Now, since our conductors form a single twisted pair, any interference will affect both conductors equally. Since our data is represented by the *differential* between the two, this remains constant and the data can be recovered correctly.

The peak differential voltage into a 100Ω resistive load is always between 2.2V and 2.8V when an *all ones* Manchester Encoded signal is used. Any harmonic measured on the transmitted data should be at least 27dB below the fundamental, and the jitter added to the signal as it passes through the MAU and twisted pair should be no more than +/-3.5ns.

- **Fiber Optic Media (10Base-FP/FB/FL)**
  In the same way that we have separate transmit and receive paths for twisted-pair media, so we do in fiber optic networks. Hence, although we are now dealing with optical rather than electrical signals, there are some similarities between our twisted-pair (copper) networks and the 10Base-Fx variants. Here however, is where those similarities cease. Optical networks are more complex, and table 6-2 outlines the major optical parameters to which our 10Base-Fx units must adhere. Many of the terms used are self explanatory, while others are described in chapter 7.

Table 6-2: MDI Optical Parameters

Parameter	Units	10Base-FP	10Base-FB	10Base-FL
Transmit Parameters				
Carrier Wavelength				
• Minimum	nm	800	800	800
• Maximum	nm	910	910	910
Spectral Width	nm	<75	<75	<75
Modulation Extinction Ratio	dB	≤13	≤13	≤13
Transmit Pulse Rise & Fall Times				
• Maximum (Data)	ns	10	10	10
• Minimum (Data)	ns	2	0	0
• Maximum Difference (Data)	ns	3	3	3
• Maximum (Idle)	ns	N/A	10	25
• Minimum (Idle)	ns	N/A	0	0
• Maximum Difference (Idle)	ns	N/A	3	25
Transmit Pulse				
• Overshoot	%	5	25	25
• Undershoot	%	5	10	10
Transmit Pulse Edge Jitter				
• Added, Data Out Circuit to MDI	ns	N/A	N/A	+/-2
• Total at MDI (Data)	ns	+/-1	+/-2	+/-4
• Total at MDI (Idle)	ns	N/A	+/-2	N/A

Table 6-2: MDI Optical Parameters (Continued)

Parameter	Units	10Base-FP	10Base-FB	10Base-FL
Transmit Parameters				
Tx Pulse Duty Cycle Distortion				
• Data	ns	+/-1	+/-2.5	+/-2.5
• Idle	ns	N/A	+/-2.5	+/-50
Transmit Average Power Range				
• Minimum	dBm	-15	-20	-20
• Maximum	dBm	-11	-12	-12
Receive Parameters				
Receive Average Power Range				
• Minimum	dBm	-41	-32.5	-32.5
• Maximum	dBm	-27	-12	-12
MAU Receive Edge Jitter (Data)				
• Received at MDI	ns	+/-4.5	+/-2.0	+/-6.5
• Added, MDI to Data In Circuit	ns	N/A	N/A	+/-8.5
• Total at Data In Circuit (MAU)	ns	N/A	+/-6.5	+/-15.0
Receive Pulse Rise and Fall Times				
• Maximum (Data)	ns	18.5	31.5	31.5
• Minimum (Data)	ns	2.0	0.0	0.0
• Maximum Difference (Data)	ns	3.0	3.0	3.0
• Maximum (Idle)	ns	N/A	31.5	41.0
• Minimum (Idle)	ns	N/A	0.0	0.0
• Maximum Difference (Idle)	ns	N/A	3.0	25.0

6.4 Collision Detection

The MAU outputs a constant Idle (IDL) signal on the Control In (CI) circuit where no collision is detected. When a collision is detected and therefore needs to be signaled to the Physical Layer Signaling (PLS) layer, the MAU then outputs a CS0 over the CI circuit. As a more general statement, we can also say that a collision signal will be output over the CI circuit whenever there are two or more MAUs transmitting, whether we are transmitting or not. Since each media type offers different collision characteristics however, it is necessary to discuss each individually as follows:

6.4.1 Coaxial Cable Types (10Base5 and 10Base2)

The actual maximum DC voltage on the cable during normal (non-collision) operation is -1293mV (max.). For collision detection using a 10Base5 topology, the MAU's detection threshold is then in the range of -1448mV to -1590mV. For 10Base2 topologies, this threshold is in the range of -1404mV to -1581mV. Two specific cases for collision assertion then exist for this general media type.

- If the MAU has been transmitting for 20 bits times or more before a transmission from another MAU is detected, then the CS0 signal must commence within 17 bits times of this second signal being detected. For coaxial media, detection of a second MAU's transmission is where the DC level on the MDI becomes more negative.

- If the MAU has been transmitting for less than 20 bit times, then the CS0 signal must be presented to the CI circuit no more than 29 bit times after the start of transmission by the MAU, and the detection of the other MAU.

Once the collision has ceased, again two specific scenarios exist for the de-assertion of the Collision presence signal:

- Where the collision occurred between this MAU and one other MAU, the IDL signal is re-instated on the CI circuit within 17 bit times of the end of either transmission. In this case, the end of transmission of the second MAU is detected by the DC level on the MDI becoming less negative.

- Where the collision was caused by more than two MAUs, the IDL signal is presented on the CI circuit within 29 bits of the end of transmission of all but one MAU.

6.4.2   Twisted Pair Media (10Base-T)

For twisted pair media, a collision is defined as being simultaneous activity on both the Data Out (DO) and Receive Data (RD) circuits. When a collision is detected, a CS0 signal is sent on the Control In (CI) circuit within 9 bit times. Once the collision has ceased, the CS0 signal is then de-asserted within 9 bit times.

6.4.3   Fiber Media (10Base-F)

The three 10Base-F specifications (10Base-FP, 10Base-FB, and 10Base-FL) each have slightly different collision function requirements. In each case, a collision is detected when we have simultaneous activity on both the transmit and receive circuits (in this case DO and ORD[2]). Equally, the collision is signaled by the presentation of a CS0 on the Control In (CI) circuit. The differences then lie in the timings at which the CS0 signal must be asserted/de-asserted, and are shown in table 6-3.

Table 6-3: Collision Presence Signal Assertion/De-Assertion

Specification	CS0 Signal	
	Assertion (Bit Times)	De-Assertion (Bit Times)
10Base-FP	3.5	3
10Base-FB	3.5	5
10Base-FL	3.5	7

6.5   Jabber Protection

Ethernet/802.3 networks were originally designed to work with *shared* media. Thus, transmissions must be deferred at any time that the medium is in use. DTEs that have failed, or are transmitting exceptionally long frames, must then be stopped or the network will be deemed unavailable for all other devices. In order to enforce this, MAUs have a built-in self-interrupt facility (Jabber Protection) which inhibits

---

[2] ORD is Optical Receive Data.

data from being transmitted over the medium. Within the MAU, there is a simple circuit that allows a transmission window of between 20ms and 150ms, during which time a normal data-link frame can be transmitted. Should any frame exceed this window, the Jabber function inhibits further transmissions from the DTE.

For normal transmission, the maximum frame size would be 1518 octets plus 8 octets of Preamble. Hence, the maximum time required to transmit this frame would be 1.2208ms (calculated as $((1518+8)*8)/(10*10^6)$). Twenty milliseconds then, should be adequate time for any transmission to take place, and any transmission that exceeds this timeframe can be considered to be in error. The MAU then activates Jabber protection at some time between 20ms and 150ms after the transmission started. In any event, the attached DTE must be inhibited from transmitting any further data 150ms from commencement of the transmission.

Once this feature is activated, the MAU next turns on the Collision Presence signal to the DTE, and continues to inhibit further transmission until it either receives a power reset, or the DTE has ceased transmission to the MAU for a period of 0.5s +/- 50%.

6.6 Signal Quality Error Test - SQE(T)

Since merely connecting a MAU (transceiver) to a DTE does not tell the DTE that the MAU is functional, the Ethernet[3] standard introduced the SQE(T) function. In operation, the MAU simply sends a Signal Quality Error signal (collision) to the DTE after the Data Out (DO) circuit has gone into the idle state once a frame has been transmitted. The DTE, on receipt of the collision signal, will interpret this as the SQE(T) function since it is not currently transmitting data, and will therefore take no further action. Thus, this *heartbeat* as it is sometimes called, is used solely to provide a basic level confidence test between the DTE and the attached MAU.

The mechanics of SQE(T) are simple. Where implemented, the MAU must start sending the collision presence signal (a CS0 over the CI circuit) within 0.6µs to 1.6µs after commencement of the IDL signal on the DO circuit. Once started, this must then continue for a time equivalent to between 5 and 15 bit times. It has to be made clear, that at no time is a collision *Jam* signal generated. This feature is purely a test signal, and has significance only between the MAU and the DTE.

Since SQE(T) is not supported by the 802.3 standard, this function is generally implemented as a switch-selectable option on most MAUs today. That said, it is common practice that, where this option is provided, all MAUs are shipped with this feature enabled. While this may seem to be perfectly innocent, it can and indeed does cause many problems where repeaters are concerned. Basically, repeaters have no concept of SQE(T), and therefore interpret this signal as a valid collision. In the case of repeaters then, the SQE(T) function must be disabled, or the repeater will log excess collisions that may result in the port to which the MAU is attached becoming partitioned.[4]

---

[3] SQE(T) is not a supported feature within the IEEE 802.3 standard.
[4] See chapter 8 for a complete discussion on Repeaters.

6.7   Other MAU Features

What we have discussed so far are the standard features found on all MAUs. There are however several other features that, while specific to certain media types and/or topologies, should be considered before leaving this subject. In addition, some vendors offer features that, while they are proprietary in nature, are important to the overall operation of a network. These are therefore also considered here.

6.7.1   Link Integrity Test

10Base-T MAUs transmit a specific sequence of idle (IDL) signals whenever there is no data to be transmitted. This IDL sequence is an IDL followed by 16ms +/-8ms of silence, and is interpreted by the receiver as link pulses. MAUs then monitor the Receive Data (RD) circuit for data and *Link Pulses*. If neither data nor link pulses are received for a time of between 50ms and 150ms the link is assumed to be inactive, and an *input_idle* is sent over the DI circuit. In this way, the attached DTE will know whether or not transmission is possible, but more importantly the MAU at the remote end of the link will know that a good transmission path exists.

10Base-Fx MAUs offer a similar link integrity test, although in this case link integrity is defined through the level of light detected at the receiver. When the level falls below that required for reliable operation, the link test fails and the *input_idle* signal is sent as before. This *low light* state is defined as being where the optical power level falls below -32.5dBm and remains in this condition for 30 or more bit times. The link test will pass where this optical level is restored for a period of 0.5s +/-0.25s.

6.7.2   Reverse Polarity Detection and Correction

You will recall that with 10BaseT we use a differential mode of data transmission. As such, each signal (transmit and receive) has two components referred to as the positive and negative sides. On the transmit side for example, the two components are Tx+ and Tx-; equally for receive we then have Rx+ and Rx-. In addition, you will remember that our 10BaseT ISO 8877 (RJ45) interface normally uses the pin assignments shown in table 6-4. With this type of technology we are working with a differential (as opposed to absolute) signal level, so it really does not concern us as to whether the two elements of each signal are reversed. Most 10Base-T MAUs are therefore able to detect where reversal has taken place, and then invert the signal electronically. For example, if Tx+ and Tx- (or indeed Rx+ and Rx-) were reversed, the MAU would correct this situation automatically. What it would not do however is convert an MDI interface to an MDI-X and switch the transmit and receive lines completely.

Table 6-4: 10BaseT (RJ45) Normal Pin Assignments

Pin	Assignment	Description
1	Tx+	Transmit positive element
2	Tx-	Transmit negative element
3	Rx+	Receive positive element
6	Rx-	Receive negative element

6.7.3 Extended Distance Working

Many vendors of MAUs and ancillary devices offer a facility that allows stations to be connected beyond the normal distances allowed in the specification. In operation, the driver circuitry within the MAU impresses a larger signal on the medium for transmission, hence the signal is able to travel a greater distance. The sensitivity of the receiver circuitry is then also increased such that weaker signals can be detected.

Many vendors claim an increase in distance of up to 40% using this technique, although it must be stressed that this cannot generally be guaranteed. The problems facing this scheme relate to the overall quality of installation of the cable plant, and indeed whether or not similar equipment is being used at each end of the link. For example, the characteristics of the cable (Category[5] 5 as opposed to Category 4 or even 3), and the quality of the terminations will play a large part as to whether we are able to reliably transfer data over these distances. Equally, driver circuitry at the remote end may be unable to recover the signal or indeed drive the signal back to the transmitter. As a rule then, while this may seem an attractive proposition, extending the distance of any connection beyond that defined within the standard should be avoided if at all possible.

6.7.4 Redundant MAUs

In the preceding sections we have discussed several features of the humble MAU that are on the periphery of its standard operation. One last feature, offered by some vendors, is that of redundant link configuration.

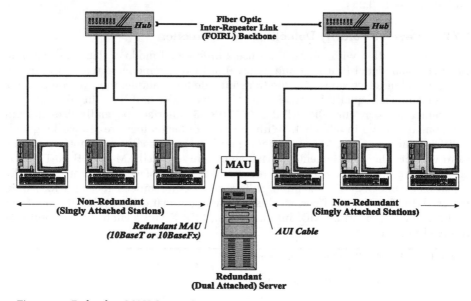

Figure 6-7: Redundant MAU Connections

---

[5] The Category of cable such as that used for 10BaseT or 100BaseTx refers to the quality and therefore the maximum transmission bandwidth to which it has been tested.

Firstly, it must be understood that this is a non-standard implementation. The principles of operation however lie in the clever use of the Link Pulse found on 10BaseT and 10BaseFx units, and is glamorous in its simplicity. In essence, the MAU is equipped with two connections which are designated as being the *Primary* and *Secondary* links. The link pulse on the Primary link is monitored by the MAU, and all the while this is present, data is barred from being sent over the Secondary. Should the MAU detect a loss of link pulse over the Primary link, it then sends data over the Secondary link instead, and bars data from being sent over the primary. Of course, once the change-over has occurred, the link pulse on the secondary link is then monitored, and loss here will cause data to be transferred back to the Primary. The one minor drawback is that if both the Primary and Secondary links are unavailable, then the MAU will endlessly toggle between links. Figure 6-7 shows how connections are made to this type of MAU, which in this case links a server to two Hubs and provides resilience even where Hub Failure occurs.

6.8 Multi-Port MAUs

Before leaving MAUs, it is worth noting that some vendors sell what have become know as Multi-Port Transceivers or Multi-Port MAUs. These devices, sometimes also referred to as *Fan-Out Units*, or a *"LAN in a Can"* are, just as their name suggests, multiple MAUs within a single enclosure.

Originally these devices were developed to overcome the limitations imposed on the number of station connections allowed on a single cable segment, and to also reduce the overall cable requirements for smaller installations. For example, with 10Base5 cabling we must maintain at least 2.5m between stations. Hence, to connect say 8 stations, we would need to use 20m of cable. Equally, with this medium we can have up to 100 node connections per 500m cable segment, but 100 stations in close proximity would still require 250m of cable. Cabling a small area with a high density of stations therefore becomes almost impossible.

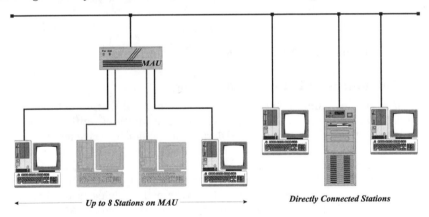

Up to 8 Stations on MAU   *Directly Connected Stations*

Figure 6-8: Multi-Port MAU - Basic Usage

The Multi-Port MAU addressed this issue since it allowed multiple stations (typically up to 8) to be connected to the backbone, yet counted as only a single connection to the cable segment. In Figure 6-8 we see an example of this type of device where we have 8 stations in a single room, together with other stations spread throughout the building.

We can now see how the Multi-Port MAU can reduce overall backbone cabling, although these devices also have another use - to create small networks where a backbone cable is not an option. In this scenario, the term *"LAN in a Can"* really does have meaning, since a collapsed backbone is created from Multi-Port MAUs, allowing up to around 64 stations to be attached. Figure 6-9 shows the Multi-Port MAU cascaded two deep (normally the maximum allowed), with the master unit feeding further units from each port. Although it must be stressed that this is not (and indeed never was) a common implementation, it could provide a cost effective solution in certain instances.

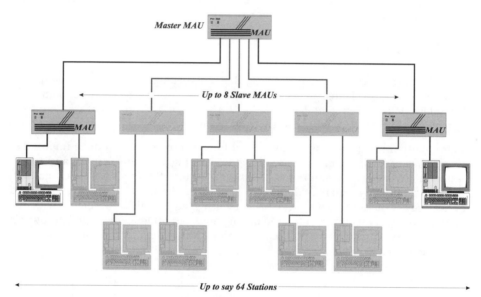

Figure 6-9: Multi-Port MAU - Cascade Configuration

6.8.1 Limitations on Multi-Port MAU Usage

While the scenarios painted above may seem extremely attractive to those trying to implement small networks, there are two major limitations with the Multi-Port MAU. Firstly, the overall length of AUI cable is generally restricted such that no station may be more than 50m (or less in many instances) away from the backbone cable. Hence, for any station connected to the MAU, the sum of the length of AUI cable between the backbone and the MAU plus the length of AUI cable from the MAU to the station is limited. In addition, where the device is used to create a complete LAN without the use of backbone cables, this overall AUI cable length limitation may be even more severe.

Finally, these devices tend to have only a single control over SQE(T). Thus, when this facility is enabled at the MAU, it will be *On* for all ports. Obvious care must therefore be taken as to what devices will eventually be connected to those MAU ports.

6.9   MAU Management

When talking of management for the humble MAU, the ISO/IEC 8802-3 standard defines a set of mechanisms that allow the management of integrated MAUs. Additionally, the standard then defines further manageable objects, allowing certain characteristics that may be detected via the AUI of the connected device (DTE or Repeater) to be observed.   At this time however, management of MAUs that are external to the device is not standardized.

Today, most management applications rely on the Simple Network Management Protocol[6] (SNMP).   Elements of this provide a means to identify, monitor, and control the functionality of the MAU. Indeed, through this protocol, application platforms are able to fetch (*GET*) information from the MAU, change the status (*SET*) of the MAU, and receive unsolicited information from the MAU (*TRAP*).

6.9.1   Managed Objects

The vehicle through which SNMP manages any device is through the objects contained within the Management information Base or MIB.[7] Table 6-5 identifies and briefly describes each of these objects available within the MAU MIB.

Table 6-5: MAU Managed Objects

Object	Description	Required
MAUID	An integer value that uniquely identifies a single MAU	Y
MAUType	An integer value that identifies the MAU type. Valid types are *global*, *other*, and *unknown*	Y
MediaAvailable	Defines whether or not the medium is currently available. Permitted types are *other*, *unknown*, *available, not available, remote fault, invalid signal.*	Y
LoseMediaCounter	A counter that reports the number of times that the MAU has left the MediaAvailable state of *available*.	N
Jabber	Defines whether the MAU is currently in the *Jabber* state.	Y
MAUAdminState	Defines the current state of the MAU. Valid states are *other*, *unknown*, *operational*, *standby*, and *shutdown*.	Y
BbMAUXmitRcvSplitType	Applicable only to 10Broad36 systems, this object defines the cable plant type. Valid values are *other*, *single*, and *dual*.	N

[6] The Simple Network Management Protocol (SNMP) is an application protocol within the Internet Protocol (IP) suite. Further discussion of this protocol is however beyond the scope of this text.
[7] The Management Information Base (MIB) is a collection of objects accessible through the Simple Network Management Protocol (SNMP).

Table 6-5: MAU Managed Objects (Continued)

Object	Description	Required
BroadbandFrequencies	An object that identifies the transmit carrier frequency used in 10Broad36 MAUs.	N
ResetMAUAction	An object used to reset the MAU in much the same way as a power cycle of at least 0.5s duration.	N
MAUAdminControl	Used to change the MAUAdminState. Valid inputs are *shutdown* and *standby*.	N
Jabber	A Trap (notification) sent to the management station whenever a MAU enters the Jabber state.	Y

6.10 Summary

In this chapter we have taken a detailed look at the operation of the Medium Attachment Unit. In essence, although relatively simplistic in nature, this device provides us with the ability to connect our station (DTE) to the network, and also provides basic medium monitoring capabilities. From this discussion, we have seen that the MAU not only transmits and receives data, but also is responsible for several other key tasks. Most importantly, the MAU is responsible for the detection of collisions, monitoring the medium itself, ensuring that DTEs do not hold the media, and of course supports the direct connection to the media via the Medium Dependent Interface (MDI).

Today, the MAU is normally internal to the device. PC Network Interface Cards (NICs) will normally incorporate the MAU, and present the MDI typically as an ISO 8877 (RJ45) connection. Equally today, since most networks have migrated to Twisted-Pair cable plant, we find that the integral MAU is capable of operation at both 10Mbps and 100Mbps.[8] Not satisfied with this, these dual speed devices will then normally be able to detect the correct speed at which to operate, choosing the highest speed that both ends of the link support through *Auto-Negotiation*.[9]

Whatever type of MAU is used, whether exposed or not, the same basic functionality remains. Differences do exist between Ethernet and 802.3 units, but these are generally overcome through switch-selectable options. Certainly care has to be taken when connecting exposed units, but the overall design criteria of simplicity, robustness, and cost-effective connectivity, are met by the humble MAU.

---

[8] 100Mbps operation is discussed in chapter 9.
[9] Auto-Negotiation is discussed in chapter 11.

10Base-F

Within the Ethernet/IEEE 802.3 standards, there exist several variants based upon Fiber Optic media. We have already briefly touched upon the most common forms of the 10Mbps fiber optic implementation, specifically 10Base-FL and FOIRL. In later chapters, we will meet those that relate to higher bandwidths such as 100Base-Fx and 1000Base-X. The purpose of this chapter however is to introduce two lesser-used 10Mbps specifications, namely 10Base-FP and 10Base-FB. Collectively, the 10Mbps fiber specifications are grouped together and are known simply as 10Base-F. It is these then, that we shall discuss here.

The first thing that we realize is that each of the 10Mbps Fiber specifications are incompatible with one another. Equally, when we examine how 10Base-F fits in with our other technologies, we learn that differences exist at the PLS and AUI[1] interface. Specifically, 10Base-F MAUs do not support the MAU *isolate* function or *Monitor mode*. Parallels can however be drawn with many aspects of the more general 10Base-X specifications. For example, as with other media types, 10Base-F MAUs do not require that an AUI is physically present. This then allows the MAU functionality to be built into devices such as Network Interface Cards (NICs). Also, since we are still dealing with a *Baseband* system, our devices will still *contend* for the network medium. In general then, although the medium itself is different, we are still dealing with a CSMA/CD system, and therefore all that we have discussed so far still applies.

7.1   Advantages of Optical Fiber

Traditionally, the biggest argument against the use of fiber media has been that of cost. Installation is more complex than that of copper, and is therefore more expensive. Certainly installers need to invest in relatively expensive equipment in order to splice and terminate fiber strands properly, and high quality test equipment is costly. The advantages can however outweigh these objections, and a shrewd network manager who installed fiber in key parts of his network is now set to take advantage of the additional benefits that this media type brings. For example:

- **Noise Immunity**
  Fiber Optics do not suffer from ingress Electromagnetic Radiation (EMI). Hence, our media can be installed in areas that are otherwise considered to be electrically hostile. These cables can be run next to high power plant and

---

[1] Physical Layer Signalling (PLS) and Attachment Unit Interface (AUI) are discussed in chapter 5.

machinery, or indeed anywhere copper cables (either coaxial or twisted-pair) would be inappropriate.

- **Lower Attenuation**
  Unlike copper cable, optical fiber suffers less from attenuation. This means that we are able to use longer segments, and can therefore connect devices without the use of repeaters to extend the LAN.

- **Security**
  In just the same way that fiber does not suffer from ingress interference, it also does not radiate any signal. Hence where security is an issue, fiber becomes the ideal choice. In addition, like its twisted-pair counterparts, this forms a point-to-point topology and therefore devices can only be added by severing the cable.

- **Scaleable Bandwidth**
  Fiber provides us with a scaleability that cannot be found with other media. Emerging Ethernet/802.3 standards, more than ever before, rely on the use of fiber. So, 10Mbps, 100Mbps, and even 1000Mbps devices can each use the same fiber type. Once again, the network manager who installed fiber rather than Category 3 Unshielded Twisted Pair, is now ready to implement those new technologies whenever he chooses.

Most importantly though, the cost of installing fiber optic cables is falling. So, by using a combination of media types, we are now able to create cost effective, complex LANs, that can cover large areas and that can take advantage of technology as it becomes available.

7.2 Optical Characteristics

The standard connector for the MDI for all 10Base-F specifications is the BFOC/2.5 (Straight Tip or *ST*) connector. Certainly, and especially in the case of FOIRL, vendors have used a variety of connectors in the past. The most common choices however, have always been either the ST connector mentioned above, the *Sub Miniature Assembly* (SMA) connector (due to its robust construction) or most recently, the Subscriber connector (SC). Equally, various fiber optic types (both single mode and multi-mode) have been employed over the years, however the most common implementation (and indeed that recommended in the 802.3 standard) uses multi-mode fiber of 62.5/125µm nominal diameters. Table 7-1 outlines some of the more important optical characteristics of the fiber and connectors.

Table 7-1: Optical Characteristics

Characteristic	Value
Attenuation	$\leq$ 3.75dB/km (λ=850nm) - See Note 1
Modal Bandwidth	$\geq$ 160MHz-km (λ=850nm)
Propagation Delay	$\leq$ 5µs/km (equivalent to 0.67c)
Connector Insertion Loss	$\leq$ 1.0dB
10Base-FP Segment Insertion Loss	16dB to 26dB (λ=850nm) - See Note 2
10Base-FB Segment Insertion Loss	$\leq$ 12.5dB (λ=850nm)

Table 7-1: Optical Characteristics (Continued)

Characteristic	Value
10Base-FL Segment Insertion Loss	≤ 12.5dB (λ=850nm)

Notes: Where links of under 5m are used, it may be necessary to use an attenuator in order to achieve the optical characteristics of the MDI discussed in the previous chapters.

This value is based upon the loss over the entire segment, including the 10Base-FP *Star*. The insertion loss across a 10Base-FP segment (excluding star) should not exceed 6dB.

7.3   10Base-FL

Certainly the most common 10Mbps fiber implementation today is 10Base-FL (where FL stands for Fiber Link). Sometimes, and erroneously, referred to as the *Fiber Optic Inter-Repeater Link* (FOIRL), 10Base-FL represents the standardization of fiber usage for station-to-repeater and repeater-to-repeater links. Early 802.3 standards permitted the interconnection of repeaters through up to 1km of fiber optic media, and hence FOIRL was born.

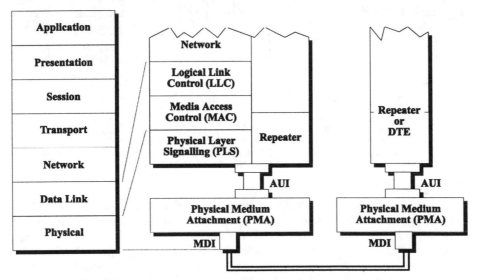

Figure 7-1: 10Base-FL and the OSI Model

The connection of stations in this way was however omitted, and it was not until September 1993, with the introduction of the IEEE 802.3j specification, that 10Base-FL was ratified, and with it station connections. Ever resourceful, many vendors produced MAUs that would connect stations using the FOIRL specification. As a result two specifications exist today, that although have many similarities, differ primarily in the maximum fiber distance that may be used. For example, FOIRL has a maximum distance of 1km per segment, while 10Base-FL may be used with segment lengths of up to 2km. Figure 7-1 shows the relationship between 10Base-FL and the OSI model.

Functionally, it has to be said that FOIRL and 10Base-FL are similar. 10Base-FL provides backwards compatibility with the older FOIRL specification, and allows communication between FOIRL and 10Base-FL MAUs, albeit with a distance limited to just 1km. From a purely practical perspective then, 10Base-FL provides for a *point-to-point* connected star topology network. This is shown in more detail in figure 7-2.

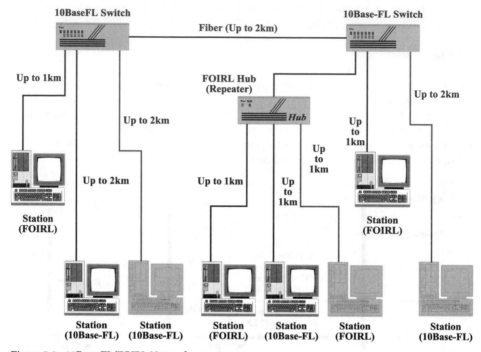

Figure 7-2: 10Base-FL/FOIRL Network

In the figure we see both standard 10Base-FL and FOIRL connections, and also connections of a hybrid nature mixing both specifications. Also notice that it is permissible to use either 10Base-FL or FOIRL as *inter-repeater* links, and as end-station connections. Such mixing and/or connections will of course be limited by distance as outlined above, and repeater-to-repeater connections will be subject to those limitations applicable to the inter-repeater link distances and maximum number of repeaters that may be employed in an end-to-end network. These parameters are detailed in chapter 8.

7.3.1   10Base-FL Signaling

With 10Base-FL little actually changes over and above what has already been discussed. In essence, any data that the MAU receives over the Data Out (DO) circuit will be sent over the Optical Transmit Data (OTD) circuit to the MDI. Whenever there is no data to be transmitted, an OPT_IDL signal that consists of 4 to 21 bit times of the lower light level followed by a periodic pulse waveform of 1MHz +25%/-15%.

7.4 10Base-FB

The *Fiber Backbone* (10Base-FB) specification is designed, as its name suggests, specifically with backbone applications in mind. Allowing segments of up to 2km, and also allowing larger numbers of repeaters to be cascaded, this specification is therefore ideally suited to that environment.

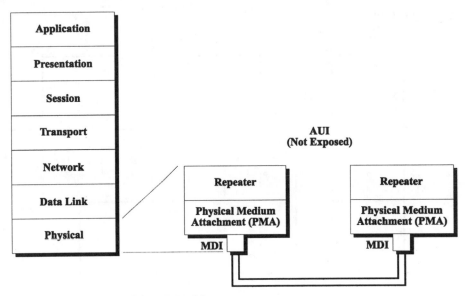

Figure 7-3: 10Base-FB and the OSI Model

10Base-FB repeaters use synchronous transmission for signaling both data and idle conditions, hence the provision for greater numbers of repeaters. In truth though, 10Base-FB is seldom implemented in today's networks. We are still limited to only 2km between devices, and since it is based on repeaters, only shared media is supported. In addition, there is no provision for higher bandwidths such as 100Mbps or 1000Mbps, and as a result most vendors have ignored this technology completely. Instead, for 10Mbps operation vendors have preferred to concentrate on the more popular 10Base-FL devices, and for network extension, use bridges, switches and routers. Sadly, what could have been introduced to extend our network came too late, and has become another cast-aside technology in our fast-changing world.

In figure 7-3 we see the relationship between 10Base-FB and the OSI model. Notice here that only repeaters are included (there is no inclusion of end station implementations within the standard), and that the AUI is not (and indeed according to the standard, should not be) exposed as with other 10Base-Fx variants. While there is really no sound reasoning for this omission, it seems unlikely that vendors will ever attempt to provide external 10Base-FB MAUs, and therefore exposed AUIs will never become a requirement.

7.4.1 10Base-FB Signaling

Slight differences do exist in the signaling that we have met so far. 10Base-FB introduces 4 further PMA to MDI signal encodings over and above the normal CD0 and CD1. These are then used in specific sequences to signal over the *Optical Transmit Data* (OTD) circuit. Figure 7-4 then shows these signals in relation to standard bit timings.

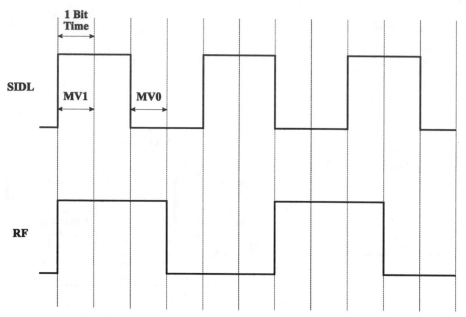

Figure 7-4:   MV0, MV1, SIDL, and RF Signaling

- **Manchester Code Violation Zero (MV0)** - A clocked bit symbol that remains low for the entire bit duration.

- **Manchester Code Violation One (MV1)** - A clocked bit symbol that remains high for the entire bit duration.

- **Synchronous Idle (SIDL)** - A repeating sequence of MV1/MV1/MV0/MV0.

- **Remote Fault (RF)** - A repeating sequence of MV1/MV1/MV1/MV0/ MV0/MV0.

Two types of fault condition can be detected, namely local and remote. Local faults are the detection of low light, *Jabber*, and invalid data. A Remote fault is detected by the receipt of the *Remote Fault* sequence. The Synchronous Idle (SIDL) is transmitted whenever the repeater sends an idle (IDL) message, or when the unit receives a Remote Fault (RF). Equally, the unit will transmit its own Remote Fault (RF) sequence whenever it detects any *local* fault condition as described above.

7.5 10Base-FP

10Base-FP defines a *passive star* topology that allows both DTEs and repeaters to be interconnected with segments of up to 500m. Being passive in nature, 10Base-FP is suited to those environments where power is not available or is unreliable. As with 10Base-FB however, 10Base-FP has very little following as is presented here purely for completeness.

The relationship of 10Base-FP to the OSI model is shown in figure 7-5. In this example, notice that DTEs or other repeaters are interconnected via a *Fiber Optic Passive Star*. This *Star* then acts as a hub, and indeed it is this device that is at the very heart of this specification.

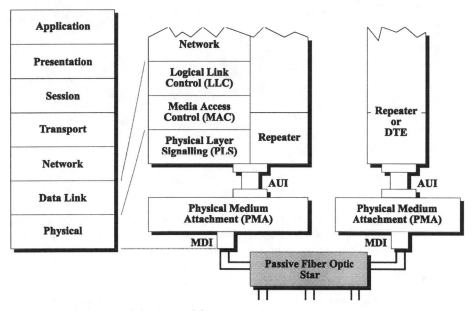

Figure 7-5: 10Base-FP and the OSI Model

As we have said, 10Base-FP typically has little application within commercial installations except where power is an issue. Certainly the military use 10Base-FP, since it provides a secure network environment with no egress radiation. Also, since it is totally passive, it can be placed where maintenance would otherwise be a problem. Operationally, the star itself functions in a similar fashion to a repeater in that signals arriving at any port are reproduced at all others. The star is not a repeater however, since no preamble regeneration or re-timing takes place. Comparing this with 10Base-FB and 10Base-FL where true repeaters are *always* used, we now see how each of the 10Base-F specifications are totally incompatible with each other.

One final difference that does require mention however, is that of definition. With 10Base-FB and 10Base-FL we talk of *Fiber Optic Link Segments* as being the fiber link between the MDIs of two communicating devices. With 10Base-FP, the term *Link Segment* is replaced by the term *Fiber Optic Mixing Segment* and includes the Passive Star hub itself. Figure 7-6 then demonstrates this final point.

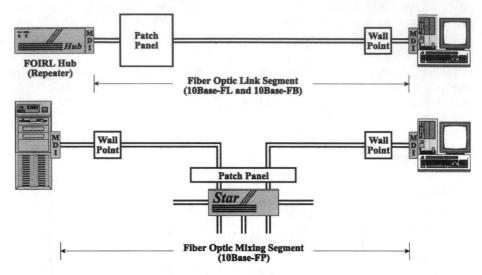

Figure 7-6:   10Base-FP Mixing Segments

7.6   Summary

In this chapter we have re-visited some of the parameters associated with MAUs as applied to the 10Base-F specifications. While the actual subject of the MAU has been discussed in detail previously, since 10Base-F is a group of technologies in its own right it therefore requires mention outside the mainstream discussion of Ethernet/802.3.

This chapter has introduced the topologies in use, and indeed expanded to some extent upon the features provided by fiber within the CSMA/CD standards. However, this chapter cannot be considered more than a simple overview, and should be read in conjunction with both chapter 6 (MAUs) and section G, which relates to media types and their physical characteristics.

10Mbps Repeaters C H A P T E R   8

As we have seen in previous chapters, regardless of the technology in use, LAN segments of infinite length cannot be constructed. Medium segment length is, as we have learned, constrained by several factors, not least of which are the electrical and/or optical characteristics, and the overall velocity of propagation. Indeed, as a result of these limitations, the number of MAUs that can be attached[1] on Bus topologies is also restricted in a similar fashion. So, where we wish to extend the distance of the LAN by adding segments, or indeed just increase the number of stations attached, we need to join segments together with special devices called Repeaters.

Repeaters are not limited to use within Bus topologies though. The *Hub* used with point-to-point topologies such as 10BaseT and 10BaseFx can also be a repeater,[2] it is just that in this case, the device has many ports.

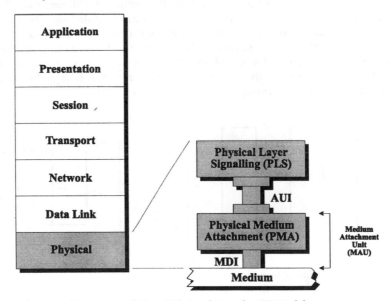

Figure 8-1: Repeaters and Their Relationship to the OSI Model

---

[1] See chapter 3 for a discussion of limitations in this regard.
[2] It is important that Repeated Hubs are not confused with their Switch counterparts. See chapter 15 for a discussion on Switching.

So what makes a repeater so special? In real terms repeaters are actually extremely simple devices, and being physical layer devices as they are, are totally transparent to stations. Repeaters are only concerned with electrical, mechanical, and timing functions, and can therefore be summarized as devices that simply Re-generate and Re-time medium signals. Figure 8-1 shows schematically the relationship between repeaters and the OSI Model.

8.1 Repeater Usage

Repeaters, as we have said, are used to join together media segments, and to act as the interconnection point for Star topology networks. It is however necessary to understand exactly why they are needed.

As we have seen previously, a station will transmit signals at a pre-determined output level. Equally, receiving stations need to see a minimum signal level, the *receive threshold*, if they are to successfully decode the data. Unfortunately, due to attenuation and distortion introduced by the medium, and attachments such as MAUs, the signal will degrade as it passes through the cable system. At some point then, the signal becomes either so weak or distorted that recovery of data is impossible. Indeed, it is actually due to the effects of attenuation and distortion that distance and station connection limitations are imposed in the first place.

8.1.1 Signal Attenuation

Attenuation is where the overall strength of the signal is reduced over distance. This reduction is due to the natural impedance, and through imperfections in the medium that may be a result of the manufacturing process. If stations are to receive data without error, then we must ensure that the signal is maintained at a level that is greater than the receive threshold mentioned earlier. Figure 8-2 shows how signal amplitude diminishes over distance and/or time, and is therefore typical of the attenuation that we are trying to overcome with repeaters.

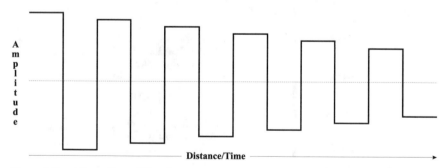

Figure 8-2: Attenuation of Signals

8.1.2 Jitter

Attenuation is not the only enemy of our signal though. We also have to look at *Jitter*, or how the harmonic content (or shape) of the signal is affected by the medium.

In an ideal world, with ideal media, Jitter would not be a problem. Unfortunately, such idealism cannot be achieved and we must work with the materials that we have. Jitter then, is caused when two (or typically more) components of the transmitted signal travel at fractionally different speeds due to imperfections that will alter the velocity of propagation (V_p).

A transmitting station will always transmit a signal with clearly defined rise/fall times. For example, in 10Base5 devices, the signal impressed on the medium must have a rise and fall time of no more than 25ns (see figure 8-3). However as this signal travels along the medium, our signal become distorted, and this clear shape is lost.

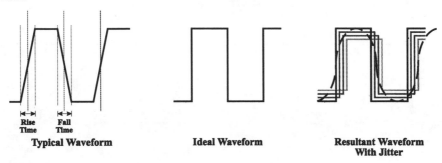

Typical Waveform   **Ideal Waveform**   **Resultant Waveform
                                                          With Jitter**

Figure 8-3: The Effects of Jitter

In the figure we see both the typical waveform with acceptable Rise and Fall times and the ideal "Square" wave. Once again, idealism is not practical and, although our *Typical Waveform* is acceptable, with the effects of jitter the signal becomes rounded and little better than sinusoidal. Failure to correctly identify the rising and falling edges of received signals then leads to misinterpretation of data. Just as with attenuation, manufacturing imperfections and the presence of taps and cable joints cause jitter. For example when a 10Base5 cable is "tapped" (even by a skilled operator), an impedance mis-match occurs, causing reflection of some of the signal. This reflection of signal then causes distortion, and Jitter is the result.

8.1.3   Typical Repeater Installations

So, since we now understand a little more of why repeaters are used, let us consider some practical examples of where these devices are typically deployed. In the following figures we see typical uses of the repeater. Figure 8-4 shows us a 10Base5 environment where, although we have used only 400m of cable, we need to increase the number of station connections. Hence we insert a repeater, which allows the addition of another 99 stations.

Equally, we may need to increase the overall cable length when the maximum station counts have not been exceeded. Consider figure 8-5 where we have a small company that has only 20 stations overall, but these stations are split between two offices on the opposite sides of a street. In this case, assuming that we were using 10Base2 cabling, we could use a maximum of 182m of cable. Local regulations would almost certainly prohibit the use of copper cable in this way, quite apart

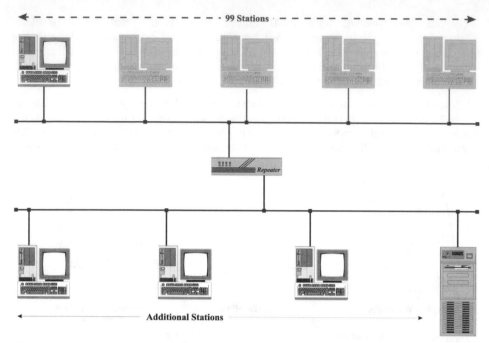

Figure 8-4: Increasing Station Count

from the fact that this cable length would possibly be insufficient to cable each office and go across the street too. A different solution must therefore be found.

In this example, we use a fiber optic cable to link the two buildings. Now we must translate our signal from electrical (in 10Base2) to optical (over the fiber) and then back to electrical again. Our repeaters perform this function and an interesting further use of repeaters is revealed. Repeaters are the only standardized way of converting between media types. Many vendors advertise what are called *media converters* that appear to perform this function, although care should be taken when implementing these. Typically, with media converters, the distances covered or station attachments allowed are much reduced, due to timing constraints or the preamble becoming shortened. This limitation then poses a problem for the unwary when the network is to be expanded at some time in the future.

Before leaving this particular example it is important to point out that where buildings are to be connected in this way, many countries prohibit the use of anything but fiber. This is because of the way in which electricity is fed into these buildings and the potential for them being connected to different electrical grounds. Hence, although repeaters must be electrically isolated from each other, in the event of a fault occurring, potentially dangerous voltages may still exist on the medium.

Finally, we should consider repeaters deployed in possibly their most common form today, that of the repeating hub. Figure 8-6, shows this typical scenario with multiple hubs (possibly on different floors of a building) linked through a fiber backbone cable. Stations then attach directly to the hubs via 10BaseT or a similar technology.

Although we have said that this is possibly the most common implementation of the repeater today, it must be stated that companies are now changing much of their network infrastructures and replacing the repeating hubs with switches.[3] Users, with their higher-powered desktop computers, are now demanding higher bandwidths that traditional *shared* networks cannot provide. Thus, it is now common to see maybe administrative staff and those that require only lower-powered machines to use shared media, and then create "server farms" and pools of higher-powered users that fully utilize high-speed *switched* Ethernet.

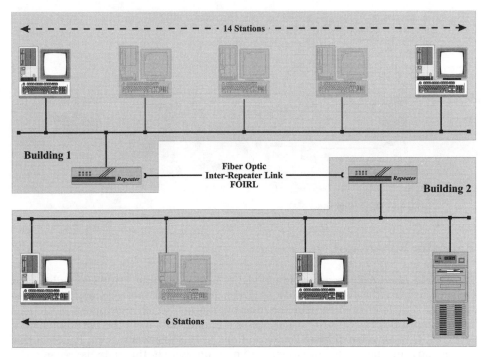

Figure 8-5: Increasing Distance

Finally, we really should realign our opinion of the lowly repeater. These hubs are now extremely intelligent, and can generally provide network administrators with vast amounts of statistics. To achieve this, they now incorporate the entire IP stack, and support Telnet and SNMP.[4] In addition, they can usually be configured such that ports can be enabled and disabled as required, and generally will be able to provide at least minimal security.[5]

---

[3] Switching is discussed in detail in chapter 15.
[4] A full discussion of IP, Telnet, and the Simple Network Management Protocol (SNMP) is beyond the scope of this book. For further information, the reader is urged to study "TCP/IP Explained" also by the author.
[5] Security is not a standardized feature of repeaters. However many vendors now offer some level of security within their repeating hubs and this facility is therefore discussed in section 8.5.

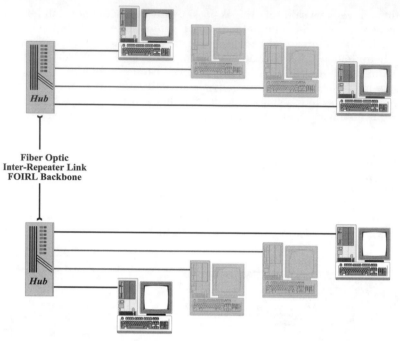

Figure 8-6: Repeating Hubs

8.2   Repeater Functionality

As we said previously, repeater functionality is quite simple. However, while it is true to say that they are generally only concerned with the regeneration and re-timing of signals, they must obey the rules of Ethernet/802.3, and indeed participate to an extent. Basically, our repeater passes a frame intact from the port on which it receives it, to all other ports. The exceptions to this are when there is contention among any of the ports, or when the port on which the data is received is *partitioned*.[6]

When repeating data in this way, we must also take into account the latency (delays) involved. The latency is defined as being the time between the first edge transition of the data on the input port, to the first edge transition of the data on the output port(s). This latency will then vary depending upon the construction of the repeater itself. For example, where the repeater has AUI connections at the input and output ports, the latency must be no more than 8 bit times. Where the MAUs on the input and output ports are built-in however, further delays are allowed as detailed in table 8-1.

Finally, when considering latency, we must also view the *variability* which is defined as being the total worst case start of packet propagation delays for successive packets separated by 96 bit times or less. In this case, for all repeaters

---

[6] See section 8.2.5 for a full discussion on partitioning.

except 10BaseFB units, we should expect less than 4 bit times, and for 10BaseFB units, 2 bit times.

Table 8-1: Start of Packet Propagation Delays

MAU Type	Input (Bit Times)	Output (Bit Times)
10Base5	6.5	3.5
10Base2	6.5	3.5
FOIRL	3.5	3.5
10BaseT	8	5
10BaseFP	3	4
10BaseFB	2	2
10BaseFL	5	5

From this discussion, it is now clear that our repeater does indeed perform a task that is more complex than is at first apparent. Thus, if we expand our original statement of functionality, we now see that this simple device provides the following:

8.2.1 Signal Regeneration, Symmetry, and Re-timing

The repeater itself is transparent to all network traffic and acquisition activity. It plays no part in transmission, back-off etc., must not alter the frame[7] in any way, and is not addressable[8] in the same way that a station is. In short, the main purpose of the repeater is to forward data on a bit-by-bit basis restoring the physical characteristics of the signal by re-timing and restoring signal strength.

The repeater therefore ensures that the amplitude, jitter, and symmetry characteristics of the output signals presented at its MDI(s), are within the specifications of the appropriate MAU type(s). Hence, any loss of signal-to-noise ratio due to losses in the cable are regained at the repeater output(s), and jitter does not accumulate over multiple segments. Of course this assumes that the input signal is within the system specifications, otherwise the repeater will be unable to pass data without error. This is particularly true where attenuation and/or jitter have increased to the point where accurate data detection has become impossible.

8.2.2 Preamble Generation

Repeaters, as we have said, work in a bit-by-bit fashion and are unconcerned with frame structure. Repeaters have no knowledge of addressing, and operate totally transparently with regard to the data field. Frames however must always have a complete preamble (the first 8 octets of the frame) and, as a consequence, repeaters are able to detect this on an input port and generate a new preamble on each output port for any received frame. This means then, that repeaters will always output a minimum of 64 bits.

---

[7] In actual fact, many modern hubs have security features built in that allow the jamming of signals and therefore do allow the modification of frames to specific ports. The method by which this is performed is however proprietary but is discussed in section 8.5.2.
[8] Most hubs today are manageable and are therefore addressable although this does not alter the basic functionality of the repeater.

8.2.3   Collision Detection and Forwarding

When a collision is detected on any port through which the repeater is transmitting, it will send a Jam signal to all ports. The Jam signal sent is the same as that sent normally, except that the first 62 bits are always an alternating pattern of 1's and 0's, and always commence with a 1. Figures 8-7 and 8-8 show collision handling for coaxial (10Base5 or 10Base2) environments. In the first example (figure 8-7), Stations A and B on Segment A are involved in a collision. The repeater then forwards this collision to Segment B.

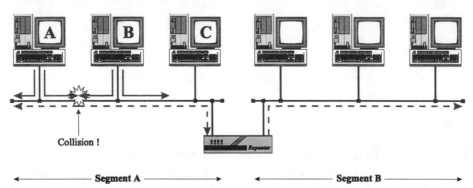

Figure 8-7:   Collision Forwarding (1)

In the second example (figure 8-8), one station on each segment is involved in the collision. Here, the data from Station B is forwarded to Segment B where it collides with the data from Station Y. Now, the collision must be passed back from Segment B to Segment A by the repeater.

Equally, repeaters work in a similar fashion for other topologies. Figure 8-9 shows a typical "Star" topology with a central Hub and several stations. In this example, Stations A and C both transmit at the same time, resulting in a collision. The repeater (Hub) sends the collision Jam signal over ALL ports so that all stations are aware of the incident.

Table 8-2: Collision to Jam Propagation Delays

MAU Type	Input (Bit Times)	Output (Bit Times)
10Base5	9	3.5
10Base2	9	3.5
FOIRL	3.5	3.5
10BaseT	9	5
10BaseFP	11.5	1
10BaseFB	3.5	2
10BaseFL	3.5	5

Note: For coaxial cable types (10Base5 and 10Base2), the input Bit Times given in the table do not include the collision rise time on the coaxial media. For the worst case round-trip delay calculation, the collision rise time plus MAU propagation delay is equivalent to 17 bit times.

In terms of delays, once a collision is detected, the repeater must commence jamming as soon as possible, in order that all stations are aware that a collision has occurred. As with the start of packet propagation delays, there are also defined maxima for the *collision-to-jam* propagation delays. Where our repeater unit has AUI connections at the input and output ports, jamming should commence within 6.5 bit times. Where internal MAUs are used, the additional allowable delays are shown in table 8-2.

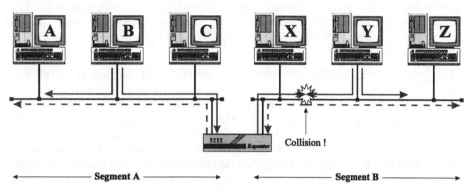

Figure 8-8:   Collision Forwarding (2)

There is an essential point that we should consider when referring to collision detection and repeaters. A repeater must not monitor a port for input for a short time after it has stopped transmitting on it. The reasoning is that if the repeater were to continue to monitor, it may well receive its own transmission and view this as new input activity. The minimum recovery time is therefore greater than the sum of all delays in the transmit and receive paths, but must be less than 10 bit times overall.

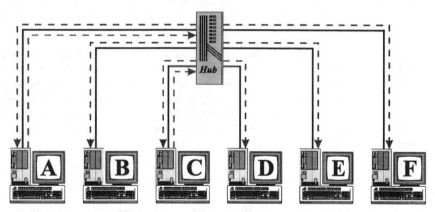

Figure 8-9:   Collision Forwarding (3)

One final element of repeater collision handling is that of fragments. It is possible that when collisions occur, small *fragments* of frames are introduced onto the network. Repeaters, on sensing these fragments, then always extend them as they pass through, such that there are 96 bits minimum. This *Fragment Extension* as it is known, ensures that all attached stations are aware of the collision and can therefore take action if appropriate.

8.2.4   Jabber Lockup Protection

You will recall from our discussion of the MAU that no device is allowed to acquire the medium for an extended period of time. For MAUs, any station that has been transmitting in excess of 150ms must be disabled, although most vendors implement the Jabber function at the lower end of the transmission window which is between 20 and 150ms.

Once the jabber function is activated, the MAU will prevent the DTE from transmitting further data until it is either power cycled or has been quiet for at least 0.5s. For repeaters with attached MAUs then, it is imperative that the port implements jabber protection before the MAU does. As such, repeaters interrupt the output of a port if it has been transmitting for longer than 5ms (equal to 50,000 bit times -20% +50%). The repeater then re-enables the port after between 96 and 116 bit times (9.6 to 11.6µs) thus ensuring that the MAU does not lock out the port.

8.2.5   Partitioning

Un-terminated network segments cause collisions due to reflections at the MDI. As a result, repeaters incorporate a feature known as *Auto-Partitioning*, where faulty segments are isolated. This then protects the remainder of the network from sensing collisions as a result of each transmitted frame.

Typically, repeaters use a simple counter on each port, which is incremented for each *consecutive* collision. When more than 30 consecutive collisions[9] have been detected at the port, or indeed if a single collision lasts longer than 30,000 bit times (3ms), the port is logically disabled and is said to be *Partitioned*. Once in this state, any collisions reported on that port will not be forwarded to the rest of the network, thereby ensuring that the faulty segment is isolated.

Every frame that is received by the repeater (on any port - including a partitioned port) will be transmitted over all of the ports as normal (including any ports that are in the partitioned state). If it is successful in transmitting over a partitioned port (i.e., there is no collision), that port is then logically re-enabled. However, a collision detected on a port that is known to be partitioned results in the port staying in the partitioned state, and the collision is not relayed through the remainder of the network.

Finally, you will recall from our discussions of the MAU, that where the Signal Quality Error Test (SQE(T)) feature is available it should not be enabled on MAUs that are connected to repeater ports. The reason for this is because SQE(T) sends a collision signal to the attached DTE (in this case the repeater port) at the end of each

---

[9] In actual fact, a port should not be partitioned at less than 30 consecutive collisions. Most vendors actually implement a simple counter that overflows at 32 consecutive collisions and then causes the port to become partitioned.

frame. Repeaters being generally non-intelligent devices, would interpret this as a collision and would eventually partition the port. Thus it is imperative that this simple rule be adhered to.

8.3 Repeater Limitations

In this chapter, we have seen that the primary uses of the repeater are in extending the physical medium segment, and increasing the number of end stations that can be attached. The uninitiated may be forgiven for believing that we could, in theory, increase the overall number of connections and distance infinitely. Sadly, of course, that is not possible and we are most certainly restricted in these areas. In the first case, *shared* Ethernet/802.3 networks should not exceed 1024 stations. As for overall network length, we must ensure that round trip delay times are not exceeded, and the shrinkage of the inter-frame gap (IFG) is limited. We must therefore remember that the physical size of any Ethernet/802.3 network is limited by the characteristics of individual components. These components include (but are not limited to) :

- Media lengths due to the associated propagation delay time(s).

- Latencies within repeater units.

- Latencies inherent in MAUs (due to start-up when data is received).

- Inter-frame gap shrinkage.

- Latencies within the DTE.

- Collision detection assertion and de-assertion times within MAUs.

Table 8-3 summarizes the delays for common network media segments and defines these as being either "Mixing" or "Link" segments. Mixing segments are those where multiple station attachments are permitted, while Link segments are more simple "point-to-point" connections. In addition, while it would be nice to be able to make broad statements as to maximum segment lengths and the maximum number of stations permitted on a segment, this is not always the case. As such, certain elements of the table require further discussion and these are highlighted through notes below.

Table 8-3: Delays associated with Common Media Types

Media Type	Max. Number of MAUs per Segment	Maximum Segment Length (m)	Maximum Medium Delay per Segment (ns)
Mixing Segment:			
10Base5	100	500	2165
10Base2	30	185	950
10Base-FP	33[1]	1000[2]	5000
Link Segment:			
FOIRL	2	1000	5000
10Base-T	2	100[3]	1000

Table 8-3: Delays associated with Common Media Types (Continued)

Media Type	Max. Number of MAUs per Segment	Maximum Segment Length (m)	Maximum Medium Delay per Segment (ns)
10Base-FB	2	2000	10000
10Base-FL	2	2000	10000
AUI:[4]			
1xDTE/1xMAU		50	257

Notes:

1. The actual number of stations connected using 10Base-FP will depend on the Passive Star characteristics as described in chapter 7.

2. A MAU to Passive Star link will not exceed 500m.

3. The actual segment length permitted when using 10Base-T will be dependent on the characteristics of the cable employed - see chapter 3.

4. While the AUI is not a segment, it is included in this table since it must form part of the calculation of round trip delay times.

The standard itself then uses two distinct models in order to validate configurations employing repeaters. In the first model, the standard describes a set of configurations that have been validated under conservative rules and are qualified as meeting the requirements of round trip delay and IFG shrinkage. With the second model, the standard then provides a set of calculation aids that allows anyone proposing a configuration to "*test*" it to see whether it is valid. These two models of operation are then described below:

8.3.1 Transmission System Model 1

In this model, a set of basic rules are outlined. These rules define a general configuration that is legal provided that the installation is sound, and that a minimum level of quality is assured throughout. In the following points, where no segment length constraints are listed, the maximum segment length (as defined for the relevant MAU) applies.

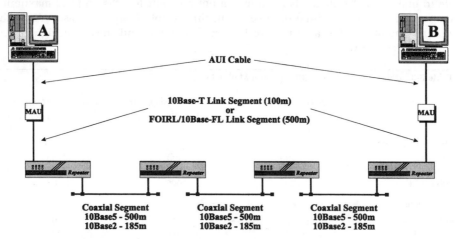

Figure 8-10: Maximum Transmission Path - 3 Coaxial Segments

- Repeaters are required for all segment interconnections.

- MAUs that are part of (integral to) the repeater count towards the maximum number of MAUs on a segment.

- The allowable transmission path between any two DTEs may consist of up to five segments. This implies four repeaters (with or without AUIs and/or integral MAUs), two MAUs (for station connection), and two AUIs (where applicable). This basic configuration is shown in figures 8-10 and 8-11.

- When the transmission path consists of four repeaters (and therefore five segments), up to three of the segments may be mixing segments. The remaining segments must be link segments (shown in figures 8-10 and 8-11).

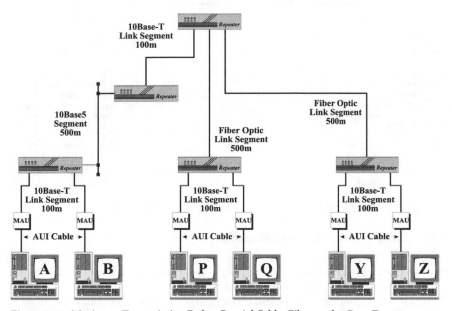

Figure 8-11: Maximum Transmission Path - Coaxial Cable, Fiber, and 10Base-T

- When five segments are in use, each fiber optic segment (FOIRL, 10Base-FB, or 10Base-FL) must not exceed 500m. Where the link segment is of type 10Base-FP, the segment should not exceed 300m.

- AUI cables for 10Base-FP and 10Base-FL should not exceed 25m. This is because two MAUs per segment are required and AUIs of 25m would result in a total AUI cable length of 50m per segment.

- If the transmission path comprises only three repeaters (and therefore four segments) as shown in figure 8-12, the following restrictions apply.

> If the inter-repeater segment is of fiber, then the segment length should not exceed 1000m in the case of 10Base-FB, 10Base-FL, and FOIRL. If the inter-repeater segment is of type 10Base-FP, then this segment length maximum is reduced to 700m.

The maximum length of fiber segment used to connect a DTE to a repeater should not exceed 400m where 10Base-FL is used. Where 10Base-FP is used, that segment should be less than or equal to 300m. Similarly, where 10Base-FL is used, the segment must not exceed 400m.

There is no restriction regarding the maximum number of mixing segments in this case.

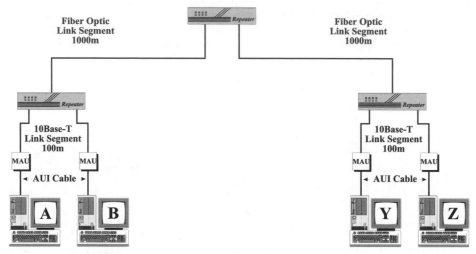

Figure 8-12: Maximum Transmission Path - 3 Repeaters and 4 Link Segments

8.3.2   Transmission System Model 2

In the first Transmission System model we saw a generalized set of rules that describe the limits to which Ethernet/802.3 networks can be extended. In actual fact, as we saw earlier, we are constrained by the round trip collision delay, and the Inter-frame Gap. Hence, any potential configuration must be validated against each of these elements separately.

In a generic model such as that in figure 8-13, we see that a network of this type will comprise the worst case path and include a "Left Segment," "Mid-Segments," and a "Right Segment." Generally, the worst case path for any network will never be the same for both the round trip delay and inter-frame gap shrinkage. They are therefore described in the following text.

The first calculation is that of the "Round Trip Collision Delay." For this, we must remember that Ethernet/802.3 networks rely on the fact that any two stations must be able to contend for the network at any time. This means that any station that is attempting to transmit *must* be notified of any contention that exists by the returned collision signal, within the "collision window".[10]   As a result, the

[10] You will recall that where collisions exist, they must be reported within 51.2μs of the start of transmission, and therefore within 511 bits after the Start Frame Delimiter. In other words, the maximum fragment size created must be less than 511 bits.

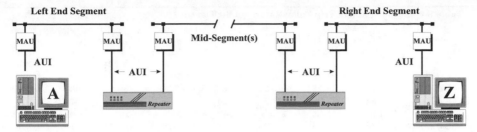

Figure 8-13: Worst Case Transmission Path

maximum physical length between DTEs (commonly referred to as the "diameter" of the network) is limited. Hence, when calculating the maximum round trip delay, the worst case transmission path will be between those DTEs that are candidates for the longest delay. The Worst Case "Path Delay Value" (PDV) is calculated using the following steps:

A. With reference to table 8-4, determine the "Segment Delay Value" (SDV) for each of the segments in the path using the formula:

SDV = Base + [Length × (Round-Trip Delay (RTD)/Meter)]

If the segment under consideration is an end segment and is of a mixing segment type, then the length is defined as being the length between the repeater and the farthest end of the segment. If the segment is a mid-segment and a mixing segment type, the length is the total length between the two repeaters.

Alternatively, if the segment length is the maximum allowed or if the true length of the segment is not known, the formula to be used simply becomes:

SDV = Max

B. Again using table 8-4, calculate the SDV for the sum of all AUI cables longer than 2m - except the AUI associated with the "Left End" DTE which does not contribute to the PDV.

C. Add all SDVs from steps A and B, and then add a margin of up to 5 bits to give the PDV. The margin may be between 0 to 5 bits (5 bits is recommended), but the PDV *must* be less than 576 overall if the network is to qualify in terms of worst case delay.

Having calculated the worst case Path Delay Value, we must now calculate the effects of Inter-frame Gap shrinkage. Inter-frame Gap shrinkage limits the total number of repeaters allowed between any two end stations, and we must once again calculate this over the worst case path. As we have already said, the worst case path here may not be the same as that used to calculate the worst case Path Delay Value (PDV). However, as before, inspection of the network should reveal the path(s) over which the calculation should be made.

Table 8-4: Segment Round Trip Delay Values (in Bit Times)

Segment Type	Max Length	Left End Base	Max	Mid-Segments Base	Max	Right End Base	Max	RTD/ Meter
10Base5	500	11.75	55.05	46.5	89.8	169.5	212.8	0.0866
10Base2	185	11.75	30.731	46.5	65.48	169.5	188.48	0.1026
FOIRL	1000	7.75	107.75	29	129	152	252	0.1
10BaseT	100^2	15.25	26.55	42	53.3	165	176.3	0.113
10BaseFP	1000	11.25	111.25	61	161	183.5	284	0.1
10BaseFB	2000	N/A^3	N/A^3	24	224	N/A^3	N/A^3	0.1
10BaseFL	2000	12.25	212.25	33.5	233.5	156.5	356.5	0.1
AUI^1	48	0	4.88	0	4.88	0	4.88	0.1026

Notes: 1. The SDV figure includes an AUI at each end of the segment (except in the case of 10BaseFB), and up to 2m of cable. In addition, the AUI associated with the Left End DTE can be ignored since this does not contribute to the overall PDV.

2. The actual maximum cable length for 10BaseT segments will depend upon the cable characteristics.

3. Not applicable; 10BaseFB does not support end connections.

When performing this calculation, we are ascertaining the worst case Path Variability Value (PVV). In this, we do not count the receive end segment. Hence where an asymmetrical network (one where the end segments are of different types) is involved, the end with the worst variability is always designated as the Transmitting end, and will therefore be used in the calculation as shown in figure 8-14. Having chosen those worst case path(s), the following steps are then performed:

A. Determine the Segment Variability Value (SVV) from table 8-5 for each segment in the path (excluding the end segment with the lowest SVV).

B. Add all SVVs from step A to determine the Path Variability Value (PVV). If the PVV is less than or equal to 49, the path qualifies in terms of variability.

Table 8-5: Segment Variability Values (in Bit Times)

Segment Type	Transmitting End	Mid-Segment
Coax	16	11
Link (except 10Base-FB)	10.5	8
10Base-FB	N/A	2
10Base-FP	11	8

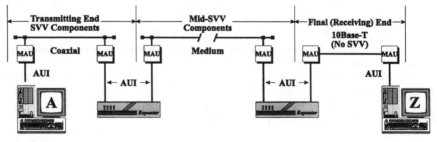

Figure 8-14: SVV Calculation - Worst Case Path

8.4 Resilient Links

One major limitation of the simple repeater is that it cannot generally be used to create resilient networks. Remember that a repeater *must* faithfully repeat all data that appears on any of its ports to all of its other ports. Thus, if we were to consider figure 8-15, we would see that any data sent from Station A would loop endlessly around the network. In short, we are never allowed to create loops in our networks.

While what we have said regarding loops in networks is true, many repeaters today do offer what is termed as *Redundant Link* facilities. These repeaters (more typically intelligent Hubs) allow the creation of multiple paths between network segments, but manage the ports such that only one path is active at any time. In figure 8-16 we see an example of this with three hubs placed in a loop such that a resilient network is created.

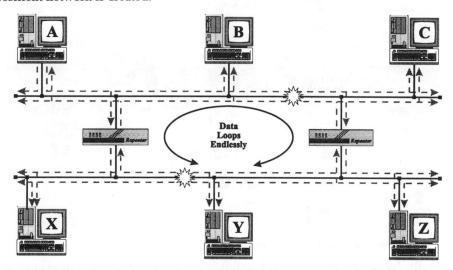

Figure 8-15: An Example of a Loop in an Ethernet Network

There is no hard and fast rule as to how redundancy is managed, and certainly no standard currently exists. Vendors use a mixture of proprietary and standards-based protocols to determine whether links are available, although they generally all have one thing in common. The one overriding factor is that both Primary and Backup paths must not be enabled at the same time. So, the ports that connect to the Backup path(s) will be disabled while the Primary path is operational, and of course, vice versa. Typically, the repeater that is controlling redundancy will *PING*[11] a device on the remote network at regular intervals over the Primary link to test for connectivity. In the example of figure 8-16 this would possibly be the *Target Server*, although it could be any device that is deemed to have 100% availability. While the Hub receives responses from the remote device, the Primary link is deemed to be functioning and therefore remains enabled and keeping the

[11] PING is the Packet Internet Groper - A simple application based upon the Internet Control Message Protocol (ICMP) used to test the reachability of network devices.

Backup path disabled. Should a response be missed a set number of times (typically 3), the Primary link is disabled, and a Backup path is enabled in its place.

In figure 8-16, both Hub 1 and Hub 2 are utilizing multiple paths to access the Target Server connected to Hub 3. In the case of Hub 1, initially the Primary link is enabled and the Backup is disabled as we have already discussed. The backup link is then used in the case of Primary link failure. Hub 2 uses not one, but two Backup paths. Here, the Primary link is normally used to carry traffic and, should this fail, the first Backup link is used in its place. Now, should this Backup link also fail, then the second Backup link (via Hub 1) will be used in its place.

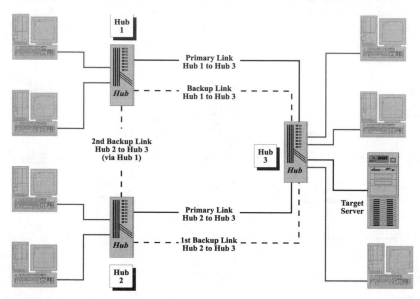

Figure 8-16:   Redundant Link Configuration

Finally, having switched to a backup link, we need to consider potential methods for rolling back to the Primary link when it becomes re-available. Vendors implementing redundant link software on their products typically allow for periodic testing of the Primary link once it is deemed to be faulty and has subsequently been disabled. One such method is that at a predetermined time (say 2am) the currently in-use backup link is momentarily interrupted and the Primary link is tested. If the link now passes, it is re-enabled, and the current Backup link is disabled so that the data paths are returned to their initial state. Equally, many vendors choose to test all configured backup links at the same time. In this way the Network Administrator can be warned of an out-of-service Backup path before it is actually needed.

8.5   Security

A further feature offered by many Hub vendors is that of security. By default repeaters, we have said, are generally dumb devices that have no idea of addressing or frame structure. Because of this, repeaters (as standardized devices) are unable to make decisions as to which stations may send data through them. Intelligent hubs, however, possess a level of sophistication that allows a high degree of management, and are therefore able to monitor traffic as it passes. This type of device can then decide the action(s) to be taken based upon the source address(es) that it sees at its ports.

8.5.1　Access Lists

One type of security commonly referred to as *"Access List," "Host Security,"* or *"Intrusion Protection"* provides protection against malicious attacks from outside. Broadly speaking, this level of security falls into two distinct areas.

- **Access to the device itself**
  Intelligent Hubs today will normally incorporate Telnet[12] server and SNMP[13] client functions that allow devices such as management stations to configure them remotely. Hubs will typically be configurable so that they only accept Telnet sessions from *trusted hosts*, i.e., those that are known to the network administrator and are typically within the network management department. Equally, these hubs will only respond to SNMP requests from pre-configured management stations that are known to them. For this particular level of security, a high degree of intelligence is required, as is an IP stack, since access will generally be granted based upon the IP address of the requesting device.

- **Port Security**
  In this type of security the device, normally on a per-port basis, can be configured with a list of those MAC addresses that are either allowed to pass data through the hub, or are denied from doing so. When an invalid source address (as determined from the Access list) is detected, the hub will then either disable the port, send a SNMP Trap to a management station, or both. Figure 8-17 shows an example of how this might be implemented.

Each of our 5 stations will have their own unique MAC address as shown in the figure. Whenever a station transmits, the hub then examines the source address field of the frame and compares it with the addresses configured in the Access list for that port. Based upon the action(s) specified, it will then either allow the frame to pass or deny access. Notice that for each port (ports 1 to 5) we have configured the hub such that the default action would be to deny access. Hence, if we were to switch stations A and C, then as soon as these stations transmitted data, the hub would take one or more of the actions described above.

One potential problem does exist and that is where two hubs are connected through a hub port. This is demonstrated in the figure (port 6) and is overcome by configuring it in the opposite way. Port 6 is configured so that the default action

---

[12] The Telnet protocol is a Network Virtual Terminal emulation protocol that is used to access devices as if connected locally.

[13] The Simple Network Management Protocol (SNMP) allows the monitoring and configuration of IP client devices. While SNMP also incorporates other facilities such as the Community String to bar access, these lists can likewise play a vital role in securing the network.

would be to allow all frames to pass. This would be required since port 6 would potentially have many different source addresses presented to it. In our example then, we have said that by default all frames will pass, but the access list then goes on to deny access to three specific station addresses. In this case it would probably be undesirable to disable the port should one of those addresses appear there, so we would normally configure the hub so that it merely sends an SNMP trap to warn of the impending security breach instead.

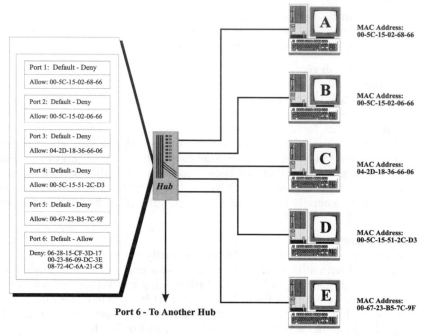

Figure 8-17:   Access List Security

8.5.2   Data Security

In a similar fashion to security based upon Access Lists, several vendors also supply hubs that will scramble data on ports that have no need to receive it (widely known as *Eavesdrop Protection*). Unfortunately most network protocols send *all* information in the clear, with no encryption of passwords or other sensitive data. Scrambling data on those ports that should not receive it then overcomes the problem where an unscrupulous employee or malicious intruder could plug an analysis tool into a spare port and monitor network activity.

The actual mechanics of operation are very similar to that of Access lists except that with this security method, the hub port must monitor both the source and destination addresses of frames as they are received. Since the hub will know which addresses legitimately reside on which ports, it will then scramble the frame as it is transmitted over all ports except the correct destination. Figure 8-18 shows this in operation.

Scrambling, as the figure indicates, is normally achieved by taking the source address, length/type, and data fields and converting them to an alternating pattern of 1s and 0s (101010101010.........). In the figure, Station A is sending data to Station D. Thus, Station D receives the data intact (as would be required) but all other stations receive corrupted Source Address, Length/Type, and Data fields.

It would not be sufficient to just not transmit the frame to those ports that should not receive it since this would break the rules of CSMA/CD. For example, if we simply did not transmit the frame, other stations would not know that the network was in use and collision detection would fail. Hence, all ports *must* receive a frame of exactly the same size as that input to the hub, even though they will be unable to decode it. Bridges and switches only transmit frames to stations that should receive them so therefore do provide a level of security by default, and also network segmentation. These devices, however, operate at a higher level (these are Data-Link or layer two devices) and are therefore more intelligent than repeaters. Bridges and Switches are discussed in chapter 15.

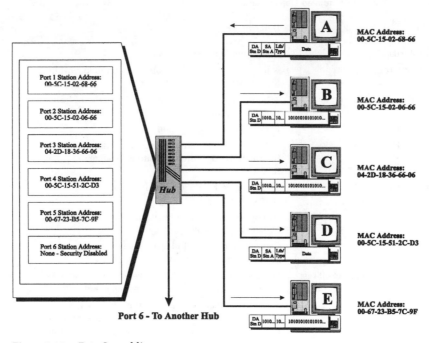

Figure 8-18:   Data Scrambling

8.6   Repeater Management

Most repeaters and hubs today are manageable through the Simple Network Management Protocol (SNMP). These *intelligent* devices therefore need to contain a set of variables or *objects* that relate to the various manageable elements, and can be broadly categorized into two main areas. In the first, management must be able to provide the means to monitor and control repeater functionality. In this, we include a method by which a repeater can be identified, the way in which a repeater can be tested and/or initialized, and a method that allows us to enable and disable individual ports. The second area of management then provides us with the means to monitor the traffic on attached segments.

8.6.1   Managed Objects

The managed objects provide the management station with a means to identify, control, and monitor a resource. Such objects might include counters to report on the numbers of frames, and/or octets that have been processed by a port, the number of collisions detected, and a means through which ports can be enabled/disabled.

Within the repeater management MIB,[14] four major sections exist, namely the Repeater Managed Object Class, the Resource TypeID Managed Object Class, the Group Managed Object Class, and the Port Managed Object Class. The following tables (8-6 to 8-9) identify and briefly describe each of these.

Table 8-6: Repeater Managed Object Class

Object	Description	Required
RepeaterID	Uniquely identifies a repeater	Y
RepeaterGroupCapacity	Number of groups that can be contained within the repeater	Y
GroupMap	A bit string that reflects the configuration of units viewed as group managed objects	Y
RepeaterHealthState	Reports on overall repeater health	Y
RepeaterHealthText	Vendor specific string that provides detailed information on the operational state of the repeater	Y
RepeaterHealthData	Vendor specific data relevant to the operational state of the repeater	Y
TransmitCollisions	A counter incremented each time a transmit collision is reported	
ResetRepeater	Causes the repeater to be reset when commanded by the management station	Y
ExecuteNonDisruptiveSelfTest	Performs a non-destructive, vendor specific self test when commanded by the management station	Y
RepeaterHealth	A sequence of repeaterHealthState, repeaterHealthText, repeaterHealthData sent as a trap to report on the operational state of the repeater	Y
RepeaterReset	A sequence of repeaterHealthState, repeaterHealthText, and repeater-HealthData sent as a trap to report on the operational state of the repeater	Y
GroupMapChange	A notification sent when a change in the group structure of the repeater occurs	Y

[14] The Management Information Base (MIB) is a collection of objects accessible through the Simple Network Management Protocol (SNMP).

Table 8-7: Resource TypeID Managed Object Class

Object	Description	Required
ResourceTypeIDName	The *named* resource Type	Y
ResourceInfo	Information pertaining to the resource	Y

Table 8-8: Group Managed Object Class

Object	Description	Required
GroupID	A unique value within the repeater to define the group	Y
GroupPortCapacity	The number of repeater ports contained within the group	Y
PortMap	A bit string that reflects the configuration of port managed objects within the group	Y
PortMapChange	A notification sent whenever a change occurs in the port structure of the group	Y

Table 8-9: Port Managed Object Class

Object	Description	Required
PortID	A value unique in the group used to identify the port	Y
PortAdminState	The state of the port, either Enabled or Disabled	Y
AutoPartitionState	Whether the port is Autopartitioned	Y
ReadableFrames	Total number of legal frames received	
ReadableOctets	A count of the total number of octets (bytes) received in valid frames	
FrameCheckSequenceErrors	A count of the number of frames received with invalid CRC fields	
AlignmentErrors	A count of the number of frames received where an alignment error has been detected	
FramesTooLong	A count of the number of frames received where the total length exceeded 1500 octets	
ShortEvents	A count of the number of times that the carrier was detected for only a *short* time where short is defined as being between 74 and 82 bit times	
Runts	A count of the number of frames received that were shorter than 64 octets	
Collisions	A count of the total number of collisions experienced	
LateEvents	A count of the number of times that a collision was detected after the collision window had expired.	

Table 8-9: Port Managed Object Class (Continued)

Object	Description	Required
VeryLongEvents	A count of the number of Jabbers experienced	
DataRateMismatches	A count of the number of times that data was received where the rate was out of specification	
AutoPartitions	The number of times that the port has become autopartitioned	
LastSourceAddress	The address of the last station seen at this port	
SourceAddressChanges	The number of times that the source address seen at the port has changed	
PortAdminControl	Allows the port to be administratively enabled or disabled	Y

8.7 Summary

In this chapter we have dealt with the way in which we can extend our network, and thereby overcome the limitations imposed in terms of numbers of attached stations and distances. Repeaters are Physical-layer devices. This means that in their standardized form, they blindly repeat all data arriving at a port to all other ports, only regenerating the signal. Repeaters also create only *shared media* networks. In operation, they are totally transparent to other network nodes, and since stations must still contend for the network medium itself, these devices do nothing to improve performance.

This is the simple repeater then. A dumb device that merely sees a signal arriving at a port and sends this with minimal delay to all other ports. Certainly at the lowest level repeaters do just this, although as we have seen, repeaters today tend to be more intelligent devices that have greater functionality than that provided simply through the Physical Layer. Management functionality, redundancy, and security are now commonplace within these devices, and our humble repeater is a key element within point-to-point topologies such as 10Base-F and 10Base-T.

100Base-Tx and -Fx CHAPTER 9

So far, our discussions of Ethernet/802.3 technologies have centered around the tried and trusted 10Mbps technologies of the past. Not content with such minuscule bandwidth availability though, designers sought to increase speeds to the dizzy heights of 100Mbps. Hence, Ethernet was now firmly back in contention against those deterministic, and indeed higher speed, LANs such as IEEE 802.5/Token Ring and even FDDI. Ethernet, however, due to its larger market share and lower-priced components easily competes on price against FDDI and, as we will see, provides an easy migration path for existing "low-speed" Ethernet installations.

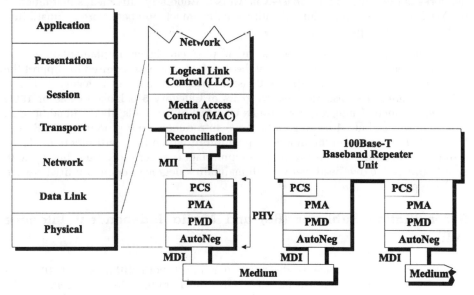

Figure 9-1: 100Base-X Architecture

IEEE 802.3u introduced this 100Mbps system, known collectively as 100Base-X, that encompasses 100Base-Tx, 100Base-Fx, and 100Base-T4.[1] Specifically, 802.3u defines a family of 100Mbps physical layers that can be used with the already scaleable MAC layer, and also introduces certain changes in the way that our model

---

[1] 100Base-T4 is discussed in detail in chapter 13.

maps to the ISO architecture in support of these new physical layers. Figure 9-1 shows these changes that, although far from major, make the overall architecture more logical, and therefore makes it easier to accommodate newer technologies as they become available.

In this new architecture, several new sublayers are introduced, such as the Reconciliation Sublayer (RS) and the Media Independent Interface (MII). Although these are discussed in some detail in the next sections, it is worthwhile providing a basic idea of their functionality here since these new sublayers provide the major change to the architecture itself. The Media Independent Interface is designed to provide us with an interconnection between the Physical Layer Entities (now known simply as the *PHY*) and the MAC. This interface is capable of running at both 10Mbps and 100Mbps through four nibble (or half octet) transmit and receive paths. The Reconciliation Sublayer then provides a mapping between the signals at the MII, and those of the MAC/PLS defined in previous chapters.

When discussing the changes to existing MAC standards, we have already said that the MAC is scaleable. This is simply achieved by having a faster bit rate and shorter bit times, thereby reducing packet transmission times and cable delay budgets. All of these changes are made in proportion to the change in bandwidth, therefore the ratio of packet duration to network propagation delay for 100Base-X networks is the same as for 10Base-X networks. Generally, this means that much of the MAC and management functionality remains intact, and backward compatibility is thus easier to implement.

We have also said that several new physical layer implementations are introduced, and it is here that much of the development was required to support the new specifications. For example, 100Base-T4 uses four pairs of Category 3, 4, or 5 balanced cable, 100Base-Tx uses two pairs of Category 5 balanced cable or 150Ω shielded balanced cable, and 100Base-Fx uses two multi-mode fibers. In addition, a new feature called *Auto-Negotiation*[2] is introduced that allows a DTE and hub/switch[3] to negotiate the mode of operation in which they will function. Thus, through this feature, we ensure that optimum data transfer rates are achieved with no administrative overhead, yet we still maintain a degree of compatibility between device types.

9.1 Reconciliation Sublayer (RS) and Media Independent Interface (MII)

The RS and MII interface is designed to support both 10Mbps and 100Mbps technologies, with the only difference being the nominal clock frequency. The functionality provided by the MII itself can be implemented in either the MAC or the PHY, although here there is a slight difference. For example, a PHY that

---

[2] Auto-Negotiation is discussed in detail in chapter 11.
[3] It should be noted that with 100Mbps Ethernet technologies, DTE connections are always made to hubs and/or Switches and that there is no Bus type architecture defined. Therefore, coaxial media is not supported for 100Mbps technologies at this time.

provides an MII is not required to operate at both 10Mbps and 100Mbps. If this is the case however, it must report the speed supported via the management interface.

So what exactly does the MII do? Simply put, the MII is designed to make the differences between the various available media types totally transparent to the MAC, which it achieves in concert with the Reconciliation sublayer. As a general statement then, we can say that the RS and MII are completely linked together in achieving this simple goal. Functionally, the Reconciliation sublayer maps the signals provided at the MII to the Physical Layer Signaling (PLS) service primitives. In figure 9-2 we see the Reconciliation sublayer inputs and outputs, and this figure also shows exactly how this mapping is achieved. In operation, the MII uses separate, four-bit wide, transmit and receive paths and, although rarely seen, could be implemented externally (as with a traditional AUI). So from the discussion thus far, it should be clear that one of the overriding motivations in the development of this standard was to build on existing technologies rather than re-design completely.

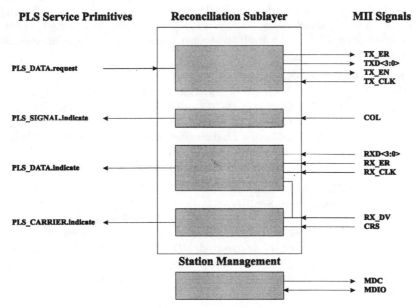

Figure 9-2: Reconciliation Sublayer Inputs and Outputs and MII

9.1.1   Service Primitive to MII Mapping

Since the motivation was to use as much of the existing technologies as possible, and since the MAC itself is used without modification, mapping between the MAC layer service primitives and the MII is required. A function of the Reconciliation sublayer, this section describes exactly how the mapping takes place.

- **PLS_DATA.request Mapping**
  This allows the PLS_DATA.request (OUTPUT_UNIT) to be mapped to the MII four data bits collectively called TXD<3:0>. The Transmit Enable

(TX_EN) and Transmit Clock (TX_CLK) signals are used to signify that data is present and to synchronize data. The PLS OUTPUT_UNIT parameter will be either a 1, 0, or DATA_COMPLETE. The MII signals TXD<3>, TXD<2>, TXD<1> and TXD<0> (TXD<3:0>) each conveys a single bit of data (that is four bits in total) while TX_EN is asserted. The value DATA_COMPLETE is then signaled by the de-assertion of the TX_EN.

Since the MII uses data paths four bits wide yet the PLS operates in single bit mode, the TXD<3:0> and TX_EN signals are generated by the Reconciliation sublayer after every four PLS_DATA.request transactions. Synchronization is achieved through the TX_CLK signal generated by the PHY.

- **PLS_DATA.indicate Mapping**
  In the opposite fashion to the PLS_DATA.request, the Reconciliation sublayer generates PLS_DATA.indicate (INPUT_UNIT) by taking data arriving from the MII (via the PHY). The synchronized data (synchronized with RX_CLK) arrives over the four signals RXD<3>, RXD<2>, RXD<1>, and RXD<0> (collectively known by the term RXD<3:0>) and each representing a single bit of data while the Receive Data Valid (RX_DV) signal is asserted. This then causes four PLS_DATA.indicate transactions to take place as the data is transferred.

- **PLS_CARRIER.indicate Mapping**
  The PLS_CARRIER.indicate (CARRIER_STATUS) primitive is generated whenever there is a change in the status of the carrier. If the RX_DV signal is de-asserted and the CRS signal transitions from de-asserted to asserted then the CARRIER_STATUS must change from CARRIER_OFF to CARRIER_ON. Equally if at any time after both CRS and RX_DV are asserted, RX_DV becomes de-asserted, then the status must change to CARRIER_OFF.

- **PLS_SIGNAL.indicate Mapping**
  In general terms, the PLS_SIGNAL.indicate (SIGNAL_STATUS) primitive can assume one of two values either SIGNAL_ERROR or NO_SIGNAL_ERROR. Whenever the MII COL signal is asserted, then SIGNAL_ERROR is assumed. Conversely, when COL is de-asserted, NO_SIGNAL_ERROR is assumed. The Reconciliation sublayer will generate the PLS_SIGNAL.indicate whenever a transition occurs between SIGNAL_ERROR and NO_SIGNAL_ERROR or vice versa.

- **TX_ER and RX_ER Mapping**
  If a frame is received where an error is detected then, since reception is in progress, the signal RX_DV will be asserted. If then the RX_ER is also asserted the Reconciliation sublayer is responsible for ensuring that the MAC detects a FrameCheckError in that frame.

  The TX_ER signal is used by the Reconciliation sublayer to ensure that frames currently being transmitted can be purposely corrupted. For example, if a repeater was to be receiving a frame on one of its ports and, during reception, it detects the RX_ER signal has been raised, then it may wish to propagate the error indication by asserting TX_ER at the MII.

- **MDC and MDIO Management Data Mapping**
  The Management Data Clock (MDC) is derived from the PHY and provides a reference for the transfer of data on the Management Data IO (MDIO) signal. MDIO is a bi-directional signal between the PHY and the Station Management Entity (STA). All Control and Status information is then transferred synchronously with respect to the MDC signal.

9.1.2 Transmit and Receive Data Encoding

Since we are dealing with a number of signals at the MII, it is important that we understand exactly which encoding of these signals is permissible. As you will appreciate, although we have a number of signals between the Reconciliation sublayer and the MII, there are in reality too few to provide all of the controls required. As such, by using the Enable, Error, and Data signals, we are able to produce a number of different indications. For example, table 9-1 shows the permissible encodings of the transmit signals.

Table 9-1: Permissible encoding of TXD<3:0>, TX_EN, and TX_ER

TX_EN	TX_ER	TXD<3:0>	Indication
0	0	0000 through 1111	Normal Inter-Frame
0	1	0000 through 1111	Reserved
1	0	0000 through 1111	Normal Data Transmission
1	1	0000 through 1111	Transmit Error Propagation

In a similar fashion we use the Receive signals, through encoding techniques, to present a number of options. Table 9-2 shows valid encoding of the RXD<3:0>, RX_DV, and RX_ER signals.

Table 9-2: Permissible encoding of RXD<3:0>, RX_DV, and RX_ER

RX_DV	RX_ER	RXD<3:0>	Indication
0	0	0000 through 1111	Normal Inter-Frame
0	1	0000	Normal Inter-Frame
0	1	0001 through 1101	Reserved
0	1	1110	False Carrier Indication
0	1	1111	Reserved
1	0	0000 through 1111	Normal Data Reception
1	1	0000 through 1111	Data Reception with Errors

9.1.3 Management Functions

Since IEEE 802.3u introduces an interface with a high degree of backward compatibility with older 802.3 specifications, the Management Functions described are considerably expanded. Management information is transferred over the MDIO signals using a specific protocol to convey this information, which is then stored in a simple register set which can be both read from and written to.

Of the registers themselves (as detailed in table 9-3) it can be seen that two registers form the *basic* register set that is mandatory for all 100Mbps PHYs. The remaining 30 registers then form an extended register set that provide additional functionality that enhances the backwards compatibility of the 100Mbps PHYs. In addition, of these 30 registers 8 are reserved for future enhancements and 16 are designated as being *Vendor Specific* thereby enabling vendors to provide proprietary extensions.

Register 0 is referred to as the *Control Register* and contains basic information that enables the MII to operate correctly. Table 9-4 provides information regarding the various bit values of the register and their operation which is then described in greater detail.

Table 9-3: Management Register Set

Register	Register Name	Basic/Extended
0	Control	Basic
1	Status	Basic
2,3	PHY Identifier	Extended
4	Auto-Negotiation Advertisement	Extended
5	Auto-Negotiation Link Partner Ability	Extended
6	Auto-Negotiation Expansion	Extended
7	Auto-Negotiation Next Page Transmit	Extended
8 - 15	Reserved	Extended
16 - 31	Vendor Specific	Extended

Table 9-4: Control Register Contents

Bit	Name	Actions	Description
15	Reset	R/W SC	1 - PHY Reset 0 - Normal Operation
14	Loopback	R/W	1 - Enable Loopback Mode 0 - Disable Loopback Mode
13	Speed Selection	R/W	1 - 100Mbps 0 - 10Mbps
12	Auto-Negotiation Enable	R/W	1 - Enable Auto-Negotiation 0 - Disable Auto-Negotiation
11	Power Down	R/W	1 - Power Down 0 - Normal Operation
10	Isolate	R/W	1 - Electrically Isolate MII from PHY 0 - Normal Operation
9	Restart Auto-Negotiation	R/W SC	1 - Restart Auto-Negotiation Process 0 - Normal Operation
8	Duplex Mode	R/W	1 - Full Duplex 0 - Half Duplex
7	Collision Test	R/W	1 - Enable COL Test Signal 0 - Disable COL Test Signal
6-0	Reserved	R/W	Set to 0 - Ignore on Register Read

Note: The *SC* designation in the *Actions* column indicates that the register contents are *Self Clearing* after the action has been performed.

Many of the register contents described above are relatively self-explanatory, however some elements do deserve further description. For example, setting bit 15 (*Reset*) ensures that both the *Status* and *Control* registers are set to their default state. Equally, by setting bit 14 (*Loopback*) we place the unit in a loopback state, such that any data sent over the transmit path will be returned over the receive path without being presented on the media. In this state, the PHY is effectively isolated from the medium in terms of reception. This should not be confused with the *Isolate* function presented by bit 10, which will cause the PHY to electrically isolate itself from the MII data paths. In this particular mode, the PHY will ignore the signals TXD<3:0>, TX_ER, and TX_EN, and present a high impedance to the signals TX_CLK, RX_CLK, RX_DV, RXD<3:0>, RX_ER, COL, and CRS. In this state, the PHY will respond only to the management signals MDC and MDIO.

Of the remaining bits, two others are worthy of a more detailed description here. Firstly bit 11 (*Power Down*) can be used to place the PHY in a low power-consumption state. In a similar fashion to the *Isolate* state, the PHY must continue to respond to management signals, although when in *Power Down*, the actual behavior of the PHY apart from this is implementation specific. The other bit is the *Collision Test* (bit 7) which when set will force the PHY to assert the COL signal. The standard itself does suggest that this function is used with some care, and indeed recommends that it is only used in conjunction with the PHY being in *Loopback* mode.

Finally, bit 13 (*Speed Selection*) simply determines whether the unit operates in 10Mbps or 100Mbps mode, and bit 8 (*Duplex Mode*) whether the unit operates in full or half duplex. Those bits dealing with *Auto-Negotiation* (bits 12 and 9) are used to ensure a high degree of backwards compatibility, and to ensure that devices supporting this function will seamlessly select the best possible data transmission modes. *Auto-Negotiation* and indeed *Full Duplex* operation are discussed in detail in chapters 11 and 12 respectively.

Register 1 (the *Status Register*) is detailed in table 9-5, and defines the functionality of the PHY and its current status. Here, all bits are read-only and bits 1 and 4 always latch high, while bit 2 always latches low.

Table 9-5: Status Register Contents

Bit	Name	Description
15	100Base-T4	1 - PHY able to perform 100Base-T4 0 - PHY unable to perform10Base-T4
14	100Base-X Full Duplex	1 - PHY able to operate 10Mbps FD 0 - PHY unable to operate 10Mbps FD
13	100Base-X Half Duplex	1 - PHY able to operate 100Mbps HD 0 - PHY unable to operate 100Mbps HD
12	10Mbps Full Duplex	1 - PHY able to operate 10Mbps FD 0 - PHY unable to operate 10Mbps FD
11	10Mbps Half Duplex	1 - PHY able to operate 10Mbps HD 0 - PHY unable to operate 10Mbps HD
10-7	Reserved	Ignored

Table 9-5: Status Register Contents (Continued)

Bit	Name	Description
6	MF Preamble Suppression	1 - PHY accepts management frames with Preamble suppressed 0 - PHY will not accept management frames with Preamble suppressed
5	Auto-Negotiation Complete	1 - Auto-Negotiation process complete 0 - Auto-Negotiation process incomplete
4	Remote Fault	1 - Remote Fault condition detected 0 - Remote Fault condition not detected
3	Auto-Negotiation Ability	1 - PHY able to perform Auto-Negotiation 0 - PHY unable to perform Auto-Negotiation
2	Link Status	1 - Link is Up 0 - Link is Down
1	Jabber Detect	1 - Jabber Condition Detected 0 - No Jabber Condition Detected
0	Extended Capability	1 - Extended Register Capabilities 0 - Basic Register Set Capabilities Only

Bits 11 through 15 identify the capabilities of the PHY in terms of speed and whether or not *Full Duplex* is supported. Bits 3 to 5 are related to the *Auto-Negotiation* process discussed in chapter 11. Bit 2 (*Link Status*) reports the actual status of the link and bit 1 (*Jabber Detect*) whether a Jabber condition has been detected. Finally, bit 0 (*Extended Capability*) reports whether registers 2 to 31 (those relating to the extended capabilities of the device) are supported.

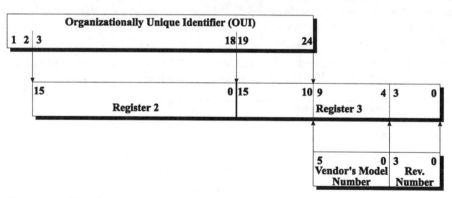

Figure 9-3: PHY Identifier

Where extended capabilities are available within the PHY, registers 2 and 3 are used to hold a 32 bit value known as the *PHY Identifier*, as shown in figure 9-3. Broadly, these registers hold the low 22 bits of the 24 bit *Organizationally Unique Identifier* (OUI) as assigned by the IEEE, a six bit *Vendor's Model Number* and a four bit *Revision Number*.

As can be seen from the figure, bits 3 through 18 of the OUI form the contents of Register 2, with the remainder of the OUI (bits 19 through 24) occupying bits 15 through 10 of register 3. The remainder of register 3 then accommodates the 6 bit Vendor's Model Number and the 4 bit Revision Number.

9.1.4 MII Frame Formats

Data transmitted over the MII has a similar structure to that of ordinary Ethernet data. The frame structure itself is shown in figure 9-4, which also shows that transmission occurs in octet order, with the order of bit transmission being one nibble (i.e., 4 bits) at a time. Each nibble is then transmitted LSB first.

The *Inter-Frame* gap is as described for standard transmissions on the media and is signified by de-assertion of both the TX_EN and RX_DV signals. The *Preamble* is 7 octets in length and once again is identical to that transmitted on the media (i.e., 7 octets of alternating 1's and 0's or **10101010...** when viewed in transmission order). The single octet *Start Frame Delimiter* (SFD) signifies the commencement of valid data and is a single octet with a value of **10101011**. The *Data* field comprises the actual data to be conveyed, although from the MAC this will include the Source and Destination Addresses that form part of the Ethernet/IEEE 802.3 frame header, and the Frame Check Sequence. Finally, the *End Frame Delimiter* (EFD) is signified by the de-assertion of either TX_EN or RX_DV (depending on the direction of data across the MII).

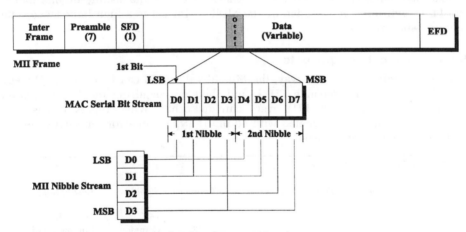

Figure 9-4: MII Frame Format and Order of Transmission

In addition to the standard MII frame format we should, for completeness, also briefly look at the Management Frame format before leaving this section. The format (shown in figure 9-5) is simple and allows each of the registers described in section 9.1.3 to be either read from or written to over the MDIO control lines.

The *Preamble* simply consists of 32 contiguous 1 bits (**11111.....11111**) on the MDIO, clocked by 32 cycles on the MDC signal. The *Start of Frame* (ST) field is a 2 bit field that comprises the binary value **01** and is used to indicate that a valid management frame is commencing. The 2 bit *Operation* field (OP) indicates whether a register Read or Write is signaled. A value of **10** indicates a Read operation, while a value of **01** indicates a Write operation. The *PHY Address* field (PHYAD) is five bits in length and is used to uniquely address any one of 32 possibly attached PHYs that may be connected. The 5 bit *Register Address* field (REGAD) is then used to uniquely address any 1 of the 32 possible registers held on the PHY.

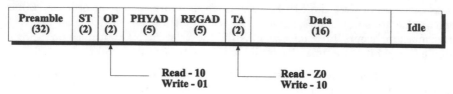

Figure 9-5: MII Management Frame Format

The *Turn Around* (TA) field of 2 bits is used to avoid contention during a Read cycle. In the case of the Read operation, the PHY presents a high impedance state (Z) for the first bit time. In the case of a Write, a 1 bit is presented in this bit time. For both operations however, a 0 is always presented during the second bit time.

The *Data* field is 16 bits in length and is used to carry the data either to or from the register addressed by the REGAD field. In this field, the first data bit transmitted represents the contents of register bit 15 and the last bit, bit 0. Finally, the *Idle* condition is represented by the MDIO being set to a high impedance state and no data is therefore valid.

9.1.5 Contact Assignments

Although rarely used in this way, the MII (like the AUI) can be exposed (thereby creating a physically separate PHY), and therefore requiring the Reconciliation sublayer to be joined to the PHY over a shielded cable. Where this is the case, the cable connections are terminated with 40 pin D-Type connectors and have the pin assignments shown in table 9-6.

Table 9-6: MII Pin Assignments

Contact	Signal	Description	Contact	Signal	Description
1	+5V	Power Rail	21	+5V	Power Rail
2	MDIO	Mgmnt IO Signal	22	Common	Common Rail
3	MDC	Mgmnt Clk Signal	23	Common	Common Rail
4	RXD<3>	Rx Data Bit 3	24	Common	Common Rail
5	RXD<2>	Rx Data Bit 2	25	Common	Common Rail
6	RXD<1>	Rx Data Bit 1	26	Common	Common Rail
7	RXD<0>	Rx Data Bit 0	27	Common	Common Rail
8	RX_DV	Rx Data Valid	28	Common	Common Rail
9	RX_CLK	Rx Clock	29	Common	Common Rail
10	RX_ER	Rx Error	30	Common	Common Rail
11	TX_ER	Tx Error	31	Common	Common Rail
12	TX_CLK	Tx Clock	32	Common	Common Rail
13	TX_EN	Tx Enable	33	Common	Common Rail
14	TXD<0>	Tx Data Bit 0	34	Common	Common Rail

Table 9-6: MII Pin Assignments (Continued)

Contact	Signal	Description	Contact	Signal	Description
15	TXD<1>	Tx Data Bit 1	35	Common	Common Rail
16	TXD<2>	Tx Data Bit 2	36	Common	Common Rail
17	TXD<3>	Tx Data Bit 3	37	Common	Common Rail
18	COL	Collision Signal	38	Common	Common Rail
19	CRS	Carrier Sense	39	Common	Common Rail
20	+5V	Power Rail	40	+5V	Power Rail

9.2 Physical Coding Sublayer (PCS) and Physical Medium Attachment (PMA) for 100Base-X

It is important to remember that the generic 100Base-X network encompasses both 100Base-Tx and 100Base-Fx, or more simply stated, both copper and fiber transmission media. It should be no surprise then, that 100Base-X networks use the tried and tested Physical Layer standards of other 100Mbps network technologies such as FDDI. For example, the ANSI X3.263 standard defining FDDI's TP-PMD describes a 100Mbps, Full Duplex signaling scheme for twisted pair wiring that forms the basis for 100Base-Tx. Similarly, ISO 9314-3 defines a scheme for transmission over fiber optic cables that forms the basis for 100Base-Fx.

The 100Base-X PCS and PMA then, simply map those characteristics of the FDDI PMD sublayer to the services expected by the CSMA/CD MAC. Figure 9-6 shows this mapping between sublayers as applied to 100Base-X.

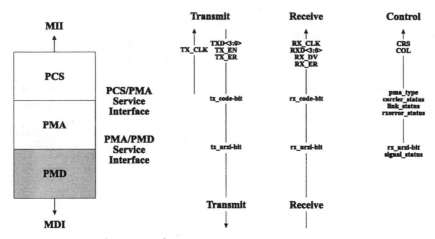

Figure 9-6: PCS and PMA Signal Mapping

9.2.1 PCS/PMA Functions

The PCS provides a uniform interface to the Reconciliation Sublayer for all potential PHYs. In general terms, the PCS provides the following functionality required by the MII in a similar fashion to that provided by the PLS/AUI of the more traditional 10Mbps systems:

- Encoding and decoding of MII data nibbles to and from five bit code groups using the 4B/5B encoding scheme employed by FDDI. This means that our 100Mbps data stream is now translated to a 125MHz signal.

- The serialization and deserialization of the code groups specified above for transmission to, and reception from, the PMA.

- Generation of the Carrier Sense (CS) and Collision Detect (CD) signals.

- Mapping of the Transmit, Receive, Carrier Sense, and Collision Detect signals between the MII and the PMA.

The PMA provides a medium independent method for the support of a range of physical media. This functionality can be generalized into the following four points that will then be expanded on later:

- Mapping of the transmitted and received coded bits between the PMA and the PMD.

- Generation of the control signals that indicate the availability of the PMD to the PCS and, where implemented, synchronize with the Auto-Negotiation function.

- Recover the clock from the embedded NRZI data from the PMD.

- Optionally generate indications of activity such as Carrier and Carrier errors from the PMD, and optionally sense receive channel failures. In addition, the PMA will transmit, and detect, the Far End Fault Indication.

Functionally, the PCS/PMA can be described in terms of the block diagram shown in figure 9-7. In this we see the major functions of the PCS and PMA and can also see the data flow between the PMD and MII.

When receiving, the PCS passes a sequence of data nibbles to the MII which have been recovered from the encoded data. Specifically, the receive function takes the data stream received from the *Receive Bits* process, and from these generates the RXD<3:0>, RX_DV, and where necessary, the RX_ER signals. When transmitting, the PCS generates the required code groups from the data received over the TXD<3:0> circuits which have been enabled through the TX_EN signal. Where the PCS is receiving data while transmitting, the PCS then also generates the COL signal. Finally, the PCS will raise *Carrier Sense* (CRS) whenever it is either transmitting or receiving. In addition, since both the transmit and receive functions are dependent upon the *link_status* signal derived from the PMD, should the link fail for any reason the PCS will cease transmission or reception immediately. Thus the *link_status* signal is constantly monitored.

9.2.2 Data Encoding

The PCS takes the 4 bit data nibbles presented by the MII (and vice versa) and encodes them into 5 bit code groups using the 4B/5B encoding scheme similar to that found in FDDI. Specifically, the difference between the encoding schemes used for 100Base-X and FDDI are as follows:

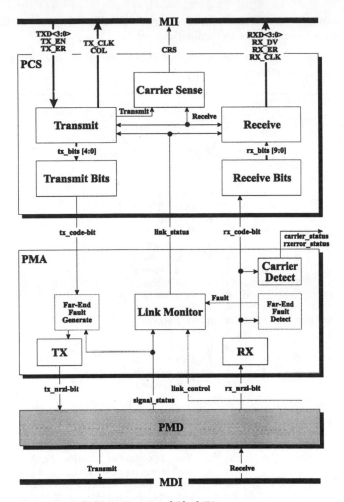

Figure 9-7: PCS/PMA Functional Block Diagram

The term *code group* is used in place of the term *symbol* used with FDDI to avoid confusion with other 100Base-X terms. The *S* and *Q* code groups are not used by 100Base-X and are therefore part of the Invalid set of codes. The *R* code group is used in the *End-of-Stream* delimiter within the 100Base-X scheme rather than as a *Reset* condition. The *H* code group, rather than signaling a *Halt Line* state, is used by 100Base-X to propagate receive errors.

Returning briefly to the use of the 4B/5B encoding scheme, it should be pointed out that what, on the surface, may seem to be a retrograde step does in fact present us with a major efficiency advantage. For example; if we consider the Manchester encoding scheme used in 10Mbps systems, we realize that since we have a transition at the mid point of each cell time, our transmission frequency is actually 20MHz maximum, providing an efficiency of only 50%. 4B/5B encoding on the other hand requires a transmission frequency of 125MHz to recover a 100Mbps data stream and therefore provides an 80% efficiency.

Table 9-7 details the MII data nibble to PCS code group encoding scheme and indicates the usage of each code group.

Table 9-7: 4B/5B Code Groups

PCS code group [4:0]					Name	MII xXD <3:0>				Interpretation
4	3	2	1	0		3	2	1	0	

Data Code Groups

4	3	2	1	0	Name	3	2	1	0	Interpretation
1	1	1	1	0	0	0	0	0	0	Data Nibble 0
0	1	0	0	1	1	0	0	0	1	Data Nibble 1
1	0	1	0	0	2	0	0	1	0	Data Nibble 2
1	0	1	0	1	3	0	0	1	1	Data Nibble 3
0	1	0	1	0	4	0	1	0	0	Data Nibble 4
0	1	0	1	1	5	0	1	0	1	Data Nibble 5
0	1	1	1	0	6	0	1	1	0	Data Nibble 6
0	1	1	1	1	7	0	1	1	1	Data Nibble 7
1	0	0	1	0	8	1	0	0	0	Data Nibble 8
1	0	0	1	1	9	1	0	0	1	Data Nibble 9
1	0	1	1	0	A	1	0	1	0	Data Nibble A
1	0	1	1	1	B	1	0	1	1	Data Nibble B
1	1	0	1	0	C	1	1	0	0	Data Nibble C
1	1	0	1	1	D	1	1	0	1	Data Nibble D
1	1	1	0	0	E	1	1	1	0	Data Nibble E
1	1	1	0	1	F	1	1	1	1	Data Nibble F

Idle Code Group

4	3	2	1	0	Name	MII				Interpretation
1	1	1	1	1	I	Undefined				IDLE - Inter-stream fill code

Control Code Group

4	3	2	1	0	Name	3	2	1	0	Interpretation
1	1	0	0	0	J	0	1	0	1	Start-of-Stream Delimiter Part 1 of 2
1	0	0	0	1	K	0	1	0	1	Start-of-Stream Delimiter Part 2 of 2
0	1	1	0	1	T	Undefined				End-of-Stream Delimiter Part 1 of 2
0	0	1	1	1	R	Undefined				End-of-Stream Delimiter Part 2 of 2

Invalid Code Groups

4	3	2	1	0	Name	MII				Interpretation
0	0	1	0	0	H	Undefined				Transmit Error - Forces signaling errors
0	0	0	0	0	V	Undefined				Invalid Code
0	0	0	0	1	V	Undefined				Invalid Code
0	0	0	1	0	V	Undefined				Invalid Code
0	0	0	1	1	V	Undefined				Invalid Code
0	0	1	0	1	V	Undefined				Invalid Code
0	0	1	1	0	V	Undefined				Invalid Code
0	1	0	0	0	V	Undefined				Invalid Code
0	1	1	0	0	V	Undefined				Invalid Code
1	0	0	0	0	V	Undefined				Invalid Code
1	1	0	0	1	V	Undefined				Invalid Code

The different code groups each have specific meaning within the 4B/5B encoding scheme. For example, the *Data* code groups (Data 0 to Data F) are used to convey individual nibbles of data between the PCS and the MII. The *Idle* code group is used as a *fill*, and is therefore transferred between PCS data streams to maintain clock synchronization. The *Control* code groups are used to delimit MAC frames and are always used in pairs. The pair JK acts as a *Start-of-Stream* delimiter (SSD), while the pair TR acts as an *End-of-Stream* delimiter (ESD). Finally, the *Invalid* code groups, with the exception of H, are not used: Their presence indicates a collision fragment and causes RX_ER to be asserted. The H code group is used only where the PCS needs to indicate a transmit error (on reception of the TX_ER signal from the MII), and may be used where, say, a repeater wishes to propagate received errors.

As we have seen, the MII passes MAC frames (via the Reconciliation sublayer) to the PCS and vice versa. This data, on reception from the MII, must be converted by the PCS into an encoded data stream and then passed to the PMA. On reception, of course, this process is reversed. Since the PCS is responsible for this encoding and decoding process, it is by its very definition transparent to the MAC and the requirement for media independence is therefore (at least partially) fulfilled.

9.2.3 Encapsulation

The PCS is responsible for producing a Physical Layer *stream* that encapsulates the MAC frame received from the MII, and for recovering the frame on reception. This *stream* has no meaning outside the 100Base-X PHY since it comprises 5 bit code groups detailed above. In addition, apart from the *Start-of-Stream* delimiter (SSD) which is used to force alignment, these code groups are undetectable. The actual encapsulation and mapping of the MAC frame to the Physical Layer stream is shown in figure 9-8.

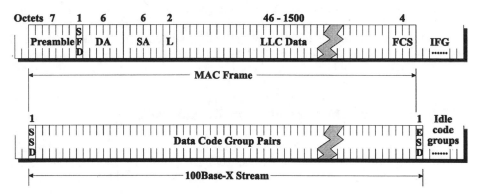

Figure 9-8: PCS Encapsulation

9.2.4 Mapping the MII to the PMA

One of the primary functions of the PMA is to convert *code bits* (individual bits from the 100Base-X stream) into NRZI format and pass these to the PMD (and vice versa). Other functions include the generation of certain status signals, such as those that indicate the status of the underlying link, and also receive error conditions. Figure 9-9 shows a simplified data flow from the MII to the PMA.

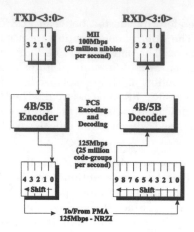

Figure 9-9:   MII to PMA Mapping

9.2.5   Comparison to Other PMAs

The major differences between the 100Base-X PMA and other, previous, 802.3 PMAs are the SQE Test and Jabber functions, neither of which are implemented here. In the first case, SQE Test was included as part of the PMA in order to test the collision detection mechanism. With 100Base-X, however, collision detection is achieved by receiving during transmission, and therefore collision detection is wholly dependent upon the health or otherwise of the PMD.

A Jabber condition is where a DTE potentially causes network failure through constant transmission. Previous PMAs implemented a Jabber control that disabled the DTE after it had been transmitting for an excessive period of time. It was important to implement this function with the DTE since it could connect to *mixing media* such as coaxial cable. With 100Base-X, however, all DTEs must connect to active repeaters or switches, so the Jabber protection feature has been moved there. Thus, the DTE circuitry has been optimized.

9.3   PMD Sublayer and MDI for 100Base-Tx and 100Base-Fx

As we have already seen, 100Base-X uses the signaling standards developed and standardized for FDDI. In other words, 100Base-X uses a 125MHz full duplex signaling system. That said, we should briefly consider how the PMD operates in the 100Base-X environment.

9.3.1   100Base-Tx PMD and MDI

One of the major problems associated with the twisted pair wiring scheme is that when signals strong enough to be reliably interpreted as data are transmitted over twisted pair cable, the wire radiates electromagnetic interference (EMI). Hence, if we were to attempt to use our 125MHz signal directly on twisted pair media, we would exceed the specifications for energy radiation as laid down by the Federal Communications Commission (FCC) and CENELEC. Quite apart from the fact that we would certainly exceed the maximum frequency specifications of the cable.

Table 9-8: UTP MDI Contact Assignments

Contact	PHY without internal MDI crossover	PHY with internal MDI crossover
1	Transmit +	Receive +
2	Transmit -	Receive -
3	Receive +	Transmit +
4	Unused	Unused
5	Unused	Unused
6	Receive -	Transmit -
7	Unused	Unused
8	Unused	Unused

In order to reduce this condition, 100Base-Tx (and indeed TP-PMD) then uses an encoding scheme known as MLT3 (Multi Level Transmission - 3 level). MLT3 reduces the frequency of the transmitted signal to 31.25MHz (125MHz/4) by basically switching between three output voltage levels. Now, our radiation is reduced to within the limitations set by the FCC and EEC, and more importantly the frequency of operation is within the specifications of the cable.

With reference to the MDI, you will recall that 100Base-Tx uses two pairs of Category 5 balanced cable or 150Ω shielded balanced cable. Where UTP cable is used, the standard connector is the modular ISO 8877 (RJ45) connector using the same pin assignments as for other 802.3 implementations and as shown in table 9-8.

9.3.2   100Base-Fx PMD and MDI

Unlike 100Base-Tx, fiber implementations can directly handle the 125MHz signaling that is presented to the PMD by the PMA. Hence, all that is required by the 100Base-Fx PMD is to take the PMA signal and convert it to NRZI prior to transmission over the media.

100Base-Fx uses two multi-mode fiber strands of, typically, 62.5/125μm construction. Standard connectors include the Low Cost Fiber Optical Interface Connector (or duplex *Subscriber Connector* (SC)), the Media Interface Connector (MIC, or more correctly the *Fixed Shroud Duplex* (FSD) Connector), and the Medium Connector Plug and Socket (or *Straight Tip* (ST) connector). In all cases, the cable strands must be crossed such that the transmitter element of one PHY connects to the receiver element of the other PHY and vice versa.

9.4   Repeaters for 100Mbps Baseband Networks

Repeaters[4] are an integral part of 100Mbps networks that encompass more than two DTEs. In a similar fashion to 10Mbps repeaters, 100Mbps units are used to extend

---

[4] In many networks today, central Hubs or Repeaters have been replaced by switches. Switches perform a radically different role to the repeater, and therefore the reader is urged to consult chapter 15 if there is any doubt as to the functionality of these devices.

the overall network diameter by interconnecting individual segments. However, since *mixing media* such as coaxial cable is not defined for 100Mbps systems, all stations in this type of network must connect to a hub of some description.

As a general rule, we can say that the repeater is designed to interconnect two or more segments (of not necessarily similar media) through individual PHYs, as shown in figure 9-10. The repeater can receive and decode data under adverse conditions such as worst case noise, distortion, and amplitude, and then restore and retransmit this data to all other attached segments simultaneously. Equally, on the detection of a collision, the repeater will propagate a Jam signal to all attached segments, and will also isolate segments when a Jabber condition is detected.

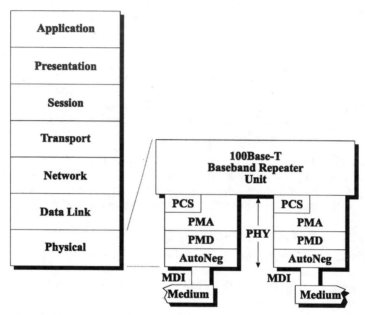

Figure 9-10: 100Base-X Repeater

9.4.1 Classes of 100Base-X Repeaters

IEEE 802.3u defines two distinct classes of repeater, known as Class I and Class II. Class I repeaters are typically designed to link dissimilar signaling systems. In these devices, the internal delays are generally considered to be too large to allow any more than one repeater to be used in a maximum segment length topology between any two DTEs within a single collision domain. Class II repeaters normally have ports that support only a single signaling system (i.e., 100Base-Tx) and therefore have less internal delays. Hence, in a maximum segment length topology, a maximum of two repeater sets may exist between any two DTEs within a single collision domain. In both cases however, segment length may be sacrificed to allow more repeaters to be added. Figure 9-11 shows these repeater types and their network design limitations.

Of course, the configurations represented above are, by their use of maximum segment lengths, the simplest. More complex networks however, can be developed where the segment length is reduced. These designs are discussed in detail in section 9.5, together with the calculations that must be performed to ensure compliance with the IEEE 802.3u standard. Equally, while we are limited to the number(s) of repeaters allowed in any single collision domain, further domains can be added with the use of Bridges, Switches, and Routers. These latter devices are beyond the scope of this chapter however, and will be discussed in later sections of this volume.

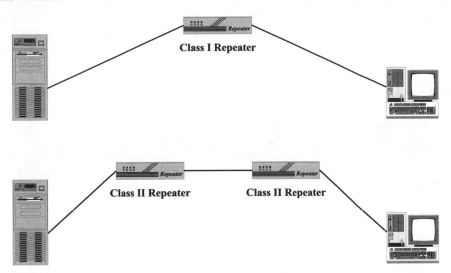

Figure 9-11: Maximum Design Limitations for 100Base-X Repeaters

9.4.2   Repeater Functionality

The functionality of the 100Mbps repeater is similar to that described in chapter 8 for 10Mbps units. The minor variations which exist allow us to accommodate the higher speed of these units, and these units always incorporate Jabber protection on their ports. In general, we can summarize the repeater functionality as being the Reception and Transmission of data, plus Collision and Error Handling.

When talking of reception and transmission, repeaters will take any data arriving at a port and re-transmit this faithfully on all other ports. During transmission, the timing and amplitude of the signal will be restored, and transmission must commence within 140 bit times for Class I repeaters and 46 bit times for Class II repeaters. In addition, signals are encoded appropriately for the port through which the transmission is taking place. The 100Base-X repeater standard does not define the PHYs used, instead the PHYs, PMAs, PCSs and MDIs used are as previously described. Finally, repeaters faithfully reproduce *any* signal, including code violations. Where a code violation is detected while receiving a frame, that violation is either repeated as received, or it is replaced by a *H* code group. In the event that substitution with a *H* code group takes place, then *H*s will be transmitted for the remainder of the frame. This is regardless of the input data, unless a collision occurs. In that case, normal collision handling then takes over.

When discussing collision and error handling, repeaters are able to detect the simultaneous reception of frames at two (or more) ports (a collision) and then propagate the Jam signal accordingly (i.e., to all connected ports). Secondly, repeaters are able to prevent links from generating streams of false data and therefore interfering with other links. Two major methods exist for this, namely the *partitioning* of ports where an excessive number of collisions are being generated, and the *jabber* function which interrupts the reception of data streams that are of excessive length. Partitioning and Jabber do differ slightly within 100Base-X units. Firstly, to enter a partitioned state there must be 60 or more consecutive collisions,[5] although as before a single successful transmission will reset the condition. Secondly, a Jabber condition is indicated at between 40,000 and 75,000 bit times.[6]

9.5 Designing 100Mbps Networks Using Repeaters

The whole point of the IEEE 802.3u standard was to devise a method of creating both homogeneous 100Mbps networks and heterogeneous 10/100Mbps mixed networks. The creation of mixed 10/100Mbps networks similar to that shown in figure 9-12 is possibly one of the most common implementations today. Here, multiple collision domains are created through the use of Repeaters, Bridges, Switches,[7] (and/or Routers[8]), and multiple service levels are available to our DTEs dependent on the type(s) of function that they will perform.

For example, we see a *Server Farm* running Switched 10/100Mbps Ethernet, a group of *super-users* running their own server on 10/100Mbps Switched Ethernet, a group of users using 100Mbps *Shared* (or repeated) Ethernet, and a group of users simply connected to a *Shared* 10Mbps Ethernet. For our discussions here, we shall of course concentrate on those users connected via the 100Mbps Repeater in the 100Mbps User group, but the figure does serve to show how flexible the technology can be.

We saw in section 9.4.1 that the IEEE 802.3u standard defines 2 separate classes of Repeater. We also saw in chapter 8, the guidelines that related to the design of *shared* 10Mbps collision domains outlined as a set of limitations and design criteria based on the numbers of repeaters that may be used. In the following sections, we will examine the design and limitations related to 100Mbps collision domains.

9.5.1 Multi-Segment Networks Within a Single Collision Domain

The overriding parameters that need some consideration when designing networks that incorporate repeaters, are the *Round Trip Propagation* and *Round Trip Collision* delays. Several characteristics have a bearing on these parameters and are listed below:

---

[5] In 10Mbps units the recommended number of consecutive collisions is 30 or more.
[6] Previously, under the 10Mbps PMA, a Jabber condition was indicated between 20ms and 150ms.
[7] Bridges and Switches are discussed in chapter 15, and allow the creation of Collision Domains.
[8] Routers are discussed in section F.

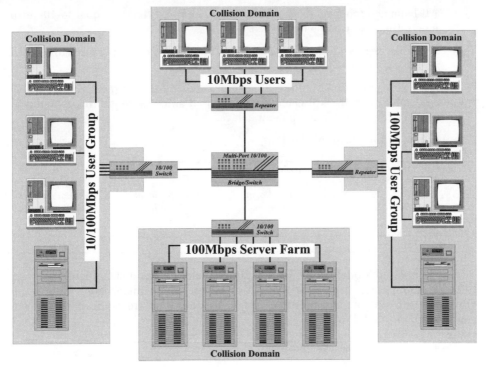

Figure 9-12: Collision Domains with 10/100Mbps Switched/Shared Services

- The length of the media in use and the propagation delay time associated with that specific media.

- The internal delays associated with devices such as DTEs, repeaters, MAUs and PHYs.

- Inter-frame gap shrinkage due to repeaters.

- Collision Detect and de-assertion times associated with MAUs and PHYs.

As with 10Mbps networks (that we saw in chapter 8), two models are defined for 100Mbps networks that allow network architects to design networks that meet the criteria for proper operation at this speed based upon those points above. These models, once again referred to as *Transmission System Model I* and *Transmission System Model II*, define design criteria based upon specific topology constraints and are described below:

9.5.2   Transmission System Model I

This model defines a set of conservative configuration rules which have been verified as meeting the requirements of a 100Mbps Collision Domain. In this model we find three simple constraints, which provided they are adhered to, will guarantee correct operation.

- All balanced (copper) cable segments must be less than or equal to 100m in length (including any patch leads).

- All fiber segments must be less than or equal to 412m in length (again including any patching).

- No MII cables (for 100Base-T) may exceed 0.5m. Typically, the delays associated with the MII cable can be ignored since these are incorporated in the DTE and repeater component delays.

These can be summarized in table 9-9:

Table 9-9: Media Delays for Transmission System Model I

Media Type	Max. No. of PHYs/Segment	Max. Segment Length	Max. Round Trip Delay/Segment
100Base-T Link Segment	2	100	114
Fiber Link Segment	2	412	412

The Maximum Model I collision domain diameter for various configurations can then be summarized in table 9-10. All distances are in meters and there is no allowance for margin. In addition, certain assumptions are made here and are stated as notes that follow.

Table 9-10: Maximum Model I Collision Domain Diameter

Model	Balanced Cable (copper)	Fiber	Balanced Cable & Fiber (Tx & Fx)
DTE to DTE	100	412	N/A
One Class I Repeater	200	272	260.8[A]
One Class II Repeater	200	320	308.8[A]
Two Class II Repeaters	205	228	216.2[B]

Notes:	A.	100m of balanced cable and one fiber link is assumed.
	B.	105m of balanced cable and one fiber link is assumed.

9.5.3 Transmission System Model II

The principal restriction related to the physical size of the network and number of devices that may be attached is the round trip collision delay. This means that to ensure that our network design is valid, it has to be possible for *any* two DTEs to contend for the network at the same time. You will remember also that any station that attempts transmission needs to be informed of a *failed* attempt by receiving a collision signal within the collision window. Thus, our maximum network diameter will be limited to the round trip delay between the two, *worst case* DTEs.

Transmission System Model II is similar to that discussed for 10Mbps systems in chapter 8 with appropriate adjustments to allow for the increased DTE, repeater and media speeds. Here, we must calculate the *Worst Case Path Delay Value* (PDV) that comprises the *Link Segment Delay Values* (LSDV), Repeater delays, DTE delays and a margin of safety. We must then ensure that this is below the collision window of

512 bit times, which is our minimum-sized frame. Hence, once we have identified the pair(s) of DTEs that represent our worst case, the PDV is calculated as follows:

$$\text{PDV} = \Sigma(\text{LSDV}) + \Sigma(\text{Repeater Delays}) + \text{DTE Delay} + \text{Safety Margin}$$

To explain this further, the following guidelines should be adhered to:

- **Link Segment Delay Value (LSDV):**
  The LSDV is calculated as being twice the Segment Length multiplied by the cable delay for the segment in question, i.e., LSDV=2(segment length × cable delay). It should be noted that the reason for doubling the value of segment length multiplied by cable delay is simply because we are calculating a round trip delay value.

  - Length is defined as being the sum of the cable lengths between the PHY interfaces at the repeater and the farthest DTE for end segments, and the sum of the cable lengths between the repeater PHY interfaces for Inter-Repeater Links.

  - Cable delays are specified by the manufacturer or the maximum value for the type(s) of cable employed. Table 9-11 shows these values specified in bit times per meter, however some manufacturers specify these relative to the speed of light. Where this is the case, table 9-12 can be used to perform the required conversion.

  - Where actual cable lengths or propagation delays for copper cable are not known, the Maximum delay time as shown in table 9-11 should be used. For fiber cables, the delay should be calculated since the values shown in table 9-11 will generally be too large.

Table 9-11: Network Component Delays

Component	Round Trip Delay (bit times per meter)	Max Round Trip Delay (bit times)
Two TX/FX DTEs		100
Cat 5 Cable Segment	1.112	111.2 (100m)
STP Cable Segment	1.112	111.2 (100m)
Fiber Cable Segment	1.0	412 (412m)
Class I Repeater		140
Class II Repeater		92

- **Repeater Delays:**
  Repeater delays will normally be available from the vendor of the device. If this information is not available, then based on the Class of repeater in use, the values found in table 9-11 should be used instead.

- **MII Cables:**
  Where the MII is exposed (physically separate), these cables should not exceed 0.5m. If this rule is complied with, then delays associated with the MII may be ignored since they will be incorporated into the relevant DTE and Repeater delay figures.

- **DTE Delays:**
  As with Repeater delays, the value used should be that supplied by the specific vendor. Where no such information is available, then the value specified in table 9-11 should be used.

- **Safety Margin:**
  The IEEE 802.3u standard recommends a safety margin of 4 bit times, although any appropriate value can be used (normally between 0 and 5 bit times). This safety margin is provided to accommodate any additional, *unexpected*, delays such as over-length cables between a DTE and the wall jack, etc.

Table 9-12: Cable Delay Conversion Table

Speed Relative to c	ns/m	BT/m	Speed Relative to c	ns/m	BT/m
0.4	8.34	0.834	0.62	5.38	0.538
0.5	6.67	0.667	0.63	5.29	0.529
0.51	6.54	0.654	0.64	5.21	0.521
0.52	6.41	0.641	0.65	5.13	0.513
0.53	6.29	0.629	0.654	5.10	0.510
0.54	6.18	0.618	0.66	5.05	0.505
0.55	6.06	0.606	0.666	5.01	0.501
0.56	5.96	0.596	0.67	4.98	0.498
0.57	5.85	0.585	0.68	4.91	0.491
0.58	5.75	0.575	0.69	4.83	0.483
0.5852	5.70	0.570	0.7	4.77	0.477
0.59	5.65	0.565	0.8	4.17	0.417
0.6	5.56	0.556	0.9	3.71	0.371
0.61	5.47	0.547			

9.6 Summary

In this chapter we have looked at the 100Mbps standards 100Base-Tx and 100Base-Fx. Other 100Mbps standards exist, such as 100Base-T4 and 100Base-T2, although it is true to say that devices conforming to these latter standards are nowhere near as common as those 100Base-Tx/Fx devices today. Certainly there was prolific activity in the race to provide the 100Mbps network based on reasonably priced, easy to acquire hardware, and many ideas were put forward. The 100Base-X technologies won through however, due mainly to vendor support.

That these technologies might claim to be superior to say 100VG-AnyLAN is somewhat doubtful with 100VG-AnyLAN providing a prioritized service. Nonetheless, the 100Base-X technologies have achieved International Standard status, support from all vendors and an extremely large proportion of the user community. Also, we must not lose sight of the fact that 100Base-Tx and 100Base-Fx have come a long way extremely quickly. Development in the 100Mbps arena was possibly the swiftest of all after the IEEE/ISO CSMA/CD standards had stagnated for many years. But even 100Mbps is not enough. Today, users hunger for more bandwidth, and are demanding faster and cheaper technologies. Thus, the next generation (Gigabit Ethernet) is born, and will be discussed in the next chapter.

Gigabit Ethernet

Gigabit Ethernet is the newest and fastest Ethernet technology to date. In real terms IEEE 802.3z (the *correct* specification for the colloquially termed Gigabit Ethernet) brings further changes to the original 802.3/8802-3 standards. In fact 802.3z defines an extended MAC, and as with our 100Mbps technologies, a set of physical layers. Architecturally our model changes once more (see figure 10-1), and although these changes may seem cosmetic, they are actually more than just changes to terminology.

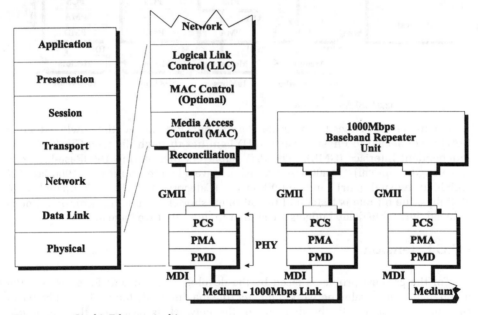

Figure 10-1: Gigabit Ethernet Architecture

Before looking at these changes and indeed the operation of the 1000Mbps system, it is worthwhile reviewing the architectures of all Ethernet/802.3 flavors. Figure 10-2 shows this evolution, and from this it is clear that backwards compatibility has been maintained wherever possible.

Working from the left, we see the *traditional* PLS/AUI/PMA architecture applicable to both 1Mbps and 10Mbps systems. The *Reconciliation* layer, introduced with 100Mbps is however applicable to both 10Mbps and 100Mbps systems as shown. At this time, the concept of the *Medium Independent Interface* (MII) was also introduced, and as we shall see later, is modified for operation at 1000Mbps. Finally, the optional *MAC Control* sublayer is introduced with our 1000Mbps system, and as we have already said, modifications to the MAC itself are also introduced.

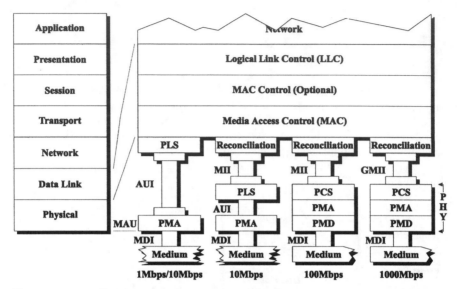

Figure 10-2: 802.3/OSI Architecture

So what changes does this new standard bring? Put simply, the newly extended MAC is connected to Physical Layer (PHY) entities through the new Gigabit Media Independent Interface (GMII). The PHY sublayers then define 1000Base-LX (long wavelength optical),[1] 1000Base-SX (short wavelength optical), 1000Base-CX (shielded twisted pair), and 1000Base-T[2] (Category 5 UTP). Compared with 100Mbps, the bit rate is faster and the bit times shorter. Frame transmission time is reduced, but cable delay budgets are similar to those that we have at 100Mbps.

10.1 MAC Extension

One of the greatest problems faced by the developers of Gigabit Ethernet was the maintenance of a usable network *diameter* (the maximum distance allowed between stations). If you recall, the diameter of the network is based on the *round trip propagation* and *round trip collision delays* of the network, and therefore if all other parameters remain constant the distance has to reduce as the speed increases. The problem that we have is that at Gigabit speeds the *Slot Time* that was 51.2µs at 10Mbps, and 5.12µs at 100Mbps, would now shrink to just 0.512µs. Obviously, since collision detection relies on the fact that we must still be transmitting when a

---

[1] Long and Short Wavelength Optical and also known colloquially as Long and Short Haul.
[2] While 1000Base-SX, 1000Base-LX, and 1000Base-CX are defined within IEEE 802.3z, 1000Base-T is defined in IEEE 802.3ab.

collision occurs, our network diameter shrinks accordingly. So what are we left with if we are to attain Gigabit speeds? How much will it affect the critical design of today's networks? And what of the future? Can we really still exist within the framework created so many years ago? Obviously things have to change if the network is to evolve, but the question is one of scale and is certainly one that requires answers. In order to understand the future then, we must first look back at our past.

In actual fact, we need not go back very far. Instead, let us consider *shared media*, and more specifically the network diameter that we found in use at 100Mbps. Here, using both *Class I* and *Class II* repeaters[3] and employing copper segments, our diameter is approximately 200m (see figure 10-3). This is approximately one tenth of the diameter at 10Mbps and it therefore follows that if we increase the speed a further 10 fold, we will naturally reduce the diameter to one tenth of this value. This now leaves us with a diameter of just 20m - unworkable for practical networks!

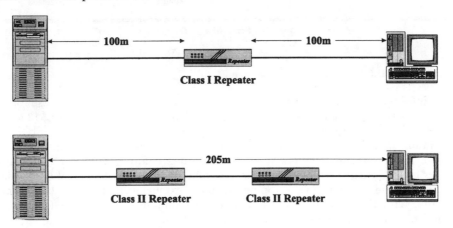

Figure 10-3: 100Base-TX Maximum Collision Domain Diameter

Having explained the problem then, the question now is how do we get around it? The technology has to be made attractive in terms of installation cost and protecting the investments already made in network infrastructures. It would be all too easy to say that Gigabit can only be used over fiber, but we would then be left with a technology that would not be widely implemented. We only have to look at how little interest was shown in Asynchronous Transfer Mode (ATM) in the early days to appreciate just how technology has to meet the users need. It has to be available, open, and fit into their existing infrastructures. Its introduction also has to be timely, and ATM was possibly light years ahead of its time. That said, the market is ready for Gigabit, but only if it is considered to be in a usable form.

The answer then, lies in the implementation of one of two possible extensions to the MAC, known simply as *Carrier Extension* and *Frame Bursting*. Either method allows us to overcome much of the distance limitation, although it has to be said

---

[3] Based upon the Transmission System Model I described in chapter 9.

that neither are required in most *practical* networks. Why are they not required? Well, they are only needed for *half duplex* media environments and few (if indeed any) networks that implement Gigabit Ethernet use this. Most (in truth, almost all) implement *Full Duplex Switched*[4] solutions instead, and with this scheme the CSMA/CD protocol is not required since collisions simply cannot occur.

10.1.1 Carrier Extension

As we have said, the real problem lies in the slot time that is used for Ethernet. With *Carrier Extension* we are able to increase the slot time without increasing the minimum frame size. What happens is simply that the minimum slot time is increased from 64 octets to 512 octets by *Padding* the frame with special *non-data* symbols called *Extension* bits. Figure 10-4 shows how this affects the MAC frame itself.

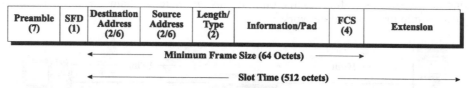

Figure 10-4: MAC Frame with Frame Extension

Frames that are 512 octets or longer do not require extension. Thus, these frames are sent normally. Frames whose length is less than this new slot time of 512 octets (4.096µs) *will* require extension, and this method would therefore apply. On reception, stations that operate in a half duplex mode must be able to detect the *real* end of the frame and therefore strip extension bits before passing the data to the upper layers. Again, if the frame is the slot time in length (or longer) then the data can be passed without any stripping since no extension bits would be present. Finally, with Carrier Extension the maximum frame size of 1518 octets remains. Thus, this whole concept relates only to short frames.

So, now we have a method that allows us to transmit at Gigabit speeds yet retain a workable network diameter. The problem now becomes one of effective use of network bandwidth, since for small frames we are now holding the channel for 8 times longer than is required to pass our data. The answer to this next dilemma is to be found in *Frame Bursting* which is discussed next.

10.1.2 Frame Bursting

In 1000Mbps systems, devices are allowed to optionally transmit multiple frames without relinquishing the transmission medium. The device transmits the first frame, and if required will pad this to the slot time by including extension bits, as previously described. If the device then has further data to transmit, it transmits further extension bits in order to fill the normal *Inter-Frame Gap* period and then transmits the next frame. This then continues with the device transmitting Extension bits as the Inter-Frame Gap, followed by real frames, until either all data

---

[4] Full Duplex operation is discussed in chapter 12 and Switching is discussed in chapter 15.

frames have been transmitted or until what is known as the *Burst Limit* has been reached (whichever is the sooner). For 1000Mbps systems, the Burst Limit is defined as 65,536 bits (8192 octets). Figure 10-5 shows an example of a transmission using Frame Bursting.

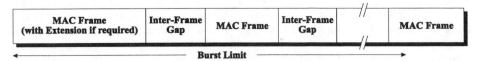

Figure 10-5: Transmission Using Frame Bursting

Frame bursting requires the device to track the number of octets that have been transmitted, so that it knows when to cease transmission due to the Burst Limit being exceeded. If the Burst Limit is exceeded during transmission of a frame, then that frame is sent and the device will then cease transmission when it is completed. It is also important to understand that only the first frame of a burst will need to be extended. Second, and indeed subsequent frames, do not require extension since the slot time (and therefore the time during which a collision should have been detected) has now been exceeded. The normal rules relating to the minimum and maximum frame sizes of 64 and 1518 octets must be adhered to, and these are the only overriding factors. In addition, since the transmitting station does not cease its transmission (even for inter-frame gaps) all other devices will detect that the medium is in use and defer their own transmissions accordingly.

As we can see then, Frame Bursting does have considerable advantage over the simpler Frame Extension, yet neither appreciably change the operation of the MAC. Frame Bursting is definitely the more popular implementation, although remember that few installations use *half duplex* gigabit technology, and therefore neither are used to any great degree.

10.1.3 A Comparison of Ethernet/802.3 Parameters

Before leaving this section let us contrast the transmission parameters of Ethernet/802.3 as shown in table 10-1. As we see, the real differences lie in the scaling of times rather than making huge demands on modifications to the MAC and other areas. In doing this, minimal changes are required, a high level of backwards compatibility is maintained, and therefore investments are protected.

Table 10-1: Ethernet/802.3 Transmission Parameters

Parameter	1Mbps	10Mbps	100Mbps	1000Mbps
Slot Time (bit times)	512	512	512	4,096
Inter-Frame Gap (µs)	96	9.6	0.96	0.096
Attempt Limit	16	16	16	16
Back-Off Limit	10	10	10	10
Jam Size (bits)	32	32	32	32
Max. Frame Size (octets)	1,518	1,518	1,518	1,518
Min. Frame Size (octets)	64	64	64	64
Burst Limit (bits)	-	-	-	65,536

10.2 Reconciliation Sublayer and Gigabit Media Independent Interface

The purpose of the RS/GMII interface is similar to that described for the 100Mbps system.[5] One major exception is that this interface is capable of supporting only 1000Mbps operation, and the other is that it is never physically separated (exposed). PHYs provide support for this speed of operation, and where other data rates are required (10Mbps or 100Mbps), other interfaces (such as a MII) must be employed. In any event, the sole purpose of this interface is to ensure media transparency to the MAC sublayer.

10.2.1 PLS Service Primitive to GMII Mapping

As with the 10/100Mbps model in the previous chapter, the Reconciliation sublayer maps the GMII signals to the PLS primitives. Figure 10-6 shows the Reconciliation Sublayer Inputs and Outputs and their relationship to the GMII that differs slightly from that shown for the 100Mbps system of chapter 9.

- **PLS_DATA.request**
  The PLS_DATA.request (OUTPUT_UNIT) will be one of five values namely ONE, ZERO, TRANSMIT_COMPLETE, EXTEND, or EXTEND_ERROR. When TX_EN is asserted, each of the TXD signals (TXD<7:0>) will convey either a ONE or a ZERO of data. Where TX_EN is de-asserted, these same signals (TXD<7:0>) convey specifically encoded eight bit equivalents of EXTEND or EXTEND_ERROR (see Table 10-2). Where the MAC has ceased transmission as signaled by the de-assertion of both TX_EN and TX_ER, TRANS-MIT_COMPLETE is signaled. In all cases, synchronization with the PHY is achieved through the GTX_CLK

- **PLS_SIGNAL.indicate**
  The PLS_SIGNAL.indicate (SIGNAL_STATUS) can assume two values, either SIGNAL_ERROR or NO_SIGNAL_ERROR. SIGNAL_STATUS will assume the value of SIGNAL_ERROR when the GMII COL signal is asserted and assumes the value NO_SIGNAL_ERROR when the COL signal is de-asserted. The PLS_SIGNAL.indicate is then generated whenever SIGNAL_STATUS transitions from SIGNAL_ERROR to NO_SIGNAL_ERROR or vice versa.

- **PLS_DATA.indicate**
  PLS_DATA.indicate (INPUT_UNIT) is used to indicate the GMII signals RXD<7:0>, RX_ER, RX_DV, and RX_CLK. INPUT_UNIT will take one of the three values; ZERO, ONE, or EXTEND and represents a single data bit as derived from RXD<7:0>. Each of these signals RXD<7:0> conveys either a ZERO or ONE while RX_DV is asserted. Where RX_DV is de-asserted and RX_ER is asserted, eight bits of EXTEND are conveyed by specific encodings of RXD<7:0> as shown in table 10-3.

- **PLS_DATA_VALID.indicate**
  PLS_DATA_VALID.indicate (DATA_VALID_STATUS) assumes the value DATA_VALID whenever the RX_DV signal is asserted. In addition,

---

[5] See chapter 9.

DATA_VALID will be assumed where RX_ER is asserted, RXD<7:0> indicates Carrier Extend or Carrier Extend Error, and RX_DV is de-asserted. DATA_NOT_VALID is assumed at all other times.

- **PLS_CARRIER.indicate**
  The PLS_CARRIER.indicate (CARRIER_STATUS) will take the value of either CARRIER_ON or CARRIER_OFF. CARRIER_STATUS assumes the value CARRIER_ON when CRS is asserted, and CARRIER_OFF otherwise.

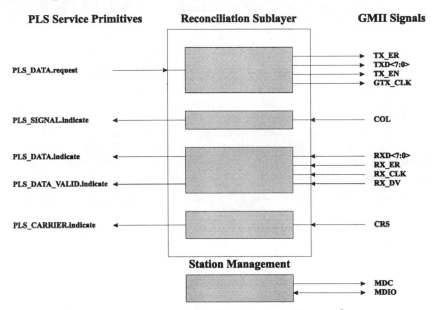

Figure 10-6: Reconciliation Sublayer Inputs and Outputs and the GMII

- **TX_ER and RX_ER Mapping**
  When TX_ER (Transmit Coding Error) is asserted while TX_EN (Transmit Enable) is also asserted, the PHY transmits one or more code groups that are not part of the valid data or delimiter set. Equally, if TXD<7:0> is carrying appropriate values and TX_EN is de-asserted and TX_ER is asserted, the PHY will generate either Carrier Extend or Carrier Extend Error code groups. Carrier Extend informs the PHY that it should transmit an end-of-packet delimiter as the initial code group of the carrier extension. Holding TX_EN de-asserted and asserting TX_ER results in transmission of Carrier Extension Error provided that the appropriate values are represented on signals TXD<7:0>.

  Receive Data Valid (RX_DV) is signaled by the PHY where data is being successfully recovered and presented on the RXD<7:0> signals. Where an error in reception occurs, RX_ER is asserted thereby informing the Reconciliation sublayer that an error has been detected. Should the PHY detect an error within Carrier Extension, RX_ER is asserted and the RXD<7:0> signals will contain the appropriate value. Assertion of RX_ER while RX_DV is de-asserted indicates that Carrier Extension is being decoded by the PHY provided that the RXD<7:0> signals contain appropriate values.

- **MDC and MDIO Management Data Mapping**

  The MDC (Management Data Clock) and MDIO (Management Data I/O) remain unchanged from that described for 10/100Mbps operation. Essentially, the MDC (derived from the PHY) provides the timing reference for the transfer of data on the Management Data IO (MDIO) signal. The MDIO is a bi-directional signal between the PHY and the Station Management Entity (STA), over which all control and status information is transferred.

10.2.2 Transmit and Receive Data Encoding

As we have seen from the preceding discussion, the Transmit and Receive GMII data paths are 8 (rather than 4) bits wide. These paths (TXD<7:0> and RXD<7:0>), apart from being used to transfer data between the MAC and the PHY, are also used to transfer control and signaling information such as Carrier Extension and Carrier Extend Error. As such, specific encoding is used to signal the function(s) required, and when used in conjunction with the signals TX_EN, TX_ER, RX_DV, and RX_ER, these can be conveyed unambiguously. Tables 10-2 and 10-3 show permissible encodings for TXD<7:0> and RXD<7:0>, respectively.

Table 10-2: Permissible Encodings of TXD<7:0>, TX_EN, and TX_ER

TX_EN	TX_ER	TXD<7:0>	Description	PLS_DATA.request
0	0	00-0E	Normal inter-frame	TRANSMIT_COMPLETE
0	1	00-0E	Reserved	-
0	1	0F	Carrier Extend	EXTEND (8bits)
0	1	10-1E	Reserved	-
0	1	1F	Carrier Extend Error	EXTEND_ERROR (8bits)
0	1	20-FF	Reserved	-
1	0	00-FF	Normal data TX	ZERO, ONE (8bits)
1	1	00-FF	TX error propagation	No applicable parameter

Table 10-3: Permissible Encodings of RXD<7:0>, RX_DV, and RX_ER

RX_DV	RX_ER	RXD<7:0>	Description	PLS_DATA.indicate
0	0	00-FF	Normal inter-frame	No applicable parameter
0	1	00	Normal inter-frame	No applicable parameter
0	1	01-0D	Reserved	-
0	1	0E	False Carrier ind.	No applicable parameter
0	1	0F	Carrier Extend	EXTEND (8bits)
0	1	10-1E	Reserved	-
0	1	1F	Carrier Extend error	ZERO, ONE (8bits)
0	1	20-FF	Reserved	-
1	0	00-FF	Normal data Rx	ZERO, ONE (8bits)
1	1	00-FF	Data reception error	ZERO, ONE (8bits)

10.2.3 Management Functions

In order to accommodate the newer technologies offered by 1000Mbps devices yet still retain a measure of backwards compatibility, the management functionality offered at the RS/(MII or GMII) interface had to be expanded. As before (in the case of the MII) management information, which is stored in a number of registers, is transferred over the MDIO using a specific protocol. The register contents however now change to allow the extended functionality offered by this new technology.

Most specifically, of the 32 available registers, Register 15 (which was previously reserved) is now used to store and convey *Extended Status* information. At the same time, the contents of Register 0 (*Control*) change, as do the contents of Register 1 (*Status*). Also, although not directly relevant to 1000Mbps operation, IEEE 802.3z defines operations for registers 8-10 (which were previously reserved). Table 10-4 shows these register designations as applicable to IEEE 802.3z.

Table 10-4: MII/GMII Management Register Set

Register	Register Name	Basic/Extended MII	GMII
0	Control	Basic	Basic
1	Status	Basic	Basic
2,3	PHY Identifier	Extended	Extended
4	Auto-Negotiation Advertisement	Extended	Extended
5	Auto-Negotiation Link Partner Base Ability	Extended	Extended
6	Auto-Negotiation Expansion	Extended	Extended
7	Auto-Negotiation Next Page Transmit	Extended	Extended
8	Auto-Negotiation Link Partner Rec. Next Page	Extended	Extended
9	100Base-T2 Control Register	Extended	Extended
10	100Base-T2 Status Register	Extended	Extended
11 - 14	Reserved	Extended	Extended
15	Extended Status	Reserved	Basic
16-31	Vendor Specific	Extended	Extended

The *Control* register (register 0) changes to support 1000Mbps operation as defined by table 10-5. Specifically, bits 13 and 6 now work in concert to enable all 3 speeds (10/100/1000Mbps) to be signaled.

Table 10-5: Control Register Contents

Bit	Name	Actions	Description
15	Reset	R/W SC	1 - PHY Reset 0 - Normal Operation
14	Loopback	R/W	1 - Enable Loopback Mode 0 - Disable Loopback Mode
13	Speed Selection (LSB)	R/W	Used with bit 6 as follows:

0.6	0.13	Meaning
1	1	Reserved
1	0	1000Mbps
0	1	100Mbps
0	0	10Mbps

Table 10-5: Control Register Contents (Continued)

Bit	Name	Actions	Description
12	Auto-Negotiation Enable	R/W	1 - Enable Auto-Negotiation 0 - Disable Auto-Negotiation
11	Power Down	R/W	1 - Power Down 0 - Normal Operation
10	Isolate	R/W	1 - Isolate MII or GMII from PHY 0 - Normal Operation
9	Restart Auto-Negotiation	R/W SC	1 - Restart Auto-Negotiation Process 0 - Normal Operation
8	Duplex Mode	R/W	1 - Full Duplex 0 - Half Duplex
7	Collision Test	R/W	1 - Enable COL Test Signal 0 - Disable COL Test Signal
6	Speed Selection (MSB)	R/W	Used with bit 13 as follows:
5-0	Reserved	R/W	Set to 0 - Ignore on Register Read

Used with bit 13 as follows:

0.6	0.13	Meaning
1	1	Reserved
1	0	1000Mbps
0	1	100Mbps
0	0	10Mbps

Note: The *SC* designation in the *Actions* column indicates that the register contents are *Self Clearing* after the action has been performed.

Register 1 (the Status register) is re-defined by IEEE 802.3z since the PHY functionality is changed to accommodate 1000Mbps operation. As with IEEE 802.3u (100Mbps operation), all bits are read-only and bits 1 and 4 latch high while bit 2 always latches low. Table 10-6 details the contents of the status register.

Table 10-6: Status Register Contents

Bit	Name	Description
15	100Base-T4	1 - PHY able to perform 100Base-T4 0 - PHY unable to perform10Base-T4
14	100Base-X Full Duplex	1 - PHY able to operate 10Mbps FD 0 - PHY unable to operate 10Mbps FD
13	100Base-X Half Duplex	1 - PHY able to operate 100Mbps HD 0 - PHY unable to operate 100Mbps HD
12	10Mbps Full Duplex	1 - PHY able to operate 10Mbps FD 0 - PHY unable to operate 10Mbps FD
11	10Mbps Half Duplex	1 - PHY able to operate 10Mbps HD 0 - PHY unable to operate 10Mbps HD
10	100Base-T2 Full Duplex	1 - PHY able to perform 100Base-T2 FD 0 - PHY unable to perform 100Base-T2 FD
9	100Base-T2 Half Duplex	1 - PHY able to perform 100Base-T2 HD 0 - PHY unable to perform 100Base-T2 HD
8	Extended Status	1 - Ext. status information in Register 15 0 - No ext. status information in Register 15

Table 10-6: Status Register Contents (Continued)

Bit	Name	Description
7	Reserved	Ignored
6	MF Preamble Suppression	1 - PHY accepts management frames with Preamble suppressed 0 - PHY will not accept management frames with Preamble suppressed
5	Auto-Negotiation Complete	1 - Auto-Negotiation process complete 0 - Auto-Negotiation process incomplete
4	Remote Fault	1 - Remote Fault condition detected 0 - Remote Fault condition not detected
3	Auto-Negotiation Ability	1 - PHY able to perform Auto-Negotiation 0 - PHY unable to perform Auto-Negotiation
2	Link Status	1 - Link is Up 0 - Link is Down
1	Jabber Detect	1 - Jabber Condition Detected 0 - No Jabber Condition Detected
0	Extended Capability	1 - Extended Register Capabilities 0 - Basic Register Set Capabilities Only

Where operation above 100Mbps is supported (i.e., 1000Mbps), the extended status register (register 15) must be implemented. As with the status register (register 1), all bits are read-only. The register contents are shown in table 10-7.

Table 10-7: Extended Status Register Contents - Register 15

Bit	Name	Description
15	1000Base-X Full Duplex	1 - PHY able to operate 1000Base-X FD 0 - PHY unable to operate 1000Base-X FD
14	1000Base-X Half Duplex	1 - PHY able to operate 1000Base-X HD 0 - PHY unable to operate 1000Base-X HD
13	1000Base-T Full Duplex	1 - PHY able to operate 1000Base-T FD 0 - PHY unable to operate 1000Base-T FD
12	1000Base-T Half Duplex	1 - PHY able to operate 1000Base-T HD 0 - PHY unable to operate 1000Base-T HD
11-0	Reserved	Ignore

Finally, as with the 100Mbps system introduced in chapter 9, where extended capabilities are available at the PHY, registers 2 and 3 contain the *PHY Identifier* as shown in figure 10-7. As before, the registers hold the low 22 bits of the 24 bit *OUI*, a six bit *Model Number* as applied by the vendor, and a 4 bit *Revision Number*.

10.2.4 GMII Frame Format

All data frames transmitted over the GMII have the structure shown in figure 10-8, which also shows the order of bit transmission. As can be seen, the one overriding

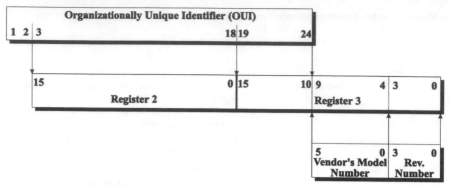

Figure 10-7: PHY Identifier (Registers 2 and 3)

difference between this format and that discussed in relation to the MII[6] is the introduction of the *Extend* field used for *Carrier Extension.*

The *Inter-Frame gap* is where there is no data activity on the interface. For example in the case of transmit, no activity is signaled where both TX_EN and TX_ER are both de-asserted. In the case of receive, either RX_DV and RX_ER are de-asserted or, RX_DV is de-asserted but RXD<7:0> contains the value 00_{16}. The *Preamble* is seven octets of alternating ones and zeroes of the form **10101010......**, and the *Start Frame Delimiter* (SFD) is a single octet of **10101011**. The *End Frame Delimiter* (EFD) is defined as being the falling edge of the RX_DV signal. Finally, the *Extend* field for transmit is where TX_ER is asserted together with the appropriate TXD<7:0> values and the TX_EN signal being de-asserted. For the receive case, *Extend* is signaled by RX_DV being de-asserted, RX_ER being asserted, and the correct coding of RXD<7:0>.

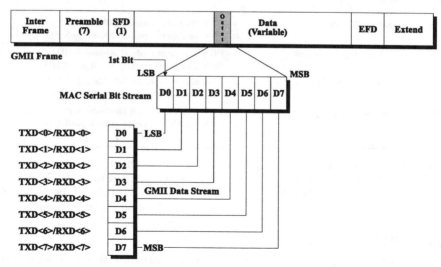

Figure 10-8: GMII Frame Format and Data Bit Order

[6] The Media Independent Interface (MII) is discussed in chapter 9.

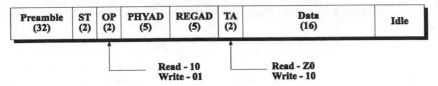

Figure 10-9: GMII Management Frame Format

Management frames as carried over the MDIO are identical to those used for the MII as shown in figure 10-9. The *Preamble* simply consists of 32 contiguous 1 bits (**11111.....11111**) on the MDIO clocked by 32 cycles on the MDC signal. The *Start of Frame* (ST) field is a 2 bit field that comprises the binary value **01** and is used to indicate that a valid management frame is commencing. The 2 bit *Operation* field (OP) indicates whether a register Read or Write is signaled. A value of **10** indicates a Read operation, while a value of **01** indicates a Write operation. The *PHY Address* field (PHYAD) is five bits in length and is used to uniquely address any one of 32 possibly attached PHYs that may be connected. The 5 bit *Register Address* field (REGAD) is then used to uniquely address any 1 of the 32 possible registers held on the PHY.

The *Turn Around* (TA) field of 2 bits is used to avoid contention during a Read cycle. In the case of the Read operation, the PHY presents a high impedance signal (Z) for the first bit time. In the case of a Write, a 1 bit is presented in this bit time. For both operations however, a 0 is always presented during the second bit time.

The *Data* field is 16 bits in length and is used to carry the data either to or from the register addressed by the REGAD field. In this field, the first data bit transmitted represents the contents of register bit 15 and the last, bit 0. Finally, the *Idle* condition is represented by the MDIO being set to a high impedance state and no data is therefore valid.

10.3 Physical Coding Sublayer and Physical Medium Attachment for 1000Base-X

The Physical Coding Sublayer (PCS) and Physical Medium Attachment (PMA) sublayers map the characteristics of the Physical Medium Dependent (PMD) sublayer to that required by the Reconciliation Sublayer (RS). In doing this, the 1000Base-LX (long wavelength optical), 1000Base-SX (short wavelength optical), 1000Base-CX (short haul copper), and 1000Base-T (twisted pair copper) PMDs are supported and in both full and half duplex modes. Essentially the PCS is an interface between the PHY and the GMII. Specifically, it is responsible for the provision of a media independent interface that manages the *Auto-Negotiation*[7] process, senses carrier signals and collisions on the media, and prepares/recovers data to/from the PMD.

The Physical Layer standards of 1000Base-X are based upon those developed by ANSI X3.230-1994 (Fiber Channel Physical and Signaling Interface). The 1000Base-X PMDs therefore use the 8B/10B encoding technique. Thus, in providing an

---

[7] See chapter 11 for a complete discussion of the Auto-Negotiation process.

interface between the GMII and PMA, the PCS must encode/decode data from/to the GMII.

The PMA is responsible for the mapping of the PCS code groups to/from the PMD before/after serialization/de-serialization. In addition, the PMA recovers the clock from the data supplied by the PMD, and where required can perform a data loopback at the PMD interface. Like the PMA, the PCS is media independent, relying on the PMD/MDI to provide this functionality as shown in figure 10-10.

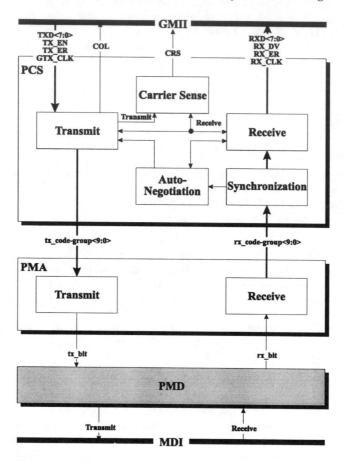

Figure 10-10: PCS/PMA Functional Block Diagram

10.3.1 Data Encoding

As we have already said, the PCS sublayer uses 8B/10B encoding. In transmit, 8 bit codes (TXD<7:0>) are translated into 10 bit code groups and passed to the PMA. For receive, the opposite is used whereby the 10 bit code groups recovered by the PMA are then decoded into 8 bit codes (RXD<7:0>) and passed to the GMII. In using an encoding scheme of this type, the 256 possible 8 bit code combinations are mapped to 1024 possible 10 bit codes. Now, through selection of appropriate 10 bit codes, we are assured of transitions within the data stream and therefore synchronization is maintained. Table 10-8 shows the encoding for the 256 possible combinations for data, and table 10-9 shows those code group combinations used for control purposes. These tables are then described further below.

The 8 bit (single octet) un-encoded data is referenced by the notation A, B, C, D, E, F, G, H, where A is the least significant bit. This 8 bit data is then translated into the 10 bit code group referenced by the bits a, b, c, d, e, i, g, h, j. Each code group is given a unique name of the form Dx.y or Kx.y where x is the decimal equivalent of bits EDCBA, and y is the decimal equivalent of bits HGF. The designation D or K then relates to whether the code group is a *Data* group, or a *Control* group - table 10-8 shows valid data groups and table 10-9 shows all valid control groups. The columns *Current RD* - and *Current RD* + relate to what is known as the *Running Disparity* (RD), a method used to assist in the detection of transmission errors. The rules for implementing RD are as follows:

- On power up, a transmitter will always assume a negative value for the initial RD. After each code group has been transmitted, a new value for the RD will be calculated (based upon the code group just transmitted) as follows:

  - RD is calculated based on what are known as *sub-blocks*. In this case, two sub-blocks exist for each 10 bit code, namely a 6 bit sub-block (comprising bits *abcdei*) and a 4 bit sub-block (comprising bits *fghj*).

  - The RD at the beginning of the 6 bit sub-block will always be the same as that at the end of the previous code group. The RD at the beginning of the 4 bit sub-block will always be the same as that at the end of the 6 bit sub-block. The RD at the end of the 4 bit sub-block will determine the RD at the end of the code group.

To calculate the RD for the sub-blocks, the following rules are applied:

- RD will be positive at the end of any sub-block if that sub-block contains more ones than zeroes. It will also be positive at the end of the 6 bit sub-block 000111 and at the end of the 4 bit sub-block 0011.

- RD will be negative at the end of any sub-block, if that sub-block contains more zeroes than ones. It will also be negative at the end of the 6 bit sub-block 111000, and at the end of the 4 bit sub-block 1100.

- If neither of the two conditions above are met, then the RD at the end of the sub-block will be the same as the RD at the beginning of the sub-block.

As an example, consider what happens when we wish to transmit the data stream 35-B7-92 and our initial RD is negative. Referring to table 10-8, we have the following data, codes, running disparity and bit patterns:

Data		35			B7			92		
Codes		D21.1			D23.5			D18.4		
	RD		RD	RD		RD	RD		RD		RD
Bits	-	101010	-	1001	-	111010	+	1010	+	010011	+	0010	+

Next, let us see what happens on receive when errors are introduced. To do this we will consider the same transmit data stream as before, only in this example we will have a single bit receive error. Notice that although the error is introduced in the first code group, it is actually detected after receiving the second group.

Tx Data		35			B7			92		
Tx Codes		D21.1			D23.5			D18.4		
RD		RD		RD		RD		RD		RD		RD

	RD									
Tx	-	101010	-	1001	-	111010	+	1010	+	010011	+	0010	+
Rx	-	101010	-	**1011**	+	111010	+	1010	+	010011	+	0010	+
Rx Codes		D21.0			*!! ERROR !!*			D18.4		
Rx Data		15			-----			92		

Table 10-8: Valid Data Code Groups

Code Group Name	Octet Value (Hex)	Octet Bits		Current RD -		Current RD +	
		HGF	EDCBA	abcdei	fghj	abcdei	fghj
D0.0	00	000	00000	100111	0100	011000	1011
D1.0	01	000	00001	011101	0100	100010	1011
D2.0	02	000	00010	101101	0100	010010	1011
D3.0	03	000	00011	110001	1011	110001	0100
D4.0	04	000	00100	110101	0100	001010	1011
D5.0	05	000	00101	101001	1011	101001	0100
D6.0	06	000	00110	011001	1011	011001	0100
D7.0	07	000	00111	111000	1011	000111	0100
D8.0	08	000	01000	111001	0100	000110	1011
D9.0	09	000	01001	100101	1011	100101	0100
D10.0	0A	000	01010	010101	1011	010101	0100
D11.0	0B	000	01011	110100	1011	110100	0100
D12.0	0C	000	01100	001101	1011	001101	0100
D13.0	0D	000	01101	101100	1011	101100	0100
D14.0	0E	000	01110	011100	1011	011100	0100
D15.0	0F	000	01111	010111	0100	101000	1011
D16.0	10	000	10000	011011	0100	100100	1011
D17.0	11	000	10001	100011	1011	100011	0100
D18.0	12	000	10010	010011	1011	010011	0100
D19.0	13	000	10011	110010	1011	110010	0100
D20.0	14	000	10100	001011	1011	001011	0100
D21.0	15	000	10101	101010	1011	101010	0100
D22.0	16	000	10110	011010	1011	011010	0100
D23.0	17	000	10111	111010	0100	000101	1011
D24.0	18	000	11000	110011	0100	001100	1011
D25.0	19	000	11001	100110	1011	100110	0100
D26.0	1A	000	11010	010110	1011	010110	0100
D27.0	1B	000	11011	110110	0100	001001	1011
D28.0	1C	000	11100	001110	1011	001110	0100
D29.0	1D	000	11101	101110	0100	010001	1011
D30.0	1E	000	11110	011110	0100	100001	1011
D31.0	1F	000	11111	101011	0100	010100	1011

Table 10-8: Valid Data Code Groups (Continued)

Code Group Name	Octet Value (Hex)	Octet Bits		Current RD -		Current RD +	
		HGF	EDCBA	abcdei	fghj	abcdei	fghj
D0.1	20	001	00000	100111	1001	011000	1001
D1.1	21	001	00001	011101	1001	100010	1001
D2.1	22	001	00010	101101	1001	010010	1001
D3.1	23	001	00011	110001	1001	110001	1001
D4.1	24	001	00100	110101	1001	001010	1001
D5.1	25	001	00101	101001	1001	101001	1001
D6.1	26	001	00110	011001	1001	011001	1001
D7.1	27	001	00111	111000	1001	000111	1001
D8.1	28	001	01000	111001	1001	000110	1001
D9.1	29	001	01001	100101	1001	100101	1001
D10.1	2A	001	01010	010101	1001	010101	1001
D11.1	2B	001	01011	110100	1001	110100	1001
D12.1	2C	001	01100	01101	1001	001101	1001
D13.1	2D	001	01101	101100	1001	101100	1001
D14.1	2E	001	01110	011100	1001	011100	1001
D15.1	2F	001	01111	010111	1001	101000	1001
D16.1	30	001	10000	011011	1001	100100	1001
D17.1	31	001	10001	100011	1001	100011	1001
D18.1	32	001	10010	010011	1001	010011	1001
D19.1	33	001	10011	110010	1001	110010	1001
D20.1	34	001	10100	001011	1001	001011	1001
D21.1	35	001	10101	101010	1001	101010	1001
D22.1	36	001	10110	011010	1001	011010	1001
D23.1	37	001	10111	111010	1001	000101	1001
D24.1	38	001	11000	110011	1001	001100	1001
D25.1	39	001	11001	100110	1001	100110	1001
D26.1	3A	001	11010	010110	1001	010110	1001
D27.1	3B	001	11011	110110	1001	001001	1001
D28.1	3C	001	11100	001110	1001	001110	1001
D29.1	3D	001	11101	101110	1001	010001	1001
D30.1	3E	001	11110	011110	1001	100001	1001
D31.1	3F	001	11111	101011	1001	010100	1001
D0.2	40	010	00000	100111	0101	011000	0101
D1.2	41	010	00001	011101	0101	100010	0101
D2.2	42	010	00010	101101	0101	010010	0101
D3.2	43	010	00011	110001	0101	110001	0101
D4.2	44	010	00100	110101	0101	001010	0101
D5.2	45	010	00101	101001	0101	101001	0101
D6.2	46	010	00110	011001	0101	011001	0101
D7.2	47	010	00111	111000	0101	000111	0101
D8.2	48	010	01000	111001	0101	000110	0101
D9.2	49	010	01001	100101	0101	100101	0101
D10.2	4A	010	01010	010101	0101	010101	0101
D11.2	4B	010	01011	110100	0101	110100	0101
D12.2	4C	010	01100	001101	0101	001101	0101
D13.2	4D	010	01101	101100	0101	101100	0101
D14.2	4E	010	01110	011100	0101	011100	0101
D15.2	4F	010	01111	010111	0101	101000	0101
D16.2	50	010	10000	011011	0101	100100	0101
D17.2	51	010	10001	100011	0101	100011	0101

Table 10-8: Valid Data Code Groups (Continued)

Code Group Name	Octet Value (Hex)	Octet Bits		Current RD -		Current RD +	
		HGF	EDCBA	abcdei	fghj	abcdei	fghj
D18.2	52	010	10010	010011	0101	010011	0101
D19.2	53	010	10011	110010	0101	110011	0101
D20.2	54	010	10100	001011	0101	001011	0101
D21.2	55	010	10101	101010	0101	101010	0101
D22.2	56	010	10110	011010	0101	011010	0101
D23.2	57	010	10111	111010	0101	000101	0101
D24.2	58	010	11000	110011	0101	001100	0101
D25.2	59	010	11001	100110	0101	100110	0101
D26.2	5A	010	11010	010110	0101	010110	0101
D27.2	5B	010	11011	110110	0101	001001	0101
D28.2	5C	010	11100	001110	0101	001110	0101
D29.2	5D	010	11101	101110	0101	010001	0101
D30.2	5E	010	11110	011110	0101	100001	0101
D31.2	5F	010	11111	101011	0101	010100	0101
D0.3	60	011	00000	100111	0011	011000	1100
D1.3	61	011	00001	011101	0011	100010	1100
D2.3	62	011	00010	101101	0011	010010	1100
D3.3	63	011	00011	110001	1100	110001	0011
D4.3	64	011	00100	110101	0011	001010	1100
D5.3	65	011	00101	101001	1100	101001	0011
D6.3	66	011	00110	011001	1100	011001	0011
D7.3	67	011	00111	111000	1100	000111	0011
D8.3	68	011	01000	111001	0011	000110	1100
D9.3	69	011	01001	100101	1100	100101	0011
D10.3	6A	011	01010	010101	1100	010101	0011
D11.3	6B	011	01011	110100	1100	110100	0011
D12.3	6C	011	01100	001101	1100	001101	0011
D13.3	6D	011	01101	101100	1100	101100	0011
D14.3	6E	011	01110	011100	1100	011100	0011
D15.3	6F	011	01111	010111	0011	101000	1100
D16.3	70	011	10000	011011	0011	100100	1100
D17.3	71	011	10001	100011	1100	100011	0011
D18.3	72	011	10010	010011	1100	010011	0011
D19.3	73	011	10011	110010	1100	110010	0011
D20.3	74	011	10100	001011	1100	001011	0011
D21.3	75	011	10101	101010	1100	101010	0011
D22.3	76	011	10110	011010	1100	011010	0011
D23.3	77	011	10111	111010	0011	000101	1100
D24.3	78	011	11000	110011	0011	001100	1100
D25.3	79	011	11001	100110	1100	100110	0011
D26.3	7A	011	11010	010110	1100	010110	0011
D27.3	7B	011	11011	110110	0011	001001	1100
D28.3	7C	011	11100	001110	1100	001110	0011
D29.3	7D	011	11101	101110	0011	010001	1100
D30.3	7E	011	11110	011110	0011	100001	1100
D31.3	7F	011	11111	101011	0011	010100	1100
D0.4	80	100	00000	100111	0010	011000	1101
D1.4	81	100	00001	011101	0010	100010	1101
D2.4	82	100	00010	101101	0010	010010	1101
D3.4	83	100	00011	110001	1101	110001	0010

Table 10-8: Valid Data Code Groups (Continued)

Code Group Name	Octet Value (Hex)	Octet Bits		Current RD -		Current RD +	
		HGF	EDCBA	abcdei	fghj	abcdei	fghj
D4.4	84	100	00100	110101	0010	001010	1101
D5.4	85	100	00101	101001	1101	101001	0010
D6.4	86	100	00110	011001	1101	011001	0010
D7.4	87	100	00111	111000	1101	000111	0010
D8.4	88	100	01000	111001	0010	000110	1101
D9.4	89	100	01001	100101	1101	100101	0010
D10.4	8A	100	01010	010101	1101	010101	0010
D11.4	8B	100	01011	110100	1101	110100	0010
D12.4	8C	100	01100	001101	1101	001101	0010
D13.4	8D	100	01101	101100	1101	101100	0010
D14.4	8E	100	01110	011100	1101	011100	0010
D15.4	8F	100	01111	010111	0010	101000	1101
D16.4	90	100	10000	011011	0010	100100	1101
D17.4	91	100	10001	100011	1101	100011	0010
D18.4	92	100	10010	010011	1101	010011	0010
D19.4	93	100	10011	110010	1101	110010	0010
D20.4	94	100	10100	001011	1101	001011	0010
D21.4	95	100	10101	101010	1101	101010	0010
D22.4	96	100	10110	011010	1101	011010	0010
D23.4	97	100	10111	111010	0010	000101	1101
D24.4	98	100	11000	110011	0010	001100	1101
D25.4	99	100	11001	100110	1101	100110	0010
D26.4	9A	100	11010	010110	1101	010110	0010
D27.4	9B	100	11011	110110	0010	001001	1101
D28.4	9C	100	11100	001110	1101	001110	0010
D29.4	9D	100	11101	101110	0010	010001	1101
D30.4	9E	100	11110	011110	0010	100001	1101
D31.4	9F	100	11111	101011	0010	010100	1101
D0.5	A0	101	00000	100111	1010	011000	1010
D1.5	A1	101	00001	011101	1010	100010	1010
D2.5	A2	101	00010	101101	1010	010010	1010
D3.5	A3	101	00011	110001	1010	110001	1010
D4.5	A4	101	00100	110101	1010	001010	1010
D5.5	A5	101	00101	101001	1010	101001	1010
D6.5	A6	101	00110	011001	1010	011001	1010
D7.5	A7	101	00111	111000	1010	000111	1010
D8.5	A8	101	01000	111001	1010	000110	1010
D9.5	A9	101	01001	100101	1010	100101	1010
D10.5	AA	101	01010	010101	1010	010101	1010
D11.5	AB	101	01011	110100	1010	110100	1010
D12.5	AC	101	01100	001101	1010	001101	1010
D13.5	AD	101	01101	101100	1010	101100	1010
D14.5	AE	101	01110	011100	1010	011100	1010
D15.5	AF	101	01111	010111	1010	101000	1010
D16.5	B0	101	10000	011011	1010	100100	1010
D17.5	B1	101	10001	100011	1010	100011	1010
D18.5	B2	101	10010	010011	1010	010011	1010
D19.5	B3	101	10011	110010	1010	110010	1010
D20.5	B4	101	10100	001011	1010	001011	1010
D21.5	B5	101	10101	101010	1010	101010	1010

Table 10-8: Valid Data Code Groups (Continued)

Code Group Name	Octet Value (Hex)	Octet Bits HGF	Octet Bits EDCBA	Current RD - abcdei	Current RD - fghj	Current RD + abcdei	Current RD + fghj
D22.5	B6	101	10110	011010	1010	011010	1010
D23.5	B7	101	10111	111010	1010	000101	1010
D24.5	B8	101	11000	110011	1010	001100	1010
D25.5	B9	101	11001	100110	1010	100110	1010
D26.5	BA	101	11010	010110	1010	010110	1010
D27.5	BB	101	11011	110110	1010	001001	1010
D28.5	BC	101	11100	001110	1010	001110	1010
D29.5	BD	101	11101	101110	1010	010001	1010
D30.5	BE	101	11110	011110	1010	100001	1010
D31.5	BF	101	11111	101011	1010	010100	1010
D0.6	C0	110	00000	100111	0110	011000	0110
D1.6	C1	110	00001	011101	0110	100010	0110
D2.6	C2	110	00010	101101	0110	010010	0110
D3.6	C3	110	00011	110001	0110	110001	0110
D4.6	C4	110	00100	110101	0110	001010	0110
D5.6	C5	110	00101	101001	0110	101001	0110
D6.6	C6	110	00110	011001	0110	011001	0110
D7.6	C7	110	00111	111000	0110	000111	0110
D8.6	C8	110	01000	111001	0110	000110	0110
D9.6	C9	110	01001	100101	0110	100101	0110
D10.6	CA	110	01010	010101	0110	010101	0110
D11.6	CB	110	01011	110100	0110	110100	0110
D12.6	CC	110	01100	001101	0110	001101	0110
D13.6	CD	110	01101	101100	0110	101100	0110
D14.6	CE	110	01110	011100	0110	011100	0110
D15.6	CF	110	01111	010111	0110	101000	0110
D16.6	D0	110	10000	011011	0110	100100	0110
D17.6	D1	110	10001	100011	0110	100011	0110
D18.6	D2	110	10010	010011	0110	010011	0110
D19.6	D3	110	10011	110010	0110	110010	0110
D20.6	D4	110	10100	001011	0110	001011	0110
D21.6	D5	110	10101	101010	0110	101010	0110
D22.6	D6	110	10110	011010	0110	011010	0110
D23.6	D7	110	10111	111010	0110	000101	0110
D24.6	D8	110	11000	110011	0110	01100	0110
D25.6	D9	110	11001	100110	0110	100110	0110
D26.6	DA	110	11010	010110	0110	010110	0110
D27.6	DB	110	11011	110110	0110	001001	0110
D28.6	DC	110	11100	001110	0110	001110	0110
D29.6	DD	110	11101	101110	0110	010001	0110
D30.6	DE	110	11110	011110	0110	100001	0110
D31.6	DF	110	11111	101011	0110	010100	0110
D0.7	E0	111	00000	100111	0001	011000	1110
D1.7	E1	111	00001	011101	0001	100010	1110
D2.7	E2	111	00010	101101	0001	010010	1110
D3.7	E3	111	00011	110001	1110	110001	0001
D4.7	E4	111	00100	110101	0001	001010	1110
D5.7	E5	111	00101	101001	1110	101001	0001
D6.7	E6	111	00110	011001	1110	011001	0001
D7.7	E7	111	00111	111000	1110	000111	0001

Table 10-8: Valid Data Code Groups (Continued)

Code Group Name	Octet Value (Hex)	Octet Bits		Current RD -		Current RD +	
		HGF	EDCBA	abcdei	fghj	abcdei	fghj
D8.7	E8	111	01000	111001	0001	000110	1110
D9.7	E9	111	01001	100101	1110	100101	0001
D10.7	EA	111	01010	010101	1110	010101	0001
D11.7	EB	111	01011	110100	1110	110100	1000
D12.7	EC	111	01100	001101	1110	001101	0001
D13.7	ED	111	01101	101100	1110	101100	1000
D14.7	EE	111	01110	011100	1110	011100	1000
D15.7	EF	111	01111	010111	0001	101000	1110
D16.7	F0	111	10000	011011	0001	100100	1110
D17.7	F1	111	10001	100011	0111	100011	0001
D18.7	F2	111	10010	010011	0111	010011	0001
D19.7	F3	111	10011	110010	1110	110010	0001
D20.7	F4	111	10100	001011	0111	001011	0001
D21.7	F5	111	10101	101010	1110	101010	0001
D22.7	F6	111	10110	011010	1110	011010	0001
D23.7	F7	111	10111	111010	0001	000101	1110
D24.7	F8	111	11000	110011	0001	001100	1110
D25.7	F9	111	11001	100110	1110	100110	0001
D26.7	FA	111	11010	010110	1110	010110	0001
D27.7	FB	111	11011	110110	0001	001001	1110
D28.7	FC	111	11100	001110	1110	001110	0001
D29.7	FD	111	11101	101110	0001	010001	1110
D30.7	FE	111	11110	011110	0001	100001	1110
D31.7	FF	111	11111	101011	0001	010100	1110

The *Special code groups* listed in table 10-9 are used either singly or in *ordered sets* to convey special control information. The /K28.5/ code group is always the first code group of all ordered sets that are repeated (see table 10-10) since this allows receivers to synchronize with the incoming bit stream. The *Comma* (see Note B, table 10-9) which is present in code groups /K28.1/, /K28.5/, and /K28.7/ is used as an easy way to locate and verify code group and ordered set boundaries within a bit stream. This *comma* is then defined as being the 7 bit string (*abcdeif*) of **0011111** (RD-) or **1100000** (RD+).

Table 10-9: Valid Special Code Groups

Code Group Name	Notes	Octet Value (Hex)	Octet Bits		Current RD -		Current RD +	
			HGF	EDCBA	abcdei	fghj	abcdei	fghj
K23.7		F7	111	10111	111010	1000	000101	0111
K27.7		FB	111	11011	110110	1000	001001	0111
K28.0	A	1C	000	11100	001111	0100	110000	1011
K28.1	A, B	3C	001	11100	001111	1001	110000	0110
K28.2	A	5C	010	11100	001111	0101	110000	1010
K28.3	A	7C	011	11100	001111	0011	110000	1100
K28.4	A	9C	100	11100	001111	0010	110000	1101
K28.5	B	BC	101	11100	001111	1010	110000	0101
K28.6	A	DC	110	11100	001111	0110	110000	1001

Table 10-9: Valid Special Code Groups (Continued)

Code Group Name	Notes	Octet Value (Hex)	Octet Bits HGF	Octet Bits EDCBA	Current RD - abcdei	Current RD - fghj	Current RD + abcdei	Current RD + fghj
K28.7	A, B	FC	111	11100	011111	1000	110000	0111
K29.7		FD	111	11101	101110	1000	010001	0111
K30.7		FE	111	11110	011110	1000	100001	0111

Notes: A. Reserved Code Group

B. Code Group contains a *comma*.

Table 10-10: Ordered Sets

Code	Ordered Set	No. of Code Groups	Encoding	Notes
/C/	Configuration		Alternating /C1/ and /C2/	
/C1/	Configuration 1	4	/K28.5/D21.5/Config_Reg	A
/C2/	Configuration 2	4	/K28.5/D2.2/Config_Reg	A
/I/	Idle			
/I1/	Idle 1	2	/K28.5/D5.6/	
/I2/	Idle 2	2	K28.5/D16.2/	
Encapsulation				
/R/	Carrier_Extend	1	/K23.7/	
/S/	Start_of_Packet	1	/K27.7/	
/T/	End_of_Packet	1	/K29.7/	
/V/	Error_Propagation	1	/K30.7/	

Notes: A. Two data code groups that represent the *Config_Reg* value.

Configuration (/C/) is the continuous repetition of the /C1/ and /C2/ ordered sets and is used to convey the 16 bit Configuration Register. Idle (/I/) is transmitted whenever the GMII is in an idle state (TX_EN and TX_ER both de-asserted). Since there is always a signal, synchronization is therefore maintained at all times. /I/ comprises one or more consecutive /I1/ or /I2/.

The Carrier_Extend (/R/) is used to extend the MAC frame as described in section 10.1. In this event, TX_EN is de-asserted and TX_ER is asserted. The extension then begins after a 2 octet delay and continues for the relevant number of GTX_CLK periods. The Start_of_Packet delimiter (SPD) (/S/) is used to indicate the commencement of data transmission and is triggered by the assertion of TX_EN. /S/ will follow an idle (/I/) if this is a single frame or if this is the first frame in a frame burst. Should this be a second or subsequent frame within a burst, then the /S/ will follow a Carrier_Extend (/R/). The End_of_Packet delimiter (EPD) (/T/) denotes the end of a frame and is signaled by the de-assertion of the TX_EN signal. Finally, the Error_Propagation (/V/) code group is used where the PCS wishes to indicate a transmission error as indicated by the assertion of the TX_ER signal. For example, a repeater may wish to propagate received errors or collisions. In this case, the code group /V/ will be transmitted.

10.3.2 GMII to PMA Mapping

Just as with 100Base-X transmissions, the 1000Base-X PCS/PMA must convert the octets presented by the GMII to code groups and pass them to the PMD. Equally, on reception, the PCS/PMA will translate the code groups received from the PMD to octets and pass these to the GMII. Figure 10-11 shows a simplified diagram that demonstrates this functionality.

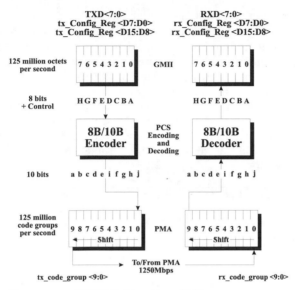

Figure 10-11: PCS/PMA Mapping to GMII

10.4 PMD and MDI for 1000Base-LX and 1000Base-SX

The purpose of the Physical Medium Dependent (PMD) sub-layer is to transmit and receive data over the Medium Dependent Interface (MDI). Four distinct specifications exist today, namely the *Short Wavelength* fiber (1000Base-SX), the *Long Wavelength* fiber (1000Base-LX), the *Short Haul Copper* (1000Base-CX), and the *Twisted Pair* (1000Base-T). Each has a specific place within the design of Gigabit Ethernet networks, although it is true to say that with the distance limitations imposed on the copper implementation of 1000Base-CX, this is rarely used.

10.4.1 General Fiber Requirements for 1000Base-SX and 1000Base-LX

Typically, network designs that incorporate 1000Base-SX and 1000Base-LX are able to cope with the generally reduced distance limitations that this higher bandwidth imposes. That said, many vendors today are able to greatly exceed these distances, a practice which (according to the standard) is perfectly acceptable provided that all other optical specifications are met. For example, today vendors are announcing their ability to run Gigabit Ethernet over distances of 100km or more. This is obviously dependent upon the quality of the fiber, the transmitter and receiver, and the overall quality of installation. Provided that the link power budget is not exceeded however, there should be no other technical limitations and problems in achieving this goal. Now, short haul WANs and campus *MANs* can certainly move into the fast lane and bring the higher bandwidth and features of this technology to a far wider user base. In any event, as a backbone technology, Gigabit will radically transform the ways in which we view our data paths.

In both cases (1000Base-SX and 1000Base-LX), the standard method of connection is via a duplex SC connector. Standard fiber types include 10/125µm Single Mode Fiber, 50/125µm Multimode Fiber, and 62.5/125µm Multimode Fiber although the 10/125µm SMF variant is supported only for 1000Base-LX operation. Connection insertion loss is then allowable at 1.5dB (worst case) for Multimode fiber and 2.0dB (worst case) for Single Mode fiber. A characteristic known as *Channel Attenuation* is extremely important here, and defines the total allowable attenuation between the two MDIs of communicating devices. Thus, the insertion loss mentioned above relates to the sum of all loses and therefore will include all splices and connectors in the entire cable run. Table 10-11 summarizes the general fiber optic characteristics.

Table 10-11: General Fiber Optic Characteristics

Description	62.5µm			50µm			10µm [1]
Wavelength	850	850	1300	850	850	1300	1310
Modal Bandwidth MHz*km	160	200	500	400	500	400/500	-[4]
Max. Attenuation (dB/km)	3.75	3.75	1.5	3.5	3.5	1.5	0.5
Channel Attenuation (dB)	2.33	2.53	2.32	3.25	3.43	2.32	4.5
Link Length (m)	220	275	550	550	550	550	5000
Link Power Budget (dB)	7.5	7.5	7.5	7.5	7.5	7.5	8.0
Channel Insertion Loss (dB)[2]	2.38	2.6	2.35	3.37	3.56	2.35	4.57
Link Power Penalties (dB)	4.27	4.29	3.48	4.07	3.57	5.08/3.96	3.27
Unallocated Margin (dB)[3]	0.84	0.60	1.67	0.05	0.37	0.07/1.19	0.16

Notes:

1. Relates to SMF - All other fiber types are MMF.

2. Nominal Wavelength of 830nm (SX) and 1270nm (LX).

3. Unallocated Margin for 50µm MMF fiber with 1300nm wavelength and Modal Bandwidth of 400 relates to the first figure. Modal Bandwidth of 500 relates to the second figure.

4. Modal Bandwidth is not specified for Single Mode Fiber. Instead, SMF is quoted in terms of what is known as Chromatic Dispersion, a much more complex figure measured in ps/km/nm.

For example, if we were to use 62.5/125µm Multimode Fiber with a Modal Bandwidth of 160 and light source of 850nm wavelength, then our Channel Attenuation is based upon the following:

(Max. Attenuation (dB/km) × Link Length (km)) + Connection Insertion Losses

or for this specific example: **(3.75 × 0.22) + 1.5 = 2.325 dB**

10.4.2 · MDI Requirements for 1000Base-SX and 1000Base-LX

Both 1000Base-SX and 1000Base-LX use the *Duplex SC* connector. By convention, the receive side of the socket is always on the left as viewed from the outside of the transceiver optical ports, and the key is on the bottom of the connector.

10.4.3 1000Base-SX

1000Base-SX transceivers are able to support both 50/125µm and 62.5/125µm multimode fiber. Distance is generally considered to be less than that available with slower technologies but, as tables 10-11 and 10-12 show, these minimum distances are still acceptable for most applications. One point to note is that SMF is not supported for SX applications. Hence, only shorter distances are specified.

Table 10-12: Minimum Operating Range for 1000Base-SX

Fiber Type	Modal Bandwidth (MHz*km)	Minimum Distance (meters)
62.5/125µm MMF	160	2 to 220
62.5/125µm MMF	200	2 to 275
50/125µm MMF	400	2 to 500
50/125µm MMF	500	2 to 550

10.4.4 1000Base-LX

As with 1000Base-SX, 1000Bae-LX transceivers are able to support both 50/125µm and 62.5/125µm multimode fiber. Additionally, however, this transceiver type is also capable of supporting 10µm single mode fiber. Thus, the maximum distance supported is far greater than that of the SX variant. Table 10-13 outlines the minimum distances supported per fiber type.

Table 10-13: Minimum Operating Range for 1000Base-LX

Fiber Type	Modal Bandwidth (MHz*km)	Minimum Distance (meters)
62.5/125µm MMF	500	2 to 550
50/125µm MMF	400	2 to 550
50/125µm MMF	500	2 to 550
10/125µm SMF	N/A - See Note	2 to 5000

Note: Modal Bandwidth is not specified for Single Mode Fiber. Instead, SMF is quoted in terms of what is known as *Chromatic Dispersion*, a much more complex figure measured in ps/km/nm.

10.5 PMD and MDI for 1000Base-CX and 1000Base-T

The most common implementations of Gigabit Ethernet today are based upon fiber optic cabling systems, and we must remember that Gigabit is generally used in the backbone. Thus, with the cost of fiber falling, and the inherent advantages that it offers, it is easy to see why there is little real interest in moving away from this scheme at this time. As our bandwidth needs increase however, there will come a time when users will demand this technology over existing copper cable plant. For this we must be ready, and indeed the IEEE is working frantically to accommodate this.

Two such standards exist today namely 1000Base-CX and 1000Base-T. IEEE 802.3z introduced the CX standard that was deemed the simpler to complete. The 1000Base-T standard was then introduced by IEEE 802.3ab.

10.5.1 1000Base-CX

The 1000Base-CX specification defines a baseband medium for what has become known as *short haul copper*. As one might expect, use of such a medium at these speeds is limited, and this limitation is related to two specific areas. Firstly, the maximum allowable distance is restricted to just 25m. Secondly, the use of copper links is restricted to those applications where a homogeneous electrical ground is available. For example, this could include connection between devices within a single rack, or between devices in two racks that share a common ground. As a result, the amount of interest shown by vendors to provide support for this specification is limited, since a fiber jumper is just as easy to implement. Indeed, most vendors have opted to support only SX and LX when interconnecting devices.

The specification itself defines that the standard *Fiber Channel* based 8B/10B coding is used with a serial line rate of 1.25GHz. The cable plant used is the 150Ω shielded balanced cable as specified in TIA 568A. Cables must then be continuous and may not contain joints or splices. Finally, each cable must be terminated by a connector where correct polarity is assured at all times.

The MDI used is specified as being either the shielded 9 pin "D" sub-miniature connector, or the 8 pin shielded ANSI Fiber Channel style-2 connector. The pin-outs of these connector types are detailed in table 10-14.

Table 10-14: Contact Assignments for 1000Base-CX MDI

Contact		
Style-1	Style-2	Description
1	1	Transmit +
2	7	Reserved (may assign the pin to power and ground) - See note
3	4	Reserved (may assign the pin to Fault Detection) - See note
4		Mechanical Key
5	8	Receive +
6	3	Transmit -
7	5	Reserved (may assign the pin as output disable) - See note
8	2	Reserved (may assign the pin to power and ground) - See note
9	6	Receive -

Note: Although many pins are reserved and may be used for other *specific* purposes, the 802.3z standard does not insist on their use.

10.5.2 1000Base-T

As we have already said, the 1000Base-T specification is part of IEEE 802.3ab. That said, existing technologies and ideas were applied wherever possible, thereby minimizing the overall effort required. For example, if we consider 100Base-X technologies we see the following:

- 100Base-TX runs over two pairs of Category 5 cable using a 125MHz symbol rate and binary encoding.

- 100Base-T4 utilizes 4 pairs of Category 3 (or better) cable with a 25MHz symbol rate and ternary encoding.

- 100Base-T2 runs over 2 pairs of Category 3 (or better) cable with a 25MHz symbol rate, quinary encoding, and DSP processing is used to handle the potential problems associated with crosstalk.

So, by using a hybrid of these existing technologies, it is possible to create a Gigabit specification that will run over four pairs of Category 5 cable and enable the use of 100m segments. This not only brings the features, bandwidth, and potential of Gigabit to the desktop, but most importantly it also serves to protect investments in existing cable plant.

1000Base-T employs 4 pairs of Category 5 cable to ensure that the symbol rate is at 125MHz or below, and use Enhanced TX/T2[8] line coding that uses 5 level Pulse Amplitude Modulation (PAM-5). By using this coding scheme, it means that we can increase the amount of data sent with each transition since TX/T2 uses 5 levels and encodes two data bits at a time. Most importantly though, the signaling frequency per pair is also reduced to below 100MHz. Figure 10-12 shows this scheme and compares it to the more normal 2 level coding. The fifth level (which is not shown) is used for redundant symbol states that are used for the encoding of error correction information.

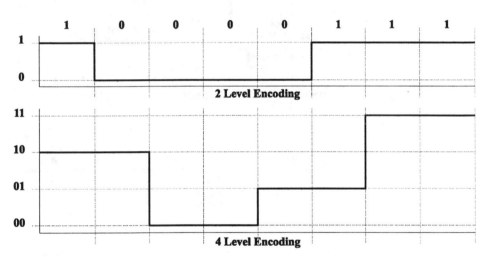

Figure 10-12: 2 and 4 Level Coding

[8] This scheme is called TX/T2 since it uses the symbol rate of 100Base-TX and the line coding used in 100Base-T2.

Now we can transmit our data at a proven rate of 125 million symbols per second since we will use 4 simultaneous transmission paths each encoding 2 bits at a time. This however is not the end of the story. Installations with existing Category 5 cable plant will no doubt need to be re-certified[9] in order to ensure that the installation is of a high enough standard to support Gigabit technologies. Indeed, it could even be argued that support of 100Mbps technologies requires re-certification if the installation is to run and remain error free. Certainly, those installing cable today would be well advised to use only cable and components of the highest standard to ensure that any future requirement is met or exceeded. Also, installation quality is key since we are now entering an era that will see UTP cable plant pushed to its absolute limits.

10.6 Repeaters for 1000Mbps Baseband Networks

In many respects the requirements for Gigabit Ethernet repeaters are superfluous, since few vendors supply them and even fewer installations actually implement them. Instead, most gigabit implementations today use switched Gigabit Ethernet, thereby making the repeater an obsolete item for this technology.

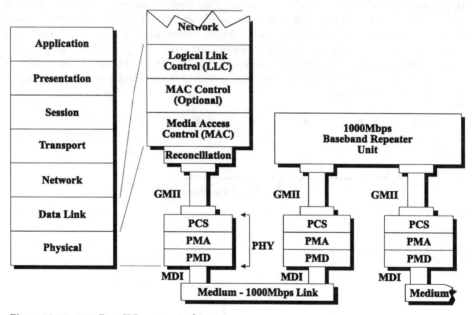

Figure 10-13: 1000Base-X Repeater Architecture

Although the previous statement is true, in order to fully appreciate the technology and all that it offers we should not ignore this device. For the sake of completeness, we will therefore briefly look at the system requirements for such

---

[9] Installations that have been tested to (and passed) a TSB-67 Level II scanner test should not require re-certification.

devices and also the design limitations associated with them. Figure 10-13 shows the basic architecture employed.

10.6.1 1000Base-X Repeater Functionality

As with all repeaters, the prime concern is to provide a capability to link two or more LAN segments. 1000Base-X repeaters, like their 10Mbps and 100Mbps counterparts, are Physical layer devices and are therefore concerned solely with the timing and amplitude of the signals presented. In practice, these units will faithfully regenerate any data presented at one port on all other ports simultaneously.

In common with the other *older* technologies, the repeaters for 1000Base-X are responsible for the *partitioning* of ports. With 10Base-X systems this was on reception of 30 or more collisions, while for 1000Base-X systems this figure is raised to 60 in line with 100Mbps technologies. In addition, as with 100Mbps units, it is the repeater that is responsible for *Jabber* protection. Jabber in the 1000Mbps system is invoked when a carrier has been present for between 80,000 to 150,000 bit times. When this condition is detected, the repeater will then suspend the repetition of data from that port until such time as either the port is reset or signal is no longer detected.

10.6.2 1000Base-X Repeater Configuration Limitations

Unlike the previous repeater units that we have seen in 10Mbps and 100Mbps systems, 1000Base-X repeaters are limited such that only one repeater is allowed within a single collision domain. These domains can of course be linked by Bridges, Switches, or Routers, and indeed a single collision domain can incorporate multiple 1000Mbps segments as figure 10-14 shows. In this way, complex networks can be designed that provide the levels of bandwidth and service individual users require, and once more investment in existing equipment is protected as much as possible.

As before, the maximum physical size (diameter) of a 1000Mbps CSMA/CD network will be limited by several factors. If we ignore the delays associated with the actual repeaters, MAUs, PHYs, and DTEs, then the diameter will be restricted by Media Lengths (which is also related to the velocity of propagation of the media) and the Inter-Frame Gap (IFG) shrinkage (as introduced by the Repeaters themselves). Table 10-15 provides information related to the delays in bit times (BT) of allowable 1000Base-X media types.

Table 10-15: Media Delays for 1000Base-X systems

Media Type	Max No of PHYs	Max Segment Length (m)	Max Round Trip Delay (BT)
Cat 5 UTP (1000Base-T)	2	100	1112
Shielded Jumper (1000Base-CX)	2	25	253
Fiber Optic (1000Base-SX/LX)	2	316 - See Note	3192

Notes: This distance may be limited by the transmission distance of the link.

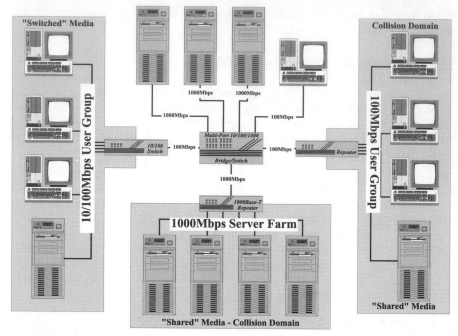

Figure 10-14: 1000Mbps Repeater Usage

Repeater usage and associated limitations are then governed by two models which are again referred to as Transmission System Models I and II. Once again, Model I provides a simple set of configuration limitations that have been validated, and therefore satisfy all of the conditions for correct operation. Model II then provides a set of calculation aids that assist in the determination of valid network configurations.

10.6.3 Transmission System Model I

Transmission System Model I defines a single repeater topology where the maximum diameter must not exceed the lesser of either 316m or the maximum allowable transmission distance for the media in use. Figure 10-15 shows allowable configurations, and table 10-16 provides the maximum diameters for different media combinations.

Table 10-16: Transmission System Model I Maximum Allowable Diameters

Configuration	Cat 5 UTP (T)	Shielded Jumper (CX)	Fiber Optic (SX/LX)	Mixed UTP/Fiber (T/SX/LX)	Mixed STP/Fiber (CX/ SX/LX)
DTE to DTE	100	25	316[1]	-	-
One Repeater	200	50	220	210[2]	220[3]

Notes:
1. May be limited by the maximum transmission distance of the media.
2. Assuming 100m of Category 5 UTP and one fiber optic link of 110m.
3. Assuming 25m of Shielded Jumper cable and a fiber optic link of 195m.

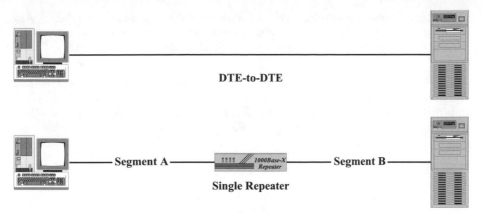

Figure 10-15: Transmission System Model I

10.6.4 Transmission System Model II

Model II defines a single repeater network whose diameter is limited by the *round-trip collision delay*. In order to test configurations for validity, the maximum round-trip delay must be calculated for all pairs of DTEs in a network. In real terms, this means that those pairs of DTEs which constitute the worst case round-trip delay must be evaluated, and the resulting delay must be less than the prescribed maximum. Calculation is then performed as follows:

A path or set of paths are identified and each are checked against the formula below. If the *Path Delay Value* (PDV) is less than 4096 then the path is qualified.

PDV = Σlink delays (LSDV) + repeater delay + DTE delays + safety margin

The *Link Segment Delay Value* (LSDV) is calculated as being:

LSDV = 2 × segment length (in meters) × cable delay for the segment

The segment length is the sum of the cable lengths between the PHY of the repeater and the PHY of the DTE. Should this length be unknown, then the maximum round-trip delays (in bit times) as specified in table 10-17 must be used in their place. The cable delay is normally specified by the manufacturer of the cable (in bit times per meter). Where this data is not available, then the value(s) can also be taken from table 10-17. Should the manufacturer specify these figures relative to the speed of light, then table 10-18 can be used to convert the figures back to bit times per meter.

Table 10-17: Network Component Delays

Component	Round-Trip Delay (BT/m)	Max. Round-Trip Delay (BT)
Two DTEs	-	864
Category 5 UTP cable	11.12	1112 (100m)
Shielded Jumper cable (1000Base-CX)	10.10	253 (25m)
Fiber Optic cable (1000Base-SX/LX)	10.10	1111 (110m)
Repeater	-	976

The total figure is multiplied by 2 since we need the total *round-trip* delay. Also, we must sum *all* segments in the path. Hence, referring to figure 10-15, we would include both Segment A and Segment B which of course could be of different media types.

Repeater delays are normally specified by the vendor. Where this detail is not available, the *worst case* value from table 10-17 can be used. Finally, an appropriate margin of safety must be decided upon. This value can typically be between 0 and 40 bit times, although the standard recommends that this value should be 32 bit times.

Table 10-18: Cable Delay Conversion Table

Speed Relative to c	ns/m	BT/m	Speed Relative to c	ns/m	BT/m
0.4	8.34	8.34	0.62	5.38	5.38
0.5	6.67	6.67	0.63	5.29	5.29
0.51	6.54	6.54	0.64	5.21	5.21
0.52	6.41	6.41	0.65	5.13	5.13
0.53	6.29	6.29	0.654	5.10	5.10
0.54	6.18	6.18	0.66	5.05	5.05
0.55	6.06	6.06	0.666	5.01	5.01
0.56	5.96	5.96	0.67	4.98	4.98
0.57	5.85	5.85	0.68	4.91	4.91
0.58	5.75	5.75	0.69	4.83	4.83
0.5852	5.70	5.70	0.7	4.77	4.77
0.59	5.65	5.65	0.8	4.17	4.17
0.6	5.56	5.56	0.9	3.71	3.71
0.61	5.47	5.47			

Provided that the PDV calculated is less than 4096, the system is then qualified in terms of worst case delay, and the network design is sound.

10.7 Summary

We have now discussed what is currently the most exciting development in Ethernet networking. Gigabit technology followed close on the heels of the 100Mbps systems (100Base-Tx and 100Base-Fx), and indeed is now fast becoming the standard to which all other technologies look. Token Ring is seriously looking at the prospect of introducing a Gigabit solution, FDDI implementers are justifiable concerned, and ATM surely looks to be replaced in many applications.

In building on the established foundation of 10Mbps and 100Mbps technologies, Gigabit Ethernet retains many of the drawbacks that are inherent in this non-deterministic system. Certainly the network diameter is no longer a problem and Gigabit supports both full and half duplex operation. So, is being deterministic really a concern? Certainly network managers have for decades been guilty of *throwing bandwidth* at bottlenecks, but normally only in the small slices that the technology has allowed. Now we have the ability to provide 10 or even 100 fold increases in performance, and therefore plug the bandwidth gap once and for all.

Gigabit Ethernet, like its predecessors, has opened networking to the masses. In common with its ancestors, it is accessible, easy to implement, and moreover less expensive than its competition. Vendors are frantically working to incorporate Quality of Service (QoS) to this important technology, and with that comes the prospect of inexpensive voice, video, and true multimedia applications. What once seemed like a far off dream is now a reality. High speed backbones really are here to stay, and things will surely only get faster still from here on in.

Auto-Negotiation C H A P T E R 11

With today's ever changing networks in terms of speed and functionality, and the fact that every desk has some measure of computing capability, it is now becoming a requirement that devices should be able to operate in a *"plug and play"* manner. Certainly, the accounts department has little need to know or understand the complexities of the network to which they connect. Their interest lies only in the speed and functionality that they have purchased and that they expect to be delivered. Hence, it is now becoming a prerequisite that devices should require little or no user interaction in terms of configuration.

For this reason, many vendors now incorporate the ability to auto-negotiate features such as whether the device will operate at 10Mbps or 100Mbps and whether *Full Duplex* operation is supported. Although not mandatory, auto-negotiation provides a standardized method through which DTEs can exchange configuration information with hubs or switches to which they are attached. Figure 11-1 shows an example of this where we have several stations, each with different capabilities but sharing the same switch. This chapter details the process of auto-negotiation, and chapter 12 then expands upon this to discuss other associated features such as *Full Duplex* operation and *Flow Control*.

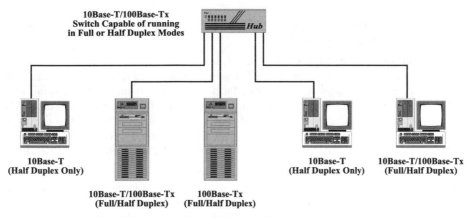

Figure 11-1: Example of Where Auto-Negotiation Is Used

Two points however must be made. Firstly, auto-negotiation is defined only for point-to-point copper implementations (i.e., XBase-T). Secondly, auto-negotiation is not infallible. Certainly, vendors strive to ensure interoperability, but with the best will in the world, this does not always work. Most vendors include management software that enables the feature or technology to be set manually, and in this way *lock* the device to operate in one single mode. This certainly does have advantages where, in the event of a power failure for example, the link will re-establish once power is restored. If there is any doubt over the functionality of auto-negotiation, manual setting of the link should be used.

11.1 Auto-Negotiation Principles

Simply put, Auto-Negotiation is a process that allows devices of different technology types, and indeed different vendors, to interoperate and provide the best possible connection in terms of data throughput. Defined in clause 28 of the IEEE 802.3u (100Mbps) standard, and then updated for new technologies as they have become available, Auto-Negotiation supports the following technologies:

- 10Base-T Half Duplex and Full Duplex
  Half Duplex operation for 10Base-T is the oldest specification supporting auto-negotiation, and allows transmission in only a single direction at any time. Thus, while receiving, the attached station may not transmit for fear of causing a collision. In Full Duplex operation, stations connected to *switch*[1] ports are able to both transmit and receive simultaneously thereby increasing the effective bandwidth of the link. Operation in Full Duplex mode is discussed in Chapter 12.

- 100Base-Tx Half Duplex and Full Duplex
  As with the 10Mbps variant, Half Duplex 100Base-Tx operation allows only transmission *or* reception at any one time. As before, simultaneous transmission and reception is possible when in a Full Duplex environment.

- 100Base-T4
  This seldom used variant of 100Mbps Ethernet always uses auto-negotiation, and is discussed in chapter 13.

- 100Base-T2 Half Duplex and Full Duplex
  As with 100Base-T4, 100Base-T2 is seldom used today, but operation in both Half and Full Duplex modes can be negotiated. In fact auto-negotiation is *required* for 100Base-T2 operation since this technology introduces the concept of *Master* and *Slave* to define DTEs, and to facilitate the timing of transmit and receive functions. Auto-negotiation is therefore considered mandatory, and this technology is discussed in further detail in chapter 13.

Notice that *Gigabit Ethernet* is currently absent from this list, and for good reason. As we said at the start, auto-negotiation is defined for point-to-point copper implementations only and at this time further work continues with regard to 1000Base-T auto-negotiation. In truth, having invested in a device that is capable of 1000Mbps operation, it is unlikely that a user would use the device in an environment that did not support this speed operation of course.

---

[1] Switches and their uses are discussed in chapter 15.

Auto-Negotiation

All other 1000Base-X implementations then either rely on fiber (1000Base-SX and 1000Base-LX) or point-to-point short haul copper (1000Base-CX). The CX variant is considered a *special case*, and therefore assumes that there will only ever be Gigabit-enabled devices at each end of the link. There is therefore no requirement to implement auto-negotiation for this variant at this time.

11.1.1 Device Operation

Auto-Negotiation is a function of the PHY, as shown in figure 11-2. Information is transferred between negotiating devices, and is observable only over the MDI or the medium itself. No information passes across the MII/GMII, and the process is therefore considered to be totally contained within the PHY.

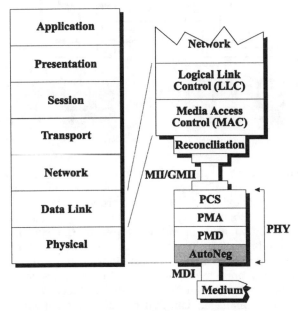

Figure 11-2: Auto-Negotiation and the OSI Model

The ability to auto-negotiate is found on most UTP-connected NICs today. Obviously 10Mbps-only cards do not have this facility. Equally, since coaxial media (i.e., 10Base-5 and 10Base-2) do not support data rates above 10Mbps, and only support half duplex operation anyway, the auto-negotiation facility will not be found on these devices.

Looking to hubs and switches, the situation is somewhat similar. Hubs, being simple repeaters and therefore capable of operating at only a single speed, rarely (if ever) incorporate the auto-negotiation facility. For example consider the situation where we have a hub with a number of devices attached at 100Mbps. Attaching a further device that is capable of operation at only 10Mbps would now mean that all existing devices would have to switch to 10Mbps in order for the devices to inter-communicate - a situation that is less than desirable. In addition, hubs are incapable of operation in Full Duplex mode, so negotiation of this facility could not arise. Switches capable of operating at multiple speeds nearly always incorporate auto-negotiation facilities. Thus, each port will negotiate with its attached device, and then select the highest common speed and the best facilities available.

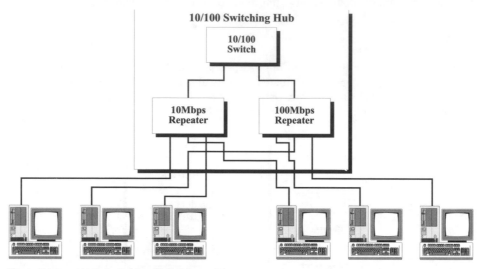

Figure 11-3: 10/100 Switching Hub Schematic

One other type of device, often referred to as a *Switching Hub* needs mention before we examine the actual operation of auto-negotiation. The switching hub itself is something of a hybrid, in that it incorporates both Hub and Switching functionality as shown schematically in figure 11-3. This device then has a number of repeaters (normally 2) each operating at one of the speeds that the device supports and a simple switch that then links the repeaters together. Operating software on the device now negotiates with stations as they are connected, and then dynamically assigns the ports to one or other of the repeaters based upon the speed selected. In this way costs are significantly reduced (compared with pure switching) yet network managers can still migrate their networks to higher speed technologies as required.

11.2 Basic Auto-Negotiation Operation

In operation, auto-negotiation relies on the *Link Pulse* which is used in point-to-point technologies such as 10Base-T and 100Base-Tx to inform the far end of the link that the device is operative. These *Normal Link Pulses* (NLPs) as they are known within auto-negotiation, are then used in a combination (known simply as a *Fast Link Pulse* (FLP) *burst*) that can identify the capabilities of the link.

The Fast Link Pulse is a sequence of 33 Normal Link Pulses that together form a *word*. Of the 33 NLPs, the 17 *Odd* numbered positions are clock pulses, and the 16 *Even* numbered positions correspond to the data of the *word*. All clock positions must contain a link pulse. Data positions however will contain link pulses where that position should represent a binary 1, and will contain nothing to represent a binary 0. Figure 11-4 shows how this is achieved by taking the most important of these words, the *Link Code Word* or *Base Page*, as an example.

The 5 bit *Selector* field allows the negotiating devices to identify the *mode(s)* in which they are capable of running. To date, only two modes are defined, these being IEEE 802.3 and IEEE 802.9, and having the bit patterns **10000** and **01000,** respectively. The other 30 possible combinations are currently reserved by the IEEE for future use.

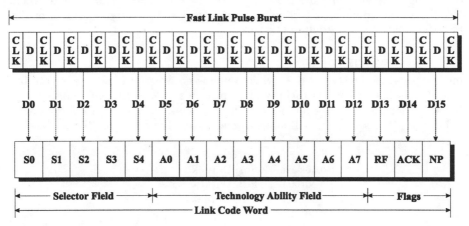

Figure 11-4: Link Code Word

The *Technology Ability* field, which is 8 bits in length, allows the devices to specify which technologies it is able to use. Table 11-1 shows these possible values, which are then interpreted simply as where the bit is set, that capability is present. For example, if the Technology Ability field were to have a value of **11110000** then the device would be capable of negotiating *any* technology except 100Base-T4, and does not implement the Pause function in Full Duplex operation.

Table 11-1: The Technology Ability Field

			Bits					
A0	A1	A2	A3	A4	A5	A6	A7	Technology
1								10Base-T
	1							10Base-T Full Duplex
		1						100Base-Tx
			1					100Base-Tx Full Duplex
				1				100Base-T4
					1			PAUSE Operation (Full Duplex Links)
						1		Reserved - Not used
							1	Reserved - Not used

You will note from the table that 100Base-T2 operation is missing. This is because 100Base-T2 configuration is through the exchange of further information based upon the *Next Page* function (see below). Equally, at this time no vendors are building 10/100/1000Base-X devices that could auto-negotiate in this way. Hence, the assumption today is that 1000Base-X devices are only ever connected to devices with similar functionality.

The *RF* or *Remote Fault* flag is used to indicate that a fault at the remote end of the link has occurred. The *Ack* (or Acknowledge) flag is used to confirm the receipt of at least 3 complete, and most importantly, consecutive and identical FLP bursts from a station. Negotiation is therefore complete when this flag is set. Finally, the *NP* or *Next Page* flag is used to indicate that the device has more information, and would therefore like to participate in a further exchange. This will delay the selection of the appropriate technology, but does allow for extended functionality. We will discuss this feature in section 11.3.

11.2.1 Technology Priorities

Under normal circumstances (i.e., where there is no *Next Page* data), once the Link Code Words have been successfully exchanged we have sufficient information to choose the technology that provides the highest common denominator for both ends of the link. In essence, we will simply choose from the following list in the order that it appears here.

1. 100Base-T2 Full Duplex
2. 100Base-Tx Full Duplex
3. 100Base-T2 Half Duplex
4. 100Base-T4
5. 100Base-Tx Half Duplex
6. 10Base-T Full Duplex
7. 10Base-T Half Duplex

The rationale is simple. 10Base-T is the lowest common denominator and therefore is of the lowest priority. Full Duplex operation is preferable to Half Duplex and therefore Full Duplex operation comes ahead of the Half Duplex counterparts. Finally, and although this may seem at variance with the Ethernet market generally, 100Base-T2 comes ahead of other 100Mbps technologies because this can run over a wider range of copper cables.

11.2.2 Timing

As we have said, the principle of Auto-Negotiation is based upon the transmission and reception of a Fast Link Pulse burst. These bursts are merely a number of Normal Link Pulses found in 10Base-T technology, and occur at the same time interval of between 8 and 24ms (typically 16.8ms). FLPs, which then contain between 17^2 and 33 pulses each have a nominal 2ms duration. Thus, it is clear that older and simpler 10Base-T devices which have no auto-negotiation facilities can easily co-exist with those newer devices which do offer a range of options/possibilities. Figure 11-5 shows the timing of the Fast Link Pulses, and then contrasts those pulses involved in Auto-Negotiation with the standard 10Base-T pulses.

---

[2] 17 pulses implies that all data positions carry binary zeroes.

11.2.3 Parallel Detection

Parallel Detection is the term used to describe how a device may use auto-negotiation to establish a link with one that supports only a single fixed speed. For example; there are many devices in operation that were manufactured before the advent of auto-negotiation, yet offer perfectly reasonable performance within the networks in which they are used. Consider the situation where we may have a switch that supports only Half Duplex 10Base-T operation, yet have stations that support 100Base-Tx (Full and Half Duplex), and 10Base-T (Full and Half Duplex) as shown in figure 11-6. In this case, our stations will send FLPs but will receive only normal link pulses in return. With Parallel Detection, the stations should then select 10Base-T as the technology to be used and establish the link accordingly.

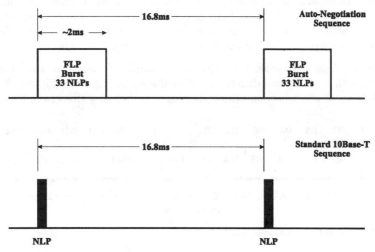

Figure 11-5: Fast Link Pulse Timing

In figure 11-6, Stations A and D will automatically establish links since they are only capable of 10Base-T (Half Duplex) operation. Station E should select 10Base-T (Half Duplex) operation, as should station B. Station C however will fail to establish a link since 100Base-Tx technology is not supported by the switch.

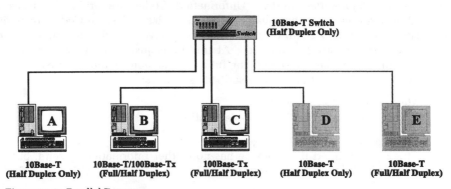

Figure 11-6: Parallel Detection

Now let us consider the case where we have a switch that is capable of providing 10/100Mbps (Full/Half Duplex) links, yet we have a station capable of operating in only 100Mbps Full Duplex mode. Our switch should now select 100Base-Tx (Full Duplex) operation on that port. In short, if a device that is capable of supporting Auto Negotiation receives 10Base-T, or 100Base-T4 Link Test pulses (NLPs), or an idle stream from a 100Base-Tx device, it should either enable the appropriate PMA if it is supported, or refuse to establish the link.

11.3 The Next Page Function

The *Next Page* bit in the Base Link Code Word indicates to the partner that additional information is available. Where this bit is set in both transmitted and received Link Code Words, then both the local device and the connection partner are able to participate in the *Next Page* exchange. If this is the case, selection of technology is delayed until after the Next Page exchange has completed.

The Next Page exchange operates in a similar fashion to that previously described, with the only real difference being the encoding used. Figure 11-7 shows the breakdown of this word, and the following text then describes each bit position.

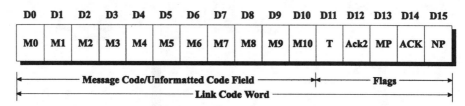

Figure 11-7: Next Page Link Code Word

As with the Basic Link Code Word, the *NP* or Next Page flag indicates that further Next Page(s) will be exchanged. The *Ack* (Acknowledgment) flag operates exactly the same as for the Basic Link Code Word by indicating acceptance of the preceding exchanges. The *MP* (Message Page) flag is used to determine whether the data in the *Message Code* field (bits D0 through D10) should be interpreted as a *Message Code*, or an *Unformatted Code*. Unformatted Codes are arbitrary pieces of information required to further qualify Message Codes. Message Codes (of which there are a theoretically 2048) on the other hand, have specific meanings and are defined within the 802.3u standard. At this time, just nine message codes are defined with two of these reserved for future expansion of the Auto-Negotiation protocol. These Message Codes are described as follows:

- **Message Code 0 - Reserved:**
  Reserved for future use by Auto-Negotiation.

- **Message Code 1 - Null Message:**
  This is transmitted if the device has no further information to send, but the partner is still transmitting information.

- **Message Code 2 - One Unformatted Message Page Follows:**
  In this case, one further unformatted page that contains a Technology Ability field will be transmitted. In this way, extensions to the base Link Code Word can be implemented.

- **Message Code 3 - Two Unformatted Message Pages Follow:**
  This is similar to the One Unformatted Message Page Follows except two pages will be used.

- **Message Code 4 - One Unformatted Page with Binary Encoded Remote Fault:**
  The following unformatted page contains Remote Fault type information; i.e., Remote Fault Test, Link Loss, Jabber, or Parallel Detection Fault.

- **Message Code 5 - Organizationally Unique Identifier (OUI) Tagged Message:**
  The Organizationally Unique Identifier followed by one Unformatted Page (proprietary information).

- **Message Code 6 - PHY ID Tagged Message:**
  PHY ID followed by one unformatted page (proprietary information).

- **Message Code 7 - 100Base-T2 Technology Message Code:**
  A 100Base-T2 Ability Page follows, using the Unformatted Next Page option.

- **Message Code 2047 - Reserved:**
  Reserved for future use by Auto-Negotiation.

The *Ack2* or Acknowledgment 2 bit is set by a receiving device to indicate that it supports the function indicated in the previous message. Finally, the *T* or Toggle bit is set by the Arbitration function within auto negotiation to ensure proper synchronization during Next Page exchanges.

Next Page exchanges are considered complete once both sides of the link have sent all Link Code Words, and have commenced sending Null messages.

11.4 The Complete Auto-Negotiation Process

The process of Auto-Negotiation itself is relatively simple, and can be described in the following steps.

- Each end of the link transmits its own FLP burst if it is capable of doing so. These bursts contain the respective Link Code Words and will not have the *Ack* flag set. Devices should be able to identify their partners as being able to participate in auto-negotiation within 6 to 17 pulses of the first FLP burst received. Once identified as auto-negotiation capable, complete exchanges can then take place. This stage is known as the *Auto-Negotiation Able Identification* state.

- Once *Able Identification* is complete, the device waits for reception of at least 3 consecutive FLP bursts that contain identical information. Once received, the end devices then enter the *Acknowledge Detect* state and commence transmission of FLP bursts that contain their Link Code Word with the *Ack* flag set.

- Once we have received 3 more complete and consistent FLPs containing the *Ack* bit in a "set" condition, the stations enter a phase known as the *Complete Acknowledge* state. In this state they then transmit between 6 and 8 more FLP bursts that contain their Link Code Word with the *Ack* bit set.

- Finally, our stations will optionally participate in a *Next Page* exchange where appropriate. This process allows the exchange of further (proprietary) information, and was discussed in section 11.3. Once this is complete the stations are able to decide upon the highest common denominator technology, and negotiate that link. Where no common technologies exist (such as where our switch supports only, say, 100Base-T4, yet our station is 10Base-T), the link will not be established.

11.5 Summary

In this chapter we have seen how the process of auto-negotiation functions. At this time, support only extends to copper point-to-point links, and even then to only 10Mbps and 100Mbps technologies. Certainly, Gigabit will be added as time goes by, but the fundamental process will remain unchanged. As an industry, we are yet to see 10/100/1000Mbps devices enter the market, but this will come in the future without doubt. At this time there is no support for fiber technologies within the auto-negotiation framework. An oversight? - No. We simply do not have the technology available that is capable of running at 10/100Mbps over this media type today. Certainly it is only time dependent, and given the speed at which this particular area of networking is changing, it cannot be far away.

So what we have is a system that is glamorous in its simplicity. Building upon the basic blocks that were provided by the architects of the earlier technologies merely proves what solid foundations the technology has. Moving forward, we see increased bandwidth capabilities and increased distances by using Full Duplex communications in a switched environment. This facet of Ethernet, however, will be discussed in the next chapter.

Full Duplex Operation

Our thirst for bandwidth increases daily. Applications handle more and more data, and with that comes the requirement to move that data from server to client and back again. In short, technology is giving us higher and higher speeds but we are filling the pipe provided almost as fast.

Certainly this should come as no shock. Knowledge of the bandwidth trap has been with us for many years, and the notion of adding higher speed technologies to bridge this gap has worked to an extent. Long ago, however, vendors sought to get more from even simple 10Mbps systems by making the communication Full Duplex, and it is this that we shall discuss here. Do not believe that this is the panacea for our bandwidth blues though. Full Duplex comes at a cost - not only financial, but potentially "network-stopping" for the unwary.

12.1 Basic Full Duplex Operation

Ethernet/IEEE 802.3 LANs in their original forms were half-duplex in operation. In general terms, the original 802.3 specifications defined a medium access protocol that could work in half duplex mode only. The reason was that it was bound by the fact that the medium (or ether) was coaxial cable, and this was shared by all stations as shown in figure 12-1. In short, just one station could transmit at any one time.

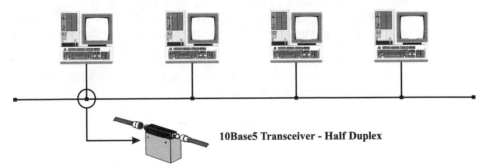

10Base5 Transceiver - Half Duplex

Figure 12-1: 10Base5 Shared Ethernet Environment

As we move forward and introduce point-to-point topologies, we can start to appreciate that there is far more potential, although this is not necessarily apparent to the casual observer. Certainly if we continue to talk of *shared* media then we gain nothing. For example, in figure 12-2 we see a familiar shared-media environment where we have multiple stations interconnected via a simple hub. As you will recall, these *hubs* perform a repeating function, and therefore we can still have only one station transmit at any time. Thus, our medium remains shared.

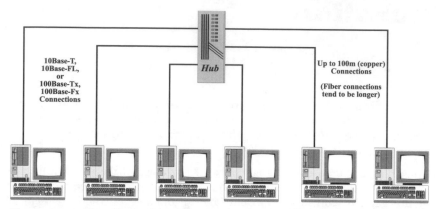

Figure 12-2: 10Mbps (or 100Mbps) Point-to-Point Connections - Shared Media

As a simple statement, we can say that a station cannot receive data from its partner while it is transmitting, since if it is transmitting then it has already acquired the channel, and a collision would result.

Replace our Hub with a Switch,[1] and the situation changes. Now our stations can simultaneously both transmit and receive, and leave the switch to relay the data to the correct port(s) (and only the correct port(s)) as required. Since our data is no longer *broadcast* to all ports, the medium between each switch port and attached device is now dedicated, and could therefore be considered its own collision domain. This, however, works only with point-to-point topologies where we have dedicated transmit and receive paths as shown in figure 12-3.

Now stations can simultaneously transfer data both to and from other devices such as servers. The switch will buffer the data transmitted from a station until it can be transmitted onto the relevant port(s), thereby allowing a greater throughput. Equally, since we have dedicated transmit and receive paths, each station can now transmit and receive simultaneously without fear of collision. Furthermore, we can say that the *Carrier Sense, Multiple Access with Collision Detection* (CSMA/CD) protocol is no longer used in this mode of operation.

12.1.1 Uses of Full Duplex Operation

At last we have a system that appears to make best use of the technologies available. Or at least it would appear that way. Does Full Duplex operation cure our problems, or does it actually raise further issues in operation though? In truth Full Duplex must be used with caution, yet one interesting by-product, that we will come to later, certainly should not be ignored.

---

[1] Switch operation is discussed in chapter 15.

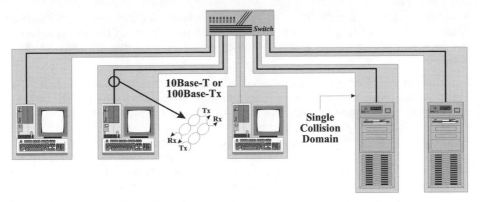

Figure 12-3: Point-to-Point Full Duplex Operation

Exercising caution when using switches has been touched on before, yet it is important enough to re-iterate here. Simultaneous transmission and reception offer the obvious possibility of increased bandwidth, and it is here where we must be careful. For example, consider figure 12-4 where we have a simple 10Mbps hub that interconnects a number of stations. Since the medium here would be shared (since we are using a hub) the overall bandwidth of the hub (and indeed the overall bandwidth of the network) would be 10Mbps.

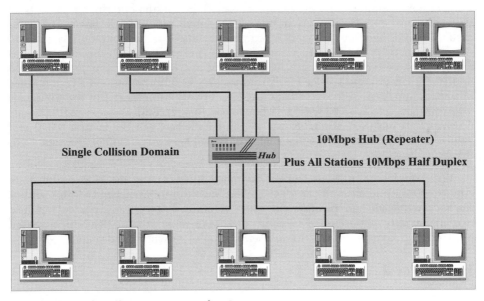

Figure 12-4: Single Collision Domain 10Mbps System

So now let us replace the hub with a simple 10 port, 10Mbps, Half Duplex only switch. Our overall bandwidth increases from 10Mbps to a potential 100Mbps, since each station would be able to transmit simultaneously. If the switch does not have the capacity to handle this load, then frames would be dropped, leading to lost data. Recovery of this data would then be the responsibility of the upper layers of the protocol, which would cause re-transmissions and an overall degradation of service.

OK, most switches could handle this load, and would even be able to handle all of the stations running Full Duplex (i.e., 200Mbps required bandwidth). But what if the switch ports were 10/100Mbps and each was running Full Duplex now? Suddenly, our 100Mbps switch that was raised to 200Mbps, now requires a bandwidth of 2Gbps - a major leap in technology. From the previous discussion it is therefore clear that, with care, we can increase overall bandwidth. Full Duplex however has one further advantage that is not necessarily so apparent, and that is the ability to run increased distances over certain media types.

You will recall that media distance limitations are based upon the *round-trip* time of the signal. In other words, if we are to detect a collision that has occurred on our own data, then we must still be transmitting when we sense the collision signal. Obviously, the maximum allowable distance is a factor of the maximum amount of data that can be transmitted, the transmission speed, and the velocity of propagation of the signal itself. If these items remain constant, then the maximum distance allowed for each medium type will also be fixed.

With copper cables there is little we can do. Signals simply cannot be guaranteed over distances greater than we have discussed so far (typically 100m), so Full Duplex operation can rarely help us here. Fiber on the other hand presents us with different parameters. With fiber our signal can reliably cover far larger distances, and therefore, in theory, maximum distances are limited to the amount of data that we wish to transmit. The more data that we transmit, the longer it will take, and therefore the medium length can be increased. Of course this would apply to shared (and therefore Half Duplex) media environments only, and since our maximum frame size is fixed anyway it is broadly irrelevant. But what happens when we do not use CSMA/CD? Remember that in Full Duplex environments CSMA/CD is not used at all. Now the link length between the station (DTE) and switch is limited only by the distance over which we can guarantee the signal. In theory, at least, fiber installations can now run with far greater link lengths.

When implementing Full Duplex Switched Ethernet the moral is really quite simple. Only purchase quality devices that have the internal bandwidth to fulfill the task required, and position the units carefully where they will deliver best overall network performance. Failure to adhere to this could lead to increased bottlenecks, lost packets, and overall degradation of network performance.

12.2 Architectural Changes

Obviously to achieve Full Duplex operation, certain changes to the architecture were required. As before, the developers were keen to ensure full backwards compatibility wherever possible, and therefore these changes are relatively minor overall. Certainly auto-negotiation[2] assists, in that devices can automatically sense

---

[2] Auto-Negotiation was discussed in chapter 11.

whether or not facilities such as Full Duplex are supported. Complete operation however also requires implementation of an optional *MAC Control* sublayer, and changes to the operation of other sublayers such as the PLS and PHY. Figure 12-5 shows how these architectural changes are implemented. The following sections will then describe the changes that have been made to the operation of what has now become an extremely versatile MAC layer.

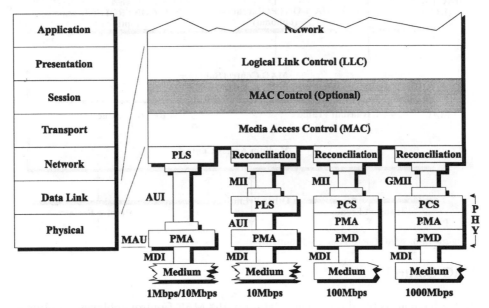

Figure 12-5: Architectural Model with MAC Control

12.2.1 Service Primitive Changes

In order to better understand the changes that the MAC Control sublayer brings, consider figure 12-6 that outlines the MAC Control service primitives and their interaction. In this figure we see that two additional primitives are added, namely MA_CONTROL.request, and MA_CONTROL.indication. In both cases, these primitives are optional, although they must be used if the optional *MAC Control* sublayer is implemented. Both primitives relate only to operation in a Full Duplex environment at this time. As we shall see though, the introduction of this *control* facility could provide for further future enhancements if required.

- **The MA_CONTROL.request**
  This primitive is used by the MAC client (the LLC layer in the case of IEEE 802.3 implementations, or the Network layer in the case of Ethernet) to indicate that MAC Control commands are being transferred. The actual data transferred is a *Destination Address* (or enough information to create the destination address of the MAC frame), an *Opcode*, and any additional parameters that are required to perform the requested operation. At this time, there is only one valid operation, *Pause*, as described in section 12.3.

- **The MA_CONTROL.indication**

  Just as the MA_CONTROL.request primitive is used by the MAC client to communicate that a specific operation should be performed, the MA_CONTROL.indication primitive allows the MAC Control sublayer to communicate status with the MAC client. The data passed is simply an *Opcode*, plus any parameters required to qualify the operation.

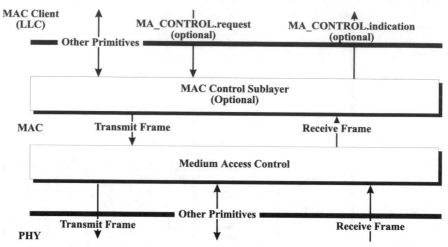

Figure 12-6: MAC Control Service Primitives

12.3 MAC Control

As we have already said, implementation of the MAC Control sublayer is optional. This does however provide for transparent, real-time control, and manipulation of the MAC. Figure 12-5 showed us the relationship between the MAC and the MAC Client (LLC or Network layer). In this section we shall examine the interaction at the MAC/MAC Control, and MAC Control/MAC Client interfaces, as well as taking a detailed look at the MAC Control operation.

12.3.1 MAC Control Frames

When looking at the MAC/MAC Control interface, the Control frames are of fixed length, equal to the minimum frame size (512 bits) minus 32 bits in length (see Figure 12-7). The MAC will then prepend the Preamble and Start Frame Delimiter fields, and after calculation, append the 32 bit FCS field. As you will see, this frame format is similar to any *normal* MAC frame, with the addition of the MAC Control Opcode and Parameters. The 6 octet *Destination Address* field is used to identify the station or stations to which the frame is directed. This can be a unicast, multicast, or broadcast address, although the address (and address type) will be defined by the operation being requested. The *Source Address* (6 octets) identifies the station transmitting the frame.

The 2 octet *Length/Type* field always contains the hexadecimal value 88-08 for this frame type. Breaking with tradition in relation to other 802.3 specifications,

Full Duplex Operation

this value is a *Type* code, akin to Ethernet usage, and has been universally assigned as *MAC Control of CSMA/CD LANs*.

The 2 octet *MAC Control Opcode* field is used to carry the operation code of the operation to be performed. Only one operation can be transferred in any one frame, and the correct (variable length) *MAC Control Parameters* for the operation must immediately follow the opcode field. At this time, just one MAC Control operation is supported, namely the *Pause* function. The operation of this operation is discussed below.

Destination Address (6)	Source Address (6)	Length/ Type (2)	MAC Control OPCode (2)	MAC Control Parameters (variable)	Reserved Always Zeroes (variable)

←——— (Minimum Frame Size (bits) - 160)/8 ———→
Octets

Figure 12-7: MAC Control Frames

The variable length *Reserved* field is used to pad the frame to the minimum frame size. This data is always transmitted as zeroes. Finally, all octets are transmitted from left to right, least significant bit first, i.e., canonical.

12.3.2 MAC Control Pause Operation

At this time only the *Pause* MAC Control operation is defined. Using an *Opcode* of $00\text{-}01_{16}$ (all other possible opcodes are reserved for future use), the *Pause* operation requests that the recipient stops transmitting *non-control* frames (i.e., data frames) for a period of time that is indicated through a two octet *pause time* parameter. This MAC Control Parameter is an unsigned integer that specifies the number of 512 bit times for which the recipient should cease transmission. The *real* time during which transmission must cease will of course be dependent upon the speed of operation. Hence, bit times are used here.

In theory, the Pause control frame could be sent to a single station, any multicast group, or indeed the broadcast address. The 802.3x standard however is very specific that frames of this type should be sent only to the multicast address **01-80-C2-00-00-01**, which has been reserved for this purpose. In this way, all devices that implement the optional MAC Control sublayer will support membership of this group, and 802.1D compliant bridges and switches will block the forwarding of these frames. In this way, flow control is maintained at a local level.

The Pause function may only be used by DTEs that have been configured to operate in Full Duplex mode. Also, the Pause function is designed purely to inhibit further transmission data frames, there being no way to inhibit the transmission of control frames.

12.4 Flow Control

As we have seen in the previous section, the MAC Control *Pause* function is designed to provide a standardized means of controlling the flow of data from a device. Typically, this would be used between switches and their attached DTEs, although as we have seen, the Pause function operates only with Full Duplex devices.

One of the major instances where we might find the need for flow control is where a switching fabric has been over-committed. Left unchecked, this would result in the switch dropping frames, and this would mean that re-transmissions were required. So, control our data flow, and we overcome the problem. Or do we? Consider what happens when we have devices that are operating in a Half Duplex mode. How can we control their data flow?

The answer here is not standardized, yet it is glamorous in its simplicity - send a collision! Put simply, switch ports that are configured to operate in half duplex mode (probably because their attached stations cannot perform full duplex operation) will normally send a collision over those ports to force the attached device to back off. In so doing, this often provides sufficient time to clear the switch's buffers, and the data can therefore be said to be flow controlled.

12.5 Summary

In this chapter we have examined the operation of Ethernet/802.3 networks in a Full Duplex environment. Full Duplex operation is important today, and indeed is becoming more so as we thirst for extra bandwidth. Do not be fooled though. Bandwidth is not the only reason for operating in a Full Duplex mode. Extended distance working with fiber cable is an equally important reason for moving to a duplex environment.

In addition, do not make the mistake of thinking that Full Duplex operation cures all of the bandwidth ills. As we have seen, operation in this mode can cause more problems than it fixes. Switches must be capable of handling the data rates, or reduced performance will result.

Network Interface Cards (NICs) that support twisted pair media will nearly all support operation at both 10Mbps and 100Mbps. Equally, these cards will almost certainly support both Full and Half Duplex operation. Take care though, and ensure that where you deploy this technology, your devices support flow control as well - both DTEs and Switches.

802.3 Variants

We have so far concentrated on the well known, tried and tested, Ethernet/802.3 technologies. Ask anyone in networking to name the different variants of Ethernet/802.3, and they will happily talk about the 10Base-X, 100Base-X, and Gigabit flavors but most will ignore the lesser known variants that are presented here. Are they really important? Possibly not, since their usage tends to be limited. Any volume that claims to cover the subject of Ethernet/802.3 however, should at least briefly describe them if only for the sake of completeness.

100VG-AnyLAN is missing from here and is discussed in the next chapter. The reasons are simple - 100VG-AnyLAN has very few similarities to Ethernet/802.3, and the subject matter is large enough to justify a chapter in its own right. This chapter then looks only at those variants standardized under 802.3.

13.1 1Base5

1Base5 is an early variant of the IEEE 802.3 specification that defines a 1Mbps system based upon the CSMA/CD access method. It has several items in common with 10Base-T, 100Base-Tx, and topologically speaking, the 802.12 (100VG-AnyLAN) standards. In more general terms, 1Base5 also uses the same MAC and PLS specifications that we saw in the 10BaseX chapters. The PMA, Hub functions, and actual medium, do however differ.

In terms of the similarities with other technologies, we should first consider figure 13-1. This figure shows that 1Base5 is built upon a Hub based architecture that we have met previously. Indeed, when we view figures 13-2 and 13-3 (shown later) this would seem to enforce this topological relationship, and as we shall see in the next chapter, this is very similar to 100VG-AnyLAN. Here however, our similarities cease.

1Base5 was originally designed to provide low cost networking in office environments, and to make use of existing telephone type (i.e., twisted pair) wiring. Indeed, one of the major attractions is that this type of technology could make use of *spare* wiring whenever available. Architecturally, there is also no minimum, typical, or maximum number of DTEs that can be connected, although this detail tends to be implementation specific. Standard telephone cabling is used, and typically consists of 600Ω, 0.4-0.6mm diameter (26-22 gauge) unshielded twisted pair cable. This is terminated in the standard ISO 8877 (RJ45) connector and even uses the standard Ethernet/802.3 pairing (pins 1/2 and 3/6) as detailed in table 13-1.

Thankfully, there are few (if any) sites that employ both 1Base5 and other Ethernet/802.3 technologies, so confusion over outlets is avoided. Certainly no vendors today supply equipment capable of operating multiple technologies that include 1Base5, and since this is extremely limited in terms of speed it is unlikely that they ever will.

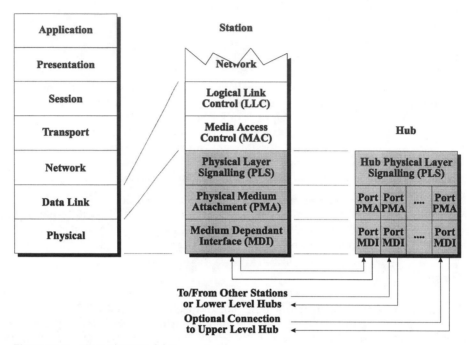

Figure 13-1: 1Base5/OSI Model Comparison

Table 13-1: RJ45 Connector Assignments

RJ45 Pin	Function
1	Data Upwards + (i.e., DTE to Hub or Lower Level to Upper Level)
2	Data Upwards - (i.e., DTE to Hub or Lower Level to Upper Level)
3	Data Downwards + (i.e., Hub to DTE or Upper Level to Lower Level)
4	Not Used
5	Not Used
6	Data Downwards - (i.e., Hub to DTE or Upper Level to Lower Level)
7	Reserved
8	Reserved

13.1.1 1Base5 Architecture

As far as layer implementation is concerned, the hubs used in 1Base5 are really just physical layer devices, and operate in a similar fashion to standard Ethernet/802.3 repeaters. Operationally, and at the simplest level, 1Base5 is as shown in figure 13-2. Here, our network comprises a minimum number of DTEs that can all be accommodated on one single Hub. In figure 13-3, we then see a more complex network that comprises multiple layers of hubs, with a larger number of stations attached.

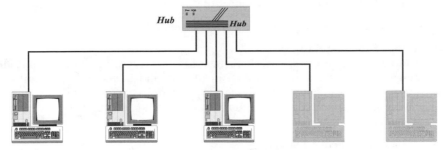

Figure 13-2: Simple 1Base5 Configuration

From figure 13-2, each station (DTE) is connected to the hub via its own cable in a Star topology. Just as with a normal repeater, our hub then regenerates and re-times incoming signals and transmits them out to all other ports. In addition, the hub detects collisions when two (or more) DTEs transmit at the same time, and then causes all stations to stop transmitting until the collision is cleared. In this way, it is the Hub that is in control rather than any or all colliding station(s).

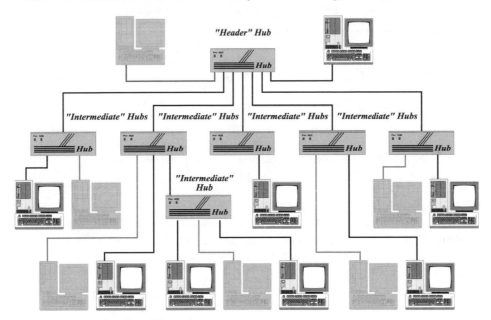

Figure 13-3: Complex 1Base5 Network

Figure 13-3 shows a slightly more complex configuration that utilizes both a *Header Hub* and *Intermediate Hubs*. With this technology, up to 5 levels of hub may be cascaded. Hubs can have 2 or more ports, and therefore can be simple repeaters (1 port upwards and 1 port downwards), or more complex devices allowing the upward and downward connection of other hubs and end stations. Typically, station to hub cable lengths are up to 250m for standard telephone cabling, although this is dependent on cable types. Indeed, some special links allow DTE-to-Hub or Hub-to-Hub distances of up to 4km.

In general, 1Base5 can be characterized by the following:

- **1Mbps Signaling Rate**
  Unlike its counterparts, 1Base5 operates at just 1Mbps. In operating at such a slow speed it is naturally limited in its use, and is certainly not suited to most of today's bandwidth hungry applications. Such slow speeds do however mean that it can function on cable plant that has a poor specification.

- **Manchester Encoded Signal**
  Just as with its 10BaseX cousins, 1Base5 uses Manchester encoding to ensure that the data is clocked correctly.

- **Twisted Pair Wiring Scheme using two pairs**
  1Base5 uses just two pairs of cable - One for the *upward* transmission of data, and the other for the *downward* path. In addition, due to the low speed that is used, and the corresponding low susceptibility to interference, Data and Voice pairs may co-exist within the same bundle. This means that 1Base5 really can make use of *any* spare telephone wiring within a building.

- **Point-to-Point connection of DTEs and Hubs**
  The *Star* topology of 1Base5 means that all connections are point-to-point. No equivalent *Bus* topology (as with coaxial cable environments) exists for this variant of 802.3, and all installations must have at least 1 hub in the network.

- **Cascading of Hubs**
  Hubs may have 2 or more ports. When equipped with just 2 ports, these devices then act simply as repeaters extending the distance of the DTE to Hub, or Hub to Hub link. When they are equipped with more ports they may also have stations attached.

13.1.2 1Base5 Operation

In order to discuss the actual operation of 1Base5 we shall use the simple example of figure 13-4. In this diagram we see just two cascaded hubs and a number of end stations. Operationally then, our hub functions as follows:

The hub is the central point for all attached devices. When hubs are cascaded as in our figure, the central point for subordinate hubs will always be the upper level. When we have no subordinate hubs and only one DTE transmits, the hub will repeat the signal (after compensating for amplitude and phase distortion or *Jitter*) to all other ports. When the hub detects two (or more) DTEs transmitting at the same time however, the hub, rather than transmitting the received frame, will transmit a *Collision Presence* (CP) signal to all ports. It will then keep transmitting this CP signal until it has received the *Idle* (IDL) signal from all devices. *Collision Presence* is easily detected by the attached DTEs, since this signal represents a violation of the standard *Manchester encoding* scheme normally used. In this way, collisions are propagated throughout the network by the Hub rather than by individual stations detecting the presence of other signals.

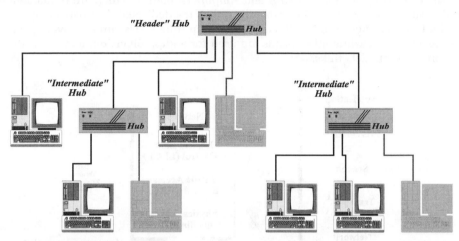

"Header" Hub

"Intermediate" Hub

"Intermediate" Hub

Figure 13-4: 1Base5 Operation

Considering figure 13-4 again, where we have a cascaded architecture, we are limited in the fact that we must never have more than one *Header Hub*. In other words, multiple top levels and loops are expressly prohibited. In a cascaded topology then, *Intermediate Hubs* propagate their signals (both *Data* and *Collision Presence*) to their attached DTEs and other (higher level) *Intermediate Hubs*. Equally, our *Header Hub* will repeat signals that it receives (again both *Data* and *Collision Presence*) down to attached DTEs and *Intermediate Hubs*. In this way, our signals travel both upwards and downwards simultaneously, eventually reaching the very extremities of the network.

One final function of the Hub is that of *Jabber* control. As you will have seen, 1Base5 uses a contention based transmission system just as our other Ethernet/802.3 specifications do. Since only one station may transmit at any time then, it is important that we have a means to cut access to a DTE that has been transmitting for too long. In 1Base5, the Jabber function will activate such that a window of between 25 to 50ms is available for the transmission of either data or the *Collision Presence* signal. If after that time the DTE (or the combined upward signal of an Intermediate Hub) is still transmitting, then the receiving Hub port will switch to sending the *Collision Presence* signal for 51 to 100ms. If the lower level still continues to transmit after this time has elapsed, the port will be disabled until such time that it becomes quiet. As you will appreciate, this is very much in common with other Ethernet/802.3 variants and it is merely timing that changes.

13.2 10Broad36

Unlike the other Ethernet/802.3 technologies that we have discussed so far, 10Broad36, as its name suggests, relates to *Broadband*, rather than *Baseband* signaling techniques. Thus, with 10Broad36, our medium is able to handle multiple transmission signals simultaneously, and uses Cable Television (CATV) technology as its medium. Terminology changes somewhat, and we now find ourselves talking about *Cable Taps* and *Amplifiers*, both of which are fundamental to this variant's operation. For example, unlike the dedicated data paths that other media types provide, 10Broad36 can support multiple LANs running over specific frequency bands, while other bands are used for audio, television, and multi-drop or point-to-point data links.

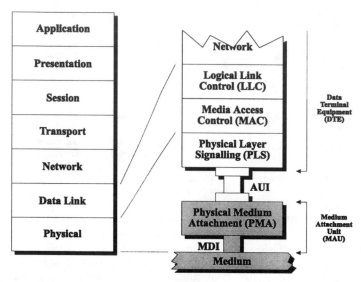

Figure 13-5: 10Broad36 and the OSI Model

In terms of the architectural relationship to the OSI model, and indeed to other forms of the technology, little changes. As figure 13-5 shows, from this perspective, changes to our model relate only to the Physical Medium Attachment (PMA), or indeed the MAU. Obviously, since our medium and transmission methods change, the Medium Dependent Interface (MDI) has to be modified accordingly. Apart from this, very few other modifications are required.

A common implementation? No. Certainly 10Braod36 has (or at least had) a place, but implementation was never widespread. 10Broad36 was one of the early specifications to come out of the 802.3 camp, and indeed even pre-dates 10Base2. Where it scored though, was in hostile environments where coaxial (10Base5) cable could not be used, or where greater distances were needed. The specification allows a network segment of 3.6km, so as you can see, if there was a niche requirement on distance - 10Broad36 could possibly fill it. In terms of *office* cabling though, it had no market at all due to the type of medium that it used.

13.2.1   10Broad36 Operation

Two forms of 10Broad36 exist, namely the *Single* and *Dual* cable systems. The operational model naturally differs between the two, but fundamentally the MAUs simply operate as modems. The MAUs translate data received from the attached station to radio frequencies in preparation for transmission over the medium, and conversely on reception, demodulate the received signal to recover the data.

Crucial to the operation of 10Broad36 is a special device known as the *Headend*. The passive MAUs simply direct their transmissions to this device that then, depending upon the cable system in use, the Headend will either convert the carrier frequency or simply join the transmit and receive legs. As figure 13-6 (A) shows, on the single cable system stations are connected to the medium by a single *Tap*. Data received from the station is then modulated and transmitted at a carrier frequency of F1. On reception by the *Headend*, this frequency is then translated to a different, higher, frequency F2, and re-transmitted. Thus the lower frequency (F1) is used for transmission, and the higher frequency (F2) for reception.

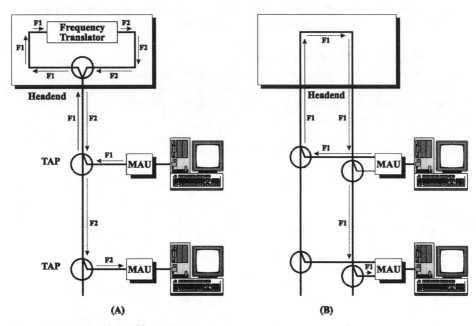

Figure 13-6: 10Broad36 Cable Systems

In a dual cable system (figure 13-6 (B)), MAUs have two connections to the medium. Here, each MAU connects to both the Transmit and the Receive side of the network, and only a single carrier frequency (F1) is used. The role of the *Headend* in this case is to connect the two legs of the medium (transmit and receive) together. Hence, the transmit path naturally becomes the receive.

During transmission, each MAU will logically compare the data transmitted with that received either at the higher frequency (in the case of the single cable system), or on the receive *leg* (in the case of the dual cable system). Any difference is then reported as a collision, although it could also be a bit error, a colliding transmission, or even an earlier transmission.

When a collision is detected in this way, the transmitting MAU will cease its transmission, and transmit a RF *Collision Enforcement* signal which is at a different frequency (adjacent to the data band). All MAUs then receive this signal and pass it back to their attached DTEs in the normal manner.

13.2.2 Transmission and Reception

Actual encoding on the medium is not Manchester Encoding as with other 10Mbps variants. Instead, 10Broad36 uses Non-Return to Zero (NRZ) encoding techniques. As a result, Manchester encoded data sent from the DTE must be decoded by the MAU and then re-encoded to NRZ format.

In actual fact the process is made slightly more complex in that for transmission, once encoded, the signal must also be modulated. Equally, when we wish to recover data from the medium, after demodulation the signal will have to be decoded and then Manchester encoded prior to transfer to the attached DTE.

13.2.3 MAU Frequency Allocations

The broadband MAU uses a data band 14MHz wide, with an adjacent *Collision Enforcement* band 4MHz wide. On a single cable system, the mid-split configuration has a frequency offset of 156.25MHz or 192.25MHz between the forward and reverse channels.

Table 13-2: Single Cable Frequency Allocations (MHz)

| | TRANSMITTER | | | RECEIVER | | |
| | | | Translation 156.25MHz | | Translation 192.25MHz | |
Data Carrier	Collision Enforce Freq.	Transmit Band	Headend Local Osc.	Receive Band	Headend Local Osc.	Receive Band
43	52	35.75-53.75	245.75	192-210	192.25	228-246
49	58	41.75-59.75	257.75	198-216	192.25	234-252
55	64	47.75-65.75	269.75	204-222	192.25	240-258
61	70	53.75-71.75	281.75	210-228	192.25	246-264
67	76	59.75-77.75	293.75	216-234	192.25	252-270
73	82	65.75-83.75	305.75	222-240	192.25	258-276

Table 13-2 lists the permissible frequency allocations for single cable systems. Although the preferred data carrier is 61MHz, and while the 156.25MHz system is listed for backwards compatibility, the 192.25MHz translation system is actually recommended.

Table 13-3: Dual Cable Frequency Allocations (MHz)

Data Carrier	Collision Enforcement Freq.	Data Band	Collision Enforcement Band
43	52	36-50	50-54
49	58	42-56	56-60
55	64	48-62	62-66
61	70	54-68	68-72

Table 13-3: Dual Cable Frequency Allocations (MHz) (Continued)

Data Carrier	Collision Enforcement Freq.	Data Band	Collision Enforcement Band
67	76	60-74	74-78
73	82	66-80	80-84
235.25	244.25	228-242	242-246
241.25	250.25	234-248	248-252
247.25	256.25	240-254	254-258
253.25	262.25	246-260	260-264
259.25	268.25	252-266	266-270
265.25	274.25	258-272	272-276

In Dual cable systems, the transmit and receive frequencies are identical. Table 13-3 lists all permissible frequency band allocations, although once again a data carrier of 61MHz is preferred.

13.2.4 Cabling (Electrical) Requirements

As we have already said, the 10Broad36 specification is based upon CATV media. As such, our cable requirements are much different from those of other Ethernet/802.3 types. The basic cable system requirements are listed in table 13-4.

Table 13-4: Cable System Electrical Requirements

Component	Value and Tolerance
Impedance	75 ohms
Return Loss	14 dB minimum
Transmit Level	+50 dBmV (+/-2 dB)
Receive Level	+6dBmV (+/-10 dB)
Maximum Receive Noise Level	-30 dBmV/14MHz
Loss Variation (per 18MHz band) - not including headend	2dB min, 52dB max.
Path Loss (between any transmit port and receive port, including loss variation)	36dB min, 52dB max.
Group Delay Variation:	
• Around data carrier	20ns/10MHz max.
• Over 18MHz band	34ns max.

Finally, connections are made between the broadband cable system and the MAU by standard "F-Series," screw-on male connectors. In the case of the dual cable system two connections are required, one each for transmit and receive.

13.3 100Base-T2

100Base-T2 provides a 100Mbps, CSMA/CD network specification that is capable of running over Category 3 (or better) twisted pair cable plant, with distances of up to 100m. The 100Base-T2 specification, as standardized by 802.3y, defines a Physical Coding Sublayer (PCS), Physical Medium Attachment (PMA), and Medium Dependent Interface (MDI). As before, and indeed as shown in figure 13-7, the PCS and PMA sublayers together form the PHY.

You will notice that support is provided for the 100Base-T MII, and Auto-Negotiation. 100Base-T2 also introduces the concept of *Master* and *Slave* operation, and it is Auto-Negotiation that is used to establish this relationship. In reality then, we should say that auto-negotiation is mandatory. In addition, 100Base-T2 is capable of running in Full Duplex mode, and supports a total collision domain diameter of up to 200m where (up to 2) repeaters are employed.

In operation, 100Base-T2 uses a *dual-duplex* baseband transmission system over two pairs (BI_DA, and BI_DB) that provide an aggregate data rate of 100Mbps. This is achieved by using a modulation rate of 25M symbols per second over each wire pair, in each direction, simultaneously, and using five-level Pulse Amplitude Modulation (PAM 5x5) over each pair.

Master/Slave operation is determined through auto-negotiation as we shall see later. The 100Base-T2 PHY can be configured in either of these modes, although in practice in a DTE-to-Repeater configuration, the Repeater will generally become the *Master* and the DTE the *Slave*. The *Master* PHY then uses an external clock to define the timing of transmitter and receiver operations, and the *Slave* then recovers the clock from the received signal and uses this to define the timing of transmitted signals. The following sections describe the operation of each sublayer individually, and where appropriate, relate to previous chapters where the functionality is similar to that of other technologies.

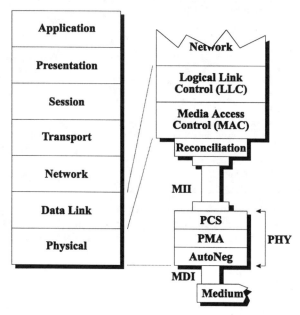

Figure 13-7: 100Base-T2 and the OSI Model

13.3.1 100Base-T2 PCS, PMA, and MDI

The 100Base-T2 PCS will, in common with the Physical Coding Sublayer of the 100Base-X system, couple the Medium Independent Interface (MII) to the PMA.

The four bit data stream to be transmitted (TXD<3:0>) is scrambled and encoded into a pair of quinary symbols. One important point is that the encoding used for data symbols differs to that used for *idles*. Idles are sent whenever one, or both, of the PHYs that share the link are operating unreliably. In operation, the link will transition from idle mode to data mode by inserting two special quinary symbols that represent a *Start-of-Stream* delimiter. Equally, when the link reverts to an idle mode from the data mode, two further special symbols are reserved as an *End-of-Stream* delimiter. By using a different encoding method then, sequences of arbitrary symbols that could represent valid data are now easily distinguished from those that are plainly idles.

The PMA transfers the messages from the PCS to the medium via the MDI. In essence, the PMA comprises two transmitters and receivers, generating and recovering the five-level, pulse-amplitude modulated signals.

In terms of the Medium Dependent Interface (MDI), the ISO 8877 (RJ45) connector is used with the contact assignments shown in table 13-5. Although the crossover function mentioned is not a requirement for basic operation, it is a functional requirement to support Auto-Negotiation.

Table 13-5: PMA Signals to MDI contacts

Contact	PHY Without Internal Crossover	PHY With Internal Crossover
1	BI_DA+	BI_DD+
2	BI_DA-	BI_DB-
3	BI_DB+	BI_DA+
4	Not Used	Not Used
5	Not Used	Not Used
6	BI_DB-	BI_DA-
7	Not Used	Not Used
8	Not Used	Not Used

13.3.2 100Base-T2 Auto-Negotiation

As we have said, 100Base-T2 relies heavily on Auto-Negotiation[1] for correct operation. When looking to this functionality, we must also refer to the 100Mbps technologies upon which this was built. In chapter 9, we saw that the MII registers 0 through 7 were used for various, specific negotiation functions. For 100Base-T2 operation, registers 8 through 10 are also used as table 13-6 shows.

Register 4, the *Auto-Negotiation Advertisement* will contain the *Base Page* that is initially transmitted. At start up then, bits 0-4[2] will reflect whether this is an IEEE 802.3 or IEEE 802.9 transmission, the *Acknowledgment* bit[2] (bit 14) will not be set, and the *Next Page* (bit 15) will be set to indicate that further page(s) follow. This *Base Page* is then followed by a *formatted Next Page* that contains the 100Base-T2 *Technology Ability Message Code* (value 7)[2] that defines that two further *unformatted* pages follow. These pages then contain the information shown in table

---

[1] The reader is urged to consult chapters 9 and 11 in order to fully understand MII Management Register usage and the full Auto-Negotiation process.
[2] See chapter 11 - Auto-Negotiation.

13-7 which, when negotiation is completed, will enable each end of the link to configure itself appropriately.

Table 13-6: Management Register Set

Register	Register Name	Basic/Extended
0	Control	Basic
1	Status	Basic
2,3	PHY Identifier	Extended
4	Auto-Negotiation Advertisement	Extended
5	Auto-Negotiation Link Partner Ability	Extended
6	Auto-Negotiation Expansion	Extended
7	Auto-Negotiation Next Page Transmit	Extended
8	Auto-Negotiation Link Partner Next Page	Extended
9	100Base-T2 Control Register	Extended
10	100Base-T2 Status Register	Extended
11 - 15	Reserved	Extended
16 - 31	Vendor Specific	Extended

Table 13-7: 100Base-T2 Technology Ability Field

Bit	Technology
Page 1	
U0	100Base-T2 Half Duplex - 1 for Half Duplex Ability, 0 for No Half Duplex
U1	100Base-T2 Full Duplex - 1 for Full Duplex Ability, 0 for No Full Duplex
U2	100Base-T2 Repeater/DTE - 1 for Repeater, 0 for DTE
U3	100Base-T2 Master/Slave Manual Configuration Enable - 1 for Enabled
U4	100Base-T2 Manual Configuration - 1 for Master, 0 for Slave
U5	100Base-T2 Master/Slave Seed Bit 0 (SB0)
U6	100Base-T2 Master/Slave Seed Bit 1 (SB1)
U7	100Base-T2 Master/Slave Seed Bit 2 (SB2)
U8	100Base-T2 Master/Slave Seed Bit 3 (SB3)
U9	100Base-T2 Master/Slave Seed Bit 4 (SB4)
U10	100Base-T2 Master/Slave Seed Bit 5 (SB5)
Page 2	
U0	100Base-T2 Master/Slave Seed Bit 6 (SB6)
U1	100Base-T2 Master/Slave Seed Bit 7 (SB7)
U2	100Base-T2 Master/Slave Seed Bit 8 (SB8)
U3	100Base-T2 Master/Slave Seed Bit 9 (SB9)
U4	100Base-T2 Master/Slave Seed Bit 10 (SB10)
U5	100Base-T2 Master/Slave Seed Bit 11 (SB11)
U6	100Base-T2 Master/Slave Seed Bit 12 (SB12)
U7	100Base-T2 Master/Slave Seed Bit 13 (SB13)
U8	100Base-T2 Master/Slave Seed Bit 14 (SB14)
U9	100Base-T2 Master/Slave Seed Bit 15 (SB15)
U10	Not Used

Once the relevant information has been transferred by the process of Auto-Negotiation, each end of the link must determine whether it should run as a Master or Slave. The process itself is simple and can be summarized by table 13-8. Logically, a Repeater will have a higher priority than a DTE, and should therefore become the Master. Where we have two devices of the same type however, the *Seed bits* are used to determine priority with the device having the largest *seed value* (where SB15 is the MSB) is declared *Master*, and the other the *Slave*. The values of these Seed bits is implementation specific, but will always be in the range of 0 to 65535.

Table 13-8: Master/Slave Configuration

| | | Resulting Resolution | |
Local Device	Remote Device	Local Device	Remote Device
DTE U2=0 and U3=0 or **Manual SLAVE** U3=1 and U4=0	**Repeater** U2=1 and U3=0 or **Manual MASTER** U3=1 and U4=1	Slave	Master
Repeater U2=1 and U3=0	**Manual MASTER** U3=1 and U4=1		
Manual SLAVE U3=1 and U4=0	**DTE** U2=0 and U3=0		
Repeater U2=1 and U3=0 or **Manual MASTER** U3=1 and U4=1	**DTE** U2=0 and U3=0 or **Manual SLAVE** U3=1 and U4=0	Master	Slave
DTE U2=0 and U3=0	**Manual SLAVE** U3=1 and U4=0		
Manual MASTER U3=1 and U4=1	**Repeater** U2=1 and U3=0		
Repeater U2=1 and U3=0	**Repeater** U2=1 and U3=0	PHY with highest Seed Value becomes Master. If both Seed Values are identical, resolution fails.	
DTE U2=0 and U3=0	**DTE** U2=0 and U3=0	PHY with highest Seed Value becomes Master. If both Seed Values are identical, resolution fails.	
Manual SLAVE U3=1 and U4=0	**Manual SLAVE** U3=1 and U4=0	Fault Detected	
Manual MASTER U3=1 and U4=1	**Manual MASTER** U3=1 and U4=1	Fault Detected	

Registers 9 and 10 are the 100Base-T2 Control and Status registers, respectively. Register 9, the Control Register, contains the device's parameters and Register 10 the status of the link. The values of bits within these registers are defined in tables 13-9 and 13-10 below:

Table 13-9: 100Base-T2 Register 9 (Control Register) Contents

Bit	Name	Actions	Description
15,14	Transmitter Test Mode	R/W	Default value is 00
13	Receiver Test Mode	R/W	Default value is 0

Table 13-9: 100Base-T2 Register 9 (Control Register) Contents (Continued)

Bit	Name	Actions	Description
12	Master/Slave Manual Config Enable	R/W	1 - Enable Master/Slave Man Config 0 - Disable Master/Slave Man Config
11	Master/Slave Manual Config Value[1]	R/W	1 - Configure PHY as Master 0 - Configure PHY as Slave
10	T2 Repeater/DTE Bit	R/W	1 - Repeater Device Port 0 - DTE Device
9-0	Reserved		

Note: 1. The actions taken as a result of this bit will depend on the values of bit 12. If bit 12 is set to zero, then bit 11 will be ignored.

Table 13-10: 100Base-T2 Register 10 (Status Register) Contents

Bit	Name	Actions	Description
15	Master/Slave Manual Config Fault	RO/SC	1 - Master/Slave Config Fault 0 - No Master/Slave Config Fault
14	Master/Slave Config Resolution Complete	RO	1 - Master/Slave Config Complete 0 - Master/Slave Config Incomplete
13	Local Receiver Status	RO	1 - Local Receiver OK 0 - Local Receiver Fault
12	Remote Receiver Status	RO	1 - Remote Receiver OK 0 - Remote Receiver Fault
11-8	Reserved		
7-0	Idle Error Count	RO/SC	The number of *Idle* Errors Detected

Note: The *SC* designation in the *Actions* column indicates that the register contents are *Self Clearing* after the action has been performed.

13.4 100Base-T4

In a similar fashion to 100Base-T2, 100Base-T4 defines the Physical Coding (PCS) and Physical Medium Attachment (PMA) Sublayers of a 100Mbps transmission system. 100Base-T4 operates over Category 3, 4, or 5 twisted pair cable - only in this 100Mbps variant, all four pairs are used. Defined within IEEE 802.3u, this specification also allows for operation of 100m segments that provide a nominal network diameter of 200m when using (up to) 2 repeaters.

Architecturally, 100Base-T4 is similar to 100Base-T2. Hence, when compared to the OSI model, there are no differences to those discussed for 100Base-T2 and shown previously in figure 13-7. The same Media Independent Interface (MII) that was used in other 100Mbps technologies is used, and seamlessly interfaces to the 100Base-T4 PCS. In the following sections, we will discuss the PCS, PMA, and the MDI, and pay particular attention to where changes are actually made.

13.4.1   100Base-T4 PCS and PMA

As with other technologies, the PCS is used to link the Media Independent Interface (MII) to the Physical Medium Attachment (PMA). For transmission, the PCS will accept 4 bit wide *nibbles* of data from the MII, encode these using an 8B6T encoding scheme, and then pass the resulting data symbols to the PMA. In reception, the opposite actions take place with data symbols recovered by the PMA being decoded by the PCS and then passed back to the MII. In addition, the PCS contains a *Carrier Sense* function, an *Error Sense* function, and a *Collision Presence* function.

The 8B6T encoding scheme maps an 8 bit octet of data onto 6 ternary symbols called a *6T Code Group*. These code groups are then fanned out over three independent channels, such that each channel carries only one third of the total 100Mbps, or 33.33333.....Mbps. The actual transmission rate of the ternary symbols is then six-eighths of the transmission rate, or 25MHz.

Physical level communication takes place over 4 pairs of Category 3, 4, or 5 unshielded twisted pair cable. Using 100Base-T4, we always leave one pair open for detecting carrier at the far end, and also for the detection of collisions. Figure 13-8 shows how these are managed.

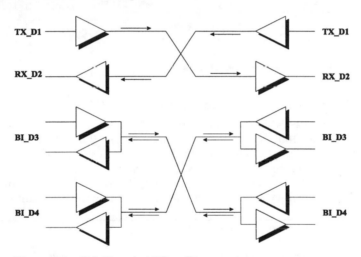

Figure 13-8:   Pair Usage in 100Base-T4

All collision detection and link integrity is achieved through the unidirectional pairs TX_D1 and RX_D2. In this way we always have three pairs in each direction for data transmission, and therefore reduce our transmission rates to 25MHz as previously described. Schematically, we can then see the PCS/PMA functionality in the block diagram of figure 13-9. In this figure, we can clearly see the unidirectional paths TX_D1/RX_D2 and the bi-directional paths BI_D3 and BI_D4 at the MDI interface. At the MII, we can then see all of the standard signals that we described when we introduced 100Mbps technologies in chapter 9. The management interface comprising MDC/MDIO is applicable to all technologies, and therefore operates in the same way as for 100Base-X. In addition, the optional link control is achieved through Auto-Negotiation as described in chapter 11.

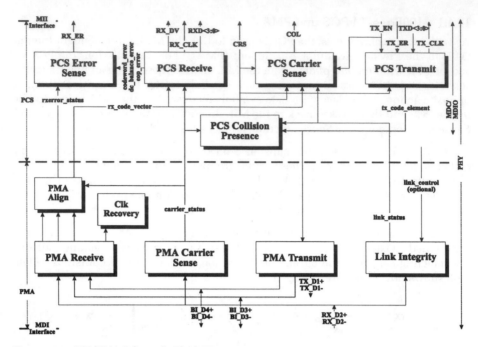

Figure 13-9: PCS/PMA Schematic Block Diagram

13.4.2   100Base-T4 Medium Dependent Interface (MDI)

The MDI for 100Base-T4 uses the standard ISO 8877/IEC 603-7 (RJ45) connector in common with other 100Mbps copper implementations. Pin utilization is as shown in table 13-11 although you will note that the pairings used for TX_D1 and RX_D2 are the same as those used for TX and RX in 10Base-T and 100Base-Tx implementations. This ensures that a high degree of compatibility can be maintained for those devices that potentially implement multiple technology types.

Table 13-11: MDI Pin Connections - 100Base-T4

Pin	PHY Without Internal Crossover	PHY With Internal Crossover
1	TX_D1+	RX_D2+
2	TX_D1-	RX_D2-
3	RX_D2+	TX_D1+
4	BI_D3+	BI_D4+
5	BI_D3-	BI_D4-
6	RX_D2-	TX_D1-
7	BI_D4+	BI_D3+
8	BI_D4-	BI_D3-

Note: PHYs without internal crossovers are recommended for DTEs while those with internal crossovers are recommended for repeaters. Hence simple, *straight-through*, cables can be employed for all connections with the exception of DTE-to-DTE and repeater-to-repeater.

13.5 Summary

This chapter has introduced some of the lesser-used Ethernet/802.3 variants. Their usage is not commonplace, yet some are significant in that they have played their role in the development of higher speed technologies. In addition, some of these have served well in terms of their usage in hostile environments, and 10Broad36 is certainly an example of this. Others, you might argue, have no place in networking. This however is only because they have not been developed beyond their original design constraints.

So what are we really left with? A mixture of odd-ball technologies for sure, but a comparison of the manner in which they operate. In real terms, the text presented here is little more than an introduction to some of these variants and the technologies that they use. In mentioning them however, we at least complete the story of Ethernet/802.3 and all of its various development stages. The final part of the story is that of 100VG-AnyLAN, which will be discussed in the next chapter. Not an 802.3 technology, but once again significant in the overall development of Ethernet generally.

100VG-AnyLAN

100VG-AnyLAN, unlike the Ethernet/802.3 standards that we have described, is defined not by any of the IEEE 802.3 (ISO/IEC 8802-3) standards, but instead by IEEE 802.12. Purists might then argue that, since this is a completely different variant, what place does it have here? The simple answer is that it is significant historically, technically, and because work continues within this area.

To understand the importance of the history surrounding the standard, one first has to understand the battles that raged while vendors fought to deliver higher and higher bandwidths. It was obvious that 10Mbps was far too slow for the applications that would run over the networks of tomorrow, yet customers had invested much in the infrastructures of their networks. Hubs, switches, and most importantly cable plant, represent tangible costs on which return is expected. Vendors then, struggled to provide higher bandwidths at reasonable cost to their customers. As is normal in these situations, the first to market a viable, cost effective, alternative to 10Mbps was bound to gain all-important advantage over their rivals.

Hewlett-Packard was, and indeed remains, the champion of the 100VG-AnyLAN cause. Leading a consortium of companies that included IBM, they developed the fundamental principles on which the 802.12 standard was founded, and which was ratified in June 1995. At the same time, other vendors struggled to produce an IEEE 802.3 alternative that provided speeds of 100Mbps - or even more. So who were the victors? Certainly in terms of pure market share, that title has to go to those vendors within the camp supporting 100Base-Tx and 100Base-Fx. Technically however, 100VG-AnyLAN could be argued to be the better option since this technology provides (at least in theory) the ability to carry multimedia application data, and is able to easily integrate with other technologies such as Token Ring. Certainly no other 100Mbps technology is as versatile, nor can it utilize the types of cable plant that this technology can. Indeed, the very name is an indicator of the media type(s) and network architectures that may be employed - 100VG-AnyLAN is a networking technology that runs at *100Mbps*, over *Voice Grade* media, with the ability to integrate *Any LAN* technology.

14.1 100VG-AnyLAN Architecture

While there are notable similarities between the IEEE 802.3 and 802.12 standards, there remains several significant differences. In order to better understand those differences, and indeed the manner in which 100VG-AnyLAN operates, it is best to compare this technology with our familiar 10/100Mbps standards. Also, as we can see from figure 14-1, comparison of this architecture with that presented by the OSI model, reveals certain major differences in terms of layer naming and functionality. Contrasting the architectures we see that much of the terminology used is similar, and indeed much of the functionality remains constant with that of our more familiar 10/100Mbps standards. 100VG-AnyLAN, however, is broadly composed of the three major sub-layers (*Media Access Control, Physical Medium Independent, and Physical Medium Dependent*) which are described in the following sections.

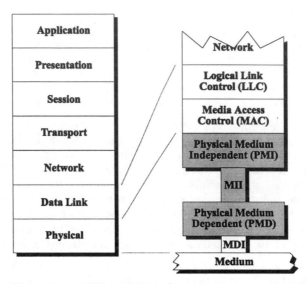

Figure 14-1: 100VG-AnyLAN Architecture

14.1.1 100VG-AnyLAN Operation

Before describing the specific layer functionality in detail, it is first necessary to understand the topology employed by 100VG-AnyLAN. Only then can we begin to appreciate the way in which data is passed between stations.

Unlike our *traditional* 10Mbps Ethernet and Token Rings of the past, 100VG-AnyLAN uses neither a Bus topology nor a *Star Wired Ring*. This architecture, in a similar vein to that of 100Base-Tx and 100Base-Fx, uses only *Hubs* to interconnect stations - although it is true to say that this is almost where the similarity ends.

Now, rather than using our familiar CSMA/CD access protocol, we use what is referred to as the *Demand Priority Protocol*. This allows the creation of high speed, shared-media LANs, while utilizing the existing media. This use of existing media is important, since as we described earlier significant money is invested in cabling infrastructures. Also, the meanings of some of the terms that we have used so far need modification, since their functions differ from our more conventional view. For example, the basic components used in a 100VG-AnyLAN environment are *End Nodes* and *Repeaters*. True, we also use *Bridges*, *Routers*, and *Switches*, and within this environment some of these devices tend to be more complex than their

CSMA/CD counterparts. In order to better understand these concepts then, let us take a look at a simple 100VG-AnyLAN network that employs several *Hubs*. Figure 14-2 shows such an example.

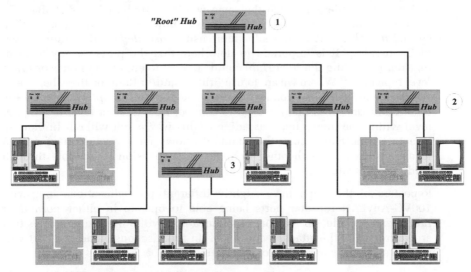

Figure 14-2: Sample 100VG-AnyLAN Network

In this figure we have a first level hub, the *Root Hub*, which feeds other, *Second Level* hubs and *End Nodes*. In addition, one *second level* hub also feeds a *Third Level* hub to which additional stations (or *end nodes*) may be connected. This *cascaded* system is typical of 100VG-AnyLAN environments, and indeed the repeaters (Hubs) are the fundamental building blocks upon which this architecture is built. Looking to the component parts in some detail then, we can describe each as follows. Although the terms used will be familiar, and much of the functionality can be likened to that of the more usual 100Base-Tx and 100Base-Fx devices, it is worthwhile pointing out where the differences lie.

- **End Nodes**
  As in *traditional* Ethernet/802.3 environments, the end node (or station) will typically be a computer system, a Bridge, Router, or Switch. Whatever the station type, it is immaterial to the overall operation of the protocol. Simply put, an end node is a device that connects to the next level of hierarchy, which in this case is a Repeater. For computer systems, connection is via a Network Interface Card (NIC), which in turn connects to the Repeater over one of the allowable media types. For other system types the interface will typically be built-in, and therefore only the media connection is required. The operation of the interface will be identical to that of a computer NIC.

- **Repeaters**
  These are the central devices within 100VG-AnyLAN environments. Unlike Ethernet/802.3 units, Repeaters here are intelligent network controllers. They manage access to the network in a *round-robin*, polling fashion checking which ports have data to transmit, and then granting access. In

addition, the repeater monitors links, ensures End Node availability, and performs any required security.

At the simplest level, a 100VG-AnyLAN network comprises a single repeater and two end nodes, in much the same way as a 100Base-Tx or 100Base-Fx network would. 100Vg-AnyLAN repeaters however are equipped with a special *uplink* port that allows the more usual *cascaded* configuration shown in figure 14-2. It is important to note here that the ports on any level of repeater (including the *Root Hub*) could connect to either end nodes or *lower level* repeaters. Where we are to use Bridges and/or Routers, these behave as standard end nodes and connect to the same ports. The *uplink* ports on the other hand, are those that are used to connect from a lower level to a higher level within the hierarchy. Cascading in this way is not without limitation. Due to timing constraints, the standard allows for a maximum of only 5 levels, although as with other technologies, expansion is possible through Bridges and Routers.

Repeaters of this type have slightly different port allocations too, with 100VG-AnyLAN repeater ports being able to operate in either *normal* or *promiscuous* mode. In the normal mode, a port will only receive frames that are addressed to the attached end node. In promiscuous mode, the port will receive all packets regardless of destination.

Finally, due to the more open nature of this technology, 100VG-AnyLAN repeaters can be configured to handle IEEE 802.3 (CSMA/CD) or Token Ring frame formats. One limitation however, is that all repeaters in the same segment *must* use the same format.

- **Bridges**
  Bridges within a 100VG-AnyLAN network perform the same basic task as in other environments. These devices are used to link multiple segments, and thereby extend the overall diameter of the network, while maintaining the same logical network addressing. The difference here, is that bridges used with 100VG-AnyLAN tend to be more complex, since they will normally be used to link different physical layer protocols and frame types. For example, a bridge in a 100VG-AnyLAN environment may well be used to link Demand Priority LANs to CSMA/CD and/or Token Ring.

- **Switches**
  Like their Ethernet/802.3 counterparts, switches perform the same basic functions as Bridges - only faster. As such, switches supporting the 100VG-AnyLAN standard (IEEE 802.12) may be used to link the Demand Protocol to 10/100Mbps CSMA/CD LANs. The levels of complexity are therefore increased, in exactly the same way as described for bridges above.

- **Routers**
  Routers within this environment operate in exactly the same way as those used in Ethernet/802.3, Token Ring, FDDI, and ATM environments. Packets are decoded at the Network Layer and routing[1] decisions are made based

---

[1] For a more complete discussion on Routers and Routing (Internetworking), see section F.

upon the destination *Network* address held within the appropriate protocol header. Once the decision is made, the packet is passed to the appropriate interface, re-framed using the relevant frame type for the attached network, and then transmitted.

14.1.2 Cable Plant and Limitations

As with other technologies, supported cable types and their associated distance limitations will vary from vendor to vendor. The IEEE 802.12 standard however, does specify several media as being acceptable. Table 14-1 lists these along with maximum allowable distances. Note that the use of flat cable is expressly forbidden as indeed it is with other technologies.

Table 14-1: Media Types and Distance Limitations

Cable Type	Category	Maximum Distance
UTP - 4 Pair	3 and 4	up to 100m
UTP - 4 Pair	5	up to 200m
STP - 2 Pair	N/A	up to 100m
Fiber	N/A	up to 2000m

A number of different technologies use Unshielded Twisted Pair (UTP) media. It is therefore important, particularly with technologies such as 100VG-AnyLAN where mixed environments are commonplace, that distinctions be made as to wiring standards. All technologies that allow the use of UTP use the familiar 8 pin (4 pair), IEC 603-7 (RJ45) modular plug. Table 14-2 identifies the cable pairings used by those common technologies.

Table 14-2: RJ45 Connector Wiring for Common Technologies

Technology	Pairs Used	Wire (Pin) Numbers
Token Ring	2 and 3	4/5 and 3/6
10Base-T	1 and 3	1/2 and 3/6
100VG-AnyLAN	1, 2, 3, and 4	1/2, 4/5, 3/6, and 7/8

Finally, and as in common with our more popular Ethernet/802.3 environments, networks must not include loops, and we are restricted to a maximum of 1024 nodes on any segment.

14.2 Media Access Control (MAC)

The *Media Access Control* (MAC) sub-layer provides a similar function to that previously described for 10Mbps Ethernet in chapter 4, and for 100BaseTx and 100BaseFx in chapter 9. As with these technologies, during transmission it is the MAC that constructs the frames in which our data will travel. Equally, when receiving, the MAC strips the header and FCS from the frame and check its integrity using the Frame Check Sequence or *Cyclic Redundancy Check* (CRC). Again, in common with these other standards, the MAC sub-layer must interface with those layers above and below. With 100VG-AnyLAN however, while the MAC sub-layer still communicates with the Logical Link Control (LLC) sub-layer above, its subordinate layer is now called the Physical Medium Independent (PMI) sub-layer.

When discussing the MAC, we must be clear as to which end of a link we are referring. All 100VG-AnyLAN networks must make use of a repeater, and this in turn leads to two separate MAC sub-layers being implemented (the MAC and RMAC) as figure 14-3 shows. Operation is similar, but different interpretations are applied to various parts of control frames.

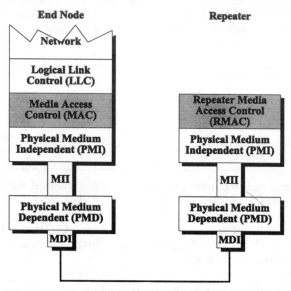

Figure 14-3: End Node and Repeater MACs

14.2.1 End Node Polling and Demand Priority

The Demand Priority Protocol used in 100VG-AnyLAN requires a substantial amount of interaction between the End Node and the Repeater. With this protocol, End Nodes issue requests (or *Demands*) to the repeater whenever they have data to send. This request is then tagged by the MAC sub-layer to request either *normal* or *high* priority data transmission. High priority data is used for time critical applications such as multimedia, and these requests are always granted before those of normal priority. Normal priority is then used for general data. Unlike Token Ring, only these two levels of priority are available. That said, accepting any prioritization system makes 100VG-AnyLAN unique within most LAN technologies, and an ideal vehicle for tomorrow's applications. Of course, to make use of this system, applications must be able to request the applicable service level and pass this request to the MAC layer. Failing to do so would render this advantage worthless.

Arbitration between repeater ports is achieved through *round robin* polling. Each repeater, regardless of level, constantly scans its ports and looks for nodes that have data to transmit, and the priority level of that data. To understand the complete cycle however, it is best explained with an example. Consider figure 14-4:

In the figure, two levels of repeater are in use. The *Root Hub* services end nodes connected to level 1 and also the second level repeater. The second level repeater services only those stations directly connected to it. Assuming that there is no high priority traffic pending transmission, the protocol allows any End Node to send just one packet during a single *round robin* scan. Where the node is replaced by a repeater however, the upper level will allow as many packets to be transmitted as there are active ports. In this way, the *Root Hub* arbitrates, such that for normal priority traffic, each End Node has use of the network to transmit an identical number of packets.

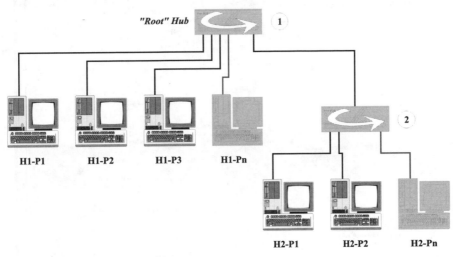

Figure 14-4: Example of *Round Robin* Polling

Returning to the example, let us consider a single scan made by the Root Hub and assume that all end nodes have *normal priority* data to be transmitted. In this case, the order of transmission would be as shown below. Remember, that this example assumes that at the precise instant that we commence polling, *all* connected end nodes are active and have data waiting. Also, although we have drawn the figure such that the second level repeater connects to the Root Hub *after* end node H1-Pn, this does not have to be the case. We shall examine the effects of moving the second level repeater to a different port in a later example.

H1-P1; H1-P2; H1-P3....H1-Pn; H2-P1; H2-P2....H2-Pn

The scan would now re-commence, and if end node H1-P1 had data to transmit it would be granted access. Round Robin polling then, allows fair access to network resources in much the same way as Token Ring and FDDI. In general, the protocol operation at this level can be summarized with the flow chart shown in figure 14-5.

- When an End Node has data to transmit it signals the hub by sending a *Request_Normal* for data of Normal priority, or *Request_High* for data of high priority. End Nodes that have no data to transmit send an *Up_Idle* signal.

- The repeater constantly polls its ports and thereby decides which have data to transmit, and at what priority.

- The repeater selects the *next* port that is indicating that high priority data is pending. In the event that none are requesting a high priority transmission, the repeater selects the next port indicating normal priority. Where no ports are indicating any data transmission, polling continues until such time as an end node has data to transmit.

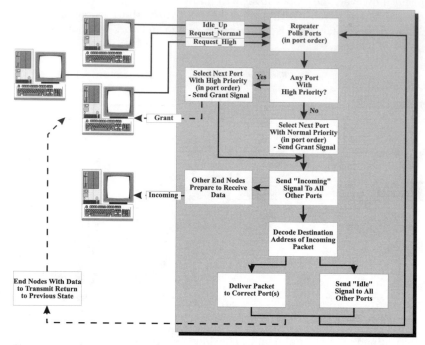

Figure 14-5: Flowchart of Packet Transmission

- Having selected the port for transmission, the repeater now indicates to that port that it is ready to accept data by issuing a *Grant* signal. To all other ports, the repeater issues an *Incoming* signal to indicate that they should ready themselves to receive data. In response to the Incoming signal, these other ports now cease transmission of requests.

- The repeater decodes the destination address of the frame as it is received. It then routes the frame to the relevant port(s) and sends an *Idle_Down* signal to all other ports.

- Once the frame transmission has been completed, all end nodes return to their previous status of either sending *Requests* or the *Idle_Up* signal.

Returning to our example once more, let us now consider the order of transmission if all end nodes had data to transmit, but the data of end nodes H1-P1, H1-P3, and H2-P2 was high priority. Now our order would be different and is shown below:

H1-P1; H1-P3; H2-P2; H1-P2...H1-Pn; H2-P1...H2-Pn

Finally, let us consider the effects of moving the connection between the Root Hub and the second level repeater. In this example (referring to figure 14-4) we shall exchange end node H1-Pn and the second level repeater. Once again, if all of our end nodes have *normal* priority data only, the order of transmission will now be:

H1-P1; H1-P2; H1-P3; H2-P1; H2-P2...H2-Pn...H1-Pn

If nodes H1-P1, H1-P3, and H2-P2 were to have high priority data as in our previous example, then the order would be:

H1-P1; H1-P3; H2-P2; H1-P2; H2-P1...H2-Pn...H1-Pn

In order to achieve this *ordered* transmission scheme, each hub maintains separate lists for normal and high priority requests. Normal priority requests are always serviced by port order until a high priority request is received. Once received, the hub will complete the current packet transmission and then service the request at the higher priority. Once all high priority requests have been serviced, the hub then resumes the transmission of normal priority traffic from where it left off. Finally, in an effort to guarantee access to normal priority traffic during sustained high priority traffic bursts, the hub monitors the time taken between requests being received and transmission being granted. If the delay involved becomes excessive, the hub will then raise the priority of the request at the port, thereby ensuring that the end node can transmit its data in a timely manner.

14.2.2   End Node Training

Demand Priority is specifically designed to operate in both Ethernet and Token Ring modes. Applications, and with them those protocols above the LLC sub-layer, believe that they are operating in one of those environments, and then leave the LLC to instruct the MAC to construct Demand Priority frames. When discussing the MAC used at the End Node, we must then discuss one important frame type known as the *Link Training* frame. Link Training is the term used to describe the procedure that allows the internal circuitry of the hub and node to be *trained* for the transmission and reception of data. In addition, this process also allows the link itself to be verified. Thus, the insertion of substandard, incorrectly wired, or noisy, media that may cause problems will be barred from use in the network.

The Link Training process requires that the node and hub exchange 24 consecutive *Training frames* without error. In passing these frames, we therefore ensure that the link is functional. Additionally, this sequence of frames allows the hub to learn important information about the attached end node. For example, the hub can determine the type of node attached (end node, hub, bridge, router, or some type of network test equipment), the operational mode of the device (normal or monitor mode), and most importantly the address of the device. The detail of this *Link Training* frame is shown in figure 14-6 and is then described below:

Start of Stream	Preamble	Destination Address	Source Address	Req. Config.	Allow Conf.	Data	FCS	End of Stream

Figure 14-6: Link Training Frame

The 16 bit *Start of Stream* field is used to indicate to the *Physical Medium Independent* sub-layer that a frame is being sent. This field is used to identify the priority of the data requesting transmission and will contain one of the two following values. In the case of *Normal* priority, the bit pattern will be **0101 1111 0000 0011**. Where the transmission request is for *High* priority data, this field will then contain **0101 1000 0011 1110**.

The *Preamble* field is 48 bits in length and simply comprises a pattern of alternating 1's and 0's, commencing with a 0, i.e., **0101 0101 01........0101**. The *Destination Address* field is of similar construction to the regular destination MAC address found in Ethernet/802.3, Token Ring, and FDDI. Firstly it is 48^2 bits long, and secondly the two highest order bits could denote whether the address is an *Individual* or *Group* address, and whether the addressing scheme is *Universally* or *Locally* administered respectively. However since the *Training* frame is never used to communicate with other stations, but only between the end node and the hub, this field will always contain the *Null* address, i.e., all zeroes.

The *Source* address, like the *Destination* address, is also 48 bits in length, and will contain the address of the end node performing the test. In actual fact, this address could either be the unicast address of the node, or the *Null* address depending upon the situation. For example, if the device performing the test is a lower level repeater, then this field will always be the *Null* address. Where the device is an end node, the field will normally contain a unique unicast address, although it is possible (albeit unlikely) that the node does not yet have an address assigned. Where this is the case, it is legal for the node to use the *Null* address during training, provided that it is assigned a unique address before joining the network.

The *Requested Configuration* field is 15 bits in length, and is used by the attached device to inform the hub about its configuration. The *Allowed Configuration* field (also 15 bits in length) is then used by the hub to inform the attached device about what activity will be allowed at the port, and to convey other pertinent information. Indeed, it is the *Requested* and *Allowed Configuration* fields that are really key to the training process. Figure 14-7 shows the *Requested Configuration* and *Allowed Configuration* fields which are then described below:

Looking first to the *Requested Configuration* field (sent from the End Node or MAC sub-layer), the bit positions have the following meanings: The *R* or Repeater bit is used to indicate whether the lower level device is a repeater or an end node. If this bit is set to **0**, then the lower level is an end node. Conversely, if set to **1**, then the lower level is a repeater. The two *P* bits are used to indicate whether the lower level will act in *promiscuous* mode, and therefore receive *all* packets rather than only those directly addressed to it. Although four bit combinations exist, only two are currently used. These combinations are **00** meaning that the lower level device will receive only those packets specifically addressed to it, and **10** where the lower level will receive *all* packets forwarded by the upper level repeater. The

---

[2] Note that unlike Ethernet/802.3 addressing, 16 bit addresses are not supported under the 802.12 standard.

seven *res* bits are reserved, always set to zero, and are ignored. Finally, the three *V* (Version) bits are used to indicate the version of the 802.12 MAC/RMAC Training Protocol. The current version is version 1, and is referenced by the bit pattern **001**.

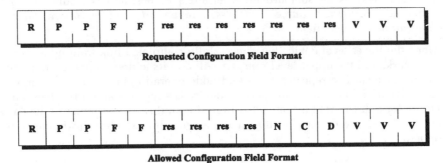

Figure 14-7: 802.12 Training Frame Configuration Fields

The format of the *Allowed Configuration* field (sent from the repeater or RMAC) is similar to the *Requested Configuration* field, except that three of those bits previously reserved are now used. The single *D* or *Duplicate Address* bit is set when the upper level repeater has detected a duplicate address. The *C* or *Configuration* bit is used to relay to the lower level whether the requested configuration is compatible with the network to which it is trying to attach. When this bit is *off* (or set to **0**), the configuration is deemed to be compatible. When set *on* (or to **1**), then the requested configuration is incompatible, and the *FF*, *PP*, and *R* bits are used to indicate the configuration that would be allowed. Finally, the *N* bit is used to convey whether access is denied due to reasons other than configuration (such as security). When the *N* bit is *off* (**0**), then access to the network is allowed where the configuration (as indicated by the *C* bit) is compatible. When this bit is *on* (**1**), then access is denied.

The Link Training frame *Data* field will contain between 594 and 675 octets of data, the first 55 octets of which may be used for *private protocol* information. The actual length of this field is however determined by the initiator of the Training frame. If the first 55 octets of the field are used to carry private protocol information, then the first 5 octets *must* contain a protocol identifier as assigned by the IEEE. The remaining octets (those from octet 56 onwards) are then all set to zero.

While this may appear both strange and wasteful, it is actually of great value. The purpose of the Training Frame is to establish that the initiator of the sequence and the medium are both operational before allowing the node to insert into the network, in a similar fashion to the Token Ring *Lobe test* function. In actual fact, 802.12 goes further, since the physical layer performs *data scrambling* on all outgoing data. Thus, the all-zeroes portion of the frame actually acts as a pseudo-random output from the transmitter, and transceivers can then use this input to characterize the frequency response of the cable. In addition, the requirement that 24 frames of this type be passed without error coupled with the length of those frames, ensures that noisy links are never inserted into the network.

The final field in the Training frame is the *Frame Check Sequence* (FCS) field. This field, in common with all technologies, is a simple *cyclic redundancy check* (CRC) that ensures error free data transmission. The value of the CRC is calculated in the same way as for standard Ethernet/802.3 frames, and is a function of the *destination address*, *source address*, *requested configuration*, *allowed configuration*, and *data* fields.

Once the lower level device has successfully completed link training it will join the network, and the upper level repeater will add its address to its internal tables. If the lower level is a repeater or an end node operating in promiscuous mode, it will receive *all* frames. If the lower level device is a repeater and it receives a frame destined for a device that is connected to it, it then directs that frame to the correct port. If the received frame is for an unknown address, then the frame will be dropped.

14.3 Physical Medium Independent Sub-Layer (PMI)

Operation at the Physical Medium Independent Sub-Layer, as its name suggests, is independent of the underlying medium. When transmitting, data passed from the MAC sub-layer is prepared for transmission, and conversely when receiving, it is this layer that prepares the data for the MAC.

The operation of the layer can be broadly split into 4 operations. Firstly, during transmission, the layer will split the MAC frame into 4 separate *streams*. Next, these streams are scrambled to remove repetitive data, and they are then encoded.

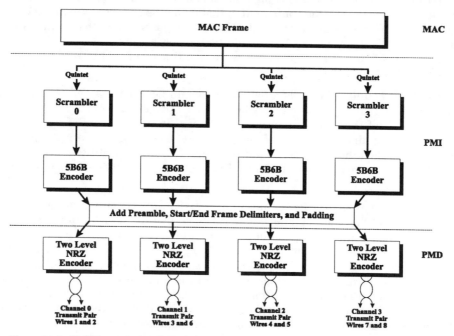

Figure 14-8: PMI Transmission Overview

Finally, the *Preamble*, *Start* and *End Frame Delimiters* are added to the channels, and *Padding* is added where the streams are not of equal length. This operation can be summarized in figure 14-8, and each of the operations are then described in detail in the following sections.

14.3.1 Quartet Channeling

The process of *Quartet Channeling* sequentially divides the data stream from the MAC sub-layer into 5 bit data *quintets*. These quintets are then distributed among the four channels that represent a transmission pair for the 4 pair UTP network. This is shown in figure 14-9.

Channel 0 will be transmitted on the twisted pair wires 1 and 2, Channel 1 on wires 3 and 6, Channel 2 on wires 4 and 5, and Channel 3 on wires 7 and 8. On *two pair* and fiber optic 100VG-AnyLAN systems, a multiplexing scheme is used that then converts the 4 channels into either two channels (in the case of two pair systems) or one channel (in the case of fiber optic).

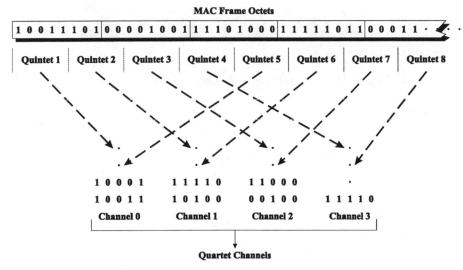

Figure 14-9: Quartet Channeling

14.3.2 Data Scrambling

Once the data has been divided into four channels of quintets, each quintet is then scrambled using a different scrambling pattern for each channel. This process randomizes the bit patterns on each transmission pair, and also serves to eliminate repetitious data such as all 0's or all 1's. In addition, random bit patterns reduce radio frequency interference (RFI) and signal crosstalk (NEXT) from one pair of wires to another within the cable.

14.3.3 5B6B Encoding

The 5B6B Encoding process is used to map the scrambled 5 bit data quintets into 6 bit symbols according to pre-determined patterns. The reasoning behind this encoding requirement is that by encoding in this way, balanced data patterns are created that contain an equal number of 0's and 1's. These then guarantee that clock transitions will occur, and that receiver synchronization will be maintained. Furthermore, encoding of this type provides for rudimentary error checking, in that those symbols that are considered invalid (i.e., those containing more than 3 0's or 1's in a row) can be detected with ease. Figure 14-10 shows an example of how 5 bit quintets are encoded using this scheme.

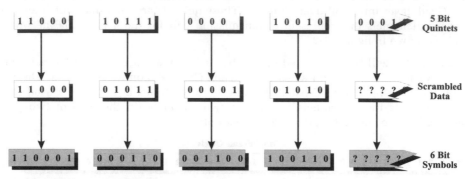

Figure 14-10: 5B6B Encoding

14.4 Medium Independent Interface Sub-Layer (MII)

The Medium Independent Interface (MII) is the logical interface between the Physical Medium Independent (PMI) and Physical Medium Dependent (PMD) sub-layers. Physically, this may be provided so as to potentially allow the interchange of PMDs, and therefore the easy reconfiguration of end nodes and repeater ports to support different link media. Generally though, this interface is built into devices, thereby making them media dependent anyway.

14.5 Physical Medium Dependent Sub-Layer (PMD)

The Physical Medium Dependent sub-layer is the link between those link dependent sub-layers and the physical medium below, and the link independent sub-layers above. The functionality of this layer can be split into the four major areas, although in more general terms it can be described as providing the control signaling, clock recovery, and data stream signaling.

14.5.1 Multiplexing

As we have already noted, 100VG-AnyLAN supports multiple media types including 2 and 4 pair Unshielded Twisted Pair, 2 pair Shielded Twisted Pair, and Single and Multimode Fiber Optic cables. Our discussions thus far have centered on the fact that this technology uses four pairs over which data is transmitted. Hence, if we are to transmit data over fewer transmission channels, multiplexing is required. That said, at the time of writing 2 pair and Fiber Optic operation are still under development, and multiplexing is therefore mentioned purely for completeness.

14.5.2 NRZ Encoding

Non-Return to Zero (NRZ) encoding is used to transmit data and link control (or status) signals. Unlike other encoding techniques such as Manchester Encoding, NRZ uses two signal levels (or states) and, as its name suggests, never returns to a "*zero*" or no signal value. 100VG-AnyLAN uses a 30MHz clock to transmit each of the four channels, which results in an encoded data rate of 120Mbits per second. When receiving, since we transmit 6 bits in order to recover 5, our decoded data rate will be 25Mbits per second per channel, or an effective transmission/reception rate of 100Mbps. In addition, since we are locked to a 30MHz clock signal, our effective maximum transmission frequency will be just 15MHz when transmitting the theoretical *worst case* data pattern of **1010101.....** 100VG-AnyLAN can therefore be safely used over existing Category 3 cable plant. Figure 14-11 shows an example of the NRZ encoding technique based upon simple binary data.

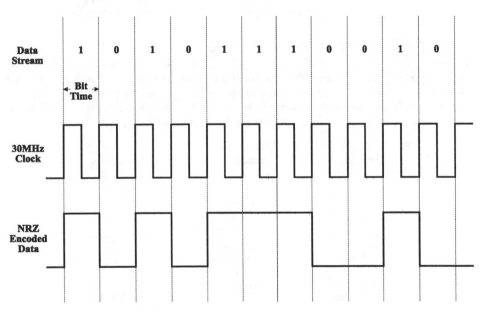

Figure 14-11: An Example of NRZ Encoding

As the figure shows, with NRZ encoding, we always transmit one data bit per clock cycle. When we detect a *high* value, a binary one is encoded, and when we receive a *low*, the data represented is a binary zero. In this way, there can be no misinterpretation of data, provided that the signal waveform does not suffer unduly from the effects of jitter or attenuation.

14.5.3 Link Status Control

Link Status Control is used to control the link between the end node and upper level repeater, or the link between an upper and lower level repeater. Control is achieved through the use of two low frequency *tones* (called *Tone 1* and *Tone 2*). The first tone, *Tone 1*, is generated by transmitting an alternating pattern of sixteen binary 1's, followed by sixteen binary 0's at 30MHz. This produces a transmission frequency of approximately 0.938MHz. *Tone 2* is approximately double the frequency of *Tone 1* at 1.875MHz, and is generated by transmitting an alternating pattern of eight binary 1's followed by eight binary 0's. Our 100VG-AnyLAN systems then use combinations of these tones (as shown in table 14-3) to communicate status between hubs and nodes.

Table 14-3: Tone Pattern Definitions

Tone Pattern Transmitted	*Meaning When Received by End Node*	*Meaning When Received by Hub*
1-1	Idle	Idle
1-2	Incoming Data Packet	Normal Priority Request
2-1	Reserved (Not Used)	High Priority Request
2-2	Link Training Request	Link Training Request

14.5.4 Full/Half Duplex Cable Operation

Transmission of data is always performed in a half duplex fashion. That is, the device can only either transmit or receive data at any one time. Where 4 pair cable operation is used, then this involves all pairs being used as previously outlined. Where 2 pair or fiber optic medium is used, then all channels will need to be multiplexed, although operation in this mode is yet to be ratified.

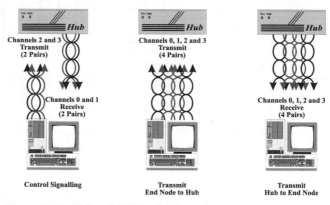

Figure 14-12: Full and Half Duplex Operation

Link status and control information always uses full duplex operation. The control tone combinations listed in the previous section are then used to relay this information. Channel 0 and 1 (pairs 2 and 3) are used for communications between the hub and the end node, and Channels 2 and 3 (pairs 1 and 4) are used between the end node and the hub. Figure 14-12 shows these operations pictorially, and can be summed up by saying that half duplex operation uses all four channels simultaneously, whilst full duplex uses two channels in each direction.

Link Status Control (as we discussed in the previous section) always operates in Full Duplex mode. Thus, if an end node receives the pattern 1-2 (Incoming Data Packet), then it is being instructed to cease transmission of control tones on channels 2 and 3, and to prepare to receive data. Equally, if a hub were to receive the pattern 1-2, or 2-1, then the attached end node is requesting permission to transmit either Normal or High priority data. Finally, if either an end node or a hub receives the pattern 2-2, then Link Training is being requested.

14.6 Medium Dependent Interface (MDI)

Just as in the more familiar technologies of 10Base-X and 100Base-X, etc., the Medium Dependent Interface in the 100VG-AnyLAN environment is that which links our device (end node or repeater) to the physical medium itself. As a result, there is a natural interdependency between the PMD and the MDI, in that they must both support the same link medium, and of course be compatible in every other way. Presently, only 4 pair Unshielded Twisted Pair media is supported, using the RJ45 connector as the MDI. Pin assignments for the connector are as recommended by the EIA/TIA 568B specification, which was described in section 14.1.2. A comparison of these pin assignments with those of other technologies is also listed in table 14-2, in that section.

As we have already said, future implementations may well allow both 2 pair Shielded and Unshielded Twisted Pair, and also Fiber Optic. These future implementations currently remain unratified, and are therefore beyond the scope of this edition.

14.7 Security

Certainly, one overriding concern of any serious Network Manager is that of security. Today security breaches are serious, and malicious attacks come not just from the Internet, but also from within. Software that can eavesdrop on networks is readily available, and at modest cost. Equally, the average user is now more computer literate than ever before, and can appreciate the wealth of knowledge that flows past his machine each and every second. Gone are the days when the only way to tap this fountain was with expensive test equipment, and a computer science degree to understand what was there. Today, the software will do the decoding work for you, and filter out all except that which is most precious.

Security, then, is an issue. Certainly in *shared* Ethernet environments all stations will listen to the network at all times, since that is a fundamental requirement. Even in Token Ring and FDDI networks data must pass through each and every station as it travels around the ring - again, purely because that is the way that it works. In 100VG-AnyLAN networks though, this is most certainly not the case.

100VG-AnyLAN has security built-in at its very core. Only those station(s) that should receive incoming data actually do. Recall that once the hub has chosen the port to transmit, it sends it a *grant* signal, and all others an *incoming* signal. The chosen port now transmits, and the destination address is decoded by the hub. Now, only the correct destination port(s) are passed the data, while all others receive an *idle*. True, each port could be configured in *promiscuous* mode and thereby breach security. However, what must be seen is the fact that 100VG-AnyLAN goes much further to address the security issue than any other technology.

14.8 Future Enhancements to 802.12

Several enhancement requests have been put before the 802.12 committee for review. In fact, in July 1995, four major enhancements were suggested. As yet none have been ratified, but in this section we shall briefly discuss them in order to give as complete coverage of the technology as possible.

14.8.1 Full Duplex Demand Priority

The desire to connect nodes in a point-to-point fashion and utilize mirrored links would naturally provide for faster links. In theory this is extremely easy to achieve since 100VG-AnyLAN node-to-node connections rely upon *Link Training* to ready the link. In essence then, by utilizing additional bits within the *Required Configuration* field, a node could advertise the fact that full duplex operation was available.

14.8.2 High Speed Demand Priority

With the thirst for greater bandwidths at end stations and servers comes the need for higher performance backbones. The High Speed Demand Priority proposal addresses this issue and is designed to provide overall increases in network performance. Currently under investigation are proposals that include 400Mbps, 1Gps, and even 4Gbps connections. Also, there are those that would like to see a *Burst* mode that would allow multiple frames to be transmitted during a single grant, up to a pre-defined time limit. If this were to become a reality, we would then see a technology that truly spanned the void between contention based Ethernet, and deterministic Token Ring networks.

Obviously much work is still required in these areas. Not least, are those parts that would mean modifications to the MAC and RMAC, and significant changes to the physical layer. Couple this with the fact that all technologies attempt to provide significant backward compatibility, and we can appreciate that this may take many years to come to fruition.

14.8.3 Redundant Link Support

Redundancy is certainly a non-standard option in most technologies. However, since the actual operation is internal to the device providing the redundant service, proprietary solutions are readily available. One recommendation before the 802.12 committee is to provide a standardized method of insuring against link and/or hub failure, through the use of multiple, redundant links. As with Full Duplex Operation, *Link Training* could be used to indicate that a secondary link was available, but which passed no data under normal conditions. Then, in the event of hub or link failure, the offending link (or that link connected to the failed hub) could be disabled, and the backup link brought on-line.

Obviously this level of resilience potentially requires multiple links and/or hubs, and therefore operational costs will rise accordingly. That said, where mission critical systems are involved, money becomes a secondary concern, outweighed totally by systems availability.

14.8.4 2-Pair Category 5 UTP PMD

As we discussed in previous sections, there is a definite move towards 2 pair operation. Certainly, one of the of the luxuries of the 100VG-AnyLAN technology is that it protects existing investments in cable plant, by allowing operation over Category 3 cables. This requires 4 pair operation in order to limit the channel bandwidth requirement, and therefore moving to 2 Pair operation will require cabling of a higher specification. As such, Category 5 is suggested, although implementation will require changes to both the PMD and MDI as we have already noted.

14.9 An Example of 100VG-AnyLAN Data Flow

Having now discussed the 100VG-AnyLAN technology in detail and introduced the basic methods of operation, it is useful to consider a complete example based upon a single hub with multiple attached end nodes. Figure 14-13 shows the example that we will use, and also a timeline diagram of how data is passed between two stations, A and B. Of course this example is kept simple purely for the sake of clarity, although, regardless of the topological complexity, the same principles will apply throughout.

In the figure, our four end nodes begin at time t_0 with no data to transmit. As a result they and the hub itself are all transmitting the *Idle* signal. As we move to time t_1, End Node A wishes to transmit data with a *Normal Priority*. Now this end node stops sending the *Idle* signal, and starts sending a *Normal Priority Request* instead.

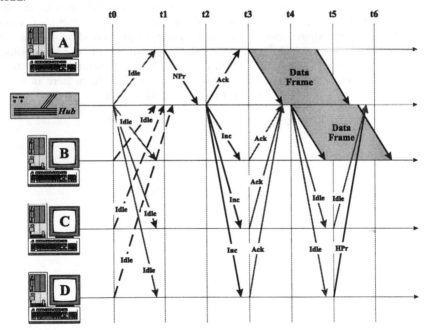

Figure 14-13: Example of Typical Data Flow in 100VG-AnyLAN Network

When our hub receives the *Normal Priority Request*, it will check its internal tables to ensure that End Node A is either next to transmit, or indeed is the only end node requesting transmission. In either case, the hub now sends an Acknowledgment to End Node A, and then readies the other stations by sending them an *Incoming* signal, shown at time t$_2$. End Nodes B, C, and D now acknowledge the *Incoming* signal by ceasing to transmit their *Idle* signals at time t$_3$, and End Node A commences transmission. By time t$_4$, the hub has decoded the *Destination Address* field of the incoming frame and found that it is directed to End Node B. The hub then recommences transmission of the *Idle* signal to nodes C and D, and forwards the frame to node B. Finally at time t$_5$, End Node D decides that it has data to transmit at a High priority. It therefore commences sending a *High Priority* request, thus reserving the transmission channel as soon as it becomes available.

14.10 Summary

100VG-AnyLAN is arguably the better 100Mbps solution when compared to say 100Base-X. Its deterministic nature allows it, at least in theory, to handle more than just data. Certainly, since there are no collisions, 100Mbps is actually achievable. Also, the advantage of using existing (low specification) cable plant is attractive, and security (particularly when compared to Ethernet) is built-in. Finally, integration with other technologies such as Token Ring means that networks employing multiple topologies can be easily integrated.

Typical future applications might include Multimedia applications such as video conferencing to the desktop, video on demand, and the transmission of high definition graphics. The major down sides however, are that smooth transition from legacy 10Mbps technologies is more difficult, and of course that means higher costs with less immediate return. Possibly more important though, the single largest drawback to 100VG-AnyLAN is that regardless of the technological improvements, marketing and fear of untried technology has meant fewer sales and therefore a weaker overall position. In real terms what we have here is a legacy technology that will almost certainly not be developed further.

Bridges and Switches

Most networks today undergo steady, yet almost imperceptible, extension. New users are added and with them servers. Simple, inexpensive, network interfaces can be added to our personal computers and laptops allowing connection to the corporate network, and remote access devices are installed for people on the move. With today's applications, networks carry an increasing amount of data. Indeed, in some cases this sheer volume exceeds the design criteria by orders of magnitude that would stagger the original architects, and leads to the increasing frustration of network users. Undeniably, it is technology that provides faster, better equipped devices with more functionality. But in truth it can be these very devices that cause congestion, create bottlenecks, or simply move these blockages around. As we saw in chapter 8, simple Repeaters and Hubs are used to add stations and increase distance. Ethernet however is non-deterministic in nature, in that we cannot accurately predict performance based on number of users. Therefore, adding stations to satisfy user demands may simply compound the problem. At some point, the network must be closely examined and, where necessary, overhauled to ensure optimum performance at all levels. After all, when purchasing a vehicle does anyone really expect it to run for ever without any thoughts of servicing?

So then, what is the answer? Obviously we need to provide increased bandwidth to cope with the quantities of data that must be moved, but here we have two problems. Firstly, we must wait for technology to provide the bandwidth that we require, and secondly, such technology is not without price. For example, taking our network from 10Mbps to 100Mbps may well require that our premises be re-cabled - and at not insignificant cost. Equally, the next step up the bandwidth ladder to Gigabit could well require further expense in cable plant - all this, and we still have no means of using our expensive infrastructure to carry information without first converting our end systems! What we need then is a method of isolating areas of high utilization, so that segments of our network only carry the data required by their associated end stations. Bridges, Switches and Routers are devices that achieve just this. Bridging, or more specifically Transparent Bridging as it is called in an Ethernet/802.3 environment, is discussed in this chapter along with Switching. Routing (or Internetworking as it is often called), being common to all technologies, is discussed separately in Section F.

15.1 Why Bridge or Switch?

In order to answer this simple question, we need to understand exactly what these devices do, and indeed the differences between them. We know that repeaters or hubs allow us to add stations and extend the network, but these also compound the problems associated with *shared* media. Repeaters are also OSI layer one devices, meaning that they have no concept of networks, but blindly *repeat* data as it arrives. Bridges, on the other hand, are more intelligent. These devices operate at the OSI Data Link layer (layer 2) and are even sometimes referred to as MAC layer bridges. This extra intelligence brings extra functionality, which in turn leads to potential improvements being made to our network traffic. Figure 15-1 shows the required layer implementation for these devices, and although a full stack is shown, layers 3 and above are required only where management protocols are implemented.

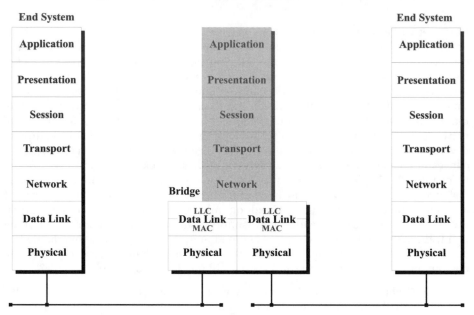

Figure 15-1:   Required Layer Implementation - Bridges

The extra intelligence that these devices have means that they can understand the structure of the MAC frame, including the maximum and minimum frame sizes, addressing, and the structure of the Frame Check Sequence. Also, bridges are often referred to as being Store and Forward devices, in that they will accept a frame through a port, which will then be buffered before making a decision as to how it should be handled. For example, if the frame is too long or too short, then it can be dropped rather than forwarded. Equally, if bridge calculates a different FCS to that provided in the frame, then again the frame would be dropped since it would be deemed to be corrupt. Most importantly though, bridges are aware of which end stations reside on the segments attached to their various ports, since they see the traffic as it passes, and read the Source and Destination MAC addresses that the frames contain. Armed with this knowledge, they can now decide whether to pass (*forward*) the frame, and also to which port(s).

Bridges, when used in Ethernet/802.3 environments, are also referred to as *Transparent* in that end stations neither have, nor need, any knowledge of their presence. Bridges also *learn* where the end stations are located automatically, thus making them *Plug and Play*. Indeed, the entire process of forwarding frames in this way is both efficient, and glamorous in its simplicity, especially when compared with their *Source Routing* counterparts in the Token Ring and FDDI worlds.

Finally, since bridges are Data Link layer devices, each port has to adhere to the rules of the CSMA/CD access protocol, and therefore each port resides in its own collision domain. In addition, bridges are protocol independent and can work with any combination of upper layer protocols (TCP/IP, IPX, DECnet, AppleTalk, etc.). Also, bridge learning logic is independent of the media transmission system used (Ethernet, 802.3, 802.3 with 802.2, or 802.3 with 802.2 and SNAP). Thus, where there is a mixture of stations on a network, the bridge is able to handle all frame types without the need for reconfiguration.

15.1.1 Bridges Vs Switches

So, now we understand a little more about bridges and what they can do, what is the difference between a Bridge and a Switch? The answer here, is essentially very little. In simple terms, Switches can do anything that Bridges can do - only switches do it faster. Typically, switches operate at (or near) *wire speed*, which means that they can process frames at the same speed that they arrive. Latency is therefore reduced, and our network should run faster.

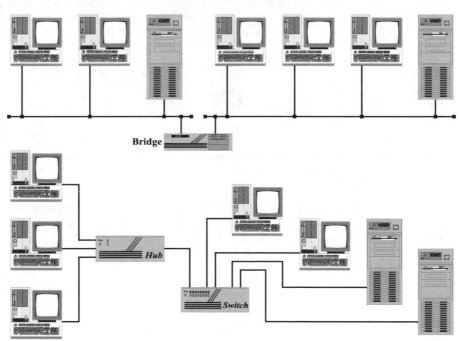

Figure 15-2: Bridge/Switch Comparison

Switches also tend to be used more to connect end systems rather than LANs, and they therefore tend to have far higher port densities than bridges. This does not have to be the case though, and depends on the size of address space that each switch port supports. In addition, Switches also support what have become known as *Virtual LANs* or VLANs[1] where stations can be grouped together into logically separate groups. In this way, broadcast traffic can be reduced, and security policies can be implemented between stations regardless of which ports they are connected to. This therefore makes the switch an incredibly versatile device. Figure 15-2 shows a simple distinction between bridges and switches, and figure 15-3 shows a simple VLAN implementation.

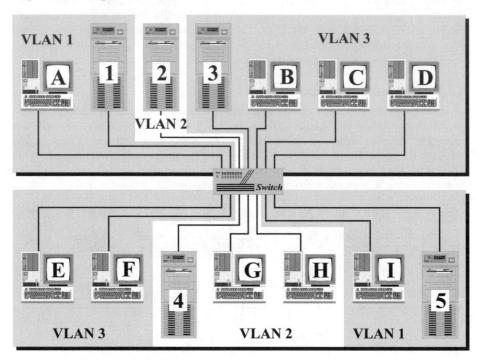

Figure 15-3:   Simple VLAN Implementation

From figure 15-3, we see that we have three specific groups of stations (VLANs) with stations A and I, and servers 1 and 5 residing in VLAN 1. We then have a second VLAN comprising stations G and H and servers 2 and 4. Finally, we have VLAN 3 which is made up of stations B, C, D, E, and F, and server 3.

Finally, before leaving this brief overview of Bridge/Switch differences, it must be pointed out that there are two major classes of switch, namely *Store and Forward*, and *Cut Through*. The basic principles of operation remain the same, although the timing of when a frame is actually forwarded differs. The differences between these two switch types are important and will therefore be discussed in Section 15.5.

[1] VLANs are important and can be complex. These will be discussed in detail in section 15.6.

15.2 Bridge/Switch Applications

We have already briefly touched on how Bridges and Switches can be used to improve our network. We have also summarized the differences between bridges and switches, and looked at the application of VLANs. Now, we should take a more detailed look at bridge/switch applications, and discuss exactly where these devices can be deployed. Certainly, it should be possible to use a Bridge or Switch in place of any Repeater in a network, although in truth this will not provide a guaranteed improvement. Indeed, it is possible that blindly placing these devices throughout a network can decrease overall performance rather than provide us with any return on our investment. The following sections therefore outline some of these applications, and also serve to show where devices such as these can improve overall network performance.

15.2.1 Isolating Areas of High Utilization

In general, bridges pass only those frames that are required. Thus, it follows that they are ideal devices to use where we wish to isolate areas of high utilization. Figure 15-4 shows a typical network where we have four LANs with widely varying traffic levels. Here, by installing bridges, we can provide improved overall throughput by isolating those areas with the highest traffic levels.

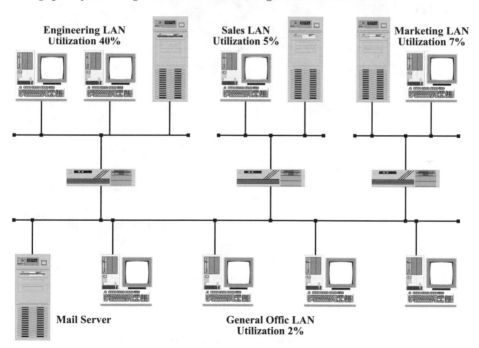

Figure 15-4:   Using Bridges/Switches to Isolate Areas of High Utilization

In our example, we have four distinct *shared media* LANs. The Engineering department has its own server, as indeed do all of the others. The Engineering LAN however suffers from extremely high utilization (40%) which implies that overall network performance will be poor. The Sales and Marketing departments do not suffer from excessive traffic in the same way, and it is important that these networks do not become *polluted* with unwanted traffic from the Engineering LAN. The General Office LAN has an average utilization of just 2%, so performance should be very good. The mail that resides on this LAN will of course be used by all departments. Thus, all users will need to access the Mail Server on the General Office LAN, on an as-needed basis. Our bridges will therefore isolate the LANs from unwanted traffic, yet allow traffic to pass when required.

One important consideration when designing networks that incorporate bridges in this way, is their placement. For example, if our Mail Server was also the main file server for the Sales personnel, then virtually all traffic from the Sales LAN could appear on the General Office LAN. In this case, the bridges (as opposed to switches) between the Sales and Marketing LANs, and the General Office LAN would be providing little in the way of traffic isolation, and could actually perform worse than a repeater due to inherent latencies.

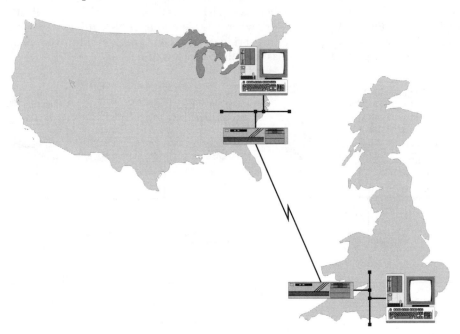

Figure 15-5:   Linking LANs Over Large Geographic Distance

15.2.2   Linking Geographically Distant LANs

As we saw in the previous example, a bridge or switch is selective as to what data it actually passes. We have seen that this works to our advantage where we wish to isolate areas of high utilization, but what of the case where we need to link LANs over large geographic distances? If we were to take an example of two LANs in say, New York and London, our choices as to the speed of link that could be employed will almost certainly be governed by cost.

Bridges and Switches

It would be impractical in all but a few cases to attempt to link these at the same speed as the LAN, and indeed it would almost certainly be undesirable to link the two such that all data from one LAN appears on the other. Thus, since our bridge forwards only those frames that are needed, the actual WAN link can be many times slower than the LANs that it connects. Figure 15-5 shows such an example.

In this case, our 10 or 100Mbps Ethernets on either side of the Atlantic are joined by say a 64kbps WAN link, allowing London and New York to communicate and transfer data as required. Obviously any transatlantic data will be slower, and therefore a client station in London connecting to a server in New York will experience significantly reduced performance. But, the point is that we can transfer data when required. The bandwidth requirements of the link are then governed by the actual amounts of data that are to be transferred, and possibly budgetary constraints since WAN costs are ongoing.

15.2.3   Creating Secure Environments

Bridges and Switches use what are referred to as *Filter Tables* to hold information about which station(s) reside on which ports. This information is based upon MAC addresses, and therefore allows the bridge/switch to make their forwarding decisions. Bridges and Switches actually learn this information dynamically, although most devices also allow this information to be added and changed manually. It therefore follows that if we can manipulate the filter table in this way, we can create secure environments.

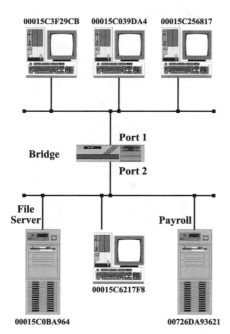

Bridge Filter Table

MAC Address	Action Port 1	Port 2
00015C3F29CB	Discard	Forward
00015C039DA4	Discard	Forward
00015C256817	Discard	Forward
00015C0BA964	Forward	Discard
00015C6217F8	Forward	Discard
00726DA93621	Discard	Discard

Figure 15-6: Creating Secure Environments

The filter table itself tells the Bridge/Switch how to handle frames as they arrive on each port. For example, a frame arriving on port 1 with a Destination Address of 00-01-5C-3F-29-CB would not need to be forwarded since that device resides on the same port. In figure 15-6, we see a network that comprises several stations and two servers. Under *normal* circumstances, the filter table entry for the Payroll server would reflect *Forward* on port 1, and *Discard* on port 2. By modifying the entry to *Discard/Discard* however, we will stop any of the three stations on the upper LAN from accessing the server.

Obviously, creating a secure environment based on MAC addresses does require a high degree of administration, and for this reason it is not common to see frames filtered in this way. For example, if the network interface card fails in the Payroll server, it means that we have to reprogram the filter table. It does however provide one of the most secure systems, since it is very difficult to spoof MAC addresses, and therefore our servers will remain relatively free from attack.

15.2.4 Constructing Resilient Networks

Generally speaking, networks provide few guarantees regarding the delivery of data, and no problem is bigger than where we experience device or link failure. When we discussed Ethernet/802.3 Repeaters we said that placing these in parallel as

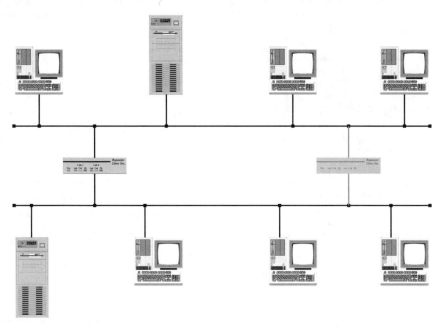

Figure 15-7: Repeaters in Parallel

shown in figure 15-7 was prohibited. A degree of resilience is normally possible in the case of link failure, but this is by the implementation of proprietary methodologies. In any event, using these devices to provide additional bandwidth is certainly out of the question.

So what of bridges, and do the same constraints that affect Repeater operation also apply to these devices? Here the answer is no, since a standardized method, known simply as the Spanning Tree Protocol (STP),[2] exists for providing redundant paths that join LANs. The protocol, which is also known as IEEE 802.1D, provides an automatic reconfiguration mechanism which guarantees that where multiple possible paths exist, only a single path actually passes data. In addition, the protocol uses the *best cost* path in terms of link speed, blocking data from using those that are inferior. Redundancy is therefore ensured, and we are protected against device and link failure.

As a variant of this subject, it is worth noting that many vendors offer what is possibly best described as Parallel path bridging. In this case, multiple paths between the same source and destination LANs carry data simultaneously. This would then appear as shown in figure 15-8, and would seem to break our golden rule where the potential for frame duplication must be avoided at all cost. Here though, the vendor applies a proprietary management system that manages the link(s), and routes each frame down either one or other of the links. Frame duplication is therefore avoided, since the same frame will never be transported across all links at the same time.

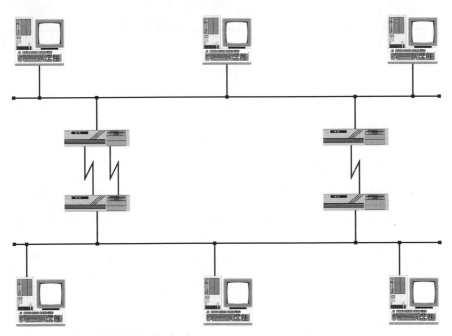

Figure 15-8: Parallel Bridging Example

Finally, we should mention that with today's wide variety of WAN technologies, we are now able to provide protection against link failure, and provide additional bandwidth on a demand basis. Figure 15-9 shows an example of this using a

[2] The Spanning Tree Protocol is discussed in section 15.4.

standard leased line of say 64kbps, which is then backed up through the ISDN network. The leased circuit is monitored by the bridge and, if it should fail, the ISDN circuit is dialed. When the leased circuit is restored, the ISDN link can then be dropped.

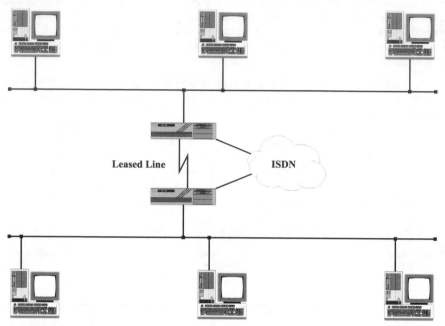

Figure 15-9: Link Backup and Bandwidth-on-Demand

In addition, the utilization of the leased circuit can be monitored, and when a pre-determined level has been exceeded, say during a file transfer, an ISDN circuit can be dialed. The extra bandwidth that this provides is then bound to the permanent link until such time as the utilization drops below another, lower, threshold. Now, since the additional bandwidth is no longer required, the ISDN link can be dropped, and the call charge stops.

This latter facility, known simply as *Bandwidth on Demand* (BonD, or BOD), is available on those devices that support the *Point-to-Point Protocol* (PPP) over their links. PPP[3] is a standard, Link Layer protocol that can be used to transport multiple upper layers, one of which is bridging. In addition, when run over multiple links, these can then be bound together using what is termed *Multi-Link PPP*, to form larger pipes and thereby provide this additional Bandwidth on Demand. Further discussion on PPP is beyond the scope of this text however, and the reader is urged to refer to the relevant standards documents or references from the bibliography.

---

[3] The development of PPP was overseen by the Internet Engineering Task Force and is standardized in a number of Request for Comments (RFCs). PPP is defined in RFC 1661, the Bridging Network Control Protocol (NCP) by RFC 1638, and Multi-Link PPP by RFC 1717.

15.2.5 Bridge/Switch Limitations

Bridges and Switches link *Collision Domains* together. Therefore, the CSMA/CD rules that relate to numbers of stations, repeaters, etc., can be extended. For example, we may already have four repeaters in our LAN, and need to increase this number further. By placing a bridge/switch in the network, we can now install four more repeaters.

We cannot continue this indefinitely though, and we are restricted to 8 collision domains within any network. This restriction is based upon round trip times, and basically implies that between any two stations, we cannot have more than 7 bridges/switches.

15.3 Bridge/Switch Method of Operation

Ethernet/802.3 are said to be broadcast networks, since all devices attached to a particular LAN segment receive all transmissions from all other stations. Bridges, at the simplest level, are merely stations that are attached to a network. Therefore they too will receive all frames that are sent, and indeed it is this very feature that enables transparent bridges to operate in the way that they do. In order to fully understand bridge operation, let us consider the Ethernet network shown in figure 15-10 which comprises two *shared* LANs joined by a Bridge.

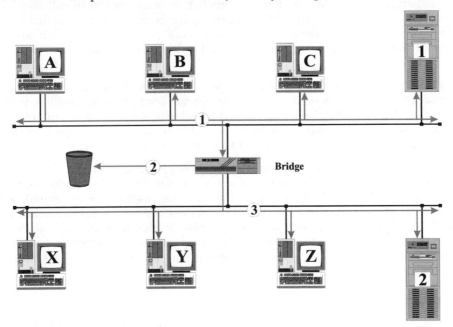

Figure 15-10: Basic Bridge/Switch Operation

In the figure, we assume that Client A sends a frame to Server 1 (Step 1 in the figure). Since this is a shared Ethernet LAN, Clients B and C will receive the frame but will discard it since the Destination MAC address is not recognized as their own. The Server (Server 1) will receive the frame and, since the Destination Address will be recognized, processes the frame further, checking that it is between 64 and 1518 octets and that the Frame Check Sequence (FCS) is correct. Assuming this to be the case, the server then processes the data. The Bridge also receives the frame and, assuming that the length is within the allowable limits, recalculates the FCS. In the event that the frame is too short, too long, or that the FCS is invalid, the frame is discarded immediately (Step 2 in the figure) on the grounds that there is little point in forwarding an invalid frame.

The bridge next consults the *Filter Table* that it maintains, telling it how it should handle the frame, and then takes that action. If the Filter table indicates that the frame should be discarded (As in step 2 in the figure), then this will be due either to the fact that the destination station resides on the same port over which the frame was received, or alternatively because some administratively assigned filtering has been applied.

From the discussion so far, clearly bridges need to have information about end station locations. So what would happen if a frame arrives at a port and the bridge has no information about the destination? Let us now assume then that the bridge has no information about Server 1 (i.e., the MAC Address of Server 1 is not in the filter table), but Client A wishes to communicate with it. Client A transmits its frame and again all stations on the upper LAN will receive it, as will the bridge. In this case though, the bridge will have no explicit information and so will *play safe* and forward the frame anyway (Step 3 in the figure) resulting in a frame that is **not** required being copied to the lower LAN. In general bridges will, by default, always forward frames to unknown destinations, and will always forward broadcasts and multicasts.

Finally, let us consider what will happen if Client A wished to converse with Server 2. In this case, assuming that the bridge has destination information, it will legitimately forward the frame. Equally, if we were to assume that it did not have the address of Server 2 stored, the bridge would forward the frame regardless (Step 3 in the figure), but in this case it would have been required anyway.

Obviously, bridge administration, even in a simple installation, would be a full time task if we needed to pre-program our units with every MAC address on our network. Particularly if we consider the way that workers move around, and especially when we consider that the MAC address of a device is hard-coded into the Network Interface at manufacture. In order to eliminate this administrative need then, bridges of this type generally *Learn* the addresses of attached stations by examining the Source Address field of frames as they arrive. From this information, we can then determine the port to which that station is attached.

15.3.1 The Filter Table

The filter table itself is essentially a list of which MAC address(es) reside on which ports, and therefore the actions that should be taken when a frame arrives with that address as the Destination. For example if we have a four port bridge with hosts distributed as shown in figure 15-11, then the actions would be as shown in table 15-1.

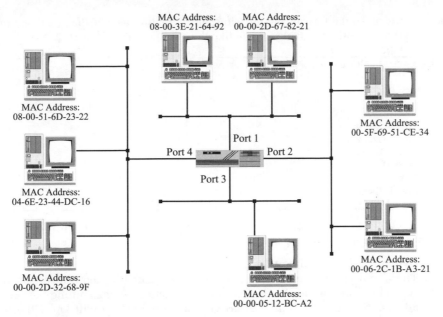

MAC Address:
08-00-3E-21-64-92

MAC Address:
00-00-2D-67-82-21

MAC Address:
08-00-51-6D-23-22

MAC Address:
04-6E-23-44-DC-16

MAC Address:
00-00-2D-32-68-9F

MAC Address:
00-5F-69-51-CE-34

MAC Address:
00-06-2C-1B-A3-21

MAC Address:
00-00-05-12-BC-A2

Port 1
Port 4
Port 2
Port 3

Figure 15-11: Simple Bridge Filtering Example

Table 15-1: Simple Bridge Filter Table

MAC Address	Action Port 1	Action Port 2	Action Port 3	Action Port 4
00002D678221	**Discard All**	Forward Po 1	Forward Po 1	Forward Po 1
005F6951CE34	Forward Po 2	**Discard All**	Forward Po 2	Forward Po 2
0800516D2322	Forward Po 4	Forward Po 4	Forward Po 4	**Discard All**
08003E216492	**Discard All**	Forward Po 1	Forward Po 1	Forward Po 1
00062C1BA321	Forward Po 2	**Discard All**	Forward Po 2	Forward Po 2
00000512BCA2	Forward Po 3	Forward Po 3	**Discard All**	Forward Po 3
00002D32689F	Forward Po 4	Forward Po 4	Forward Po 4	**Discard All**
046E2344DC16	Forward Po 4	Forward Po 4	Forward Po 4	**Discard All**
FFFFFFFFFFFF	Forward All	Forward All	Forward All	Forward All

For example, if a frame arrives on port 1 with a destination address of say 00-00-2D-67-82-21, this frame should be discarded since that device resides on the same port. If this frame were to arrive on say port 3 though, then it should be forwarded to port 1. Notice that our filter table includes an entry for the broadcast address FF-FF-FF-FF-FF-FF, and also the ports through which these frames will be forwarded. Obviously if we have a frame destined for all devices (broadcast), then this frame must be propagated throughout our entire network. Equally, multicasts (which are unlikely to be known to our bridge) must also be forwarded, so we would probably also see these addresses in the filter table of a real bridge.

While it is common practice for vendors to display the filter table as shown in table 15-1, at the simplest level the only information that needs to be held is the address and the port on which frames from that station are received. In that way, we can still make the forwarding decision, but the table takes up far less memory. This can then simplify our table to look like the one shown in table 15-2.

Table 15-2: Simplified Bridge Filter Table

MAC Address	Port
00002D678221	1
005F6951CE34	2
0800516D2322	4
08003E216492	1
00062C1BA321	2
00000512BCA2	3
00002D32689F	4
046E2344DC16	4

Filter Table entries themselves take several forms. In particular, we should consider the following four types:

- **Dynamic (or Learned) Entries**

  These entries are Source Addresses that are learned by the bridge. Bridges typically learn the relative locations of end stations by examining the source address field of frames as they arrive. Since the bridge will know the port through which the frame arrived, it will now know what actions to take when a frame arrives with this address as the destination.

  These entries are said to be dynamic since they do not need to be pre-programmed. Equally, it is clear from our previous discussions that, in order to function optimally, bridges and switches need to know the locations of every end system. Thus, in an effort to ensure that the device always works with the best, most up-to-date information, these entries are typically aged out over a 5 minute (300 second) period. Entries that are older than this and have not been used within the *Discard* timer period, are then deleted.

- **Static Entries**

  Unlike their dynamic counterparts, Static entries are permanently assigned in the Filter Table and are therefore never aged out. These entries include certain reserved addresses, the MAC addresses of the bridge/switch own ports, and also any source or custom entries that may have been administratively applied.

  Typical *Reserved* addresses include (but are not limited to) those specified by the 802.1D standard. Here, frames that contain the addresses shown in table 15-3 as the destination address, must be never be forwarded. The bridge may however use the information contained in the frame to create its own frames, as would be the case for the 802.1D Spanning Tree Algorithm.[4]

  Bridges and switches are assigned a number of MAC addresses - one for each port. Frames received by the device that are addressed to itself (i.e. via one of its own MAC addresses) obviously need not be forwarded. Thus, it is also

---

[4] The Spanning Tree Protocol or Algorithm will be discussed in detail in section 15.4.

Bridges and Switches

common practice to include these addresses (with an action of discard) as Static entries.

Table 15-3: Reserved Multicast Addresses	
Destination Address	Description
01-80-C2-00-00-00	Reserved for IEEE 802.1D Spanning Tree Protocol
01-80-C2-00-00-01	Reserved for IEEE 802.3y Full Duplex Pause Function[5]
01-80-C2-00-00-02 to 01-80-C2-00-00-0F	Reserved for IEEE 802.1 Committee Future Use.

Finally, custom entries are used to enforce traffic policy, and thus control over the network. For example, if in figure 15-10 we wished to stop station A accessing Server 2, we might apply a filter that forced any frame with a destination MAC address of station A to be discarded if it were to arrive at port 2.

- **Source Entries**
  Typically bridges make their forwarding decisions based upon the Destination address of the frame. Most bridges however, also allow us to filter based upon the Source address, thereby expanding the bridge capabilities further. These entries are generally termed Source filters or source entries, and are typically used where we wish to customize or control access through our network. Addresses of this type are normally manually entered, and are therefore treated as static entries in that they are never aged out.

- **Custom Entries**
  The previous points have already touched upon the subject of custom entries in the sense of both Static and Source filters. Customization however goes much further. Bridges and switches, as we have already discussed, make decisions after first buffering the frame.[6] Therefore since the entire frame has been received, we can make a filtering decision based upon any element of the frame, be it an address, a protocol type, or indeed some bit pattern buried deep within the frame.

  The implementation of this type of filter tends to be very vendor specific, although it is true to say that most will offer some measure of this in their products today. Once again, since these entries are entered manually, they become static entries, which are not aged. For a full discussion of this type of feature, see section 15.2, Bridge Applications.

From our discussions above, it is clear that the filter table itself comprises several, potentially overlapping, sections. Figure 15-12 shows this interaction, and shows that Source and Custom filters are always static, while Destination filters may be either learned or static. Obviously, some of this can be considered to be implementation specific, since it is not a requirement to implement custom

---

[5] The Pause function is discussed in chapter 12.
[6] This is not true of Cut Through switches which are discussed in section 15.5.

filtering. However, most vendors do provide some means of manually administrating the filtering task.

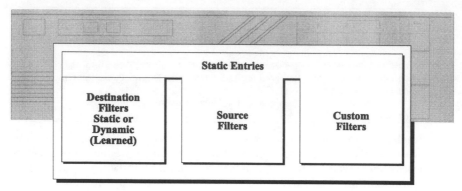

Figure 15-12: Bridge/Switch Filters

15.3.2 Bridge/Switch Address Learning

Bridges and Switches will normally learn about attached devices by default, although in most cases this can be disabled on a per-port basis. Typically, the only reason why anyone would wish to disable learning is where the device is being used to provide some measure of security, and where a number of custom filters have been previously defined. Such devices will then normally forward frames to certain pre-defined locations, and discard all other traffic.

The bridge/switch learns which stations are where, by examining frames as they arrive. Since the frame will contain the source address of the station, the bridge/switch will now know to which port that station is connected. Hence, the device will *learn* where stations are.

15.3.3 Protocol Prioritization

Although not part of any bridging standard, most vendors today offer levels of prioritization for bridged traffic. Bridges (as opposed to switches) typically have a number of output queues on which frames are placed for forwarding, and these queues will then generally have a priority associated with them. The priorities are normally High, Medium, and Low, and a forwarding algorithm is applied during the forwarding process.

The actual algorithms themselves are very much implementation specific, but a simple example might be to take say three frames from the High priority queue, two from the Medium priority queue and one from the low priority queue. Alternatively, the High priority queue might be cleared before the Medium priority queue, which is then cleared before the Low priority queue. In any event, traffic is prioritized, although the criteria are also vendor specific. For example, traffic is generally prioritized by protocol type, with frames being identified by the EtherType field as shown in figure 15-13. This then raises a problem in that 802.3 frames (since they do not carry a Protocol ID directly) cannot be treated in this way.

Vendors implementing prioritization in this way therefore normally allow Ethernet frames to be prioritized by protocol type, while 802.3 frames have to be treated with the same priority.

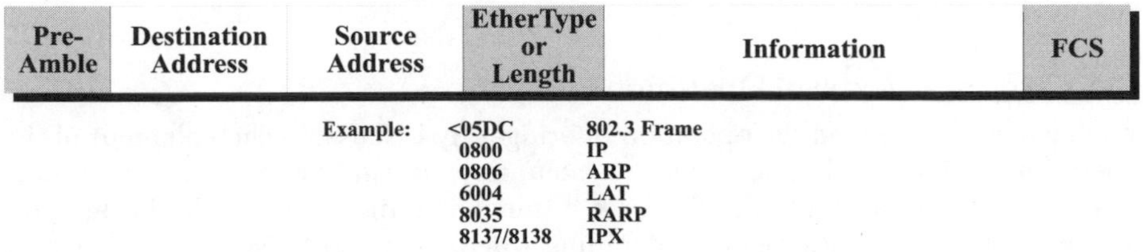

Pre-Amble	Destination Address	Source Address	EtherType or Length	Information	FCS

		Example:	<05DC	802.3 Frame
			0800	IP
			0806	ARP
			6004	LAT
			8035	RARP
			8137/8138	IPX

Figure 15-13: Ethernet/IEEE 802.3 Frame Types

In addition to the type of protocol prioritization detailed above, many vendors also allow bridged traffic to be discarded by protocol type. As such, should we wish to discard all IPX traffic carried in say Ethernet frames, we can do this by applying a single protocol filter. Our bridge configuration may then be as shown in table 15-4.

Table 15-4: Sample Protocol Priorities

Protocol Name	EtherType	Priority
DEFAULT	-	Medium
LAT	6004	High
IP	0800	Medium
IPX	8137	Discard

15.3.4 Frame Ordering

As we have seen, bridges and switches operate at the MAC layer. As a result, since this layer provides no sequencing information, it is imperative that these devices relay information in exactly the same order as it is received. True, unordered information is no problem to some protocols, but others such as LAT rely on information being received at the destination in the same order that it was transmitted. There can therefore be no compromise to the basic premise that data is always passed based on the first-in, first-out (FIFO) principle.

15.3.5 Transit Delays

In order to guarantee the correct operation of upper layer protocols, it is necessary to limit the transit delay experienced by frames as they pass through bridges and switches. Here though, we have two problems. Firstly, MAC frames do not contain any information that indicates the accumulated delay so far, and secondly we cannot accurately determine the additional delays that will be introduced in processing the frame by the bridge. In order to ensure that the overall transit delays experienced are not exceeded, and that the maximum frame lifetime is enforced, it may be necessary for the bridge to discard frames where they cannot be processed within a specified time frame.

The actual value of this time, known as the *Maximum Bridge Transit Delay*, is based on the maximum delays imposed by all bridges in the network and on the required maximum frame lifetime. The IEEE 802.1D standard recommends that this value should be set at 1 second, and that the absolute maximum value should not exceed 4 seconds.

15.3.6 Bridge Model of Operation

We have now examined the operation of bridges by discussing each element of their operation. Putting this together, we can now create the model of operation described by figure 15-14. Here we see a frame arriving at one of the bridge ports, followed by each major process in deciding whether this frame should be forwarded

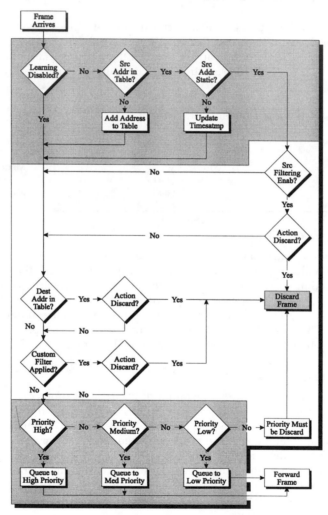

Figure 15-14: Bridge Basic Model of Operation

or not. The top section of the figure deals with the learning process, and how, when enabled, the source address is either added to the filter table or the timestamp is refreshed to ensure that the entry is not timed out. Of course, since the whole frame will have been received before any filtering decisions are taken, should the frame be invalid (too short, too long, invalid FCS, etc.) it will be discarded immediately. No indication that the discard has taken place will be passed to the source station, which will rely on the upper layers (e.g., the Transport Layer) to detect that this discard has taken place.

The center section deals with the filtering decision process, based on the Source and/or Destination address and any custom filters that may be employed to enforce traffic policies. Finally, the bottom section deals with the prioritization of traffic as it is passed to the forwarding process. Here, this example assumes 3 output queues, and also allows traffic to be discarded based upon the EtherType of the frame.

15.4 IEEE 802.1D Spanning Tree Protocol and Algorithm

In section 15.2.4 we mentioned that it was possible to create resilient networks by using bridges (or switches) running the *Spanning Tree Protocol* (STP). For example, if we consider the network topology shown in figure 15-15, we see that there are potentially three data loops. Spanning Tree is then used to *automatically* configure the bridges such that only one path exists between any two LAN segments. Hence, one of Bridges A and B, and one of Bridges C and D will block user data, leaving just one path open. In fact, we can summarize the operation of the Spanning Tree Protocol as follows:

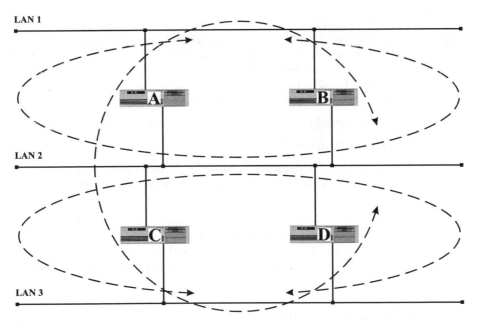

Figure 15-15: Resilient Network Without Spanning Tree

- Spanning Tree will configure the *active* topology of a bridged (switched) LAN such that there is no more than one route between any two end stations. Loops are therefore eliminated and frame multiplication is avoided.

- Spanning Tree provides for fault tolerance through the automatic re-configuration of the topology as a result of bridge (switch), or link failure.

- The entire topology will stabilize in *any* sized bridged (switched) network within a short, calculable, time period.

- The resultant *active* topology will be predictable and reproducible. In addition, the topology may be selected through certain, modifiable, management parameters.

- The operation of the protocol and algorithm is transparent to end stations, and the network bandwidth consumed by the operation of the protocol is a small percentage of that available overall.

15.4.1 Bridge/Switch Port States

As we have seen from the previous discussion, bridge (switch) ports need to be *turned-off* by the Spanning Tree algorithm if we are to ensure a *loop-free* topology within our network. Ports that do not pass user data are said to be in a *Blocking* state although in practice there are many states that port can be in. Listed below are those states and the action(s) that are taken when the port is in that state. In the next section, we will then discuss the operation Spanning Tree itself and how these states are entered and exited.

- **Blocking**
  In this state, a port does not forward any *user* frames, thereby preventing frame duplication. Bridge Protocol Data Units (BPDUs) that are used to convey Spanning Tree information are received are processed, however all other received frames are discarded. In addition, the *Learning* process does not add station location information to the *Filtering* database. Ports enter this state whenever any of the following are true:

  - The bridge (switch) is initialized.

  - The port is initially enabled.

  - The port receives information that indicates that another bridge (switch) is the *Designated Bridge* for the LAN to which the port is attached.

- **Listening**
  This state is only ever entered from the *Blocking* state, and only where the algorithm has determined that the port should prepare to participate in the forwarding process. In this state, the port will not pass any *user* data, but will process BPDUs. In this state, no station location information is added to the filtering database.

- **Learning**
  In the Learning state, the port is still preparing to participate in the forwarding process. The port still discards received data frames, still acts

upon BPDUs that are received, but here will also add station location information. In this way, when the port enters the *Forwarding* state, it will do so with at least rudimentary filtering information.

- **Forwarding**

  In the Forwarding state the port is fully participating in the process of forwarding data frames. In this state, the port will forward data frames that are received, it will act upon received BPDUs, and will add station location information to the filtering database. This state is only ever entered from the *Learning* state.

- **Disabled**

  This state can only be entered through management. In this state, the port does not participate in *any* bridge forwarding, or learning, and it ignores all received BPDUs.

15.4.2 Spanning Tree Operation

In order to better understand the operation of the protocol and algorithm, it is useful to consider a specific example such as that shown in figure 15-16. Although this is a relatively simple example, and relies on *shared* Ethernet segments joined by bridges, it is equally applicable to switched point-to-point segments. In addition, it is complex enough to show each of the elements of the algorithm itself without over complication, and will therefore suffice for our discussions below.

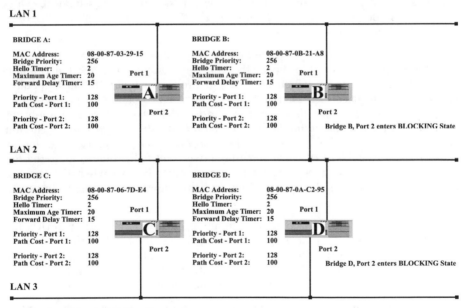

Figure 15-16: Spanning Tree Parameters

You will notice that each bridge has associated with it a number of parameters. It is the exchange of these, via the Spanning Tree Protocol, that enables the algorithm to construct a loop free topology. This information is transferred through two types of Bridge Protocol Data Units (BPDUs) namely *Configuration* BPDUs, and *Topology Change Notification* BPDUs. The format of these BPDUs are shown in figure 15-17. The *Configuration BPDU* is used by bridges to advertise their Spanning Tree parameters, and the *Topology Change Notification BPDU* is used by bridges to notify others that a topology change has been detected. These BPDUs are then discussed together with the protocol and algorithm below.

Protocol Identifier (2)	Vers (1)	BPDU Type (1)	Flags (1)	Root Identifier (8)	Root Path Cost (4)	Bridge Identifier (8)	Port ID (2)	Msg Age (2)	Max Age (2)	Hello Time (2)	Fwd Delay (2)

Configuration BPDU

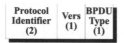

Topology Change Notification BPDU

Figure 15-17: Bridge Protocol Data Units (BPDUs)

The two octet *Protocol Identifier* field is always set to all zeroes for both formats., as is the one octet *Version* field. The *BPDU Type* field (one octet) assumes the value of all zeroes (00000000) for *Configuration BPDUs* and **10000000** for *Topology Change Notification BPDUs*.

The remaining fields are applicable to only *Configuration BPDUs* as follows: The one octet *Flags* field is used to encode the *Topology Change Flag*, and the *Topology Change Acknowledgment*, which are used to propagate the fact that a topology change is taking place (see section 15.4.4). The eight octet *Root Identifier*, and *Bridge Identifier*, carry the Ids of the *Root Bridge* (discussed later), and the bridge responsible for the transmission of this *Configuration BPDU* respectively. The four octet *Root Path Cost* is the *Accumulated Path Cost* between the Root Bridge, and the bridge transmitting the BPDU. The remaining two octet fields then contain the *Port Identifier*, and various timers that relate to how ports behave when the topology changes. The *Port ID* is discussed below, and the timers are discussed in section 15.4.4.

In operation, bridges will communicate amongst themselves using BPDUs that are sent to the reserved *multicast* address 01-80-C2-00-00-00. The bridges then use this address as the Destination Address, and the address of the bridge port as the Source Address. The frame format itself is IEEE 802.3 with IEEE 802.2 (LLC),[7] and uses DSAP and SSAP addresses of 42 (IEEE Management).

Initially, if we imagine that all of the bridges in our example are turned on simultaneously, each bridge will transmit *Configuration* BPDUs through each of its ports. At this time no user data is forwarded, and our network will be flooded with

---

[7] See section E for a complete discussion of IEEE 802.2 (LLC).

these management frames. Naturally, each device will receive the Configuration BPDUs of each of the other bridges. Based on the information that these frames contain, the bridges will then take action accordingly. These actions, and indeed the process through which the loop-free topology is created and maintained, is then summarized in the steps below:

- Firstly, the bridges elect what is known as the *Root Bridge*. This is the bridge that will determine the timing used by all other bridges and can be said to be in control. The *Root* Bridge will be the one that has the *lowest* Bridge Identifier, which is an 8 octet, hexadecimal value that comprises a 2 octet *Priority* field, and the 6 octet *MAC Address*.

  In essence any bridge can become the root, although by administratively setting the *Bridge Priority* we have ultimate control. Equally, since all MAC Addresses are unique, the election of the Root Bridge is always clear cut even when all bridges use the same value of Bridge Priority. Based on our example of figure 15-16, Bridge A would become the Root since this has the lowest Bridge ID.

  Most importantly, all bridges transmit their own Configuration BPDUs over each of their ports, until they receive information from another device that supersedes theirs. In effect then, all bridges assume themselves to be the Root Bridge until they hear information to the contrary. From then on, they receive information from the Root Bridge, and then propagate this throughout the network. With reference to figure 15-17, we can see that there are fields that contain the ID of this bridge, and also the ID of which bridge is believed to be the Root.

- All *non-Root* bridges will identify one of their ports as being a *Root Port* - the port through which the bridge will receive traffic from the Root Bridge. Naturally, this port should be the port that is topologically closest to the Root in terms of accumulated *Path Cost*, and therefore will be the fastest route between the Root Bridge and *this* bridge. The *Path Cost* of any network is defined by the standard as being:

  Path Cost = 1000Mbps/(Speed of the attached network)Mbps

  So, for 10Mbps networks, the Path Cost will always be 100. Most vendors allow this value to be administratively set, although by using the standardized formula above, we ensure that the *least cost* path is always selected.

  Referring to figure 15-17, we see that there is a *Root Path Cost* field. This is the accumulated path cost mentioned above, and will be modified by successive bridges as the Configuration BPDU travels away from the Root Bridge.

  For our example of figure 15-16, it is clear that Bridges C and D would both elect port 1 as being the *Root Port* since these ports each have an Accumulated Path Cost of 100 back to the Root Bridge. For Bridge B however, both ports have an equal path cost since these ports attach to the same LANs as the Root Bridge. To break this deadlock, the port with the lowest *Port Identifier* will become the Root Port. The Port Identifier is a 2 octet hexadecimal number comprising a 1 octet *Port Priority*, and a 1 octet *Physical Port Number*. In our example, Port 1 of Bridge B will therefore become the *Root Port*.

- In order to create a *loop-free* topology, it is important that we have only one path for passing data between any two networks. To achieve this, for each network there will be one *Designated* Bridge that will carry all traffic for that network. The Root Bridge will become the *Designated Bridge* for all networks to which it attaches, so in our example Bridge B will play no part in the final topology. For LAN 3 however, either Bridge C or Bridge D will become the *Designated Bridge*. In actual fact it will be the bridge with the least accumulated path cost back to the Root or, where there are multiple units, the one with the best (lowest) Bridge ID. In our case the Designated Bridge for LAN 3 would be Bridge C, since both C and D have the same accumulated Path Costs but C has a better Bridge ID.

- The ports on a Designated Bridge that attach to the LAN(s) for which that bridge is the Designated bridge, become what are known as *Designated Ports*. All ports that are neither *Root Ports* nor *Designated Ports* are then placed in *Blocking* mode, and we are left with a loop-free topology.

- Finally, once the topology is stable, the Root Bridge continues to send Configuration BPDUs every *Hello* time. These *Hellos* are received and propagated by all bridges throughout the network, which ensures that that all bridges know that the Root bridge is functioning, and also that all links to the Root are available.

15.4.3 Spanning Tree Parameter Values

Before we consider what happens when a Bridge or link fails, it is worth noting the various parameters that are used, the range of values that they can assume, and the recommended value of each. In every case, *all* bridges within the network will use the timer values that the Root bridge uses. Thus, although each bridge could be configured differently, the values configured on any particular bridge will only be used if that bridge becomes the Root.

- **Bridge Hello Time**
  This is the time interval at which *Configuration* BPDUs are transmitted by the Root Bridge. The standard recommends that the value can be between 1 and 10 seconds, and recommends that the default value is 2 seconds.

- **Bridge Forward Delay Time**
  The Forward Delay Time is the amount of time that a bridge port will remain in the *Listening* or *Learning* states as it transitions from *Blocking* to *Forwarding*. The allowable range of values is between 4 and 30 seconds, and the recommended default value is 15 seconds.

- **Bridge Maximum Age Time**
  The Maximum Age Time is the length of time during which a bridge *must* receive a *Configuration* BPDU that originated from the Root Bridge. If a

Configuration BPDU has not been received within this period, the Root bridge (or one of the links to the Root Bridge) is deemed to be down. It is also a requirement that the following relationships are met:

Bridge Maximum Age Time $\geq$ 2 × (Bridge Hello Time + 1 second)
Bridge Maximum Age Time $\leq$ 2 × (Bridge Forward Delay Time - 1 second)

The allowable range is between 6 and 40 seconds, and the recommended default value is 20 seconds.

- **Bridge Priority**
  The Bridge Priority, used in conjunction with the MAC address of the bridge, defines the Bridge Identifier. This value is therefore is instrumental in determining which bridge will be elected as the Root Bridge. The permissible range is from 0 to 65,535, and the recommended default value is 32,768

- **Port Priority**
  The Port Priority is used to break deadlock situations where more than one port of a bridge can act as the Root Port. When this situation occurs, a *Port Identifier* (a concatenation of the Port Priority and the Physical Port number) is used. The port with the *lowest* Port ID, will then be elected as the *Root Port*. Allowable values are between 0 and 255, and the recommended default value is 128.

15.4.4   Loop Detection and Topology Changes

Assuming that we now have a stable, loop-free topology in figure 15-16, we will now consider what happens when either the Root Bridge or a Designated Bridge fails, or indeed when a link fails. Where the Root Bridge (or a link to that bridge) fails, bridges beyond the failure will stop receiving Configuration BPDUs on a regular basis, and the entire network topology from the point of failure outwards will be re-negotiated. Obviously failure of the Root Bridge is the worst case scenario, yet is possibly easier to understand. Let us take a simple example based upon figure 15-16, where Bridge C (the Designated Bridge for LAN 3) fails, and Bridge D has to become the Designated Bridge.

Bridge D will have port 2 in a blocking state. It will, however, be receiving BPDUs from the Root Bridge (across LAN2) through Port 1, and would have been receiving BPDUs from Bridge C through Port 2. Note that although Port 2 of this bridge was blocking, and would therefore not be forwarding any user data, it would still expect to receive BPDUs from the Designated Bridge for that LAN.

Now, assuming that the timer values in use are the recommended default values, we would expect to receive BPDUs every *Hello* time (2 seconds), and each time we receive a BPDU, the *Maximum Age Timer* is reset. In the event that the Maximum Age Timer expires (i.e., we have not received a BPDU within 20 seconds), Bridge D will transition its blocked port from *Blocking* state to *Listening* state. At this point, the *Forward Delay Timer* is also started, and the bridge continues to listen for BPDUs. If a BPDU, indicating that a Designated Bridge exists on LAN 3 is now received through Port 2, the port will immediately revert to *Blocking* state. If the

Forward Delay Timer (15 seconds) expires though, then Port 2 of Bridge D will transition from *Listening* state to the *Learning* state, and the *Forward Delay Timer* will be restarted. In this state, the bridge port is learning the addresses of stations connected to the same LAN, and also listening for a BPDU from a Designated Bridge. Once again, if a BPDU is received, the port will immediately transition back to a *Blocking* state. In the event that no BPDUs have been received when the Forward Delay Timer expires, the port transitions from the *Learning* state to the *Forwarding* state, and Bridge D becomes the Designated Bridge for LAN 3.

Having discussed what happens where we have a failure, let us now discuss what happens if a loop is introduced. For example, let us take figure 15-16, and this time simply place a repeater between LANs 2 and 3. Obviously we now have a loop, and Bridges C and D will now receive BPDUs from the Root Bridge over their lower ports. This will not affect Bridge D since it is already in a *Blocking* state. Bridge C however would expect to receive BPDUs from the Root only through Port 1. Since it is now receiving them through both ports, it will transition one of its ports to the *Blocking* state to create a loop-free topology. Which port will become blocked will depend upon the *Port Priority*. Using the values of figure 15-16 though, it will be Port 2.

Finally, let us now consider a slightly different scenario where we revert to figure 15-16, and assume that we have a stable topology. What would happen if we now replace Bridge D with one whose MAC address is numerically lower than that of Bridge A? If we assume that all other parameters remain constant, what we will now see is that our *new* bridge D becomes the Root, since it's *Bridge Identifier* is lower. Remember, all bridges assume themselves to be the Root Bridge unless they receive information to the contrary. Our new Bridge D will therefore assert that it is the Root, and will cause a complete topology change.

Before leaving this topic, let us finally consider when *Topology Change Notification* BPDUs are transmitted. These BPDUs are transmitted in order to notify a bridge on the path towards the Root, that an extension of the topology has been detected by the transmitting bridge. Bridges transmits this BPDU type, whenever they detect, or receive notification of a topology change from any bridge other than the Root. Eventually then, this results in the Root bridge being notified of the topology change as these BPDUs are propagated backwards towards the Root.

15.4.5 Spanning Tree Domains

One of the major problems of Spanning Tree, is the length of time that it takes to create a stable, loop-free topology, and the fact that *NO* user data flows while this is taking place.

For example, consider what would happen if we were to add Bridge C to the existing, *stable*, network topology shown in figure 15-18. From our previous discussions, our *new* bridge would believe itself to be the Root bridge and immediately send Configuration BPDUs. In the event that this bridge actually does have a better claim than the existing Root, the entire network will then need to go through the whole Spanning Tree process, and of course no data will flow while this is happening! Now consider the fact that regardless of what happens in the

London domain, there is absolutely no chance of this creating a loop in *New York*. Unfortunately Spanning Tree is not intelligent enough to know this, so it will play safe and stop data flow throughout the entire network.

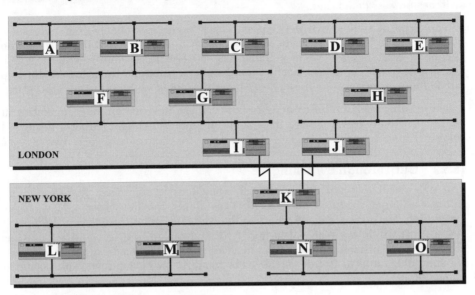

Figure 15-18: Sample Spanning Tree Split by Domain

Some vendors, seeing this as a problem, have come up with what is really a proprietary solution. We have said that bridges use the multicast address 01-80-C2-00-00-00 to communicate, but in truth it could be *any* multicast address. The only criteria, is that *all* bridges must agree on which address will be used. In actual fact, Bridge C would not need to run Spanning Tree at all. Similarly, provided that Bridges K, L, M, N, and O all agree on the administratively assigned multicast address to use, it definitely does not need to be the same as that used in London.

It must be stressed that this is not standardized, but it nonetheless does form a simple solution to the biggest problem of Spanning Tree - the time it takes to operate.

15.5 Switch Types

We have now discussed the operation of Bridges and Switches at some length, and have said that they operate in broadly the same fashion. In truth, this view has been somewhat simplified since there are several types of Switch. Each type operates slightly differently, and each has its own set of advantages and disadvantages. In this section, we will therefore discuss the relative merits of each.

15.5.1 Store and Forward Switching

The Store-and-Forward Switch is the *classical* method of switching. These devices operate in exactly the same manner as bridges, storing each frame as it arrives, and then making forwarding decisions only when the entire frame is buffered. Indeed, our discussions thus far have centered around this method of operation, and we have made little distinction between bridges and switches except to say that switches process data faster.

This type of switch will never pass illegal frames. It checks that frames are within the legal limits in terms of size, that the FCS is correct, and that there are no alignment errors. Only when a frame has satisfied these simple criteria will a decision be made as to whether it should be forwarded or discarded. Failure to satisfy these criteria results in the frame being discarded without further processing.

The result of this buffering activity is that these devices, although operating at *wire speed*, tend to be slower than some of their other counterparts discussed below.

15.5.2 Cut Through Switching

You will recall that the Ethernet/802.3 frame header comprises the *Destination Address*, *Source Address*, and *Length/Type* fields in that order. Now, since forwarding decisions are made based on the contents of the *Destination Address*, it follows that we do not really need to defer that decision until the entire frame has been buffered. Instead, once we have received the full 6 octet *Destination Address*, we should be able to decide on how the frame must be handled, and act on it immediately.

In the case of *Cut Through* Switches then, our data is handled faster because we can actually be forwarding a frame even as it is still arriving. The down side is that we run the risk of propagating *bad* frames. For example, since we are making our forwarding decision based on only the first 6 octets of the frame, we do not know whether the frame is validly formed. The frame may be of illegal length, it may be a collision fragment, it may have an invalid FCS, or it may contain alignment errors. The price that we pay for extra speed is that we may propagate bad frames.

15.5.3 Fragment Free Switching

Fragment Free Switches address one of the problems that *Cut Through* switches introduce, that of the propagation of *Runt* frames (those frames less than 64 octets long). In essence, a Fragment Free switch behaves in a similar fashion to a Cut Through switch, except it buffers at least 64 octets *before* it makes its forwarding decision. In this way, our network is protected from Runt frames and collision fragments, although there is no protection against *Giant* frames (those larger than 1518 octets), or frames with alignment errors or invalid FCSs.

15.5.4 Adaptive Switching

In the same way that *Fragment Free* switches improve on the basic *Cut Through* principles, *Adaptive* Switches bring the best of all worlds to the fore. In operation these switches behave as *Cut Through* devices, although they also monitor the number of *bad* frames that are being forwarded. When this number exceeds a certain threshold, the switch stops acting as a *Cut Through* device and behaves as a *Store-and-Forward* device until the error rate drops.

15.6 Virtual LANs (VLANs)

Possibly one of the most significant features of modern switches, is the ability to create *closed* user communities called *Virtual LANs*, or VLANs. In operation, a VLAN is a group of stations that the network administrator assigns as a single, *logical*, network. Once the VLAN is created, no traffic can then cross its perimeter, and that group of users then becomes isolated from the outside world. VLANs therefore help to address the problems associated with broadcast/multicast traffic on large networks, and also security issues. Figure 15-19 shows a simple example of a switch configured with a number of VLANs, each of which operate totally independently of each other.

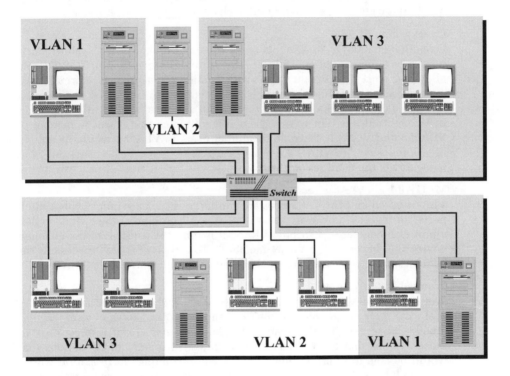

Figure 15-19:   Simple VLAN Example

Of course, there is nothing to stop an external connection being made between VLANs. Indeed, in many cases administrators will set up their VLANs such that each represents a separate *subnet*.[8] Where communication is required between VLANs, an external connection is made to a router, and the router will incorporate filtering to ensure that security is maintained. In this way we achieve both a reduction in broadcast/multicast traffic across a single switch, and the ability to share resources, yet we maintain security.

---

[8] The concepts of subnets and routing are discussed in section F.

15.6.1 VLAN Types

As if to confuse the issues, vendors today now talk about several different VLAN types. Although similar, each is subtly different and therefore worthy of note here.

- **Port-Based VLANs**

  These are the simplest of all VLAN types to understand, and are offered by all vendors. The switch port(s) are configured so that the attached device is a member of that VLAN in much the same way as shown in figure 15-19. Broadcast/Multicast traffic is reduced, and security is maintained. The disadvantage is that VLANs of this type will typically only exist on a single switch unless Inter-Switch VLANs (ISVLANs) are supported. Inter-Switch VLANs are significant in order to create large, scaleable, networks. As a result, these are discussed later in this chapter.

- **Overlapping VLANs**

  One other element of VLANs that some vendors implement is the ability for a port to be a member of multiple VLANs. Known as *overlapping* VLANs, this allows a port to communicate with stations that would normally be considered to be out-of-bounds. This facility is extremely useful with servers. For example, consider figure 15-19, and most specifically the server in VLAN 3. If this port were to be configured such that it was a member of VLAN 3 and VLAN 2, it would mean that users in VLAN 2 would be able to access the server in VLAN 3, yet users in VLAN 3 would be restricted from using any of the facilities of VLAN 2.

- **MAC Address VLANs**

  VLANs based on MAC Addresses are similar to those based on simple switch ports. In this case however, rather than simply configuring the switch so that a port is a member of a specific VLAN, it is the MAC address of the attached device that becomes the VLAN member. This type of VLAN represents far better security, since now an attached device cannot simply be substituted.

- **Protocol Based VLANs**

  Protocol Based VLANs are useful in reducing the traffic created by *chatty* protocols. For example, AppleTalk and NetWare servers send regular broadcasts advertising their services. These frames are of interest only to those stations that use the servers, and indeed it is only those stations that would be able to interpret them anyway. For example, an IP station would have no interest in an AppleTalk or NetWare advertisement, so therefore does not need to receive it. Hence, large performance improvements can often be made where protocol based VLANs are created.

15.6.2 Inter-Switch VLANs

As we briefly mentioned earlier, one of the biggest problems with VLANs (and in particular Port-based VLANs) is the fact that it is difficult to span multiple switches. Certainly, until the ratification of the IEEE 802.1Q standard, vendors used all types of proprietary extensions to overcome this problem. The issue is simple - how to encapsulate VLAN information within a standard frame? The answer is equally simple - VLAN Tagging. This does not require major changes to end station architecture, and in all cases the end station is totally unaware of any VLAN implications. VLANs are transparent to end stations, and they will simply transmit their frames in exactly the same way as they always have. Consider figure 15-20 where we have three switches and two VLANs.

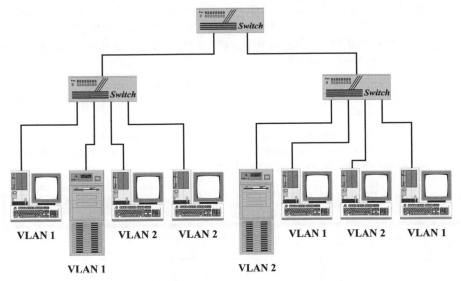

Figure 15-20: Inter-Switch VLAN Example - 1

Let us assume that a station in VLAN 1 on the left hand side sends a broadcast to all stations. The frame itself will be constructed normally, and will be received by the switch on the left. Only those stations that are members of the same VLAN on this switch will receive the frame - this is standard. The switch will now need to *Tag* the frame with VLAN information, and then transmit it onwards. The port through which ISVLAN traffic is transmitted and received is known as a *Trunk* port, and indeed it is this port that is responsible for the Tagging and Un-tagging of frames. When the switch on the right receives the *Tagged* frame through its *Trunk* port, it will need to examine the *Tagging* information and then *Un-tag* the frame. Finally, it will pass it to the relevant port(s).

Tagging a frame naturally changes its overall format. This modified format which is standardized by IEEE 802.3ac, and used by IEEE 802.1Q, increases the overall size of the Ethernet/802.3 frame by four octets and is shown in figure 15-21. The fields are then described below:

Firstly, the two octet *Length/Type* field that follows the *Source Address* always contains a *Type* value and is referred to as the *Tag Protocol Identifier*. The value of this field is always $81\text{-}00_{16}$ for *Tagged* frames. The two octet *Tag Control Information* field is new to *Tagged* frames and comprises the following sub-fields:

- A three bit *User Priority* field that is capable of representing eight *priority* levels (0 through 7). This now means that *Tagged* frames can be prioritized, and this priority information can be carried across individual LAN segments.

- A single bit *Canonical Format Indicator* (CFI). This field is used to signal the bit order of address information when encapsulated frames (such as Token Ring/Source Routed FDDI frames) are carried.

- A 12 bit *VLAN Identifier* (VID) which is then used to uniquely identify the VLAN to which this frame belongs. The VID is encoded as an unsigned binary number, and can take any value with the exception of the following:

  0   The *Null* VID indicates that the *Tag Header* of the frame contains only *User Priority* information.

  1   This is the *Default* VID and is used as the default VID for each Bridge/Switch port. This value can be administratively set on a per-port basis.

  FFF   The hexadecimal value FFF is reserved for *implementation use*. That is, this value will have *internal* significance within the Bridge/Switch only and cannot be used outside of the device.

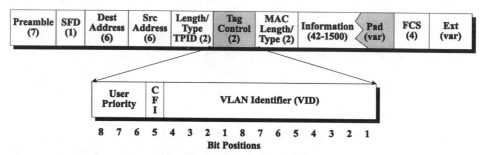

Figure 15-21: Tagged Ethernet/802.3 Frame Format

The two octet *MAC Length/Type* field now becomes the standard Ethernet/802.3 *Length/Type* field as described previously. Our frames can therefore be Ethernet format and use this field to define the upper layer protocol being carried, or IEEE 802.3 and use this field to define the length of the *Information* field.

Before leaving the subject of *simple* Tagged Ethernet/802.3 frames, it is worth noting one final difference to standard 802.3 frames. You will recall that in the standard frame the minimum length is 64 octets, and hence the length of the combined *Information* and *Padding* must be a minimum of 46 octets. With *Tagged* frames however, since we have increased the overall length by 4 octets, our minimum *Information* and *Padding* is now reduced to 42 octets.

It has to be said that IEEE 802.1Q does allow for the length to be padded to such that the frame is a minimum of 68 octets, thereby allowing a *downstream* bridge/switch to *Un-Tag* a frame without the need to adjust the frame length in any way. This is not a requirement of the standard however, merely a means by which both standard bridges/switches and those with ISVLAN support can easily co-exist.

Finally, since we have discussed only the *Tagging* of Ethernet/802.3 frames, we must consider one other frame type - frames that carry the *Sub-Network Access*

Bridges and Switches

Protocol (SNAP)[9] header. In this frame type, the *SNAP Header* will have the value AA-AA-03, the *SNAP PID* will have the value 00-00-00, and this will then be followed by the 802.1Q *Tag Protocol Identifier* of 81-00.

15.7 Embedded Routing Information Field (E-RIF) Format

The subject of the 1 octet *CFI* field mentioned in the previous section needs further explanation if we are to fully understand the rationale behind its inclusion. Certainly this *flag* can, and indeed is, used to define the bit ordering of addresses embedded within the frame, but what we need to understand is why this is necessary in the first place.

Our discussions so far have revolved around the fact that Ethernet/802.3 networks use what has become known as *Transparent* bridging. In truth, until the advent of 802.1Q/802.3ac, this was in fact the only bridging method available. Now, things have changed though, and the standards have allowed a higher degree of overlap between technologies. Broadly, an *Embedded Routing Information Field* (E-RIF), can appear in an *Ethernet encoded Tag Header* and therefore allow Ethernet/802.3 networks to carry Token Ring/FDDI frames and vice versa. Where the E-RIF field is present, it immediately follows the 2 octet *MAC Length/Type* field, and comprises a two octet *Route Control* (RC) field, and two or more octets of *Route Descriptors* (RDs) as defined by the RC. Where RDs are present, these can be up to a maximum of 28 octets in length. The format of the E-RIF is shown in figure 15-22.

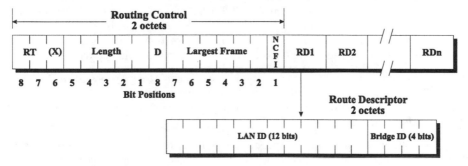

Figure 15-22: E-RIF Field

The three bit *Routing Type* (RT) field is used to define whether the frame should be forwarded through the network along a single route, or through multiple interconnected LANs. The potential value(s) of this field are similar to those discussed in the Token Ring section of this volume, with one addition. These are:

- **Specifically Routed Frame (SR) - Routing Type (RT) value 0XX**
  Where the most significant bit of the RT field is 0, this implies that the RD field(s) contained in the E-RIF will determine the specific route that the

---

[9] The Sub-Network Access Protocol (SNAP) is discussed in detail in section E.

frame should take through the network. The two least significant bits of the field are then preserved as the frame passes through the bridges en-route to the final destination.

- **All Routes Explorer Frame (ARE) - Routing Type (RT) value 10X**
  Where the two most significant bits of the RT field are set to 10, the frame is treated as an *All Routes Explorer* frame and will follow as many routes to the destination as are allowed by the ARE forwarding decision. For this type of frame, the source station will not use any Route Descriptors, but these will be added by *Source Route Transparent* (SRT) bridges[10] along the route. This also results in as many frames arriving at the destination as there are routes between the source and destination.

- **Spanning Tree Explorer Frames (STE) - Routing Type (RT) value 11X**
  Where the two most significant bits of the RT field are set to 11, the frame is treated as a *Spanning Tree Explorer* frame. This means that the frame is forwarded only by *Source Route Transparent* (SRT) bridges whose ports are in the *Transparent* bridging *Forwarding* state. With the frame following the *Spanning Tree path*, it will appear only once for each LAN on the network, and will therefore only appear once at the destination station. Once again the source station will transmit the frame without *Route Descriptors* (RD). Each SRT bridge that forwards the frame will then add a RD as with the All Routes Explorer.

- **Transparent Frame - Routing Type (RT) value 01X**
  It is this value that is added by IEEE 802.1Q, and is used to indicate that a Transparent Frame is being carried. This value also indicates that with the exception of the *NCFI* field, the remainder of the E-RIF is discarded if the frame is forwarded using IEEE 802.5 (Token Ring) media access methods.

  As such, the E-RIF will contain no *Route Descriptors* (the frame is *Transparent*), and will always be 2 octets long. There are four rules that are applied to ensure that the RT field of VLAN and non-VLAN aware devices remains unambiguous.

  - Where we have an *untagged*, Source Routed frame that is received from a Token Ring or FDDI LAN that needs to be forwarded over an Ethernet/802.3, or Token Ring/FDDI LAN, then if the value of the RT field was 0XX, it will be converted to 000 in the E-RIF.

  - If the frame is received from a Token Ring LAN, and it is an *untagged*, transparent frame that is to be forwarded as a tagged frame over either an Ethernet/802.3 or FDDI LAN, then the *Tag Header* will carry an E-RIF field where the value of the RT field is 010.

  - If a VLAN aware source station on a Token Ring/FDDI LAN sends a *Source Routed*, *Tagged* frame where there is no E-RIF in the *Tag Header*,

---

[10] Source Route Transparent bridges are generally used in mixed Ethernet/Token Ring environments. These bridges allow frames to be passed between the two technologies and forwarded through the network using Transparent or Source Route bridging as the technology dictates.

then the station should not use the values 010 or 011 in the *Routing Type* (RT) field of the *RIF*.

- If a VLAN aware source station on an Ethernet/802.3 LAN generates a Source Routed, tagged, transparent frame (i.e., where there is Source Routing information carried in the E-RIF in the Tag Header), then the station will not use the values 010 or 011 as Routing Types in the E-RIF.

The 5 bit *Length* (LTH) field indicates the length of the Routing Information field. The values will always be even and be between 2 and 30, except in the case where the E-RIF Routing Type field indicates that the frame is a Transparent frame. In this case, the LTH field indicates a value of zero to ensure that these frames cannot be misinterpreted by devices that are capable of performing Source Routing.

The 1 bit *Direction* (D) indicator defines the order in which the *Routing Descriptors* are read. Where the bit is set to 0, the RDs are read in the order RD1, RD2, RD3,.....RDn. The frame then travels from LAN to LAN in a *forward* direction. Conversely, where the bit is set to 1, the RDs are read in the order RDn, RDn-1, RDn-2,.....RD1, and the frame travels in the *reverse* direction. The D bit only has meaning where the Routing Type indicates a *Specifically Routed* frame. Hence, this will always be set to 0 for *Spanning Tree Explorer* (STE), and *All Routes Explorer* (ARE) frames.

The 6 bit *Longest Frame* (LF) field defines the longest information field that can be exchanged between devices. A station sending an explorer frame will set this field to the largest value that it can accept. Bridges en-route to the destination can then reduce this value, as can the final destination station. The field itself is split into two halves, known as the *Base*, and the *Extension*. The actual longest frame can then be determined from table 15-5.

Table 15-5: Length Field Values

		Extension							
		000	*001*	*010*	*011*	*100*	*101*	*110*	*111*
	000	516	635	754	873	993	1112	1231	1350
	001	1470	1542	1615	1688	1761	1833	1906	1979
B	*010*	2052	2345	2638	2932	3225	3518	3812	4105
A	*011*	4399	4865	5331	5798	6264	6730	7197	7663
S	*100*	8130	8539	8949	9358	9768	10178	10587	10997
E	*101*	11407	12199	12992	13785	14578	15370	16163	16956
	110	17749	20730	23711	26693	29674	32655	35637	38618
	111	41600	44591	47583	50575	53567	56559	59551	>59551

Finally, the single bit *Non-Canonical Format Indicator* (NCFI) flag indicates the *type* of address(es) that may be carried. When the bit is set to 0, this indicates that all MAC address information that may be carried as MAC data is in non-canonical form. Conversely, when set to 1, all MAC address information carried as MAC data will be in canonical form. In Source Routed RIF frames this bit is reserved, and its value is preserved across bridges.

15.8 The Generic Attribute Registration Protocol (GARP)

The Generic Attribute Registration Protocol (GARP) as standardized by IEEE 802.1P, provides devices the ability to disseminate information about GARP applications among themselves. At the present time, two major GARP applications exist, namely the GARP Multicast Registration Protocol (GMRP), and the GARP VLAN Registration Protocol (GVRP), both of which will be discussed later in this section.

15.8.1 GARP Protocol Operation

In operation, GARP participants make *Declarations*, or withdraw *Declarations*, relative to particular attribute values. These declarations (or withdrawals) are then propagated throughout the active topology, and result in the registration (or de-registration) of those particular parameter values for other GARP participants within the bridged LAN. For example, in figure 15-23 we see a typical application where a GARP-capable end station (A) registers an attribute. The arrows on the links then show the direction of attribute declaration by participating bridges.

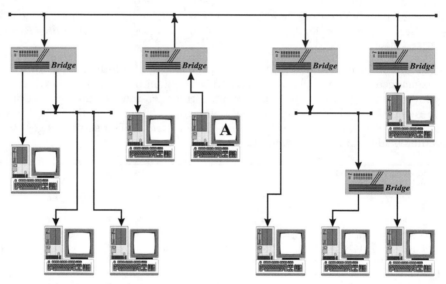

Figure 15-23: GARP Attribute Propagation

The protocol itself is based on the general principle that GARP participants communicate their current state, rather than send directions. In total five Attribute specific messages, and one general message, are used to convey this information as follows:

- **JoinEmpty**
  This means that the device is declaring the particular attribute value. It has not registered it, but it is interested in whether there are any other participants that wish to declare it.

- **JoinIn**

  This means that the device is declaring the particular attribute value. It has either registered it itself, or it is not interested in whether there are any other participants that wish to declare it. In other words, in using this message type the device is behaving as if there are other participants that would like to declare it.

- **LeaveEmpty and LeaveIn**

  LeaveEmpty and LeaveIn are the opposite of JoinEmpty and JoinIn, and mean that the device is de-registering that particular attribute value.

- **Empty**

  The device is neither declaring the attribute value, nor is it registering the attribute. It is however interested in whether there are other participants that might wish to declare it.

- **LeaveAll**

  This means that all registrations will shortly be de-registered. Hence if any participants have an interest in continuing any of their registrations, they must rejoin.

For each application, there is a uniquely defined group (Multicast) MAC address which is known as the GARP Application address. GARP does however make use of the same LLC address as the Spanning Tree Protocol. The use of distinct MAC addresses and protocol identifiers in this way ensures that the particular PDUs are delivered to the correct protocol entities. The structure of the GARP Protocol Data Unit (PDU) is then shown in figure 15-24.

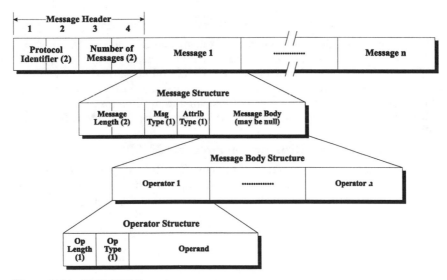

Figure 15-24: GARP PDU Format

As far as the GARP PDU header is concerned this comprises 4 octets, two of which are used as the *Protocol Identifier*, and two which are used to indicate the number of messages that follow. For messages, the format is such that each has a header of a two octet *Message Length* field, a one octet *Message Type* field, and a one octet *Attribute Type* field - all of which are encoded as unsigned integers. Where the *Message Type* contains a value of one, the message is a *LeaveAll* message as previously defined. Where this octet is zero, this implies that the message is a *Packed Message* and therefore contains one of the other *Join*, or *Leave* messages. All other values of *Message Type* are currently reserved. Where the *Attribute Type* field contains the value zero, then the message applies to all attribute types defined by the specific GARP application concerned. Where the *Attribute Type* field is any other value, then this implies that the message applies only to a specific attribute type as defined by the specific GARP application concerned.

The *Message Body* is made up of a number of variable length *Operators*, each of which has a single octet *Operator Length* field, a single octet *Operator Type* field, and a variable length *Operand*. The *Operator Type* and *Operator Length* fields are encoded as unsigned integers. The *Operator Type* will then assume one of the values shown in table 15-6, each of which have been defined previously. The *Operand* encoding and value depend on the specific GARP application being conveyed, and are therefore not discussed here.

Table 15-6: Attribute Operator Types

Operator Type	Description
0	JoinEmpty Operator
1	JoinIn Operator
2	LeaveEmpty Operator
3	LeaveIn Operator
4	Empty Operator

Finally, we should discuss the format of the special case, *LeaveAll* message. For this message type, the message is structured with a *Message Length* of 4, a *Message Type* of 1, and an *Attribute Type* of either 0, or any other value that is valid for the specific GARP application. If the *Attribute Type* value used is 0, then the message applies to all attributes of all types defined for the application. Any other value indicates that the message applies only to those attributes of that specific type.

15.8.2 GARP Multicast Registration Protocol (GMRP)

The GARP Multicast Registration Protocol (GMRP) allows *Multicast Group* membership information to be propagated throughout a Bridged network. In many respects, this protocol can be likened to the a combination of the *Internet Group Management Protocol* (IGMP)[11] that allows devices to declare membership of IP multicast groups, and *Multicast OSPF* (MOSPF)[12] that allows this group information

---

[11] The Internet Group Management Protocol allows the registration of IP multicast group information. Thus, Layer 3 (IP) multicasts can be propagated throughout an internet being directed only to those subnets that contain group members. Discussion of this protocol is beyond the scope of this text, but it is discussed fully in the volume "TCP/IP Explained" also by Philip Miller.

[12] Multicast OSPF is a routing protocol that allows Multicast Group information to be exchanged between routers. As with IGMP, explanation of this protocol is beyond the scope of this text, but is fully discussed in the volume "TCP/IP Explained" also by Philip Miller.

to be propagated. Thus, although GMRP is standardized through IEEE 802.1P and operates at Layer 2, there is a striking similarity. Two specific types of information are carried by GMRP, namely *Group Membership* information, and *Service Requirement* information.

The Group Membership information that is carried by GMRP indicates that one or more GMRP participants are members of a particular group, and therefore carries the MAC address(es) associated with that group. Registering group information in this way enables GMRP aware devices to forward frames destined for those MAC address(es) in the direction of the registered group members only. Multicast traffic is now reduced throughout the bridged network, and performance may well improve as a result.

Service Requirement information indicates that one or more GMRP participants require *Forward All Groups*, or *Forward Unregistered Groups* to be the *default* filtering behavior. Ports that forward frames in the direction from which the Service Requirement information was received, modify their default group forwarding behavior. The ability to dynamically manipulate the default group forwarding behavior then allows devices to interact with non-GMRP aware devices.

GMRP uses the Group Address **01-80-C2-00-00-20** to propagate its information. Within the GARP message format, two *Attribute Types* are then defined as follows:

- **Group Attribute**
  The Group Attribute carries Group Membership information. The one octet *Group Attribute Type* field has the value **0000 0001**, and *Operators* contained within the Message Body are eight octets in length (including the one octet *Operator Length*, and one octet *Operator Type* fields). The actual *Operand* is then six octets and contains the group MAC Address.

- **Service Requirement**
  This attribute carries Service Requirement information with the one octet *Group Attribute Type* field containing the value **0000 0010**. The *Operators* in the Message Body are then three octets (including the one octet *Operator Length* and one octet *Operator Type* fields), and two single octet *Operands* are defined. The first, *All Groups* Operand is encoded as **0000 0000**, and the second Operand which is *All Unregistered Groups*, is encoded as **0000 0001**. All other Operand values are currently reserved.

15.8.3 GARP VLAN Registration Protocol (GVRP)

The GARP VLAN Registration Protocol (GVRP) allows the propagation of Dynamic VLAN Registrations throughout a Bridged network. In operation, it is similar to the GARP Multicast Registration Protocol (GMRP) except that GVRP carries 12 bit VLAN Identifiers (VIDs) rather than 48 bit (6 octet) Group MAC Addresses.

Defined by IEEE 802.1Q, GVRP uses the group address **01-80-C2-00-00-21**, and defines a single Attribute Type (referred to as the *VID* attribute), encoded as **0000 0001**. The *Operator* then carries a two octet *Operand* that represents an unsigned binary number equal to the VLAN ID that is being propagated.

15.9   Port Trunking

Port Trunking is a feature provided by many vendors, that allows the aggregation of multiple ports into a single group. Although not standardized, and therefore highly proprietary, it is significant in that it effectively combines bandwidth into a single connection. Thus, it is worthy of note here.

Typically only available on higher bandwidth ports, Port Trunking allows an administrator to create multi-gigabit pipes to transport traffic through the areas of highest utilization in the network. For example, four separate one-gigabit ports could be aggregated into a single four-gigabit trunk port. Furthermore, most vendors provide these ports with additional features, over and above simple load sharing. These might include:

- Address based traffic sorting that keeps the frames in the correct order.

- Fault tolerance. Should a port within a *Trunk group* fail, the remaining ports will continue to forward the traffic. Recovery from a failed port is therefore not based upon Spanning Tree convergence times.

15.10 Layer 3 Switches

One of the burning issues facing the network architect today is the need for speed. Speed of operation in both end stations and infrastructure devices is paramount, and our network users demand more and more from the devices that they use. Higher speed networks certainly help, but they do not go far enough. LAN segments must be joined, and for this we need devices such as Bridges, Switches, and Routers.[13] Certainly our *wire speed* Switch means that there is so little latency that we can ignore the fact that it is there for all practical purposes, and bridges have been superseded by their higher powered switch counterparts. These devices however, have one major drawback - they rely totally on Layer 2 information, and therefore create a *flat* addressing scheme. To get around this we require routers, but these too have a problem - these devices are software based and therefore introduce very high latency. So what is the solution? Certainly networks of any size will typically employ a combination of Switches (Bridges) and Routers, but if the router is not to become a bottleneck it will need to be replaced. Thus, seeing the potential of this huge market, vendors strove to develop the next generation router - enter the Layer 3 Switch. There are no standards that relate to the operation of these devices, but they typically work by analyzing the correlation between Layer 2 and Layer 3 addresses. Once this correlation between two end-points is established, the device can then simply switch traffic between ports using the Layer 2 information rather than having to process information at Layer 3. Our devices now have less information to process, and the switching itself can take place in hardware. The net result is that we retain the advantages of Routing, without the introduction of further latency.

---

[13] The concept of Routing (Internetworking) is discussed in section F.

A full discussion of Layer 3 Switching is impossible without an understanding of the workings of Layer 3 of the OSI Model (the Network Layer). Thus, although we can broadly outline the operation of these devices here, this concept will be discussed further in section F (Internetworking).

15.11 Layer 4 Switches and Beyond

In exactly the same way that there is no defined standard for Layer 3 switching, there are no standards laid down for switching at Layer 4, or indeed at any higher layers. Certainly several vendors claim to be able to *switch* based on information from these layers, but what do they really mean? In essence, what really happens is that the switches themselves identify data *Streams* based upon information contained within the *Transport* layer, and then just as with Layer 3 switches, correlate this with Layer 2 addressing. Now these devices can switch this data at layer 2, and of course at wire speed. Is it hype, or is it for real? Many vendors are claiming to be able to switch at the *Application* layer (Layer 7), so the concepts of upper layer switching are taking shape. Certainly, *Any Layer* switching as it is rapidly becoming known, will improve network throughput, but until there is a viable standard to which all vendors can adhere, interoperability will remain the biggest issue.

15.12 Problems Associated with Bridges/Switches

From our discussions so far, one might be excused for thinking that bridges and/or switches are the cure for our network ills. Sadly, this is not the case, since they do not address all of the problems, and indeed fail to address the one fundamental problem of most networks - broadcast and multicast traffic! Certainly VLANs will confine this traffic type, and IEEE 802.1P will allow multicast traffic to be directed to only those devices that have registered to receive it. Fundamentally, though, our networks still suffer from broadcasts that propagate throughout them in what have become known as *Broadcast Storms*.

The Broadcast Storm is possibly the biggest problem that faces our network architect today. The problem revolves around the fact that many protocols, and in particular *legacy* protocols such as IPX, AppleTalk, and LAT, rely on broadcasts or multicasts to *advertise* services. Thus, if we were to have a predominantly IP network with a small number of IPX and/or AppleTalk users, all of the bridges and switches in the world would not stop the IP users from receiving the IPX and AppleTalk advertisements. Placing users for each protocol on separate VLANs will help, but without this our broadcast will eventually percolate throughout the entire network. Too many broadcasts, and our network will literally be on its knees. Another limitation that must be considered is the amount of *Address Space* that the bridge/switch has. Remember that these devices work on the fact that they know which MAC address(es) reside on which ports. Thus, if we are to cascade our switches, as we might in the case of a large backbone switch, we may have a large number of devices (and therefore MAC addresses) ultimately connected to a single switch port. So, since a bridge/switch will always forward a frame to all ports if it has no knowledge of where it should send it, we must make sure that the device has enough address space for the number of devices that we wish to deploy.

Finally, we must not forget that all too many devices of this type are over-committed. Where these devices are deployed, we must ensure that there is sufficient backplane bandwidth. Always remember that 20 ports of 10/100Mbps Ethernet that runs at Full Duplex requires a backplane bandwidth of 4Gbps if it is to run at 100% utilization. Of course few networks do run at anything close to 100% constantly, but a backplane bandwidth of 2Gbps would mean that the network could not run higher than 50% without dropping frames. Failure to consider these simple facts when sizing the network, can lead to disaster just a little further down stream.

15.13 Summary

We have now discussed the most popular way to join network segments together, and certainly the best and most cost effective method of improving network performance. Bridges have been around a long time, and they have served us well. They have allowed us to segment our network, and given us the ability to connect geographically distant LANs. They have provided us with a means to implement security, and through the Spanning Tree Protocol have made it possible to create resilient networks. Their days are numbered though, since they have introduced latencies that are totally unacceptable today.

Switches are the latest devices that we can use to improve performance, although these are really just super fast bridges of course. A switch is normally implemented in hardware using Application Specific Integrated Circuits (ASICs), and thus *wire-speed*, or near *wire-speed* operation is possible. But this is not all that switches bring. Switch development continues and we can now see real benefits. We can create *Virtual LANs* (VLANs) which allow us to have closed user groups where we cut down broadcast and multicast traffic. We can implement 802.1P and create multicast groups, and of course with our improvements in technology, Layer 3 switching is a reality, albeit non-standardized.

So where do we go from here? Our vision of the future must be for higher speed switches to match our ever increasing bandwidth demands, and higher and higher *wire-speeds*. Backplane bandwidths will also need to increase in line with the demands for higher port densities, coupled with the higher port speeds. Finally, as these devices take over the network backbone, resilience will also become ever more important.

Section C

Token Ring/IEEE 802.5
(ISO 8802-5)

Token Ring Introduction

This section aims to explain the fundamentals of the token passing protocol and look at how Token Ring has developed from a passive technology into one based very much on active equipment. It includes detailed explanations on station operation, protocol theory and ring management. Having established the method of operation we will then explore the physical composition of Token Ring LANs from a simple passive network through to today's more complex switched networks.

16.1 A Brief History of Token Ring

The Token Ring access protocol dates back prior to 1970, in fact it was first proposed to the IEEE for standardization as early as 1969. It was developed by IBM as a high speed method (relative to other technologies at that time) of interconnecting mainframe computers. This proposal to the IEEE was at the time not acted upon, but was revisited in 1980 upon the development of the personal computer. Much of the initial development undertaken by IBM was used as the foundation for the IEEE 802.5 sub-committee to initiate research into a LAN access method based upon Token Passing. The potential for Token Ring to become a suitable access protocol for forthcoming LANs based on low cost desktop machines had been realized and work commenced towards producing some level of standardization.

The IEEE deliberated on the first draft of their 802.5 Token Passing Ring standard until its release in 1985. During this period a number of significant events took place to guarantee the future development of Token Ring. Among the most notable were firstly, the declaration by IBM that Token Ring was to be its LAN strategy for the future, and secondly the joining forces of IBM and Texas Instruments (TI) to develop the chip set to run the access protocol. Within weeks of the release of the IEEE 802.5 standards document, IBM was shipping standards compliant products with the TMS 380 chip set from TI at the heart of the product suite.

Since the release of the first standard, Token Ring has come a long way. In the first release the technology was based upon two speeds, namely 1 Mbps and 4 Mbps. Later updated versions of the standard have long since dropped 1 Mbps operation and introduced 16 Mbps in its place. Other enhancements include the introduction of Early Token Release, enhanced media support incorporated unshielded twisted pair and fiber optic cabling solutions, and Dedicated Token Ring.

16.2 Basic Method of Operation

In the previous section we saw that Ethernet was based on a bus topology. Token Ring, as the name suggests, is based on a ring topology but is implemented over a physical star. The ring consists, if the transmission path were to be traced, of a number of point to point links between the output of each station and the input of its downstream neighbor. This introduces the first fundamental difference between a Token Ring station and one attached to Ethernet, that of the data path in relation to the station. In Ethernet, a bus topology network, each station is required to listen to data as it flows past on the bus. In a Token Ring environment made up of point to point links between stations, the data path is through each and every station. This means that as each station is ultimately responsible for receiving and then re-transmitting all data on the ring, it is able to perform basic repeater functionality of signal regeneration and re-timing. Figure 16-1 below demonstrates the logical topology of the ring and highlights how data flow takes place.

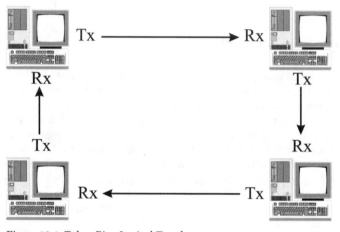

Figure 16-1: Token Ring Logical Topology

Token Ring is based upon a deterministic protocol of token passing providing permission to gain access to the ring. This requires the continual circulation of a token (a special three octet sequence easily identified by all stations), which stations are able to "capture" thus allowing them to transmit. This then, will ensure that only one station is able to transmit data on to the ring at any given moment, assuming, that is, that only one token exists. As with any baseband digital technology a fundamental principle is to ensure that only a single data signal exists on the cable at any moment in time. Token Ring achieves this very simply by only allowing transmission if the station is in possession of the token.

So, taking the basic points mentioned thus far, what is the normal method of operation on the ring? As previously mentioned, a token circulates continuously. Any node with data queued for transmission must wait to receive this token before it may transmit its data. Upon receipt of the token, the node will "remove" it from the ring and replace it with its data frame. This will be transmitted downstream to the next node on the ring. Like other technologies, Token Ring frames include address information regarding the intended destination and the source of the data. This will ensure that only the intended target(s) will process the data contained within the frame.

Based on figure 16-2, assuming node A was the source of the transmission and node C the intended destination, the following text describes the basic events taking place in the transmission of a single data frame. Node A, having data queued for transmission, waits for, then captures the token and replaces it with its data frame. This frame will then be received on the incoming port by node B who will copy the

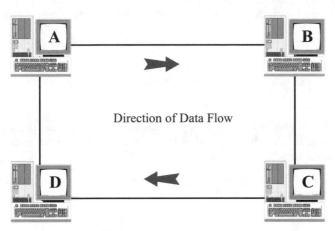

Figure 16-2: Basic Token Ring Operation

frame into both its repeat and frame buffers. Node B at this point is responsible for onward transmission to its downstream neighbor, node C. It must however, also determine whether this frame is in fact destined for itself, and would thus require further processing. In addition, while forwarding and potentially processing the frame, node B will perform basic error checking on the arriving data to ensure that what does arrive is complete and error free. These processes are separate but inextricably linked, in that, the results of destination address determination and error checking could force a modification of the repeated data frame. As this frame is destined for another node, and assuming no errors were detected, the frame will be repeated unmodified downstream to node C.

Node C will ultimately receive the incoming frame and again will copy it to its frame and repeat buffers. This time the receiving node will recognize the destination address as matching its own and will copy the entire frame in to its frame buffer for further processing. Simultaneously, the frame will also be repeated onward to the next downstream node. However, as the destination station, it will modify certain flags at the end of the frame to indicate that it has both recognized its address and managed to successfully copy the frame. This provides Token Ring with a confirmation of delivery service unseen in the Ethernet environment. You will notice at this point that the receiving station has no responsibility for the removal of the frame from the ring. This is an important point as it is quite possible that the frame could in fact be destined for more than one recipient. Node D will be the next recipient of the frame on its continuing circulation of the ring. Its response to receiving this particular frame will ultimately be the same as node B as it is not an intended recipient.

The frame will eventually be received back by node A, the source of the frame on the ring. Initially, A will start repeating the frame, at least the first few fields, until it recognizes its own address in the source address field. Upon recognition it will start to strip the frame from the ring and issue a new token. While stripping, node A will check the flags at the end of the frame to see whether the frame had been successfully received and copied by the destination. If not then steps can be taken to resolve the problem. It may be that the destination station is not available, it may be on another ring, it may not even exist. In any case, the Token Ring node is actually aware that a problem exists and can take steps to solve it if required.

Some thought based on just this simple description of the Token Ring protocol will highlight potential problems that could occur. For example, consider the following:

- What would happen to the transmission path, should a member of the ring be switched off or fail in some way? Could the transmission path heal itself to maintain ring integrity?

- What would happen if a node were to be removed from the ring while in possession of the token?

- What happens when a node is removed from the ring before it can remove any data frames it placed on the ring?

- What happens when there is a protocol failure and nodes need to be re-initialized?

Each of these needs to be addressed if Token Ring is to provide any level of resilient performance. One solution taken is to assign a single station on the ring to monitor the token passing protocol and to take steps towards recovery if some form of protocol breakdown occurs. This station is known as the Active Monitor and has a number of specific responsibilities.

Each node on the ring has the ability to assume the role, but only one will be elected to do so. Should protocol breakdown occur then the Active Monitor will be able to detect the problem and initiate error recovery. Every other station will assume the role of Standby Monitor ensuring that the Active Monitor fulfils all of its responsibilities. Each of these two functions requires a method by which it can check correct protocol operation. With Token Ring, the role of timers, counters, and flags is crucial to normal protocol execution. In this way, everything from the presence of the Active Monitor to the circulation of the token is timed, and error recovery procedures are put in place should any of these timers expire prematurely, or indeed overrun, depending on purpose.

Token Ring can only function successfully if a fair degree of sophistication is built in to the technology. This sophistication provides a LAN access technology that is both reliable and extremely resilient. For this reason Token Ring is well favored in city institutions, the financial sector, and manufacturing automation, in fact, any application where resilience, not budget, is the overriding concern. This resilience is discussed in detail in the chapters that follow.

16.3 4Mbps and 16Mbps Operation

Token Ring, when first developed, operated at speeds of either 1 or 4 megabits per second (Mbps). The 1989 release of the IEEE 802.5 standard dropped 1Mbps and introduced 16Mbps operation. Today, both 4 and 16Mbps Token Ring are still widely installed and are often both existent on the same LAN. The method of operation for both is the same with only the speed of transmission varying. This difference is enough however, to make direct communication between two stations operating at different speeds impossible. Where stations do exist on the same network operating at 4 and 16Mbps then either a Bridge or a Router must be used to separate the two on to different rings.

The introduction of 16Mbps operation has highlighted a potential problem in larger networks. One of the fundamental rules of Token Ring, is that any station transmitting data is not allowed to release the token back onto the ring until it starts to receive back the last frame it has transmitted. This may seem fairly sensible, in that it guarantees that no other station can transmit data until the currently transmitting station is in the throws of stripping off the last of its own frames. The potential problem lies in the period of time between transmitting the last frame and receiving it back so that you can release the token. During this period, the transmitting station must generate a fill pattern on the ring (the ring must not be quiet as in Ethernet). During the time the fill pattern is being generated the ring is effectively not being used for useful transmission, and thus bandwidth is being wasted. This can impact the efficiency of the ring, and therefore some steps are obviously required to overcome the problem.

16.4 Early Token Release

Early Token Release (ETR) is the solution provided to overcome this problem. When enabled (normally an option on today's NICs), the station will release the token downstream immediately after transmitting the last of its data frames rather than waiting for the frame to return. The token will then be available to the next node downstream as soon as it has repeated the incoming frame. This node is then free to transmit data onto the ring. This could lead to multiple frames on the ring at the same moment. For this reason it is sometimes known as the multiple frame single token protocol.

The phenomenon of wasting bandwidth due to waiting for frames to return prior to releasing the token is only significant in a 16Mbps Token Ring rather than 4Mbps. For this reason, ETR is only implemented at the faster speed and even then will only be beneficial on larger rings that transmit a significant number of fairly small frames.

16.5 Summary

Although serving only as a brief introduction, we have seen this chapter potentially raise more questions than it answers. Token Ring has been around now for over twenty five years and still has a loyal, if shrinking, user base. This is essentially focused in financial, manufacturing, and retail environments due to its inherent resilience, predictable response times, and available bandwidth. All of these features are available due to the sophisticated mechanisms within Token Ring that provide the points of discussion in the following sections. Chapter 17 discusses the Physical Layer operation of Token Ring covering such points as media, connectivity, timing, and latency. Chapter 18 on the other hand looks closely at the protocol itself at the MAC Layer, where most of the sophistication is provided. As with many networking technologies, management is a key aspect of successful operation, and Token Ring is no different. Chapter 19 therefore details the management functions within the technology and the benefits they provide. Chapters 20, 21, and 22 look beyond the basic IEEE 802.5 based original protocol operation covering extending network design through Source Route Bridging, Dedicated Token Ring, and High Speed Token Ring, respectively. When combined, these chapters provide an in depth coverage of Token Ring technology including modern advances designed to improve service levels to the user.

The Physical Layer

This chapter examines the Physical Layer operation with a Token Ring station, which is separated into two distinct sublayers. The upper sublayer, the Physical Signalling Components (PSC), interfaces directly with the MAC layer and is completely independent of media type being used. This includes aspects such as symbol timing, encoding/decoding, latency on the ring, and the detection of physical errors such as burst errors[1] . The lower sublayer, however, the Physical Media Components (PMC), is media dependent covering topics such as media specifications, Jitter, and electrical characteristics and is discussed in detail in the latter part of this chapter.

17.1 Physical Signalling Path

The function of the PSC is primarily to couple the PMC to the Media Access Control (MAC) at layer two. In other words it provides the interface between the MAC protocol, where data is encapsulated into datalink frames, and the physical port, where electrical/light signals are transmitted and received. Obviously, a transition from MAC frame to electrical signal or vice versa requires a level of sophistication not to mention predefined encoding and decoding mechanisms. The diagram shown in figure 17-1 shows the components that constitute the PSC and how it interfaces with both the MAC and the PMC, while the text below describes the primary functions of these components.

- ***PHY Receiver/Transmitter***
  These provide the direct interface to the ring, transmitting or receiving electrical/light signals depending on the media type. The sole purpose of the PHY receiver is to correctly receive signals and pass them to the PSC for interpretation. Likewise, the transmitter transmits signals passed to it by the PSC. Both of the components are media dependant as you would expect.

- ***Delimiter Detector***
  As the name suggests, the Delimiter Detector is there to detect start and end delimiters and signal their presence to the MAC. This is important for the purposes of token detection and frame start/end detection. As Token Ring uses nonstandard symbols to indicate

---

[1] Burst errors are discussed in detail in section 17.4.1.

start and end delimiters, it is a very easy physical layer function to detect them.

- **Symbol Decoder/Encoder**

  The Symbol decoder is used to convert Differential Manchester[2] encoded signal elements to MAC recognizable Data or Non-data symbols. Likewise, the encoder takes symbols from the MAC and encodes them into differential Manchester format before passing the encoded signal through the PSC towards the PHY transmitter.

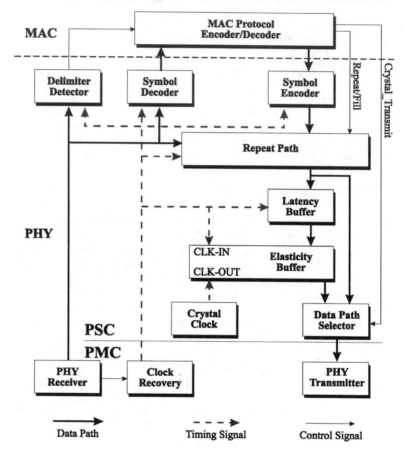

Figure 17-1:   Internal Data Path

- **Repeat Path**

  The Repeat path is controlled by the MAC and through it flows all data, whether it be repeated data or station generated. The idea on which this is based is fairly simple, in that by having all data flow

---

[2] Differential Manchester encoding is discussed in section 17.2.

The Physical Layer

through a single point it is easy to control the output, i.e., if only a single output from this point exists, then a station cannot repeat if the MAC is transmitting, therefore frame stripping will occur. Likewise, if not transmitting the MAC can order a fill pattern to be generated to allow for frame stripping.

- ***Latency Buffer***
  The Latency buffer is only inserted in the data path on the station if it is the Active Monitor. In all other instances it is not used. The function of the Latency Buffer is to ensure that an entire token can exist on the ring. How this is achieved and why it is necessary is described in detail in section 17.3.1.

- ***Elasticity Buffer***
  As with the Latency Buffer, this is only used by the Active Monitor for the purpose of adjusting the overall ring latency in harmony with its own internal clock. Described in more detail in section 17.3.2.

- ***Internal Clock***
  The internal crystal clock is also only used by the Active Monitor and is directly linked to the Elasticity Buffer. The Active Monitor is responsible for the overall ring latency as compared with this internal clock. All other stations derive their clocking information from the received data signal as shown in the diagram and explained in section 17.2.

- ***Data Path Selector***
  As the diagram shows, signal elements can arrive at the Path Selector either direct from the Repeat Path or via the Elasticity Buffer. The Path selector defines which signal stream is sent to the PHY Transmitter and which is cut off.

17.2 Encoding Techniques

Some form of encoding is required to convert data symbols into electrical signals prior to transmission. However, when considering encoding, another aspect comes to the fore to complicate matters, namely that of synchronization. The problem is straightforward; if a transmitter transmits a signal, how can you be sure that the receiving element maintains synchronization with the transmitted signal? If synchronization is not maintained, then interpretation of the received signal will be corrupt when compared with the original data. So therefore options need to be considered as to how this problem can be overcome.

A simple method to maintaining synchronization is to transmit a separate timing signal in parallel with the data signal. Clocking for the incoming data can then be derived from this distinctly separate received input. This method however, requires the use of an additional transmission circuit distinct from the data path.

Although this may be possible in a multi-pair cable, it becomes totally impractical across fiber as it would require two duplex patch cords per connection. Another method, and one preferred by most LAN technologies, is to build a timing element into the data signal in such a manner that the receiving end could derive clocking, and therefore maintain synchronization, from the data signal received. This has the distinct advantage that only one communications channel is required as well as ensuring that all receivers utilize the same timing source when decoding the signal. A number of different encoding mechanisms exist which allow timing information to be included within the data signal, with differential Manchester encoding being the method employed by Token Ring.

17.2.1 Differential Manchester Encoding

Manchester encoding dictates that there should be two signal elements per data symbol, with a transition between the two elements at the mid point as shown in figure 17-2. As the diagram shows, for data one and data zero symbols, a mid point transition to the opposite polarity is made. The purpose of this transition is to incorporate a timing element into the signal. This is achieved by the fact that no

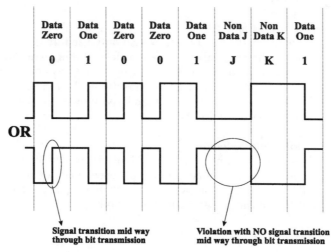

Figure 17-2:   Differential Manchester Encoding

matter what the data stream, a signal transition is guaranteed to occur at a predefined interval equating to one bit time, i.e., from the mid point of one bit to the mid point of the next. Any signal transitions at the full bit boundary are used to determine the value of the bit being transmitted based on the following rules.

- A Data-One symbol is denoted by the first signal element being of the same polarity as the second signal element of the preceding bit. Therefore, there is no signal transition at the initial bit boundary.

- A Data-Zero symbol is transmitted with the first signal element of the opposite polarity to the second element of the preceding bit. Therefore, there is a signal transition at the start of the symbol.

- For all data symbols there is a mid bit transition from the first to the second signal element.

- Non-Data symbols J & K exist as violations to Differential Manchester encoding for the purpose of immediate recognition within the data stream. They do not include mid bit signal transitions and as such are instantly recognizable to receiving devices. Their purpose is to act as start and end delimiters to both tokens and frames. Remember that on the ring the signal is continuous (data or fill), so it is therefore essential that stations can recognize, within this continuous stream, where tokens/frame start and finish.

- A J violation is denoted by both signal elements being of the same polarity as the second element of the preceding bit. While a K violation has both signal elements of the opposite polarity to the latter half of the preceding bit. You will note that the lack of mid bit signal transitions means that when these are being transmitted, no timing information is included. This proves not to be a problem as they are only ever transmitted as JK symbol pairs and are always separated by a data symbol. Therefore, a receiving station will never experience more than three bit times between mid bit transitions. All stations can maintain synchronization for a period this short.

It should be noted that while Differential Manchester encoding is similar to Manchester encoding, described in the Ethernet section, there is the subtle difference in how data-one and data-zero symbols are defined. In addition, the Ethernet standard does not recognize non-data symbols as used within Token Ring.

17.3 Ring Latency

Ring Latency on a Token Ring network is an important feature that must remain consistent when the ring is in normal operation. It is defined as the cumulative latency of the ring plus the internal latency of the Active Monitor. The cumulative latency of the ring is further defined as being the time it takes a signal element to travel around the ring from the Active Monitor's transmitter back to its receiver. As each station on the ring derives its clocking information from the Active Monitor, it is thus the responsibility of the AM to maintain a consistent ring latency.

Under normal protocol operation, only one station, the Active Monitor utilizes the internal Crystal Clock. The diagram shown in figure 17-1, shows the clock interfacing directly with the Elasticity Buffer. This buffer is one of two employed within the Active Monitor which are both inserted within the data path, and as such add to the overall ring latency.

17.3.1 Fixed Latency Buffer

The Fixed Latency Buffer is utilized by the Active Monitor for the sole purpose of ensuring that an entire 24-bit token can exist on the ring. Imagine the situation where there are only a few devices on the ring. In these circumstances it is possible that the overall physical transmission path is not very long. If the physical path is shorter than is required to accommodate an entire token, then the transmitting device will actually be stripping the token from the ring while it is still transmitting the back end of that token. Therefore, the token cannot possibly circulate as it would continually need to be regenerated. This may sound as though it is not a major consideration until you understand how much physical cable is required to accommodate one token. The formula below gives some idea as to the physical requirements:

Ring Speed $= 4Mbps$
Time taken to transmit 1 bit $= 1/4,000,000 = 2.5 \times 10^{-7}$
Time taken to transmit 24 bits $= 2.5 \times 10^{-7} \times 24 = 6$ *microseconds*
Velocity of propagation of Type 1 STP $= 76\%c$ *(c = speed of light in vacuum)*
$= .76 \times 3 \times 10^{8}$ *approx.*
$= 2.28 \times 10^{8}$ *approx. m/s*

Therefore, using D = S × T, the cable requirement for a single 24 bit token is:
$2.28 \times 10^{8} \times 6 \times 10^{-6}$ $= 1368$ *m approx.*

While the above calculation is based on some approximations, it does serve to demonstrate just how long the transmission path needs to be in order to accommodate a single token. As this is a mandatory requirement i.e., to accommodate the token, another method must be used to ensure the physical transmission path is long enough to satisfy the criteria. Hence, the need for a Fixed Latency Buffer within the Active Monitor. This buffer is inserted into the data path and is predefined at 24 bits in length. In this way it is possible to guarantee that the data path exceeds the minimum requirement as the buffer itself will accommodate the token while any cabling or internal transmission paths that exist on the ring are in excess of the minimum requirements.

17.3.2   Elasticity Buffer

The purpose of the Elasticity Buffer on the Active Monitor is to compensate for variations in the cumulative latency on the ring. This is achieved by inserting a buffer into the data path that has the ability to grow or shrink depending on whether the arriving data stream is faster or slower than the internal crystal clock. The buffer, initialized at 3 bits for 4Mbps or 15 bits for 16Mbps operation, will shrink accordingly if the data stream is slower than the internal clock, and grow if it is faster. The net effect is to speed up or slow down the overall ring latency to bring it into line with the crystal clock of the Active Monitor. The buffer has the range to shrink to nothing or increase to double its initial size in an effort to maintain the ring latency. Should the signal frequency be outside this range then an underflow/overflow is said to have occurred and a frequency error will be noted.

17.4   Physical Error Detection

For Token Ring to be considered reliable, it has to have built in error detection capability to overcome potential problems. It is possible that errors could occur at the Physical layer i.e., signalling errors due to faulty Network Interface Cards

(NICs), or at the MAC layer due to protocol irregularities. Protocol errors are dealt with in chapter 19, while Physical layer error detection is discussed below.

17.4.1 Burst Errors

We have seen that the encoding mechanism employed, Differential Manchester encoding, implements polarity changes in the signal to denote Data-one or zero and Non-data symbols. We also know that Differential Manchester encoding places a polarity change at the mid-point of each data symbol encoded thus creating two distinct signal elements per symbol. Therefore, a normal transmission signal should never have more than three signal elements in succession without a polarity change. In fact, the only time three signal elements of the same polarity in succession do occur is when a Non-data J symbol is transmitted. Therefore, if four or more signal elements arrive in succession of the same polarity, it is considered an error condition.

When a receiving station detects four signal elements arriving of the same polarity in succession it will indicate a Burst4_error to the MAC. If the next signal element arrives still of the same polarity, a Burst5_error is reported and the PSC inverts the signal before repeating it. By inverting the signal, the PSC never repeats more than four signal elements of the same polarity and thus ensures that the downstream station does not detect the same Burst5_error. In this way, burst errors are said to be isolating, as the cause must be immediately upstream from the station detecting the Burst5_error.

17.4.2 Frequency Errors

Although rare, frequency errors can occur whereby the received signal is outside the acceptable clocking thresholds of the receiving station. Because the data stream is clocked via the crystal clock within the Active Monitor, should this problem arise it is normally due to a faulty NIC in the station upstream from the detecting device. Detection occurs through monitoring overflow/underflow of the elasticity buffer, whether or not it is actually in the data path (remember, only the Active Monitor inserts the elasticity buffer into the data path). For a frequency error to occur, the average bit rate over a 32 ms period must be outside the range of +/- 10% of the required bit rate of 4 Mbps or 16 Mbps whichever is implemented.

17.5 Media Types

Token Ring makes use of different media types to suit different customer requirements. Although cabling is covered in more detail in chapter 38, it is also relevant to discuss specifics applicable to Token Ring in this section. As with Ethernet, Token Ring has embraced new media types as and when technology allowed. It all started with Shielded Twisted Pair (STP) from the IBM Cabling System, with Unshielded and Foil Screened Twisted Pair (UTP/FTP) being added to the allowable media list in recent years. Like Ethernet, Fiber is also utilized, initially only for trunk cabling, however the 1998 version of the ISO 8802-5 standard includes an Amendment defining direct station attachment over fiber optic cabling.

One major difference between Ethernet and Token Ring media is the omission of any form of Co-axial support within Token Ring. The reason for this is straightforward in that co-ax only provides a single transmission path, while a Token Ring station requires two paths, one to connect its transmitter to the downstream receiver, and one to connect its receiver to the upstream transmitter. Therefore, the only media supported are twisted pair and fiber, each of which can provide duplex connections.

17.5.1   IBM Shielded Twisted Pair (STP)

IBM was the first organization to define a structured cabling system in 1984 after the deregulation of the US Telecoms market. The system was based on high quality Shielded Twisted Pair (STP) cable and a connector, which is widely known as the IBM MIC (Media Interface Connector). IBM STP comes in a number of different forms, as defined below, each of which has slightly different construction, thereby offering different transmission characteristics. The idea being that each cable type provides different advantages in different environments, i.e., a solid core cable is better for distribution purposes, while a strand core cable makes a better patch cable.

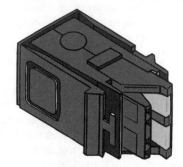

Figure 17-3:   IBM MIC Connector

In all their STP cable forms, the same basic construction method is adhered to. That is a two pair cable, with each individual pair being twisted together and foil screened. The two screened bundles are then enclosed in an overall braided metal screen within the PVC jacket. This provides for excellent transmission characteristics due to the high quality materials and excellent immunity to Electro-Magnetic Interference (EMI). The main types are described below:

- **Type 1A**
  Superseding Type 1, Type 1A is based on 2-pair STP utilizing 22AWG (0.6mm) solid core conductors. It is capable of supporting a signalling rate up to 350 Mhz making it a very high performance cable. It is primarily used for distribution cabling and trunk cables.

- **Type 2A**
  Type 2A is a hybrid cable based on Type 1A with the inclusion of four pairs of UTP between the outer braided shield and the PVC jacket. The idea being that the STP inner can be utilized for data connectivity, while the outer UTP can be used for voice connections. Although popular in the US, this cable type is not used in some parts of the world as running voice and data on the same physical cable is frowned upon by some Telecoms organizations.

- **_Type 6A_**

  Again superseding an earlier version, Type 6A is also rated to 350 Mhz. Based on 26AWG (0.4mm) stranded conductors, this cable is designed to be flexible and is ideal for patch cables and work area fly leads. It should be noted that the normal connector used when attaching to an end user device is the nine pin DB9 connector.

- **_Type 9A_**

  This is a smaller, space saving version of Type 1A. It is based on the same construction method as Type 1A but has 26AWG (0.4mm) solid conductors. This means it can be used for all the same applications as Type 1A but typically only supports ⅔ the distance.

All the cable types defined above have a characteristic impedance of 150 ohms. They are the media on which Token Ring was designed and still account for a large proportion of the installed Token Ring base.

17.5.2   Unshielded Twisted Pair (UTP)

UTP is fast becoming the media type of choice to the desktop. This is because it provides the performance levels required while remaining relatively low cost by comparison to other media types. Chapter 39 provides an in depth discussion on UTP and structured cabling systems, however some specifics are worthy of mentioning while considering Token Ring technology. ISO/IEC 11801 standard defines UTP categories 3, 4 and 5 for use with structured cabling systems. While it remains perfectly possible to run some forms of Token Ring over Cat3 and Cat4 (4 Mbps operation), only Cat5 cable has the

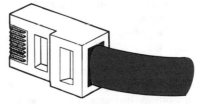

Figure 17-4:   UTP RJ45 Connector

performance capability to run all forms of Token Ring. It is therefore advisable when considering UTP, to implement Cat5 for this technology.

Category 5 UTP is constructed of four pairs of 24AWG (0.5mm) solid core (for distribution cable) or stranded conductors (for patch leads). Each pair is twisted together to minimize the effects of EMI. These are then enclosed within a PVC jacket. The standard connector is the 8-pin modular jack defined in ISO 8877 but more commonly known as the RJ45 connector. This is available in different forms for both stranded and solid core conductors. There are two wiring options available for the RJ45 jack as defined in ISO/IEC 11801. These are laid out in table 17-1, however it should be noted that Token Ring only utilizes two pairs namely on pins 3 & 6, and 4 & 5. Pins 1, 2, 7, & 8 are not used and remain redundant.

When utilizing UTP, some factors require important consideration within the network design. The main one being reduced ring lengths when compared to Type 1 STP. Another important aspect is that Token Ring was designed for 150 ohm cabling infrastructure. UTP has an impedance of 100 ohms and therefore would create an impedance mismatch unless some form of matching device was also included within the design. The device used for this purpose is known as a media filter and is discussed in more detail in section 17.5.4.

Table 17-1: RJ45 Wiring Options

Pin	EIA T568A	EIA T568B	Signal (As seen by station)
1	White/Green	White/Orange	Not Used
2	Green	Orange	Not Used
3	White/Orange	White/Green	Transmit - A
4	Blue	Blue	Receive - A
5	White/Blue	White/Blue	Receive - B
6	Orange	Green	Transmit - B
7	White/Brown	White/Brown	Not Used
8	Brown	Brown	Not Used

17.5.3   Foil Screened Twisted Pair (FTP)

Foil Screened Twisted Pair (FTP), also known as UTP-S or S-UTP, is similar in construction to UTP but also includes a foil screen surrounding all four pairs to provide greater immunity to EMI. It is becoming more popular in some countries as legislation becomes tougher on emissions and immunity. From a performance perspective, it is categorized in the same fashion as UTP and offers the same performance levels. Its popularity is due to the myth that to conform to current EMI regulations, some form of screening is required. In reality, a properly installed cabling infrastructure utilizing quality components should comply whether it is screened or not.

An important factor to consider when implementing a screened cabling solution is the continuity of the screening and the quality of the grounding. The current guidelines indicate that screening should be continuous from earth point to end user equipment, but grounded at only a single point, to avoid earth loops. For a full discussion on screening see chapter 39.

17.5.4   Media Filters

When utilizing "standard" Token Ring Network Interface Cards (NICs) or I/O Controllers on devices such as Bridges and Routers, most transmitters have been designed for operation over 150 ohm impedance cabling. Should it be desired to connect these devices to 100 ohm UTP/FTP cabling then it is likely that a large impedance mismatch will occur. This will cause signal reflections within the cable, likely to create signal distortion, and could also lead to excessive radiated EMI.

The answer would seem to lie with an impedance matching transformer however, this would also pose a problem. The matching transformer would allow AC data signals through without problem and it would also match the impedance levels. Unfortunately the transformer would block all DC signals. This would be a big problem as stations rely on a DC Phantom signal[3] to open the bypass relay with

---

[3] Phantom Signals are covered in section 17.6.2.

the MSAU[4] to gain access to the ring. It is therefore imperative for DC signals to pass unhindered. One way of doing this would be to use an active transformer that was powered. The drawback here is that this device would require a power supply and would inevitably be more expensive and cumbersome. The solution is to use a media filter. A media filter does not provide impedance matching, for the reasons discussed above, it merely "softens" or attenuates the signal to minimize the effects of the mismatch. In this way DC current is not blocked and the impedance mismatch does not cause a problem with regard to excessive

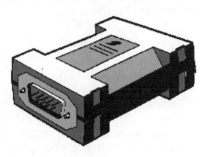

Figure 17-5: Media Filter

reflections or EMI. The device can remain small and unpowered, which means that it is cheap and easy to use. It normally comes with DB9 connectivity on one side to connect to the station and RJ45 connectivity on the other side to interconnect with the UTP cabling system.

17.5.5 Fiber Optic Cable

Until recently, fiber optics has only been utilized for trunk connections within Token Ring. The 1998 release of the ISO 8802-5 standard however, includes an amendment defining fiber use for station attachment. In both cases, the fiber defined is 62.5/125 μm multimode fiber, although 50/125 μm is a viable alternative.

As with many other LAN technologies, Token Ring has a standard distance limitation over fiber of 2Km. This allows for larger ring design or building interconnection. The standard connector used has been the ST (bayonet) connector, however, current equipment releases are now utilizing the new SC (Subscriber) connector as specified in the ISO/IEC 11801 cabling standard, and shown in the lower part of Figure 17-6, and described in detail in chapter 39.

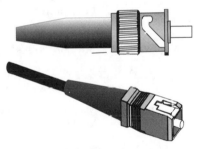

Figure 17-6: Fiber ST and SC Connectors

Due to the nature of fiber, it requires active equipment but this does not exclude its use in a passive network design. Signal conversion is required from electrical to optical (light) signals, therefore the ideal device is a Token Ring repeater at either end of the trunk connection. This unit is typically an external box in a passive environment, or built into the trunk port in an active MAU. In many cases, active MAUs provide modular Trunk ports allowing a "mix and match" approach to suit local cabling plant. This is possible as only the functions of the PMC differ between various media types. Therefore the PSC remains media independent.

---

[4] MSAU (Multi-Station Access Unit) is discussed in section 17.6.1.

The use of fiber optics for station attachment is discussed in section 17.6.9 on Fiber Optic MAUs.

17.6 Physical Topology

Token Ring is a classic example of how the logical topology of the network can differ from the physical topology. Logically, the technology operates as a ring. However, it has already been mentioned that a physical ring can have potential problems. For example, if the transmission path is through each station, what happens should a station be turned off? This would seem to break the transmission path thus damaging the integrity of the ring. There is also the complexity of trying to cable the network such that each station has its transmitter connected to the receiver of its downstream neighbor. To simplify connectivity, and to overcome some of the potential problems, Token Ring is installed with a physical star topology with point to point links between stations and a central concentrator known as a Multi-Station Access Unit (MSAU). The ring then exists within the MAU so that the logical topology of Token Ring can prevail.

17.6.1 Multi-Station Access Units (MSAUs or MAUs)

Token Ring allows for two different type of MAU known as the Passive MAU and the Active MAU. Both provide the following basic functionality:

- Allow stations to couple to the ring via their lobe[5] cables.

- Provide interconnection between ports (known as Trunk Coupling Units TCUs) to allow a star wired network topology to be built.

- Support both 4Mbps and 16Mbps operation.

- Allow TCU detection by the end station to allow monitoring for physical faults such as open/short circuits.

- May include Ring In and Ring Out ports to interconnect multiple MAUs.

The basic difference between the two types of MAU is in the circuitry within the unit and what that does to the data signal. The Passive MAU, as the name suggests, is completely passive and simply provides a signal path between stations, reliant upon each station to drive the signal to its downstream neighbor. On the other hand, the Active Retiming MAU is fully powered and provides embedded repeater functionality within the data path of each port. This means that each station only needs to be able to drive a signal as far as the MAU port before it is actively repeated. This has the distinctive advantage of extending the maximum physical size of the ring.

A MAU consists of two distinctly different types of ports, Lobe ports for station connectivity and Ring In/Out ports for MAU interconnectivity. The diagram in

---

[5] Lobe Cables are the cables that connect devices to the MAUs and can include patch, distribution, and fly cables.

figure 17-7 shows the basic data path through the MAU. When operating in a single MAU ring, the primary path automatically wraps to the backup path, thus constructing an internal ring within the MAU.

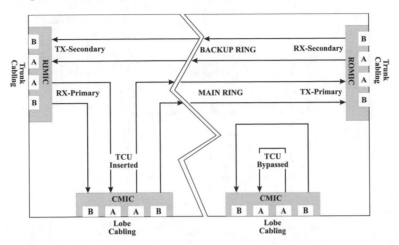

Figure 17-7: Data Transmission Path within a MAU

Figure 17-8 shows a more detailed view of the internal construction of a Shielded Twisted Pair Passive MAU, which for many years was the basic building block of Token Ring networks. As you can see the unit consists of a number of TCUs for lobe attachment and a Ring In and a Ring Out port for ring extension. Each TCU includes a bypass relay such that if a station is not inserted and an active member of the ring, the relay is closed and the port is bypassed. This overcomes the problem of a break in ring integrity being caused by a station removing itself from the ring.

Concentrators are available today in many forms, supporting three different media types, with many port count variations, and as we have seen, active and passive varieties. All include lobe ports for station connectivity and some also include Ring in/Out trunk ports for ring extension.

Although only STP is shown in the diagram, three variations of the Media Interface Connector (MIC) exist for the lobe port. These are the CMIC_S for STP (as shown), the CMIC_U for UTP cabling, and a new version the FMIC for fiber optic attachment. The CMIC_S lobe connector is defined in the standard to support the IBM MIC connector[6] widely used with Shielded Twisted Pair (STP) cabling. This cable type has two pairs of conductors, each twisted together and individually screened. This provides excellent transmission characteristics as described in section 17.5.1. One pair (Black/Orange) is utilized for transmission while the other (Red/Green) is used for reception. The CMIC_U is based on the RJ-45 connector traditionally used with Unshielded Twisted Pair (UTP). Although based on a four pair cable, only pins 3, 4, 5, & 6 are used with pins 3 & 6 used to transmit and 4 & 5 for receive. Pins 1, 2, 7, & 8 are not used in Token Ring. The latest version (1998)

---

[6] The IBM MIC Connector is described in section 17.5.1.

of the standard also defines the FMIC. One of the main considerations here is the inclusion of electrical to optical conversion within the TCU. This is considered in more detail in Section 17.6.9 on Fiber Optic MAUs.

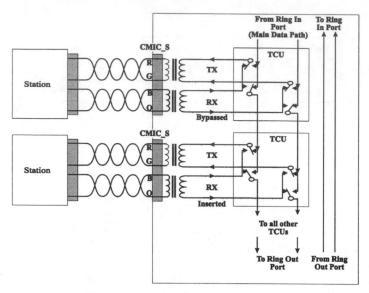

Figure 17-8:   Inserted and Bypassed State

17.6.2   Phantom Current

The process by which the relay within the TCU is opened is part of the Ring Join process and involves the application of a "Phantom Current" by the end station. This is a DC current applied by the station along the lobe cable to the TCU. This current is known as Phantom because as it is DC by nature it is "invisible" to the data signal which is AC in nature. It is however enough to open the relay and allow access to the ring. Two circuits exist, on TX-A/RX-A and TX-B/RX-B. This ensures that all conductive paths within the lobe cable are part of the transmission path for the Phantom Current. In this way, should a fault exist within the cable or transmitter/receiver hardware of the station, the Phantom Current will not be able to open the relay, thus ensuring that faults are not introduced onto the ring. The voltage level of the DC current should not exceed 7.0v differential between the source and return. In addition, the current should be no greater than 20mA.

As we have seen, the main purpose of the Phantom Current, in conjunction with the TCU, is to allow stations to join and leave the ring as and when required without damaging ring integrity. It also provides another valuable service, in that continual wire fault detection is maintained within each station's transmission path. The Phantom has to be maintained all the while a station is attached to the ring. Therefore, should cable failure occur or even hardware failure within the station, the Phantom will disappear and thus the relay will close. Figure 17-9 shows both Phantom circuits and it can be seen that wire faults such as open or short circuits can be readily detected at either end of the connection. Some MAUs

The Physical Layer

also include LED indicators to show when Phantom is applied and successfully allowing the device to be inserted in the ring.

17.6.3 Trunk Ports

Most, but certainly not all, concentrators include two additional ports known as Trunk ports to allow MAU interconnection to extend the ring. These trunk ports, labelled Ring In and Ring Out, must not be used as station attachment ports as they do not include bypass relays and therefore do not have the protective element offered by the TCU. Typically, but not exclusively, passive MAUs will have MIC connectors as these are self wrapping when unconnected. What this means is that the transmit pair will short to the receive pair if a connection is not made. In this way the ring is contained within the MAU. Once connected, the short circuit is removed and the ring is extend to the additional MAU.

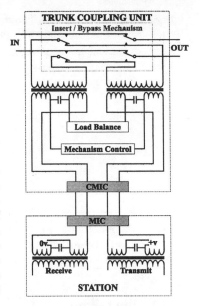

Figure 17-9: Phantom Circuits

With Active MAUs, the choice of media type for the trunk ports is more flexible as the port effectively becomes a repeater[7] . This allows for media conversion as well as extended drive distances, thus a lot of vendors provide modular Ring In/Out ports allowing the end user to decide on the media type best suited to their network.

The diagram in Figure 17-10 shows how, when interconnecting MAUs with full Ring In/Out connectivity, a primary and a secondary ring are created. Although it is not necessary to use both Ring In and Ring Out, it is certainly advisable as the secondary ring is only created when both connections are made. The purpose of the secondary ring is to provide a backup path in the event of connection failure on

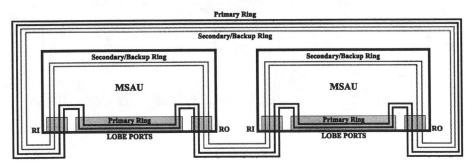

Figure 17-10: MAU Interconnectivity

---

[7] A repeater provides signal regeneration and retiming in much the same manner as an Ethernet repeater.

one of the trunk paths. Table 17-2 shows the pin connectivity to each of the transmission paths at the trunk port.

Table 17-2: Trunk Port Pin Assignments

UTP RI & RO	STP RI & RO	Ring In Signal	Ring Out Signal
1	-	Not Used in ISO 8802-5	
2	-	Not Used in ISO 8802-5	
3	B	TX-Secondary-A	RX-Secondary-A
4	R	RX-Primary-A	TX-Primary-A
5	G	RX-Primary-B	TX-Primary-B
6	O	TX-Secondary-B	RX-Secondary-B
7	-	Not Used in ISO 8802-5	
8	-	Not Used in ISO 8802-5	

Also demonstrated in Table 17-2 is the fact that, like lobe ports, trunk connections only utilize two pairs, even in a four pair UTP. The Red/Green pair connect to the Primary ring while the Black/Orange pair connect to the Secondary ring.

17.6.4 Ring Wrap

The true resilience of the physical ring is demonstrated with a dual ring configuration created when interconnecting multiple MAUs with both Ring In and Ring Out connectivity, as demonstrated in Figure 17-10 with both a primary and a secondary ring being created. The purpose of the primary ring is obviously data transmission, while the secondary ring is not used under normal circumstances.

The secondary (backup) ring is utilized when a failure occurs on one of the trunk paths. If a trunk cable is removed, then the primary ring will automatically wrap onto the secondary ring to maintain a continuous path, as shown in Figure 17-11. This wrapping feature is achieved by shorting the transmit signal channel onto the

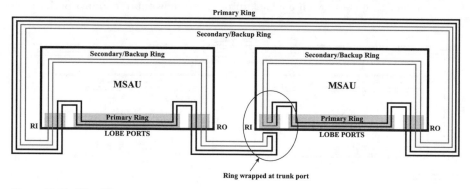

Figure 17-11: Ring Wrap

receive channel, thus maintaining a signal path. The method utilized to achieve this varies depending on the media type, and whether the MAU is Active or Passive.

For STP trunk ports on a Passive MAU, the wrap facility is achieved through the use of MIC connectors on both the port and the trunk cable. This connector, described in detail in section 38.3.2, automatically shorts transmit to receive internally when disconnected. Therefore, should one end of the cable be removed, then the ring will wrap at two points, namely at the trunk port and at the connector itself. This ensures that both open paths are wrapped to the secondary ring. This mechanism is ideal in a passive environment, but does rely on trunk cable removal. It is incapable of wrapping should a cable breakage occur thus leaving the ring damaged and requiring user intervention.

For all media types used when interconnecting Active MAUs, the situation is a little simpler, or is it? Most Active MAUs implement repeated trunk ports which will include some form of wire fault detection on the trunk cable. This normally takes the form of a "phantom" like current being passed down the trunk cable, which is then detected at the far end, with a similar current being passed back. The existence of the current automatically informs the MAU that the circuit is active and a cable fault does not exist. Sounds simple doesn't it? The problem lies in the fact that most vendors implement a proprietary form of wire fault detection leading to a scenario where it is only likely to work correctly when connected to equipment from the same vendor. This means that in a multi-vendor environment, cable breakage can cause downtime requiring user intervention. The answer is to implement an Active ring network with a single vendor supporting wire fault detection.

The wrap facility should be regarded as an extremely useful resilience feature within Token Ring, which in most cases provides an added level of protection not found in some other technologies implemented today.

17.6.5 Drive Distances

When implementing Token Ring, one of the most important factors to consider is the maximum drive distance supported. We have seen that a station is responsible for driving a signal around the ring to the next device downstream. In an active network it is aided by the repeater functionality within the TCU. However, in a passive network, the transmitting station is totally responsible for driving the signal to its downstream neighbor. If you consider the situation where a station is the only one on the ring, it becomes more apparent why drive distance is an important consideration. In this scenario, the transmitting station must drive the signal around the entire ring and back to itself without suffering excessive attenuation[8]. The situation of having a single station on the ring is made even worse if the ring should wrap as this effectively doubles the ring length. This then is the worst case scenario and must be catered for in the network design if Token Ring is to be reliable under all circumstances.

Many factors affect the maximum supported drive distance including; ring speed, media type, and attenuation. Each of these is explained in the text that follows:

---

[8] Attenuation is the weakening of the signal amplitude over distance.

- **Ring Speed**

  Drive distance is reduced as the signalling rate increases due to increased attenuation. Therefore the distance supported at 16Mbps will be less than at 4Mbps.

- **Media Type**

  Due to the transmission characteristics of different media types, different maximum drive distances can be obtained from each cable type. For reference, the following limits can be applied for each form of cabling at the two main ring speeds.

Table 17-3: Maximum Drive Distances

Media Type	4 Mbps	16 Mbps
IBM Type 1 & 2 STP	770 meters	346 meters
IBM Type 6 & 9 STP	579 meters	260 meters
Category 5 UTP	400 meters	100 meters
Multimode Fiber	2 Km	2 Km

- **Attenuation**

  All transmission media suffer from attenuation, which can be best described as signal power loss over distance. The greater the distance, the greater the signal loss. With copper cabling, the signalling rate also affects the attenuation, again with higher rates suffering the worst. The key aspect is that a signal must not be attenuated to such an extent that the signal strength is below the minimum sensitivity of the receiver at the far end. With fiber optics, signalling rate has no effect on attenuation, hence the same maximum drive distances for both operating speeds.

17.6.6   Adjusted Ring Length (ARL)

When designing a passive Token Ring network, drive distance is important in the design, but to allow for all conditions, a wrapped ring condition must be catered for. Figure 17-11 demonstrated how, under this condition, the transmission distance practically doubled in length. It is paramount that this is allowed for in a network design otherwise the ring will fail to operate when wrapped.

The Adjusted Ring Length is the term used to describe the ring in a wrapped condition and is calculated by adding the lengths of all the trunk cables and then subtracting the shortest one. This provides the worst case ARL which, if within specification, should ensure the ring continues to operate when wrapped. Tables have been published, shown in section 17.7, which can be used to calculate the allowable ARL if the longest Lobe cable is known, or alternatively, using the known ARL, calculate the longest allowable Lobe cable. To ensure the network continues operation when wrapped, these calculations must be carried out, and if the figures do not add up then the network must be re-designed. Examples of calculating ARLs and allowable designs are given in a later section on Network Design.

17.6.7   Station Counts

There are no fixed limits on station counts in Token Ring in the same way as there are in Ethernet. There are however, limits on overall Jitter and Attenuation allowable on the ring, which indirectly limits the station count. This is especially true of Jitter (timing irregularities that occur through timing recovery within stations) which effectively limits the station count to a maximum of 250 on a ring.

The maximum station count actually depends on whether Active or Passive MAUs are used to build the network. The figures in Table 17-4 can be used as a guideline as to the limits that can be achieved, although in reality networks today are getting smaller rather than larger as administrators segregate their corporate networks to increase bandwidth available to the end user using techniques such as bridging and routing.

Table 17-4: Maximum Station Counts

Passive MAUs	4 Mbps	16 Mbps
Max. Number of Stations	250	250
Additional other Repeating Elements	50	125
Active MAUs		
Max. Number of Stations	144	180
Max. Number of Re-timing TCU Ports	144	180
Additional other Repeating Elements	12	15

The station count for Active Token Ring is much reduced from the Passive variety due to the active retiming circuitry within the TCU, which in itself is a source of Jitter. These figures can only be used as a guideline because no hard and fast rules exist. For example, if the station count is reduced, then the number of repeater elements can be increased accordingly. In addition, many vendors actually state maximum station numbers for rings built with their equipment, which in some cases is much less than the figures stated above. Therefore the rules are simple, if the manufacturer of your equipment states a maximum figure, do not exceed this amount. If no figure is stated, then the guidelines in this text can be used.

17.6.8   Active vs Passive

The question of whether to build a network based on Active or Passive equipment is one open to debate. However, some of the points highlighted below may help in making the decision:

- Passive networks require detailed design calculations to ensure that drive distances are not exceeded, even under a wrapped condition.

- Active networks are simpler to design as drive distance is not as important a consideration, rather maximum cabling distances are often specified by the manufacturer of the equipment which need to be adhered to.

- Active MAUs often have modular trunk ports allowing more flexible implementation with existing cable plant.

- Active MAUs are often manageable, providing network administrators more control over the network.

- Active MAUs often combine more features such as Automatic Ring Speed Detection and Automatic Beacon Resolution.

- Passive MAUs are cheaper.

The conclusion seems to be that assuming cost is not the major issue, Active Token Ring provides more benefits than Passive. It is certainly true that it provides more features and tends to be more flexible.

17.6.9 Fiber Optic MAUs

Fiber optic station attachment may seem a simple extension to supported configurations, after all it has been available in an Ethernet environment since 1992. In Token Ring, however, there were some problems that needed to be overcome before a standardized version could be released. Essentially there are two main considerations when connecting stations via fiber cable. The first is electrical to optical signal conversion. This particular problem is fairly easily solved due to modern communications circuitry, in fact many technologies use signal converters. The second problem is potentially more of an issue and specific to Token Ring. In a copper MAU, a phantom current is used to open the bypass relay in the TCU. Should the station want to disconnect or a fault develop then the phantom current would disappear and the bypass relay would close, thus preserving the integrity of the ring. For a fiber optic MAU to provide the same level of resilience, it must have a mechanism whereby the station can signal insert or bypass, as well as an automated method to detect faults so that stations can be removed from the ring.

It is obvious that a phantom current does not provide the answer with fiber. The alternative used is a mechanism based on out-of-band command signalling. This provides the ability to toggle or "key" command signals that in turn instruct the TCU to insert or bypass the ring. An echo mechanism is also used to return the command signals to the station so that wire fault conditions can be detected. The text that follows describes this process in a little more detail.

The 1998 version of ISO 8802-5 Amd 1 defines two new interfaces for Token Ring, namely the Fiber Media Interface (FMI) and the Fiber Media Interface Connector (FMIC). Both are designed to support 62.5/125 μm multimode fiber, but 50/125 μm and 100/140 μm fiber are also specified as an alternative. The supported wavelength for the light source is 850nm providing distance support of up to 2km. All insertion and removal procedures are controlled by the station through the use of "insertion" and "bypass" keys. When not inserted, the TCU must provide a repeat path from the transmit to the receive fiber to allow stations to carry out lobe tests prior to requesting to insert in the ring.

When the station wishes to insert in to the ring it must send an Insertion Key (a specific signal pattern) to the TCU, effectively requesting the TCU to insert into the ring. Upon recognition of the Insertion Key, the TCU will perform the necessary switching to insert the station into the ring. The TCU will also echo the insertion key back to the station that sent it (Insertion key Echo). This provides two functions, firstly the receipt of the Insertion Key back at the station provides lobe integrity checking and secondly it provides insertion confirmation. Should the Insertion Key not be received back at the station, via the Echo, then the station should transmit a Bypass Key (a different command signal also with a unique signal pattern) to the TCU requesting removal from the ring. This in turn will also be echoed back to the station. The Bypass Key is also used at any stage if the station wants to remove itself from the ring, either through choice or as dictated by the MAC protocol. Again the procedure is for the station to control the process by issuing the Bypass Key which informs the TCU to switch to Bypass State and the Bypass Echo informs the station that this has been completed.

The only differences ultimately between fiber optic MAUs and copper MAUs are at the PMC level of the PHY as described above. In all other respects the fiber MAU performs the same functions as previously described for active MAUs including signal retiming and regeneration.

17.7 Network Design

Designing a Token Ring network can be quite a tricky operation, as already described, especially if the network is based on passive MAUs. This section is designed to provide a few guidelines to ensure your networks will always be successful and eliminate errors that create unsuccessful designs. The design process is effectively split into a six stage procedure that progesses from the initial stages through to design validation, ensuring the final implementation is both correct and suits the requirements.

Stage 1
An accurately scaled drawing of the proposed physical layout of the area within which the network will be laid out is essential if accurate calculations are to be made. As well as being drawn to scale, it should also include every device which will be connected to the network.

Stage 2
Decide on key elements such as cable type, network speed and whether active or passive MAUs are to be used. If active MAUs are to be used then stage 3 considerations plus the following of manufacturers guidelines will normally be enough to complete a successful design. If passive MAUs are preferred then the full six stage implementation plan will be required.

Stage 3
Divide the total number of devices on the network by the number of lobe ports per MAU to define the minimum number of MAUs that will be required. Factors such as location, expansion, and flexibility may require this number to be increased.

Stage 4
With reference to the scale drawing, decide upon the location for the wiring closet(s) that will house the MAUs. Mark the locations on the drawing and note the

number of wiring closets; we will need this number later as part of the design verification process.

Stage 5

Mark on the drawing the cable runs between wiring closets as accurately as possible so that distances can be measured. It is also important to measure the cable run distance from the device that is furthest away from any MAU, i.e., the longest lobe cable.

Stage 6

The network is essentially now designed and needs verification before implementation can take place. To verify the design, some variables already established will be required. These are: the number of MAUs, the number of wiring closets, the longest lobe cable, and the yet to be calculated Adjusted Ring Length. To calculate the ARL, add up the distance between the wiring closets and subtract the shortest one. Do not worry about including the patch cables between the RI and RO ports within each wiring closet (these are allowed for in the calculations that follow).

Table 17-5: 4Mbps Token Ring over Type 1 & Type 2 Cable

Number of Wiring Closets

MAUs	2	3	4	5	6	7	8	9	10	11	12
2	367										
3	358	353									
4	349	345	340								
5	340	336	331	326							
6	332	327	322	318	313						
7	323	318	314	309	304	300					
8	314	309	305	300	295	291	286				
9	305	301	296	291	287	282	277	273			
10	296	292	287	282	278	273	269	264	259		
11	288	283	278	274	269	264	260	255	250	246	
12	279	274	270	265	260	256	251	246	242	237	232
13	270	266	261	256	251	247	242	238	233	228	224
14	261	257	252	247	243	238	234	229	224	219	215
15	253	248	243	238	234	229	225	220	215	211	206
16	244	239	234	230	225	221	216	211	206	202	197
17	235	230	226	221	216	212	207	202	198	193	189
18	226	222	217	212	208	203	198	194	189	184	180
19	218	213	208	203	199	194	190	185	180	176	171
20	209	204	199	195	190	186	181	176	171	167	162
21	200	195	190	186	181	177	172	167	163	158	154
22	191	186	182	177	173	168	163	158	154	149	145
23	182	178	173	168	164	159	154	150	145	141	136
24	174	169	164	160	155	150	146	141	136	132	127
25	164	160	155	151	146	142	137	132	128	123	118
26	155	151	147	142	137	133	128	123	119	114	110
27	146	142	138	133	129	124	119	115	110	105	101

If using Type 6 or Type 9 cable, divide the number in the table by 1.33 when calculating.
Distances are in meters

Select either Table 17-5, 17-6, 17-7, or 17-8 depending on ring speed and media type and read off the value in the table that applies to the number of wiring closets and the number of MAUs in your design. This value is equal to the maximum combined value of the ARL and the longest lobe cable, so subtract your ARL from this figure and then subtract the length of the longest lobe cable from the remainder. If the sum produces a negative result then the design is invalid and will not work. If it produces a zero or positive result then the design is valid.

Table 17-6: 16Mbps Token Ring over Type 1 & Type 2 Cable

Number of Wiring Closets

MAUs	2	3	4	5	6	7	8	9	10
2	163								
3	157	151							
4	150	145	140						
5	143	138	133	128					
6	136	131	126	121	116				
7	130	125	120	114	110	105			
8	123	118	113	108	106	98	93		
9	116	111	106	101	96	91	86	81	
10	110	105	99	94	89	84	79	74	69
11	103	98	93	88	83	78	73	67	62
12	96	91	86	81	76	71	66	61	56
13	83	78	73	68	63	58	53	48	42
14	70	65	60	55	50	45	40	34	30
15	57	52	47	42	37	31	26	21	16
16	44	38	34	28	23	18	13	8	3
17	30	26	20	15	10	5			
18	17	12	7						

If using Type 6 or Type 9 cable, divide the number in the table by 1.33 when calculating.
Distances are in meters

Table 17-7: 4Mbps Token Ring over UTP

Number of Wiring Closets

MAUs	1	2	3	4
1	225			
2	219	209		
3	213	203	198	
4	207	197	192	186
5	201	191	186	181
6	195	185	180	175
7	190	179	174	169
8	184	174	168	163
9	178	168	162	157
10	172	162	157	151

Distances are in meters

Table 17-8: 16Mbps Token Ring over UTP

Number of Wiring Closets

MAUs	1	2	3
1	55		
2	46	39	
3	36	30	23
4	26	20	
5	16		

Distances are in meters

Invalid designs should be redesigned such that the verification process produces a positive result.

It is quite common that an initial design may fail to meet required specifications and need to be redesigned, especially in larger installations. If necessary, consider the use of repeaters to overcome large distances between MAUs.

17.8 Summary

It is clear that at the Physical Layer, Token Ring does not have the same level of detail specified as there is in the Ethernet standards. Early versions of the IEEE 802.5 standard were in fact very light on definition at the physical level. This has improved somewhat over time but is still not as well defined as some other technologies. In the past, design guidelines have been issued by IBM when implementing Token Ring over STP cabling and network designers have followed these. With the advent of structured cabling and the widespread implementation of UTP cables, it is important to follow International design guidelines for structured cabling. For Token Ring to survive in this environment, it must operate over a compliant cabling infrastructure. By opting for structured cabling and following either manufacturers, or published design guides, it should not be too much of a problem to implement a successful infrastructure capable of supporting Token Ring technology.

The Media Access Control (MAC) Layer

Chapter 16 discussed, in basic format, the method of operation of a Token Ring Network. In this chapter we will delve a little deeper into the mechanics of a participant of the ring and look at the processes involved in controlling access to the network. It is worth remembering exactly what the role of the Media Access Control (MAC) is. Its responsibilities are essentially two fold, namely to provide equal, fair, and speedy access to all, while ensuring that only one station has access to the medium at any given moment. This is essential to maintain the integrity of the transmitted data and ensure corruption does not occur. Coupled with this, it is also the responsibility of the MAC to provide some means of error recovery in the event of protocol breakdown or data corruption.

The figures used in the following sections depict the formats of the various fields of both the token and data frames in the order in which they are transmitted, i.e., from left to right as shown in the diagrams. Unlike Ethernet, Token Ring transmits all data most significant bit first (Non-canonical format). Therefore all data flow is as shown in the figures that follow. The same can also be said for bit comparisons made by receiving stations, which will compare bits in order of arrival.

18.1 The Token

The token is the crux of the Token Ring Protocol as it is the means by which nodes gain the right to transmit their data onto the ring. Without possession of the token, a node must repeat all incoming data and queue its own data until the token has been received. It is possible for the token to occur at any point in the data stream and it is therefore essential that all stations can detect it on any single bit boundary. For this to be true it is important that the token starts with an instantly recognizable sequence. As you will see below in section 3.1.1 the token uses special non-data symbols to signify both the starting sequence and end of the token. In this way recognition by the receiving station is guaranteed.

It is the responsibility of the Active Monitor to ensure the first token is placed on the ring and then all stations continually monitor its presence to ensure circulation continues. The placement of the first token is the final phase of the Claim Token process[1] in which the Active Monitor is elected. Once token passing has been established, the ring stations will set a timer (Timer, No Token, default 2.6s) before

---

[1] The Claim Token process is the method used to elect the Active Monitor and is discussed in detail in section 19.3.

the expiry of which they expect the token to arrive on their receive port. On arrival, the timer is reset in order to check the next circulation and so on. Should the token not arrive prior to the expiry of the timer then the detecting station can initiate error recovery.

18.1.1 Token Format

The 24 bit token has the following format as shown in Figure 18-1 below. It comprises of three one octet fields namely the Starting Delimiter, Access Control, and Ending Delimiter. The purpose and format of each of these fields are described in the text that follows.

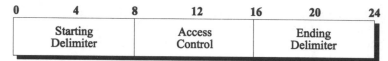

Figure 18-1:   Token Format

18.1.2 Starting Delimiter

The Starting Delimiter is a one octet field that can be detected at any point in the data stream. The format is fixed, as shown in Figure 18-2, utilizing a combination of non-data J and K symbols in conjunction with data symbol 0. This symbol sequence is only found in a Starting Delimiter and cannot be duplicated at any other point of a data transmission. Receiving stations check for the arrival of the entire eight bit sequence before considering the Starting Delimiter valid.

Figure 18-2: Starting Delimiter

18.1.3 Access Control Field

The role of the Access Control field is primarily to allow a priority system[2] to be implemented on a Token Ring network. The three Priority (P) bits are used to indicate the priority of the token. Being three bits in length, this allows for eight priority levels from 000_2 up to 111_2. Stations with data frames queued for transmission can only capture the token if the priority of that token is equal to or lower than the priority of the frame queued for transmission. The T bit is transmitted as 0_2 if this is a token and 1_2 if part of a Start of Frame Sequence (SFS). The Monitor (M) bit is used to stop frames or high priority Tokens from endlessly

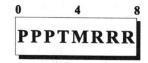

Figure 18-3: Access Control Field

circulating the ring. It is transmitted by the sending station as 0_2 and as the high priority token or frame passes through the Active Monitor it is changed to a 1_2. Should a frame or high priority token arrive at the Active Monitor with this bit already set to 1_2, then it must have circulated the entire ring at least once. Under normal operation, the transmitting station is responsible for stripping its own

---

[2] Access Priority is discussed in detail in section 18.6.

The Media Access Control (MAC) Layer

frames from the ring after one complete circulation, and high priority tokens should have had their priority reduced prior to a second circulation. Therefore, if the Active Monitor sees an Access Control Field with the M bit set to 1_2 then some form of breakdown must have occurred. The Active Monitor will then strip the frame or token from the ring, initiate a Ring Purge[3] , and finally issue a new normal priority token. The three R bits or Reservation bits at the end of the field are also used as part of the Access Priority system. They can be set in any frame or token to a value from 000_2 to 111_2 by any repeating station to request the next token be released at a corresponding priority level.

18.1.4   The Ending Delimiter

The Ending Delimiter is the final octet of the 3 octet token sequence. The format, as shown in figure 18-4, has six fixed bits plus two indicators. The sequence JK1JK1 is fixed and instantly recognizable due to the inclusion of the J and K non-data symbols. The I bit is used as an Intermediate bit which, if transmitted as a 1_2, indicates that this is the first or intermediate frame in a transmission sequence and there are more frames to follow. If this is the last or only frame in a sequence then this bit is transmitted as 0_2. In a token this indicator has no significance. The Error (E) bit is always transmitted by the source as 0_2. Should any repeating station

Figure 18-4: Ending Delimiter

detect an error in a token or frame then it modifies the E bit to a 1_2. The detecting station will then increment its error counter and periodically report detected errors to the Ring Error Monitor (REM)[4] . By setting the Error bit all subsequent stations are instantly aware that this token or frame is erroneous, and it also stops these stations from reporting the same error.

It is also the case that the three fields of a token can be found in a Token Ring frame. Therefore, some indicators i.e., the I bit in the Ending Delimiter, have significance in frames only, while others, such as the E bit in the same field, have significance in both frames and tokens.

18.1.5   Token Validity

For a token to be considered valid for use for data transmission it must satisfy the following criteria:

- Start with a valid Starting Delimiter.

- The T (Token) bit must be set to 0_2.

- No code violations must exist in the P (Priority) bits.

---

[3] The Ring Purge Process is a management function carried out by the Active Monitor and is discussed in section 19.2.2.
[4] The Ring Error Monitor is an optional server designed to collect error statistics for management purposes. See section 19.1.3 for further details.

At the point at which the decision to use the token is made, with all the above criteria satisfied, only part of the token has been received. Therefore, additional checks, such as to the length of the token are not made prior to its use. If the token is not to be used and is simply being repeated around the ring then the check on token validity is somewhat more extensive. In this instance the token must satisfy the following criteria to be considered a good token:

- Start with a valid Starting Delimiter.

- It is three octets in length.

- The token comprises of only 1_2's and 0_2's between the SD and ED.

- The T (Token) bit must be set to 0_2.

- The third octet must be an Ending Delimiter.

Failure to meet the above criteria would result in the repeating station setting the E bit in the Ending Delimiter showing this token to be in error.

18.1.6 Token Holding Time

The token holding time is the amount of time after receiving the token that a station may continue to transmit its data frames prior to releasing the token back onto the ring. The time is not directly monitored by a specific timer, but by a counter. The Counter, Transmitted Octets (CTO) is used to determine whether the next frame queued can be transmitted in the available time remaining. The total period allowed to remain in receipt of the token is set at 9.1mS which at 4 Mbps is equivalent to a total of 4,550 octets while at 16 Mbps is equal to 18,200. The value of CTO is pre-set depending on the data rate, and is decremented as each octet is transmitted. Therefore, only frames with a total length smaller than the remaining value of CTO will be transmitted, with longer ones being deferred until the next token capture. Stations may implement any starting value for CTO not exceeding the already stated maximums, and additionally are not required to transmit multiple frames per token capture. This indicates some leeway for vendor-specific implementations, however multiple frame transmissions per capture and maximum CTO values obviously allow for a more efficient system.

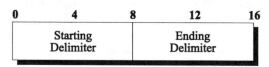

Figure 18-5: Abort Sequence

18.2 Abort Sequence

The abort sequence, as shown in Figure 18-5, is used by transmitting stations to prematurely terminate frame transmission. When the sequence is received by ring stations it is an immediate indication that the frame currently being received is invalid. It is possible that the abort sequence may occur at any point during data

The Media Access Control (MAC) Layer

transmission so therefore, must be recognizable on any bit boundary. This is again achieved via the use of non-data J and K symbols in the starting and ending delimiter fields.

18.3 Frame Formats

For token ring frames to be successfully interpreted by receiving stations a pre-set format is required. This format, shown in figure 18-6, is understood by all ring stations and includes all the necessary MAC-level information to allow successful delivery and processing of the transmitted data.

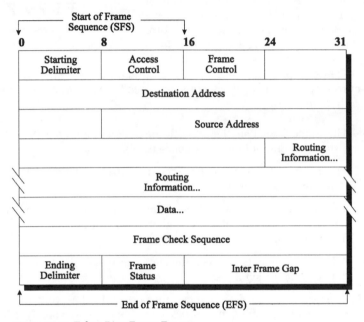

Figure 18-6: Token Ring Frame Format

The individual fields and their formats are discussed in the text that follows:

18.3.1 Starting Delimiter (SD)

The starting delimiter is in fact the same as that found in a token as the token itself is modified to form the Start of Frame Sequence (SFS). It therefore follows that the bit sequence of $JK0JK000_2$ is the same as previously described in section 18.1.1.

18.3.2 Access Control Field (AC)

Like the starting delimiter before it, the access control field is also modified from the circulating token to form a part of the start of frame sequence. One modification in the format from that of the token is the T bit which is modified from a 0_2 to a 1_2 to indicate this is an SFS.

18.3.3   Frame Control Field (FC)

The frame control field is a single octet in length and is used to indicate what type of frame this is. The format, as shown in figure 18-7, is separated into two areas, the F bits indicate the frame type bits, while the Z bits provide control. The two F bits have the following significance:

$$00_2 \quad = \quad \text{MAC Frame}$$
$$01_2 \quad = \quad \text{LLC Frame}$$
$$1x_2 \quad = \quad \text{Undefined (reserved for future development)}$$

MAC frames are part of the in built management capability of a token ring network and are discussed in detail in section 18.5. LLC frames are normal user data frames and as such are normal token ring transmissions. The undefined format leaves the standards bodies some scope to further define the token ring protocol to add yet more functionality. Although any future format is currently undefined, there are some specific rules that any future frame type must adhere to:

Figure 18-7: Frame Control Field

- The frame format shall start with the already defined SFS and end with a standard End of Frame Sequence (EFS).

- The positioning of both the Access Control and Frame Control fields will remain unchanged.

- The SFS and the EFS will be separated by a whole number of octets where the minimum is 1 and the maximum is defined by the constraints of the token holding time.

- All signal elements between the start and end delimiters shall be either data 0 or data 1 symbols.

The Z bits, as said, are used for control purposes. In the event that the frame type bits denote a MAC frame, the six Z bits are used to specify MAC frame handling. This is discussed in detail in section 18.5. If the frame type bits indicate an LLC frame, then the six control bits have the following designation; rrrYYY. In this instance, the rrr bits are reserved for future development and always transmitted as 000_2. The YYY bits indicate user priority of the transmitted data.

18.3.4   Destination Address (DA)

The destination address field is six octets in length and contains the MAC address of the intended recipient. Addressing is discussed in detail in the next section.

18.3.5   Source Address (SA)

As with the destination address, this field is six octets in length and uniquely identifies the source of this frame. Due to the format of the address[5], the first bit of this field is redundant from an addressing point of view, and is therefore used for

---

[5] Address field formats are discussed in detail in section 18.4.

an alternative purpose. As you may note from figure 18-6, the diagram shows a Routing Information field following the source address. This field may or may not exist depending on the network environment. To inform receiving stations of the existence of the routing information field, the first bit of the source address is transmitted as 1_2. If the field is not present then the same bit is transmitted as 0_2. For this reason, the most significant bit is called the Routing Information Indicator (RII).

18.3.6 Routing Information Field (RIF)

The routing information field provides information to source route bridges[6] as to the path this frame should take through the network. In a non-source route bridged network, this field has no meaning and will not exist. Where it does exist, it is important for receiving stations to know two things. Firstly, the presence of the field, achieved via the Routing Information Indicator (RII) as detailed above, and secondly, how long the field is, so that they are aware as to the position of the data field that follows it. This is achieved via a length indication in the RIF itself. The purpose and format of the RIF are covered in a later chapter.

18.3.7 Data Field

The data field, like the RIF before it, is a variable length field containing zero or more octets. Unlike Ethernet networks, in a token ring environment there is no minimum length for this field. The maximum is set by the limits of the token holding time as previously discussed. This field can contain either MAC data or LLC (user) data as defined by the frame type bits in the FC field. If the data is MAC data then it follows the strict formats described in section 18.5. If on the other hand the data is LLC then the format is undefined in the 802.5 standard as it will be application specific, but will contain a higher layer Protocol Data Unit (PDU).

18.3.8 Frame Check Sequence (FCS)

The *Frame Check Sequence* (FCS) field is used by receiving stations to ensure that the frame has been received intact. The 32 bit (4 octet) field is actually a Cyclic Redundancy Check (CRC) computed over the entire frame excluding Start/End Delimiters and Frame Status Field. This value is then calculated and encoded using the following generating polynomial:

$$G(x) = x^{32}+x^{26}+x^{23}+x^{22}+x^{16}+x^{12}+x^{11}+x^{10}+x^8+x^7+x^5+x^4+x^2+x+1$$

Stations transmitting frames calculate the Frame Check Sequence and place the CRC value calculated in the FCS field of the frame. This field is then transmitted *Most Significant Bit* (MSB) first.

On reception, stations receiving the frame perform a similar calculation as the frame arrives, and then compare the newly computed value with that of the FCS received. By using a 32 bit CRC, it has then been calculated that the chances of not detecting bad data as it is received are reduced to 2^{32-1} (or 4.3 billion) to 1.

---

[6] Source Route Bridging is covered in some detail in chapter 20.

18.3.9 Ending Delimiter (ED)

The ending delimiter in a frame is of the same format as described for a token in section 18.1.4. The JK1JK1 sequence is fixed, however, the I and the E bits do have significance in frame transmissions. The Intermediate (I) bit is used to denote whether their are further frames to follow in this transmission sequence. If transmitted as 1_2 then this is the first or intermediate frame of a sequence. If transmitted as 0_2 then this frame is the last or only frame and there are no more to follow. The Error detected (E) bit is always transmitted as 0_2 by the source station and amended to 1_2 by a receiving or repeating station if an error is detected. Errors include failure to match the frame check sequence and invalid frames (see section 18.3.12).

18.3.10 Frame Status Field (FS)

The purpose of the frame status field is to provide confirmation of delivery to the source station. The A and the C bits are always transmitted as 0_2 and amended to 1_2 by the receiving station if set criteria are met. The criteria specified are firstly the receiving station must recognize its own unique or group address in the destination address field. If so the Address Recognized (A) bits are set to 1_2. If the station copies the frame from the ring and the frame is valid then the Frame Copied (C) bits are also set to 1_2 on the repeated copy. This will then inform the source station upon its receipt that successful delivery has been accomplished. The A and the C bits are duplicated because the FS field is beyond the scope of the FCS and as such cannot be determined to be error free. Therefore, by duplicating the information it is far less likely that signal distortion will corrupt both instances. The receiving station can accept with reasonable confidence the accuracy of the A and C bits if both instances match.

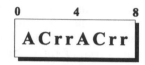

Figure 18-8: Frame Status Field

18.3.11 Inter-Frame Gap (IFG)

After each frame transmitted, a mandatory inter-frame gap must be imposed by the transmitting station. This IFG is composed of a composite sequence of 1_2's and 0_2's which at 4Mbps should be a minimum of one octet in length (two is preferred) or at 16Mbps, five octets. Receiving stations may not receive the full IFG as transmitted, as the Active Monitor has the ability to modify it as part of it responsibility to maintain cumulative ring latency.

18.3.12 Frame Validity

For transmitted frames to be processed by receiving stations they must satisfy the following criteria:

- Must start with a valid starting delimiter

- Must have a whole number of octets

- The frame type (FF) bits must be equal to 00_2 or 01_2

- All symbols between the SD and ED must be equal to 0_2 or 1_2

- The T bit within the AC field is equal to 1_2

- A valid ED exists

- Consists of a minimum of twenty one octets

- Includes and computes a valid FCS

Frames failing to meet the above criteria are deemed to be in error and are not processed. Failure to meet the criteria stated would result in the detecting station setting the error bit in the ending delimiter so that all subsequent stations, including the source, would be aware of the error condition.

18.4 MAC Addressing

For successful delivery of data frames in a LAN environment it is important to implement an addressing scheme. This addressing occurs at the MAC level so that the destination and source addresses can be included when frames are generated.

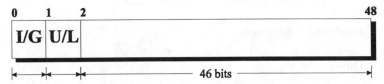

Figure 18-9: Destination Address Format

In line with other popular technologies such as Ethernet and FDDI, Token Ring addressing utilizes six octet MAC addresses. There has been, in past standards, the ability to implement two octet addressing if desired, but this has now been dropped. The format for the destination address field is shown in figure 18-9. Here you can see the most significant bit, denoted I/G, is used to determine whether this frame is intended for an individual or a group of stations. In addition, the next most significant bit, the U/L bit, also has special meaning. It specifies whether this address is locally or universally administered. The forty six bits that constitute the rest of the address field are used to ensure duplicate addresses do not exist.

18.4.1 Unicast Addresses

A Unicast address is one that denotes a specific station, and is signified by the Individual or Group (I/G) bit being transmitted as 0_2. It is important that this address is unique on the LAN, in the case of locally administered addresses[7] , or globally, if universally administered. Duplicate addresses cannot be tolerated as they can cause confusion and security problems. It is therefore paramount that all stations have their own unique address.

18.4.2 Multicast Addresses

A Multicast address is used when the transmission is destined for a group of, but not all, stations. When used it allows stations in that group to all process the single

[7] See section 18.4.6 for a discussion on administering addresses.

frame as it passes around the ring. This provides far greater efficiency in the use of available bandwidth than addressing individual frames to each station in that group. Source stations will set the I/G bit to 1_2 to signify this frame is a Multicast and therefore destined to a group of stations. The format of the following forty seven bits will then signify which group. The use of multicasting as a means of addressing is becoming more widespread, with more and more protocols taking advantage of its efficiency. For this reason it is essential for stations to support the functionality if they wish to operate in a multi-protocol environment.

18.4.3 Broadcast Addresses

A broadcast is a variation of the Multicast in that the group is all stations. It is therefore an ideal mechanism for functions that wish to simultaneously communicate information to all stations on the LAN. The broadcast address is denoted by transmitting all forty eight bits as 1_2, i.e., FF-FF-FF-FF-FF-FF in hex format. In addition, stations in token ring must also recognize C0-00-FF-FF-FF-FF$_{16}$ as a broadcast address. This latter address is used as the broadcast address for MAC frames and its use for other functions should be avoided.

18.4.4 Functional Addresses

Functional addresses are used to denote a functional entity such as the Active Monitor. This allows stations to address frame to the entity without the need to know their Unicast MAC address. This can be extremely useful as the following example will demonstrate.

When ring stations join the ring they are required to ask the Ring Parameter Server (RPS) for any defined ring parameters (such as ring number). At this stage of joining, the ring station has no idea as to the MAC address of the RPS or even if the entity exists on this ring. It is therefore extremely useful to address its requests to a functional address recognized by the RPS rather than trying to discover its associated unique address.

Functional addresses are identified through the use of a Functional Address Identifier (FAI) which consists of the most significant seventeen bits of the address

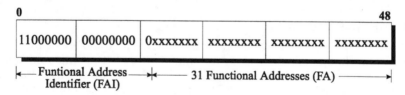

Figure 18-10: Functional Address Format

field. The least significant thirty one bits are then used to represent each of thirty one different functional addresses. Figure 18-10 shows the format of the functional address identifier, while table 18-1 shows functional addresses used for MAC frames and their associated management entity.

The Media Access Control (MAC) Layer

Table 18-1: Functional Addresses

Functional Address 11000000 00000000 0xxxxxxx-	Function Name	Hexadecimal Address
-xxxxxxxx-xxxxxxxx-xxxxxxx1	Active Monitor	C0-00-00-00-00-01
-xxxxxxxx-xxxxxxxx-xxxxxx1x	Ring Parameter Server (RPS)	C0-00-00-00-00-02
-xxxxxxxx-xxxxxxxx-xxxx1xxx	Ring Error Monitor (REM)	C0-00-00-00-00-08
-xxxxxxxx-xxxxxxxx-xxx1xxxx	Configuration Report Server (CRS)	C0-00-00-00-00-10

Each six octet address identifies an individual function, however, multiple functions can be addressed by combining the functional addresses. For example, C0-00-00-00-00-12 would address both the ring parameter server and the configuration report server.

18.4.5 Null Address

The address 00-00-00-00-00-00$_{16}$ is defined in the 802.5 standard as a null address not used to define any station. This means any frame destined for this address should return to source with the address recognized (A) and frame copied (C) bits in the frame status field still set to 0$_2$.

18.4.6 Administering Addresses

Token ring allows two methods for administering addresses for ring stations. These are Universally administered and Locally administered. The method in use is shown by the U/L bit which is the second bit in the destination address field. If transmitted as 0$_2$ then the address is universally administered, if transmitted as 1$_2$ then it is locally administered. The paragraphs that follow describe each method in detail.

Universal administration of addresses is when individual station addresses are administered from a single registration authority. This will ensure that each and every station has a unique address, not only on the LAN, but on a global basis. This is ensured by a combination vendor identification and unique station number as figure 18-11 shows below. Each manufacturer of network interface cards and other token ring products is assigned a three octet prefix by the IEEE. This prefix forms the first three octets of the MAC address of each device they manufacture. It is therefore possible to tell the manufacturer simply by comparing the vendor ID prefix with the published list from the IEEE[8] . It is the responsibility of each vendor to ensure that, for each product they manufacture, the final three octets of the address field are unique. In this way it is possible to guarantee the uniqueness of the address.

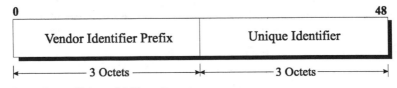

Figure 18-11: Universal Address Format

[8] A full list of vendor ID prefixes is contained in appendix A.

Local address administration is specified with the U/L bit being transmitted as 1_2 and means that addresses are assigned by the network administrator of the LAN. This provides a range of conceivable addresses between 40-00-00-00-00-00$_{16}$ and 7F-FF-FF-FF-FF-FF$_{16}$. Early versions of the 802.5 standard allowed for an hierarchical address structure where the least significant fourteen bits of the most significant two octets were used to denote Ring ID. The latest version of the standard omits this option and, in fact, actively discourages this practice in future implementations. It is obvious from this description that the responsibility lies solely with the network administrator to ensure duplicate addresses do not exist anywhere on the LAN. There is, however, no need to be concerned about duplication beyond the boundaries of the local network.

Locally administered addresses are allowed for in technologies such as Ethernet and FDDI, but are only implemented in Token Ring. This is primarily due to IBM influence as networks requiring connectivity in an all IBM environment are the only ones that implement this form of addressing and these are principally token ring networks. In fact, manufacturers of Network Interface Cards (NICs) normally do not allow the specification of locally administered addresses in non-token ring environments. With the potential for duplication, and the increased administration for normally busy personnel, it makes sense for most networks to implement universally administered addressing if given the option.

18.5 MAC Frames

The token ring protocol utilizes special frames known as MAC frames to control and manage the ring. The use of these frames is described in more detail in sections to which they relate, for example the Beacon MAC frame and its function is described in section 19.4 on Beaconing. This section concentrates on the format and field content of the 23 defined MAC frames in the IEEE 802.5 standard.

Ring stations are informed that the arriving frame is a MAC frame via the content of the Frame Control (FC) field. Any value in the range 00$_{16}$ to 3F$_{16}$ denotes a MAC frame and therefore management information contained within the data field. If the value is 00$_{16}$ then stations are only required to copy the frame if they have sufficient available buffering. For values from 01$_{16}$ to 3F$_{16}$, every attempt should be made by the receiving station to copy the frame. The frame, when copied, will have the format as shown in figure 18-12.

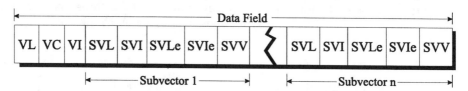

Figure 18-12: MAC Frame Data Field Format

Table 18-2 describes each of the fields shown in the above for the MAC frame.

Table 18-2: MAC Frame Fields

Identifier	Description	Function
	Vector	This is the basic unit of management information and contains a length field, an identifier field, and zero or more subvectors. Each MAC frame is only permitted one vector.
VL	Vector Length	A two octet field that provides the length of the vector.
VC	Vector Class	A single octet field that identifies the function of both source and destination entities. The field is divided into two four bit subfields with the first identifying the destination entity and the second the source entity. Table 18-3 shows documented vector class values that could be found in either source or destination class fields.
VI	Vector Identifier	This is a single or three octet field used to identify uniquely this vector. If the value of the VI is less than FF_{16} then this is a single octet field. If the value of the first octet is equal to FF_{16} then it is a three octet field, with the following two octets identifying the vector.
SVL	Subvector Length	This field is one octet in length and identifies to recipients the length of the subvector. If the length reaches FF_{16} then the length is specified in the extended Subvector Length field (SVLe).
SVI	Subvector Identifier	This is also a one octet field and is used to uniquely identify the subvector. However, if the value is FF16 then the identification is made via the extended Subvector Identifier field (SVIe).
	Subvector	MAC frames contain a single vector and one or more subvectors. It is these subvectors that contain any MAC data being transmitted. There is no order dependency for subvectors within the vector as long as each can be identified via its own identifier.
SVLe	extended Subvector Length	This field is only functional if the SVL field contains the value FF_{16}, in which case it is two octets in length. In this instance it is this field that is then used to identify the precise length of the subvector including SVL, SVI, SVLe, SVIe, and SVV fields. If the SVL field contains any value other than FF_{16} then this field is non-existent.
SVIe	extended Subvector Identifier	This field also only exists if its parent (SVI) is equal to FF_{16}, in which case it is also two octets in length and uniquely identifies the subvector. Currently, this field is unused; codes for it are undefined and reserved for future development
SVV	Subvector Value	The subvector value field is of variable length and contains the actual management data to be transported. Precise definitions as to the contents of this field are contained in table 18-4.

The current release of the IEEE 802.5 standard defines twenty three different vector types and twenty two subvector types. In the tables that follow, table 18-3 describes the different vectors, table 18-4 the different subvectors, and table 18-5 provides a cross-reference to show which subvectors correspond to each vector, plus other useful information regarding both source and destinations for each MAC frame.

Table 18-3: MAC Vectors

Identifier	Description	Function
00_{16}	Response (RSP)	The RSP MAC frame is used either in acknowledgement of receipt, or to report an error in a received MAC frame. It is only sent by receiving stations if the received MAC frame was either a unicast, or they were the first recipient of a broadcast/multicast MAC frame.
02_{16}	Beacon (BN)	The BN MAC frame is sent by a station detecting a continuous signal loss. It is a fundamental element of the beaconing process described in detail in Section 19.4.
03_{16}	Claim Token (CT)	Used by stations electing a new Active Monitor to the ring.
04_{16}	Ring Purge (RP)	The RP MAC frame is used by the Active Monitor to ensure ring integrity prior to generating a token. It is part of a recovery sequence in the event of ring failure. Receipt by ring stations causes resetting of certain timers and flags to indicate the ring is about to become operational. If the Active Monitor receives the RP back then it is successful and a new token is generated.
05_{16}	Active Monitor Present (AMP)	The AMP MAC frame is transmitted according to the Timer, Active Monitor (TAM). This equates to transmission every 6.8 to 7.0 seconds. Its purpose is two-fold; firstly it provides other ring stations evidence of the existence of the AM, and secondly to initiate the neighbor notification process. This process is covered in some detail in section 18.7.6.
06_{16}	Standby Monitor Present (SMP)	The SMP MAC frame is generated by each ring station not currently fulfilling the Active Monitor role. The frame is transmitted between 10 to 20 mS after the reception of an AMP frame or an SMP with the A & C bits set to 0_2. This forms part of the neighbor notification process
07_{16}	Duplicate Address Test (DAT)	The DAT MAC frame is used by ring stations as part of the process of joining the ring. By addressing the DAT frame to themselves, stations can discover whether their own MAC address is unique simply by interrogating the address recognized bits in the FS field when the frame returns.
08_{16}	Lobe Media Test (TEST)	The TEST MAC frame is used in two instances, for the same purpose. Firstly, it is part of the joining process stations go through prior to becoming active members of the ring. Secondly, it is also used when testing of the transmission path is required (i.e., during the beaconing process). The TEST frame is transmitted via the transmit link and returns directly via the receive link of the lobe cable, never actually reaching the main ring. In this way if returned without error it provides proof of the stations ability to transmit and receive without error.
$0B_{16}$	Remove Ring Station (REMOVE)	The REMOVE MAC frame is used by the Configuration Report Server (CRS) or by network management to force a station to remove itself from the ring.

Table 18-3: MAC Vectors (Continued)

Identifier	Description	Function
$0C_{16}$	Change Parameters (CHG_PARM)	The purpose of the CHG_PARM MAC frame is to allow the CRS to inform stations of the current ring operating parameters. The stations would then typically respond with a RSP MAC frame.
$0D_{16}$	Initialize Station (INIT)	The INIT MAC frame is sent by the Ring Parameter Server (RPS) to ring stations in order to initialize their operating parameters. Once again stations would normally respond via the use of the RSP MAC frame.
$0E_{16}$	Request Station Addresses (RQ_ADDR)	Used by a management function, for example the CRS, the RQ_ADDR MAC frame requests a ring station to respond with the addresses recognized by that station.
$0F_{16}$	Request Station State (RQ_STATE)	The RQ_STATE MAC frame is also used by management functions, to request data regarding the state of the station.
10_{16}	Request Station Attachments (RQ_ATTCH)	The RQ_ATTCH MAC frame is used by management functions, such as the CRS, to request information about functions running within the station.
20_{16}	Request Initialization (RQ_INIT)	The RQ_INIT MAC frame is used as part of the ring joining process by a station to inform the RPS that the station has joined the ring and requests ring operating parameters.
22_{16}	Report Station Addresses (RPRT_ADDR)	The RPRT_ADDR MAC frame is used by ring stations in response to the RQ_ADDR frame.
23_{16}	Report Station State (RPRT_STATE)	The RPRT_STATE MAC frame is used as response by stations to the RQ_STATE request.
24_{16}	Report Station Attachments (RPRT_ATTCH)	The RPRT_ATTCH MAC frame is used by stations as a response to RQ_ATTCH request from a management function.
25_{16}	Report New Active Monitor (NEW_MON)	The NEW_MON MAC frame is used by a station to report to the CRS that it has assumed the role of Active Monitor following a successful Claim Token process.
26_{16}	Report SUA Change (SUA_CHG)	The purpose of the SUA_CHG MAC frame is to allow stations to report to the CRS when a change occurs in their Stored Upstream Neighbors Address (SUA) due to the neighbor notification process.
27_{16}	Report Neighbor Notification Incomplete (NN_INCMP)	The NN_INCMP MAC frame is only generated by the Active Monitor and is sent to the Ring Error Monitor (REM) if the AM detects the neighbor notification process is incomplete.
28_{16}	Report Active Monitor Error (ACT_ERR)	The ACT_ERR MAC frame is sent to the REM under two circumstances; firstly if the Active Monitor detects another on the ring or alternatively if a station detects a malfunction of the Active Monitor process and initiates Claim Token.
29_{16}	Report Error (RPRT_ERR)	The RPRT_ERR MAC frame is sent to the REM periodically by ring stations to report all errors detected since the last report.

Table 18-4 identifies all published subvectors listed in numerical order of their SVI values. The lengths shown are for the subvector value field only.

Table 18-4: MAC SubVectors

Identifier	Description	Function
01_{16}	Beacon Type	This is 2 octets in length and its purpose is to indicate to recipients the type of fault detected in a beaconing condition. The SVV field can have one of the following values: 0001_{16} Issued by a dual ring station during reconfiguration 0002_{16} Signal loss 0003_{16} Timer TCT expired during Claim Token, no claim frames received 0004_{16} Timer TCT expired during Claim Token, claim frames received
02_{16}	Upstream Neighbor's Address (UNA)	This subvector value is 6 octets in length and contains the upstream neighbor address of the sending station. The transmitting station inserts the value of SUA (Stored Upstream Address). The receiving station refers to this as the RUA (Reported Upstream Address).
03_{16}	Local Ring Number	2 octet value indicating the local ring number of the transmitting station. Value is assigned during request for initialization or through the Change Parameters MAC frame.
04_{16}	Assign Physical Drop Number	A 4 octet value specifying the location of the target station. Assigned via the RQ_INIT or CHG_PARM MAC frame.
05_{16}	Error Report Timer Value	States the value of the Timer, Error Report (TER) in 10ms increments. The value itself is 2 octets in length.
06_{16}	Authorized Function Classes	2 octet value used to indicate the function classes that are authorized to be active within the station. Valid range for this subvector is $0000\ 0000\ 0000\ 0000_2$ to $1111\ 1111\ 1111\ 1111_2$. Defined function classes are: xxxx 1xxx xxxx xxxx Configuration Report Server (CRS) xxxx x1xx xxxx xxxx Ring Parameter Server (RPS) xxxx xx1x xxxx xxxx Ring Error Monitor (REM) xxxx xxxx 1xxx xxxx Network Management (NM) All other function classes are reserved for future standardization.
07_{16}	Authorized Access Priority	This 2 octet subvector can be set by the system administrator to reflect the maximum allowable access priority a station may set non-MAC frames.
09_{16}	Correlator	The correlator subvector is 2 octets long and is used to associate responses with requests. The correlator subvector value of a response should be the same as that of the request.
$0A_{16}$	Source Address of Last AMP or SMP Frame	This 6 octet subvector value forms part of the Report Neighbor Notification Incomplete MAC Frame. If the value is set to null it indicates the AMP frame was not received, if set to the station address it indicates either the AMP was not received or no SMP frames were received. Any other condition is indicated by the source address of the last SMP received.

Table 18-4: MAC SubVectors (Continued)

Identifier	Description	Function
$0B_{16}$	Physical Drop Number	This SVV is 4 octets in length and identifies the physical location of the sending station.
20_{16}	Response Code	This 4 or 6 octet SVV is used in Response MAC frames to identify to the other station the result of its original request. It consists of a 2 octet response code followed by a 1 octet VC and 1 or 3 octet VI from the received MAC frame to allow the receiving station to associate this response to the original request.

Valid 2 octet response codes are:

0001_{16}	Positive acknowledgement
8001_{16}	MAC frame data field incomplete, has no VL or VI
8002_{16}	Vector length error, VL different from that of the frame
8003_{16}	Unrecognized Vector Identifier
8004_{16}	Inappropriate source class, source class is not valid for the transmitted VI
8005_{16}	Subvector length error
8006_{16}	Reserved
8007_{16}	Missing Subvector, a required subvector was missing from the frame
8008_{16}	Subvector unknown, received subvector is unknown by the station
8009_{16}	MAC frame too long, received MAC frame exceeded maximum length
$800A_{16}$	Function requested was disabled, frame rejected

Identifier	Description	Function
21_{16}	Individual Address Count	This subvector value is 2 octets in length and defaults to 00 00_{16} meaning only a single individual address is supported by this station. Any non-zero value indicates the number of individual addresses supported by the station.
22_{16}	Product Instance ID	This SVV is used by the manufacturer to indicate station characteristics such as serial number, machine type, etc. The length is not specified.
23_{16}	Ring Station Version Number	This subvector value and length are not specified in the standard but the SV can be used in either an RQ_INIT or RPRT_STATE MAC frame.
26_{16}	Wrap Data	This SV is used in the TEST MAC frame and is implementation specific.
28_{16}	Station Identifier	This 6 octet SVV is used in the RPRT_STATE MAC frame to uniquely identify the station. The universally administered station address is recommended.
29_{16}	Ring Station Status	This subvector is used in the RPRT_STATE MAC frame and is implementation specific. However, its format should be defined in the Product Instance ID (SV 22_{16}), as defined earlier in this table.

Table 18-4: MAC SubVectors (Continued)

Identifier	Description	Function
$2B_{16}$	Group Addresses	A 4 or 6 octet value containing the group address of the sending station. If 4 octets are used then they are the low order octets of the group address. If a value of all 0's is sent it means either group addresses are not supported on this station or none are set. If multiple group addresses are supported, any may be reported.
$2C_{16}$	Functional Addresses	A 4 octet value specifying the functional addresses that are currently active in the sending station. See section 18.4.4 for a full description of functional addresses.
$2D_{16}$	Isolating Error Counts	A 6 octet value indicating the types of isolating errors detected since the last error report. Used in the RPRT_ERR MAC frame. See section 19.1 for a more detailed description of Token Ring errors.

Each octet represents an eight bit counter as follows:

Octet 0   Line Errors (CLE)

Octet 1   Internal Errors (CIE)

Octet 2   Burst Errors (CBE)

Octet 3   AC Errors (CACE)

Octet 4   Abort Sequence Transmitted (CABE)

Octet 5   Reserved (00_{16})

Identifier	Description	Function
$2E_{16}$	Non-isolating Error Counts	Another 6 octet subvector used in the RPRT_ERR MAC frame, this time to indicate counts of non-isolating errors since the last error report.

Each octet represents an eight bit counter as follows:

Octet 0   Lost Frame Errors (CLFE)

Octet 1   Receive Congestion Errors (CRCE)

Octet 2   Frame Copied Errors (CFCE)

Octet 3   Frequency Errors (CFE)

Octet 4   Token Errors (CTE)

Octet 5   Reserved (00_{16})

30_{16} Error Code

Table 18-5: MAC Frame Reference

Vector Name (VI)	Priority	Destination	Source	Subvector Name (SVI)	
Response	0 or 7	SA of requester	RS	09_{16}	Correlator
				20_{16}	Response Code
Beacon	**	Broadcast	RS	01_{16}	Beacon Type
				02_{16}	UNA
				$0B_{16}$	Physical Drop Number

The Media Access Control (MAC) Layer

Table 18-5: MAC Frame Reference (Continued)

Vector Name (VI)	Priority	Destination	Source	Subvector Name (SVI)	
Claim Token	**	Broadcast	RS	02_{16}	UNA
				$0B_{16}$	Physical Drop Number
Ring Purge	**	Broadcast	AM	02_{16}	UNA
				$0B_{16}$	Physical Drop Number
Active Monitor Present	7	Broadcast	AM	02_{16}	UNA
				$0B_{16}$	Physical Drop Number
Standby Monitor Present	3 or 7	Broadcast	RS	02_{16}	UNA
				$0B_{16}$	Physical Drop Number
Duplicate Address Test	3 or 7	Self	RS	None	
Lobe Media Test	3 or 7	Null	RS	26_{16}	Wrap Data
Remove Ring Station	3 or 7	Target RS	CRS	none	
Change Parameters	3 or 7	Target RS	CRS	09_{16}	Correlator
				03_{16}	Local Ring Number
				04_{16}	Assign Physical Drop Number
				05_{16}	Error Timer Value
				06_{16}	Authorized Function Classes
				07_{16}	Authorized Access Priority
Initialize Station	3 or 7	Target RS	RPS	09_{16}	Correlator
				03_{16}	Local Ring Number
				04_{16}	Assign Physical Drop Number
				05_{16}	Error Timer Value
Request Station Addresses	3 or 7	Target RS	&&	09_{16}	Correlator
Request Station State	3 or 7	Target RS	&&	09_{16}	Correlator
Request Station Attachments	3 or 7	Target RS	&&	09_{16}	Correlator
Request Initialization	3 or 7	RPS	RS	02_{16}	UNA
				21_{16}	Individual Address Count
				22_{16}	Product Instance ID
				23_{16}	Ring Station Version Number
Report Station Addresses	0 or 7	SA of Request	RS	09_{16}	Correlator
				02_{16}	UNA
				$2B_{16}$	Group Address
				$2C_{16}$	Functional Address(s)
				21_{16}	Individual Address Count
				$0B_{16}$	Physical Drop Number
Report Station State	0 or 7	SA of Request	RS	09_{16}	Correlator
				28_{16}	Station Identifier
				29_{16}	Ring Station Status
				23_{16}	Ring Station Version

Table 18-5: MAC Frame Reference (Continued)

Vector Name (VI)	Priority	Destination	Source	Subvector Name (SVI)	
Report Station Attachments	0 or 7	SA of Request	RS	09_{16}	Correlator
				06_{16}	Authorized Function Classes
				07_{16}	Authorized Access Priority
				$2C_{16}$	Functional Address(s)
				21_{16}	Individual Address Count
				22_{16}	Product Instance ID
Report New Active Monitor	3 or 7	CRS	AM	02_{16}	UNA
				$0B_{16}$	Physical Drop Number
				22_{16}	Product Instance ID
Report SUA Change	3 or 7	CRS	RS	02_{16}	UNA
				$0B_{16}$	Physical Drop Number
Report Neighbor Notification Incomplete	3 or 7	REM	RS	$0A_{16}$	SA of Last AMP or SMP Frame
Report Active Monitor Error	3 or 7	REM	AM or RS	30_{16}	Error Code
				02_{16}	UNA
				$0B_{16}$	Physical Drop Number
Report Error	3 or 7	REM	RS	$2D_{16}$	Isolating Error Count
				$2E_{16}$	Non-isolating Error Count
				02_{16}	UNA
				$0B_{16}$	Physical Drop Number

Notes: Priority - indicates frame priority as transmitted in the Frame Control (FC) field

**	Transmitted without waiting for a token	
&&	Any non-zero function class (CRS, RPS, REM, or NM)	
RS	Ring Station	
AM	Active Monitor	
CRS	Configuration Report Server	
REM	Ring Error Monitor	
RPS	Ring Parameter Server	

When stations receive a MAC frame addressed to their unicast, broadcast, or functional address, they will process the frame only if it is valid. This validity check is designed to enable the station to make an informed choice as to whether the frame should be processed or ignored. The actions taken are as follows:

RI_INVALID Any MAC frame containing a Routing Information Field may be ignored.

VI_UNK Unrecognized vector ID: The station will reject the MAC frame if it contains an unrecognized vector ID value.

VI_LTH_ERR Vector length error: Reject any MAC frame if the vector length does not agree with either the length of the frame, or the sum of the length of all the SVLs plus the VL, VC, and VI fields

The Media Access Control (MAC) Layer

SHORT_MAC	MAC frame too short: MAC frames may be rejected if, based on the VI value, the frame is too short to contain all required subvectors. As a minimum, MAC frames should contain subvectors as shown in table 18-5.
LONG_MAC	MAC frame too long: MAC frames may be rejected if the vector length field indicates a length longer than that required to contain all the allowable subvectors.
SV_LTH_ERR	Subvector length error: The station will reject any MAC frame if the subvector length is either longer or shorter than that specified in table 18-4.
SV_MISSING	Missing required subvector: The station will reject any MAC frame which does not include all required subvectors.
SV_UNK	SVI value unknown: Any MAC frame may be rejected if it contains an unrecognized SVI value. However, knowledge of all SVI values contained in table 18-5 is mandatory.
SC_INVALID	Invalid source class: The MAC frame will be rejected if its source does not match that stated in table 18-5.
FUNCTION_ DISABLED	Function disabled: The function requested has been disabled by management.

If the validity check is passed the MAC frame is processed and acted upon in accordance with the VI included within the frame.

Specific processes or functions that are reliant upon the use of MAC frames are described throughout this text and will therefore not be covered at this point. This section does however provide a point of reference for all subsequent management process descriptions.

18.6 Station Operation

As we have seen thus far, a station's access to the ring is controlled by a continuously circulating token. At any stage, under normal operation, a station can be in one of three modes: transmitting data, repeating, or transmitting a fill pattern. Each of these is discussed in turn in the text that follows.

18.6.1 Transmitting

When stations have data to transmit, this data is passed down the internal communications stack to the MAC layer where frames are constructed and queued for transmission. These frames must remain queued until the MAC receiver element signals the reception of a valid token, thus releasing the queue.

We have seen in section 18.1.5 the checks undertaken by the station in order to ascertain the validity of the token. Even if the token itself passes all these validity checks, it does not guarantee the station is able to use it for data transmission. The access control field within the token will indicate its priority level. If the priority level of the token is equal to or less than that of the queued data frame then it can be used. If the priority level is higher than that of the queued frame then the token must be repeated onwards. In the case where multiple frames are queued for transmission, then only those equal to or higher in priority than the token can be transmitted. Other frames within the queue must wait until a token arrives holding a lower priority level.

Assuming the arriving token is of suitable priority level, the MAC transmitting element will change the token to a Start of Frame Sequence (SFS) by altering the access control field. It does this by changing the T bit from a 0_2 to a 1_2, and setting the M and R bits to 0_2. Having repeated the original token SD field followed by the modified AC, the MAC transmitter will cease repeating mode and start transmission by adding the FC, DA, SA, RI (if required), and DATA fields. While these are being transmitted, the MAC will compute the FCS and add it after the DATA, before concluding the frame with the End of Frame Sequence (EFS). As part of the EFS, the access control field will be transmitted with the A and C bits set to 0_2. The MAC will then introduce the required interframe gap prior to transmitting the second frame (if multiple frames are queued).

18.6.2 Token Transmission

A station is responsible for releasing the token back onto the ring once transmission of the last frame is complete. The policy for the release of the token back onto the ring is determined by the Flag, Early Token Release Option (FETO). This flag if set to 1, indicates that ETR is active, and if set to 0, ETR is inactive. This policy is normally set by the network administrator as part of the initial station setup. Most NIC manufacturers allow ETR to be chosen as an option on 16Mbps adapter installation programs. The station will release the token, based on the FETO, using the following guidelines:

- Early Token Release - The token is released by the transmitting station as soon as it has completed the inter-frame gap following the last frame.

- Normal Token Release - The token is only released once the return of the last transmitted frame has been verified. This is achieved by matching the source address of the frame being stripped to that of the last frame transmitted. If the match is made then the token can be released.

18.6.3 Fill Pattern

A station's transmitter can be in any one of three states; transmitting data frames or a token, repeating data frames or a token, or transmitting a fill pattern. Fill is transmitted by the station when there is essentially nothing else to send and ensures that the ring is never "quiet", as this is an illegal condition in a Token Ring network. The fill pattern can consist of any combination of data 1_2 and data 0_2 symbols, although data 0_2's are preferred.

The Media Access Control (MAC) Layer

18.6.4 Repeating

When a frame is transmitted, all other stations (including the destination) must repeat the frame around the ring. This is done on a bit by bit basis (similar to the way an Ethernet repeater repeats), with modifications being made if necessary. The modifications that can be made are detailed below, including the circumstances in which they can occur. All other bits are repeated as received.

- The *M* bit
  Originating stations will always transmit frames and tokens with the Monitor (M) bit in the AC field set to 0_2. As the frame circulates the ring the Active Monitor[9] will modify this bit to 1_2. All other stations repeat this bit as received.

- The *R* bits
  Again, originating stations will transmit these bits in the AC field as 000_2. Stations will repeat these bits as received, unless they have frames queued for transmission. In this instance, they are free to modify the R bits to match the priority of any queued frames to reserve the next token to be released at that priority level.

- The *E* bit
  Stations originating frames or tokens will always transmit them with the E bit set to 0_2. Any station in the repeat path can modify this to a 1_2 upon detecting an error[10], marking the frame/token invalid.

- The *A* bits
  When transmitted, the A bits in the AC field are always set to 0_2. Stations in the repeat path can modify these to a 1_2 if the frame is addressed to that station, either as a unicast, multicast, or broadcast, and it is a valid frame.

- The *C* bits
  Also part of the AC field, these bits too, are transmitted as 0_2 and modified to a 1_2 by any repeating station that recognizes its address and successfully copies the frame, assuming it is valid.

18.6.5 Frame Reception

All active stations on the ring will inspect incoming data streams to ascertain if this is a frame that needs to be either copied or acted upon in some other manner. The main indication is the destination address, which could potentially match either the receiving stations unique MAC address, relevant multicast address, supported functional address, or broadcast address. If a match to any of these is achieved, the station will, in addition to repeating the frame, copy it to its internal frame buffer, to be passed up the relevant communications stack. If the copy process is successful then the station is free to modify the C bits, having already modified the A bits, in the AC field.

---

[9] The purpose of the Monitor bit is described in section 18.1.3.
[10] What constitutes an invalid frame or token was discussed in sections 18.3.12 & 18.1.5, respectively.

All receiving stations, whether copying or not, will monitor frame validity by checking and computing the FCS, and ensuring that there are no violations to Differential Manchester encoding. Should either of these conditions exist then the A and C bits are not set, rather the E bit will be modified to 1_2 and the station will increment its error counter.

18.6.6 Frame Stripping

Frame stripping, while essentially a straightforward process, can be complicated by the use of early token release and the existence of bit errors in the data stream. Stations rely heavily on counting the start and end delimiters of frames to strip the same number of frames from the ring as were transmitted. Any errors in the start or end delimiter could result in a miscount and therefore under or over stripping could occur. Assuming no errors, stations strip their data from the ring by simply transmitting a fill pattern while counting the received frames arriving. Once the number of frames arriving matches the number transmitted the station will cease transmitting fill pattern and return to repeat mode.

Where problems can occur is when a station miscounts the number of frames received, either resulting in understripping (counts too few actual frames) or over stripping (counts too many). Of these two conditions, understripping is far less desirable and should be avoided even at the cost of overstripping. It may seem a simple process - count the frames out and then count them back in again - but consider the method of counting. This is based on counting start and end delimiters, which could be corrupted due to burst errors[11], or even false delimiters created due to things such as noise generated by noisy TCUs. This can mislead a station into a miscount. The paragraphs that follow describe the processes used by stations to compensate for both under and overstripping, as well as lost frames, which would also affect the count.

Accounting for Lost Frames
Each frame transmitted increments a frame counter, and likewise each frame received decrements the same counter. In addition, the source address of the last frame transmitted is temporarily stored for future comparison. At all times while the frame counter is greater than 1, all received frames are automatically stripped. If the frame counter is equal to (or less than) 1 then the station compares the incoming source address with the one stored earlier. If all is well then the two should be equal and the station will complete the stripping of that frame before returning to repeat mode. If the source addresses do not equate then the station stops stripping, thus allowing the ending delimiter to be repeated. This is an indication to the next transmitting station that overstripping has occurred.

Accounting for overstripping by the previous station
If a station transmits a frame and before receiving back a start delimiter it receives an end delimiter, the station will take this as an indication of the end of its frame and decrement its frame counter accordingly. Thus, if only one frame was transmitted, the frame counter would then be equal to

[11] Burst errors are discussed in section 19.1.3

0 and the station would return to repeat mode. The only exception to this rule is if a burst error is detected.

To prevent understripping

Stations counting received frames do not decrement their frame counter if an end delimiter is received prior to the transmission of their first end delimiter (and therefore their first complete frame). After the first end delimiter has been received, only complete frames are subsequently counted. Should an error be detected within a frame, that frame may be counted but the station should continue to strip until after the next start delimiter has been received, thus potentially overstripping (remember this is much preferred to understripping). Stations can use the value of the stored source address to determine if overstripping has occurred, should this condition happen on the last or only frame transmitted.

As you can see, procedures are in place to account for all eventualities. In addition, should a station fail to remove its frames from the ring, there is always the Active Monitor scrutinizing the value of the M bit, ready to intervene if required.

18.6.7 Station Counters

As stated somewhat earlier in this chapter, Token Ring as a protocol relies heavily on the use of tools such as counters, flags, and timers to indicate the state of a vast array of different elements that contribute to the protocol as a whole. One of the simplest methods of tracking transmissions or receptions is through the use of counters. Within Token Ring there are essentially two groups of counters, one group monitoring aspects of protocol operation, and another monitoring errors. In the table 18-6 protocol operational counters are described; error counters are discussed in section 19.1.3.

Table 18-6: Operational Counters

Counter	Description
Counter, Beacon Circulating (CBC)	Used to count the number of Beacon frames from the upstream neighbor before activating beacon frame detection.
Counter, Beacon Repeat (CBR)	A station uses this counter to monitor the number of Beacon MAC frames received from its downstream neighbor before removing itself from the ring.
Counter, Claim Receive (CCR)	Counts the number of received Claim Token MAC frames that were transmitted by this station. Used to resolve the claim token process.
Counter, Claim Transmit (CCT)	Used during Claim Token to count the number of Claim Token frames transmitted.
Counter, DAT Failure (CDF)	Used by a station to count the number of times a Duplicate Address Test MAC frame returns with the address recognized bit $A=1_2$
Counter, DAT Good (CDG)	Counts the number of times a Duplicate Address Test MAC frame returns with the address recognized bit $A=0_2$ and frame copied bit $C=0_2$

Table 18-6: Operational Counters (Continued)

Counter	Description
Counter, Error Report (CER)	Used to control the amount of times the Error Report MAC frame is re-transmitted.
Counter, Frame (CFR)	As previously described, this counter is used to monitor the number of transmitted frames that are still circulating the ring.
Counter, Neighbor Notification Requests (CNNR)	Counts the number of neighbor notifications since the last ring purge.
Counter, Request Initialization (CRI)	A stations uses this counter to restrict the number of Request Initialization MAC frames sent to the Ring Parameter Server that return with the A bit = 1_2, i.e., recognized.
Counter, Request Initialization Not recognized (CRIN)	A stations uses this counter to restrict the number of Request Initialization MAC frames sent to the Ring Parameter Server that return with the A bit = 0_2, i.e., not recognized.
Counter, SUA Change (CSC)	A station uses this counter to limit the number of times the SUA Change MAC frame is re-transmitted.
Counter, Transmitted Octets (CTO)	The CTO counter is used to restrict the time a station can hold the token after capture. A simple method of determining the token holding time would be to use a timer, but by using a counter instead, the amount of processing required is reduced. For example, the counter is pre-loaded with a value once the token has been captured (4550 @ 4Mbps or 18200 @ 16Mbps Maximum), and decremented every 8 symbols (1 octet) transmitted. In this way, if multiple frames are transmitted, the station simply needs to compare the octet count of the next pending frame to the value of the counter. If the frame is smaller then there is time for the transmission, if not, then the frame is held over until the next capture. The figures of 4550 and 18,200 octets at 4 and 16Mbps respectively reflect maximum values and equate to a token holding time of 9.1mS.

Note: Counters can be pre-set to a value and/or incremented or decremented depending on their purpose and actions specified by station operation.

18.6.8 Station Flags

Flags have long been an important method used in computers and networking either to remember an occurrence of an event or alternatively to set a policy or parameter. Token Ring is no different, making wide use of the feature within the protocol, both within the MAC level with protocol flags, and external to the MAC indicating MAC policy. The differences between the two groups are fairly straightforward. The MAC protocol flags are always set to 0_2 during the station initialization phase when joining the ring, and can be changed to 1_2 by the station to remember that a specific event has occurred on the ring. For example, the Flag, Active Monitor is set to 1_2 if a station is successful in the claim token process and becomes Active Monitor. Station Policy flags however, are different; they define the way in which the MAC actually operates, and cannot be altered by the MAC itself. Typically, the setting of these flags is either due to the operational characteristics of the network itself, or sometimes by external network management. Table 18-7 details policy flags used to determine MAC operational characteristics, while table 18-8 describes those flags used by the MAC protocol for event indication.

Table 18-7: Station Policy Flags

Flag	*Description*
Flag, Beacon Handling Option (FBHO)	This flag indicates at what stage the station is able to participate in the beaconing process prior to that station actually completing the join ring process, i.e., should beaconing occur while the station is joining the ring or wait until the process completes. This can have an effect on speed of fault resolution.
	FBHO = 0 once neighbor notification is complete
	FBHO = 1 not until request initialization is complete
	FBHO = 0 is recommended
Flag, Claim Contender Option (FCCO)	Indicates how a station behaves during the Claim Token[12] process. Normal operation would be for a station to transmit its own claim if it receives a claim from a station with a lower numerical value for its MAC address. If the FCCO is set to 1 then normal operation ensues. If FCCO is set to 0 then the station will not transmit its own claim frame, but simply repeat the received claim. In this way it is possible for management to ensure any given station does not become Active Monitor.
Flag, Early Token Release Option (FETO)	Indicates whether Early Token Release is set as an option on a 16Mbps station.
	FETO = 0 Early Token Release is not selected
	FETO = 1 Early Token Release is selected
	This flag has no meaning in a 4Mbps station.
Flag, Error Counting Option (FECO)	A station reports all detected errors upon expiry of the Error Report Timer. This flag determines when this timer is reset and thus begins countdown. If FECO is set to 0 the timer is reset upon the reception of the first error and all errors are reported upon expiry. If FECO is set to 1 then the timer is immediately reset upon expiry and the error report is sent.
Flag, Medium Rate Option (FMRO)	Indicates the speed at which the station is set to operate.
	FMRO = 0 4 Mbps
	FMRO = 1 16 Mbps
Flag, Multiple Frame Transmission Option (FMFTO)	This flag dictates how a station handles token reservation while transmitting multiple frames. A value of 0 for FMFTO will result in a lower latency for higher priority traffic, while a value of 1 will increase the latency as the transmitting station will complete its transmission sequence before releasing the token

[12] Claim Token is the process used for selecting the Active Monitor and is discussed in section 19.4.

Table 18-7: Station Policy Flags (Continued)

Flag	Description
Flag, Reject Remove Option (FRRO)	Indicates how a station will respond to the receipt of a REMOVE MAC frame. If the flag is set to 0 then the station will remove itself from the ring. If the flag is set to 1 then the station will send a RESPONSE saying the function is disabled.
Flag, Token Error Detection Option (FTEO)	This flag indicates how a station will handle token errors. FTEO = 0 Isolation/reporting of token errors supported. FTEO = 1 Isolation/reporting of token errors not supported. FTEO = 0 is recommended
Flag, Token Handling Option (FTHO)	Determines how the Active Monitor detects the lack of a frame or token on the ring. If set to 0, the Active Monitor will use the Timer, Valid Transmissions solely. If set to 1, the FAT[13] flag is used in conjunction with the TVX timer.
Flag, Good Token Option (FGTO)	Dictates the policy for detecting the presence of a token. FGTO = 0 A valid token with priority 0 or a valid token priority greater than 0 followed by a frame. FGTO = 1 Any valid token

The MAC protocol flags, detailed in table 18-8 are, in general, always set to 0 when a station joins the ring. Each is then used to indicate the occurrence of a specific event by changing to the set condition (1) when the event takes place. Any set flags will then be reset to 0 when either the condition no longer exists or other appropriate action takes place. A ring purge can force some flags to be reset, but others are impervious even when the ring is re-initialized via the purge procedure. The purpose of most of the following flags is fairly self-evident from the description, however some relate to procedures discussed in later sections, and cross referencing will enhance understanding.

Table 18-8: MAC Protocol Flags

Flag	Description
Flag, Active Monitor (FAM)	This flag is set to 1 if a station is elected Active Monitor via the claim token process and 0 for all other stations.
Flag, Await New Monitor (FANM)	FANM is only set to 1 in one circumstance, when it joins the ring and has yet to detect the presence of an Active Monitor. The flag set to 1 indicates to the station that it may participate in the Claim Token process, useful if it is the only station on the ring.
Flag, Any Token (FAT)	The FAT flag is only used by the Active Monitor in its role of ensuring correct ring operation. When a frame or token is received by the Active Monitor it will set this flag to 1. At the same time the TVX timer is reset. The flag is then tested and reset if TVX expires, indicating the token is lost and ring recovery is required.

---

[13] The FAT flag is discussed in table 18-8.

Table 18-8: MAC Protocol Flags (Continued)

Flag	Description
Flag, Beacon Repeat (FBR)	This flag is an integral part of the beaconing process and is set to 1 when a station enters the test state as a result of receiving BEACON frames. Once set the station will refrain from entering the test state and thus ensure multiple entries in this condition do not occur.
Flag, Beacon Test (FBT)	Also used as part of the beaconing process, this flag is set on by the transmitting station once it enters the test state to ensure it too does not re-enter the test condition more than once.
Flag, Claim Token (FCT)	FCT is set to 1 on the reception of a Claim Token MAC frame to assist the determination of the correct subvector (Beacon Type)[14] when entering the transmit beacon state.
Flag, Duplicate Address Test Complete (FDC)	Set to 0 on joining the ring, FDC is set to 1 on completion of the Duplicate Address Test (DAT) thus allowing transition into the next phase, Neighbor Notification.
Flag, Ending Delimiter (FED)	This flag is used during frame transmission to indicate when the frame counter can be decremented upon the receipt of incoming End Delimiters. It is set to 0 when a station first captures a token and begins transmission. It is then set to 1 upon transmission of the first frames ED. Once set, all arriving frames can be decremented from the frame counter to ensure the same number transmitted are stripped from the ring. It is important in that it effectively tells the frame counter when to start counting, and as such prevents understripping.
Flag, Error Report (FER)	FER is set to 1 upon detection to the first reportable error and indicates that any subsequent errors should not reset the error report timer. Once the timer has expired and the errors reported, the flag is reset to 0.
Flag, Insert Delay (FID)	This flag is set to 1 by any station re-entering from the beacon test state to ensure that the PHY has sufficient time to re-insert into the ring. When set the station must wait for: a) TID timer to expire, or b) reception of a frame, or c) detection of signal loss Once one of these conditions is detected, FID is reset to 0 and the station is free to continue with resolution of the beaconing process.
Flag, Inserted (FINS)	Initially set to 0, FINS is then set to 1 when a station is able to participate in the beaconing process. The point at which this flag is set is dependent on the FBHO policy flag (see table 18-7).
Flag, Join Ring (FJR)	Initially set to 0, FJR is set to 1 upon completion of the Request Initialization phase of the joining process, thus indicating the station has completed the joining process and is now a full participating member of the ring.

[14] Refer to MAC frame subvectors in table 18-4.

Table 18-8: MAC Protocol Flags (Continued)

Flag	Description
Flag, Lost Frame (FLF)	FLF is used in conjunction with the lost frame error counter to count lost frames. Set to 1 when the station, having detected the failure of the frame to return, stops stripping, and reset to 0 once the counter has been incremented.
Flag, My Address (FMA)	The FMA flag indicates to the station if the frame currently being stripped is the last frame it transmitted. Set to 0 after capture of the token but prior to any transmission, this flag is only set to 1 if the last frame being stripped (frame counter = 1) has a source address equal to that of this station.
Flag, Monitor Present (FMP)	This flag is set during the joining phase to indicate the presence of an active monitor on the ring.
Flag, Neighbor Notification Complete (FNC)	FNC, initially 0, is set to 1 once the neighbor notification part of the join ring process is complete, to indicate the station is aware of its upstream neighbor's address.
Flag, Not My Address (FNMA)	The opposite of FMA, this flag is used to prevent overstripping. Set to 0 upon token capture, this flag is set to 1 if the last frame being stripped has a SA that is not equal to that of the station. If this flag is set to 1 then the station immediately returns to repeat mode as it has obviously just started to strip a frame transmitted by another station. This ensures the other station will receive the correct number of ending delimiters and thus match its frame counter to the number transmitted.
Flag, Neighbor Notification (FNN)	Only used by the active monitor, FNN indicates when the neighbor notification process is complete. Set to 0 when the process is started, FNN is then set to 1 when the active monitor receives either an AMP or SMP frame with the A and C bits both set to 0.
Flag, Neighbor Notification Waiting (FNW)	Used during the join phase, this flag is initially set to 0. As a station is unable to participate in neighbor notification until it has completed the DAT test, it sets this flag to 1 should it receive a neighbor notification frame to indicate that its neighbor is waiting.
Flag, Operational (FOP)	Indicates the station is operational, i.e., it has completed a lobe test and inserted into the ring. It is set to 0 initially and when the station removes itself from the ring.
Flag, Priority Token (FPT)	This flag simply indicates the presence of a token with a priority greater than 0. If a token is received with P>0 then FPT is set to 1. If a frame or token arrives with P=0 the FPT is set to 0.
Flag, Remove Hold (FRH)	Default 1, this flag is set to 0 once the station has waited the required minimum time before removing itself from the ring.
Flag, Signal Loss (FSL)	FSL indicates the reception of a valid signal from the ring. FSL is set to 1 if signal loss has occurred for the duration of the signal loss timer and 0 if a valid signal is being received.
Flag, Signal Loss Detected (FSLD)	FSLD is set to 1 when loss of signal is detected, activating the signal loss detection process. Ultimately this can lead to beaconing.

Table 18-8: MAC Protocol Flags (Continued)

Flag	Description
Flag, Standby Monitor Present (FSMP)	Only used by standby monitors, it is used to detect failures in the neighbor notification process and stop excessive notification frames. FSMP is set to 0 when a standby monitor receives an AMP frame with A and C bits not equal to 0. It is set to 1 when the station receives an SMP or AMP frame with A and C bits set to 0. Any subsequent SMP frames arriving with A and C bits set to 0 (before the next notification cycle) would indicate an error.
Flag, Starting Delimiter (FSD)	The FSD flag is used by all stations when they are counting their transmitted frames. It is set to 0 when a station enters the transmit state and 1 when it receives a starting delimiter.
Flag, Test Wait (FTW)	Used by a station during the beaconing process to ensure the concentrator has fully completed its insertion cycle prior to the station executing a Remove_Station. Set to 0 during normal operations, FTW is set to 1 by the beacon test function when it detects the need to enter beacon test mode.
Flag, Transmit Idles (FTI)	When FTI is set to 0, this indicates the station is in repeat mode and will repeat incoming data. When set to 1, the station will transmit fill (idles) and not repeat received data.
Flag, Transmit from Crystal (FTXC)	Stations will under normal conditions use the incoming signal as a timing reference and phase lock loop to that signal. There are three conditions however that demand a station to use its own crystal as a timing source for transmission. These are, the station is the Active Monitor, or transmitting Claim Token frames, or Beaconing. In these conditions, FTXC is set to 1 and the station uses its own crystal timing source.
Flag, Transmit Immediate (FTXI)	Indicates whether a station should wait for a token before transmitting frames. When set to 1, the station transmits without waiting for the appropriate token. When set to 0, a token must be captured first and released after transmission.
Flag, Wire Fault (FWF)	Set to 1 if a wire fault is present or 0 if not.
Flag, Wire Fault Active (FWFA)	Wire fault detection is activated (1) or deactivated (0) using this flag.

Note: FTXC and FTI require further specific actions when set.

18.6.9   Station Timers

Timers are used extensively in Token Ring to control how long a particular condition can exist. Timers can be reset, expired or counting down, depending upon circumstances on the ring. Invariably, the term reset is used to describe the initiation of the timer, expired means the time has run out, which often leads to another action. Table 18-9 describes the system timers used by the protocol.

Table 18-9: System Timers

Timer	Description
Timer, Active Monitor (TAM)	Although each station has a TAM, only the Active Monitor uses it to ensure an AMP MAC frame is transmitted every 6.8 to 7.0s.
Timer, Beacon Repeat (TBR)	Used by each station in Beacon Repeat state and reset each time a Beacon MAC frame is received. Monitors the absence of Beacon Frames forcing the station into Claim Token if the timer expires.
Timer, Beacon Transmit (TBT)	Used to determine how long a station transmits Beacon MAC frames before moving to the Beacon Test state. Can be between 15.8 and 26s although 18s is recommended.
Timer, Claim Token (TCT)	This timer is used to detect the failure of the Claim Token process. Reset upon entry into the process, the process should complete before expiry. Values between 1.0 and 1.2s.
Timer, Error Report (TER)	Used to determine the intervals at which errors should be reported to the Error Monitor. The default value is between 2.0 and 2.2s after which all error counters are reset.
Timer, Insert Delay (TID)	This timer is used after the Beacon Test to delay the station recognizing its own Beacon frames until sufficient time has elapsed to ensure re-insertion in to the ring. The default value is between 5.0 and 20.0s.
Timer, Join Ring (TJR)	Used to detect the failure of the Join Ring process. The default is between 17.8 and 18.0s prior to the expiry of which the station should have completed the ring join process.
Timer, No Token (TNT)	TNT, default value between 2.6 and 5.2s (2.6s recommended), is used by the Active Monitor to monitor the Token circulating on the ring. It is reset each time the Token rotates and expiry requires the ring to be re-initialized before normal protocol operation can continue.
Timer, Queue PDU (TQP)	With a recommended value of 20ms, this timer is used to schedule the following events: The queuing of SMP MAC frames during Neighbor Notification. The transmission of Beacon MAC frames during the Beaconing state. The transmission of Claim Frames during Claim Token.
Timer, Remove Hold (TRH)	Defaulting to between 5.0 and 7.0s, this timer delays a station from issuing a remove request immediately after insertion. This allows the TCU adequate time to complete the insertion process prior to receiving a request for removal.
Timer, Remove Wait (TRW)	This timer forces a station to remain in Repeat state while the TCU completes a remove request. The default is set at 200ms.
Timer, Request Initialize (TRI)	Used during the Ring Join process, this timer should not expire before a response to the Request Initialization MAC is received. If it expires, it forces the station to queue another after Neighbor Notification is complete. The default is 2.5 to 2.8s.
Timer, Return to Repeat (TRR)	Ensures transmitting stations return to the Repeat state after 4.0 to 4.1ms.

Table 18-9: System Timers (Continued)

Timer	Description
Timer, Ring Purge (TRP)	Used by the Active Monitor, this timer is used to detect the failure of a Ring Purge MAC frame to return and thus indicates to move to Claim Token. Default value is between 1.0 and 1.2s.
Timer, Signal Loss (TSL)	Used to detect whether a signal loss condition is steady and therefore initiate Beaconing. Value between 200 and 250ms.
Timer, Standby Monitor (TSM)	Active in all stations apart from the Active Monitor, this timer detects the presence of the Active Monitor on the ring by resetting each time a AMP, SMP or Ring Purge MAC frame is detected. Each of which proves the presence of the Active Monitor. Expiry of the timer will force Claim Token. Default value between 14.8 and 15.0s.
Timer, Valid Transmission (TVX)	Only used by the Active Monitor, this timer helps detect the absence of valid frames or tokens. With a default value of between 10.0 and 11.0ms expiry causes the Active Monitor to purge the ring.
Timer, Wire Fault Delay (TWFD)	Used to delay the detection of wire fault after joining the ring or re-inserting after the Beacon Test. Defaults to 5 to 10s. TWFD + TWF must be greater than 7.0s.
Timer, Wire Fault (TWF)	Used to determine the sampling period for wire fault, with the default being 0 to 10.0s with 5s recommended.

The use of so many counters, flags, and timers may seem to increase the complexity of the protocol, but it is this very complexity that provides the benefits of Token Ring. Consider the potential problems highlighted in chapter 16 and you will begin to understand many of the reasons for such a sophisticated protocol. Furthermore, consider some of the shortcomings of other protocols, such as Ethernet, that can really struggle should network utilization reach or exceed 35-40%. In contrast Token Ring, with its complexity and ability to cope with almost all eventualities, is probably running at its optimum with utilization rates in excess of 75-80%. The powers of recovery that Token Ring offers, for virtually any form of failure, makes it a favorite in environments, such as the financial industry, where network downtime in considered an inconceivable option, and also automation environments, such as manufacturing, because of bandwidth and "slot-time" predictability. Sophistication is built in to all aspects of Token Ring, especially at the MAC level, as the process required simply to join the ring clearly demonstrates.

18.7 Station Insertion

Joining the ring would seem a simple proposition, but in reality it has the potential for causing a number of problems if a set procedure is not undertaken. Consider for a moment some of the pitfalls that could occur. Firstly, there is a need to break the ring to allow a new member; other stations could and most likely will be using the ring at that moment to transmit their data. Then there are other considerations such as: is another station on the ring already using the same address?; does an active monitor exist on the ring?; is the ring integrity likely to be compromised by the additional station? All of these lead to the conclusion that the ring is sacrosanct and stations must do all in their power to ensure its continued operation. This process is nowhere more evident than when joining the ring.

For a station to become a valid member of the ring it must first join that ring. This process involves seven separate stages through which the station must pass, in effect tests, the aim of which is to ultimately preserve the integrity of the ring. Each stage is described in the text that follows, with full access to the ring denied until all have been completed.

18.7.1   Lobe Test

The first stage of ring entry involves testing the station itself and its associated cabling to ensure that addition to the ring will not introduce a fault in the data path around the ring. It is therefore necessary to check the functionality of the transmitter, receiver, and associated cabling of any station wishing to become a member. The simplest way to achieve this is to take advantage of the fact that prior to ring entry the TCU at the MAU is in bypass state, therefore the station is in effect on a ring of its own that consists of itself, the lobe cable, and the bypassed TCU. The station wishing to join must transmit a TEST MAC frame, which will obviously travel around this self contained ring, i.e., down the transmit pair in the lobe cable and straight back via the receive pair. Successful reception by the MAC receiver indicates that the transmit and receive elements are functioning correctly, as is the associated cabling. A successful conclusion to this test leads the station to stage 2, while failure would be reported to a higher level entity for rectification.

18.7.2   Phantom Current

Stage two in the ring joining process is the application by the joining station of phantom current. The process itself is described in Section 2.6.2. By applying phantom current, the TCU is opened and the station becomes part of the transmission path of the ring. As the TCU opens and the station inserts, the ring will in effect be broken. It is imperative that this "breakage" occurs for the minimum amount of time, therefore the station is limited to a maximum of 5.0mS in which to insert. At this point the station is part of the ring path and must therefore repeat all incoming data, but is not an active member, so cannot transmit its own data.

18.7.3   Ring Speed Test

As part of the ring it is obviously important for a new member to satisfy itself as to the data speed of the ring. A station inserting at 4 Mbps onto a 16 Mbps ring or vice versa can cause problems. The immediate downstream station will detect a problem because incoming data will be at the wrong speed, as will the newly inserted station. In both cases, the stations will see the fault as a signal fault and instigate signal fault resolution (beaconing). The problem, however, is that for beaconing to work, the upstream neighbor (the new station is immediately upstream from the beaconing station) must be able to interpret the incoming beacon frames, not very likely if they are transmitted at a different data speed to the one you are operating at. The net result is that once beaconing starts in this instance, it will not cease until the problem, in this case the new station, is removed from the ring. Unfortunately, this will not happen automatically as the new station does not know it is the cause of the problem.

Many newer active MAUs incorporate ring speed detection circuitry that prevents stations of the wrong speed inserting in the ring, precisely to overcome the problems outlined above.

18.7.4 Active Monitor Test

Stage four involves checking for the existence of an Active Monitor on the ring. This is an important stage for two reasons. Firstly, we have seen previously the importance of the Active Monitor to the ring, and normal operation cannot be carried out without it. Secondly, it is possible that the joining station may actually be the first station on the ring, therefore no Active Monitor exists. The test itself is straight forward and simply involves monitoring the frames on the ring for the existence of an Active Monitor. Simply put, there are three types of MAC frame that can only be generated if an Active Monitor exists on the ring. Therefore, if the joining station sees one of these frames then it knows that the test is successful. The three MAC frames in question are RP, AMP, and SMP. The first two, RP and AMP, can only be generated by an Active Monitor, while SMP MAC frames are only generated by ring stations immediately after an AMP has circulated. In either case existence of any of these would provide conclusive evidence that the test has been passed.

Obviously a time limit needs to be applied to the detection process. This limit is governed by the Timer, Standby Monitor (TSM) and is set between 14.8 and 15.0 seconds. In reality, should an Active Monitor exist, then a maximum of 7.0 seconds should be all that is required to detect it. If the process fails, i.e., the timer expires before an Active Monitor is detected, then the joining station initiates the Monitor election process Claim Token.

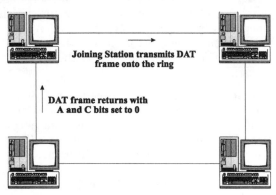

Joining Station transmits DAT
frame onto the ring

DAT frame returns with
A and C bits set to 0

Figure 18-13:   Duplicate Address Test

18.7.5 Duplicate Address Detection

Stage five is the detection of any other station on the network using the same MAC address as the one assigned to the joining station. This is important as the IEEE

802.5 standard outlaws duplicate addresses, for obvious reasons. The joining station initiates the process by issuing a Duplicate Address Test (DAT) MAC frame. The MAC frame is issued with both source and destination addresses equal to that of the sending station. As with all transmitted frames, the A and C bits in the frame status field are set to 0_2. As the frame circulates the ring, any station with a MAC address equal to the destination address field will process the frame and set the A and C bits to 1_2. Should the frame return to the sender with the A and C bits set, then this is an immediate indication the address used is already in use on the network. If this is the case the station will withdraw from the ring. If universally administered addressing is being used then this should never happen (in theory), however, there is more chance of duplicate addresses on a locally administered addressing scheme.

18.7.6 Neighbor Notification

Stage six is the Nearest Active Upstream Neighbor (NAUN) Notification process. In which all participating stations notify their downstream neighbors of their MAC addresses. This is especially important for the fault tolerance implementation on the ring. The reason being, that a station detecting a fault will be downstream of that fault. If the ring is to have the ability to initiate error recovery, then the station upstream of the fault must also be notified, so that the fault domain is isolated, and stations either side can determine and eliminate the problem. It is therefore imperative that stations can address their upstream neighbors to inform them of signal loss/fault conditions.

The neighbor notification process is initiated approximately every 7.0 seconds by the Active Monitor who issues an AMP MAC frame. This is issued with a source address equal to the MAC address of the sender and a broadcast destination address. As the destination address is a broadcast, the immediate downstream neighbor is guaranteed to process the frame, as will all the others. However, the first station will be aware it is the first by the fact that on reception, the A and C bits are still set to 0_2. As the AMP frame is repeated on by this station it will set the A and C bits to 1_2, immediately indicating to other stations that they are not the first to see this frame. As the frame is repeated by this initial station, knowing it is the first, it can simply read off the source address of the AMP as being that of its upstream neighbor.

The MAC protocol indicates that 20mS after seeing an AMP frame a station must issue its own SMP frame. This too, is issued as a broadcast and will be read by all stations. However, in the same way as the downstream neighbor of the Active Monitor was able to determine its upstream neighbor address, so to will the downstream neighbor of the station issuing the SMP frame. Thus, all stations will issue, in turn, an SMP allowing their downstream neighbor to note their address. The whole process is complete in a few milliseconds depending on the number of stations on the ring and has little or no impact on ring performance.

18.7.7 Request Initialization

The final stage to full participation is the issuing of a Request Initialization MAC frame by the joining station. This is issued to the Ring Parameter Server (RPS) functional address C0-00-00-00-00-02$_{16}$. If the RPS is present on the ring, a fact indicated by the request returning with A and C bits set to 12, the station will expect to receive either an Intialize Station or Change Parameters MAC frame. This will complete the joining process. If not, then the station will accept default values and still complete.

This entire process, all seven stages, can take in excess of 15 seconds to complete due to the necessary timers at various stages. This, however, is far more preferable than introducing a potential problem station that can cause far more problems once it joins the ring.

18.8 Access Priority

As a protocol, Token Ring offers a priority mechanism through which ring stations with high priority PDUs can gain access to the token faster than if they were to wait their normal turn. This level of prioritization is well beyond the capabilities of simpler protocols such as Ethernet. The main function of the system is to allow for more efficient ring management as user data normally has a priority level of 0, while MAC frames can have differing levels depending on their importance.

The mechanism is based on exclusive use of the (P)riority and (R)eservation bits in the Access Control field of a frame/token. There are three P and three R bits giving rise to eight possible levels of priority from 0 (lowest) to 7 (highest). Under normal conditions these bits are transmitted as 0$_2$, but they can be modified by stations to indicate either that they want to reserve the next token at a higher priority (R bits), or that this is a high priority token (P bits).

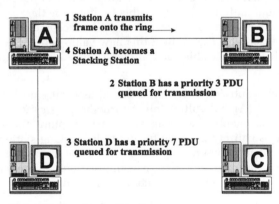

Figure 18-14: Access Priority

In figure 18-14, four stations are involved in normal ring participation. However both stations B and D have high priority PDUs awaiting transmission. The text that follows attempts to explain the access priority mechanism and starts from the point at which station A is transmitting.

As the frame from A circulates the ring it will be seen first by station B. In this instance B is not the intended recipient so it's main function is to repeat the frame back onto the ring. However, station B has a high priority PDU awaiting transmission (as shown in this example as priority 011_2 or 3). As the frame is repeated by station B, it will modify the R bits in the AC field to 011_2 to reflect this. The frame will continue is path around the ring to D via C. Although C was the recipient in this instance, it has little effect on the priority mechanism as a copy will be repeated on around the ring to D. Station D also has a high priority PDU queued, in this instance priority 7. As this is higher than the currently reserved value, it will modify the R bits to 111_2 to request the next token be released at priority 7. When the frame returns to station A, the station will obviously strip it from the ring. During this process it will note the value of the R bits within it and store this as Rr. When the new token is generated by A it will be with a priority level of 7 to reflect Rr. The old service priority level will be stored as Sr while the new higher level will now be stored as Sx. Station A is now referred to as a Stacking Station and is the only station able to reduce the ring priority back to its previous level (apart from the Active Monitor should A fail to do so).

Both stations B and C are unable to capture the resulting token as its priority level is higher than that of any queued PDUs. The token will in fact go via B and C, directly to station D to allow transmission of its high priority PDUs. Station B of course still has a priority 3 PDU queued and must again request, via the R bits, a priority 3 token. This is achieved in the same fashion as described above by modifying the AC field in circulating frames/tokens. Station A, being a stacking station, has the ability to capture every token that has a priority equal to Sx in order to examine the R bits to allow the service level to be lowered if required.

Once station D has completed its transmission, it will release a new token still with a priority of 7 but a reservation level set to 3 to reflect the request of station B. The stacking station, station A, is responsible for lowering the ring priority level. In this example, A will POP the Sx value of 7 from its stack and STACK the new value of 3 as Sx. The token will then reflect this new value and continue its circulation with a priority level of 3. This then allows station B to capture the token and transmit its data.

Once the token is subsequently released, and assuming no further reservations, the stacking station (A) will ultimately return the ring service level back to its original value of 0, enabling all ring stations to capture the token for normal transmissions. It is entirely possible for multiple stacking stations to exist on the ring at any one time with one raising the priority level from say 0 to 3 and another from 3 to 7. In this instance each of the stacking stations can only return the service priority level back to the level from which they raised it.

The Active Monitor is responsible for monitoring the entire process to ensure that high priority tokens do not continually circulate the ring, thereby stopping normal data flow. This is achieved via the M bit within the AC field in the same fashion as frames are stopped from continued circulation. The M bit, originally set as 0_2 by the station transmitting the token, is reset to 1_2 by the Active Monitor. Should a high priority token be received by the Active Monitor with the M bit already set to 1_2, then the token will be stripped from the ring and a new standard token issued.

18.9 Summary

In this chapter we have seen much of the complexity of the Token Ring protocol. The token and frames all have significance down to bit level to provide additional information to the receiving/sending station, as well as others on the ring. Much of the complexity comes from the extensive use of timers, flags, and counters that keep complete control on every aspect of protocol operation. This use of so many timers, etc., is necessary to provide the features which put Token Ring in front of other technologies, such as Ethernet, when it comes to reliability and resilience. We have seen for example, how timers such as the Timer, No Token is used to ensure tokens continually circulate the ring and how the expiry of which triggers recovery procedures by the controlling station, the Active Monitor. In addition to the use of timers, flags, and counters, Token Ring also offers the mind comforting feature of restricting access to the ring to functionally correct stations only, by ensuring all devices trying to access the ring undergo extensive insertion tests prior to becoming fully active participants.

The developers of the technology have without doubt provided a robust protocol with many attractive features, especially to those who require high availability and predictable response times. In subsequent chapters we will discover how this sound platform can be built upon to provide high bandwidth, multi-segmented networks that can offer users much well into the future.

Ring
Management

As we have seen thus far, Token Ring is essentially a simple protocol, complicated by the need for fault tolerance and resilience. An essential aspect to this is ring management, which provides the necessary functionality to overcome nearly all conceivable problems with a single ambition, i.e., to maintain the integrity of the ring. Many responsibilities in this area fall to the Active Monitor; however, as we will see in this section, the remaining Standby Monitors also play an important part in keeping the ring running efficiently.

19.1   Token Ring Errors

Error conditions do occur within a Token Ring network, and can be classified as either hard or soft errors. Hard errors are defined as errors that prevent frames or tokens from circulating the ring, i.e., signal failure. Soft errors on the other hand are errors that cause corruption to the data but do not prevent frames and tokens from circulating the ring. Error detection, reporting, and recovery require that stations are able to identify and isolate the fault condition, and under some circumstances may require the station causing the fault to remove itself from the ring.

Error conditions can be isolated into fault domains, by use of the neighbor notification process. They are then reported via either Beacon MAC frames or Error Report MAC frames, depending on the condition. Recovery processes are then managed in strict formation, as shown in figure 19-2, using the Ring Purge[1] process, Claim Token, and the Beacon process.

19.1.1   Fault Domain

The idea of a fault domain is to isolate the location of a fault condition prior to taking corrective action to rectify the problem. A fault domain consists of the following entities:

- The station downstream of the fault condition, the one that detects the error. This is station G in figure 19-1.

- The station upstream to the one reporting the error. Station F in the diagram.

- All components between the two stations, i.e. MAU, ring media, etc.

---

[1] These processes are discussed in detail later in this chapter.

It is important for accurate problem determination that all stations are able to identify the fault domain when a fault condition is detected. This obviously implies that at any given moment in time all stations are required to be aware of their upstream neighbor's MAC address. Hence, the importance of the neighbor notification process which, as well as being part of the ring joining procedure, is repeated approximately every 7 seconds.

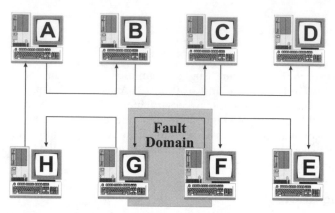

Figure 19-1: Fault Domains

19.1.2 Fault Reporting

Two reporting schemes are available, one for hard errors such as signal loss and one for soft errors such as a missing token. The following text explains the reporting process in both cases using figure 19-1 to highlight the fault domain.

Hard Errors
- Token Ring uses the Beacon process to recover from hard errors and attempt to restore normal operation. If this is not possible, then the Beacon MAC frame will identify the failure domain for further analysis by network management functions.

- If station G detects a hard error, it will identify the fault domain as being between F and G (itself), and start transmitting Beacon MAC frames. The MAC frame contains the source address of G and the upstream neighbor's address of F. This MAC frame identifies the fault domain, alerts the rest of the ring stations that normal operation is suspended, and alerts network management functions.

Soft Errors
- Token Ring uses either the Ring Purge process or the normal token protocol to recover from such errors.

- Again using figure 19-1, if station G detects an error it will generate an Error Report MAC frame containing its own source address and the upstream neighbor's address (F). This error report is sent to the Ring

Error Monitor for analysis by network management functions and identifies the fault domain.

19.1.3 Error Counters

Error counters are used to monitor the number of instances of all soft errors prior to them being reported to the Ring Error Monitor (REM). Each counter is initially set to 0 and counts to 255. It is reset back to 0 when the errors are reported and freezes at 255 if the number exceeds this value. Currently ten error counters are defined, one for each of the soft error conditions. Table 19-1 defines these counters along with the soft error conditions each monitors.

Table 19-1: Error Counters

Counter	Description
Counter, Abort Error (CABE)	This counter is increment whenever a station prematurely terminates a transmission prematurely by sending an abort sequence.
Counter, AC Error (CACE)	Incremented each time a station receives an AMP or SMP MAC frame with the A and C bits set to 0, and then receives another SMP MAC frame with the A and C bits also set to 0 without first receiving an AMP frame. This would indicate the upstream neighbor is sending SMP frames out of sequence and could jeopordize the integrity of the neighbor notification process.
Counter, Burst Error (CBE)	If Differential Manchester Encoding is violated in that there are no signal transitions within five half bit times, the detecting station will force a transition (thus preventing other stations detecting the same fault) and increment the CBE counter. Forced transitions will continue until a transition is received from the ring.
Counter, Frame Copied Error (CFCE)	Should a station receive a frame destined for its unique address with the A bits already set to 1 it would indicate a duplicate address on the network, and as such an error. Stations are only required to increment the counter if the frame is a MAC frame or includes a RI field.
Counter, Frequency Error (CFE)	The CFE counter is incremented whenever the receive signal is outside acceptable clocking thresholds. This may well be caused by excessive jitter or even a faulty network adapter.
Counter, Internal Error (CIE)	CIE is incremented each time a station recognizes any form of recoverable internal error. Multiple reports of this error condition could isolate a station in marginal operating condition.
Counter, Line Error (CLE)	The counter CLE is incremented each time a frame is received by a station with the E bit set at 0, but the frame contains an error, i.e., the FCS does not compute. The station will set E=1 to stop other stations reporting the same error and to isolate the fault domain.
Counter, Lost Frame Error (CLFE)	Each time a frame is transmitted, the TRR timer is reset. If this timer expires before the frame returns to be stripped from the ring, then the frame is said to be lost and CLFE is incremented.

Table 19-1: Error Counters (Continued)

Counter	Description
Counter, Receive Congestion Error (CRCE)	CRCE is incremented when a receiving station sets the A bits but is unable to copy the frame and therefore does not set the C bits in the AC field.
Counter, Token Error (CTE)	The CTE counter is only incremented by the Active Monitor to count the occasions it has had to purge the ring and issue a new token. This could be due to the TVX timer expiring or frame/tokens arriving with the M bit already set.

19.2 Active Monitor Functions

The role of the Active Monitor can be separated into two distinct areas, namely those functions that operate at the Physical Layer, and those at the MAC Layer. The Physical Layer functions, such as Latency Buffering were discussed in chapter 17, so it is the MAC Layer functionality which is of primary concern in this section.

We have seen that the Active Monitor is responsible for various routine management tasks, such as initiating and monitoring the Nearest Active Upstream Neighbor notification, and monitoring the circulation of frames and tokens via the M bit in the Access Control field. Another of the general management functions includes the detection of lost frames or tokens via the Timer, Valid Transmission (TVX, default 10mS) before the expiry of which the Active Monitor should see either a Start of Frame Sequence or a token. If TVX expires, or another fault manifests itself, the main weapon in the Active Monitor's arsenal is the Ring Purge. However, as discussed in the text that follows, the Active Monitor, the election of the Active Monitor, and the functions it performs, play pivotal roles in ring recovery in event that problems occur.

19.2.1 Ring Recovery

The concept behind token ring recovery is a simple one. Once the protocol has detected the interruption of the normal token passing process it will move up and down the recovery hierarchy without exception, based on the following rules.

- If a process proves successful it will move up the hierarchy.

- If a process proves unsuccessful it will move down the hierarchy.

As an example, should the Active Monitor detect the loss of the token it will initiate the Ring Purge process. If this proves successful then normal operation will resume. Should it fail, then Claim Token is initiated. Likewise, on the way back up the hierarchy, if Claim Token is successful then Ring Purge is executed before the ring can return to normal operation.

19.2.2 Ring Purge

The Ring Purge has one purpose, that of cleaning up the ring and releasing a new token to recommence normal token passing operation. The Ring Purge, initiated by the Active Monitor, takes place in any of the following circumstances as seen by the Active Monitor:

- A station wins the Claim Token process.[2]

- The token no longer exists on the ring, i.e., TVX has expired without seeing a token or frame.

- A station fails to strip its own frame from the ring after transmission (i.e., the frame is received with the M bit already set to 1).

- A high priority token is received with the M bit set to 1 (i.e., a stacking station has failed to lower the token priority).

The Ring Purge process is initiated by the Active Monitor by transmitting Ring Purge MAC frames. The description that follows describes the process:

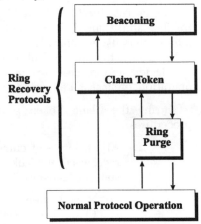

Figure 19-2: Ring Recovery Hierarchy

The Active Monitor transmits a Ring Purge MAC frame and resets the Timer, Return to Repeat (TRR default 4.0 mS). Should TRR expire before receiving a valid purge frame then it transmits another Ring Purge.

If the SA of the received Ring Purge MAC frame is not equal to to that of the stations MAC address, then it will disable its own Active Monitor functions and return to the repeat state.

When the Active Monitor receives its own purge MAC frame back it will move to the repeat state and release a new token of a priority level equal to that of the reservation bits set in the purge MAC frame. If the priority is greater than 0 then the Active Monitor becomes a stacking station.

The whole process is monitored by the Timer, Ring Purge (TRP) which is reset to a value between 1.0 and 1.2s. If this timer expires before the Ring Purge process is complete then the Active Monitor has effectively failed to correct the problem on the ring, and will initiate Claim Token to move to the next stage in fault recovery.

19.3 Claim Token

The Claim Token process is used to determine which station becomes the Active Monitor. The election process, using Claim Token MAC frames, is designed to be a

---

[2] The process by which the Active Monitor is elected.

fast and efficient way to decide the new Active Monitor. Claim Token is effectively stage two in ring recovery, entered into when one of four conditions occur:

- A Standby Monitor detects that TNT (2.6s) has expired, indicating that no token has been seen in this time period.

- A Standby Monitor detects that TSM (15s) has expired, indicating that no Active Monitor currently exists.

- The ring purge process fails, requiring escalation to stage 2 of ring recovery.

- The beacon process completes (stage 3), requiring rising to stage 2.

The process itself is initiated by the station detecting the problem, which enters the Transmit Claim Token state by transmitting Claim Token (CT) MAC frames at 20mS intervals, as controlled by the timer TQP. The process that follows is well defined so as to ensure one of two possible outcomes; either an Active Monitor will be elected and proceed to stage 1 recovery and thus back to normal protocol operation, or stage 3, Beaconing, will be entered.

During the Claim Token process, all stations operate using the following procedures:

1. All stations not currently involved in the Claim Token process that receive a Claim Token MAC frame enter either the Repeat Claim Token state, or Transmit Claim Token state, based upon the following:

   (a) If the station is currently the Active Monitor it enters the Repeat Claim Token state, as the very fact that Claim Token has been initiated indicates this station is incapable of providing proper Active Monitor functions and should therefore be excluded from this election.

   (b) If the station is not the Active Monitor but has the Flag, Claim Contender Option (FCCO) set to 0, it is also excluded from the election and must enter the Repeat Claim Token state.

   (c) If the station is not the Active Monitor and has FCCO set to 1 it will interrogate the incoming Claim Token MAC frame to check the Source Address (SA). Its subsequent actions are based on one of the following:

      If the SA is numerically higher than the MAC address of the station interrogating the frame, then that station will enter the Repeat Claim Token state and wait for the Claim Token Process to complete.

      If the SA is equal to the MAC address of the station, it will also enter Repeat Claim Token state, as this is an indication that another station on the ring has the same address - a fault that has to be rectified, but not at this stage.

If the SA is lower than its own MAC address, then the station will enter the Transmit Claim Token state and transmit its own Claim Token MAC frames until it either receives its own MAC frames back, or receives Claim Token MAC frames with a higher numerical address.

It can be seen that by using the procedures as currently described, only those stations that are eligible will enter Transmit Claim Token state to continue through the election process.

2.   Stations in Repeat Claim Token state do not take any direct part in the Claim Token process, except for repeating the Claim frames forward around the ring. They must, however, continue to monitor as the receipt of a Ring Purge MAC frame would indicate that they can move to normal Repeat state, whereas the receipt of a Beacon MAC would force them into Repeat Beacon state.

3.   The Claim Token Process is monitored by all stations through the use of the Timer, Claim Token (TCT), which is reset once a station enters either Repeat or Transmit Claim Token state. Should this timer expire before the Claim Token process is complete, then it is said to have failed and the station will move into Beacon state.

4.   For those stations in Transmit Claim Token state, the election process is effectively carried out as follows:

(a)   Stations transmit fill pattern if they are not transmitting a Claim Token MAC frame and do not repeat frames. In addition, Claim Token MAC frames are transmitted at 20mS intervals without the need to wait for the token. This is because this routine is part of ring recovery and is therefore not required to maintain, nor could maintain, normal token passing.

(b)   All stations in Transmit Claim Token state interrogate incoming Claim Token MAC frames to check the SA field to compare with their own MAC address. Depending on the result of this comparison the following actions are undertaken:

If the received SA is numerically higher than its own then the station enters Repeat Claim Token state and waits for completion of the process.

If the received SA is lower than its own then the station remains in its current state.

If the received SA is the same as its own MAC address, but the reported Upstream Neighbor's Address (UNA) within the frame does not equal the Stored Upstream Address (SUA) of the station, there is another station on the ring with the same MAC address as this station, an obvious fault condition. Should this occur, the station enters Repeat Claim Token state and waits for the process to complete.

If the received SA is the same as its own MAC address, and the reported Upstream Neighbor's Address (UNA) within the frame does equal the Stored Upstream Address (SUA) of the station, but the M bit within the AC field is set to 1, then an Active Monitor is still functioning on the ring and the station will remain in Transmit Claim Token state. Remember, the M bit within the Access Control field is used by the Active Monitor to indicate that it has seen this frame and therefore can be used to stop frames from endlessly circulating the ring.

If the received SA is the same as its own MAC address, and the reported UNA within the frame does equal the SUA of the station, and the M bit within the AC field is set to 0, then the station wins the Claim Token process. Thus it is essentially the station with the highest numerical value for its MAC address that will win the Claim Token process.

Successful completion of the Claim Token process is ensured once the newly elected Active Monitor has confirmed its election by typically transmitting three successive Claim frames, all of which circumnavigate the ring. At this stage the Active Monitor will release a Purge MAC frame, the reception of which forces all other stations still in the Repeat Claim Token state to move to the normal Repeat state, ready for the release of a new token and the resumption of normal operation.

At first sight, this may appear to be an over detailed process but it is vital to ensure that ambiguity is removed from the Claim Token process. These procedures, if followed, ensure two critical facts; firstly only one Active Monitor is elected, and therefore, only one token released, and secondly, the ring is physically intact and is capable of resuming normal operation. Even with such complexity, the Claim Token process is completed in less than a second and is unlikely to affect end users, as any data frames lost will be resent.

19.4 The Beacon Process

Failure to complete the Claim Token Process automatically leads to stage three of the recovery process, Beaconing. The Beacon process is used to recover from a number of fault conditions, each using its own Beacon Type subvector within the Beacon MAC frame. Four Beacon Types exist as described below:

- **Type 1**   Beacon Type 1 is only implemented by stations operating the IEEE 802.5c Dual Ring protocol and is the highest priority Beacon Type. As such, all stations not implementing the 802.5c protocol will not interfere with Type 1 Beacon MAC frames.

- **Type 2**   Type 2 Beacon frames indicate signal loss on a long term basis. This is denoted within the station by the Flag, Signal Loss (FSL) being equal to 1. Examples of conditions that cause Type 2 Beacons include; medium failure, receiver failure, transmitter failure on the upstream neighbor, stations inserting at the wrong speed, etc.

- **Type 3**   Type 3 Beacon frames indicate the upstream neighbor is bit streaming, i.e. stuck transmitting fill. This is indicated by the status of the flag, claim token (FCT) being set to 0, i.e., no claim frames have been received; remember the beaconing condition is entered if Claim Token fails, therefore Claim frames should have been received during the Claim Token Process. In addition FSL is equal also to 0, indicating that signal is being received. The received data obviously does not correspond to the expected protocol.

- **Type 4**   Similar to Type 3, but this time FCT is equal to 1 indicating Claim frames have been received. This is an indication that the upstream neighbor is streaming Claim frames continuously.

Irrespective of the Beacon Type, all stations within the process operate as described below using Figure 19-3 for reference.

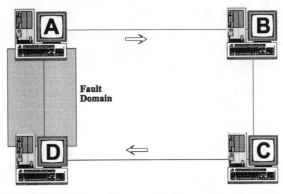

Figure 19-3:   Beacon Process

The station immediately downstream from the fault (station A in figure 19-3) will be the first to detect a fault and as such shall enter the Beacon Transmit state. In this condition, the station begins to broadcast Beacon MAC frames that contain both the Beacon type (the reason for beaconing) and the Stored Upstream Address (SUA). The reason for including the SUA is simply that the Beacon MAC frames are ultimately directed to that station. As shown in figure 19-1, a fault domain consists of the detecting station, its upstream neighbor, and the cabling between the two. The beaconing station releases Beacon MAC frames without regard for the token and at intervals set by Timer, Queue PDU (TQP), which defaults to 20ms.

All stations not in Beacon Transmit state which receive a Beacon MAC frame enter the Beacon Repeat state. This causes all stations downstream from the beaconing station to ultimately enter the repeat state. Any station newly attached to the ring, which has not completed the join process, i.e., not completed neighbor notification, immediately removes itself from the ring so as not to hinder the recovery process. The idea being to maintain the fault domains established during the last neighbor notification process.

Each station in Beacon Repeat state compares the transmitted UNA within the Beacon MAC frame with its own unique station address. The one station with which a successful comparison should be made is the upstream neighbor of the beaconing node. This station will count the number of Beacon frames received and when the figure reaches eight (160ms approx.), it will remove itself from the ring and perform a full self test to verify whether or not it is the cause of the problem. Should it prove to be the cause it will remain off the ring, alternatively, should it pass all internal tests it will re-insert.

At any stage during the process, should station A (the beaconing station) receive its own Beacon frames back the process is deemed complete and it will immediately move to Claim Token. Timer, Beacon Transmit (TBT) is initiated at the beginning of the beacon process by the transmitting station with a recommended value of 16s. Should TBT expire without the beaconing station receiving its own Beacon frames back, then this station could be the cause of the problem and will immediately remove itself from the ring for verification. In this way the stations on either side of the fault domain will have removed themselves from the ring and verified the correct operation of their receivers and transmitters as well as their lobe cables before re-inserting.

The beacon process contains two monitoring functions to ensure that the process completes should an unexpected event occur during the process. The first involves the use of the Timer, Beacon Repeat (TBR), which runs on all stations with a value of 200ms. This timer is reset every time a Beacon frame is received, and should never expire during the beaconing process. However, should the beaconing station withdraw from the ring during the process and not return, Beacon frames will stop and TBR will expire. Should this happen, Claim Token will immediately be initiated. This is an indication that the beaconing station was the cause of the problem. The second monitoring function is carried out by the station immediately downstream of the beaconing node and is designed to stop Beacon MAC frames from continuously circulating the ring. The monitoring station identifies itself by comparing the Source Address (SA) of the Beacon frame with its (SUA); if a match occurs, then this station (station B in figure 19-3) must monitor the beacon process in the following manner. When first entering Beacon Repeat state, Counter, Beacon Circulating (CBC) is set to an initial value; each time a Beacon MAC frame is received where the SA is equal to the stations SUA, the counter is decremented. When CBC reaches zero, all subsequent Beacon frames from the upstream neighbor will have the M bit in the AC field set to 1. If the station should then receive a Beacon frame with the M bit already set, this frame would have already completed a circulation of the ring rather than being a newly generated frame. In this instance the monitoring station will immediately initiate Claim Token.

19.5 Automatic Beacon Resolution

There are some circumstances that would initiate the Beacon process from which the process may be unable to recover. An example is port failure on the MSAU, when the stations on either side of the fault domain would verify they are functioning correctly, but the fault would remain. Another example would be a station inserting into the ring at the wrong speed. In this instance the Beacon process would be unable to resolve the fault as the wrong speed station would be unable to participate. Most manufacturers of Token Ring equipment, especially active MAUs, now implement some form of Automatic Beacon Resolution, although the feature is often marketed under slightly differing names. The main essence of this feature is to monitor Beacon activity and to ensure some form of resolution occurs. This is often achieved by timing the process and should resolution not be completed within a specified time then simply bypass the offending ports on the MAU. Some manufacturers can isolate individual offending ports, while others isolate groups or alternatively a whole card within a modular chassis. It is obviously more desirable to isolate offenders on a per port basis, but in either instance the main focus is to re-establish normal ring protocol operation for non-offending stations.

19.6 Standby Monitor Functions

In addition to normal station functions, Standby Monitors must ensure that the Active Monitor is functioning correctly in its tasks. This is achieved primarily through timer functions monitoring token circulation and Active Monitor existence. The Timer, No Token (TNT), which defaults to 2.6s, is used to recover from token related error conditions. The timer is reset each time a token is detected and should never count down to zero. Any token related faults that occur should be detected and rectified by the Active Monitor well within this time period. Should TNT expire then the Active Monitor has failed in its task and Claim Token is initiated. Timer, Standby Monitor (TSM) is set at 15s and is used to monitor the presence of the Active Monitor. Every 7 seconds the Active Monitor generates an Active Monitor Present (AMP) MAC frame. This serves two purposes, one by way of a "hello" to inform others of its existence, and secondly by initiating the NAUN process. If by the time TSM expires the Standby Monitor has failed to see an AMP, SMP, or RP MAC frame then the Active Monitor has again failed in its duties (or does not exist) and therefore Claim Token is initiated.

In addition to monitoring the Active Monitor, Standby Monitors also have two other functions, namely claiming to be the Active Monitor (used during the Claim Token process), and beaconing to enable recovery from ring faults. During the Claim Token and Beaconing processes ALL stations on the ring use these Standby Monitor functions.

19.7 Additional Server Functions

For more complete management purposes, addition server functionality can be configured on the ring, typically on a management node. One major difference between management of an Ethernet network compared to Token Ring is that information can only be monitored or gathered provided that the gathering device is actually inserted in the ring as an active station. Each of the server functions described briefly below is not mandatory, but if in existence can greatly enhance the manageability of the network.

19.7.1 The Ring Parameter Server (RPS)

The Ring Parameter Server (RPS) is used to ensure that all stations on the ring use compatible options. All stations make a request for various ring parameters from the RPS during the joining process. If in existence, the RPS will respond with the required parameter values, if not, the stations will use default values instead.

19.7.2 The Configuration Report Server (CRS)

The Configuration Report Server (CRS) is used to monitor and maintain the configuration of the ring. In this role, all stations must report any changes to their upstream neighbor address (which, of course, is detected during the Neighbor Notification process). This enables the CRS to be alerted to stations inserting or removing from the ring. Management applications that are capable of reporting a ring map with station positions on the ring gain their information from the CRS.

19.7.3 The Ring Error Monitor (REM)

The Ring Error Monitor (REM) is used to maintain information about all errors occurring on the ring. Each station maintains error counters and a Timer, Error Report (TER). When TER expires, a station sends an Error Report MAC frame to the REM with the values of the error counters and identification of the fault domain. Management applications that can interrogate the REM can provide valuable information regarding the state of the ring, and through analysis of the statistics can help isolate potentially faulty nodes.

19.8 Summary

With a continuous transmission path that includes each attached station, there is no doubt that Token Ring requires some element of ring management to allow recovery from failure scenarios. The three stage process starting with the Ring Purge, encompassing Claim Token, and the Beacon Process if all else fails, is designed to allow recovery from a wide range of potential soft and hard error conditions. Protocol errors can and do occur on the ring, however, in most circumstances a ring purge from the Active Monitor should be enough to re-initialize the ring and restore normal operation. Failure to do so forces escalation in the fault recovery hierarchy to claim token and finally to beaconing if required.

While error recovery is considered the most important process within ring management, error monitoring is also a necessary function. Within Token Ring this task is performed by an additional server entity, the Ring Error Monitor. Although this server entity is entirely optional on the ring, when configured the REM provides network managers valuable statistical information regarding the health of their network.

Source Route Bridging

We have discussed so far, the mechanism by which Token Ring operates in a single ring environment. It is the case, however, that due to ever increasing user populations and their bandwidth demands, multiple ring networks are probably more common than single ring networks today. With the existence of multiple rings in a single network environment it is obviously important that communications between rings be simple, efficient, and reliable. We have already seen in chapter 15 how bridges are used to link multiple Ethernet networks together to create an extended LAN. In a Token Ring environment the same is true, we can also use bridges to interconnect rings to create an extended Token Ring network. The difference, however, is the mechanism used to achieve this. In the Ethernet Bridging section we saw how the bridges were in effect "transparent" to the end stations, hence the name Transparent Bridging. In Token Ring, the most common method employed is based around the source station establishing a route to the destination, hence the name Source Route Bridging. It is important not to confuse this with any form of routing, which operates at OSI Layer 3 of the protocol stack. Source Route Bridging is a form of bridging very firmly based around Layer 2 activity. In this chapter we will explore the method employed by Source Route Bridging to achieve the goal of providing seamless communications between rings, while maintaining traffic isolation wherever possible.

20.1 What Is Source Route Bridging (SRB)?

As already mentioned, the philosophy behind Source Route Bridging (SRB) is completely different from that of Transparent Bridging. With SRB, the emphasis of route discovery and maintenance is placed squarely on the source station, with the bridge acting merely as a relay device. This change of responsibility (Transparent Bridges, remember, provide all the intelligence with no participation from the end station) gives a more flexible and adaptive solution when bridging between end points. This flexibility comes from the ability to utilize not only the quickest path but also the capability to implement many different design options such as parallel paths or meshed rings.

Source Route Bridging relies on end stations to supply the route information to the bridges so that they can pass the data onto the next leg towards the destination. This in itself opens up a number of questions such as: how do source stations know that a particular frame needs bridging? how do they know the route to take? how do they pass this information to the bridges? etc. To be able to best answer these and other questions, it is necessary to follow the event flow in a sample network such as the one in figure 20-1. In the diagram we see there are five networks (Ring 1 to Ring 5) inter-connected by five Source Route Bridges (Bridges A to E). Throughout this chapter we will continually refer back to this as the reference network. Before delving into the specifics of SRB, it is important to understand the basic concepts. Take the situation above, Station X wishes to send data to Station Y. The first thing to note is that both stations are aware they are in a bridged network. This is established during NIC configuration, SRB must be enabled on that device. Once enabled, as each station wishes to communicate with another, it will send out an XID test frame on its local ring to try and establish a response. If the destination device is local, then this frame will return with the A and C bits in the Frame Status field set to 1_2. In the example in figure 20-1, Stations X and Y exist on different rings, therefore an XID test frame sent out by X, destined for Y, will return to the sender with the A and C bits not set.

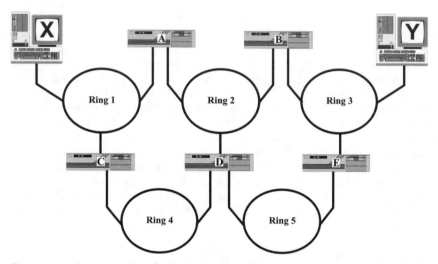

Figure 20-1: Source Route Bridged Reference Network

When Station X receives its test frame back with the address indicators not set it immediately knows that Station Y does not exist on its local network. It does not necessarily mean Station Y is somewhere else within the extended LAN, after all it may not exist at all. However, since it does not exist on the local ring, Station X must try and discover if Station Y exists somewhere else within the network. This discovery process is essentially the crux of Source Route Bridging. The bridges have no internal tables detailing station locations, therefore individual end stations must discover for themselves where other devices are. This in itself is an advantage, as at the time of communication, and therefore the time of discovery, one station can find the most efficient route to another. For example, although a route through bridges A and B (from our reference network) may appear the shortest path, the route through C, D, and E may be quicker due to current traffic loads.

The discovery process is discussed in detail in section 20.1.2, but essentially involves a discovery frame being sent out across the extended network, addressed to the intended recipient, Station Y in our example. The discovery frame contains a special field known as the Routing Information Field (RIF) which allows the bridges to fill in information as to the route the frame takes. This discovery frame is sent to all networks, so will ultimately reach Station Y, who will turn it around and send it back. On reception of its own discovery frame back, Station X will interrogate the RIF for the route taken. This is then placed in a Route Cache for future use. All frames between Stations X and Y are then able to be sent with route information to ensure delivery across the extended network.

20.2 Routing Information Field (RIF)

In section 18.3 we saw that a Routing Information Field (RIF) may exist immediately after the Source Address Field. The presence of the RIF is indicated by the Routing Information Indicator (RII) being set to 1_2. To recap, the RII is the most significant bit of the first octet of the Source Address field. Used as a multicast indicator within the Destination Address, this bit had no significance in the Source Address so therefore lends itself to this alternate use. All stations (and bridges) are immediately aware of the inclusion of the RIF if the RII is set.

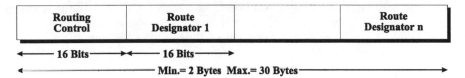

Figure 20-2: Routing Information Field (RIF)

The RIF, shown in figure 20-2, consists of a 2 octet Routing Control field and a number of Route Designators. This number can range from 0 up to 14, although in practice, rarely exceeds 8 as the typical maximum bridge hop count is 7.

20.2.1 Routing Control Field

The purpose of the Routing Control Field, shown in more detail in figure 20-3, is to inform participating devices how to handle the information contained within.

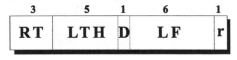

Figure 20-3: Routing Control Field

The indicators contain within the Routing Control field are described in more detail below:

Routing Type - RT
The purpose of this field is to inform devices how to route the frame through the network, that is, does it follow a single route or multiple routes. There are three types of source routed frames with this field being the type indicator.

Specifically Routed Frame (SRF) RT = 0XX$_2$
If the most significant bit is set to 0$_2$ then the RIF contains a specific route within the Route Designators which must be followed explicitly by the bridges within the network. The bits XX$_2$ have no significance and are preserved as their transmitted values throughout the network.

All Routes Explorer Frame (ARE) RT = 10X$_2$
The All Routes Explorer frame is used in route discovery and is forwarded by all SRBs in an attempt to locate the destination. In the process, the frame is duplicated on each forwarding port, resulting in the destination station receiving as many ARE frames as there are routes between source and destination. The source station sends an ARE in search of the destination with standard source and destination MAC addressing but with no Route Designators within the RIF field. These are added to the ARE by the bridges as it progresses through the network.

Spanning Tree Explorer Frame (STE) RT = 11X$_2$
As with Transparent bridging, spanning tree can be employed in a source route environment, although the net result is slightly different. When implemented, a source station can send a STE frame in place of an ARE which will be forwarded only once onto each LAN. The result is that no matter how many physical paths there are from source to destination, only one STE will reach that destination, thus cutting the amount of explorer traffic on the network.

Length - LTH
The purpose of this field is to indicate the length of the RIF. Therefore valid values are even numbers between 2 and 30 inclusive. All explorer frames are created with just a routing control field, and therefore a length value of 2 is inserted in this field. As these explorer frames traverse the network and bridges add route designators to the RIF, the length field is incremented accordingly, such that it reflects the new overall length of the RIF.

Direction - D
This bit, the direction bit, only has significance in specifically routed frames; (RT = 0XX$_2$), in all other cases it is transmitted as 0$_2$ and ignored. Within SRFs the purpose is to inform bridges in which direction to read the routing designators within the RIF. For example, if set to 0$_2$ the designators are read in the order RD1, RD2, ... RDn. Whereas, if the D bit is set to 1$_2$, the order is reversed and read as RDn, ... RD2, RD1. This allows a discovered route to be used in both directions rather than just one.

Largest Frame - LF
The purpose of this 6 bit field is to indicate the largest frame that may be transmitted between a particular source and destination over a specific route. The field only has significance in ARE or STE frames, and is ignored in SRF frames. The purpose being that during route discovery, source stations can also discover the maximum frame size that the route can support. Factors that may influence this figure include; source station frame size support, intervening networks, and destination station, any of which are able to modify this field downwards during

discovery if the value is above the maximum supported at that point in the route. Modification upwards is not allowed at any point. Note that this field indicates the maximum length of the Info field within the frame, rather than the overall frame length as shown in figure 20-4.

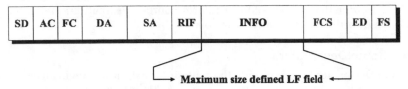

Figure 20-4: Maximum Frame Size Definition

The LF field is coded with a 3 bit base code and a 3 bit extended code as shown in figure 20-5. All bridges that comply with the latest version of IEEE 802.1d standard will have an indicator allowing the administrator to select whether base coding or extended coding should be used. Tables 20-1 and 20-2 show largest frame values for base coding and extended coding, respectively.

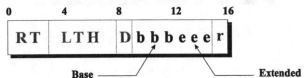

Figure 20-5: Base And Extended Bits Within Largest Frame Field

Table 20-1: Largest Frame Base Values

Base	Value	Rationale
000	516 Octets	ISO 8473, Connectionless Network Protocol, plus LLC
001	1470 Octets	ISO 8802-3, CSMA/CD LAN
010	2052 Octets	80 × 24 character screen with control
011	4399 Octets	ISO 8802-5, FDDI, 4Mbps Token Ring
100	8130 Octets	ISO 8802-4 Token Bus LAN
101	11,407 Octets	ISO 8802-5 4-bit burst errors unprotected
110	17,749 Octets	ISO 8802-5 16Mbps Token Ring
111	> 17,749 Octets	Base for extending to 65,535 octets

Table 20-2: Largest Frame Extended Values

Base	Extended							
	000	*001*	*010*	*011*	*100*	*101*	*110*	*111*
000	516	635	754	873	993	1112	1231	1350
001	1470	1542	1615	1688	1761	1833	1906	1979
010	2052	2345	2638	2932	3225	3518	3812	4105
011	4399	4865	5331	5798	6264	6730	7197	7663
100	8130	8539	8949	9358	9768	10,178	10,587	10,997
101	11,407	12,199	12,992	13,785	14,578	15,370	16,163	16,956
110	17,749	20,730	23,711	26,693	29,674	32,655	35,637	38,618
111	41,600	44,591	47,583	50,575	53,567	56,559	59,551	>59,551

Reserved - r

The last bit of the routing control field is currently undefined, and is reserved for future development. It is thus given the r designation and transmitted as 0_2.

It can be seen then that with just a few fields within the Routing Control Field, a wealth of information is available to inform source, destination, and intervening bridges, on how the frame should forwarded.

20.2.2 Route Designators

The Route Designator fields provide the route information for the bridges to follow. In fact the bridges themselves are the source of this information in the first place. Each designator is 2 octets in length, as shown in figure 20-6, and contains the following fields:

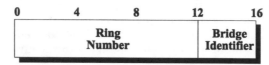

Figure 20-6: Route Designator

Ring Number

The Ring Number is a 12 bit numerical identifier that is user configurable on all SRBs. The parameter is configured on each port of the bridge, with each ring having a unique identifier within the bridge. Although it is not necessary for ring numbers to be unique within a network, the following rules apply:

- All bridge ports attaching to the same ring should have the same ring number applied to them.

- All ports within a bridge should attach to rings with different identifiers.

Bridge Identifier

This four bit field is used to identify a bridge and is a global parameter on the device, that is also user configurable. To insure successful bridging throughout the network, bridge IDs should be unique. In this way a combination of ring number and bridge ID will uniquely identify part of a route.

Route designators are used to provide a complete path description from source to destination in the fashion Ring Number/Bridge ID/Ring Number/Bridge ID/etc. In this way a frame can be forwarded along a specific route, ensuring it ends up on the destination station's local ring. It is the purpose of ARE and STE frames to gather Route Designators describing a path, while specifically routed frames have the end to end sequence within the RIF for the bridges to read.

20.3 Route Discovery

For the purpose of route discovery, we will refer to the reference network as shown in figure 20-1. In the example, Station X wants to communicate with Station Y.

Although, briefly discussed in the opening paragraphs of this chapter, the processes involved in route discovery and data transfer are covered in detail in the sections that follow.

When Station X wishes to communicate with Y, the first step in the process is to establish whether the destination is based on the local ring or not. This is established through the transmission of a test or XID (eXchange IDentification) frame. Transmitted by the Source (X), this frame is addressed to Station Y on the local ring. Obviously, in our example, Station Y is not based on the local ring, therefore the frame will return with the Address Recognized and Frame Copied flags unset. Station X is now aware that Station Y is not accessible on the local ring, it must therefore try to discover its whereabouts on the extended network.

The discovery process is initiated by Station X transmitting a frame destined for Station Y, but this time including a RIF field to indicate that this is a Source Route frame. The Routing Control field will be as shown in figure 20-7, indicating this to be a All Routes Explorer (ARE) frame. The length field will be set to 00010_2 to indicate the RIF is two octets in length, because at this stage no route designators exist.

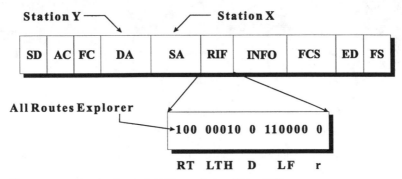

Figure 20-7:   Routing Control At Transmission Of An ARE

Also shown in the routing control field in figure 20-7, the Direction (D) bit is set to 0_2, indicating that route designators, when added, should be read by the bridges from left to right. Additionally, the largest frame size supported by the local station/ring is also indicated, in this instance set to 110000_2 (17,749 octets).

By referring to our sample network, you will see that this ARE will encounter bridges A and C on the local ring. Bridge A will receive the frame first, and due to the inclusion of the RIF will process the frame and make a decision as to whether to forward it or not based on the contents of the routing information contained within. In this instance, the bridge will detect that this is an ARE due to the Routing Type field, and will therefore be aware that it needs to forward the frame to all locally attached rings. With this in mind, the bridge will set the A and C bits in the Frame Status field of the locally repeated copy, which will then continue to circulate the local ring (Ring 1). In this way, a copy will reach Bridge C, which will also be aware through the information contained within the RIF of its responsibilities to forward the frame. As per the standard Token Ring protocol, the bridge will again repeat a local copy thus ensuring Station X receives its original frame back and may strip it from the ring. The fact that the frame returns with the A and C bits set indicates to the Station that the discovery process is under way and that at least one bridge has forwarded the ARE frame to another ring within the extended LAN.

At this stage, it is apparent that two copies of the original ARE frame are now in existence on the LAN, one at Bridge A and one at Bridge C. In fact, during the entire discovery process, this number will increase to reflect the number or possible paths to which the frame could be forwarded. Based on the our reference network, the total number of copies generated throughout the network would actually be eleven. This number is based on each bridge forwarding the frame to each ring to which it is connected as long as the ring number does not already exist within the RIF. In this way the frame will continue to explore in a forwards direction and not go backwards towards the source. For simplification, given the large number of discovery frames generated, we will track the route of just one copy, based on the path shown in figure 20-8. It should be noted, however, that the processes described will be carried out to each and every ARE copy during the discovery process.

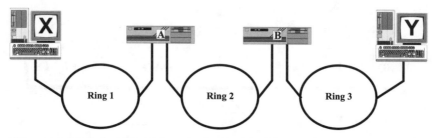

Figure 20-8:   Sample ARE path between Stations X and Y

At this stage in the discovery process, Bridge A has a copy of the ARE in its buffer, and a responsibility to forward this to Ring 2. The bridge will amend the RIF prior to forwarding, to add route designators which indicate this part of the frames path. The bridge will add not one, but two route designators, as it is the first bridge in the path for this ARE. This is established by the bridge by checking the length of the RIF. As it is currently only 2 octets in length, this must be the first bridge.

The purpose of adding two designators is to show both the originating ring number and the ring number to which the bridge is about to forward the frame. Without this the path would never be complete; you will notice that there are always more rings than bridges between two stations. Bridge A will therefore add route designators 1 and 2 to the RIF, with 1 showing Ring 1/Bridge A and 2 showing Ring 2/Null Bridge ID. A null Bridge ID must be added to the second designator as bridge A has no idea of the identifier of the next bridge in the path, or even of its existence.

As well as adding the route designators to the RIF, the bridge must also increase the length field to 6 to reflect its increased length. In addition, the bridge may well modify the LF field if either it, or the ring on which it is about to transmit the frame,

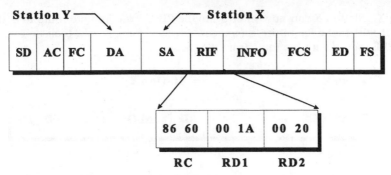

Figure 20-9: RIF as transmitted on to Ring 2

will only support a smaller frame size. Finally, the bridge will re-calculate the FCS for the frame and forward it onto Ring 2. At this stage the RIF will look like that shown in figure 20-9. Note that the RIF is shown in Hexadecimal.

The ARE frame will circulate Ring 2 and will be picked up by bridge B. Again, like bridge A, bridge B will be aware of its responsibilities to forward the frame through the RIF contents, so will therefore set the A and C bits within the Frame Status field of the locally repeated copy, and buffer its own copy internally. The local copy will obviously circulate Ring 2 completely, being copied also by bridge D. Bridge A will ultimately strip this copy from Ring 2 once it completes its circulation of the ring.

Meanwhile, Bridge B will prepare its copy of the ARE prior to forwarding onto ring 3. This will include modification of the RIF in a slightly different fashion to that of bridge A earlier. As the length of the RIF is not 2 octets, Bridge B is not the first bridge in the path. Therefore, it will add only a single route designator to the Routing Information Field. Bridge B will modify the null Bridge ID in RD2 to reflect its own Bridge ID, and then add RD3 which will include the next ring number (ring 3) and a null Bridge ID. It will of course increase the length field to 8 and set the LF field if necessary. You will notice from figure 20-10 that the LF field has been modified to show a largest supported frame size of 4399 octets (011000_2). Again the bridge will re-compute the FCS before forwarding the frame onto ring 3. At this stage the frame is on the last part of its journey, as it will reach Station Y which will recognize its own MAC address in the Destination Address field, and will therefore copy it into its frame buffer while acknowledging the locally repeated copy so that Bridge B can strip it from the ring, satisfied that another device (bridge or station) has assumed responsibility. The arriving frame at Station Y will have a RIF field as shown in figure 20-10.

Station Y will cache the route, but its ultimate responsibility is to turn the frame around and return the route back to Station X. This it does by swapping the Source and Destination Addresses, changing the RT field within the RIF to 000_2 to indicate a Specifically Routed Frame (SRF), and altering the D bit to a 1_2 to inform bridges to read the route designators from right to left. The frame is then dispatched onto Ring 3 and will be picked up by Bridge B, which seeing the RT field and its own Bridge ID within the RIF will forward the frame as per the route designation onto Ring 2. Likewise Bridge A will forward the frame back to Ring 1, thus ensuring its return to

Station X. Station X can now interrogate the RIF for a complete route to Station Y, which it will cache for future reference. All data transfer can then be carried out using SRF frames with the route from the cache.

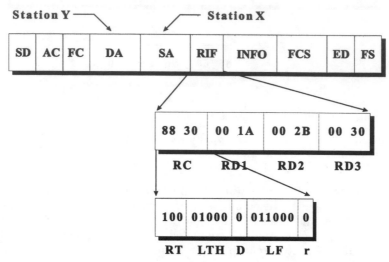

Figure 20-10:   RIF field as seen by Station Y

20.4 Multiple Path Networks

Referring back to our reference network in figure 20-1, it is apparent that Station Y will, in fact, receive four ARE frames for each discovery frame transmitted by Station X. This is because four different routes exist between the devices as described below and shown in figure 20-11.

- Ring 1 - Bridge A - Ring 2 - Bridge B - Ring 3

- Ring 1 - Bridge A - Ring 2 - Bridge D - Ring 5 - Bridge E - Ring 3

- Ring 1 - Bridge C - Ring 4 - Bridge D - Ring 5 - Bridge E - Ring 3

- Ring 1 - Bridge C - Ring 4 - Bridge D - Ring 2 - Bridge B - Ring 3

It is incumbent upon Station Y to return each of the ARE frames as they arrive back to Station X. Each will return along the path via which it arrived, back to the source, Station X, who will cache only the most efficient route, i.e., that which arrives back first.

Most stations involved in Source Route Bridging will only cache a route for a short period, after which, if not used, the route will expire. This is because it is more efficient for the station to rediscover the route than maintain large tables of different routes which would require large memory overheads. The additional advantage is that at the time of rediscovery, the most efficient route of the moment can be established. This may or may not be the same route as was discovered first time around. For example, from the reference network, it would be assumed that the route Ring1/Bridge A/Ring 2/Bridge B/Ring 3 would be the most efficient. Now assume that Bridge A is heavily utilized by other traffic on the LAN. It may be the case that the route Ring 1/Bridge C/Ring 4/Bridge D/Ring 5/Bridge E/Ring 3 is the least utilized so at the time of discovery, the most efficient. Therefore, Station X would be able to use this route and thereby effect an element of load balancing on the bridges when multiple paths exist.

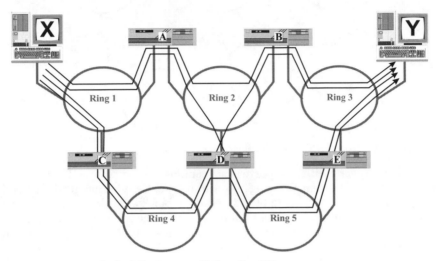

Figure 20-11:   Multiple Paths Between Stations X and Y

20.5 Spanning Tree in Source Route Bridged Networks

In section 20.3 we saw that during route discovery a total of 11 ARE frames were generated in our sample network to discover a single route. This figure does not include the 15 that would be generated in returning the four possible routes back to Station X. This means that across the five rings, a total of 26 frames would circulate in the discovery process of a single route. Imagine the traffic load if 100 stations were all discovering routes at the same time. This unnecessary traffic burden is also duplicated when broadcasts are generated in the network. Bridges are responsible for forwarding broadcast frames, and do so to all ports. As networks in a Source Route environment are often of a meshed or parallel path design, this can also lead to much heavier traffic loads than is actually required, especially in networks where broadcasts are frequent.

The solution is to employ the Spanning Tree Algorithm in much the same fashion as it is employed in a transparent bridged environment. Disabled by default in most SRB implementations, once enabled bridges will construct a network topology such that only a single path exists to all network segments. All other ports are set to blocking. A typical example would be that as shown in figure 20-12, where ports on Bridges C and E have been greyed out to reflect their blocking state. In this way all duplicate paths are removed, which in turn removes duplicate frames during discovery or broadcasting.

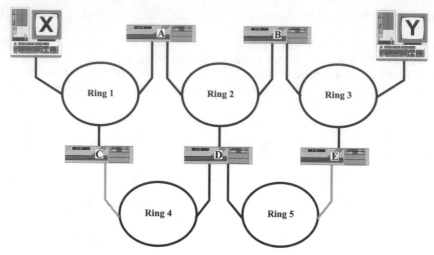

Figure 20-12: Spanning Tree in Operation

There is however a difference between Spanning Tree in Source Route Bridging as opposed to Transparent Bridging. In a transparent environment, the spanning tree algorithm forces ports into a blocking state to block all user traffic. This is not quite the case for a source route environment. In source routing, the spanning tree blocked ports, shown greyed out in the diagram, only block non-source-routed traffic and Spanning Tree Explorer (STE) frames. What this means is that frames which include a RIF field in which the blocked port is part of the path, will still be forwarded, as will ARE frames.

So what is the advantage of Spanning Tree in source route bridging? The answer is simple; firstly, broadcast frames do not include a RIF, so will therefore not be duplicated unnecessarily throughout the network, reaching each ring once only, and secondly, stations can use STE frames for route discovery rather than ARE frames. Utilizing the example in figure 20-12, should station X send out an ARE as before, 26 copies of that frame will exist at some point through the network and all four possible routes would be discovered. On the other hand, if an STE was generated instead then the number of frames would be 8 and only one route would be discovered, that via Ring 1/Bridge A/Ring 2/Bridge B/Ring 3, thus bringing about a significant reduction in explorer traffic within the network.

20.6 Source Route Bridging vs Transparent Bridging

Source Route Bridging is the most common method of bridging in a Token Ring environment and offers many advantages over its counterpart, Transparent Bridging. The main advantages are outlined below, along with what may be perceived as counter arguments in favor of Transparent Bridging.

- Source Route Bridging allows the selection of optimum routes at the time of discovery, especially where parallel paths exist. This provides for more efficient use of redundant bridges, as ports are not placed in standby and a level of load sharing can be achieved.

- Source Route Bridges do not contain forwarding tables, and have no requirement for updating tables when devices are added or removed. This provides for speedier convergence in the event of additions or subtractions from the network.

- There are no fixed routes with an SRB network. This allows devices to discover alternative paths in the event of device failure.

- Source Route Bridges allow the implementation of many more design options for the network, with parallel paths and meshed rings being the norm in Token Ring.

- Transparent Bridges are very much plug and play devices that allow implementation with little or no configuration. Their Source Route counterparts require a degree of configuration before they are able to operate, thus leaving them open to misconfiguration and potential problems.

- Source Route Bridges place far more emphasis on the intelligence of the client. This inevitably leads to more expensive client interface cards. The biggest reason behind the success of Ethernet is the cost of implementation being that much lower than other technologies.

20.7 Source Route Transparent Bridges

The two types of bridging technology discussed in this book are very different, and each is predominantly associated with a particular networking technology, hence the positioning within technology chapters in the book. Many organizations however, implement mixed technology networks and require an easy to implement and reliable method of interconnectivity between them as well as the ability to link up networks of similar technology. The answer is based around a hybrid of the two technologies, namely Source Route Bridging and Transparent Bridging. The name of the device, not surprisingly, is a Source Route Transparent Bridge. The method of operation is basically very simple, if a frame arrives with source routing information, i.e., a RIF, then the frame is source routed accordingly. If however, a RIF does not exist, then the bridge will forward the frame based on its own internal forwarding tables, as with a standard Transparent Bridge. Spanning Tree can be employed to eliminate bridging loops, thus the network topology would likely be similar to that employed with standard Transparent Bridges.

20.8 Summary

In this chapter we have discussed Source Route Bridging, an alternative to Transparent Bridging, and the most common method in a Token Ring Network. There is no doubt that source route bridging offers more flexibility in design of the network, but at a price, namely that of the increased intelligence required in the client, thus increasing the price of Token Ring NICs. The ability to load balance, and to find more efficient and diverse routes, make SRB an attractive option, but one that has only been taken up in token passing technologies, such as Token Ring and FDDI.

Dedicated Token Ring

With the ever increasing deployment of personal computers and local area networks, computer applications are being developed to provide ever increasing functionality and productivity. Applications such as; Client-Server computing, Email, groupware, and conferencing are all increasingly found in the workplace. All have one thing in common, an increasing hunger for LAN bandwidth. Over the last 10 years LANs have increased in size, complexity, and importance, as most organizations have come to depend on them as vital components of their business. Token Ring, as a technology, has grown with the requirements to provide 16Mbps of reliable, and predictable bandwidth, along with the sophistication of a priority access mechanism and guaranteed response times. However, even taking into consideration Token Ring's ability to prioritize messages, to fairly and efficiently carry these messages from all attached devices at 16Mbps wire speed, applications requirements are demanding more. One solution to ever increasing bandwidth, and the most popular, is LAN switching. Dedicated Token Ring (DTR) is the method employed to introduce switching into a Token Ring environment.

The main objectives for Dedicated Token Ring are summarized in the list below:

- Provide a migration path based on evolution to increase available bandwidth for classic Token Ring hardware.

- Provide dedicated bandwidth for each attaching classic Token Ring station.

- Provide dedicated bandwidth for each DTR station allowing simultaneous transmit and receive, i.e., full duplex.

- Address the bandwidth requirements of emerging applications like multimedia.

- Provide a standardized migration path from a shared to a switched LAN environment.

- Preserve basic Token Ring principles such as priority handling, direct path routing via the RIF, and a broadcast/multicast capability.

- Provide a solution that can interoperate with present Token Ring hardware via existing installed media.

Based on these requirements, the IEEE 802.5 committee have released the IEEE 802.5 AMD 1 standard, formulating DTR at both Physical and MAC layer operation.

Much of the initial work has been done by such organizations as the Alliance for Strategic Token Ring Advancement and Leadership (ASTRAL), but inevitably standardization is the only way any technology gains universal acceptance. Much work has been done to achieve the benefits of LAN switching in a Token Ring network, while maintaining compatibility with existing Token Ring technology. As can be seen from the list below, a DTR station must conform to many aspects of the original standard as well as those specifications outlined in the rest of this chapter.

- Implementation of the same frame formats - while some bits that are significant in the standard Token Passing Protocol (TKP) have no significance in DTR, the same formats are used.

- Support for 48 bit locally or universally administered addressing.

- Recognize the RII bit within the source address field as an indicator of a Routing Information Field (RIF) - The ability to generate or respond to frames with source routing information is considered optional.

- Support of data rates of 4 or 16Mbps - Implementations may chose to support either or both data rates.

- Encoding of data as defined in section 17.2.1.

- Support for UTP and STP cabling media as defined in chapter 17.

- Meet the signalling specifications such as Phantom Current, wire fault detection, jitter and timing specifications, also specified in chapter 17.

Although this list is a sample, it does highlight some of the main conformance characteristics, and outlines a desire to maintain compatibility with classic Token Ring. To further underline this, figure 21-1 shows the structure of a DTR network and how it can interoperate with an existing infrastructure.

21.1 Structure of a DTR Network

A basic DTR network is constructed from DTR concentrators, lobe cables and stations, as demonstrated in figure 21-1. A DTR concentrator is made up of C-Ports and a Data Transfer Unit (DTU). The C-Ports allow for connectivity between the concentrator and stations, or other DTR concentrators directly via lobe cables, in a similar fashion to the method used for interconnecting to Ethernet LAN switches. In addition, DTR concentrators also typically support a high speed data transfer service (such as ATM or FDDI) via dedicated ports, as an alternative method of connectivity between concentrators.

In preceding chapters we have established that classic Token Ring is a half duplex technology reliant on token passing as an access method, the consequence of which is that all users gain only a share of the available LAN bandwidth. Dedicated Token Ring is a whole new concept based on the same physical topology and media. Each DTR station connecting to a C-Port, essentially forms a two node ring that can take advantage of this fact by dropping the requirement to repeat frames and utilize a token. DTR stations can therefore implement a new transmission protocol, known as Transmit Immediate (TXI), which negates the requirement for a token and allows them to transmit at will. At the same time, DTR stations have the ability to receive simultaneously, thus providing full duplex operations. Within the concentrator, signals received at each C-Port are "switched" to the Data Transfer Unit (DTU), hence the name "Switched Token Ring". The DTU is in fact equivalent to a switch, or high speed multi-port bridge, allowing data to be transferred between C-Ports via its own internal bus.

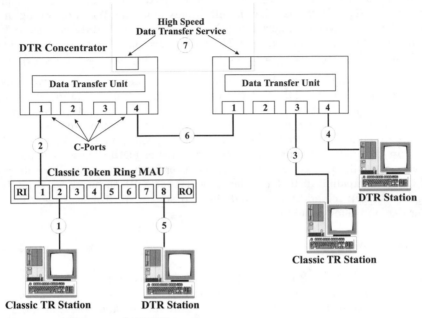

Figure 21-1:   Structure of a DTR Network

The performance increases available when using DTR are substantial, however a wholesale migration from a Classic Token Ring to a Dedicated Token Ring environment is not practical for most organizations. Realizing this the developers and standards bodies have developed a flexible protocol that allows for many types of interconnections as shown below and cross referenced with figure 21-1. The connection of a Classic Token Ring Station to a standard MAU ① is included for completeness:

- ②Attachment of DTR C-Ports directly to Classic MAU ports

- ③Direct attachment of Classic Token Ring Stations to DTR Concentrator

- ④Direct attachment of DTR stations to C-Ports

- ⑤Attachment of DTR stations to Classic MAU ports

- ⑥Attachment of DTR Concentrator C-Ports to each other

- ⑦Accommodation of a high speed interconnect, i.e., ATM, FDDI

The DTR standard defines a number of operating modes as discussed in detail in section 21.2. These include a Port Mode and a Station Emulation Mode. It is these modes that provide for the flexibility of connection as shown above. Take for example connection ②, which shows a Classic TR MAU connected directly to a DTR Concentrator C-Port. This is achieved by the port entering Station Emulation Mode, thus allowing that port to participate in the ring emulating a Classic Token Ring Station. The philosophy here is to allow the smooth migration from a Classic to a Dedicated Token Ring environment without the need for an initial wholesale equipment change. In the same way, Classic Token Ring Stations can connect directly to a DTR C-Port operating in half duplex mode ③. When operating in Port Mode, DTR stations can connect using the TXI protocol in full duplex mode ④ and benefit from dedicated bandwidth. DTR stations also have the ability to run in half duplex mode for connectivity to a C-Port or alternatively to a Classic TR MAU ⑤.

Interconnectivity between DTR Concentrators can be achieved in two different ways. The first is by using the C-Port's ability to run Station Emulation and connect it directly to a C-Port running in Port Mode ⑥. The C-Ports enter a sort of "discovery" process that gives them the ability to learn that they are interconnected. The other method of interconnectivity is by high speed Data Transfer Service Ports that support high throughput services such as ATM or FDDI. These have the ability to connect to the C-Ports via the Data Transfer Unit. It is this flexibility and backwards compatibility that the developers hope will convince existing Token Ring users requiring additional bandwidth to stick with Token Ring technology rather than move towards Ethernet.

21.2 Operating Modes

With Dedicated Token Ring, from here on known as DTR, being designed as a flexible migration path from a shared to a dedicated bandwidth allocation, it is important to distinguish between the various station types and operating modes.

21.2.1 Classic Token Ring Station

A Classic Token Ring Station is one that operates according to the protocol described in chapter 18 of this section of the book. It therefore fully utilizes the token passing method, as described, and fully supports the frame and token formats laid out on sections 18.1 and 18.3. The method of operation for these stations within a DTR environment is unchanged, allowing smooth migration from a legacy shared environment to a higher bandwidth "switched" topology.

21.2.2 DTR Station

A DTR station is one that has the ability to register and request use of the TXI access protocol, described in section 21.3, if the concentrator provides support, or alternatively, operate as a Classic Token Ring Station, providing fallback in the event of connection to a non-supporting port, i.e., a standard MAU.

21.2.3 C-Port Operation in Port Mode

There are two modes of operation for C-Ports in a DTR environment, the first of which is Port Mode. When in this mode there are two further sub-modes based on the access protocol employed, TKP for token passing or TXI for transmit immediate.

The TKP mode is employed for Classic Token Ring Stations (CTRS) or DTR Stations operating as their CTRS counterparts. The TXI mode is for the sole use of DTR Stations with the ability to implement that protocol. In the event the C-Port does not allow the TXI protocol, maybe through configuration, any attempt to connect may fail or cause fallback to the TKP access method.

21.2.4 C-Port Operation in Station Emulation Mode

The second mode of operation for a C-Port is Station Emulation Mode, within which two sub-modes also exist as before, TKP access or TXI access. These have specific uses identified as itemized below:

When operating in Station Emulation Mode using the TXI access protocol, the C-Port is designed to interconnect to another DTR concentrator, the connecting C-Port must be in Port Mode.

When operating in TKP access mode, the C-Port can connect to another DTR concentrator or a Classic MAU lobe port. When connecting to another DTR concentrator, the connecting C-Port must be in Port Mode.

Much effort has gone into the development of DTR to provide a smooth migration from one environment to the other, however a few anomalies do exist and are worth noting, as with some applications it is possible that they may affect responses:

It is possible that the lobe test repeat path may cause the A and C bits in the Frame Status field to be set on repeated frames when addressed to a Broadcast or the C-Ports MAC address.

Any frames transmitted via the TXI protocol are not received by the transmitting station, even if the destination address is one that would normally be recognized. TXI operation therefore provides an explicit loop-back facility, rather than depending upon normal PHY layer operation as would be the case with Classic Token Ring.

The repeat path provided by the C-Port during a lobe test is based on the assumption that the station will conduct its lobe media test at the same speed as it intends to insert into the ring. Failure to do so can cause access problems.

Finally, if a C-Port is configured for TXI protocol support only, then that port will not provide a reliable repeat path during registration. Therefore, if a CTRS or DTR station configured for TKP support tries to connect, it will fail the lobe media test and will be unable to differentiate between this and cable/connectivity failure.

As you will note, these potential problems are minor but do have the ability to disrupt normal operation on a mixed environment if not considered.

21.3 DTR Access Protocol Support

As we have already seen, in a DTR network a number of different configurations are supported. Determination as to the correct configuration for station and C-Port is crucial for successful operation. This determination is made based upon the condition of certain policy flags, the results of the registration process, and phantom signalling detection made by the C-Port. When a C-Port is operating in port mode and utilizing the TKP protocol, operation is identical to that described in chapter 18. Therefore, this section will concentrate on TXI protocol support and refer to the TKP protocol operation only if the reference enhances understanding of the operation.

When operational, a DTR station/C-Port have, in effect, three different states, a Join State, a Transmit State, and a Monitor State. The interaction between C-Port and DTR station during each of these states provides the key to understanding DTR and the TXI protocol. Figure 21-2 shows each of the states mentioned and some of the key functions within them.

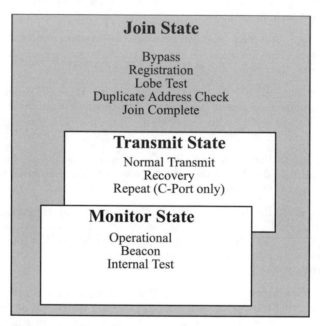

Figure 21-2: Station/C-Port Operational States

Prior to delving into the mechanics of these processes, it is probably best to introduce some of the timers, flags, and policy variables that are unique to DTR and widely used in its implementation.

21.3.1 DTR Timers

In previous chapters we have seen that Token Ring makes extensive use of timers to control various aspects of the protocol. Dedicated Token Ring is no different, and introduces a series of new timers, not seen in Classic Token Ring, which are discussed in this section. These timers are subdivided into two sections, labelled SMAC (Station MAC) timers and PMAC (C-Port MAC) timers, and are detailed in tables 21-1 and 21-2.

Table 21-1: SMAC Timers

Timer	Description
Timer, Station Insert Process (TSIP)	This timer is used as part of the Registration and Join process to control the rate at which Registration MAC frames can be sent. A default value of 200ms is recommended by the standard.
Timer, Station Initial Sequence (TSIS)	Also part of the Registration and Join Process, this timer dictates the length of time a station transmits idle transmission prior to the transmission of the first Registration Request MAC frame. It is during this period that the C-Port acquires phase lock on the station's clock. A default of 40ms is recommended.
Timer, Station Internal Test (TSIT)	This timer is an integral part of the TXI Hard Error Recovery process. It is used to delay the dropping of the phantom current to insure that possible wire fault conditions are detected. Default 7s.
Timer, Station Join Complete (TSJC)	Used as part of the Join process to limit the time which the station will wait for an Insert Response MAC frame. Expiry indicates a failure of the Join process. A value between 17.8s and 18s is required.
Timer, Station Lobe Media Test (TSLMT)	An integral part of the Hard Error Recovery process, this timer is used to delay a station from starting its Lobe Media Test for a period of 10s as recommended.
Timer, Station Lobe Media Test Complete (TSLMTC)	Designed to limit the time a station spends undergoing its LMT. Set between 2.3s and 2.5s, should it expire prior to the end of the test then the test is deemed to have failed and the station will close it connection.
Timer, Station Lobe Media Test Delay (TSLMTD)	This timer was introduced to allow enough time for the C-Port to configure a repeat path before the station initiates its Lobe Media Test. A period of 200ms to 250ms is recommended.
Timer, Station Queue Heart Beat (TSQHB)	A new concept for the TXI protocol, the Heart Beat requires a Station Heart Beat MAC frame to be queued every 1s for transmission.
Timer, Station Queue PDU (TSQP)	This is a pacing timer used to pace the transmission of Beacon MAC frames when in a Beacon Transmit state. A value between 10ms and 30ms is required with 20ms recommended.
Timer, Station Registration Request (TSREQ)	Used during the Registration and Join process, this timer paces the rate at which Registration MAC frames are sent by the station. A value of 40ms is recommended.
Timer, Station Receive Heart Beat (TSRHB)	This timer is part of the Heart Beat process and is used to detect a hard error condition. Initiated at 5s each time a Heart Beat MAC frame is received by the station, should it expire then the Hard Error Recovery process is started.
Timer, Station Registration Wait (TSRW)	Used during the Registration Query process to allow the C-Port enough time to configure itself to receive the station's Registration MAC frame. A minimum value of 200ms is required, however implementations may employ a value higher than this.

Table 21-1: SMAC Timers (Continued)

Timer	Description
Timer, Station Signal Loss (TSSL)	Used to determine whether the Stations PHY (SPHY) "signal_loss" condition is in a steady state, indicating a signal loss has occurred. A value between 200ms and 250ms is required.
Timer, Station Wire Fault (TSWF)	Implemented on stations that support wire fault detection to specify the sampling rate. A value between 0s and 10s is required with 5s recommended.
Timer, Station Wire Fault Delay (TSWFD)	Implemented on stations that support wire fault detection to delay detection after Join Completion or following insertion after the Hard Error Recovery process. A value between 5s and 10s is required with the sum of TSWF and TSWFD being a minimum of 7s.

Table 21-2: PMAC Timers

Timer	Description
Timer, C-Port Break Lobe Test (TPBLT)	Used when the C-Port is set not to support the TKP access mode to disrupt the lobe media test such that a station configured for TKP does not open as a single station on the ring. A value between 10ms and 30ms is required.
Timer, C-Port Disrupt Lobe Test (TPDLT)	Again used to disrupt the station's lobe test when TKP access is set as not supported by the C-Port. The standard requires a value between 2.6s and 2.8s.
Timer, C-Port Error Report (TPER)	Used to determine when to report errors that have been detected by the C-Port. Set between 2s and 2.2s, this value can be changed during station initialization or via the Change Parameters MAC frame.
Timer, C-Port Insert Request Delay (TPIRD)	Used during the Duplicate Address Check process to support clocking requirements.
Timer, C-Port Internal Test (TPIT)	Part of the Hard Error Recovery process, while this timer runs, the C-Port transmits Beacon frames. Default 600ms.
Timer, C-Port Lobe Media Test Failure (TPLMTF)	Set between 15s and 18s, this timer helps to further define the LMT. The duration of the test, while not controlled in Classic Token Ring, cannot exceed the value of this timer.
Timer, C-Port Lobe Media Test Running (TPLMTR)	This timer is also used during the Lobe Media Test, it is started when the C-Port initializes its support for the LMT, which is said to have failed should it not complete before the timer expires. Between 6s and 7.4s is recommended.
Timer, C-Port Queue Heart Beat (TPQHB)	Used as part of the Heart Beat process, each time it expires the C-Port queues a Heart Beat MAC frame for transmission. Defaults to 1s.
Timer, C-Port Receive Heart Beat (TPRHB)	Used to aid the detection of hard errors, this timer has a default value of 5s. Should it expire before a Heart Beat MAC frame is received from the station then the Hard Error Recovery process will be initiated.

Table 21-2: PMAC Timers (Continued)

Timer	Description
Timer, C-Port Registration Query Delay (TPRQD)	Used during the Registration Query process, this timer allows sufficient time for the station to drop the phantom signal and for the C-Port to detect the event. A value between 20ms and 200ms is required.
Timer, C-Port Signal Loss (TPSL)	Determines whether the C-Port's PHY (PPHY) "signal_loss" condition is in a steady state, indicating a signal loss has occurred. A value between 200ms and 250ms is required.

21.3.2 Policy Flags and Variables

In addition to the timers mentioned above, the DTR standard also introduces a series of new policy flags and variables to support the new access protocol. Again, to aid the descriptive sections that follow, an understanding of the flags and their use will prove useful. Station flags and variables are detailed in table 21-3, while those applicable to the C-Port are shown in table 21-4. The station policy flags and variables detailed in tables 21-3 and 21-4 are used by both DTR stations and C-Ports operating in station emulation mode and using the TXI access protocol. The port policy flags and variables are used by a C-Port operating in port mode and using the TXI access protocol.

As with Classic Token Ring, the role of the policy flag is to determine the fashion in which the MAC will operate, and is therefore not able to be changed by the MAC itself. Typically, the operator or network manager will define station policies, such as access method (DTR or Classic Token Ring), and this definition determines the state of the flags in question. The MAC will simply read the flag setting to determine its correct mode of operation.

Table 21-3: Station Policy Flags and Variables

Flag	Description
Flag, Station Error Counting Option (FSECO)	This flag is used to determine how the station uses its error report timer (TSER). If set to 0 then TSER is reset when the first error is received and an error report generated when it expires. If set to 1 then TSER is reset immediately when it expires, and a report generated when it expires again only if errors have been encountered.
Flag, Station Medium Rate Option (FSMRO)	FSMRO determines the operating speed of the station. When set to 0 it operates at 4Mbps, if set to 1 it operates at 16Mpbs.
Flag, Station Open Option (FSOPO)	This flag is used to control how the station reacts should it not receive a registration response during the Registration process. If set to 0 the station will switch from TXI access support to TKP access and enter the Lobe Test. If set to 1 then TKP access is forbidden and the station enters Bypass state.

Table 21-3: Station Policy Flags and Variables (Continued)

Flag	Description
Flag, Station Registration Denied Option (FSRDO)	Determines how the station will react if it receives a response to its registration request denying use of the TXI protocol. A 0 indicates it will revert to the TKP protocol and enter Lobe Test. A 1 forces it into Bypass state.
Flag, Station Registration Option (FSREGO)	This flag is used to determine whether the station registers itself with the C-Port requesting the use of an access protocol. A value of 0 means that registration does not take place and the station joins using the TKP access protocol. If set to 1 then registration does take place and TXI is requested.
Flag, Station Registration Query Option (FSRQO)	Used to indicate whether the station supports the registration query protocol. If set to 0 then the protocol is not supported and the station will ignore all received Registration Query MAC frames. If set to 1 the protocol is supported and the station responds to received Registration Query MAC frames.
Flag, Station Reject Remove Option (FSRRO)	This flag is used to determine how a station will behave when it receives a Remove Ring Station MAC frame. If set to 0 then the station will remove itself from the ring. If set to 1 then the station will respond with a Response MAC frame indicating that the function is not supported/disabled.
SPV(AP_MASK)	This policy variable indicates which access protocols are being supported. 0001_{16} TKP Protocol 0002_{16} TXI Protocol 0003_{16} Both TKP & TXI Protocols No other value of SPV(AP_MASK) is supported
SPV(IAC)	This variable represents the number of individual addresses supported by this station. 0000_{16} Indicates that only the station's MAC address is supported.
SPV(MAX_TX)	Represents the maximum transmit octet count supported by the station. The station may support any value as long as it does not exceed the maximum frame size permitted for the applicable operating speed. 4Mbps 4550 octets 16Mbps 18,200 octets
SPV(PD)	This policy variable is used to describe which form of phantom signalling and wire fault detection is supported by the station. 0001_{16} As specified in ISO/IEC 8802-5 and as is described in earlier sections of this text. All other values are reserved for future use.

Table 21-4: C-Port Policy Flags and Variables

Flag	*Description*
Flag, C_Port AC Repeat Path Option (FPACO)	Determines whether the C-Port shall set the A and C bits within the frame status field on its repeat path when a non-null destination address is recognized. A value of 0 indicates that the C-Port will not set the A and C bits while a value of 1 indicates that it will.
Flag, C-Port Abort Sequence Option (FPASO)	Used to control the ending sequence of oversize frames when cut-through mode is used. When set to 0 the over-size frame is ended with an abort sequence. When set to 1 it is ended with an invalid FCS and with the E bit set.
Flag, C-Port Beacon Handling Option (FPBHO)	Used to indicate how the C-Port will participate in the beaconing process while completing the join process when using the TKP access protocol. If set to 0 then it can begin after completion of neighbor notification, if set to 1 then it cannot start until the join process is complete.
Flag, C-Port Error Counting Option (FPECO)	This flag is used to determine how the C-Port uses its error report timer (TPER). If set to 0 then TPER is reset when the first error is received and an error report generated when it expires. If set to 1 then TPER is reset immediately when it expires, and a report generated when it expires again only if errors have been encountered.
Flag, C-Port Frame Control Option (FPFCO)	Used to control frame forwarding to the DTU. If set to 0 a complete valid frame must be received before it is indicated to the DTU. When set to 1 only a frame header needs to be received before indicating to the DTU. If the C-Port is set to cut-through then FPFCO must be set to 1.
Flag, C-Port Medium Rate Option (FPMRO)	Determines the operating speed of the C-Port. When set to 0 it operates at 4Mbps, if set to 1 it operates at 16Mpbs.
Flag, C-Port Operation Table Option (FPOTO)	Used to determine the mode of the C-Port. When set to 0 the C-Port operates in Station Emulation mode. When set to 1 it operates in Port mode.
PPV(AP_MASK)	This policy variable indicates which access protocols are being supported. 0001_{16} TKP Protocol 0002_{16} TXI Protocol 0003_{16} Both TKP & TXI Protocols No other value of PPV(AP_MASK) is supported
PPV(MAX_TX)	Represents the maximum transmit octet count supported by the station. The station may support any value as long as it does not exceed the maximum frame size permitted for the applicable operating speed. 4Mbps 4550 octets 16Mbps 18,200 octets
PPV(PD_MASK)	This policy variable is used to describe which form of phantom signalling and wire fault detection is supported by the station. 0001_{16} As specified in ISO/IEC 8802-5 and as is described in earlier sections of this text

As previously stated, DTR and the TXI protocol make extensive use of these new timers, flags, and policy variables in its operation. The text that follows attempts to unravel the complexities of the protocol by looking at the method employed for normal operation. Figure 21-2 highlighted the three operational states of the DTR station/C-Port, and the key processes within each one.

As with most ring based technologies, and certainly Token Ring, it is necessary to join the ring in order to become a participating member. The same is true with DTR, albeit on a ring that may only comprise of the station involved and the C-Port to which it is attached (in effect a two device ring). This then is the first state a DTR station can be in, the Join State, which comprises a series of processes to effect successful joining of the ring. The first of these processes is the Bypass state.

21.4 TXI Join Process

The Join process for a DTR station operating the TXI protocol is based on an exchange of MAC frames, providing control information in a sequence monitored by timers. The purpose of a structured sequence is to establish the compatibility between station and C-Port and to ensure that the station is not about to introduce potential problems onto the network.

21.4.1 Bypass State

The Bypass State is the initial state of all devices, whether they are running TKP or TXI protocols, on power up. It is also the state devices are in when removed from the ring. It is a requirement that the following conditions are met before leaving the Bypass State and attempting registration.

- All Counters are set to 0.

- All Event Flags are also set to 0.

- All Stored Values (e.g., Stored Upstream Address SUA) are set to 0.

- C-Port and Station Operational Policy Variables and Policy Flags are set as these will determine the connection configuration.

- All Timers are not running.

If these conditions are met then stations/C-Ports can move to the Registration State to attempt joining.

21.4.2 DTR Registration

Registration is the term used to describe the process of C-Port and station swapping address information and determining access protocol support. During the registration function, the C-Port and station exchange the following information about themselves:

- The station will save the C-Port's source/MAC address (PMAC Address) as its Stored Upstream Address (SUA)

- The C-Port will save the station's source/MAC address (SMAC Address) as its SUA.

  With DTR this is the equivalent of the Neighbor Notification function seen with Classic Token Ring.

- The C-Port will also store the station's Individual Address Count (IAC). The station may support multiple individual addresses, whereas the C-Port will not.

As well as neighbor notification, the registration process is also used to determine compatibility between C-Port and station (i.e., they are able to support the same access protocols). If they are compatible, the C-Port registration function initiates a Registration Response (REG_RSP) MAC frame with an Access Protocol Response (AP_RSP) subvector value of 0002_{16}, indicating that the Transmit Immediate (TXI) access protocol, phantom signalling, and wire fault support method have been accepted. If they are incompatible, the C-Port will notify the station via a Registration Response (REG_RSP) MAC frame with an Access Protocol Response (AP_RSP) subvector value of 0000_{16} indicating access denied. This means that the access protocol, or the phantom signalling, or the wire fault support method is unsupported by the C-Port in its current mode, either by design or through management configuration. The C-Port will then remain in the Registration State while the station will return to the Bypass State and notify its internal management function. Of the timers, flags, and policy variables described previously, those shown in table 21-5 are used to control the registration process.

Table 21-5: Flags, Policy Variables, and Timers Used to Control the Registration Process

Station Policy Flags & Variables	Description
FSOPO	Flag, Station Open Option
FSRDO	Flag, Station Registration Denied Option
FSREGO	Flag, Station Registration Option
SPV(AP_MASK)	Station, Access Protocol Mask
SPV(IAC)	Station, Individual Address Count
C-Port Policy Flags & Variables	
FPOTO	Flag, C-Port Operation Table Option
PPV(AP_MASK)	C-Port, Access Protocol Mask
Station Timers	
TSIS	Timer, Station Initial Sequence
TSJC	Timer, Station Join Complete
TSREQ	Timer, Station Registration Request

The registration process is initiated by a station once it has completed its own internal testing and received instructions to open from its internal management. The station will examine its policy flags in order to determine how it is supposed to operate, i.e., which access protocol to use TKP or TXI. This is set by management and cannot be reset by the Station's MAC. The registration sequence is then started by the station transmitting an idle sequence for a period controlled by the initial sequence timer (TSIS), which defaults to 40ms. The purpose of this is to allow the C-Port to phase lock on to the clocking recovered from the signal, and thus synchronize with the station's clock. For any meaningful data transfer to take place this is an essential part of the process.

The Station then generates and transmits a Registration Request MAC frame to the C-Port[1] . The purpose of the MAC frame is to request service from the C-Port, and it contains operating information such as address and access protocol details that the C-Port will require. If a C-Port is present at the other end of the link it will respond with a Registration Response MAC frame. This response will indicate acceptance or rejection based on such parameters as access protocol, phantom signalling, and wire fault detection. Should the Response MAC frame indicate acceptance of the station's request, then the Duplicate Address Check process is initiated automatically by the C-Port's response. This process is discussed in section 21.4.4.

To ensure an outcome each time a station initiates the registration process, the DTR standard includes specific actions to monitor the exchange of registration frames between station and C-Port. These include the Registration Request Timer that paces additional Registration Request MAC frames should a response not be forthcoming from the C-Port. This could be due to either the request or response being lost in transmission. Up to six requests can be sent, and the C-Port will respond to each one it receives. If an acceptance response is sent by the C-Port, then the internal data path within the C-Port configures itself to support the Station's Lobe Media Test (LMT). This involves providing an internal repeat path such that Test MAC frames are looped back to the originating station via the attached lobe cable. This is an additional function, automatically provided by classic Token Ring MAUs prior to the application of phantom signalling, that needs to be incorporated within the functionality of the C-Port.

Successful completion of the registration process is when a response is received by the station to its Registration Request granting access. This then leads to the next stages of the Join process, the LMT and Duplicate Address Check processes. A failed registration can occur when the station fails to receive a response to its Registration Request MAC frame, or the response received denies access. Failure to receive a response is perhaps the most obvious reason for the process not to complete. In this instance the station will have transmitted six successive Registration Request MAC frames without receiving a reply from the C-Port (perhaps the port only supports TKP access or is misconfigured or malfunctioning). The steps then taken by the station are controlled by the policy flag Station Open Option and the Access Protocol Mask[2] . If the options for the policy flag and protocol mask have been set to support both TXI and TKP protocols, then the station will immediately switch to TKP access and initiate its LMT in an attempt to access the ring. If the options set do not allow TKP access then the station will

[1] DTR specific MAC frames are discussed in table 21-7.
[2] See table 21-3 for details.

Dedicated Token Ring

close. A station's reaction in the event of a registration denial by the C-Port is also governed by a policy flag and the Access Protocol Mask. The flag, Station Registration Denied Option, if set accordingly, allows the station to revert to the TKP protocol and initiate its LMT. Again, if the options are set to TXI only, then the station will close.

21.4.3 Lobe Media Test (LMT)

The Lobe Media Test (LMT) is an inherent aspect of the TXI join process, as it is with the TKP protocol. For TXI however, it is necessary to further the LMT process and add some restrictions not applicable within TKP. That said, the main function of the LMT process remains the same, that is to determine whether the lobe is operating at an acceptable bit error rate (BER) and not about to introduce unacceptable errors into the transmission path. Typically, a station will use the TEST MAC frame for this purpose, however other frames are, with the TKP protocol, allowed to be used for the same purpose. With the TXI protocol not supporting functions such as the Active Monitor or Standby Monitors, some MAC frames must be restricted from use. The restrictions applied to the LMT process when operating the TXI protocol are:

- For the purposes of the LMT the transmission of Claim Token, Beacon, Ring Purge, AMP and SMP MAC frames is prohibited. The reason for this is that these MAC frames do not form part of normal operation within the TXI protocol, and are therefore used by the station to detect that it has been moved from a dedicated to a shared Token Ring environment.

- A time limit is also imposed on the LMT process for the first time. Some networks have experienced issues regarding the duration of the LMT with TKP access, so it was seen as a step forward to restrict the amount of time allowed for the process to complete. To this end the timer LMT Complete is used with a required value of 2.3s to 2.5s. The timer is initiated at the same time as the LMT process, and should it expire before the process completes then LMT is said to have failed.

- Due to the nature of the C-Port within a DTR concentrator it is also necessary to add a delay factor to the LMT process. The purpose of the delay is to allow enough time for the C-Port to reconfigure itself to construct a repeat path for the station such that LMT can be carried out. The delay is controlled by the SMAC timer, LMT Delay, which has a value between 200ms and 250ms.

- The bit error rate (BER) defined as providing an acceptable transmission path, and therefore a successful completion to the test is less than or equal to 10^{-7}.

Successful completion of the LMT allows the station to move to the next stage of the join process, the issuing of an Insert Request MAC frame. Failure of the LMT process would cause the station to close. From the station's perspective, the issuing of the Insert Request is also the initiation of the Duplicate Address Check (DAC) process. However, the C-Port starts its part of the DAC process during registration, in advance of the station. This is demonstrated in figure 21-3, which shows a state representation of the join process.

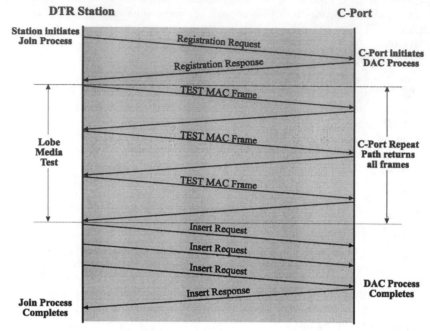

Figure 21-3: DTR Join Process

21.4.4 Duplicate Address Check (DAC)

The Duplicate Address Check (DAC) process varies somewhat from that described in section 18.7.5, earlier in this text, but is important for all the same reasons, i.e., the appearance of two or more devices with matching addresses will cause delivery and operational problems on the network. Within DTR, when using the TXI protocol, the DAC process consists of a joint co-operative effort between C-Port and DTU (Data Transfer Unit) within the concentrator to establish whether the attaching station is using an address already in use on the network. This process starts when the C-Port receives the REG_REQ MAC frame from the station, and finishes when the C-Port transmits an INS_RSP MAC frame back to the station as shown in figure 21-3.

The Registration Request (REG_REQ) MAC frame produced by the station to initiate the Join process contains two parameters used by the C-Port as part of the DAC procedure. The Source Address is the obvious one, and the Individual Address Count (IAC) policy variable is the other. This variable specifies the range of individual addresses supported by the station, which would typically be a single address, but the facility exists for multiple addresses. The values within these fields are passed by the C-Port to the DTU for it to determine from its forwarding tables whether or not the address range conflicts with other known addresses on the network.

Having made a comparison, the DTU will provide the C-Port with a response indicating a positive or negative result. For the C-Port, the process concludes when it receives both a response from the DTU and an Insert Request (INS_REQ) MAC frame from the station. The C-Port will provide the station with the conclusion in its Insert Response (INS_RSP) MAC reply. Should the DAC process provide a negative result then the C-Port will include the subvector 8020_{16} in its response, and terminate the station by moving directly to a Bypass state. Should the result be favorable then the C-Port includes the subvector 0000_{16} in its response, and completes the Join process by entering the Join Complete TXI state.

From the station's perspective, should it receive an INS_RSP MAC frame that includes the subvector 8020_{16} in it, then it will not remain attached, and it too will enter the Bypass state and notify the appropriate management functions. Should the response include the subvector 0000_{16} the station will enter the Join Complete state.

The duration of the DAC process is controlled by timers running in the station to ensure the process completes. The Timer Station Join Complete (TSJC) is used as part of the Join process to limit the time which the station will wait for an Insert Response MAC frame. Should it expire prior to the reception of an INS_RSP MAC frame then the station will enter Bypass state and notify management functions. Likewise, if the Timer Station Receive Heart Beat (TSRHB) expires during the DAC process it is possible an error has occurred and the station will also enter Bypass state and notify management functions.

21.5 TXI Transmit Operation

The method of transmission used by the TXI protocol, i.e., the concept of no token, has been around since the inception of Classic Token Ring, where a token has never been required during the Beacon process. Therefore the concepts are not new, but simply expanded to the normal transmit operation. This has been made possible by the dedicated nature of the link rather than the shared media environment of Classic Token Ring. Within the TXI protocol the transmit function is supported by a number of different states, two in the case of a station, and three for a C-Port.

Station Transmit Normal State

This is the normal condition for a station's transmit function when operating the TXI protocol. In this condition, the station will either be transmitting idle symbols generated by its internal clock, or a recovered clock. When a transmit request is made, the station provides the necessary start of frame sequence and changes to a Transmit Data state.

Station Transmit Frame Data State

This state is adopted by a station or C-Port (in station emulation mode), when transmitting data frames. The state is maintained until one of the following conditions is met:

- The station or C-Port (in station emulation mode) has no more data to transmit and releases an end of frame sequence. It will then return to the Transmit Normal state.

- The station or C-Port (in station emulation mode) detects a transmission error. In this instance the action taken depends on the following:

  If the transmission error is correctable, then an Abort Sequence will be transmitted and the station will return to the Transmit Normal state.

  If the transmission error is uncorrectable, then the transmission of an Abort Sequence is optional prior to returning to the Transmit Normal state. The Join function of the station or C-Port (in station emulation mode) will then enter the Bypass state.

  If the transmission error is caused by a frame exceeding the maximum supported length, then the action taken depends on the value of the flag FPASO. This flag is used to control the ending sequence of oversize frames when cut-through mode is employed. When set to 0 the oversize frame is ended with an abort sequence. When set to 1 the frame is ended with an invalid FCS and with the E bit set.

  All the above actions will cause the receiving device to either stop reception or to discard the frame.

C-Port Transmit Normal State

This is the normal operating state of the C-Port's transmit function when using the TXI access protocol. In this state the C-Port is transmitting idles generated by its internal clock. When a transmit request is made, and a repeat request is not made, then the C-Port transmits the start of frame sequence and moves to the Transmit Data state. When a repeat request is made then the C-Port turns its internal clock source off to derive clocking from received data, and moves to Transmit Repeat state, repeating all received data.

C-Port Transmit Data State

In this state the C-Port will transmit data until one of the following conditions applies:

- The C-Port has no more data to transmit and releases an end of frame sequence. It will then return to the Transmit Normal state.

- The C-Port detects a transmission error. In this instance the action taken is the same as described for a Station Transmit Data state.

C-Port Transmit Repeat State

This state is used when the C-Port must provide a repeat path to support the station's TXI LMT. This state is entered when the Transmit Normal state detects the flag FPRPT (Flag, C-Port Repeat) being set to 1. The repeat path is maintained until the flag is reset to 0, and the C-Port returns to Transmit Normal state.

21.5.1 Transmit Functional Model

The functional model of the transmit function when operating the TXI protocol is shown in figure 21-4. In this model two queues are defined; one for LLC user data and management traffic, and one for MAC traffic primarily responsible for the establishment and maintenance of the link.

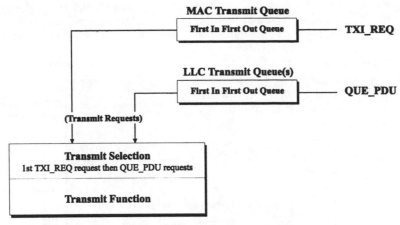

Figure 21-4: Functional Model of TXI Transmit Operation

The MAC protocol is responsible for establishing and maintaining lobe connections, and uses the MAC transmit queue for Transmit Immediate frames that have priority over LLC user data. This means that frames placed in the MAC queue are always transmitted before those within the LLC transmit queue. In addition, any frames placed in the MAC queue are transmitted without regard for the operational state of the MAC.

All user data frames and management traffic are placed in the LLC transmit queue, which is only available once the MAC reaches an operational condition (FSOP/FPOP = 1 Operational), and all frames from the MAC queue have been transmitted. A MAC is said to be operational once the Join process is complete, and remains this way until it either closes, or the MAC enters Hard Error Recovery. Figure 21-4 shows the LLC queue as a single queue, which may or may not be the case. The standard leaves the option open for implementers to establish multiple queues, although it does not describe how this should be achieved. The main advantage of multiple queues for user traffic is in allowing some form of priority mechanism to be employed. Classic Token Ring already allows for priority traffic with use of the user priority bits within the Frame Control field. By implementing multiple queues, for example two, it would allow for frames with a priority level of between 0-3 to be presented to a low priority queue, while those with priority levels between 4-7 could be mapped to a high priority queue. This priority queuing mechanism would then provide added flexibility and functionality to any implementation. The user priority part within the Frame Control field is used to determine which queue the frame is sent to.

It should be noted that once the Join process is complete, the transmit function within station and C-Port is either transmitting frames, or else it is transmitting idles. There is not a "quiet" time on the link, it is always active, with the C-Port providing the required clocking.

21.5.2 TXI Heart Beat

The concept of a "Heart Beat" protocol is not new, and has been implemented in many technologies over the years. Its purpose is to provide each end of a point to point link with acknowledgement that the other end is functioning and the link is operational. The same is true with the Heart Beat function operating within the TXI

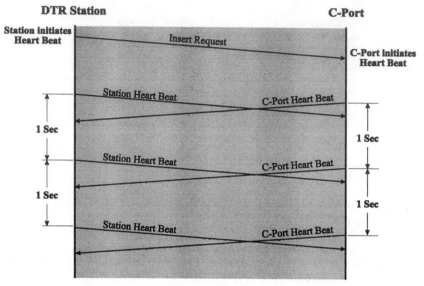

Figure 21-5: Heart Beat Process

protocol. Its presence is used as an indication that the link is functioning correctly. The Heart Beat protocol is based on the exchange of Station and C-Port Heart Beat MAC frames between the two devices. This is a continual process, with frames queued at one second intervals providing an ongoing mechanism for fault detection. Each time a station or C-Port detects a Heart Beat MAC frame from the other entity, it resets its timer TPRHB or TSRHB (Timer, C-Port/Station Receive Heart Beat), and the function continues. Figure 21-5 shows a representation of the Heart Beat process.

Station support of the Heart Beat facility becomes active when it detects the successful conclusion of its Lobe Media Test. At this point it resets TSRHB (default 5s) and sets it own internal flag, Station Heart Beat Active (FSHBA) to 1. When this flag is set, the station queues Heart Beat MAC frames for transmission, paced by the timer, Station Queue Heart Beat (TSQHB) which defaults to 1 second pacing intervals. If the station receives a Heart Beat MAC frame from the C-Port prior to the expiry of TSRHB, it resets the timer and the TXI Heart Beat process continues uninterrupted. If however, TSRHB should expire before a Heart Beat MAC frame is received, then a TXI Heart Beat failure condition is said to have occurred. Under these circumstances, the station will take one of two options; firstly, if the Join process has completed then the Heart Beat process is disabled and the station initiates Hard Error Recovery; alternatively, if the Join process is not complete, then the station moves to a Bypass state and informs management functions.

A C-Port's support of the TXI Heart Beat Function becomes active once the C-Port detects the end of the stations LMT, by receipt of an INS_REQ MAC frame. When a C-Port receives a Heart Beat MAC frame from the station it will reset its timer, C-Port Receive Heart Beat (TPRHB), and the process will continue as normal. It is only when TPRHB expires without the receipt of a Heart Beat MAC frame from the station that a TXI Heart Beat failure condition is said to have occurred. In this condition the C-Port adopts the same options as described for a station above, depending on the whether the Join process has completed or not.

21.5.3   TXI Hard Error Recovery

Hard Error Recovery is a fairly simple process, designed to allow the TXI protocol to recover from such faults as lobe or station failure. The process, shown in a high level representation in figure 21-6, is described in the text that follows.

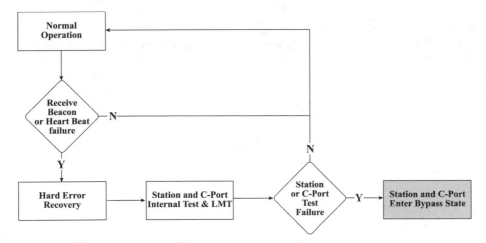

Figure 21-6:   Hard Error Recovery Process

The TXI Hard Error Recovery process consists of a number of different machine states. These states are: the C-Port and Station Beacon Transmit states, the C-Port and Station Internal Test states, and the Station's Wire Fault Delay state. Each of these is described below:

Beacon Transmit State

The Beacon Transmit state is entered by the C-Port and the station when a failure in the Heart Beat process occurs. On entering this state both devices transmit Beacon MAC frames that contain both the reason for the beaconing (Beacon Type) and the address of the upstream neighbor (UNA). Once the Beacon Transmit state has been entered, both C-Port and station follow a strict procedure in an attempt to resolve the problem. The C-Port will reset its timer, C-Port Internal Test (TPIT) to a value of 600ms (default) and transmit Beacon MAC frames while the timer is running.

Should the timer expire without connection recovery, the C-Port will initiate its internal test procedure. The station also resets a timer on entry to the Beacon Transmit state, timer Station Internal Test (TSIT). This has a default value of 7s, to delay the dropping of the phantom current, to ensure that possible wire fault conditions are detected. Again, if the timer expires without recovery occurring then the station will enter its own internal test state.

The Beacon MAC frame contains the detected cause of the Beacon condition within a subvector in the frame. This is primarily for management reporting purposes, with two causes (Beacon Types) existing.

> **Beacon Type 2:** The C-Port or station has detected a long term signal loss e.g., a break in the network medium (lobe) making it impossible to detect a signal on its receive port.

> **Beacon Type 5:** The C-Port or station has detected a breakdown in the Heart Beat function but not a long term signal loss e.g., one of the devices is stuck transmitting fill, and therefore not operating correctly.

Station Wire Fault Delay State

The Station's Wire Fault Delay state is enabled when the station receives a Beacon MAC frame that includes a Stored Upstream Address (SUA) equal to its own source address, and thus indicating the station to be upstream of the fault. The purpose of the delay is to allow the station sufficient time to detect a wire fault condition that may be the cause of the C-Port's beaconing. On entry to the wire fault delay state, the station resets both TSIT and TSLMT timers to effect the delay. Upon expiry of TSIT, if the station has not detected a wire fault, it will continue with its internal test. TSLMT is then used to start the execution of the Lobe Media Test.

Internal Test States

The station and C-Port both enter their Internal Test state when their respective timers, TSIT and TPIT expire. The precise requirements for the internal test are implementation-specific and are thus beyond the scope of the standard. However, it is recommended that they test as much of the internal circuitry as possible in an attempt to trace the detected fault. If either the C-Port or station's internal tests prove unsuccessful, the failing entity will remove itself from the lobe connection and report the failure to its own internal management process.

It should be noted that it is entirely possible for either the C-Port or the station to disconnect itself from the TXI lobe connection without the knowledge of the device at the other end of the link. In order to provide diagnosis of the cause of a failure of this kind, an outside agent is required to co-ordinate error reports from both devices. Unfortunately, the definition of such an agent is also outside the scope of the standards and is therefore implementation-specific.

If the internal test procedures prove successful, both devices prepare to resume normal operation by undergoing the Join phase prior to normal transmit state. This involves the C-Port providing a repeat path such that the station can undertake its Lobe Media Test, followed by the rest of the Join procedure.

21.6 DTR Frame Format

Dedicated Token Ring (DTR) when using the TXI access protocol makes use of the frame format, abort sequence, and fill as described in chapter 18 of this text. As the protocol is based on full duplex, transmit immediately technology, it does not have any requirement for the token, which was also described in the same chapter. There are, however, some subtle differences in the significance of some of the fields within a data frame when compared to its use in Classic Token Ring, as described below. Although differences in significance do occur, the same format is maintained to allow seamless integration between Classic and Dedicated Token Ring environments, and therefore provide a distinctive advantage to existing users.

21.6.1 DTR Frame Fields

The basic format of a DTR frame is unchanged from that of Classic Token Ring as shown in Figure 21-7. The variations in field significance are then described below.

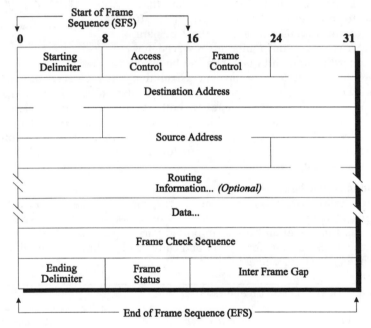

Figure 21-7: Dedicated Token Ring Frame Format

Start Delimiter

The Start Delimiter (SD) remains unchanged from a Classic Token Ring environment and is transmitted with the unique bit pattern of JK0JK000$_2$.

Access Control Field

The Access Control (AC) field is essentially redundant when using the TXI protocol. As only two devices exist on the "ring" and both can transmit simultaneously, there is no requirement for a prioritization mechanism to reserve the right to transmit. This means that the P and R bits within the field are not used and will be transmitted as 0_2 and ignored by all DTR devices. Likewise, there is no

requirement for the T bit to distinguish between frames and tokens, as the latter do not exist when using TXI, and therefore this will always be transmitted with a value of 1_2. The M bit, normally used by the Active Monitor, is also redundant as there is no such entity in DTR. This is transmitted with a value of 0_2. The expectation therefore, is that the AC field will be transmitted as 00010000_2 and any other value will be ignored.

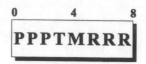

Figure 21-8: Access Control Field

Frame Control

The Frame Control (FC) field maintains all of its functionality from the Classic environment. As previously described, the F bits are used to differentiate between

MAC frames and LLC user data. The significance of the remaining Z bits are determined by the type of frame. If the frame is a MAC frame then they are coded to indicate the type of MAC frame. If the frame carries LLC user data, then the Z bits are coded rrrYYY, where the r bits are reserved for future standardization, and the Y bits can be used

Figure 21-9: Frame Control Field

to indicate the priority level of the data. Given that 3 bits are available, this equates to 8 priority levels that can be used. The DTR standard allows for manufacturers to implement multiple transmit queues in both station and C-Port, such that high priority traffic can be placed in a high priority queue and transmitted in front of data placed in a low priority queue. Although allowed for in the standard, the mechanics for achieving this are not defined, and therefore any implementation is likely to be vendor-specific.

Destination/Source Address Fields

The address fields within a DTR frame are the same as those described for Classic Token Ring in chapter 18. Given that DTR does not support the Active Monitor function, the functional addresses supported vary slightly as shown in table 21-6. DTR has the same support for locally and universally administered addresses as a Classic Token Ring environment.

Table 21-6: DTR MAC Functional Addresses

Functional Address 11000000 00000000 0xxxxxxx-	Function Name	Hexadecimal Address
-xxxxxxxx-xxxxxxxx-xxxxxx1x	Ring Parameter Server (RPS)	C0-00-00-00-00-02
-xxxxxxxx-xxxxxxxx-xxxx1xxx	Ring Error Monitor (REM)	C0-00-00-00-00-08
-xxxxxxxx-xxxxxxxx-xxx1xxxx	Configuration Report Server (CRS)	C0-00-00-00-00-10
-xxxxxxxx-x1xxxxxx-xxxxxxxx	Lobe Media Test (TEST)	C0-00-00-00-40-00

Routing Information Field (RIF)

The Routing Information Field (RIF) remains an optional field, dependent on the implementation of Source Route Bridging on the network.

Frame Check Sequence (FCS)

The Frame Check Sequence (FCS) also remains unchanged from the Classic Token Ring environment, providing rudimentary error checking at the MAC level.

Ending Delimiter (ED)

Although the Ending Delimiter (ED) maintains the same format with DTR, the significance of the Intermediate Frame (I) and Error Detected (E) bits varies from the classic environment. With DTR, a receiving device shall consider the ED as valid if it receives the first six bits as JK1JK1$_2$ without regard to the I and the E bits at the end of the field. The

Figure 21-10: Ending Delimiter

Intermediate Frame (I) bit is not used in the TXI protocol and shall always be transmitted as 0$_2$. The Error Detected (E) bit is not used by a station operating the TXI protocol and again shall be transmitted as 0$_2$. A C-Port will also transmit the E bit as a 0$_2$, unless an oversize frame is being transmitted and the flag, C-Port Abort Sequence Option is set to 1.

Frame Status Field (FS)

The Frame Status Field (FS) has little meaning during normal transmit operations with the TXI protocol, as frames are not normally repeated back to the sender.

However, they are always transmitted as 0$_2$, by both station and C-Port, and only modified if the C-Port transmit mode is repeating frames back to the station, provided that its flag, C-port AC Repeat Path Option, is set to 1, and that the frame is copied by the C-Port. The reserved (r) bits are set aside for future standardization and always transmitted as 0$_2$. Receiving devices will ignore these bits within the field.

Figure 21-11: Frame Status Field

21.7 DTR MAC Frames

Dedicated Token Ring (DTR), like its predecessor Classic Token Ring, makes extensive use of MAC frames to control network operation. When operating the TXI protocol, a new suite of MAC frames are employed, as shown in table 21-7, while when operating in a Classic Token Ring environment the MAC frames are as described in chapter 18.

Table 21-7: DTR MAC Vectors

Identifier	Description	Function
00$_{16}$	Response (RSP)	The Response MAC frame is sent by either a station or a C-Port to acknowledge an error in, or the receipt of a received MAC frame. This MAC frame is never sent to a ring station.
02$_{16}$	Beacon (BN)	The BN MAC frame is sent by a station detecting a continuous signal loss.

Table 21-7: DTR MAC Vectors (Continued)

Identifier	Description	Function
05_{16}	C-Port Heart Beat (PHB)	This MAC frame is used by the C-Port as part of the Heart Beat process described in section 21.5.2. You will notice that the Vector Identifier value of 05_{16} is the same as that used for the AMP MAC frame in Classic Token Ring and which is not used in DTR with the TXI protocol.
06_{16}	Station Heart Beat (SHB)	The SHB MAC frame is used by the station as its part of the Heart Beat process. It too uses a VI value borrowed from the TKP protocol and redundant in a TXI environment. 0616 is the same value as used by the SMP MAC frame.
08_{16}	Lobe Media Test (TEST)	The TEST MAC frame is used during the LMT process and at any other time at which the station needs to test its lobe connection, such as during hard error recovery
$0B_{16}$	Remove DTR Station (REMOVE)	The REMOVE MAC frame is used by the Configuration Report Server (CRS) or by network management to force a station to remove itself from the ring.
$0C_{16}$	Change Parameters (CHG_PARM)	The purpose of the CHG_PARM MAC frame is to allow the CRS to inform stations of the current ring operating parameters. The stations would then typically respond with a RSP MAC frame.
$0D_{16}$	Initialize Station (INIT)	The INIT MAC frame is sent by the Ring Parameter Server (RPS) to ring stations in order to initialize their operating parameters. Once again stations would normally respond via the use of the RSP MAC frame.
$0E_{16}$	Request Station Addresses (RQ_ADDR)	Used by a management function, for example the CRS, the RQ_ADDR MAC frame requests a ring station to respond with the addresses recognized by that station.
$0F_{16}$	Request Station State (RQ_STATE)	The RQ_STATE MAC frame is also used by management functions, this time to request data regarding the state of the station.
10_{16}	Request Station Attachments (RQ_ATTCH)	The RQ_ATTCH MAC frame is used by management functions, such as the CRS, to request information about functions running within the station.
11_{16}	Registration Request (REG_REQ)	The Registration Request MAC frame is used by the station to register its operating parameters with the C-Port. The frame carries information regarding the access protocol requested, phantom signalling and wire fault detection. The C-Port will accept or reject this request via its Registration Response MAC frame.
12_{16}	Registration Response (REG_RSP)	Used by the C-Port to respond to a REG_REQ MAC frame from the station indicating either acceptance or rejection of its registration request.
13_{16}	Insert Request (INS_REQ)	The INS_REQ MAC frame is sent by the station, when operating the TXI protocol, to the C-Port to try and complete the Join Process.
14_{16}	Insert Response (INS_RSP)	The INS_RSP is sent from the C-Port to the station to indicate whether its INS_REQ has been accepted or rejected. Acceptance completes the Join Process.

Table 21-7: DTR MAC Vectors (Continued)

Identifier	Description	Function
15_{16}	Registration Query (REG_QRY)	This MAC frame is used as part of the Registration Query protocol so that a C-Port may indicate to a station, attached using the TKP access method, that TXI is supported.
22_{16}	Report Station Addresses (RPRT_ADDR)	The RPRT_ADDR MAC frame is used by ring stations in response to the RQ_ADDR frame.
23_{16}	Report Station State (RPRT_STATE)	The RPRT_STATE MAC frame is used as response by stations to the RQ_STATE request.
24_{16}	Report Station Attachments (RPRT_ATTCH)	The RPRT_ATTCH MAC frame is used by stations as a response to RQ_ATTCH request from a management function.
29_{16}	Report Error (RPRT_ERR)	The RPRT_ERR MAC frame is sent to the REM periodically to report all errors detected since the last report.

The RPRT_ERR MAC frame shall be used by:

> A station using either TKP or TXI access protocols

> A C-Port in Station Emulation mode and using the TKP access protocol

The RPRT_ERR MAC frame can also optionally be used by;

> A station using the TXI protocol

> A C-Port in Station Emulation mode using the TXI access protocol

> A C-Port in Port mode using the TKP access protocol

The RPRT_ERR MAC frame shall not be used by;

> A C-Port in Port mode and using the TXI access protocol

Some MAC frames exist in a TKP environment, that do not exist when operating the TXI access protocol. These MAC frames, detailed in table 21-8, are recognized by the receiving C-Port or station, and indicate that a protocol mismatch has occurred; i.e., one entity is using the TXI protocol while the other is using TKP.

Table 21-8: TKP MAC Vectors Unused with TXI Protocol

Identifier	Description	Action
03_{16}	Claim Token (CT)	This MAC frame is recognized by a TXI device but indicates a protocol mismatch. This causes the C-Port and station to return to the Bypass State.
04_{16}	Ring Purge (RP)	As Above
05_{16}	Active Monitor Present (AMP)	As Above
06_{16}	Standby Monitor Present (SMP)	As Above

This MAC frame recognition is required because any station operating the TXI protocol that was "inserted" into a shared Token Ring would break the ring. This obviously needs to be avoided, hence the actions detailed above.

21.7.1 Management Routing Interface (MRI)

The Management Routing Interface (MRI) is essentially a set of services within a DTR concentrator that provide the ability to forward MAC frames to and from such management services as the Configuration Report Server (CRS), the Ring Error Monitor (REM), and the Ring Parameter Server (RPS). This is required as the C-Port in itself does not have the ability to provide this function, as it typically forwards frames based on MAC address or RIF field and therefore may not have the required information within the forwarding database to know how to forward the frames. In these circumstances the frames are sent by the C-Port to the MRI, which determines whether the port should transmit the frame or not.

A MAC frame must meet certain criteria in order to be determined as a management MAC frame that needs to be sent to the MRI. These criteria are;

- The MAC frame contains a source address equal to that of a management function, i.e., a functional address, and a destination address not recognized by the C-Port.

- The MAC frame is from a station, and the destination address is neither that of another station nor the C-Port.

The MRI makes its decisions on whether a frame needs to be forwarded, and where to, based on a set of management objects that are used to support the MRI function. Specifically, the dtrMRITable contains the required information to forward management MAC frames between the concentrator's C-Ports. In most cases, network administrators have the ability to configure the MRI such that management traffic is directed specifically to stations that house the management functions, or alternatively to broadcast the frame to all C-Ports.

21.8 Summary

In this chapter we have discussed a new concept in Token Ring networking, that of a switched environment with dedicated bandwidth per station. This involves the implementation of a new access protocol, Transmit Immediate (TXI) that allows devices to operate in full duplex mode, without the need for a token. In many respects, Dedicated Token Ring is an extension of concepts seen in a Classic Token Ring, but further defined to allow continual operation. An example of this is transmission without a token as seen in the TXI protocol. This is merely an extension of the transmission process used during the beaconing function in Classic Token Ring.

Much of the focus during development of DTR has been on the integration of Classic and Dedicated Token Ring environments. By providing seamless migration from the older Classic Token Ring technology to the newer Dedicated technology, the developers have ensured that existing Token Ring users can protect their current investment, while benefiting from an upgrade path should they require additional bandwidth in their network. This approach has obvious advantages over the alternatives that would require wholesale changes to infrastructure equipment, the cost of which would most likely be prohibitive to many organizations.

High Speed Token Ring

High Speed Token Ring (HSTR) operating at speeds of 100Mbps or even 1000Mbps (not yet finalized), has come about purely through market forces and the marketing hype surrounding 100/1000Mbps Ethernet technology. For many Token Ring networks, the ability to grow from a shared 4/16Mbps environment, through a 16Mbps switched technology, and onto 16Mbps full duplex (32Mbps) switched network, provides the scalability and flexibility they require. But for larger networks, or those with large amounts of network traffic, the need for a faster and more scalable solution means that if their continued investment in Token Ring technology is to be maintained, then it must offer the ability to provide more bandwidth. Enter HSTR, developed solely to maintain the loyalty of existing users and head off a wholesale migration to faster Ethernet technologies. For these customers, the ability to stay with Token Ring is a preferable option for many reasons. Firstly, there is investment protection; the ability to keep much of their current infrastructure means that upgrade costs are kept to a minimum. Secondly, and probably more importantly, is the reason that many of these users chose Token Ring as their networking technology in the first place, that is, its superior reliability and manageability over Ethernet. Many of these organizations have SNA[1] based traffic, produced by the computer systems on which much of their mission critical operations are based. Token Ring is specifically suited to SNA traffic, far more so than Ethernet.

For Token Ring networks there are many upgrade stages that can be implemented before there is a need for a faster solution. For example, a simple, single shared ring can be segregated via bridges linked by a backbone ring. For some, this may well be enough to aid throughput, but as many networks are moving away from the old 80/20 scenario where 80% of network traffic remained local and 20% went over the backbone, more bandwidth is required. Modern networks include Internet and Intranet traffic, and corporate-wide applications such as Email. These applications have seen traffic patterns reverse the old rule to something more akin to 20/80, with 80% of the traffic traversing the backbone. With this in mind, it becomes necessary to look at the bandwidth available in the backbone to avoid it becoming a bottleneck on the network. The most logical next step is the adoption of DTR technology and the implementation of backbone switches with high speed backplanes. An example of this is shown in figure 22-1, which demonstrates how a multiswitch backbone can be implemented. If cut-through switching is employed,

---

[1] System Network Architecture is an IBM protocol used by their micro/mini/mainframe computers.

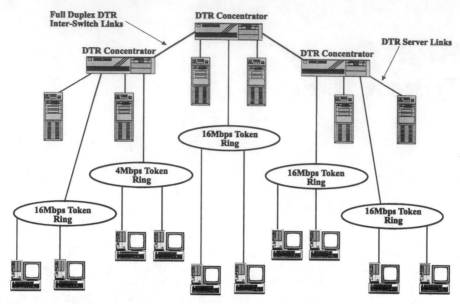

Figure 22-1:   DTR Multi-Switch Backbone

the internal latency of the switches can be minimized and a radical improvement in overall network throughput can be achieved.

However, even this design has its limitations. The overall throughput is limited to the speed of the inter-switch links and those of the servers. Even with full duplex DTR technology, this only equates to 32Mbps. With much hype and a lot of quality marketing, higher speed Ethernet technology posed a serious threat to Token Ring manufacturers only able to deliver 32Mbps at best. It is also obvious that should a more hierarchical design be required, such as that shown in figure 22-2, then a need for higher speed uplinks was a definite requirement.

An organization known as the High Speed Token Ring Alliance (HSTRA), comprising many of the leading manufacturers, was created in August 1997 to push for the rapid development of standards-based high speed Token Ring solutions. Within months, this consortium put a technical proposal in front of the IEEE 802.5 committee for ratification of a 100Mbps High Speed Token Ring standard. In addition to this, most of the vendors within the HSTRA had also gone on record, saying that they would have products to demonstrate by May 1998. This extremely aggressive schedule was set due to the extremely competitive nature of the advance in Ethernet technology in the market place.

The problems before the HSTRA were how to develop a new higher speed Token Ring technology such that it could reach the market within a very short time frame, and maintain the loyalty of existing Token Ring users. This latter point being absolutely crucial given the investment required by the participating vendors. Before any real development could take place, some fundamental questions had to be answered, so that a focus could be given to that development. These questions included such issues as:

High Speed Token Ring

- At what speed is the new High Speed Token Ring to operate?

- What cabling media options are to be supported?

- Is a shared and switched environment to be supported, or switched only?

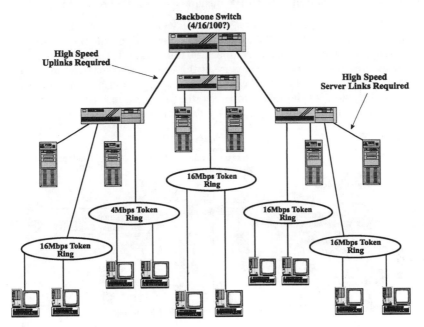

Figure 22-2:   Hierarchical Network Design

The issue of speed raises an interesting debate, as it did so at the time. Several speeds were suggested, 100Mbps, 128Mbps, 155Mbps, or even directly to 1Gbps technology. Several members of the consortium perceived little to be gained by adopting 100Mbps as the supported speed, as it offered nothing by way of direct advantage over the already released Fast Ethernet technology. Many therefore, wanted an increase to 128Mbps, 155Mbps or even the gigabit technology. Ultimately, the decision was taken to adopt the same speed as Ethernet, 100Mbps. The reason was based again on a marketing, as well as a technical point of view. By adopting 100Mbps, HSTR could use the 100Mbps Ethernet PHY[2] directly, thus providing a quicker route to market. Some thought, however, was required regarding the media support, as traditionally Token Ring networks have predominantly been based on 150Ω IBM STP cabling systems, not the Category 5 UTP more often found in an Ethernet environment, not to mention the vast majority of structured cabling systems. It was decided that support for both copper cabling systems was required, as well as fiber optic support.

With speed and media support decided, the last fundamental question is whether HSTR should be based on a shared media technology (as with Classic Token Ring), a switched technology (as with Dedicated Token Ring), or both (as with 100Mbps

[2] The 100BaseX Ethernet PHY is discussed in chapter 9.

Ethernet). The decision taken was based on market research at the time, which indicated that there was likely to be little interest in a shared solution, especially if switch ports were aggressively priced. With this in mind HSTRA embarked on the development stage with their design brief being a MAC layer based on DTR technology, in conjunction with a PHY design based on that of 100Mbps Ethernet.

So what does HSTR actually offer? The answer is a seamless migration path to add more bandwidth to a Token Ring network, without the need to adopt alternative technologies. The developers of the original Token Ring technology, back in the late 70's and early 80's, were at the time slated for over engineering the technology. This had a disadvantageous effect at the time, making Ethernet much simpler and cheaper to deploy. However, the work done all those years ago has provided tremendous benefits to latter day developers of HSTR, as the technology is

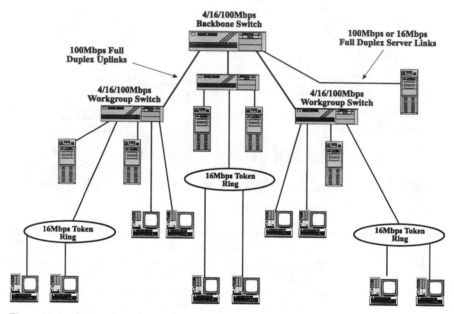

Figure 22-3:   Integrating HSTR with DTR and Classic Token Ring

capable of being scaled easily to faster speeds. In fact, it is expected that Gigabit Token Ring, when it is ratified (expected later this year), will adopt the same MAC architecture as that used for 100Mbps, which in turn was developed directly from DTR technology at 16Mbps. Figure 22-3 shows a typical network with HSTR adopted where potential bottlenecks may have occurred before, but still mainly based on 16Mbps technology to the desktop. This is because Token Ring, unlike its Ethernet counterpart, is able to offer almost 100% utilization of available bandwidth, without suffering any form of performance degradation or protocol breakdown. Therefore, 16Mbps is likely to provide adequate bandwidth to the desktop for some time to come. If additional resource is required for servers, or power users, then full duplex (32Mbps) or 100Mbps (full/half duplex) DTR technology can be deployed for these users.

22.1 Summary

HSTR has been developed primarily to suit market demands for additional bandwidth on inter-switch links and high performance server connections. As such, it has been developed as a switched-only technology, although a shared environment could be forthcoming if the market demands. Because of the switched-only nature of HSTR, it has been developed directly from DTR technology running at 100Mbps speeds. To further aid speed to market and to keep product costs low, the 100Mbps Ethernet PHY has been adopted to operate with the HSTR MAC architecture.

By adapting existing technology, the HSTRA has ensured that the efficiency benefits already enjoyed by Token Ring users have been maintained with the new higher speed offering. This means that full support of native frame formats, source routing technology, and larger frame sizes is maintained with HSTR. The first generation of HSTR, 100Mbps, offers a sixfold speed increase over existing Token Ring networks, and is capable of running in either full or half duplex modes. Given the efficiency of Token Ring over Ethernet, 100Mbps Token Ring is seen as a credible alternative to Fast Ethernet, with Gigabit speeds to follow in the near future.

Section D

Fiber Distributed
Data Interface
(FDDI)

FDDI
Introduction

This section takes a look at FDDI as a technology which builds on the foundations set by Token Ring and introduces many new concepts that make this technology both more sophisticated and flexible than either Token Ring or Ethernet. The approach taken is to provide a general overview in this chapter, and then build up the detail on a layer by layer basis, in relation to layers within the OSI Model, in subsequent chapters. By starting at the Physical Layer and building through the MAC Layer, and then finishing by taking a look at the management functions that help control the whole operation, it is hoped that a thorough understanding can be gained in a step by step fashion.

23.1 What Is FDDI?

Fiber Distributed Data Interface, or FDDI as we will call it for the rest of this section, is a technology born out of a desire to produce a high speed technology which would take full advantage of the benefits of the bandwidth, distance, and speed offered by fiber optic cabling plant. It was in 1982 that developers and standards organizations, in particular the American National Standards Institute (ANSI), began work to develop what we now know as FDDI. At this point, for the first time, fiber optic cabling became a commercially viable alternative to traditional copper cabling for the purposes of computer interconnectivity. This was primarily due to advances in cable production techniques that allowed manufacturers to produce fiber optic cable at a price and quality that made it affordable in the market place.

One of the primary decisions to be made, apart from basing a technology solely on fiber, was to determine how the access protocol would operate. As we have seen in preceding sections, the two main technologies of the time (and still in the early stages of development) were Ethernet and Token Ring, both of which utilize completely different access mechanisms to control medium access. FDDI could easily have been based on yet another method, however the token passing protocol employed by Token Ring offered many of the features desired by the developers in that it was reliable, deterministic, and had resilience capabilities. It was therefore decided that FDDI would be designed as a technology based on a token passing protocol, very similar to Token Ring in many aspects, but with added sophistication providing additional benefits to application developers of the future. So in a nutshell, FDDI is a ring based networking technology that employs a token passing mechanism similar to that of Token Ring. It does however, operate at a much higher speed, 100Mbps, and can incorporate an overall ring length of 100km. As you will see in subsequent chapters however, it is far more sophisticated than its predecessor and yet this complexity makes it easier for network administrators to implement it.

23.1.1   FDDI and the OSI Model

As with most LAN technologies, FDDI has been developed based on a layered architecture, with each layer providing services to the layer above and receiving services from the layer below. The most well known architecture of this type is the 7-Layer OSI Reference Model developed by the International Standards Organization (ISO). This particular model, however, was very much based around WAN technologies and does not directly map to the LAN counterparts as can be

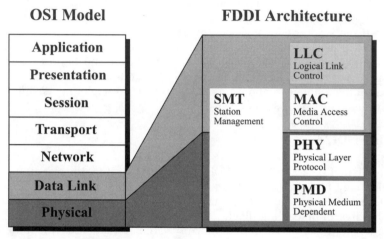

Figure 23-1:   FDDI Architecture

seen in figure 23-1. It can be seen that the Physical Layer is subdivided into two sublayers, the Physical Medium Dependent (PMD) and the Physical Layer Protocol (PHY), while the Data Link Layer is also sudivided into Media Access Control (MAC) and Logical Link Control (LLC). With FDDI there is also a fifth entity, that of Station Management (SMT), that operates in parallel to the lower three sublayers. The purpose of each sublayer is described in detail in the text that follows.

Physical Medium Dependent Layer (PMD)
The Physical Medium Dependent (PMD) is the lowest layer in the FDDI architecture and as such provides a direct interface to the cabling infrastructure.   To provide flexibility there are currently three PMD standards defined, one for Singlemode Fiber, one for Multimode Fiber, and one for Twisted Pair copper cabling. The standards define such things as transmitters, receivers, cables, connectors, signalling, and loss budgets.

Physical Layer Protocol (PHY)
The Physical Layer Protocol (PHY) is the upper sublayer of the Physical Layer and defines physical aspects that are medium independent such as decoding incoming bit streams to symbol streams in a form supported by

the MAC. The PHY is also responsible for establishing clock synchronization with the incoming bit stream. The PHY provides services to and receives services from the sublayers immediately above and below, i.e., the PMD and the MAC.

Media Access Control (MAC)

The primary responsibility of the Media Access Control (MAC) sublayer is to provide fair and deterministic access to the network medium. As already mentioned, this is achieved via a token passing protocol similar to that of Token Ring. In addition, the MAC is also responsible for such things as data framing structure and rudimentary error checking. The additional sophistication of the FDDI MAC allows for advanced features such as data priority, guaranteed bandwidth, and restricted tokens, all of which are discussed in more detail in chapter 27.

Station Management (SMT)

The Station Management (SMT) entity interfaces with all three previously mentioned sublayers to provide monitoring, support, and control for the functions these sublayers undertake. There must be an SMT entity within every FDDI node.

23.1.2 FDDI Network Environments

One of the important criteria for the physical design of FDDI during development was that it should be flexible in implementation so as to support a number of different environments each with differing needs. Three main environments were identified as being those that FDDI would be designed to support, each is discussed below:

Data Center Environment

In this environment there are likely to be relatively few FDDI devices but throughput will be high. It typically comprises of a small number of very powerful computers (i.e., mainframes, mini-computers, etc.), all of which require high levels of reliability and fault tolerance as they will provide key functions within an organization. It is also likely that these devices will be operational for very long periods but will require occasional scheduled down time for maintenance purposes.

Campus Environment

A typical campus would include multiple buildings, some of which may be some distance from others (up to 2km). In this environment large volumes of data may need to be transferred in a reliable and fault tolerant manner. It is likely that there may be a reasonably large number of devices that are expected to remain stable and operational for long periods of time.

Office/Building Environment

A typical office includes a large number of devices in a relatively small area, all of which are likely to be power cycled on a daily basis. These devices may well be connected via some form of structured cabling distribution scheme and be subject to many moves and changes.

From the requirements of each of the three environments it can be seen that a wide range of flexibility is required to provide a single technology that ideally supports the high throughput, highly fault tolerant computer center, as well as the up-down, on-off nature of a standard office, while at the same time providing the distance requirements of the Campus LAN. It is the flexibility of the FDDI topology that allows such diverse environments to happily co-exist, operating on a single FDDI LAN.

23.2 FDDI Topology

To provide the requirements of the design specification, FDDI needed a flexible topology. In fact the resulting development produced a technology that could operate over different topologies depending on the implementation requirements. The basis for the FDDI topology is a ring, and has to be so to accommodate the type of token passing protocol employed. However, the adoption of a single ring would not provide the fault tolerance required, so a dual ring is used configured as a primary and backup ring for resilience purposes. Even this does not provide all the solutions required; for example consider an average office with many devices concentrated in a relatively small area. In this environment a dual ring would provide a mass of cables with little need for the benefits a dual ring provides. In this instance a concentrator unit with single links to each device makes far more sense, but creates an entirely different, more tree like, topology. For these reasons FDDI supports dual ring, tree, and dual ring of trees' topologies, as shown in figure 23-2.

In the diagram all three topologies are demonstrated. In box A we can see the dual ring topology, which although shown at the heart of the network (where it is normally employed), could be operating entirely on its own, without connectivity to the rest of the network. The same is true of the tree configuration in box B, as this could also operate in isolation. One important thing to remember about the tree topology is that although connections are singular and point to point, they are in fact duplex links providing a transmit and a receive path, with the concentrator forming an internal ring in exactly the same fashion as the Token Ring technology. This ensures that a ring is maintained even in the point to point orientated tree. When interconnecting the dual ring to the tree topologies (consider the network as a whole), a dual ring of trees is formed. In this configuration only one dual ring exists, which can have a single or multiple trees attached. Note how the primary ring extends down the branches of the trees to incorporate all attached devices. It should also be noted that it is not possible to create a tree of dual rings.

Another important aspect of FDDI highlighted in figure 23-2 is the different device connections and port types. Although these are discussed in greater detail in chapter 24, they are worth a mention at this stage. The first and most apparent difference between devices is the number of rings to which they attach. The diagram shows some (Box A) which attach to both rings and are known as dual attached, and some (Box B) that attach to the primary ring only, and are known as single attached. For a device to be dual attached it must have two ports, with a total of two transmitters and two receivers, one of each for each ring. The data within each ring travels in opposite directions (known as counter rotating rings), therefore each physical port must have a transmitter for one ring and a receiver for the other. This leads to a differentiation between the two ports, with one transmitting on the primary and receiving on the secondary ring, while the other does the opposite. These are known as A and B ports, respectively. There is also a differentiation between ports in a tree, with one end of the link providing connectivity functions, while the other is typically (but not exclusively) a station of some description. Ports at either end of a link operate in a Master/Slave configuration, and are known as M and S ports accordingly. All these different device and port types lead to many different connectivity options. It is the number of these options that provides the flexibility in the FDDI topology already mentioned. It can also lead to some invalid connection scenarios, which are detailed in section 24.5.1.

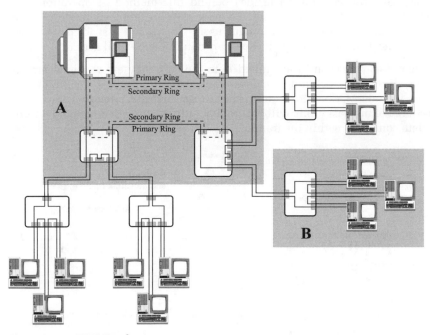

Figure 23-2:   FDDI Topology

Also apparent in figure 23-2 are the two different device types, namely stations and concentrators. All devices connecting onto an FDDI network fall into one of these two categories, with Computers (of all sizes), bridges, routers, etc., all being categorized as FDDI stations. Devices allowing other FDDI nodes to connect into them, thus providing network connectivity, are called concentrators.

23.3 Basic Method of Operation

The basic operation of an FDDI network is essentially very similar to that of Token Ring, as described in the earlier section. It is very much based on the token passing principle established by IBM. Each station wishing to transmit data must wait to capture a circulating token prior to transmission. This token is, as you would expect, a special sequence of octets not duplicated during normal transmission, and therefore instantly recognizable. Having captured the token, a station is free to transmit queued data, until either the queue is empty or the holding timer expires, whichever is the sooner. The duration of the Token Holding Timer is not fixed as it is in Token Ring, but is subject to a ring scheduling algorithm that operates on a principle of early or late token arrival. Described in detail in section 27.2, the method is based on an expected rotation time for each token circulation of the ring. If the token arrives in advance of this rotation timer expiring it is said to be early, and the station can use it for the amount of time by which it is early (the token holding time). If the time taken for a single rotation is greater than the target rotation time then it is said to be late and the station may not capture it at all for normal data transmission. The idea behind this method of operation is that it proves to be fairer to all users when the network is heavily loaded, with heavy users being "penalized" in favor of the light user. This is not a strict penalty as such, merely a mechanism whereby all users can gain fast and equal access.

When data frames are transmitted onto the ring they are repeated around that ring by all stations, including the destination station. Like other technologies, FDDI frames include MAC address information regarding the intended destination and the source of the data. This will ensure that only the intended target(s) will process the data contained within the frame.

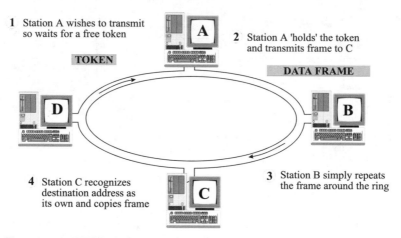

Figure 23-3:   FDDI Basic Operation I

Based on figure 23-3, assuming node A is the source of the transmission and node C the intended destination, the following text describes the basic events taking place in the transmission of a single data frame. Node A, having data queued for transmission, waits for, then captures the token and replaces it with its data frame. This frame will then be received on the incoming port by node B who will copy the frame into its repeat buffer. Node B at this point is responsible for onward transmission to its downstream neighbor, node C. It must, however, also determine whether this frame is in fact destined for itself, and would thus require further processing. In addition, while forwarding and potentially processing the frame, node B will perform basic error checking on the arriving data to ensure that what does arrive is complete and error free. These processes are separate but inextricably linked, in that the results of destination address determination and error checking could force a modification of the repeated data frame. As this frame is destined for another node, and assuming no errors were detected, the frame will be repeated unmodified downstream to node C.

Node C will ultimately receive the incoming frame, and will copy it to its frame and repeat buffers. This time the receiving node will recognize the destination address as matching its own, and will copy the entire frame into its frame buffer for further processing. Simultaneously, the frame will also be repeated onward to the next downstream node. However, as the destination station, it will modify certain fields at the end of the frame to indicate that it has both recognized its address and managed to successfully copy the frame. This provides FDDI with a confirmation of delivery service as previously seen in the Token Ring environment. You will notice at this point that the receiving station has no responsibility for the removal of the frame from the ring. This is an important point as it is quite possible that the frame could in fact be destined for more than one recipient.

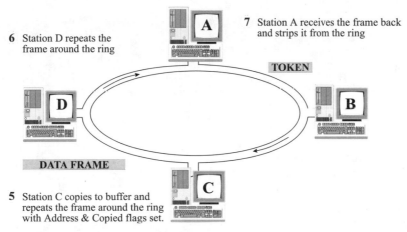

Figure 23-4: FDDI Basic Operation II

Node D will be the next recipient of the frame on its continuing circulation of the ring. Its response to receiving this particular frame will ultimately be the same as node B as it is not an intended recipient. The frame will eventually be received back by node A, the source of the frame on the ring. Initially, A will start repeating the frame, at least the first few fields, until it recognizes its own address in the source address field. Upon recognition it will start to strip the frame from the ring and issue a new token. While stripping, node A will check the fields at the end of the frame to see whether the frame had been successfully received and copied by the destination. If not, then steps can be taken to resolve the problem. It may be that the destination station is not available, it may be on another ring, it may not even exist. In any case, the FDDI node is actually aware that a problem exists and can take steps to solve it if required.

As you may well have determined from this description, FDDI is almost identical in basic operation to Token Ring. There are however, many small but not insignificant differences, which provide the added level of sophistication required to support a data rate of 100Mbps compared with the standard 16Mbps offered by Token Ring. In addition to this increased data rate, the maximum device count is greatly increased to 1000 FDDI entities per ring, where an entity is typically a physical port. As it typically requires 2 entities per connection, this roughly equates to 500 stations on a single ring. The overall ring length is also vastly increased, primarily because this is a fiber technology, to 200km, although because FDDI supports a wrap facility similar to Token Ring, a ring should be designed to a maximum of half distance, 100km. Additionally, devices should be no more than 2km apart[1] (depending on media).

23.3.1   Wrap Mode

With fault tolerance being one of the key design goals for the FDDI technology, the ability to restore the ring to operational state in the event of segment failure, station removal, or port failure is considered a key point. In the event of cable failure, the

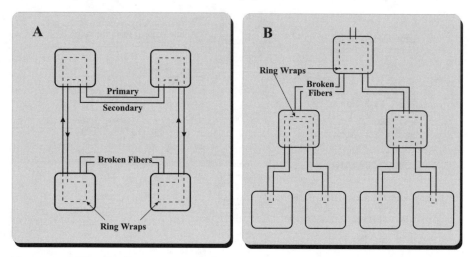

Figure 23-5:   Wrap Facility

SMT entity within the adjoining devices will detect the signal loss and immediately wrap the transmit and receive ports internally on either side of the broken cable. This will then continue to provide a continuous path around the network, now encompassing the secondary ring, in much the same manner as the Token Ring wrap facility. The ring length will also increase to encompass the secondary ring, hence the need to design the network to a maximum of 100km. If the segment failure is not in the dual ring but in part of a tree, then the same events occur,

[1] 2km is the maximum separation based on Multimode Fiber.

isolating the broken segment. The problem is, however, that this is likely to segment the network into two as a secondary path does not exist in tree topologies.

Figure 23-5A demonstrates how two devices either side of a broken segment within a dual ring wrap the primary onto the secondary ring to maintain a consistent path around the network. Figure 23-5B shows the same wrap facility but this time in a tree topology, and demonstrates how the two parts of the network become isolated from each other. Although a dual ring configuration offers the fault tolerance of wrapping without segmenting the network, it is worth noting that if the ring were to wrap a second time, due to another fault, then it would segment the network into two as with the tree topology. It is for this reason that devices which are likely to be turned off on a regular basis, i.e., workstations, are not normally placed on a dual ring, as each time the device was powered down it would cause the ring to wrap. Such devices are better placed in a tree configuration connected to a concentrator.

23.4 Summary

FDDI, as we have established, is based on a token passing protocol similar to that of Token Ring. Designed to take advantage of the superior bandwidth and distances offered by fiber cabling, FDDI supports a ring speed of 100Mbps and an overall ring length of 100km. These properties make this technology ideal for LAN backbone applications, and potentially Metropolitan Area Networks (MAN) applications as well. Critical design aspects in the development of FDDI were flexibility and fault tolerance, and we have seen through the varied topology and wrap facility some of the features that enabled these design goals to be achieved. In subsequent chapters we will explore the technology in greater detail, highlighting many more features that make FDDI a highly sophisticated technology, which many network managers trust to provide high speed services in their corporate networks.

Physical Medium Dependent (PMD)

CHAPTER 24

The Physical Medium Dependent (PMD) represents the lowest sublayer of the FDDI architecture, and is equivalent to the lower part of the OSI Physical Layer. As such it defines the physical interface to the network, encompassing aspects such as cables, connectors, signalling levels, loss budgets, and transmitter/receiver characteristics. All devices attaching to an FDDI network must have at least one PMD, however dual attached devices will have two, while concentrators will have one per port. This leads to an interesting concept, because the PMD stands independent of the upper layers and can therefore be mixed within a device. For example, a concentrator could have a user defined mix of copper and fiber PMDs to suit their own requirements.

Currently, three separate PMD standards have been ratified, and are in widespread use around the world. The first we will consider is Singlemode Fiber (SMF-PMD), which due to the properties of the media is ideal for long distance applications. As a cheaper, and in many cases a more practical, alternative, Multimode Fiber (MMF-PMD) is available, and is by far the widest installed fiber media. To allow for the fact that fiber to the desktop has not yet become an

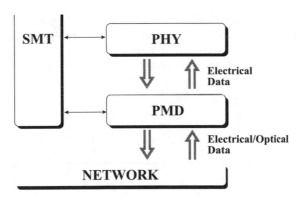

Figure 24-1: PMD/PHY Interaction

attractive option for most people, a copper PMD has also been developed, using Twisted Pair cabling (TP-PMD). Within this standard allowances are made for twisted pair cabling in either the unshielded (UTP) or shielded (STP) variety. This standard also replaces proprietary implementations widely known as CDDI or CuDDI.

The primary responsibility of the PMD is to ensure data signals are transmitted/received from the network medium and passed to the PHY for decoding. To ensure an error rate of less than 1 in 10^{10} bits transmitted, every aspect of the physical infrastructure must be closely defined. Figure 24-1 demonstrates the interaction between the PMD, the PHY, and the SMT, which closely controls their operation.

24.1 Multimode Fiber PMD (MMF-PMD)

As already mentioned, three separate PMD standards exist, with the Multimode Fiber PMD being the original. Designed to support link distances up to 2km, the MMF-PMD is by far the widest implemented in FDDI LANs. The optical fiber communication uses what is known as a bi-polar coding scheme, requiring two different levels of light. This means that in FDDI, neither signal level employs a "no light" condition, but uses a "less light - more light" scheme, which enables the no light condition to be used to detect cable breakages.

When considering fiber, distances are not rigidly defined in terms of length because signal losses on a link can vary. The loss budget is the acceptable losses, due to attenuation, that a link can suffer and still remain viable. The loss budget is determined by calculating the difference between transmitter output power and receiver input sensitivity. For multimode fiber these figures are given below:

	Min.	Max.
Transmit Output Power	-20dBm	-14dBm
Receive Input Threshold	-31dBm	-14dBm

The maximum allowable loss budget can therefore be calculated as:

$$-20dBm - -31dBM = 11dB$$

It is this figure of 11dB which is ultimately more important than a defined maximum distance, which is only *implied* at 2km. Within each link, losses can and will occur over the fiber itself, and also at coupling points such as patch panels and splices. The sum of all losses must therefore be ≤ 11dB for each link.

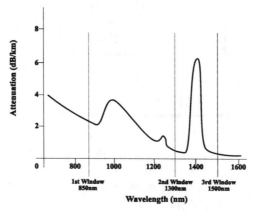

Figure 24-2:   Fiber Spectral Response Curve

The wavelength of the light source used within FDDI is also different than that specified in Ethernet or Token Ring. Figure 24-2 shows a typical spectral response curve for fiber and demonstrates the three optimum wavelength for light sources so that losses are minimized on the link. The shorter 850nm wavelength is typical of Ethernet/Token Ring, while 1300nm is used for FDDI. With the longer wavelength, greater distances or lower losses can be achieved. However, some small variation in the wavelength of a light source is inevitable leading to added attenuation. To minimize this effect, FDDI imposes a restriction stipulating light sources should be able operate within the limits of 1270nm to 1380nm maximum. Light sources not capable of staying within these constraints should not be used.

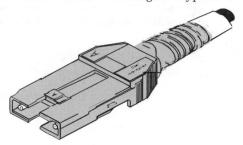

Figure 24-3:   FSD Connector

The standard cable size is specified as 62.5/125µm[1] with 50/125µm as an acceptable option. This falls into line with international structured cabling standards that make the same recommendations. The connectors used vary depending on location within the cabling plant. For example, the standard connector when attaching to an FDDI device is the Fixed Shroud Duplex (FSD) connector shown in figure 24-3. On the other hand the SC or ST connectors as shown in figure 24-4, are far more common in a patch panel environment, although not exclusively so. The FSD connector provides simplicity in that it is a duplex connector, keyed for correct orientation that guarantees transmit always connects to receive. It is important when connecting to backbone cabling within a patch panel using single connectors such as the SC or ST, that this cross-over is maintained.

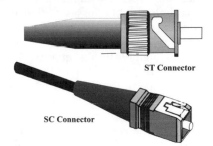

ST Connector

SC Connector

Figure 24-4: ST and SC Fiber Connectors

24.2 Singlemode Fiber PMD (SMF-PMD)

The singlemode fiber (SMF) PMD specifies two categories of SMF link, category I and category II, for medium and long link lengths respectively. Both categories use the same type of fiber, typically 8/125µm fiber, although the core diameter can vary from 7-9µm. Although category I is defined as medium length, it does in fact allow for distances up to 15km with a maximum loss budget of 10dB. Category II SMF links utilize a class II transmitter with a greater output power, thus providing a

---

[1] Fiber specifications are covered in chapter 39.

greater allowable loss budget, up to 32dB. This allows distances up to 60 km to be achieved with a category II link. Both transmitter and receiver can be specified to be either category I or category II, and mixing on the same link is allowed with varying resulting loss budgets defined as specified in table 24-1. Category I and II transmitters are distinguished by their associated output power capability and thus maximum achievable link lengths. Category I and II power output are defined as:

	Min.	Max.
Category I Transmit Output Power	-20dBm	-14dBm
Category II Transmit Output Power	-4dBm	0dBm

The same is also true of receiver sensitivity with category I and II receivers being defined as:

	Min.	Max.
Category I Receive Input Threshold	-31dBm	-14dBm
Category II Receive Input Threshold	-37dBm	-15dBm

Based on these figures, a natural assumption would be to use category II links for all connectivity beyond the scope of multimode fiber (2km). However care should be taken with category II links not to swamp the receiver, therefore a minimum link loss of -15dB must be guaranteed to ensure proper operation. When mixing different category transmitters and receivers, table 24-1 can be used to select the most appropriate combination for any given link. This selection relies on the pre-calculation of the losses of that link. The following factors should be taken into consideration in calculating those losses. Typically for singlemode fiber the fiber itself will account for most of the losses at a rate of 0.4dB per kilometer approximately (cable quality varies and you should check individual cable specifications). On top of the accumulated cable losses 0.1dB should be added for each splice in the link and 0.5dB for any connector coupling. The sum total of all these losses can be compared with the figures in the table to provide the combination best suited for that particular link. Connectors used with singlemode fiber are the same as those used with the original MMF PMD. This includes the FSD, SC, and ST connectors. Splices are nearly always of the fusion variety as mechanical splices are not accurate enough for the very small 7-9μm optical core.

Table 24-1: Link Category Combinations

Combination	Min. Loss Budget	Max. Loss Budget	Transmitter	Receiver
A	0dB	10dB	Category I	Category I
B	1dB	16dB	Category I	Category II
C	14dB	26dB	Category II	Category I
D	15dB	32dB	Category II	Category II

24.3 Twisted Pair PMD (TP-PMD)

The Twisted Pair (TP) PMD was developed to allow low cost attachment to an FDDI network. It is designed to run over Category 5 UTP or IBM STP cabling, while presenting the same level of service to the PHY as either of the fiber PMDs. This ambition presented some technical difficulties, the most notable of which was meeting published RF Emissions standards, such as the FCC Class B Emissions limits in the US and EN 55 022 Class A emissions standards in Europe. It is now possible, utilizing the cable types specified, to implement TP-PMD up to a maximum link distance of 100m and successfully achieve emissions targets.

In many aspects, especially fucntionality, the TP-PMD is the equivalent to its fiber counter parts. However, one notable exception to this is in the encoding mechanism employed. Both the fiber PMDs make use of a bipolar encoding mechanism called NRZI[2] in conjunction with 4 bit to 5 bit conversion[3] , known as NRZI 4B/5B, leading to a line signalling rate of 125MHz. This presents a problem, as Category 5 UTP is only rated to 100MHz and signalling at this rate would almost certainly cause emission limits to be exceeded. It was therefore necessary to reduce the line signalling rate when transmitting over copper, while maintaining a consistent service to the PHY.

24.3.1 MLT-3 Coding

The mechanism chosen to overcome signalling rate issues is Multi-Level Transmit 3 (MLT-3). This is a tri-polar encoding mechanism based on three different signal levels. Its purpose within TP-PMD is to encode the data in such a manner that the signalling rate is reduced and with it the emissions that radiate from the cable.

MLT-3 encoding is essentially very simple, operating with a positive signal level, a negative one, and a zero level. It does however require a binary input rather than the normal NRZI encoded signal normally passed from the PHY. Therefore an NRZI decoder is placed within the PMD to produce a binary output suitable for MLT-3. The transition between levels is what differentiates between a binary 1_2 and 0_2. In addition to the ability to transition between three signal levels, a counter is required. This can be a single bit counter as it is only necessary to determine between odd and even. The rules for encoding are:

- The transmitter can only transition between adjacent signal states, i.e., from positive to zero, zero to negative, zero to positive. A transition from negative to positive is not allowed.

- A transition only takes place when a 1_2 is transmitted. No transition takes place when a 0_2 is transmitted.

- If a 1_2 is transmitted, the signal will transition from its current state to an adjacent state, i.e., from positive to zero, negative to zero.

- If the current state is zero and a transition is required then it will be positive if the counter is even or negative should the counter be odd.

- The counter is incremented when the zero state is left.

These rules are demonstrated in figure 24-5 which shows a example of MLT-3 encoding. The receiver function is the opposite to that described above, with the

---

[2] Non Return to Zero Inverting (NRZI) is described in section 25.1.1.
[3] 4B/5B conversion is described in section 25.1.2.

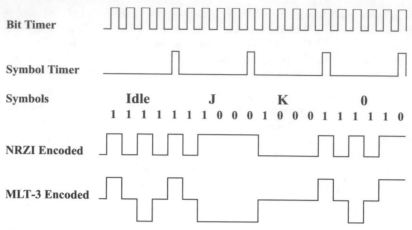

Figure 24-5:   Sample MLT-3 Encoding

decoded MLT-3 signal being passed through an NRZI encoder before being handed to the PHY. The benefit produced by this system is the much reduced signalling rate, down from 125Mhz on fiber to 31.25Mhz over copper. This produces much lower radiated emissions allowing the technology to stay well within published guidelines.

24.3.2 Cables and Connectors

The cable plant for TP-PMD is based on Category 5 UTP and IBM Type 1 STP. These provide the high quality transmission characteristics required for the high signalling rate coupled with the extremely low allowable physical error rate defined. This error rate is no greater than that defined for fiber PMDs at $<2 * 10^{-10}$.

The physical connector specified varies between cable types. For UTP, the RJ45 connector is specified in common with other technologies and, more importantly, structured cabling systems. Within the connector, two

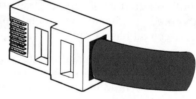

Figure 24-6:   UTP Connector

pairs are utilized for transmit and receive, with transmit on pins 1 & 2 while receive is on pins 7 & 8. For STP, the DB9 connector is used, with transmit and receive on pins 1 & 6 and 5 & 9, respectively.

24.4 FDDI Node Types

When discussing FDDI topology, we made the distinction between devices that attach to both the Primary and Secondary Ring, and those that attach only to the Primary. These devices are known as Dual Attached and Single Attached, respectively. To further aid the distinction between device types, each group is sub-divided into sub-groups known as Stations and Concentrators. This gives rise to four main categories of FDDI device, Dual and Single Attached Stations, and Dual and Single Attached Concentrators. In addition, a fifth category exists, Null Attached Concentrators, which provide user connectivity but have no eternal ring connections and therefore form the root of a tree topology. Each of these device types is discussed in the sections that follow.

24.4.1   Dual Attached Station (DAS)

Dual Attached Stations (DAS) can range from computer and peripheral devices to bridges and routers. They are categorized as DAS devices because they are not

concentrators and they connect to both the Primary and the Secondary ring. To achieve this dual connectivity two physical ports are required, and therefore two PMDs and two PHYs, one for each port, as shown in figure 24-7. Each port is physically identical but logically different. You will notice in the diagram that one port supports Primary inbound and Secondary outbound, while the other has Secondary inbound and Primary outbound. Each port is given a designator to denote the difference, with the former known as an A port and the latter as a B port.

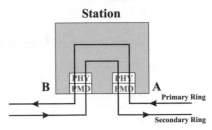

Figure 24-7:   Dual Attached Station

24.4.2   Single Attached Station (SAS)

A Single Attached Station (SAS), shown in figure 24-8, has only a single physical port, supporting Ring inbound and outbound via a duplex link. Known as a Slave

or S port, connectivity to the FDDI is achieved via a concentrator in a tree topology. SAS devices are the most common type in most FDDI networks, as it is the simplest method by which to connect workstations to the LAN. You will note that as with all FDDI connections, a duplex fiber connection is required for each physical link. This is to provide transmit and receive functions on separate fibers due to the baseband nature of the technology. To aid with connectivity, FDDI makes extensive use of a duplex fiber connector known as the Fixed Shroud Duplex

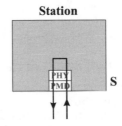

Figure 24-8: Single Attached Station

(FSD) connector or Media Interface Connector (MIC). This is discussed in more detail in section 24.1. Single Attached Devices are increasingly being connected via twisted pair cable instead of fiber.

24.4.3   Dual Attached Concentrator (DAC)

A Dual Attached Concentrator (DAC) is used to connect single attached devices to the main FDDI dual ring. It consists of an A and B port as the DAS, and also a number of Master or M ports as shown in figure 24-9. M ports provide the ability for Slave devices (Via S ports) to connect or to be isolated from the ring. This isolation feature is very important in protecting the main ring from devices that are faulty, powered down, or exceeding acceptable error rates. It should be noted that this is a feature of all concentrators, not just those that are dual attached. There is no fixed limit on the number of M ports a concentrator should have, however they are typically available with up to 32 ports.

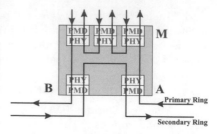

Figure 24-9: Dual Attached Concentrator

24.4.4 Single Attached Concentrator (SAC)

A Single Attached Concentrator (SAC) is similar to a DAC (described above), but does not have dual ring connectivity via A and B ports. These are replaced with a single Slave (S) port which can be linked to any M port within the network. This means that SAC devices are used to extend a tree topology by cascading from other concentrators. There is in fact no limit to how many levels are cascaded, but some thought must be given to resilience if considering this form of design. All single attached devices, stations or concentrators, have no physical resilience should link failure occur. The result would be isolation from the rest of the network. For this reason, while Single Attached Stations are common,

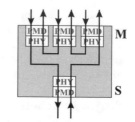

Figure 24-10: Single Attached Concentrator

their concentrator counterparts are fairly rare, with most network managers preferring the fault tolerant capabilities of a Dual Attached Concentrator. Figure 24-10 shows a SAC device and the logical data path through it.

24.4.5 Null Attached Concentrator (NAC)

Null Attached Concentrators (NAC) are those that provide M port connectivity only, thus forming the root of a tree topology, as shown in figure 24-11. These are often concentrators that have the ability to dual or single attach but have had the function of these ports changed via management to provide a greater volume of M ports. A typical implementation would be a self contained, high speed workgroup. As with the other concentrator types, a NAC device can have other concentrators cascaded from its M ports to form a more extensive tree topology. The diagram shown in figure 24-12

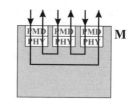

Figure 24-11: Null Attached Concentrator

shows many of the device types mentioned in this section and displays how the primary ring finds path to all attached devices to ensure the continuous data path necessary for a token passing protocol.

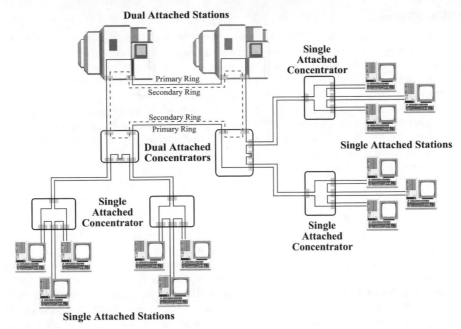

Dual Attached Stations

Primary Ring

Secondary Ring

Single Attached Concentrator

Secondary Ring

Primary Ring

Dual Attached Concentrators

Single Attached Stations

Single Attached Concentrator

Single Attached Concentrator

Single Attached Stations

Figure 24-12: FDDI Device Types

24.5 Port Types and Connections

In the previous section we introduced the concept of port types, and configurations which they can achieve. Four port types are defined, with each having a specific role within the FDDI network, these being A, B, S, and M ports. All ports are duplex in nature, with a transmit and a receive capability. The difference between them is based on their specific role and the ring(s) they connect to. With so many different port types, there is the possibility to create both legal and illegal configurations. Section 24.5.5 details all the possible connections, and whether they are legal.

24.5.1 A Port

The A port is one of the two ports that are used to connect a dual attached device to the dual ring. It is defined as having a receiver connected to the primary ring and a transmitter connected to the secondary ring. To ensure correct orientation of the duplex connector, it is keyed, normally with modular keys. This key, shown in figure 24-13a is usually colored red to ensure easy recognition by network administrators when implementing the LAN. For most implementations, the A port (and B port) will be fiber. Although not illegal, copper implementations of a dual ring configuration are rare. Many devices have the ability to configure the A port (and the B port) as additional M ports, thus changing these devices to null attached concentrators.

24.5.2 B Port

The B port is functionally the opposite of the A port, with a receiver for the secondary ring and a transmitter connecting to the primary. Again, a modular key, colored blue to differentiate it, is often used to ensure correct orientation of the duplex connector. This is shown in figure 24-13b, and as you can see is keyed on the opposite side to the A port key. To connect correctly a complete dual ring, it simply a case of connecting each A port to the B port of its neighbor. Once all A ports are connected to all B ports, two functional, counter rotating rings should be achieved. To aid the process, if all A and B ports keyed appropriately, and patch cords also have appropriate keys, i.e., a red at one end and a blue at the other, misconfiguration will not be possible.

24.5.3 M Port

The Master (M) port is so known because it provides connectivity to slave devices such as other concentrators or end stations. All concentrators have differing amounts of M ports, which are often modular in nature. By being modular it enables end users to mix and match PMD types to suit their own cabling requirements. For example, a mix of some multimode fiber and some UTP may provide the best solution for a given implementation. By allowing different PMD types within a single concentrator it makes that device more flexible to the user. M ports are normally used to connect to S ports on slave devices, however, a special configuration known as Dual Homing, described in section 24.6, allows the connection of A and B ports to M ports for a resilient tree topology. As with previous port types, connector keying is also common and normally colored green to differentiate it from the A and B keys. This is shown in figure 24-13c.

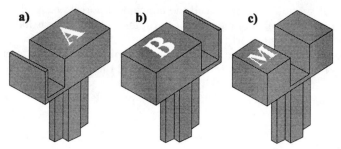

Figure 24-13:   Port Keys

24.5.4 S Port

A Slave (S) port is the port on any single attached device that is used to connect that device to the M port of a concentrator, and thus to the ring in a tree topology. S ports can only be used in this way when connecting to a larger ring. The only other legal configuration is to connect two S ports together to create a single ring of two devices, i.e., back to back. S ports are not usually keyed, but where they are, the M port key is used.

24.5.5   Valid Connections

Different connection types fall into different categories, namely preferred, special, undesirable, and illegal. Table 24-2 lists possible connection combinations and the category they fall into, as well as their use. You will note that there is only one illegal combination which is actually prevented, if not by connector keying (which can be circumvented), then by SMT (Station Management) which does not allow this configuration.

Table 24-2:   Valid Connection Combinations

Combination	Category	Function
A → B & B → A	Preferred	Normal dual ring connection
M → S & S → M	Preferred	Normal tree configuration
A → M & M → A	Special	Used for Dual Homing
B → M & M → B	Special	Used for Dual Homing
A → A & B → B	Undesirable	Creates twisted rings
A → S & S → A	Undesirable	Creates wrapped ring
B → S & S → B	Undesirable	Creates wrapped ring
S → S	Undesirable	Creates a single ring of two nodes
M → M	Illegal	Creates a tree of rings

It is worth remembering that correct connector keying can alleviate any potential connectivity problems.

24.6   Dual Homing

We have seen the flexibility of FDDI in its ability to support multiple topologies, but what about resilience? With one of the initial design goals being to produce a highly fault tolerant architecture, does FDDI provide the levels of resilience desired? The answer to this question is yes, to a certain extent. Within a dual ring topology, we know that the ring can wrap either side of a faulty component, and services are maintained. However, should the ring wrap a second time, then it will

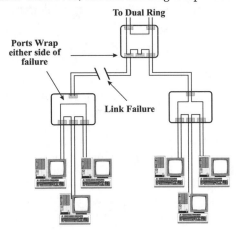

Figure 24-14:   Link Failure

be segmented into separate rings causing isolation of devices. Within a tree topology, however, only a single physical link is utilized to connect devices. Should this link fail, as shown in figure 24-14, then devices are certainly going to be isolated from the main ring.

To overcome this problem, a method of connectivity has been devised, known as Dual Homing. With dual homing, a tree topology is maintained but with the provision of redundant links to maintain connectivity should the primary link fail.

So how is this achieved? As with all physical connections within FDDI, the solution is quite simple. Under normal operation, single attached devices are cascaded from concentrators with S ports being connected to the concentrator M ports. This cascading can, if required, drop through as many levels as necessary producing many single points of failure. With dual homing, single attached devices are swapped for dual attached devices which are connected via their A and B ports to the same concentrator M ports as before. In this configuration the dual attached device does not behave as either dual or single attached (as previously described), but more as a hybrid device that uses one of its ports as a slave for connection purposes to the tree, and the other in a "hot" standby mode. In this way, should the primary link fail, the standby link will take over thus maintaining normal ring operation. Dual homing is shown in figure 24-15.

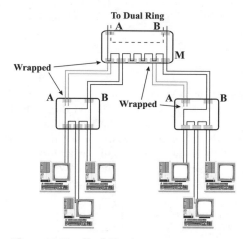

Figure 24-15: Dual Homing

Under normal operation it is the device's B port that provides connectivity to the ring, with the A port being the standby port. Station Management (SMT) controls the link initiation procedure that will force the B port into slave mode, and make the A port wrap internally. This is achieved via the Configuration Element Management (CEM) entity within SMT, which is responsible for initializing and maintaining paths. Should the primary path fail, switch-over to the standby link is achieved via SMT forcing the B port to warp internally, while the A port changes to a through state. Although the diagram shows all A and B ports connected to M ports within the same concentrator, this is not a necessity. The ports of a dual homed device can be connected to different concentrators if a higher level of resilience is required.

As already mentioned, the primary goal of this type of architecture is to improve the fault tolerance within the network. Certainly for concentrators and servers this is an attractive method of connectivity, for two reasons. The first is that by minimizing the number of devices on the dual ring, you actually increase the number that can be taken offline easily for maintenance or other purposes. The second, especially useful for server devices, is the media employed. With dual homing to a tree topology, it is easier to utilize twisted pair media for the server connectivity rather than requiring fiber media as would be the case within a dual ring. Therefore servers can be added to the LAN at lower cost, in the knowledge that the fault tolerance capability is not reduced.

24.7 Optical Bypass Relay (OBR)

Optical Bypass Relays (OBR) provide an added level of resilience and flexibility to a dual ring configuration. Consider for a minute a dual attached device. This is normally a device that would remain in an up state for long periods without the need to remove it from the ring. However, what would be the normal result of taking such a device offline for routine maintenance? During this down state period the dual ring would be wrapped either side of the removed device. Therefore, the

ring would remain operational. The problem lies in that should an unrelated failure now occur, the ring would wrap again, causing segmentation, an obviously undesirable state of affairs. By placing an OBR in between dual attached devices and the network, as shown in figure 24-16, you stop the dual ring from wrapping if it were necessary to remove the dual attached device from the ring, thus maintaining the same high level of resilience enjoyed during normal connectivity. For this reason, an OBR is often inserted between key servers and the network.

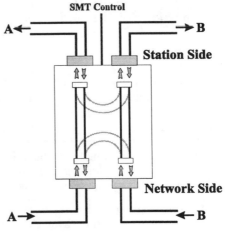

Figure 24-16: OBR in Pass Through Mode

An OBR has A and B connectivity either side of the device, as shown in the diagram. It is also connected to the device it is protecting, normally via a UTP cable, to receive control signals from SMT. All the time a signal is being received, the OBR operates in a straight through manner, passing optical signals directly to the dual attached device. Should this device be powered off for some reason, then the OBR would revert to a bypass state, passing inbound signals directly to the outbound port, as shown in figure 24-17. This protects the dual ring and prevents it from wrapping.

Care should be exercised when implementing Optical Bypass Relays, as they suffer from high signal attenuation due to the fact that they provide no signal generation and are passive devices. This means that by placing an OBR in a link you will be introducing up to 2.5dB of signal loss on that link. With an allowable loss budget of only 11dB per link, this is a considerable percentage for a single point on that link. Remember that should a device be removed from the network, the link distance between the two adjoining devices either side must remain within the allowable parameters for a single link. This means that some thought should be given to maximum link distances before OBRs are implemented in the network.

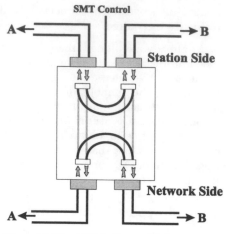

Figure 24-17:   OBR in Bypass Mode

For example, station A is connected to stations B and C in a dual attached fashion. The link distance from A to B is 2km, and from A to C is also 2km. Should A be removed from the ring with an OBR in place, then stations B and C would be 4km apart, obviously outside the allowable specification, and the ring would wrap as a valid connection would not be established, the one event the OBR was designed to prevent! By shortening the distances between A and B, and between A and C, this would be avoided as the distance between B and C would be reduced.

24.8 Summary

In this section we have looked a little closer at many of the physical aspects of FDDI, and seen the flexibility and scaleability it provides. Although one of the more complex technologies, it is this complexity that makes it simple to implement at the Physical Layer for the user. For example, building a dual ring could not be simpler than connecting A ports to B ports. The same is true for a tree topology, with S ports connecting to M ports. In fact the only real variation from this is when implementing dual homing devices, when A and B ports are linked via M ports. Beyond these few connections, all others should really be avoided.

Of the original design goals, a fault tolerant network was key to successful implementation. At the Physical Layer we have seen a number of features which make this possible. Both dual attachment and dual homing are two such features, each providing alternate paths in the event of link failure. Another key goal was that of flexibility. Here we have seen many features designed to achieve this particular goal. Flexibility in topology, in media selection, and even in media mixing within a concentrator, all add to the user friendliness of the technology. All in all, FDDI provides us with a highly flexible, fault tolerant network environment, with a performance level far exceeding its early counterparts of 10Mbps Ethernet and 16Mbps Token Ring, and even 100Mbps Fast Ethernet.

CHAPTER 25

Physical Layer Protocol (PHY)

The Physical Layer Protocol (PHY) provides the interface between the MAC and the various PMD standards. By isolating the PHY, rather than grouping it with the PMD, it can remain independent and unchanged regardless of which PMD is implemented. The primary task of the PHY is to receive data from the MAC and encode it prior to passing to the PMD for transmission, and receive data from the PMD and decode prior to passing it up to the MAC. Therefore, encoding of data is the main ingredient of this chapter. One thing that will become apparent during subsequent sections, that may at first be a little surprising, is the fact that although FDDI operates at a data transfer rate of 100Mbps the signalling rate on the fiber is in fact 125Mbps. This is explained in detail later in this chapter, but is basically due to the encoding mechanism utilized by the FDDI PHY. For every 4 bit Hex symbol passed to the PHY by the MAC, a 5 bit symbol is produced and passed to the PMD. Why? Primarily to overcome the possibility of synchronization errors at the receiving end of the link. As with other technologies, the synchronization between transmitter and receiver is paramount if successful transmission of data is to occur.

25.1 Encoding/Decoding

The basic function of the PHY is to provide the necessary interface between PMD and the MAC. The MAC will pass/receive data as 4 bit Hex symbols representing a MAC frame. The PMD on the other hand needs to pass/receive coded 5 bit data to and from the medium. The role of the PHY is thus defined as taking 4 bit Hex data from the MAC and encoding it into a format ready to pass to the PMD, alternatively, taking 5 bit coded data from the PMD and decoding it back to 4 bit Hex symbols for the MAC to reconstruct the frame.

The five bit encoded data is known as a symbol, a term used extensively within FDDI. A symbol is simply the 5 bit encoded representation of a 4 bit Hex data symbol. Therefore it takes two symbols to represent a single octet of data, meaning that 10 bits (2 symbols) will be transmitted for each octet of data passed from the MAC. This is why the signalling rate is 25% higher than the actual useable data rate. If the data transfer from MAC to MAC is 100Mbps, the rate between PMDs must be 125Mbps, equating to a signalling rate of 125MHz. Why? Is the obvious question. To understand this, an explanation of the encoding mechanism is needed and provided below.

25.1.1   Non-Return to Zero Inverting (NRZI)

We have seen in other technologies, such as Ethernet and Token Ring, the need to encode data such that clocking information can be derived from the transmission signal. The same is true of FDDI but with an added problem of the increased transmission rate. The increased speed requires a more simplified encoding mechanism if error rates are to fall within allowable constraints. For this reason,

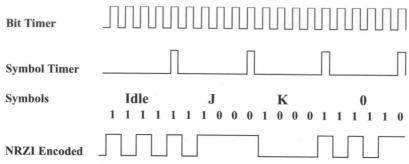

Figure 25-1: Sample NRZI Encoding

and the fact that fiber was the media on which transmission was taking place, a mechanism other than Manchester encoding was chosen. This mechanism, known as Non-Return to Zero Inverting (NRZI) is very simple in that the signal state only changes when a 1_2 is transmitted, as shown in figure 25-1.

Unlike Manchester encoding where a transition at each mid-bit time allowed clock recovery, and thus transmitter-receiver synchronization, with NRZI the transition only takes place after each binary 1 element. Therefore, as long as there is never too many 0_2's in succession the receiver can maintain perfect synchronization with the sending transmitter. The problem, as highlighted, is too many 0_2's in succession. So what constitutes too many? Even with modern electronics, synchronization can only be guaranteed if timing information can be retrieved within no more than three bit times. This means that a maximum of 3 successive 0_2's can be transmitted before a 1_2 must be received, to generate the necessary signal transition. This transition can be used by the receiver to sync its local clock. Given the sometimes random nature of data, a method must be implemented to guarantee that at no point in the data stream are more than 3 successive 0_2's transmitted. The method employed is known as 4B/5B encoding.

25.1.2   4 Bit/5 Bit Encoding

4B/5B encoding provides a mechanism whereby any data stream can be transmitted with the guarantee that no more than 3 consecutive 0_2's exist. The method by which this is achieved is very straightforward. Consider an 8 bit octet, which when passed to the PHY can be broken down as two halves, each represented as a four bit hexadecimal data symbol. These hex data symbols take the values 0-9 & A-F thus representing each of the sixteen possible combinations of four bits. This is shown in table 25-1.

There are a number of possible four bit combinations, which when combined produce a data stream with more than 3 consecutive 0_2's, for example $C1_{16}$ produces a data stream of 11000001_2. However, if a five bit symbol were used, also shown in the table, there are thirty two possible combinations, at least sixteen of which can be combined and meet the requirements limiting consecutive 0_2's. The answer then is to translate the four bit hex symbol into a qualifying five bit symbol. For example, $C1_{16}$ which would initially be passed from the MAC as $1100\ 0001_2$ would be translated by the PHY to $11010\ 01001_2$ thus ensuring the transmission signal as passed to the PMD does not contain too many consecutive 0_2's.

Table 25-1: 4B/5B Encoding

Decimal Value	Hex Value	4 Bit Code	5 Bit Code	Assignment	
0	0	0000	11110	Data	
1	1	0001	01001	Data	
2	2	0010	10100	Data	
3	3	0011	10101	Data	
4	4	0100	01010	Data	
5	5	0101	01011	Data	
6	6	0110	01110	Data	
7	7	0111	01111	Data	
8	8	1000	10010	Data	
9	9	1001	10011	Data	
10	A	1010	10110	Data	
11	B	1011	10111	Data	
12	C	1100	11010	Data	
13	D	1101	11011	Data	
14	E	1110	11100	Data	
15	F	1111	11101	Data	
			00000	Q	Quiet Line Symbol
			11111	I	Idle Symbol
			00100	H	Halt Line Symbol
			11000	J	Start Symbol
			10001	K	Start Symbol
			01101	T	End Symbol
			00111	R	Reset Symbol
			11001	S	Set Symbol
			00001	Invalid	
			00010	Invalid	
			00011	Invalid	
			00101	Invalid	
			00110	Invalid	
			01000	Invalid	
			01100	Invalid	
			10000	Invalid	

25.2 Symbol Types

FDDI takes advantage of the fact that five bit encoding is used by making use of additional symbol types above and beyond the sixteen hexadecimal data symbols. With 5 bit encoding, there are 32 unique bit combinations from which to choose. Sixteen (0-F) represent semi-octets of data, an additional five (J, K, T, R, and S) are used as control symbols, while a further three (Q, I, and H) represent line states and are used for signalling purposes at various stages of operation. Of the control symbols, the J and K always operate as a pair, forming the bit pattern 11000 10001. This bit pattern is unique, and cannot be duplicated in a normal data stream. For this reason the JK symbol pair is ideal for a start delimiter, as the combination is easily detected at any point in the transmission flow. Unlike Token Ring, FDDI has an end delimiter defined which does not involve either the J or K symbol. The T symbol is used for this purpose, and is again unique. The last of the control symbols are the R and the S symbols. These are used as flags with a frame to demonstrate a Set or Reset status. For example, in Token Ring we saw the Address Recognition flag within the Frame Status field represented by a single bit within the field. The same flag is part of an FDDI frame but is represented by an entire symbol. This would be transmitted as R by the sender and changed to S if the recipient recognized its address, i.e., S=On and R=Off.

25.3 Line States

Line states refer to the physical state of the link between devices, by determining and controlling the physical condition. They are signalled by the PHY transmitter under the control of SMT, and likewise, are received by the corresponding PHY receiver and notified to SMT. Line state detection is performed continuously in order to ascertain the current status of the link. There are six defined line states, each of which is mutually exclusive, but these are not totally exhaustive as conditions can exist which do not fulfil the criteria of any line state. When this arises the line state is said to be unknown.

25.3.1   Quiet Line State (QLS)

The Quiet Line State is entered by transmitting Q symbols and is used legitimately as part of the link establishment procedure. Slightly less legitimately, QLS can also be entered should PMD detect a loss of signal from its associated PMD. QLS is exited upon receipt of any other symbol.

25.3.2   Idle Line State (ILS)

Idle Line State is entered by transmitting I symbols and is used as part of link establishment. In addition, it is also used to establish and maintain clock synchronization with its ideal alternating 0, 1 signal pattern. As with QLS, ILS is exited on receipt of any other symbol type.

25.3.3   Halt Line State (HLS)

Halt Line State is also part of the link establishment process and is entered by transmitting H symbols. Receipt of another symbol type will cause exit from HLS.

25.3.4   Master Line State (MLS)

The last of the line states contributing towards link establishment, Master Line State is entered by the continuous transmission of alternating Q and H symbols and exited through the receipt of any other symbol combination or the loss of signal.

25.3.5 Active Line State (ALS)

Active Line State is entered upon the transmission of "normal" data, and thus indicates that symbols 0-F, J, K, R, S, or T are being transmitted. This then is the standard line state during normal operation. ALS is exited on the receipt of any other symbol (Q, I, or H) or the loss of signal.

25.3.6 Noise Line State (NLS)

The Noise Line State is never knowingly entered by PHY, and occurs when consecutive noise events are detected which do not fulfill the criteria for any other line state. Noise events are implementation specific, but could typically include such things as:

- Elasticity buffer error

- decoding of a mixed pair of control and data symbols

- decoding of 0-F, R, S, or T symbol when the last known line state is not either ILS or ALS.

Typically 16 noise events are required to enter NLS, the counter for which is reset when another known line state is entered.

The use of Line States allows PHY to establish, monitor, and control the physical link. This provides additional abilities beyond those typically available to most LAN technologies. For example, the link can be fully qualified for link integrity during the establishment phase, likewise line states can also be used for link recovery in the event of failure. The trace function, the final stage of link recovery and described in section 26.10, is an example of this.

25.4 Elasticity Buffer

Each link within an FDDI ring is in effect a point to point connection and is, therefore, to some extent, independent of the rest of the ring. This is particularly true of signal timing, where each link is timed independently. The transmitting station fixes the signal timing for the link by clocking the output signal with its own internal fixed frequency oscillator. The receiving station must then derive signal timing from the received signal. This station will then transmit the "data" to its downstream neighbor. This subsequent transmission is timed by this station against its own oscillator. With this type of mechanism there is a possibility of a small discrepancy between incoming signal timing and local fixed frequency oscillator, resulting in an excess or deficiency of bits being transferred from input to output. To overcome this some form of compensation needs to be introduced.

This compensation is provided by an Elasticity Buffer similar to that encountered within an Active Monitor on a Token Ring network. The main difference being that in FDDI, every station provides the functionality. The buffer is automatically inserted into the data path within the device, from which the data can be removed earlier if the incoming clocked data is slower than the frequency of the output, or later if the incoming frequency is greater.

Should the inbound frequency be identical to that of the output, then the buffer would be continually half full. It should be noted that if the differential between the incoming and outbound frequency is too great, then the buffer may well not be large enough to cope and bits will be deleted. To cope with this, stations should ensure that a minimum of sixteen idle symbols are inserted at the start of a frame, to provide non-critical bits which can be manipulated by the receiving station, and removed if additional compensation is required.

The minimum elasticity buffer size is calculated using the following algorithm:

The maximum FDDI frame size = 9000 symbols (4.5Kb)

9000 symbols = 45,000 bits

Maximum allowable difference between TX/RX frequencies = +/- 0.01%

0.01% of 45,000 bits = 4.5 bits

+/- 4.5 bits = 9 bits

As you can see, a buffer of only 9 bits can fill extremely quickly. However, the standard defines the accuracy of the fixed frequency oscillators to within 0.01% so the buffer should be sufficient.

25.5 Summary

FDDI separates the PHY functionality from that of the PMD within the Physical Layer. This separation of responsibilities allows a level of modularity to be introduced to the PMD, while a consistent service is provided by the PHY. This service revolves primarily around the encoding and decoding of data to a consistent format prior to passing it to the PMD, or MAC in the case of decodes. The encoding takes the form of translation from 4 bit data symbols to 5 bit code symbols, and the encoding to NRZI format. NRZI provides the simplicity to ensure errors are not introduced at high data rates, but suffers from synchonization problems if consecutive 0_2s are transmitted. Using the 4B/5B translation overcomes this problem. It should be noted however, that this mechanism induces a 25% overhead on the transmission signal, leading to a signalling rate of 125Mhz for a useable data rate of 100Mbps.

Media Access Control (MAC)

The Media Access Control (MAC) sublayer constitutes the lower half of the Data Link Layer (Layer 2) of the OSI model. In line with other MACs, its primary responsibilities revolve around controlling access to the medium, and frame generation/reception. It is also important that the FDDI MAC provides a standard service to the upper sublayer at layer 2, Logical Link Control[1] (LLC). This is because it is a function of LLC to maintain control of the exchange of data between two devices on the same physical network. This is done without regard for the type of MAC in place, as the LLC is technology independent. Therefore the MAC service to LLC must be consistent across all types of MAC.

Data requiring transmission by the MAC is passed by LLC as an integer number of octets, and is known as a Service Data Unit (SDU). In addition, the MAC address of the destination device, and some indication of the priority of the data, will also be passed to the MAC by the LLC. The MAC is then responsible for constructing a Protocol Data Unit (PDU) that contains the necessary addressing and control information as well as the SDU. This is also known as a MAC frame, the detailed contents of which are described in section 26.2. The MAC is then responsible for queuing the frame for transmission by the PHY and PMD.

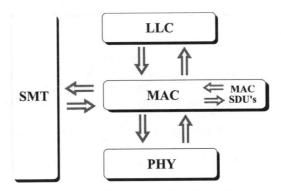

Figure 26-1:   MAC Interaction with Adjacent Layers

In earlier chapters we established that transmission is dependent on the capturing of a usable token. The determination of whether a token is usable or not is based on a ring scheduling algorithm, and introduces the concept of early and

---

[1] LLC is discussed in detail in chapter 30.

late tokens. For normal user data a usable token is one which is early, while a late token is unusable. The scheduling algorithm and the basis of how tokens are determined as early or late is discussed in section 27.3.

In addition to the LLC, the MAC may also receive SDUs from SMT, and have the ability to deliver received information to SMT for management purposes. Control information is contained within the frame header to indicate whether a received frame is intended for LLC or SMT. This control information is contained within a field known as Frame Control, which also has the ability to specify one other source, the MAC itself. The MAC can generate MAC frames, in much the same manner as those seen in a Token Ring environment, for control and co-ordination purposes on the ring. Figure 26-1 shows the various interfaces to the MAC and highlights the different sources of SDU for transmission by the MAC.

26.1 The Token

The token is very much at the heart of FDDI operation, with possession of a usable token being essential in order to transmit frames queued by the MAC. The token is circulated continuously on the ring, but in variance to Token Ring, each circulation is timed in order to determine its usability. As no Active Monitor exists in an FDDI environment, a mechanism is required to establish which station is responsible for placing the first token on the ring. This is determined by a Claim Token[2] process each and every time a device inserts into the ring, after which every device is responsible for the well being of the token.

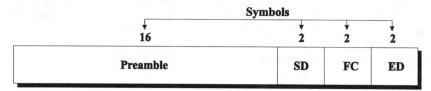

Figure 26-2:   Token Format

The token, shown in figure 26-2, is always preceded by a preamble of a minimum of 16 symbols. These are Idle (I) symbols that produce an alternating signal pattern ideal to establish synchronization. The preamble also allows receiving devices to make best use of their elasticity buffers, by using the preamble, rather than useful data, to drop symbols in the event of buffer overrun. You will notice that field sizes are defined in terms of the number of symbols, rather than number of octets. This is the case for all definitions within FDDI, and will remain consistent throughout subsequent diagrams. The remaining fields within the token format are described below:

26.1.1   Start Delimiter (SD)

The Start Delimiter (SD) consists of a JK symbol sequence that is not reproduced at any other point in normal transmission and thus makes an ideal and uniquely

---

[2] Claim Token is discussed in section 27.4

Media Access Control (MAC)

identifiable sequence for indicating the start of tokens and frames. Neither the J nor K symbols are used at any other point in normal transmissions.

26.1.2 Frame Control (FC) Field

The Frame Control (FC) field is represented as a single octet and as such is submitted for transmission as 2 symbols. The field however has bit level significance with identification between SMT, MAC, and LLC frames, as well as distinguishing between restricted[3] and non-restricted tokens. At the MAC level the FC field bit significance is shown in figure 26-3 and described in table 26-1.

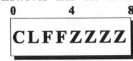

Figure 26-3: Frame Control Field

Table 26-1: Frame Control Field Definition

CL	FF	ZZZZ	Description
0x	00	0000	Void Frame
10	00	0000	Non-restricted Token
11	00	0000	Restricted Token
0L	00	0001 to 1111	SMT Frame
1L	00	0001 to 1111	MAC Frame
CL	01	r000 to r111	LLC Frame
CL	10	r000 to r111	Reserved for Implementation Specific Requirement
CL	11	rrrr	Reserved
KEY:		C = Class (0 = asynchronous, 1 = synchronous[4])	
		L = Address Length (0 = 16 Bit, 1 = 48 Bit)	
		x = 0 or 1 - not specific	
		r = reserved	

It can be seen from the table above that the Frame Control field is multi-functional, in that it provides the receiving station with information about what follows this field. In terms of MAC and SMT frames it can distinguish between 16 types of each, as well as accommodating 8 different priority levels of LLC data.

26.1.3 End Delimiter (ED)

The End Delimiter for a Token is represented by a pair of T symbols which, much like the SD, is unique and an easily identifiable sequence. The ED is important within a token, as without it the token would be deemed invalid.

26.2 Frame Format

The frame format for FDDI, shown in figure 26-4, is also preceded by a minimum of 16 Idle (I) symbols in the form of a preamble, again for the same purposes of synchronization and elasticity buffer operation. Specified in symbols, the minimum frame size is 28 symbols (if 16 bit addressing is employed), while the

---

[3] Restricted and Non-restricted tokens are discussed in section 27.3.
[4] Class of service is discussed in section 27.1.

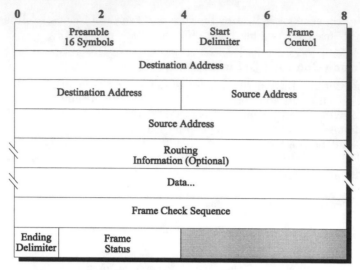

Figure 26-4:   FDDI Frame Format

maximum is equal to 9000 symbols (equating to 4.5kB). The only variable length field within the frame is the Data field which can be as small as 0 symbols or as large as 8956 symbols. All other fields are fixed in size as shown in the diagram.

26.2.1   Preamble

The Preamble is, as with the token, a minimum of 16 Idle (I) symbols, allowing line synchronization and elasticity buffer operation to be established.

26.2.2   Start Delimiter (SD)

Again, the same as the Token, with the JK combination producing a bit pattern that can be unambiguously recognized at any point within the data stream, without the need to reference symbol boundaries.

26.2.3   Frame Control (FC)

The Frame Control field has bit level significance, and is described in detail in section 26.1.2. Within a frame it distinguishes between frames generated by the MAC, SMT, or passed down from LLC.

26.2.4   Destination Address (DA)

This field contains the Data Link address of the MAC entity that is the intended recipient of the frame. The format is exactly the same as with other LAN technologies such as Ethernet and Token Ring. In line with these technologies, 16 or 48 bit addressing is accommodated, with 48 bit being the predominant format. The length of the address field is indicated by the L indicator within the FC field. This field can legitimately contain either a unicast[5] , multicast or broadcast address.

---

[5] Address types are covered in section 26.3.

26.2.5 Source Address (SA)

This field indicates the address of the MAC entity that originated the frame. The first bit of the field is known as the Routing Information Indicator (RII) and when set to 1_2, indicates the presence of a Routing Information (RI) field immediately after the Source Address field. The Source Address field can only contain unicast addresses, any other form of address would not only be physically impossible, but would be an indication of a fault.

26.2.6 Routing Information (RI)

This field is optional and only exists if the Source Route Bridging protocol is operational on the network. For a full discussion of source route bridging and the format of this field see the Token Ring section, chapter 20.

26.2.7 Data

The Data field contains the SDU as passed by the LLC, SMT, or generated by the MAC itself. It is variable in length and can be as small as 0 symbols, or extend up to 8060 symbols.

26.2.8 Frame Check Sequence (FCS)

The Frame Check Sequence (FCS) is 8 symbols in length and is used to provide rudimentary error checking at the MAC level. The 32 bit (4 octet) field is actually a Cyclic Redundancy Check (CRC) computed over the entire frame, but excluding Start/End Delimiters and the Frame Status Field. This value is then calculated and encoded using the following generating polynomial:

$$G(x)=x^{32}+x^{26}+x^{23}+x^{22}+x^{16}+x^{12}+x^{11}+x^{10}+x^8+x^7+x^5+x^4+x^2+x+1$$

Stations transmitting frames calculate the Frame Check Sequence and place the CRC value calculated in the FCS field of the frame. This field is then transmitted *Most Significant Bit* (MSB) first. On reception, stations receiving the frame perform a similar calculation as the frame arrives, and then compare the newly computed value with that of the FCS received. By using a 32 bit CRC, it has been calculated that the chances of not detecting bad data as it is received are reduced to 2^{32-1} (or 4.3 billion) to 1.

26.2.9 Ending Delimiter (ED)

The End Delimiter for a frame differs from that of a token in that it is a single T symbol rather than two successive T symbols. Frames are only considered valid if a legitimate end delimiter is received.

26.2.10 Frame Status (FS)

The Frame Status field is an arbitrary number of R and S control indicators used to indicate specific events. Three control indicators are mandatory, the Error Detected (E), Address Recognized (A), and Frame Copied (C). Each is transmitted as an R symbol by the originating station and changed to an S symbol, if applicable, by subsequent stations on the ring. The use of other control indicators is implementation specific and is not defined in the standards, except that although stations may not recognize additional indicators, they must repeat them in their entirety.

26.3 FDDI Addressing

For successful delivery of data frames in a LAN environment it is important to implement an addressing scheme. This addressing occurs at the MAC level so that the destination and source addresses can be included when frames are generated. In line with other popular technologies such as Ethernet and Token Ring, FDDI addressing normally utilizes 48 bit MAC addresses. FDDI also allows 16 bit addressing and is the only common LAN technology that permits a mixture of 16 and 48 bit addressing on the same physical network. In all other respects, FDDI addressing is similar to that found in Ethernet or Token Ring networks.

26.3.1 Unicast Addresses

A Unicast address is one that denotes a specific station, and is signified by the Individual or Group (I/G) bit (the most significant bit in the address field) being transmitted as 0_2. It is important that this address is unique on the LAN, as duplicate addresses cannot be tolerated since they can cause confusion and security problems. It is therefore paramount that all stations have their own unique address.

26.3.2 Multicast Addresses

A Multicast address is used when the transmission is destined for a group of, but not all, stations. When used it allows stations in that group to all process the single frame as it passes around the ring. This provides far greater efficiency in the use of available bandwidth than addressing individual frames to each station in that group. Source stations will set the I/G bit to 1_2 to signify this frame is a Multicast and therefore destined to a group of stations. The format of the following forty seven bits will then signify which group. The use of multicasting as a means of addressing is becoming more widespread, with more and more protocols taking advantage of its efficiency. For this reason is essential for stations to support the functionality if they wish to operate in a multi-protocol environment.

26.3.3 Broadcast Addresses

A broadcast is a variation of the Multicast in that the group is all stations. It is therefore an ideal mechanism for functions that wish to simultaneously communicate information to all stations on the LAN. The broadcast address is denoted by transmitting all forty eight bits as 1_2, i.e., FF-FF-FF-FF-FF-FF in hex format.

26.4 MAC Receiver/Transmitter States

MAC operation is essentially divided into two separate but inter-dependent functional entities, the MAC receiver and the MAC transmitter. These two entities are independent and are able to communicate via signals defined by FDDI, but are implementation specific in the way they are realized within a particular device. It is important to understand that in FDDI the stations are continuously transmitting, although what they are transmitting depends on their current status; it could be their own frames, repeating another stations frames, or transmitting Idle symbols. The discussion that follows explains the different states of the MAC receiver and transmitter, and the events that cause them to change from one state to another. It also describes how the transmitter and receiver communicate, as an event in the one can cause a state change in the other.

26.4.1 MAC Receiver

In its initial state, the MAC receiver is monitoring the incoming data stream, awaiting a start delimiter which would indicate the arrival of either a frame or a token. When a J symbol arrives, the receiver signals to the transmitter that a J symbol has arrived, and then checks to establish whether it is followed by a K symbol, which would indicate a valid start delimiter. The receiver must also check that the following two symbols are valid data symbols indicating the FC field. Should either of these conditions not be met as specified, then the receiver must signal to the transmitter to strip the incoming symbols. This it can achieve easily by transmitting Idles instead of repeating.

If the frame control field indicates a token, then the receiver must check that the next two received symbols are T symbols, indicating a valid end delimiter and thus a valid token. The last part of the receiver's responsibility towards the token is to establish whether it is restricted or not, and then signal to the transmitter that a token has been received as shown in figure 26-5.

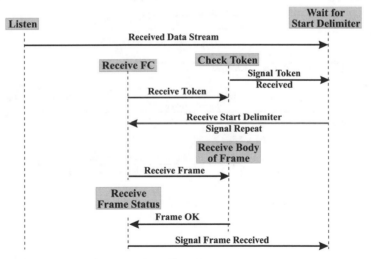

Figure 26-5:   MAC Receiver State Changes

Should the FC field indicate that a frame is being received, the receiver will check the destination address field to establish if it is the intended recipient. If the destination MAC address matches its own then it will set a flag to indicate that this frame should be copied into a receive buffer for delivery to SMT or LLC. The next check is made on the source address field to verify whether or not this station was the originator of the frame, if it matches the stations own address then the MAC receiver will immediately signal the transmitter to strip the frame by transmitting Idles.

The receiver continues to scan the rest of the frame, calculating the FCS and checking the length for validity. Failure of either of these checks would cause the receiver to set the E (error) indicator in the FS field to S (set), assuming it had been received as R (reset). If the E indicator is received already set to S then the receiver does nothing and the indicator is repeated as received. If the destination address matched the stations own address, the receiver would change the A indicator to S to indicate Address Recognized and the C indicator also representing Frame Copied. The receiver will then return to inactive state, waiting for the next start delimiter.

26.4.2 MAC Transmitter

The MAC transmitter is, in the absence of circulating frames or the token to allow transmission, transmitting Idle (I) symbols. It will always return to this state unless more gainful tasks require its attention. Once it receives a signal from the receiver that a J symbol has been received, the transmitter immediately moves to the repeat state, in which it onward repeats symbols to its downstream neighbor. If the receiver signals that a token has been received, and that it is usable, the transmitter immediately reverts back to transmitting Idles so as to strip the token from the ring, i.e. capture it ready for use.

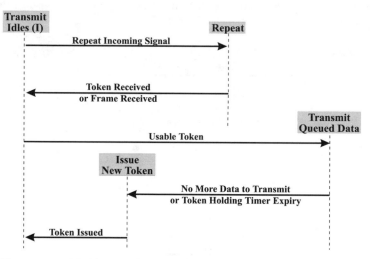

Figure 26-6: MAC Transmitter State Changes

If the token received is both valid and usable, the receiver will signal this to the transmitter, which will move to the transmit state and start transmitting queued data. The transmitter will continue to output queued data until it either has nothing left in the queue, or the token holding timer expires, whichever happens first. The duration of the token holding timer is based on the ring scheduling algorithm discussed in section 27.3. While the transmitter is transmitting its own queued data it is not repeating any incoming data from its upstream neighbor. Therefore it is actually stripping all incoming symbols from the ring. These will either be Idle symbols or the data symbols from this station's transmitted frames. Once the data queue is empty, or the token holding timer expires, the transmitter will immediately release a new token on to the ring. Upon completion of this task it will move back to idle state, transmitting Idle Symbols.

26.4.3 Runts and Other Spurious Symbols

Runts, or partial frames for want of a better term, are a fact of life on an FDDI network and are caused during normal operation. We have seen that as soon as the MAC receiver detects a JK symbol pair, it indicates to the transmitter to start repeating. This is necessary to ensure correct repeat operation on the ring. It is not until the FC field is received that the receiver is aware whether this inbound symbol stream is a token or a frame. Assuming it to be a frame, the next check is on the source address. If the receiver detects the SA matches its own address, i.e., it was the originator, it will immediately signal the transmitter to return to Idles. In doing so, the transmitter will strip the frame from the ring. However, by this time the SD, FC, DA, and SA fields have already been repeated, immediately followed by a stream of Idle symbols. This sequence is known as a runt, and is part of normal operating procedures. They do not cause any form of operational problems as they will be stripped automatically by the first device they encounter that is transmitting. All other devices they encounter prior to this will have repeated them unwittingly.

When a token is received, a transmitter will automatically begin to repeat the initial J symbol before the receiver determines that this token can be captured, at which point the transmitter will begin transmitting Idles. This leaves a spurious J symbol on the ring, followed by a sequence of Idles. Again this causes no problems as a receiver seeing the J symbol and indicating to the transmitter to repeat, will immediately spot the following I symbols and tell the transmitter to return to Idles. Other spurious and erroneous symbol sequences can occur, but are ignored by MAC receivers unless a J symbol is received, in which case it will act as described above.

26.5 Summary

In this Chapter we have examined the FDDI MAC, with particular emphasis on Token and Frame formats, describing the functions of the fields contained within. Additionally we have taken a look at the MAC receiver and transmitter, and the state changes they go through, coupled with the events that cause them. There is little difference between FDDI and Token Ring at this level, with many similarities quite noticeable. For example, the Frame Control field serves a similar purpose in both technologies, as does the Frame Status field. Start and end delimiters contain unique bit sequences in both technologies. The most startling difference is the existence of the preamble at the start of every token or frame in FDDI. As we have said, the need for synchronization, and especially the existence of an elasticity buffer within each device, make the preamble an essential part of FDDI MAC operation. In the next chapter we will explore FDDI ring operation, where the differences between the two technologies become easier to define.

FDDI Ring Operation

As we have seen thus far, FDDI has many similarities to a Token Ring network. In this chapter we will examine areas of ring operation that differ from Token Ring, and introduce more of the sophistication offered by FDDI technology. Features covered in this section include the introduction of different classes of traffic, the restriction of tokens, and the method by which the timed token protocol operates. In addition, the Claim Token and Beacon processes also differ from their Token Ring counterparts, so need some explanation to describe the method of operation.

27.1 Service Classes

FDDI introduces the concept of classes of data transfer service. Two classes are specified, Asynchronous and Synchronous. Not to be confused with the terms as used in a serial communications environment, these classes define the guarantees in place for data transfer and are described below.

27.1.1 Asynchronous Service

Asynchronous service defines dynamic bandwidth allocation, and applies to much of the data transfer that takes place over a LAN. Data is presented for transmission in a sporadic fashion, and bandwidth is allocated dynamically based on its availability. Traffic using asynchronous service is known as asynchronous data, and has to contend with all other users data on the network. A typical asynchronous profile is demonstrated in figure 27-1, where it can be seen that data is presented at random intervals in random amounts, there is often little consistency. Asynchronous traffic accounts for most, if not all, LAN traffic on most of today's FDDI networks. It should also be noted that asynchronous carries lower priority than synchronous traffic.

27.1.2 Synchronous Service

Synchronous service, and the synchronous data that uses it, is guaranteed bandwidth. A station wishing to use synchronous service requests bandwidth from the Bandwidth Allocation Manager[1] , which then allocates a percentage of the total bandwidth available. This bandwidth is then available for use on every token rotation. The idea is based on providing a guaranteed level of service to constant

---

[1] The Bandwidth Allocation Manager is a service provided by SMT and is described in chapter 28.

bit rate applications such as voice or video. Normal data applications are far too variable to take advantage of this type of service.

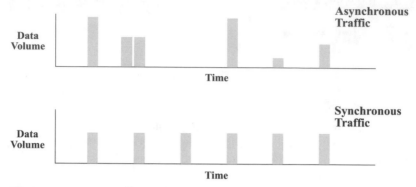

Figure 27-1:   FDDI Service Classes

A ring scheduling algorithm is used within FDDI to allow for the provision of synchronous bandwidth, while also providing bandwidth dynamically for asynchronous data. This algorithm, described below, is based on a timed token protocol, in contrast to the fixed timers used within Token Ring.

27.2 Ring Scheduling Algorithm

The ring scheduling algorithm is, as already stated, based on a timed token protocol. Each MAC maintains a timer known as the Token Rotation Timer (TRT) that records the amount of time taken for each token circulation on the ring. TRT is set in such a way that it is due to expire after a period of time known as the Target Token Rotation Time (TTRT). This second timer, TTRT, is based on a figure negotiated between all stations during ring initialization.

The concept of the protocol is essentially very simple. Tokens are deemed to be either early or late, based on the two timers mentioned above. If a token arrives before TRT reaches TTRT then it is said to be early. Early tokens can be used to transmit asynchronous and synchronous traffic. A token arriving after TRT has reached TTRT is said to be late, and can only be used to transmit synchronous data. This algorithm thereby guarantees an average rotation time equal to TTRT, and a maximum of twice TTRT, thus guaranteeing both average and maximum response times to devices (applications).

A counter, Late_Ct (Late Count), is also involved in determining whether a token is early or late. When TRT expires (TTRT seconds), the timer is reset and Late_Ct is incremented. This counter is reset each time a token arrives, whereas TRT is only reset on token arrival should the token be early. Thus establishing whether the token is early is a simple case of checking the value of Late_Ct on token arrival. If it is 0 then the token is early, if not it is late. In addition, as TRT is not reset on the arrival of a late token, the subsequent rotation has even less time to complete as TRT is left to accumulate the lateness of the token.

Late tokens can only be used to transmit synchronous data, and only for a period equal to the percentage of bandwidth allocated by the Bandwidth Allocation Manager. Therefore, if the allocation is 10% this is equal to 10% of TTRT. If TTRT is negotiated to be equal to 50ms, then synchronous data can be transmitted for a maximum period of 5ms by this device on each token rotation, early or late.

Early tokens can be used for asynchronous or synchronous data. When a token is deemed to be early, Late_Ct is cleared, TRT is reset, and the value left on TRT when the token arrives copied to a new timer, the Token Holding Timer (THT). In this way THT reflects the amount of time by which the token was early, and it also indicates the maximum amount of time for which the device can transmit asynchronous data. It is important to note that the value of THT reflects transmission time for asynchronous data. It is entirely possible that a station may have synchronous and asynchronous PDUs queued. When this occurs, the synchronous allocation is in addition to the THT period, and as these PDUs could be queued internally in any order, the MAC must be capable of stopping and starting THT while synchronous PDUs are transmitted.

In the interests of fairness to others, a limit is placed on the amount of time a station may hold on to the token. Consider this example; if a device has a 20% synchronous allocation where TTRT is equal to 50ms, it is guaranteed to hold the token for 10ms on each rotation for synchronous data. Should the token circulate the ring in only 5ms, then TRT will be equal to 45ms when the token arrives thus THT will also be equal to 45ms. In theory this means that the station will be entitled to hold the token and transmit data for 10ms + 45ms = 55ms. This would cause an unfair delay on other devices TRT timers during this circulation. Therefore a limit of TTRT has been placed on the amount of time the token can be held, in this example 50ms, after which the token must be released. Another aspect, also in the interests of fairness, is that once TRT is reset when a token arrives early, it begins retiming the next circulation immediately, without waiting for THT to expire and the token to be released. Therefore, while transmitting, a device is actually encroaching on the next token rotation time. Thus, when eventually releasing the token, it has less time to complete its rotation before being considered late on it next arrival. This provides a mechanism whereby a station with a high level of transmissions cannot constantly grab the asynchronous bandwidth to the detriment of others in a highly utilized network.

27.2.1 Asynchronous Data Priority Mechanism

A further benefit of FDDI, linked to the token holding timer, is the ability to prioritize asynchronous traffic. Eight priority levels are defined from 000_2 to 111_2, and indicated to the MAC by LLC when passing the PDU for transmission. This optional facility operates by setting thresholds on THT after which frames of lower priority levels cannot be transmitted. The idea being that as THT gets closer to expiry, only high priority frames are transmitted, with lower priority ones awaiting the next token rotation.

Figure 27-2 shows the general principles of the data priority mechanism with thresholds being passed as THT moves closer to expiry. Obviously, some thought needs to be given to threshold values, as setting them too low would cause many

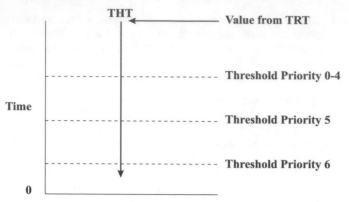

Figure 27-2: Asynchronous Data Priority

transmissions to be deferred, and could result in a station being unable to capture a token because THT is not long enough to transmit low priority frames before the low priority threshold is breached. If data priorities are not implemented, all asynchronous data can be transmitted in the order that it is queued.

27.3 Token Types

FDDI defines two types of token, Restricted and Non-restricted Tokens, only one of which may be on the ring at any one time. The different types are distinguished via the Frame Control field, where non-restricted tokens are coded 10000000_2 while restricted ones are 11000000_2.

27.3.1 Restricted Tokens

Restricted tokens are issued when a station wishes to enter into an extended dialogue with another device(s), utilizing all of the available asynchronous bandwidth. The decision to enter into this kind of dialogue is made by higher layer applications, FDDI simply provides the mechanism to make it possible. The process is initiated by the station capturing a non-restricted token, transmitting its initial dialogue data, and then releasing a restricted token. The destination device will receive the initial frames, and it too will enter restricted mode, allowing it to capture a restricted token. All other stations on the ring remain in non-restricted mode, and therefore unable to capture the restricted token. This automatically guarantees all of the asynchronous bandwidth to this dialogue session. All frames, including SMT frames, are barred from using the token unless involved in the extended dialogue. Termination of the extended dialogue session is achieved simply by releasing a non-restricted token.

Support for restricted token mode is entirely optional, however all stations, whether they support restricted mode or not, must respect the requirement not to use a restricted token. To ensure devices do not remain in restricted mode too long and thus deny access to other stations, SMT monitors the process through a negotiated maximum duration time. Should the extended dialogue exceed this duration, SMT will abort the process via its interface with the MAC.

FDDI Ring Operation

27.3.2 Non-restricted Tokens

Non-restricted tokens are essentially normal tokens available to all for the transmission of asynchronous data, within the confines of the scheduling algorithm.

27.4 Claim Token Process

The Claim Token process is used in part to determine the negotiated value of TTRT and to decide which station is responsible for releasing the token onto the ring. Claim Token occurs every time there is a change in the topology of the ring including the addition or removal of stations from the ring.

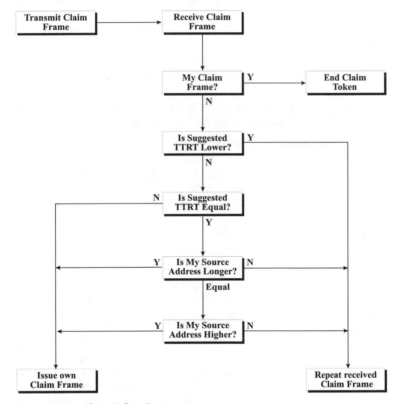

Figure 27-3: Claim Token Process

The Claim Token process is initiated when a station transmits a Claim Token MAC frame, identified by a FC field of $1L000011_2$. The transmitting station addresses the MAC frame to itself, as all other stations are required to process claim frames without regard to the destination address. Within the data field of the MAC frame, the transmitting station inserts its preferred value for TTRT. The station should then continue transmitting subsequent claim frames with no regard for the token. While transmitting, the station will monitor incoming frames, expressly looking for arriving claim frames. The Claim Token process is described below, and shown in figure 27-3.

Any station receiving a claim frame will clear its Ring_Op (Ring Operational) flag and join the claim process. Remember the primary purpose of Claim Token is to negotiate a value for TTRT and select the station to issue the first token. To do this, all stations must be participating in the process and analyze claim frames in the following manner:

> If a claim frame arrives with suggested TTRT value that is lower than the stations own, the station should copy the value to its T_neg parameter and repeat the incoming frame.

> If a claim frame arrives with a suggested TTRT value greater than its own the station should strip the incoming claim frame and continue transmitting its own.

> If a claim frame arrives with a suggested TTRT value equal to the stations own suggested value, the station will compare the source address of the inbound frame with its own address. The longer of the two addresses (16 or 48 bits) will take precedence, or the numerically greater address if the lengths are the same. The station will copy the suggested TTRT value into T_neg and repeat the frame if the inbound claim takes precedence, if not it will continue to transmit its own claim frames.

The process completes when one station receives its own claim frame, i.e., when it has traversed the entire ring. From the process described above, only one station can possibly receive its own frame back, and that is the station with the lowest suggested value for TTRT, or in the event of a tie, the longest and numerically greatest address. This station is said to have won the claim token process. You will also notice from the steps above, that during the process, all stations will have the negotiated value for TTRT stored in their T_neg parameter.

27.4.1 Ring Initialization

Once the claim token process has completed, the task of initializing the ring remains. The station that won the claim process is responsible for this, and starts by copying the new negotiated value for TTRT, currently held in T_neg to T_opr (TTRT Operational), and setting TRT to equal T_opr. Once the new timers are initiated, the station releases a non-restricted token onto the ring. When the downstream station receives the token, it too will copy T_neg to T_opr and reset TRT to the new value. It will also set Late_Ct to 1 and Ring_Op (Ring Operational) flag to indicate the operational status of the ring. Having initialized, it will repeat the token around the ring. All subsequent stations undergo the same initialization sequence until the token returns to the station that won the claim token process.

Once the token has returned to the initial station, it too will set the Ring_Op flag showing the ring to be operational, and the Late_Ct to 1. The purpose of all stations setting Late_Ct = 1 on this first rotation is so that on the second rotation, all stations will consider the token late and thus only use it for synchronous traffic. This allows unused synchronous bandwidth to be accumulated for the transmission of asynchronous data due to the token arriving very early on the third and subsequent rotations. It is not until the third rotation of the token that the ring is effectively back to "normal".

27.5 Error Recovery

The responsibility for error recovery lies with both the MAC and SMT; the MAC for ring inactivity and token errors; SMT for physical link errors affecting the device. The MAC utilizes a timer know as Timer, Valid Transmissions (TVX) to detect inactivity and lost tokens. The default value for TVX is 2.5ms, which is reset each time a valid frame or token is received. Should TVX expire, then no valid transmissions or tokens have been received in 2.5ms, causing the ring to be re-initialized. The Late_Ct counter is also used to monitor token errors, based on the guarantee by the ring scheduling algorithm that the maximum duration between token arrivals is twice TTRT. Therefore, as Late_Ct is incremented each time TRT expires, should Late_Ct = 2 then the token is assumed lost and the ring re-initialized.

When either of these events occur, the re-initialization process is based on the station entering claim token. In doing so the station will reset TRT to the maximum supported by the device and issue claim frames. If TRT should expire before the claim token process completes, then it is deemed to have failed, probably because of either an internal station fault on the ring or physical link problems.

SMT is ultimately responsible for physical link configuration, although the port is monitored at the physical level. If a port detects link failure or cable problems, it will signal to SMT that an error condition exists, and SMT will wrap the port by reconfiguring the configuration logic within the port such that it is removed from the ring. This ensures that the integrity of the ring is maintained even to the detriment of the device reporting the problem. It is possible for two cable faults to cause the ring to be segmented into two rings; under such conditions both rings will remain fully operational but separate. SMT also has the ability to signal to the MAC to enter the next stage of error recovery, the Beacon Process, a condition also entered should the claim token process fail as described above.

27.5.1 The Beacon Process

The Beacon Process is designed to signal to the other stations on the ring that a significant break has occurred, and to provide the diagnostic assistance required by SMT to recover the ring. It is initiated when a station detects the failure of the claim token process, or otherwise requested by SMT, normally due to a global reconfiguration of the ring, i.e., if a single ring is partitioned into two, or separate rings joined into a single ring. The steps involved in the beacon process are shown in figure 27-4 and described below.

When entering the beacon state, the station will transmit beacon MAC frames continuously, without regard for the token. These beacon frames are distinguished by a frame control field which is set to $1L000010_2$, and an information field of at least four octets. The first octet is used to demonstrate the beacon type, with 00_{16} indicating a failed claim token process. All stations receiving a beacon MAC frame will repeat it to its downstream neighbor until only one station on the ring is generating beacon frames, the station immediately downstream from the logical break causing the problem.

When the station downstream from a beaconing station receives the first beacon MAC frame it will reset its TRT timer. The purpose of this is that should the process not complete prior to the expiry of TRT, this station will attempt to enter claim token and remove spurious beacon frames from the ring. This overcomes the situation that the error, or break in the data path, is actually within the station that is beaconing.

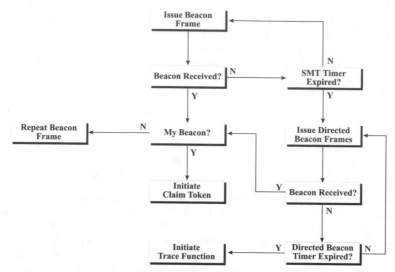

Figure 27-4:   The Beacon Process

Should a beaconing station receive its own beacon frames back, the ring has recovered, the process ends, and claim token is initiated. Failure to receive the beacon frames back indicates a more serious problem. SMT maintains a timer, default 8s, that should it expire, indicates the station is in a Stuck Beacon Condition. Once this condition is reached, SMT directs the station to send out Directed Beacon frames which indicate to all others, for management purposes, that a stuck beacon condition exists. These directed beacon frames are transmitted for a period long enough to ensure they have sufficient time to circle the entire ring, default 370ms. This period is deemed long enough to ensure smooth operation of the recovery process, allowing for the fact that interruptions may occur due to new stations destroying beacon frames as they enter the ring. Failure of the ring to recover before this period has expired leaves FDDI with only one further option to effect ring recovery, and that is to initiate the Trace Function.

27.5.2   Trace Function

The Trace Function, although controlled by SMT, consists of PHY level signalling that attempts to recover the ring from a stuck beacon condition. The purpose is to localize the fault to a single link within the fault domain. Figure 27-5 shows that the fault domain extends from the beaconing MAC to its upstream neighboring MAC. It also shows how the path between these two MACs can consist of several links, both physical and internal to concentrators. To allow fault rectification, the fault must be localized to a single link, around which the ring can wrap if necessary if recovery is not possible.

The trace function is initiated by the station in the stuck beacon condition by transmitting Master Line State (MLS) through the port that is feeding it, i.e., upstream. MLS consists of a continuous series of Q and H symbols. If the station is dual attached, these are transmitted upstream on the secondary ring, if single attached the station transmits them to the concentrator through which it is attached. Any device receiving the MLS signal that was previously active, will immediately transition to the trace state and establish what precisely was providing the input to the port on which the MLS was received. This input will either be provided by the output from a MAC, or in the case of a concentrator, the output from another port. In the case of the MAC providing the output, the trace has found its target, alternatively, if the output is caused by a port then the trace must be propagated further upstream. The ultimate target for this trace (MLS) is the MAC that is immediately upstream from the beaconing MAC, thus encompassing all possible links within the fault domain.

If a device receives the MLS that does not contain a MAC, i.e. a concentrator, it simply passes the signal on through the appropriate port. The trace signal will eventually reach the upstream MAC, which will cause its SMT to remove the station from the ring to carry out a full internal self test. In doing so, Quiet Line State (QLS) is transmitted from all ports to indicate the station is leaving the ring. This QLS signal propagates back downstream towards the MAC, initiating the trace function.

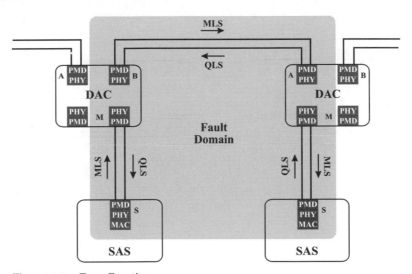

Figure 27-5:   Trace Function

Any port currently in the trace state (all ports in the fault domain) that receives the QLS signal interprets this as a completion of the trace function, and will leave the ring and carry out a full internal self test. As QLS propagates back to the station initiating the trace function, every device in the path carries out its own self test, including all concentrators. In this way, the device, station, or concentrator, or physical link, that is the root cause of the problem can be isolated, allowing the ring to recover around it. To protect against errors in propagating the trace function, SMT maintains a timer, default 7s. Should the trace function not complete before the expiry of this timer, the station will leave the ring. This allows the rest that are left on the ring to recover and re-activate the ring.

27.6 Summary

In this chapter we have discussed some of the features that sets FDDI apart from other technologies such as Ethernet and Token Ring. The support of two different classes of service, synchronous and asynchronous, allows application developers to introduce new applications with the ability to take advantage of the guaranteed bandwidth offered. Although most applications still fall into the asynchronous category, due to their variable nature, even these can have a similar facility through the use of restricted tokens on the asynchronous bandwidth. When developed, FDDI was designed to be flexible and robust. The flexibility is apparent at all levels, not least in the application support outlined above. The robustness is provided by FDDI's ability to recover from both protocol and physical errors. SMT and MAC keep close control on protocol operation, while SMT in conjunction with the PMD and PHY monitor and maintain the physical links. This is no more clearly demonstrated than the Claim Token, Beacon Process, and Trace Function series of processes designed to recover the ring from any protocol or physical error. In the next chapter we will take a closer look at SMT and the processes it uses to maintain control of the FDDI.

Station Management (SMT)

Many of the advanced features provided by FDDI, and much of the fault tolerance the technology provides, are due to the internal management capability within each FDDI device. Station Management, (SMT) as it is known, interfaces directly with all layers within the FDDI architecture, the PMD and PHY, as well as the MAC level. SMT itself is described as a set of functional parts, known as entities, that provide the control and the support for various functions operating within the FDDI layers.

28.1 SMT Architecture

SMT provides four different areas of management within an FDDI device, as shown in figure 28-1: frame based management services, Connection Management (CMT), Ring Management (RMT), and device implementation management. The first three

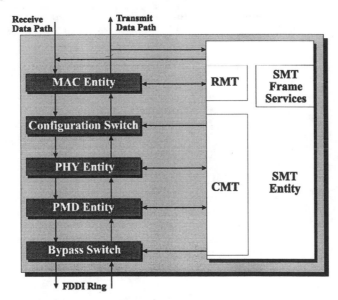

Figure 28-1:   SMT Architecture

of these are completely specified in the FDDI standards, while the fourth, device implementation management, is only outlined. The reason for this is that in some instances there are specific actions that must be performed; these are detailed in the standards, but just how the device performs these actions is implementation specific and therefore beyond the scope of the standards.

SMT interaction with other functional elements is by means of a well defined interface that allows SMT to request actions to be taken by other elements, and also allows those other elements to indicate to SMT that an event has occurred. This interface is internal to the FDDI device and not normally visible to either the user or management application, or even to standards based management such as SNMP, which would employ its own agent to run on the device with some other form of interface to SMT. The details of this interface are described in fairly abstract terms within the standard so as not to unduly constrain implementation by manufacturers.

28.2   Frame Based Management

SMT offers a series of frame based services that are used by higher level management functions to gather detailed information or to exercise control over the FDDI network. SMT requests the MAC to generate a frame based on the SDU passed to it by the SMT. This frame is generated using the standard FDDI frame format, as shown in section 26.2, with a frame control field specified by SMT and passed to the MAC along with the SDU. Two types of SMT frame exist:

SMT Information   - FC = 01000001_2
Next Station Addressing   - FC = 01001111_2

The SMT SDU is contained within the Data field of the frame. The format of the SDU, and therefore the frame data field, is shown in figure 28-2 and explained in

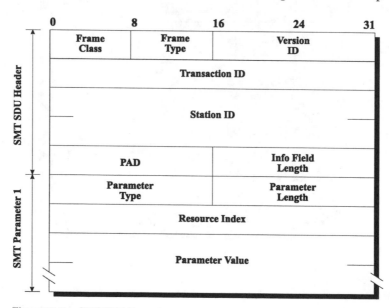

Figure 28-2:   SMT SDU Format

the text that follows. For the sake of clarity, only one SMT parameter is shown in the diagram, the reader should note however, that the SDU may have multiple parameters, in which case they will all follow one after the other in the format shown.

SMT SDU Header

Frame Class   Used to identify the function of the frame.

Frame Type   Identifies the frame as an Announcement, Request, or Response.

Version ID   Identifies the version of SMT and therefore the structure of the information field. Ensures interoperability between different implementations.

Transaction ID   A unique identifier used to match responses to requests, implementation specific.

Station ID   Used to identify the station generating the SMT frame. The six least significant octets represent the stations MAC address, the two most significant octets are free for implementation specific usage.

PAD   Aligns the SMT info field on a 32 bit boundary, transmitted as 0000_{16}.

Info Field Length   Used to indicate the length of the info field not including the SMT header. This can be variable and any value from 0-4458 octets.

SMT Information Field

The SMT information field contains a string of zero or more parameters/attributes as determined by the SMT frame class.

Parameter Type   Identifies the parameter or attribute

Parameter Length   The total combined length of the Resource Index and Parameter Value fields.

Resource Index   Only included if the Parameter Type field indicates a parameter/attribute associated with a MAC, a PATH, or a PORT, as defined within the FDDI MIB.

Parameter Value   The specific SMT information that is associated with this parameter or attribute.

Currently there are ten different frame classes defined, each specifying a different frame function. Of these ten functions, many offer different sub-types as defined by the frame type field. To uniquely identify the specific function of an SMT frame you must therefore combine the frame class and the frame type fields within the SMT PDU. Table 28-1 summarizes the SMT PDU types and specifies their requirement within an SMT implementation.

The purpose of these various SMT PDU types is to support a series of frame based protocols. Each of these protocols performs a specific service, either directly to SMT or indirectly to the performance of the FDDI. The sections that follow describe the protocols employed and specific details of the SMT frame types that are used.

Table 28-1: Summary of SMT Frames

Frame_Class	Code	Frame_Type	Requirement
Neighbor Information Frames (NIF)	01_{16}	Announcement	Optional
		Request	Mandatory
		Response	Mandatory
Configuration Status Information Frame (SIF)	02_{16}	Request	Optional
		Response	Mandatory
Operation Status Information Frame (SIF)	03_{16}	Request	Optional
		Response	Mandatory
Echo Frames (ECF)	04_{16}	Request	Optional
		Response	Mandatory
Resource Allocation Frames (RAF)	05_{16}	Announcement	Optional
		Request	Optional
		Response	Optional
Request Denied Frame (RDF)	06_{16}	Response	Mandatory
Status Report Frame (SRF)	07_{16}	Announcement	Mandatory
Get Parameter Management Frame (PMF)	08_{16}	Request	Optional
		Response	Mandatory
Set Parameter Management Frame (PMF)	09_{16}	Request	Optional
		Response	Optional
Extended Service Frame (ESF)	FF_{16}	Announcement	Optional
		Request	Optional
		Response	Optional

28.2.1 Neighbor Notification Protocol

The Neighbor Notification Protocol is used to perform three major functions. Firstly it provides the mechanism for an FDDI station to discover both its upstream and downstream neighbor's MAC addresses, which are important for fault rectification. In addition it also provides a duplicate address check mechanism when the ring is not operational (a function normally carried out by another part of SMT), and it also provides a periodic handshaking allowing for verification of MAC's transmit and receive functionality in the absence of "real" traffic.

Every 30 seconds (default period), a NIF request is generated by SMT, and transmitted by the MAC with the A and C indicators in the frame status field set to R symbols. The downstream neighbor will be the first to see this frame and will record the source address as being that of its upstream neighbor. Within an additional 30 seconds the downstream station must construct a NIF response addressed to the original station. Upon reception, the originating station can record the MAC address of its downstream neighbor. The original station can also check the status of the A indicator in the frame status field, and assuming it arrives as an R symbol, knows that no duplicate address exists on the ring.

A benefit of this protocol is that all stations can use NIF responses to generate a map of the ring, providing the ability for any station to know both upstream and downstream neighbors. NIF protocol information is shown in table 28-2.

Table 28-2: Neighbor Notification Protocol Frame Information

	MAC FC Field	Dest. Address	SMT Frame_Class	SMT Frame_Type
NIF Request	01001111	FF-FF-FF-FF-FF-FF	01_{16} (NIF)	02_{16} (Request)
NIF Response	01000001	Received SA	01_{16} (NIF)	03_{16} (Response)

28.2.2 Status Report Protocol

The Status Report Protocol is used by SMT to periodically report station status information, particularly changes in configuration and error conditions. The protocol is based on a report timer, which triggers an SRF frame if reportable information exists when it expires. The SRF frame is addressed to well known multicast address 01-80-C2-00-01-10, which allows any station configured to listen to SRFs to access the information contained within the frame. This can be particularly useful for management purposes.

Status reportable conditions and events are detailed below, while frame information is shown in table 28-3:

Conditions

Excessive Frame Error Rate - activated if the frame error ratio exceeds the threshold defined in the FDDI MIB.

Excessive Link Error Rate - activated if a port detects link errors exceeding the threshold defined in the FDDI MIB.

Duplicate Address Detected - this condition is activated if a MAC detects that its own, or its upstream neighbor's address, is a duplicate MAC address.

Peer Wrap Condition Exists - activated if a dual attached device is wrapped on its A or B port and the other end of the link is not an M port.

Not Copied Threshold Exceeded - activated when the ratio of frames not copied to those successfully copied exceeds the ratio defined in the FDDI MIB.

Elasticity Buffer Error Condition Exists - activated when a station's elasticity buffer errors exceed an implementation specific defined threshold.

Events

MAC Path Change - generated should the path through a MAC in the device change.

Port Path Change - generated should the path through a port in the device change.

MAC Neighbor Change - generated if a MAC detects a change to its upstream or downstream neighbor's address.

Undesirable Connection - generated if a port detects it has been connected to another in an undesirable fashion.

Table 28-3: Status Report Protocol Frame Information

	MAC FC Field	Dest. Address	Frame_Class	Frame_Type
SRF Announce	01000001	01-80-C2-00-01-10	07_{16} (SRF)	01_{16} (Announcement)

28.2.3 Status Information Protocol

This protocol is designed to allow FDDI stations to request status information from any other FDDI station on the ring, using a request and response type mechanism. The information required is requested using a Status Information Frame (SIF) Request, to which the destination station must respond with a SIF Response.

Status Information Frames can be subdivided into two categories; SIF Configuration frames and SIF Operation frames. SIF Configuration frames are used to carry connection and configuration parameters, while SIF Operation frames carry statistical information. Information for both frame categories is shown in table 28-4.

Table 28-4: Status Information Protocol Frame Information

	MAC FC Field	Dest. Address	Frame_Class	Frame_Type
SIF Configuration Request	01000001 or 01001111	Individual or group	02_{16} (SIF)	02_{16} (Request)
SIF Configuration Response	01000001 (SMT Info)	Received SA	02_{16} (SIF)	03_{16} (Response)
SIF Operation Request	01000001 or 01001111	Individual or group	03_{16} (SIF)	02_{16} (Request)
SIF Operation Response	01000001 (SMT Info)	Received SA	03_{16} (SIF)	03_{16} (Response)

Table 28-5 shows SMT configuration and operation parameters requested in the SIF requests outlined above.

Implementation of the SIF configuration response and the SIF operation response are mandatory on all FDDI stations, while support for SIF configuration and operation request frames are entirely optional, and dictated by the implementors. The main purpose behind the Status Information Protocol is to gather information regarding the status of the node's MAC and ports for managerial purposes. This allows SMT to provide network management with information regarding the status of any node on the ring. Utilizing this facility, network management applications can provide more in depth status monitoring over FDDI stations than with most other legacy technologies.

Table 28-5: Status Information Protocol Parameters

Configuration Response		Operation Response	
SMT Parameter Type	*Code*	*SMT Parameter Type*	*Code*
Station Descriptor	0002_{16}	Time Stamp	0004_{16}
Station State	0003_{16}	MAC Status	0009_{16}
Time Stamp	0004_{16}	Link Error Status	$000A_{16}$
Station Policies	0005_{16}	MAC Frame Counters	$000B_{16}$
Path Latency Contribution	0006_{16}	MAC Frame Not Copied Count	$000C_{16}$
MAC Neighbors	0007_{16}	MAC Priority Values	$000D_{16}$
Path Descriptor	0008_{16}	Port Elasticity Buffer Status	$000E_{16}$
SMT Supported Versions	0014_{16}	Manufacturer	$000F_{16}$
		User Data	0010_{16}
		Set Count Value	1035_{16}

28.2.4 Parameter Management Protocol

The Parameter Management Protocol is designed to allow remote management of FDDI devices via a request-response mechanism. Any attribute or parameter defined in the FDDI MIB can be subject to remote management using PMF Get Request frames or PMF Set Request frames. Any request is responded to using a PMF Get Response or PMF Set Response frame. The Parameter Management Protocol allows a certain amount of access control through an authorization parameter which is implementation specific, so therefore varies from one implementation to another. If implemented, an access control policy defined by the responder may allow or deny access based on certain criteria, again implementor defined. If no access control policy is defined, then the responder should carry out the requested action without regard for the authorization parameter.

Table 28-6 shows more detail on the Parameter Management frame information, whilst table 28-7 specifies the actual parameters used.

Table 28-6: Parameter Management Protocol Frame Information

	MAC FC Field	*Dest. Address*	*Frame_Class*	*Frame_Type*
PMF Get Request	01000001 or 01001111	Individual or group	08_{16} (PMF)	02_{16} (Request)
PMF Get Response	01000001 (SMT Info)	Received SA	08_{16} (PMF)	03_{16} (Response)
PMF Set Request	01000001 (SMT Info)	Individual	09_{16} (PMF)	02_{16} (Request)
PMF Set Response	01000001 (SMT Info)	Received SA	09_{16} (PMF)	03_{16} (Response)

Table 28-7: Parameter Management Protocol Parameters

Get Request		Get Response	
SMT Parameter Type	*Code*	*SMT Parameter Type*	*Code*
Get Parameter	FDDI MIB Object	Reason Code	0012_{16}
		Message Time Stamp	1033_{16}
		Set Count Value	1035_{16}
		Last Set Station ID	1036_{16}
		Get Parameters	FDDI MIB Objects
Authorization	0021_{16}	Reason Code	0012_{16}
Set Count Value	1035_{16}	Message Time Stamp	1033_{16}
Set Parameters	FDDI MIB Object	Set Count Value	1035_{16}
		Last Set Station ID	1036_{16}
		Set Parameters	FDDI MIB Objects

28.2.5 Echo Protocol

The Echo Protocol provides a simple SMT to SMT loop back testing facility on the FDDI ring. An FDDI station initiates an Echo Request frame, which can be any size up to the SMT maximum frame size of 4458 octets. A station receiving an Echo Request must reply with an Echo Response frame, which includes the information field from the request. This request-response mechanism is demonstrated in the frame information shown in table 28-8.

Table 28-8: Echo Protocol Frame Information

	MAC FC Field		*Dest. Address*	*SMT Frame_Class*	*SMT Frame_Type*
Echo Request	01000001	or	Individual or	04_{16} (Echo)	02_{16} (Request)
	01001111		Group		
Echo Response	01000001		Received SA	04_{16} (Echo)	03_{16} (Response)
	(SMT Info)				

28.2.6 Resource Allocation Protocol

The Resource Allocation Protocol is a frame based service designed to support the allocation of synchronous bandwidth, and ongoing monitoring, to ensure that over allocation does not occur, i.e., if two rings join to form one. In essence, the protocol provides three key functions; managing the allocation of synchronous bandwidth, monitoring of bandwidth allocated, and recovery from instability when over subscription of available bandwidth occurs. The protocol, like many others, is based on a request and response mechanism shown in table 28-9, and uses Resource Allocation Frames (RAF) to carry the necessary parameters to establish the service. One of the primary parameters carried is a Synchronous Bandwidth Allocation (SBA) command that specifies the bandwidth allocated. Once established, the bandwidth allocation is continuously monitored via a management process within SMT that polls for information from the participating stations.

Table 28-9: Resource Allocation Protocol Frame Information

	MAC FC Field	Dest. Address	SMT Frame_Class	SMT Frame_Type
RAF Request	01000001 (SMT Info)	Individual or Group	05_{16} (RAF)	02_{16} (Request)
RAF Response	01000001 (SMT Info)	Received SA	05_{16} (RAF)	03_{16} (Response)

Table 28-10 shows the parameters used by the Resource Allocation Protocol.

Table 28-10: Resource Allocation Protocol Parameters

RAF Request SMT Parameter Type	Code	RAF Response SMT Parameter Type	Code
Synchronous Bandwidth Resource	0015_{16}	Synchronous Bandwidth Resource	0015_{16}
SBA Command	0016_{16}	SBA Command	0016_{16}
Path Index	$320B_{16}$	Reason Code	0012_{16}
SBA Payload Request	0017_{16}	Path Index	$320B_{16}$
SBA Overhead Request	0018_{16}	Current Payload	$320F_{16}$
Current Payload	$320F_{16}$	Current Overhead	3210_{16}
Current Overhead	3210_{16}	Allocation Address (Usually SA)	0019_{16}
Allocation Address (Usually SA)	0019_{10}	Category of Allocation	$001A_{16}$
Category of Allocation	$001A_{16}$	SBA Remaining	$001D_{16}$
Maximum TTRT Value for Source	$001B_{16}$		
Minimum Segment Size for Source	$001C_{16}$		

28.2.7 Extended Frame Services Protocol

The Extended Frame Service (EFS) is designed for extending the range of services provided by SMT. This is a request and response type protocol, in which frames can be either Request, Response, or Announcement, as shown in table 28-11. Each service as it comes along is assigned a unique identifier (ESF_ID) which is defined by the IEEE. This identifier will then be included in all service frames to uniquely identify the service. Recipients are not required to support all service types, implementation is entirely optional. However, should ESF frames generally, or a particular service, not be supported by a recipient then it must ignore the request.

Table 28-11: Extended Frame Services Protocol Frame Information

	MAC FC Field	Dest. Address	SMT Frame_Class	SMT Frame_Type
ESF Announcement	01000001 or 01001111	Individual or Group	FF_{16} (ESF)	01_{16} (Announcement)
ESF Request	01000001 or 01001111	Individual or Group	FF_{16} (ESF)	02_{16} (Request)
RAF Response	01000001 or 01001111	Individual or Group	FF_{16} (ESF)	03_{16} (Response)

28.3 Connection Management

SMT Connection Management provides control of both internal configuration and external connectivity to other devices.

The primary areas of responsibility for Connection Management include:

- Initialization of physical connections
- Connection continuity testing
- Establishing local loop with neighboring MAC
- Control of optical bypass switch
- Detecting and reconfiguring around fault conditions
- Testing link confidence
- Continual monitoring of link quality
- Support for line states for maintenance purposes
- Support of the trace function

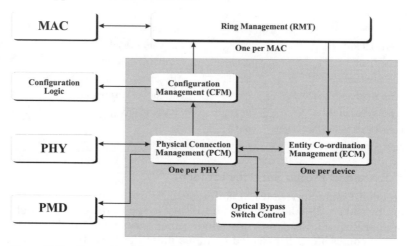

Figure 28-3:   Connection Management

Connection Management is itself subdivided into three key areas: Entity Co-ordination Management (ECM), Physical Connection Management (PCM), and Configuration Management (CFM).   ECM co-ordinates the activity of ports associated with a physical connection, and is found as a single instance per FDDI node.   PCM is responsible for the physical connection between a port and its neighboring FDDI node, and as such there is one instance of PCM per port on an FDDI node. CFM provides management of the configuration of both MAC and port entities within the FDDI node. There is one instance of CFM per node.

28.3.1   Entity Co-ordination Management (ECM)

Entity Co-ordination Management (ECM) is responsible for responding to SMT connect and disconnect requests, and starting/stopping PCM entities corresponding to each port as required. As such, the ECM becomes responsible for the control of the optional Optical Bypass Relay (OBR), and the co-ordination of the trace function. This includes the propagation and termination of the trace signal, as well as the initiation of the path test required, once the trace has completed, to locate potential internal faults.

The path test is also conducted during station initialization, prior to the ECM starting the PCM.

28.3.2   Physical Connection Management (PCM)

Physical Connection Management (PCM) includes all the signalling necessary to initialize connections, withhold invalid connections, and support required maintenance. In section 24.5.5 we saw that there are many possible combinations of port connectivity, some valid, some invalid. Table 28-12 shows a complete connection matrix for all combinations of two ports, whether they be A, B, S, or M ports.

Table 28-12: Port Connectivity Matrix

Local Port	Remote Port			
	A	*B*	*M*	*S*
A	U	V	W	U
B	V	U	W	U
M	V	V	I	V
S	U	U	V	V

V - A valid connection

U - A valid but undesirable connection, notification to SMT required

I - An invalid connection, notification to SMT required

W - A valid connection but wrapping would occur on the A or B port - B would take preference

You will note that some connections, while valid, are marked as undesirable and require notification to SMT. An example would be connecting an A port to another A port. This would create twisted primary and secondary rings, a condition that would be detrimental to correct ring operation.

Connection Initialization is one of PCM's primary responsibilities, and extensive use of PHY line states enables PCM to signal to and receive information from its peer PCM. Information required includes; port type, link confidence testing information, MAC local loop test requirements, and configuration information for the local port. The purpose is to ensure that the physical link is valid, and that the physical error rate on the link is within acceptable limits.

The initialization sequence is started by ECM generating a signal to PCM to indicate that the medium itself is available. This PC_Start signal forces PCM to enter what is known as the Break state, where Quiet Line State (QLS) signals are transmitted to the peer PCM. Reception of these QLS signals will then force the peer PCM into the Break state also. QLS is transmitted for sufficient time to ensure Break state is entered by the PCM entities at both ends of the link, default 5ms. Reception of either QLS or HLS (Halt Line State) at the end of this period will make the PCM enter the next phase, the Connect state.

In the Connect state, the primary aim is to allow the remote PCM to retrieve clocking information from this node. This is achieved via the transmission of HLS signals for a default period of 480ns. The peer PCM can derive a clock signal from the transmission signal received. At the end of the default period, reception of HLS causes PCM to move to the Next stage. At this stage the PCM has established clock synchronization with its peer PCM, but is not yet at a stage where SMT can include the link within the FDDI ring. First, port connectivity and link confidence must be verified. To achieve this, PCM will signal 10 bits to its peer, using HLS to represent a 1_2 and MLS (Master Line State) to represent 0_2. The 10 bits, their meanings and values are shown in Table 28-13 below.

Table 28-13: Initialization Bit Sequence

Bit	Name	Description
0	Escape Bit	Always transmitted as 0_2 in current SMT standard; allows for future development of the standard.
1 & 2	Port Type	Used to indicate the local port type Bit 1 Bit 2 Type A 0 0 Type B 0 1 Type S 1 0 Type M 1 1
3	Compatibility Flag	Set to 1_2 if local compatibility rules allow the connection based on the transmitted and received values of bits 1 & 2. The connection is allowed when either the transmitted or the received Compatibility Flag is set.
4 & 5	Link confidence test duration	Used to indicate the duration of the link confidence test Bit 4 Bit 5 Short (default 50ms) 0 0 Medium (default 500ms) 0 1 Long (default 5s) 1 0 Extended (default 50s) 1 1
6	MAC available for LCT	If set to 1_2, the local MAC will be made available for the Link Confidence Test (LCT). Should a MAC not be available at the other end, this local MAC can optionally source PDUs for the LCT. If no PDUs are available, any sequence of Idle Line State (ILS) or Active Line State (ALS) symbols can be used. If set to 0_2, or there is no MAC available at either end, both ends transmit ILS for the LCT.
7	LCT Fail Flag	Normally 0_2, this flag is set to 1_2 by SMT if it considers LCT to have failed. If received by either end of the link, the link is restarted and a longer duration for LCT is used.
8	MAC for Local Loop	Used to indicate whether a MAC is available for a local loop test.
9	MAC output on Port	Indicates whether a MAC output will be connected to the PHY that is associated with this port once initialization is complete.

Once the PHY to PHY signalling is complete, SMT will issue a PC_Join signal to PCM. This will cause PCM to move to the next state, the Join state. In this state

PCM transmits HLS to indicate to the peer PCM that the signalling process has completed. After a default period (50μs) PCM moves to the Verify state.

The main purpose of the Verify state is to check that the just received HLS does actually indicate that inclusion within the FDDI ring is imminent. In this condition, PCM transmits MLS for a default period of 50μs. Having transmitted (and received) MLS for this period, the Active state is finally entered. This is the last stage before the link is actually available for data transfer. In the Active state, PCM will transmit (and receive) ILS for a period of 50μs. Once completed, PCM will issue a CF_Join signal to CFM to complete the process and have this link included within the ring.

28.3.3   Configuration Management (CFM)

Configuration Management (CFM) is primarily responsible for performing PHY and MAC interconnection to allow port configuration within the node. It makes use of implementation specific internal data paths to interconnect the PHYs and MACs. These paths are specified by SMT as the primary path, the secondary path, and local paths. The primary path is the internal path through which the primary ring would interconnect, and likewise the secondary path performs the same function for the secondary ring. Local paths, on the other hand, are not part of either the primary or secondary rings, but segments of other rings that may pass through the station on occasion, e.g., to connect a MAC to a port for a Link Confidence Test.

Connections within the device are established via the use of Configuration Control Elements (CCEs). Each CCE provides a link between the port of MAC to which it is associated, and the primary, secondary, or local path in order to provide the configuration required. In normal operation, a dual attached station operates with the primary ring being received on the A port and transmitted on the B port, and the secondary ring being received on the B port and transmitted on the A port. In this condition the device is said to be in a through ("thru") condition, while should it wrap then the condition is reported as wrap_a or wrap_b depending upon the port on which the device wrapped. Most FDDI management tools provide information to show the state of the device configuration, and often display this state in the native terms just specified.

One other important function provided by CFM is the provision of the Scrub Function, designed to remove PDUs generated by MACs that are no longer part of the data path. It is possible these MACs have been removed by a network topology change or internal action taken by the device. The Scrub Function guarantees that all PDUs currently on the data path (ring) have been created since the last reconfiguration. The precise implementation of the Scrub Function is implementation specific, as with much in FDDI, but there are, however, a number of mechanisms that can be used.

- Continual transmission, for a sufficient amount of time, of claim or beacon MAC frames.

- Continual transmission of ILS for sufficient time to remove old PDUs.

- Removal of PDUs originated by MACs which are no longer part of the ring.

The first two of these methods effectively block the data path, thus stripping the unwanted PDUs from the ring. The third may only be performed by the station containing the MAC, which simply strips the PDUs from the ring.

28.4 Ring Management

Ring Management (RMT) is responsible for correct ring operation, participating in error recovery when a Stuck Beacon condition occurs, detection of duplicate addresses, and ongoing monitoring of restricted token dialogues. Each of these is discussed below.

28.4.1 Duplicate Address Detection

RMT is responsible for detecting duplicate addresses on the ring that may prevent correct ring recovery. Any of the following could be used as evidence that a duplicate address exists:

- Receiving a Beacon frame with a source address equal to its own while being in the claim state for more than double the maximum ring latency. The duplicate is therefore beaconing.

- The reverse of above, receiving a claim frame with a source address equal to its own while being in a beaconing state for more than twice the maximum ring latency. The duplicate has entered the claim state.

- Receiving a claim frame with a source address equal to its own having not been in a claim or beaconing state for than twice the maximum ring latency. This indicates the duplicate has continued claiming while the local MAC has issued a token.

Should a duplicate be detected, FDDI does not require the detecting station to remove itself from the ring, as with some other technologies, merely that RMT takes action to ensure the ring remains operational. This may involve one of the following:

- Remove all frames with a source address equal to the duplicate address, then change the local MAC address to a unique universally administered address.

- Remove the duplicate MAC via the use of SMT frame based services.

The only safe way is to remove the duplication, which can be achieved via either method, although it is unlikely that the local MAC will have an alternate address to change to.

28.4.2 Stuck Beacon Recovery (Trace Initiation)

As we have already seen in previous sections, the beacon process is initiated when a MAC detects the failure of the claim process. During this beacon process, all stations enter a repeat mode with the sole aim of attempting the resolve errors in the data path and restore the ring to an operational state.

A flag, Ring_OP, is used by RMT to demonstrate when the ring is operational. This flag is automatically reset by the MAC when claim token is entered, and therefore RMT is aware that the ring is in a non-operational state and error recovery is under way. If this condition exists for a period in excess of 1s, RMT changes to a Detect state to monitor for duplicate addresses or a stuck beacon, either of which would prevent ring recovery.

28.5 Summary

Station Management (SMT) is a complex entity within each device, and consists of three main areas and responsibilities. Frame based services provide detailed status information and allows SMT to exercise control over the network, Connection Management (CMT) provides internal configuration and external connectivity, while Ring Management (RMT) is used to control potential fault conditions on the FDDI. SMT is in effect the "brains" behind FDDI that allows for the sophistication and fault tolerant options that this technology provides.

Bridging
in FDDI
Networks

Traditionally, FDDI has been widely deployed as a high speed backbone technology used to interconnect lower speed LANs such as Ethernet 10BaseX. This allowed network designers to maximize the available bandwidth to users by minimizing potential traffic bottlenecks on the main transition route, the network backbone.

In the early days of FDDI deployment there was no official standardized approach to FDDI bridging and a number of issues needed to be overcome to successfully establish communications links. Consider the network layout shown

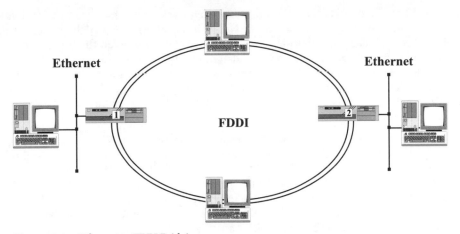

Figure 29-1:   Ethernet to FDDI Bridging

in figure 29-1. Here we see two Ethernet networks interconnected with an FDDI backbone using Ethernet to FDDI bridges. The diagram also shows both Ethernet and FDDI attached stations. Many issues exist in establishing communications across the LAN, as detailed below:

- Ethernet and FDDI networks each have different maximum frame sizes, namely 1518 and 4500 octets, respectively.

- Ethernet and FDDI each transmit data in different orders, Ethernet transmits least significant bit first (non-canonical), while FDDI transmits most significant bit first (canonical).

- How does the FDDI LAN deal with the A and C indicators in a frame originating from the Ethernet?

- If a frame originates from the Ethernet side of the network, what device is responsible for stripping it from the FDDI LAN?

- How does a bridge deal with an Ethernet frame in order to successfully transmit it over an FDDI network?

Obviously these issues needed to be overcome to allow any form of interconnection between Ethernet networks and FDDI.

Early products adopted a technique known as Encapsulation Bridging to overcome some of the problems outlined above. Although relatively successful, some issues remained, not least the fact that Ethernet stations were unable to communicate with their FDDI counterparts. This meant that the FDDI could only be used as a high speed highway between Ethernet LANs. A later technique, and one that overcomes this problem, is known as Translational Bridging, and this is the method that is widely adopted today when bridging between different LAN technologies.

29.1 Encapsulation Bridging

As already mentioned, Translational Bridging was the first type of bridging available for interconnecting access LANs such as Ethernet via high speed FDDI. This method is based on Ethernet to FDDI bridging, and involved the bridges taking the Ethernet frame transmitted by the end station and encapsulating the entire thing within the data field of an FDDI frame before it was forwarded across the FDDI network. The far end bridge would then de-encapsulate the Ethernet frame and forward it to its local Ethernet segment. This method of operation is shown in figure 29-2 and described in more detail below.

In the example shown, Node X is transmitting to Node Y, both on separate Ethernet segments linked via an FDDI backbone. Node X would transmit the frame locally in the normal fashion for an Ethernet network. Due to the broadcast nature of Ethernet, Bridge 1 will automatically receive the frame, and will have to decide whether to forward it or not. Encapsulation bridges typically have the ability to learn local MAC addresses on their Ethernet ports, as previously described in the Ethernet bridging section of this book. As Bridge 1 will be aware that Node Y does not reside on the same local segment it will make the decision to forward the frame. Depending on the implementation, Bridge 1 may be aware that Node Y exists on the far side of Bridge 2 or it may not. Most encapsulation bridges run proprietary protocols over the FDDI link that make the bridges aware of each other, and may or may not advertise the bridge's forwarding tables.

If the implementation supports forwarding table advertisement, Bridge 1 will create an FDDI frame addressed to Bridge 2, and encapsulate the entire Ethernet frame within the Data field. Should the implementation not support the feature then Bridge 1 will have to create a frame addressed to each bridge on the FDDI LAN as it does not know which one serves the target node. The proprietary nature of encapsulation implementations is one of its biggest disadvantages, as interoperability between vendors is nearly always impossible. Assuming only two bridges on the FDDI, Bridge 1 will address its frame to Bridge 2. As this is an FDDI frame destined to and sourced from FDDI devices, problems such as acknowledging the A and C bits and frame stripping do not arise. Bridge 2 will receive the frame, strip off the FDDI header and trailer, and transmit the original Ethernet frame over its local segment to be received by Node Y.

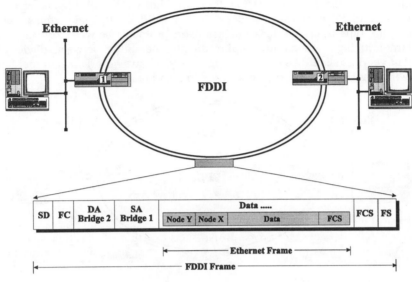

Figure 29-2:   Encapsulation Bridging

The main advantage of Encapsulation Bridging was that it functioned well and avoided many of the complications outlined at the beginning of this section. Frame size was not a problem, as these were only ever originated from an Ethernet device and would comfortably fit within the data field of an FDDI frame. In addition, there was no interaction between Ethernet and FDDI, as the latter was merely used as a relay between Ethernets. This allowed the FDDI protocol to operate independently and without complication.

The main disadvantages were two fold. Firstly, as mentioned above, these devices would operate proprietary protocols over the FDDI and would therefore not provide interoperability between vendors. Secondly, and perhaps in some ways more importantly, Ethernet devices were incapable of communicating with FDDI attached Nodes. In the early days this had not proved too significant, but as the proliferation of FDDI attached stations and servers increased this became a major issue. This issue was the biggest single reason why it became apparent that an alternative solution was required to allow full interoperability between Ethernet and FDDI devices, as well as between devices from different vendors. The technique that emerged and was finally standardized is known as Translational Bridging, which has become the *de facto* method used in all inter-technology bridging and switching implementations today. Most current vendors of internetworking equipment now support this method of bridging/switching when connecting networks of differing technologies.

29.2 Translational Bridging

Translational Bridging is exactly as the name suggests, a translation between two different technologies within the bridge such that bridging can be carried out as specified within the IEEE 802.1D standard. In other words, a bridge is expected to receive a valid Ethernet frame and produce a valid FDDI frame from it, or vice versa. This type of bridge does not use extra protocols between bridges, and as standard bridging methods are employed, interoperability between devices from different vendors should be ensured. Figure 29-3 shows how Translational Bridges can be implemented, and is then discussed in detail below.

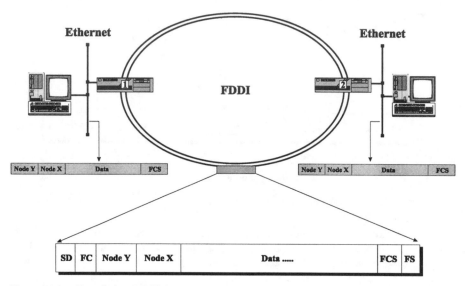

Figure 29-3:   Translational Bridging

We saw in the Ethernet bridging section how bridges learn their environment and the location of other devices in relation to themselves. Translational bridges are no different, also having the ability to autolearn the topology and location of stations. This provides the ability to forward or filter frames based on the destination address with a high degree of accuracy. This leaves the primary issue as being the translation of Ethernet frames to FDDI frames, or viceversa. The detail on how this is achieved is covered in section 29.3 for Ethernet-FDDI translation, and in section 29.4 for Token Ring-FDDI translation.

Figure 29-3 shows two Ethernet networks inter-linked via an FDDI backbone, with two Ethernet/FDDI translational bridges providing the connectivity. When Node X transmits a frame to Node Y located on the second Ethernet subnetwork, it does so by transmitting a standard Ethernet frame addressed to the other station. This will be picked up by Bridge 1, which will translate the frame to an FDDI format and forward it across the backbone. The decision to do this is based on the internal forwarding tables of Bridge 1. The frame that is forwarded on to the FDDI is a precise translation of the original Ethernet frame, and retains the addressing information, i.e., a destination address of Node Y and a source address of Node X, even though neither station exists on the FDDI subnetwork. Bridge 2 will ultimately receive the frame, and again make a decision to process it and forward it to the local Ethernet based on the destination address and the contents of its forwarding tables. As can be seen in the diagram, the frame that is forwarded is an exact match of the original Ethernet frame generated by Node X. Once the frame is forwarded by Bridge 2, its receipt by Node Y is assured.

There is still outstanding the issue of removing the locally repeated copy of the frame from the FDDI ring, in order to comply with FDDI MAC procedures. The complication is that the FDDI version of this frame does not include a source address of any device on the FDDI network, therefore normal FDDI MAC procedures, detailed earlier in this book, will not provide the functionality required to strip the frame. It is therefore necessary for the bridges to implement specific mechanisms to ensure they are able to remove frames they forward across the FDDI. The standards are less than specific on this particular issue, simply stating the requirement to strip frames rather than the precise mechanism to achieve this. This is not unreasonable, as it is entirely a local matter on the bridge and can easily be left to different implementations. Two such mechanisms exist: firstly, maintaining a database of source addresses in frames that have been transmitted; or secondly, transmitting a marker frame addressed to itself at the end of each transmission and stripping everything up to and including that marker. The first method, that of compiling a database of source addresses transmitted, would obviously require a level of processing overhead and additional memory, and would require all received frames to be checked against the database to determine whether they should be stripped or not. The second method, the marker frame, is less processor intensive and would also require less memory.

Although not common, translational bridges can, due to their rather general definition within the standards, come in a variety that supports Token Ring to FDDI translation and can therefore be used to link such networks together. In this variety, it is quite possible that source routing could be used as the bridging protocol. Another distinct advantage of translational bridges, apart from their LAN technology support, is the very fact that stations on either network type have the ability to communicate with each other, a feature not available with encapsulation bridging. A station connected to an Ethernet segment can quite easily converse with one attached to an FDDI segment if the two segments are inter-connected via a translational bridge. This is due to the fact that during the translation the addressing information remains intact, allowing the two devices to directly address each other.

29.2.1   Bit Transmission Ordering

Initially, due to the canonical and non-canonical nature of Ethernet and FDDI, respectively, the issue of bit order transmission may seem likely to cause a potential problem. Remember that Ethernet transmits its data least significant bit first, while FDDI converts Hex data into 5-bit symbols and transmits them most significant bit first. The diagram in figure 29-4 shows the functional design within a translational bridge, and from it you can clearly see that the two sides of the bridge (Ethernet and

FDDI) contain their own independent MAC. Data is passed between the MACs via the bridge relay mechanism, which operates a separate MAC service to each MAC. Frames are passed to the MAC layer as an SDU (Service Data Unit) along with the necessary addressing information to successfully transmit the frame. This SDU is passed to the MAC by the MAC service as a stream of octets in the order in which they are to be transmitted on the network.

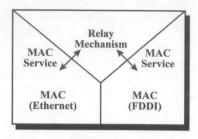

Figure 29-4: Bridge Functional Layout

29.3 Ethernet - FDDI Bridging

Before getting involved in the frame translation process it is important to understand the differences between the various frame types available in both Ethernet and FDDI networks. We have seen in earlier sections of this book that rather than just one, four possible different frame construction types exist in an Ethernet environment. Figure 29-5 shows the differences (highlighted in grey) between the frame types which are then discussed below.

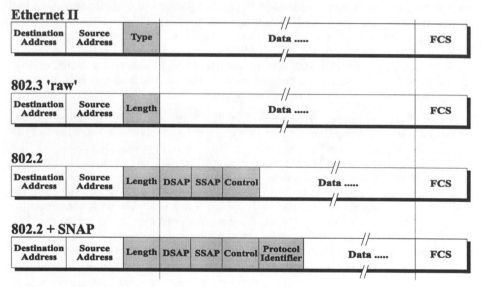

Figure 29-5: Ethernet Frame Types

Ethernet II Frame Format

Ethernet II or "DIX" Ethernet has a format that includes Destination and Source Address fields (each 6 octets in length), immediately followed by a Type field (2 octets) which contains a Type code detailing the type of data within the Data field. This type code (a full list is shown in appendix B) refers to the upper layer protocol generating the data and therefore required for processing that data at the destination device. The Data field is the only variable length field within the format, ranging from 46-1500 octets. This field is padded with null data if the actual data is less than 46 octets. A 4 octet Frame Check Sequence completes the frame for rudimentary error checking. For a full discussion of Ethernet frame formats and the fields therein see the Ethernet Section of this book.

Ethernet "Raw" Frame Type

Ethernet "raw" or 802.3 (without 802.2) is only used by Novell Netware, and then typically on implementations prior to Version 4.0 of the network operating system. It is in effect the IEEE 802.3 implementation without LLC, and as such does not truly conform to the standards. However, being quite widely implemented, it must be allowed for in a translational bridge environment. The frame differs from Ethernet II in only one respect, that of the Type field previously mentioned. With Ethernet "raw" this field denotes the Length of the Data field and not the type of data. It can therefore contain any value between 46 and 1500, or $002E_{16}$ and $05DC_{16}$ in Hex. The lack of a type field for the data does not represent a problem as Novell's IPX is the only protocol to use this frame type. Identification can be made from the fact that the first 2 octets of the data field are coded $FFFF_{16}$ which can be easily spotted by a translating bridge. Please note that IPX does not exclusively utilize Ethernet "raw" frame formats, the protocol can equally make use of the other formats (and often does).

Ethernet 802.2 Frame Format

802.2 frame format complies with the true spirit of the IEEE 802.3 standard which includes an 802.2 (LLC) header within the first part of the Data field. The name may seem confusing but is so called because of the colloquial use of 802.3 to describe Novell's proprietary implementation detailed above. As can be seen from figure 29-5, the format retains the standard address fields and the Length field described above, but also includes DSAP (Destination Service Access Point - 1 octet), SSAP (Source Service Access Point - 1 octet), and Control fields (1 octet), which form the 802.2 header. These fields are used to provide information to the receiving device as to the upper layer protocol from which the data derived. For a more detailed discussion on these fields and the operation of LLC (Logical Link Control) please refer to the LLC section.

Ethernet 802.2 + SNAP Frame Format

The 802.2 + SNAP (Sub-Network Access Protocol) builds upon the 802.2 format by adding a 5 octet protocol identifier field immediately after the 802.2 header. The idea behind this is to overcome the limitations of the 802.2 DSAP/SSAP which only allow for a maximum of 256 different protocols. In fact, the Protocol Identifier field provides a direct correlation to the Ethernet Type field in the Ethernet II format, and will normally contain exactly the same type code prefixed with 3 octets of 00_{16}.

With four different formats from which translation may need to take place, the situation is further complicated by the possibility of two different formats that are used in a FDDI environment. These are shown in figure 29-6 and described below.

FDDI 802.2 Frame Format

The FDDI 802.2 frame differs from the Ethernet 802.2 format only in respect of technological differences. That is the Ethernet header and trailer differs from the FDDI, but the 802.2 header is consistent between the two. The FDDI version contains Frame Control Field, but no Length or Type field, and also Start of Frame and End of Frame Delimiters due to the nature of FDDI. As with Ethernet, the Data field is also variable, containing up to 4478 octets.

FDDI 802.2

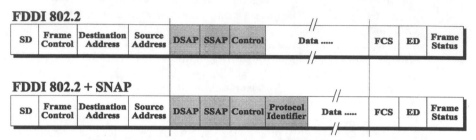

Figure 29-6: FDDI Frame Types

FDDI 802.2 + SNAP Frame Format

As with the Ethernet 802.2 with SNAP frame, the FDDI 802.2 plus SNAP version builds on the 802.2 (LLC) frame with the addition of a Protocol Identifier field. This is a 5 octet field, of which the first three octets would provide a vendor ID space for the layer three protocol (more typically the vendor ID from the first 24 bits of the MAC address), or be coded 000000_{16}. The last 2 octets would contain the protocol type information in the same fashion as the Ether-Type field in Ethernet II.

29.3.1 Ethernet to FDDI Translation

A translational bridge has to cope with the possibility of receiving any one of up to four different frame types and converting these to one of two FDDI formats for transmission on to the FDDI ring. It is therefore essential that the bridge establish

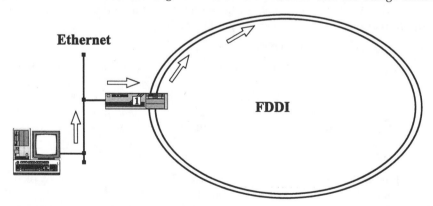

Figure 29-7: Ethernet to FDDI Translation

which of the Ethernet frame types it is receiving before deciding on the translation required. The diagram shown in figure 29-7 shows a typical scenario in which, through the paragraphs that follow, the detail of the translation process for each of the frame types encountered is discussed.

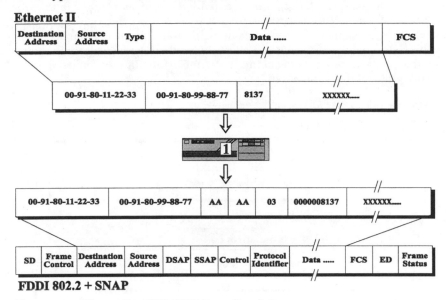

FDDI 802.2 + SNAP

Figure 29-8: Ethernet II to FDDI SNAP Frame Translation

The first process in establishing Ethernet frame type is to investigate the value of the 2 octet field immediately following the Source Address. If this value is greater than 1500 (O5DC$_{16}$) then the field must contain an Ethernet type code, as a length in excess of this value would be invalid. If this is the case and a type code is present then the frame type must be Ethernet II. If the value is less than 1500 (05DC$_{16}$) then the field represents the length of the Data field and this frame is one of the "802.3 suite". Assuming the bridge detects an Ethernet type code in this field, it will insert a SNAP header to represent this type code and format the frame into FDDI 802.2 + SNAP format. This involves removing the Type field, and adding FDDI specific fields such as the Start Delimiter, Frame Control, End Delimiter and Frame Status fields. It will then re-calculate the Frame Check Sequence and insert the new value in the FCS field. This process is shown in figure 29-8, where you will notice the DSAP and SSAP fields have been set to AA$_{16}$ and the Control to 03$_{16}$. This is standard if a SNAP header follows. The Ethernet Type field displayed shows a value of 8137$_{16}$ (Novell's IPX) which equates to 33079 in decimal. This is much larger than 1500, indicating this to be an Ethernet II frame. As also shown in the diagram, the address information fields have remained unchanged through the translation process. Once completed, the frame is ready for onward transmission over the FDDI network.

Translation of Ethernet 802.3 "Raw" frames to FDDI is a somewhat more complex issue, as the frame contains neither a Type field nor 802.2 or SNAP header information. This means that the translation bridge cannot create an FDDI frame with either 802.2 or SNAP header information. The frame that will be created is an FDDI frame containing an FDDI header and trailer plus a Data field, as shown in figure 29-9. This type of frame is, strictly speaking, invalid on an FDDI network as all frames should contain at least an 802.2 header in addition to the FDDI specific header and trailer. Problems are overcome by the bridges being able to recognize this type of frame as translated Ethernet 802.3 "Raw" and deal with it accordingly. Not all bridges support this by default, with some requiring the facility to be "enabled" through management. In effect this frame type is dealt with as a special case, due to its wide implementation in early Novell IPX environments (which is the only protocol that supports it).

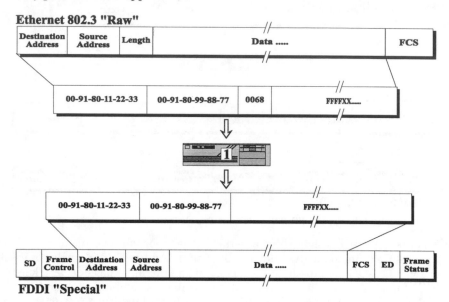

Figure 29-9: Ethernet 802.3 "Raw" to FDDI Translation

Ethernet 802.2 frames are somewhat more straightforward than either of the preceding cases, as they already contain 802.2 LLC header information, and thus require the bridge to simply convert directly from the Ethernet frame format to that of FDDI, keeping the addressing, LLC, and data information intact. This translation is shown in figure 29-10. You will notice the DSAP and SSAP fields contain the value $E0_{16}$ which is the assigned identification number for Novell IPX, indicating that to be the required protocol to process the data contained in the Data field. Identification of the frame type is solely based on the length field. As this contains a value of 0068_{16}, which is equivalent to 104 in decimal, the field displays the length of the data field and is therefore obviously part of the "802.3 suite". With this determined, the bridge simply translates the frame to FDDI format, leaving all relevant fields intact, thus a 802.2 frame in Ethernet format remains an 802.2 frame once converted to FDDI. The same process applies for Ethernet 802.2 + SNAP frame types, as the LLC and SNAP fields remain intact throughout the translation process with only the format changing from Ethernet to FDDI. This involves the removal of the length field and the introduction of the FDDI start and end of frame

Ethernet 802.2

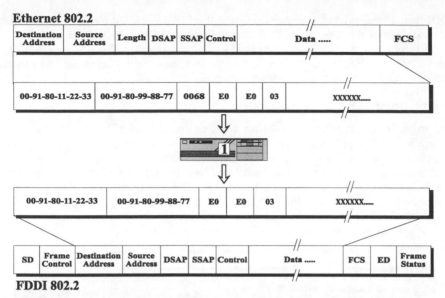

FDDI 802.2

Figure 29-10:   Ethernet 802.2 to FDDI 802.2 Frame Translation

sequences. This is demonstrated in figure 29-11, in which the DSAP and SSAP values have been set to AA_{16} to indicate that a SNAP header follows, and the Protocol Identifier field displays an organizational code of 000000_{16} followed by the type field of 8137_{16} (Novell's IPX).

It is entirely possible for a translation bridge to encounter any or all of the various Ethernet frame types, and to provide consistent translation to an acceptable

Ethernet 802.2 + SNAP

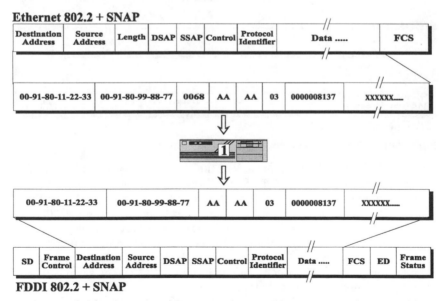

FDDI 802.2 + SNAP

Figure 29-11:   Ethernet 802.2 + SNAP to FDDI 802.2 + SNAP Frame Translation

FDDI format for onward transmission over the FDDI network. This is achieved by interrogation of the 2 octet field immediately after the source address to determine frame type. All other relevant fields are left unchanged. This may seem to be a simple process, but the complications begin to appear when bridging these frames from the FDDI back on to an Ethernet segment.

29.3.2 FDDI to Ethernet Translation

The major concern when translating a frame back from FDDI to Ethernet is to maintain the same format as the frame originated in, so as not to cause communication problems, in other words if the frame was originally generated by an Ethernet II node and was then translated to FDDI 802.2 + SNAP, it is important that it is correctly translated back to Ethernet II and not Ethernet 802.2 + SNAP. The same is true for each of the four possible Ethernet frame types from either of the two FDDI frame formats. To achieve this the bridge must follow a defined set of guidelines such that consistency is maintained, even within mixed vendor environments.

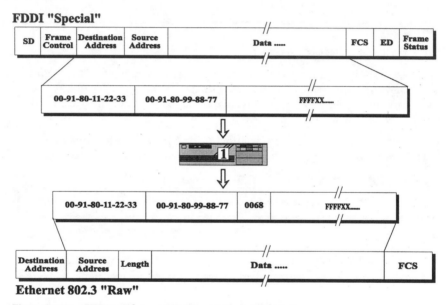

Figure 29-12: FDDI to Ethernet 802.3 "raw" Frame Translation

In this section we will examine each of the examples discussed in the previous section, and discover how the FDDI frame derived from each is translated back to its original Ethernet format by the translation bridge on the other side of the FDDI backbone. Two cases are relatively straightforward, namely Ethernet 802.3 "raw" and Ethernet 802.2. The first of these, Ethernet 802.3 "raw", as we have already said, is treated as a special case by the FDDI as it does not contain an 802.2 header. Because of this, frame recognition is simple for the bridges, and translation back to the original format can take place as shown in figure 29-12. The same is true of the Ethernet 802.2 frame. It is the only frame type that is translated in to an FDDI 802.2 frame, and therefore the bridge can easily determine the format which it must be translated back to, as is shown in figure 29-13. In either instance, as with the other frame formats, the bridge is aware that it must translate and forward the frame onto the Ethernet segment due to matching the destination address with its own internal forwarding tables.

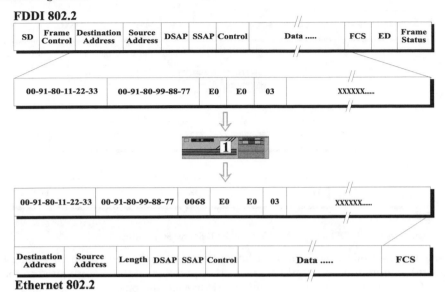

FDDI 802.2

SD	Frame Control	Destination Address	Source Address	DSAP	SSAP	Control	Data	FCS	ED	Frame Status

00-91-80-11-22-33	00-91-80-99-88-77	E0	E0	03	XXXXXX......

00-91-80-11-22-33	00-91-80-99-88-77	0068	E0	E0	03	XXXXXX......

Destination Address	Source Address	Length	DSAP	SSAP	Control	Data	FCS

Ethernet 802.2

Figure 29-13:   FDDI 802.2 to Ethernet 802.2 Frame Translation

The bridge, in order to determine whether the received FDDI frame is an 802.2 or 802.2 + SNAP frame, will interrogate the 2 octets immediately following the Source Address field. If these octets contain the values $AAAA_{16}$ then a SNAP header follows. If not, then this is an 802.2 frame (with the exception of the 802.3 "raw" special case already mentioned). If no SNAP header exists, as we have said, conversion takes place by removing the FDDI specific fields such as the SFS, EFS and Frame Control field, and adding a length field and recalculating the FCS. A problem arises however, when a SNAP field is included. Does the bridge convert the FDDI SNAP frame to Ethernet 802.2 + SNAP or does convert it to Ethernet II format?

In order to maintain the integrity of the communications link it is important that frames translated from Ethernet to FDDI and then back to Ethernet retain a consistent format on either side of the translating devices. Both Ethernet II and Ethernet 802.2 + SNAP frames are translated to FDDI 802.2 + SNAP and therefore, if these are to re-emerge on another Ethernet, must be translated back to their original format. The translating bridge must therefore make a decision as to which Ethernet format to translate back to. Most Ethernet/FDDI bridges use the following rule in order to make this decision. FDDI + SNAP frames are translated to Ethernet II unless the last 2 octets of the SNAP Protocol Identifier field are equal to $809B_{16}$ or $80F3_{16}$. These two values equate to the protocol identifier (or Ethernet type codes) of AppleTalk over Ethernet and AppleTalk ARP, respectively. These two protocols are the only ones that predominantly use the Ethernet 802.2 + SNAP frame format.

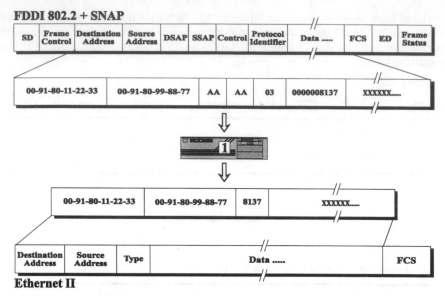

FDDI 802.2 + SNAP

SD	Frame Control	Destination Address	Source Address	DSAP	SSAP	Control	Protocol Identifier	Data	FCS	ED	Frame Status

00-91-80-11-22-33	00-91-80-99-88-77	AA	AA	03	0000008137	XXXXXX......

00-91-80-11-22-33	00-91-80-99-88-77	8137	XXXXXX......

Destination Address	Source Address	Type	Data	FCS

Ethernet II

Figure 29-14:   FDDI 802.2 + SNAP to Ethernet II Frame Translation

As Ethernet 802.2 or Ethernet II frame formats are the most favored among the network community, it is unlikely that other protocols will be configured to make use of the Ethernet 802.2 + SNAP format. However, the possibility exists and must be considered when designing Ethernet/FDDI bridged networks. Figures 29-14 and 29-15 show how the FDDI to Ethernet translation takes place for FDDI 802.2 + SNAP frames.

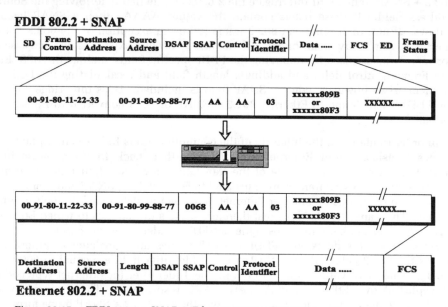

FDDI 802.2 + SNAP

SD	Frame Control	Destination Address	Source Address	DSAP	SSAP	Control	Protocol Identifier	Data	FCS	ED	Frame Status

00-91-80-11-22-33	00-91-80-99-88-77	AA	AA	03	xxxxxx809B or xxxxxx80F3	XXXXXX......

00-91-80-11-22-33	00-91-80-99-88-77	0068	AA	AA	03	xxxxxx809B or xxxxxx80F3	XXXXXX......

Destination Address	Source Address	Length	DSAP	SSAP	Control	Protocol Identifier	Data	FCS

Ethernet 802.2 + SNAP

Figure 29-15:   FDDI 802.2 + SNAP to Ethernet 802.2 + SNAP Frame Translation

Table 29-1 shows a summary of how an Ethernet/FDDI translation bridge handles frame translation between all of the various formats available. The table is constructed to portray the translations involved in a frame being generated on an Ethernet segment, being bridged onto an FDDI and then back to another Ethernet in order to reach its destination.

Table 29-1: Ethernet/FDDI Frame Translation Synopsis

Ethernet 1		FDDI Ring		Ethernet 2
Ethernet II	⇔	FDDI 802.2 + SNAP	⇔	Ethernet II
Ethernet 802.3 "raw"	⇔	FDDI "Special"	⇔	Ethernet 802.3 "raw"
Ethernet 802.2	⇔	FDDI 802.2	⇔	Ethernet 802.2
Ethernet 802.2 + SNAP *AppleTalk/AppleTalk ARP*	⇔	FDDI 802.2 + SNAP	⇔	Ethernet 802.2 + SNAP *AppleTalk/AppleTalk ARP*

29.3.3 Possible Complications

Translational bridging between Ethernet and FDDI networks has been around for many years, but still has the ability to cause problems if not carefully implemented, due to the various frame combinations that may be in existence on the network. The main complications are highlighted below, which, with sensible implementation, can be avoided.

- With most bridges on the market translating all FDDI 802.2 + SNAP frames to Ethernet II (with the exception of those where the last 2 octets of the Protocol Identifier field are equal to $809B_{16}$ or $80F3_{16}$), it is important that no other protocol is configured to use Ethernet 802.2 + SNAP frame format. Failure to adhere to this will result in frames originally generated as Ethernet 802.2 + SNAP being translated on to their destination network as Ethernet II frames, and thus result in a loss of communication.

- Care must be taken when implementing Novell File Servers as FDDI attached devices. Any FDDI directly attached device will only generate and respond to FDDI 802.2 or FDDI 802.2 + SNAP frame formats. With many early versions of the Network Operating System (NOS) defaulting to the Ethernet 802.3 "raw" format for Ethernet attached clients, this could result in a communications failure. The recommendation from Novell is to reconfigure all clients such that they use the Ethernet 802.2 frame format and avoid problems. Later versions of the NOS (version 4.0 and above) now default to this format.

- It is also possible to experience problems when routers are configured on the same ring as the bridges. It is important that the routers are configured to use both FDDI 802.2 and FDDI 802.2 + SNAP frame types if clients exist on Ethernet segments that may utilize any or all of the available Ethernet formats.

Maintaining a consistent frame format throughout the network, and being aware of the frame types generated, will help to avoid many of the potential pitfalls that can be encountered.

29.4 Token Ring - FDDI Bridging

Token Ring - FDDI translation bridges are few and far between in the networking world but they do exist, mainly within routers as a sub-function. When considering the translation process, the possibilities are somewhat fewer than in an Ethernet environment due to the frame formats that exist in Token Ring. As with FDDI, only two formats exist, Token Ring 802.2 or Token Ring 802.2 + SNAP. These of course, are the same formats that exist in an FDDI environment and therefore translation is straightforward, involving a simple replacement of the Token Ring specific fields within the frame, i.e., the Start Delimiter, Access Control, End Delimiter, and Frame Status fields. The Address and Data fields, including the 802.2 (LLC) header and SNAP header (if it exists) will remain intact. This is shown in figure 29-16, in which the SNAP specific fields are shown in grey to indicate that they may or may not exist. Obviously if they do then the DSAP and SSAP fields within the LLC header will change to AA_{16} to reflect their presence.

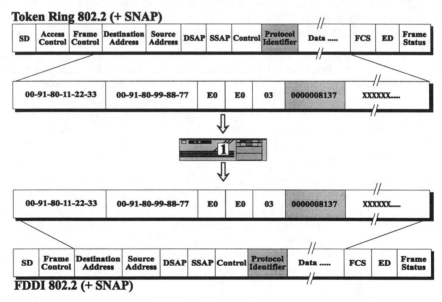

Figure 29-16:   Token Ring to FDDI Frame Translation

Care should be taken when implementing Token Ring to FDDI bridging, with regard to the maximum frame size supported by the clients on the Token Ring Network. 16Mbps Token Ring supports frames up to 17,749 octets, which is nearly four times larger than the maximum supported on FDDI. Therefore, should frames larger than the 4500 octets that FDDI supports be generated and attempt to be bridged, they will be discarded by the bridge which is unable to fragment frames at layer 2. Frame fragmentation is a layer 3 function supported by routers, and the net result will be extremely poor performance or loss of communications.

Another area to be considered is that of the bridging mechanism employed by the two networks. Most Token Ring networks employ Source Route Bridging, and while this can also be implemented on FDDI, it is not uncommon to find FDDI networks utilizing Transparent Bridging. This leaves a small matter of the Routing Information Field within the Token Ring frame, and how to handle things like route discovery and specifically routed frames. In circumstances such as these, most vendors apply the following guidelines. The bridge will contain two databases, a forwarding database as is common to all transparent bridges, and a routing information database to track routes to all known devices on the source routed network. In addition, the transparently bridged network will be assigned a ring number as if it were a source routed network. This ring number is common to the entire transparent network, such that it appears as a single ring to the source route devices. Should a source route device originate a frame to a device on the transparently bridged side of the network, the bridge will translate it, minus the RIF field, and forward it according to its forwarding database. Should that receiving device respond then it will be forwarded again by the bridge according to its forwarding database, this time however a RIF must be added to reach its destination. This RIF is compiled by the bridge from the information in its routing information database and added during the translation process. Thus the frame has the required RIF in order to traverse the source route bridged network. As implementations can vary slightly between vendors, the reader is advised to consult the implementation notes applicable to their own installation.

29.5 FDDI Switching

Switches have tended to replace bridges in all networking environments in recent years, and the same is true for FDDI. Ethernet/FDDI switches are common, and are in essence beefed up bridges designed to provide maximum throughput on each of their ports. The mechanisms involved in switching between technologies is identical to that of bridging, and is based on store and forward principles as the entire frame must be buffered in order to perform the translation process. Switching FDDI/FDDI is also a function available from some vendors providing high throughput backbone switches. In the main these devices operate using transparent bridging principles in cut-through mode, allowing the high throughput of frames necessary when switching between multiple FDDI networks. For a more detailed explanation of transparent bridging and cut-through principles, please refer to the Ethernet bridging section.

29.6 Summary

In this section we have looked at bridging in an FDDI environment, mainly with regard to bridging traffic from another technology across an FDDI backbone. Of the two methods discussed, encapsulation bridging is more historical than actual on today's networks, as the method of preference now is translational bridging. This provides the benefit of allowing devices from alternative technology networks to communicate directly with FDDI attached devices, a feature not available when using encapsulation technology. It should be remembered that when implementing translational bridges, especially in an Ethernet network, care should be taken with the frame types on either side of the bridge in order to maintain communications.

Section E

Logical Link Control ANSI/IEEE 802.2 (ISO 8802-2) The SubNetwork Access Protocol (SNAP)

Logical Link Control CHAPTER 30

When discussing network technologies, the first thing that must be realized is that there are a number of different technologies and access methods from which to choose. In this volume alone, we have discussed the CSMA/CD access method used in Ethernet and 802.3, and Token Passing methods used in Token Ring/802.5 and the Fiber Distributed Data Interface. Also recall that since the initial introduction of the 7 Layer ISO Reference Model, it has had to be refined in order to accommodate LANs. In short, since upper layer protocols must be able to be transported across any network technology, we can say that the Network Layer requires a consistent interface regardless of which MAC we decide to use. It is the task then of the Logical Link Control sub-layer to ultimately provide this consistency as figure 30-1 shows.

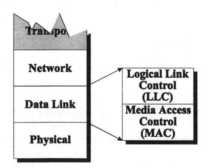

Figure 30-1: The LLC Sub-Layer

Logical Link Control (LLC) is a derivative of *High-Level Data Link Control* (HDLC) and, as its name implies, controls the link. As we saw in the early chapters, and indeed throughout this text, there are a number of different Medium Access methods. Each of these provides broadly the same functionality, in that they allow host systems to access the network medium for the purpose of data transmission. Each also has its own methodology defining whether access is by a connectionless or connection-oriented mechanism, depending upon the overall reliability required.

In addition, when looking at the data to be transferred, we see that with today's LANs there are a number of protocols that need to be transported. Hosts of the past tended to be single protocol devices, and indeed many organizations built their entire communications infrastructures on a single internetworking platform such as

TCP/IP. Today this is not the case, with companies using say TCP/IP for electronic mail and Internet access, and Novell NetWare with IPX, and/or Windows NT with NetBEUI for file transfer and printing. Now, our LANs must carry these multiple protocols seamlessly. What is more important though, our stations are now multi protocol devices that must de-multiplex data as it arrives, and pass it to the correct protocol module for processing. Thus, a method of identifying the protocol carried is of paramount importance to the correct operation of the network.

You will recall that with Ethernet the protocol identifier forms part of the header as the "Type" field, but in other technologies such as Token Ring, FDDI, and indeed 802.3, the protocol must be defined elsewhere. It is the Logical Link Control (LLC) protocol then, that is responsible for this, as indeed it can be for the establishment, maintenance, and closing of the link.

30.1 LLC PDU Structure

The LLC PDU immediately follows the MAC Header as figure 30-2 shows. Here we see the LLC PDU itself depicted as the payload of the MAC frame, which of course it is. If we then further examine this structure applying it to a technology such as say 802.3, we can see that the LLC Header could actually be considered as an extension to that of the existing MAC layer. Of course when applied to technologies such as 802.3, the LLC PDU immediately follows the *Length* field of the MAC Header. In 802.5 however, it is possible that a Routing Information Field (RIF) may be present. Where this is the case, the LLC follows the *RIF*.

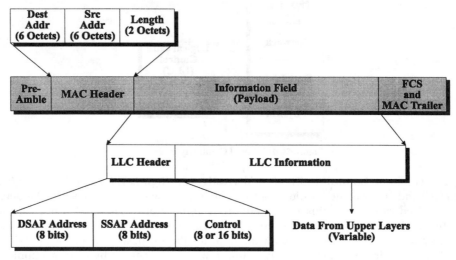

Figure 30-2:   MAC/LLC Relationship for 802.3

The headers of LLC PDUs are always sent to and received from the MAC layer least significant bit first, regardless of the underlying MAC layer itself. The *Information* field of the PDU however, is always transmitted in the order in which it was received. Thus, on receipt of a LLC PDU from the MAC layer, data will be delivered to the Network layer in the same bit order that it was received from the

MAC. Equally, data for transmission from the Network Layer will be submitted to the MAC layer in the same bit order that it was received from the Network layer.

One of the most significant things from the figure is that the LLC PDU contains no Frame Check Sequence (FCS). This in itself presents no problem, since the FCS of the entire MAC frame is used here to ensure that data arrives intact. More specifically, we see that the LLC PDU comprises 16 bits of addressing, the *DSAP* and *SSAP*[1] and 8 or 16 bits of Control information. The xSAP fields (known collectively as the *LSAP*) represent the Destination and Source *Service Access Points* respectively, i.e., an identifier for the entities on both the destination and source systems. The Control field is either 8 or 16 bits in length, and is discussed in detail in section 30.1.2. In general though, 16 bit Control fields are used in formats that include sequence numbering, while 8 bit fields are used in all other cases.

30.1.1 LLC Addressing

LLC Addressing is achieved through LSAPs. These Service Access Point addresses (DSAP and SSAP) take a similar form to those of the MAC layer, although shorter in length as figure 30-3 shows. Here we see that, just as with MAC Addresses, the Destination Address (DSAP) has an Individual or Group Address bit, used to identify whether this PDU is destined for a single Service Access Point (SAP) or a group. When this bit is set to 0, the DSAP specified is that of an individual DSAP. When this is set to 1, a group address is implied.

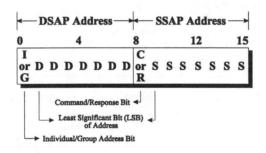

Figure 30-3:   LLC Addressing

DSAP and SSAP addresses are normally of the form X0DDDDDD and X0SSSSSS, where X is either the I/G or C/R (Command/Response) bit, and 0DDDDDD and 0SSSSSS are the actual DSAP and SSAP addresses. Addresses X1DDDDDD and X1SSSSSS are considered invalid at this time (except in the case of the global LSAP), being reserved for future definition by the ISO. In addition, a *Null* address (where all bits are set to 0), and a *Global* address (with all bits set to 1) are defined. The Global address is valid only as a DSAP, and is used to address all active DSAPs. In this, the I/G bit is set indicating that a group of DSAPs are being addressed. The Null address on the other hand can be used as either a DSAP or SSAP address, and is used to indicate that no SAPs at the Network layer are addressed.

---

[1] A Service Access Point is an address used within an OSI environment.

Table 30-1: Common LSAP Address Assignments

IEEE Administered LSAPs

Address (Hex)	Assignment
00	Null LSAP
02	Individual LLC Sub-Layer Management Function
03	Group LLC Sub-Layer Management Function
06	ARPANET Internet Protocol (IP)
0E	PROWAY (IEC 995) Network Management and Initialization
42	IEEE 802.1 Bridge Spanning Tree Protocol
4E	EIA RS-511 Manufacturing Message Protocol
7E	ISO 8208 (X.25 over IEEE 802.2 Type 2 LLC)
8E	PROWAY (IEC 955) Active Station List Maintenance
AA	Sub-Network Access Protocol (SNAP)
FE	ISO Network Layer Protocol
FF	Global LSAP

Manufacturer-Implemented LSAPs

04	IBM SNA Path Control (Individual)
05	IBM SNA Path Control (Group)
18	Texas Instruments
80	Xerox Network Systems (XNS)
86	Nestar
98	ARPANET Address Resolution Protocol (ARP)
BC	Banyan Vines
E0	Novell NetWare
F0	IBM NetBIOS
F4	IBM LAN Management (Individual)
F5	IBM LAN Management (Group)
F8	IBM Remote Program Load (RPL)
FA	Ungermann-Bass

Finally, two further addresses (01000000 and 11000000) are used to indicate the individual and group addresses, respectively, for *LLC Sub-layer Management* and an address of 01100101 is designated as the *Route Determination Entity* (RDE)[2] SAP address. Table 30-1 lists some *Well Known* LSAP Address assignments which, although not exhaustive in terms of manufacturer implemented LSAPs, does list those that are most common.

The *Command/Response* (C/R) bit in the SSAP is used to indicate how the data contained should be treated. An understanding of the various *Types* and *Classes* of LLC is required to fully appreciate how this bit is applied however, and is therefore discussed later.

30.1.2 LLC Control

The *Control* field in the LLC PDU differs depending upon which specific operation is being performed and, as we have already seen, can be either 8 or 16 bits in length. This field then yields three distinct Control field formats as shown in figure 30-4.

---

[2] The Route Determination Entity and its operation is discussed in section 30.3.

The 7 bit *N(S)* field is used as a sequence number supplied by the transmitting station and indicates the number of this PDU in modulo 128. This field is only present in *I-Format* PDUs. The 7 bit *N(R)* field is used by the receiving station for acknowledgements by indicating the sequence number of the next expected PDU (again in modulo 128). This field is present in both *I-Format* and *S-Format* PDUs. The meaning of the *P/F* (Poll/Final) bit (used in all PDUs) is dependent on whether the PDU is a Command or a Response, and is referred to as the *Poll* bit in Commands, and the *Final* bit in Responses. In essence, frames with the P bit set are used to solicit responses from the receiving LLC, which will respond with a PDU with the F bit set. Only one PDU with the Poll bit set should be outstanding in a given direction at any given time on a data link connection. A single exception to this however is where a PDU has been sent with the P bit set and no response has been received within a specified timeout period. In this instance, retransmission of the original PDU is allowed for error recovery purposes.

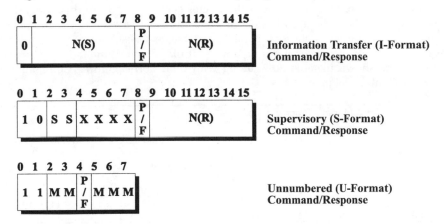

Figure 30-4:   LLC PDU Control Fields

In the S-Format PDU, the *S* bits are used to indicate the type of supervisory function. The bits marked as *X* are reserved, and must always be set to zero. Finally, for *Unnumbered* (U-Format) PDUs, the 5 *M* bits are used as Modifier bits, and describe the type of operation to be performed. The actual PDUs themselves, and how the Control field relates to them, are then described in the following sections.

30.2 Types and Classes of LLC

The IEEE 802.2 and ISO/IEC 8802-2 standards define three types of operation for data communication between Service Access Points (SAPs). *Type 1* operation is the simplest form of LLC operation and uses a Connectionless, Unacknowledged system. Any implementation that then claims conformance with the 8802-2 standard must also implement this LLC type as a minimum.

Type 2 LLC uses a Connection Oriented, Acknowledged system that requires the establishment of a *logical* connection before any data is transmitted. *Type 3* operation, which was introduced in the 1994 version of the standard, then enhances Type 1 operation by providing a Connectionless, Acknowledged system. Implementation of LLCs Type 2 and/or Type 3 is however optional.

When quoting compliance to LLC, a device will conform to one of the four possible classes defined in the 8802-2 standard. *Class I* devices support only Type 1 operation and, as stated above, this is considered to be the minimum level of conformance. *Class II* devices support both Type 1 and Type 2 operation. *Class III* devices support only connectionless operation in that they support Types 1 and 3 only. Finally, *Class IV* devices support all three types of operation.

30.2.1   Type 1 LLC

This simple type of LLC is used in technologies such as 802.3. In this system, data is exchanged without the need to establish a connection between LLCs, and only U-Format PDUs are used. Data sent using Type 1 LLC is not acknowledged, and there are no error recovery mechanisms or flow control. Three command structures are supported as shown in table 30-2, along with their corresponding Command and Response Control fields.

Table 30-2: Type 1 I-Format Protocol Data Units

Command	Response	Description	Command Control Field 11MMPMMM	Response Control Field 11MMFMMM
UI	-	Unnumbered Info.	1100P000	-
XID	XID	Exchange Id.	1111P101	1111F101
TEST	TEST	Test Frames	1100P111	1100F111

- **Unnumbered Information Frames**
  The *Unnumbered Information* Command does not require the establishment of a Data Link connection and has no associated Response. It is however this PDU that is used to transport actual data. With no Connection established, and no requirement for either Acknowledgments or Flow Control systems, Responses here would be superfluous. One obvious shortcoming of such a system though, is that data can be lost. We then rely on the upper layers of whatever protocol stack is being used to detect when this has occurred. For this type of PDU, an individual, group, global, or null address can be used as the DSAP, while the SSAP always contains the individual address of the originator. The Control field in the Command is always 1100P000.

- **Exchange Identification (XID) Frames**
  The *XID* command PDU is used to communicate the types of LLC supported, and the size of the receive window to the destination LLC. On receipt of such a frame, the target LLC then responds with similar information related to itself. The *F* bit in the Response is always set to the same state as the *P* bit in the Command. In the Command, the DSAP can be an individual, group, global, or null address, and the SSAP is always the senders' individual

address. In the Response, both the DSAP and SSAP will always be an individual or null address.

The *Information* field of the PDU is as shown in figure 30-5. Here a simple 8 bit *Format Identifier* is followed by a 16 bit Parameter field used to indicate the supported LLC services and the *Receive Window*. The Information field, in common with the preceding fields, is always transmitted Least Significant Bit (LSB) first.

The Format Identifier is always of the form 10000001_2 indicating the IEEE Basic Format. The 5 bit LLC Types/Classes field however varies depending on whether the Null LSAP is used. Table 30-3 shows valid values for the LLC Types/Classes field for differing values of LSAP.

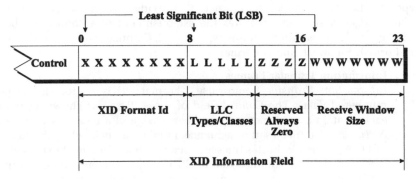

Figure 30-5:   LLC XID Information Field Format

Table 30-3: LLC Types/Classes

Null LSAP:

LLC Types/Classes Value	Type/Class Supported
10000	Class I LLC
11000	Class II LLC
10100	Class III LLC
11100	Class IV LLC

Non-Null LSAP:

10000	Type 1 LLC
01000	Type 2 LLC
00100	Type 3 LLC
11000	Type 1 and Type 2 LLCs
10100	Type 1 and Type 3 LLCs
01100	Type 2 and Type 3 LLCs
11100	Type 1, Type 2, and Type 3 LLCs

- **Test Frames**

The *Test* Command PDU is used to solicit a response (Test Response) from the target LLC, thereby checking the path between the two units. In the Command, an Information field containing arbitrary data is optional. Where present however, this should be returned intact in the corresponding

Response. It is possible that the sending unit may create a TEST PDU where the information field is longer than receiving unit is prepared to accept. In this case, a Response PDU with no Information field would also be acceptable.

For the Command, the DSAP address can be an individual, group, global, or null address, and can be used with an individual, group, or global Destination MAC Address. In responses, the F bit is always set to the same state as the P bit in the Command. The following trace shows a simple 802.2 Test exchange.

30.2.2   Type 2 LLC

Type 2 LLC is more complex since it provides for a *Connection Oriented, Acknowledged* system that requires the establishment of a connection before any real data can be transmitted. In this type of LLC, Command and Response PDUs can be I-Format, S-Format, and U-Format.

- **Information Transfer Frames**
  Information Transfer frames use I-Format PDUs to transfer sequentially numbered data. The *Control* field of these PDUs (as shown in figure 30-6) each contain a send sequence number $N(S)$, and a receive sequence number $N(R)$. $N(S)$ indicates the sequence number associated with this I-Format PDU. $N(R)$ then indicates the sequence number of the next expected I-Format PDU and therefore implies that all PDUs with sequence numbers up to (but not including this number) have been successfully received.

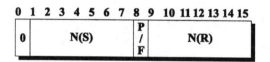

Figure 30-6:   I-Format PDU Control Field Format

The Poll/Final (*P/F*) bit is used to indicate whether this PDU contains a solicitation or a response. For example, in Command PDUs this bit is referred to as Poll (*P*), and in Response PDUs as Final (*F*). Where the F bit is set, this indicates that the PDU was sent as a result of a previous solicitation.

Only one PDU with the P bit set can be outstanding at any time. In the event that a corresponding PDU with the F bit set is not received within some timeout period however, the sending station can then re-send the original command PDU in an effort to recover from the error.

- **Supervisory Frames**
  Supervisory frames use the S-Format PDU in order to perform numbered supervisory functions. These functions include Acknowledgments, Error Recovery, and the temporary suspension of information transfer. S-Format frames never include an information field, therefore the inclusion of a send sequence number $N(S)$ is not required. These frames however need to indicate the sequence number of the next expected PDU and therefore do

include the *N(R)* field. The *Control* field for this type of frame is shown in figure 30-7. The *S* bits indicate the type of Supervisory frame as indicated by table 30-4. These S-Format PDU types are then described below:

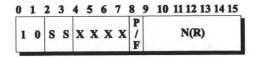

Figure 30-7: S-Format PDU Structure

Table 30-4: S bit Interpretation in S-Format PDUs

S Bits	Frame Type	Description
00	RR	Receive Ready
01	REJ	Reject
10	RNR	Receive Not Ready

- **Receive Ready (RR)**
  This type of PDU indicates that the station is ready to receive I-Format PDUs, and that all PDUs up to (but not including) that indicated by *N(R)* have been received correctly.

- **Reject (REJ)**
  The *Reject* PDU is used to request that the I-Format PDUs from *N(R)* are re-sent.

- **Receive Not Ready (RNR)**
  The *Receive Not Ready* PDU is used to temporarily suspend information transfer possibly as a result of congestion at the receiving station. These PDUs are sent to indicate that no further I-Format PDUs can be accepted, but that all PDUs up to (but not including) *N(R)* have been successfully received. Once the congestion has been cleared, a Receive Ready (RR) PDU is sent to indicate that further I-Format PDUs can now be received.

- **Unnumbered Frames**
  Unnumbered (U-Format) PDUs, when used in Type 2 operation, add further control functions by using the *M* bits of the *Control* field to indicate the function required. The Control field of U-Format PDUs, as shown in figure 30-8, have no sequence numbering associated with them (no *N(S)* or *N(R)* fields) therefore no sequence numbering is ever conveyed in these frames. The types of PDU, with their associated Control fields, when used in Type 2 LLC are shown in table 30-5.

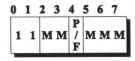

Figure 30-8: U Format Command/Response PDUs

Table 30-5: Type 2 U-Format Data Units

Command	Response	Description	Control Field
SABME	-	Set Asynch. Balanced Mode Extended	1111P110
DISC	-	Disconnect	1100P010
-	UA	Unnumbered Acknowledgement	1100F110
-	DM	Disconnect Mode	1111F000
-	FRMR	Frame Reject Response	1110F001

- **Set Asynchronous Balanced Mode Extended (SABME)**

  The *SABME* command is used to establish a connection in Asynchronous Balanced mode. An affirmative response to this is to receive an Unnumbered Acknowledgment, at which time the connection is established. No Information field (data) is ever passed during the connection establishment process (SABME/UA), and upon successful establishment, the Send and Receive sequence numbers are zeroed. As such, all outstanding I-Format PDUs remain unacknowledged. Having sent a SABME PDU, the sending station will not enter Asynchronous Balanced Mode until after the receipt of the UA PDU.

- **Disconnect (DISC)**

  The *Disconnect* PDU is sent to terminate a connection previously established with a SABME/UA sequence. The response to a Disconnect request is an Unnumbered Acknowledgment. As with connection establishment, no information field is present in either the DISC or UA PDUs, and any I-Format frames that are outstanding when the DISC PDU is issued will remain unacknowledged.

- **Unnumbered Acknowledgment (UA)**

  The *Unnumbered Acknowledgment* (UA) PDU is used to acknowledge the receipt (and acceptance) of both SABME and DISC PDUs only. As previously discussed, no information field is ever present in these PDUs.

- **Disconnect Mode (DM)**

  The *Disconnect Mode* PDU is sent to indicate a logical disconnection from the connection. In this case the system is then said to be in *Asynchronous Disconnected Mode* (ADM). No Information field is ever present in the DM PDU.

- **Frame Reject (FRMR)**

  The *Frame Reject* (FRMR) PDU is used to report that an uncorrectable error condition has occurred. Such errors are as follows:

  1. A Command or Response PDU was received that included either invalid or unsupported information. For example, a Supervisory or Unnumbered PDU might be received that contained an unsupported Information field, an unsolicited Response PDU may have been received where the *F* bit is set, or an unexpected Unnumbered Information field may have been received.

2. An I-Format PDU may have been received where the Information field exceeded the maximum amount of data that is supported for that connection.

3. A PDU was received with an invalid *N(R)* field. For example, the *N(R)* field may indicate an I-Format PDU that has previously been sent and acknowledged, or one that has either not been sent or is not the next sequential numbered PDU.

4. A PDU was received with an invalid *N(S)* field.

The FRMR PDU is only ever used in the Asynchronous Balanced Mode and, on receipt, the station will initiate any actions required such as initializing or terminating the link with SABME/DISC PDUs, etc. FRMR PDUs always contain an Information field, the format of which is shown in figure 30-9.

The 16 bit *Rejected PDU Control Field* field is the Control field taken from the PDU that caused the exception to occur. If the PDU causing the problem was a U-Format type, then the first 8 bits will contain the Control field of the rejected PDU, and bits 8 to 15 are set to zero. The 7 bit *V(S)* and *V(R)* fields contain the current values of *N(S)* and *N(R)* at the station that initiated the FRMR. The *C/R* field (1 bit) indicates whether the PDU that caused the exception was a Command or a Response. Where this bit is 0, the PDU was a Command, and where the bit is 1, it was a Response.

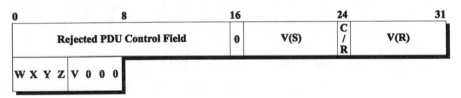

Figure 30-9: FRMR PDU Information Field Format

The five flags, *W*, *X*, *Y*, *Z*, and *V* indicate the type of error that was found and can be set either individually or in specific patterns. The *W* bit, when set, indicates that the Control field in the offending PDU (and returned in bits 0 through 15) was invalid. The *X* bit is used to indicate that the received PDU contained an Information field that was unsupported for that type of Command or Response. In this case, the *W* bit will also be set since the Control field indicates the type of PDU. When the *Y* bit is set, this indicates that the Information field received exceeded the maximum Information field length supported on the connection. Finally, the *Z* and *V* bits are used to indicate invalid values of *N(R)* and/or *N(S)*, respectively. The *N(R)* and/or *N(S)* field in error is of course returned in the Rejected PDU Control Field held in the first 16 bits.

30.2.3 Type 3 LLC

Type 3 LLC was introduced after the original edition of the 8802-2 standard. With this type of LLC, PDUs are exchanged without the need to establish a data link connection, but each command PDU is acknowledged. Only U-Format PDUs, the Control field of which is shown in figure 30-10, are used in this type of LLC.

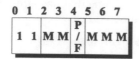

Figure 30-10: U-Format PDU as Used in Type 3 LLC

The encoding of the Control field for Type 3 LLC is listed in table 30-6, and results in a total of two commands and two responses, as described below:

Table 30-6: Type 3 U-Format Data Units

Command	Response	Description	Control Field
AC0	-	AC0 Command	1110P110
AC1	-	AC1 Command	1110P111
-	AC0	AC0 Response	1110F110
-	AC1	AC1 Response	1110F111

The receipt of an *ACn* Command always results in an acknowledgment by an *ACn* Response at the earliest opportunity. *ACn* Commands are sent with either an individual, group, or global DSAP address, and the originator's individual SSAP address. The information field will then contain either a *Link Service Data Unit* (LSDU) or will be of zero length (null). Table 30-7 describes the different functions performed by the *ACn* Commands and Responses depending on whether the information field is of zero length or contains a LSDU.

Table 30-7: Summary of Type 3 PDU Functions

	Commands			Responses	
P Bit	LSDU	Function	F Bit	LSDU	Function
0	Null	Re-Synch.	0	Null	Ack of re-synch. or ack of received data
0	Non-Null	Sending Data	0	Non-Null	Reserved (Illegal)
1	Null	Requesting Data	1	Null	Ack requested, data unavailable
1	Non-Null	Exchanging Data	1	Non-Null	Ack with requesting data

ACn Responses are used to reply to *ACn* Commands. These PDUs always contain a sub-field in the first octet of the information field as shown in figure 30-11, and may or may not also contain a LSDU. The bits in the Status Sub-field, *CCCC* and *RRRR*, reflect the success or failure of information transfer in commands and responses, respectively. These codes are then described in table 30-8.

The Category of "Success" indicates that the requested action was performed successfully. "Temporary Errors" indicate that the operation was unsuccessful, possibly due to resource exhaustion of some kind. Retrying the operation may then result in success. "Permanent Errors" are generally the result of programming or hardware errors and retrying the operation is unlikely to result in the operation being performed.

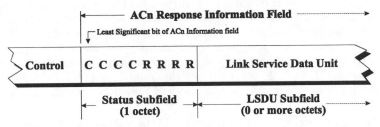

Figure 30-11: ACn Response Information Field

Table 30-8: ACn Response Status Sub-field CCCC and RRRR values

Status Subfield C Bits:

CCCC	Mnemonic	Category	Description
0000	OK	Success	Command Accepted
1000	RS	Permanent Error	Un-implemented/inactivated service
1010	UE	Permanent Error	LLC user interface error
0110	PE	Permanent Error	Protocol error
1110	IP	Permanent Error	Implementation-dependent error
1001	UN	Temporary Error	Resource temporarily unavailable
1111	IT	Temporary Error	Implementation-dependent error

Status Subfield R Bits:

RRRR	Mnemonic	Category	Description
0000	OK	Success	Response LSDU present
1000	RS	Permanent Error	Un-implemented/inactivated service
1100	NE	Permanent Error	Response LSDU never submitted
0010	NR	Success	Response LSDU not requested
1010	UE	Permanent Error	LLC user interface error
1110	IP	Permanent Error	Implementation-dependent error
1001	UN	Temporary Error	Resource temporarily unavailable
1111	IT	Temporary Error	Implementation-dependent error

Note: The *CCCC* and *RRRR* fields are represented **Most** Significant Bit first, although in reality these are transmitted **Least** Significant Bit first.

For commands, the *CCCC* bits indicate several unique error conditions. *RS* indicates that the responding LLC or the specified LSAP does not support the reception of data that was contained in the command PDU. *UE* indicates that there has been a failure at the interface between the responding LLC and its user. As such the data contained in the command was not passed up. *PE* indicates that the received *ACn* command PDU has violated the requirements of the standard. *UN* indicates that the command could not be completed due to a temporary resource failure. Finally, *IT* and *IP* are used to indicate either a temporary or permanent condition in the case that a specific standard code does not exist for the error encountered.

The *RRRR* bit status codes are similar in use to the *CCCC* bits. Here, the *RS* code is used to indicate that either the responding LLC or the specified DSAP does not support the inclusion of data in the response PDU. *NE* indicates that the responding LLC has never (since power up) received a request to associate a reply LSDU with the specified LSAP. *UE*, as before, is used to indicate that, due to a failure at the interface between the LLC and its user, the responding LLC is unable to obtain the required response data. *UN* indicates that due to temporary resource failure, the responding LLC is unable to include the requested LSDU in the response PDU. Finally, *IT* and *IP* are used by the implementation to indicate either temporary or permanent errors where a standard code does not exist for the error.

30.3 Route Determination and LLC Route Determination Entity

Source Routing Transparent (SRT) Bridges are a special type of bridge used to connect two (or more) network segments into a single bridged network. These bridges then, are capable of forwarding data either via Source Routed paths, or Transparently as required. With Source Routing (unlike Transparent) Bridges, the source station specifies the exact path that a frame will take through the network by specifying the segments that must be traversed. This path is communicated through a special field in the frame called the Routing Information Field (RIF). The Route Determination Entity, which is optional in 802.2 (8802-2) environments, then uses the MAC service to discover the route and uses that route to transfer data.

Specifically, Source Routing Transparent bridges allow four different methods of routing traffic through the bridged network. These are classified as follows:

- **Specifically Routed Frames (SRF)**
  Frames sent this way take the route specified in the Routing Information Field (RIF) and only appear on those segments that are specified in the RIF.

- **Non-Source Routed Frames (NSR)**
  NSR frames only ever travel along the Spanning Tree path, and always adhere to the rules of Transparent Bridging.

- **Spanning Tree Explorer Frames (STE)**
  These frames are forwarded throughout the entire bridged network, but follow the Spanning Tree path and the rules for SRT bridges. Specifically, these frames are not forwarded by bridges that do not support Source Routing. It is either this frame type or the All Routes Explorer that is used to determine the route that is represented in the Routing Information Field.

- **All Routes Explorer Frames (ARE)**
  ARE frames are forwarded to all segments within the bridged network. It is either this frame type or the Spanning Tree Explorer that is used to determine the route that is represented in the Routing Information Field.

30.3.1 LLC Support in Route Determination

As we saw when we discussed LLC Addressing, when implemented, RDE has been assigned its own LLC address (01100101_2). With Route Determination then, the

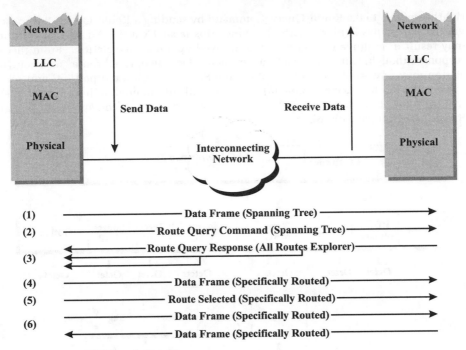

Figure 30-12:   RDE Sample Data Flow

RDE LLC address is used as both the source and destination. RDE also makes use of three Unnumbered Information (UI) PDUs as follows. Figure 30-12 then shows a typical data flow between two stations during route discovery.

- **Route_Query_Command**
  This is sent from the source station to the target or destination station in the route discovery process. In essence, this PDU informs the target that route discovery is in progress and that a Route_Query_Response is required. These PDUs are always sent via the Spanning Tree Route, i.e., via Non Source Routed (NSR) or Spanning Tree Explorer (STE) frames.

- **Route_Query_Response**
  This PDU is returned to the source station (from the target) in response to a Route_Query_Command PDU through an All Routes Explorer (ARE) frame.

- **Route_Selected**
  The Route_Selected PDU is sent from the source station to the target to inform it that a route has been selected. This PDU is always sent as a Specifically Routed Frame (SRF).

In figure 30-12, our source station (to the left) sends a data frame (1). At this point, the station has not selected a route, thus the frame is sent via the Spanning Tree path. The source station also sends a Route_Query_Command via a Spanning Tree Explorer (2) to discover the optimal path to use. Our target station (to the right) responds to the Route_Query_Command by sending a Route_Query_Response via the All Routes Explorer path (3). Since this is sent via the All Routes path, it may result in multiple responses being received by the source station. From these responses though, our source station can then select the optimal route. The source station may now send data frames along the Specifically Routed path (4) and will also send a Route_Selected frame (5), again Specifically Routed, to inform the target that a route has been selected. Our stations can now converse using that Specifically Routed path (6).

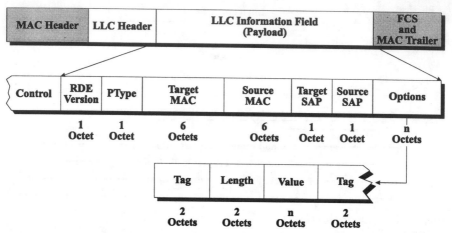

Figure 30-13: RDE PDU Encoding

30.3.2   RDE PDU Encoding

As we have already said, all RDE PDUs are Unnumbered Information (UI) type frames. Here the DSAP is always the RDE LLC address (with the I/G bit set to 0), and the SSAP is the RDE LLC address (with the C/R bit set to 0). The Control field is then set to 11000000_2 and the Information field is encoded as shown in figure 30-13. The 1 octet *RDE Version* field is used to indicate the version of the RDE protocol. The current version is 1 which is then encoded, least significant bit first, as 10000000_2. PType (also 1 octet) is used to denote the type of RDE PDU and is encoded as shown in table 30-9 (note that, as before, the binary values in this table are shown least significant bit first).

Table 30-9: RDE PDU Type Encoding

Value (Binary)	Value (Hex)	RDE PDU Type
10000000	01	Route Query Command (RQC)
01000000	02	Route Query Response (RQR)
11000000	03	Route Selected Command (RSC)

The *Target* and *Source MAC* fields, each of which are 6 octets in length, are used to identify the MAC addresses of the Target and Source stations, respectively. Again, these are presented least significant bit first. The *Target* and *Source SAP* fields denote the SAP Addresses of the target and source SAPs, respectively. In both cases these fields are 1 octet in length and are represented least significant bit (i.e., the *I/G* bit) first. Finally, the variable length *Options* field is used to convey options where applicable. This field, as shown in the figure, is then encoded in the form of *Tag-Length-Value*.

30.4 The Sub Network Access Protocol (SNAP)

The biggest drawback of 802.2 (8802-2) is that the DSAP and SSAP fields are only 8 bits long, thereby limiting the potential number of protocols that can be defined to 256. Compared to Ethernet II where a 16 bit Type field is used, this is indeed a limitation. One only has to view the vast number of Ethernet protocols represented in appendix B, even ignoring any future protocol evolution, to appreciate that 802.2 is restrictive.

The Sub Network Access Protocol was developed by the IEEE in order to support the coexistence of multiple standards, and to provide backwards compatibility with Ethernet II. In essence, SNAP expanded the SAP address space, making it compatible with the 16 bit EtherTypes employed in Ethernet II and potentially extended it. This required a new header to be employed as shown in figure 30-14.

For SNAP operation, the LLC DSAP and SSAP addresses are always set to AA$_{16}$ and UI-Format, Unnumbered Information frames are always used, with the Control field always set to 03. The 5 byte SNAP header is then organized as a 3 octet Vendor ID, that was originally intended to carry the ID of the organization that the Network Layer protocol came from. In actual fact, this ID is the same as the 24 bit Organizationally Unique Identifier (OUI) found as the first 24 bits of the 48 bit MAC Address. Alternatively, and indeed more commonly, this field is normally encoded as all zeroes (000000).

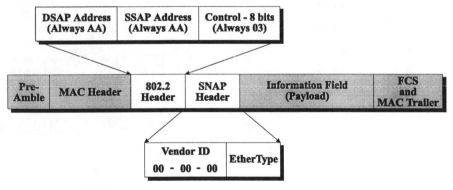

Figure 30-14: SNAP Header Format

The 2 octet EtherType field then contains the encoded Protocol ID in exactly the same format as that used by Ethernet II. Thus, compatible protocol IDs are employed, and an expanded LSAP address space is available for any future protocol additions.

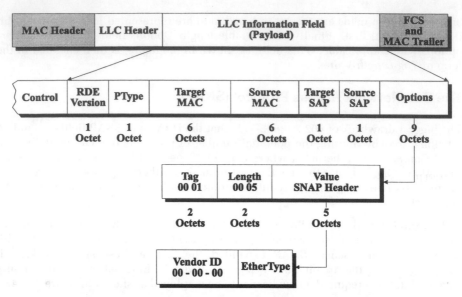

Figure 30-15: Option Usage for LLC/SNAP with the Route Determination Entity

30.4.1 SNAP Support for the Route Determination Entity (RDE)

Where we have a LLC Route Determination Entity that supports SNAP addressing, the options field of the RDE PDU is encoded as shown in figure 30-15. Here the *Tag* field always assumes the value 0001_2 and the *Value* field is the 5 octet SNAP header as described above. The *Length* field always reflects a length of 5.

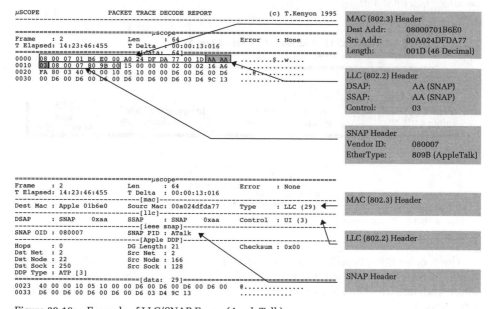

Figure 30-16: Example of LLC/SNAP Frame (AppleTalk)

Logical Link Control

30.4.2 Examples of LLC/SNAP Usage

Figure 30-16 shows a common LLC/SNAP implementation in the AppleTalk protocol. In this figure we see a detailed raw frame together with the same frame fully decoded.

30.5 Common Implementations

There are many topologies and applications that employ some form of LLC to transport data. Most commonly, Token Ring/802.5 and FDDI topologies use LLC, along with network applications such as Novell's NetWare and Microsoft's NetBEUI. In addition, Transparent bridges that employ the IEEE 802.1D/(ISO/IEC 10038) Spanning Tree Protocol (STP) all use this type of encapsulation.

- **Novell NetWare**

  NetWare servers using versions 3.12 and above that employ Ethernet connections default to using 802.3 with 802.2 encapsulation, simply referred to as 802.2. This has, in the past, presented problems where users have upgraded from earlier releases which used a raw 802.3 encapsulation, since in this latter case no protocol identifier was present. Instead, with the raw 802.3 frame type, the Novell IPX header immediately followed the *Length* field of the 802.3 frame. Identification of the protocol was then achieved through the assumption that Novell did not use the 2 octet *Checksum* field that occurred first in the IPX header, and was always set to $FFFF_{16}$. Problems occurred however when client stations that supported only raw framing wished to converse with servers that supported only 802.2 and vice versa.

  Figure 30-17 shows a single Novell IPX frame as both raw hexadecimal data and also decoded:

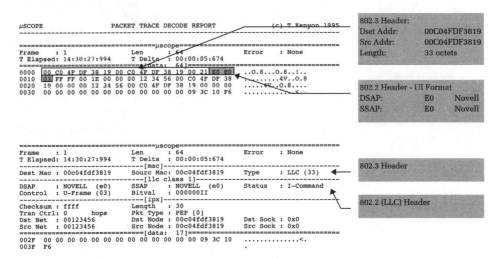

Figure 30-17: Novell IPX Packet Showing 802.3/802.2 Framing

- **NetBIOS**

  NETwork Basic Input/Output System (NetBIOS) can be run over a number of protocols, and has been widely adopted in PC network operating systems.

```
µSCOPE                 PACKET TRACE DECODE REPORT          (c) T.Kenyon 1995
------------------------------------------------------------------------

==========================µscope==========================
Frame     : 7               Len      : 64           Error    : None
T Elapsed: 14:30:28:026     T Delta  : 00:00:00:000
--------------------------[mac]--------------------------
Dest Mac : 00a024dfda77     Sourc Mac: 00c04fdf3819   Type     : LLC (3)
------------------------[llc class 2]--------------------
DSAP     : NETBIOS (f0)     SSAP     : NETBIOS (f0)   Status   : I-Command
Control  : U-Frame (7f)     Bitval   : 0IIIIIII
Mbits    : SABME 1b         PFbit:1
------------------------[data:    47]--------------------
0011   00 00 00 00 00 00 00 00 00 00 00 00 00 00 00 00   ................
0021   00 00 00 00 00 00 00 00 00 00 00 00 00 00 00 00   ................
0031   00 00 00 00 00 00 00 00 00 00 00 00 3B 1D B9 6C   ............;..l
```

The Source station sends an Unnumbered UI-Format frame with the M bits set to indicate SABME.

```
==========================µscope==========================
Frame     : 8               Len      : 64           Error    : None
T Elapsed: 14:30:28:026     T Delta  : 00:00:00:000
--------------------------[mac]--------------------------
Dest Mac : 00c04fdf3819     Sourc Mac: 00a024dfda77   Type     : LLC (3)
------------------------[llc class 2]--------------------
DSAP     : NETBIOS (f0)     SSAP     : NETBIOS (f0)   Status   : I-Response
Control  : U-Frame (73)     Bitval   : 0III00II
Mbits    : UA    18         PFbit:1
------------------------[data:    47]--------------------
0011   D6 73 D6 73 D6 73 D6 73 D6 73 D6 73 D6 73 D6 73   .s.s.s.s.s.s.s.s
0021   D6 73 D6 73 D6 73 D6 73 D6 73 D6 73 D6 73 D6 73   .s.s.s.s.s.s.s.s
0031   D6 73 D6 73 D6 73 D6 73 D6 73 D6 08 9D D1 BC       .s.s.s.s.....
```

The Destination responds with an Unnumbered Acknowledgement indicating that Asynchronous Balanced Mode has been Entered.

```
==========================µscope==========================
Frame     : 9               Len      : 64           Error    : None
T Elapsed: 14:30:28:026     T Delta  : 00:00:00:000
--------------------------[mac]--------------------------
Dest Mac : 00a024dfda77     Sourc Mac: 00c04fdf3819   Type     : LLC (4)
------------------------[llc class 2]--------------------
DSAP     : NETBIOS (f0)     SSAP     : NETBIOS (f0)   Status   : I-Command
Control  : S-Frame (0101)   Bitval   : 0000000I0000000I
Sbits    : RR   (00)        N(R)     : 0             PFbit:1
========================[data:    46]====================
0012   00 00 00 00 00 00 00 00 00 00 00 00 00 00 00 00   ................
0022   00 00 00 00 00 00 00 00 00 00 00 00 00 00 00 00   ................
0032   00 00 00 00 00 00 00 00 00 00 CD 25 94 98          ...........%..
```

The Source station sends a Supervisory frame indicating Receive Ready (RR) and sets N(R) to zero.

```
==========================µscope==========================
Frame     : 10              Len      : 64           Error    : None
T Elapsed: 14:30:28:026     T Delta  : 00:00:00:000
--------------------------[mac]--------------------------
Dest Mac : 00c04fdf3819     Sourc Mac: 00a024dfda77   Type     : LLC (4)
------------------------[llc class 2]--------------------
DSAP     : NETBIOS (f0)     SSAP     : NETBIOS (f0)   Status   : I-Response
Control  : S-Frame (0101)   Bitval   : 0000000I0000000I
Sbits    : RR   (00)        N(R)     : 0             PFbit:1
========================[data:    46]====================
0012   01 01 01 01 01 01 01 01 01 01 01 01 01 01 01 01   ................
0022   01 01 01 01 01 01 01 01 01 01 01 01 01 01 01 01   ................
0032   01 01 01 01 01 01 01 01 01 01 EC C7 BC 7F          ..............
```

The Target station sends a Supervisory frame indicating Receive Ready (RR) and indicates N(R) of zero.

```
==========================µscope==========================
Frame     : 11              Len      : 64           Error    : None
T Elapsed: 14:30:28:026     T Delta  : 00:00:00:000
--------------------------[mac]--------------------------
Dest Mac : 00a024dfda77     Sourc Mac: 00c04fdf3819   Type     : LLC (18)
------------------------[llc class 2]--------------------
DSAP     : NETBIOS (f0)     SSAP     : NETBIOS (f0)   Status   : I-Command
Control  : I-Frame (0001)   Bitval   : 000000000000000I
N(S)     : 0                N(R)     : 0             PFbit:1
------------------------[netbios]------------------------
Head Len : 14               Delimiter: EFFF
Command  : Session End (0x19)
Data1    : 0x8f             Data2    : 0x05bc
TxCorrtor: 0x0000           RxCorrtor: 0x0000
========================[data:    32]====================
0020   00 00 00 00 00 00 00 00 00 00 00 00 00 00 00 00   ................
0030   00 00 00 00 00 00 00 00 00 00 00 00 F1 C7 02 59   ..............Y
```

The Source station sends the first Numbered Information frame with sequence N(S) of zero.

```
==========================µscope==========================
Frame     : 12              Len      : 64           Error    : None
T Elapsed: 14:30:28:026     T Delta  : 00:00:00:000
--------------------------[mac]--------------------------
Dest Mac : 00c04fdf3819     Sourc Mac: 00a024dfda77   Type     : LLC (4)
------------------------[llc class 2]--------------------
DSAP     : NETBIOS (f0)     SSAP     : NETBIOS (f0)   Status   : I-Response
Control  : S-Frame (0103)   Bitval   : 0000000I000000II
Sbits    : RR   (00)        N(R)     : 1             PFbit:1
========================[data:    46]====================
0012   01 03 01 03 01 03 01 03 01 03 01 03 01 03 01 03   ................
0022   01 03 01 03 01 03 01 03 01 03 01 03 01 03 01 03   ................
0032   01 03 01 03 01 03 01 03 01 03 02 6F 1F 15          ...........o..
```

The target sends an Acknowledgment indicating that it has a sequence number of zero (N(S)=0) and expects to receive a sequence of 1 from the source station in the next frame.

Figure 30-18: Sample NetBIOS Trace Showing I-Format Frame Usage

Although not officially a protocol, but more an Application Programming Interface (API) that can be called to provide network access, NetBIOS provides a datagram service between peer applications. Figure 30-18 shows a sample NetBIOS trace and details UI and I-Format frames.

- **IEEE 802.1D/8802-1D Spanning Tree Protocol**

  Bridges are able to run what is commonly referred to as a *Spanning Tree*[3] in order that they can guarantee a loop free topology exists. Here all bridges communicate with each other through multicasts, and exchange certain information that ensures that where such loops exist, only the best paths are utilized. This Spanning Tree Protocol, as standardized by IEEE 802.1D/ISO 10038 uses a simple 802.2 encapsulation and uses the LSAP addresses of 42 as the protocol fragments in figure 30-19 show.

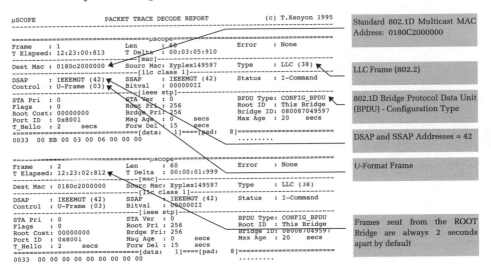

Figure 30-19:   Protocol Trace Showing 802.1D/ISO 10038 Spanning Tree Protocol Packets

30.6 Summary

In this chapter we have discussed the function of the LLC layer, and explored its use and indeed its structure. In short, the LLC provides us with a means of protocol identification through Service Access Points, and then further provides a method for data transfer in either connectionless, or connection oriented modes.

LLC is not without its shortcomings, however, and although this is the favored method of data encapsulation within Internationally standardized network access methods, it is limited in the number of protocols that it can support. As a result, Subnetwork Access Protocol encapsulation (always intended as a stop-gap until the network community was ready to migrate to full OSI compliance) has been adopted

---

[3]   See chapter 15 for a full discussion on the IEEE 802.1D Spanning Tree Protocol.

by many common protocols, since this provides an *Ethernet like* protocol identification.

LLC is key to LAN access methods such as Token Ring and FDDI, and so is used extensively within the network community as a whole. SNAP then tends to be employed where upper layers that traditionally ran across Ethernet (such as TCP/IP) are used with the newer 802.X access methods, and those built on them.

Section F

An Introduction to Internetworking

Internetworking Introduction

So far, we have concentrated our efforts on networking at Layer 2 (the *Data Link Layer*), and as we have seen, there are some quite major differences when we consider the topologies and access methods employed. Ethernet runs over cable plant that comprises coaxial cable, unshielded twisted pair cable, and fiber optic. It runs at 10, 100, and 1000Mbps, and is totally non-deterministic in nature. Token Ring uses no coaxial cable, but uses both shielded and unshielded twisted pair cables besides fiber. This technology runs at 4 and 16Mbps, and is highly deterministic. Vendors are moving to standardize 100Mbps Token Ring (and beyond), but today the upper limit in speed remains at 16Mbps. FDDI, like Token Ring, uses fiber and twisted pair, and works at 100Mbps only. There are no serious plans to improve on this, but again, this is a deterministic technology when viewed from the perspective of performance.

So what is *Internetworking*, and what relevance does this have to those technologies mentioned above? To answer this, we really need to consider networks themselves in a little more depth, and indeed the problems that they bring with them. The view that we have taken so far, is that networks are a collection of LANs and that they are always of the same basic technology. In practice this is not always true. In reality, networks are collections of systems that have a common interface or element of software that allows the exchange of information with each other. These may be printers, or servers that house common data in a database. The purpose in creating the network is so that these resources can be shared.

Consider for a moment the evolution of most networks. Few companies are static, and this means that resources are added as required - normally with little thought for the network infrastructure. With the addition of new resources, many companies tend to implement newer technologies - after all, there is little point in adding a new *super-server*, and then run it on 10Mbps *shared* Ethernet. Now, add to this the fact that takeovers and mergers mean that different systems and network types need to be embraced under a common control. Finally, consider that business today relies on the ability to use the resources of other companies and institutions, and needs to exchange electronic messages world-wide. What we have here is a recipe for disaster, unless it is carefully controlled

Enter *Internetworking*, the name given to the ability to communicate between disparate systems and network technologies in a way that is transparent to the user. Internet access is a prime example. If you access the Internet from a single, stand-alone PC using a dial-up connection, then you normally make the connection manually. As such, you may be aware of some of the processes that take place. If you access the Internet from your PC connected to a LAN however, do you concern yourself with whether the LAN is Ethernet, Token Ring, or even whether you are using an *internet*[1] that is a mixture of both? Indeed, would the connection be any different at the user level if it were one or the other, and even remembering the differences in frame structure? And of course, although you might make a manual connection using a dial-up link, can you do any more (or less) as a result? The answer is of course not - the difference will possibly be in speed alone, and even that is not guaranteed.

The key to understanding what provides us with this transparency requires knowledge of Layer 3 of the OSI model - the *Network* Layer - and much of what we will discuss in this section relates to just that. Certainly, Network Layer functionality is more complex than Layers 1 and 2, and indeed this is generally true as you rise upwards towards the Application itself. What we have discussed so far is purely Layer 3 protocol independent. Apart from defining the access method and physical characteristics, we have not concerned ourselves with the *type(s)* of networks that we have discussed at all. Moving to Layer 3 and we must now define the protocol carried by the physical frame on the LAN, since this layer is totally protocol dependent. Now, we must talk of IP networks, IPX networks, and so on, and although they may all happily co-exist over the same LAN infrastructure, stations that use different Layer 3 protocols most certainly cannot talk to each other. Grasping this simple principle allows us to begin our discussion of internetworking, which is best served by examining one protocol in particular, the Internet Protocol or IP. The reason for choosing this protocol specifically, is simply that it forms the backbone of the most widely implemented suite of protocols, better known as TCP/IP. Do not be fooled into thinking that this is the *only* protocol of note, nor that all others are of little significance. Certainly other suites exist, and these will be briefly described later. Of particular importance is the Internetwork Packet eXchange (IPX) that was introduced by Novell. This is important not only because of the number of networks that still use IPX today, but also because it has a legacy of issues that can seriously impair network performance. We shall discuss IPX in chapter 36, but for the moment we will concentrate our efforts on TCP/IP alone.

31.1 TCP/IP

TCP/IP, or more correctly, the *Internet Protocol Suite*, is in fact a whole suite of protocols that allow cooperating computer systems to communicate. With the *Transmission Control Protocol* (TCP) and the *Internet Protocol* (IP) being two of the major components, it is thus given its colloquial name - TCP/IP.

As we said above, TCP/IP is not the only protocol suite in use today. Many other protocols are used to varying degrees, but it is true to say that the *Internet* protocols

---

[1] Note here, the difference between "The Internet" and "an internet." The Internet (capital I) is the world-wide collection of machines and networks that have generally open access. An internet (small i) on the other hand is a collection of private networks that are interconnected so that users on one network may access data on another. Also, the term "internetworking" is used to describe the ability to communicate across network boundaries in this way.

are the most widely implemented overall. The protocols that make up what we know as TCP/IP have never received International standard status, but it is true to say that they have become *de facto* standards, and will be with us for many years to come. Finally, the TCP/IP protocols are certainly not new. The core protocols have been around for many years, and although the supporting protocols are always being added to and improved, many of these have been around in one form or another since the beginning as well.

So what we really have is a complete, coherent, suite of protocols that provides us with the functionality that is demanded by internetwork users globally. It provides us with basic functionality that provides a naming service, and allows the exchange of mail messages and files. We can connect our machine to another, geographically distant machine, as if we were locally attached through *Virtual Terminal* packages. It allows us to create extremely complex *internets*, connect to the Internet itself, and create *intranets*[2] , and *extranets*[3] . All-in-all, TCP/IP is a general purpose protocol suite that does most of whatever you would need. It is no better, or worse than many others, but it is universally accepted.

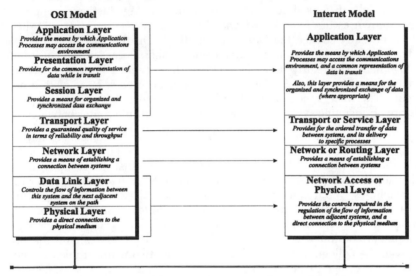

Figure 31-1: A Comparison of the OSI and Internet Architectural Models

As we have said, TCP/IP is certainly not new, it pre-dates many protocols that have claimed a wider following yet it is interesting to note that it implements a *layered* approach. It does not use seven layers as does the OSI model, but instead uses four. Many may argue that this is insufficient, but then again keeping the overall architecture simple is also seen as one of its major advantages. Figure 31-1

---

[2] The value of the Internet and the ease with which information can be exchanged using Internet tools, is without question. Recognizing this, many companies have now created intranets that that provide Internet type services to internal personnel.

[3] Just as intranets provide Internet type services internally to companies, extranets can be used to provide customers with privileged access to the company's resources. This might be to look up stock levels, place orders, or check credit details, etc.

shows a comparison of the OSI Model and that used by TCP/IP, and also briefly describes the functionality of each layer.

Let us not be fooled, TCP/IP does not introduce new *Physical Layer* access methods. This architecture is built purely upon those that already exist, and those new and emerging technologies tend to naturally adapt to encompass TCP/IP. Also, the actual protocol stack is less feature rich than say OSI. This can be easily rationalized by merely examining the market share of TCP/IP networks against its competition though, and the rate at which new networks are being added.

31.1.1 A Brief History of TCP/IP

Before continuing our discussion of the protocol suite itself, it is worth briefly looking at the history of this significant cornerstone of networking heritage. As we have said, TCP/IP is not new by any stretch of the imagination, and indeed we can trace this particular history back to the 1960s.

It was US Department of Defense that first saw the potential of linking what had become widely dispersed resources. As a result, they instigated a project that became known as the *Defense Advanced Research Projects Agency* (DARPA) that would eventually change the face of computing. On the face of it, the task was simple - link all of the various research centers, laboratories, and of course, defense sites together. The reality however was that these centers housed a diverse set of computing platforms, and whatever solution was eventually employed, it had to be resilient. The interconnection methods therefore had to be totally independent of hardware or operating system, and had to support multiple routes between sites.

The result was the creation of the *Advanced Research Projects Agency Network* (ARPANET), and was the first large scale network of dissimilar machines. But just linking them together would of course not be enough. Instead, this project required the development of a whole host of protocols that formalized the manner in which these machines would communicate. These protocols were developed during the late 1970s and became known as the *Internet Protocol Suite*, or *IP Suite*. The migration of the ARPANET to IP then continued, and was completed in 1983. Development continued with the protocol suite itself of course, and the suite was then given the colloquial name of TCP/IP after the two main protocols - the rest is really history, except that development in this area continues today of course.

31.1.2 TCP/IP Related Protocols

As we said previously TCP/IP is not a single protocol, but is instead a whole suite of protocols that work in concert to provide the rich functionality that we now take for granted. Figure 31-2 shows many (but by no means all) of the protocols, and also serves to show just some of the interdependencies. Each protocol is then briefly described below,[4] although those that are shaded receive further discussion in later sections and chapters.

---

[4] A full discussion of the entire Internet Protocol suite is beyond the scope of this book as is a complete discussion of routing. Later chapters will introduce many of the protocols and routing concepts, but for further information the reader is urged to read TCP/IP Explained also by Philip Miller.

- **Network Access or Physical Layer Protocols**

As we have already said, TCP/IP does not introduce any new underlying network technologies. Instead, existing technologies such as Ethernet, Token Ring, and FDDI are used. Indeed, provided that there is a means of protocol identification, there is no reason why the Internet Protocol suite cannot be used over *any* underlying network. When talking of existing technologies, there is a requirement for address translation since these technologies rely on an addressing structure that is incompatible with that used by the Internet Protocol (IP). To accommodate this, a protocol known as the Address Resolution Protocol (ARP) is introduced.

IP can also run over a multitude of WAN technologies including packet switched networks such as Frame Relay, and point-to-point links using the Point-to-Point Protocol (PPP). With these possibilities, the Internet Protocol suite is ideally suited to both LAN based and wide area applications

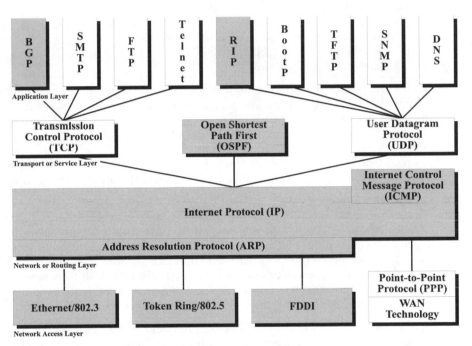

Figure 31-2: The Major Protocols of the Internet Protocol Suite

- **The Network or Routing Layer**

At the very heart of the Internet Protocol suite, is the Internet Protocol (IP) itself. This is the only protocol that is supported at this layer, and provides us a *connectionless* communications environment, and an addressing scheme that is exceptionally well suited to routing. By connectionless, we mean that no *handshaking* takes place between end systems at this layer, and we have no acknowledgment facilities at all. In short, the protocol relies on other, *upper*, layers to build any additional reliability as required.

IP is a general purpose Network layer protocol and is complimented by the Internet Control Message Protocol (ICMP) that provides an error messaging capability, and rudimentary routing and reachability functionality. So interlinked are IP and ICMP, that although ICMP is a totally separate protocol, most people consider it to be integral to IP itself.

Overall then, IP provides us with a low overhead, *connectionless*, delivery system. If we couple this with the address translation capabilities of ARP, and low level control reporting mechanisms of ICMP, we have an excellent protocol on which to build networked applications.

- **Transport or Service Protocols**
  Although the figure may indicate to the contrary, there are in fact only two *Transport* protocols - the *Transmission Control Protocol* (TCP), and the *User Datagram Protocol* (UDP). TCP provides a guaranteed, *connection oriented* transport system that is key to many user applications. UDP, on the other hand, is favored by the *services* where a compact, low overhead, transport system is required. UDP is therefore *connectionless*, and provides no additional reliability over that provided by IP. Instead, UDP relies on the application to provide reliability where it is required, normally through simple hand-shaking procedures.

  There are several other protocols that are *direct* users of IP and therefore occupy the same layer as true *Transport* protocols. These protocols such as the Open Shortest Path First (OSPF) routing protocol should more reasonably be referred to as *Service* protocols because of the tasks that they fulfill. In addition, they provide none of the functions normally associated with transport protocols, such as sequencing or quality of service. Nonetheless, they do provide invaluable functionality and should therefore not be ignored.

- **Application Protocols**
  The culmination of the underlying protocols is to provide services to the applications themselves. Do not be confused, Applications may share the same name as Application Protocols, but there is a distinction. The protocols are there to provide a standardized interface to the communications environment for a specific type of data. The Application itself then provides a user interface to that environment. The Internet Protocol suite supports a large number of application protocols a few of which are mentioned below:

  - *Telnet* is a *Network Virtual Terminal* protocol that allows a station to be connected to another (remote) machine as if connected locally. Stations may now run applications on remote machines, and access data in *real-time*. A variant, the Remote Login (Rlogin) protocol, extends the functionality of Telnet such that a host, once trusted, can attach to another machine without the need to login. Although this raises security issues, Rlogin is an extremely useful application where we have the need to attach to multiple servers continuously.

  - Two file transfer protocols are supported. The first, the *File Transfer Protocol* (FTP), provides a reliable means of transferring files between machines across a TCP/IP internet. The second is the *Trivial File Transfer*

Protocol (TFTP) which, as its name suggests, is a more basic method of transferring files. TFTP is favored by developers who need to download operating system image files to devices. Because of its simplicity and corresponding size, it can easily be programmed into ROM, and therefore allows a device to download a file prior to booting.

- The *Simple Mail Transfer Protocol* (SMTP) is used by mail servers and clients to transfer electronic mail messages. Taken for granted, and buried deep within most Graphical User Interface (GUI) mail applications, SMTP is at the core of all Internet email.

- The *Bootstrap Protocol* (BootP) is used by many devices in an almost seamless manner. BootP, which has been with us for a long time, allows a device to query a server so that it can obtain information as to what its IP address is, where it can find its boot image, and indeed which router it should use. Today, this has also been extended and enhanced so that it is now in use on many PCs. The *Dynamic Host Configuration Protocol* (DHCP) extends BootP and allocates IP addresses from address pools.

  This should really be described as a service rather than an application, although since it relies upon the *Transport or Service* layer, the definition of application is met. In any event, BootP/DHCP provides an invaluable service to the infrastructure of many IP internets today.

- The *Simple Network Management Protocol* (SNMP) is possibly the most widely implemented management protocol today. As its name suggests, SNMP provides network administrators and managers with the ability to manage and control devices that comprise the network itself. Keeping the overall network traffic that it uses at a minimum, SNMP operates using a simple command/response mechanism. The network management station that implements the management application queries the device for information, or sets a particular value within the device. The device then responds with the appropriate information, or acknowledges that the change has taken effect.

- The most common applications of the *Domain Name Service* (DNS) are to translate names to addresses, and to direct email to the correct mail servers. Working almost transparently yet through a global network of DNS servers, "www.*acme.co.uk*" is translated to 192.168.5.206, and email for phil@acme.co.uk will find itself delivered to mailserver.acme.co.uk so that user "phil" can download it next time he logs on. DNS is therefore a cornerstone of the Internet itself since without this service, we would have to remember the IP addresses of every machine that we wanted to communicate with.

- Although not shown in figure 31-2, the *Hyper-Text Transfer Protocol* (HTTP) as used by Web browsers is possibly one of the most significant protocols in use today. Each time that we surf the Internet looking for information or amusement, it is HTTP that is used to download the web pages themselves. In truth, HTTP could now be said to be *the* major application protocol of the entire suite.

31.1.3 Routing Protocols

Routing, which is at the core of the Internet Protocol, is the task of finding the best path from a sender to a desired recipient. Network topologies change due to device and link failure, and undergo transformation due to expansion. This task then becomes naturally more difficult. In order that networks can be *adaptive* it is important that we can detect changes that occur, and react accordingly. Routing protocols allow us to do this, in that they allow our routers to communicate with one another, and propagate reachability information. Two families of routing protocols exist, namely the *Interior Gateway Protocols* (IGPs), and the *Exterior Gateway Protocols* (EGPs), and each has a specific role within any internet.

IGPs are used within what is known as an *Autonomous System* (AS) which is a group of networks that implement common administrative policies. EGPs then link these Autonomous Systems together, and define the policies that we wish to apply between these administrations or domains. As a result, IGP implementations are far more common than EGP implementations, although this does not make them any less complicated. Many AS's are extremely large and complex, and comprise huge numbers of separate, heterogeneous, networks. This means that the AS itself may well be sub-divided into Areas making administration easier, and reducing the overall amount of routing traffic itself. Some examples of routing protocols are:

- **The Routing Information Protocol (RIP)**
  This is one of the original routing protocols of the Internet Protocol suite. It uses what is known as a *Distance Vector* algorithm to determine the quality of routes that are discovered, and simply propagates these as being a number of *Network Hops* away. RIP is extremely simple to implement, administer, and is equally simple in its operation. It is ideal for small internets, but it does not scale well, and it is not generally used in larger installations.

- **The Open Shortest Path First (OSPF) Protocol**
  OSPF is a vast improvement on RIP in that it limits routing exchanges, and scales extremely well from the smallest installation to the largest. OSPF uses what is known as a *Link State* algorithm, and defines the quality of the path to the destination network in terms of the true *link* costs (speed) rather than a simple hop count. It can be complex to implement and administer in larger installations since it provides the ability to split the internet into *Areas*, and therefore reduce overall routing traffic. That said, most vendors today have made it relatively simple to implement in the smaller installations.

- **The Exterior Gateway Protocol (EGP)**
  This is not shown in figure 31-2, although if it were, it would be shown as a direct user of IP in the same way as OSPF is. EGP is the original *Exterior Gateway* protocol, and for many years was the only standardized method of inter-connecting Autonomous Systems together. In use, it is relatively easy to implement, but it has no route aggregation[5] capabilities. Hence, it has now been superseded by the new *Border Gateway Protocol* (BGP).

---

[5] Route Aggregation allows us to combine multiple routes together such that we are able to use less specific addressing. This concept requires a basic understanding of the IP Address structure, and therefore will be expanded on in chapter 34 - Routing Principles.

- **The Border Gateway Protocol (BGP)**

  The newest of all routing protocols, BGP allows the connection of Autonomous Systems in a similar way to EGP. BGP is newer and is more feature rich than its EGP counterpart, with the most significant improvement being the ability to aggregate routes. In truth, no EGP is widely implemented. Only those with extremely large internets, or Service Providers that need to link to the Internet need to concern themselves with the operation of these protocols. For all others, OSPF is more than adequate.

31.1.4 Supporting Services

Before leaving this discussion, it is worth briefly revisiting the role of the supporting services that form part of the Internet Protocol suite, and indeed those that we both rely on, and take for granted. We have already mentioned the *Domain Name Service* (DNS), and the *Simple Mail Transfer Protocol* (SMTP), without which we would almost certainly not be able to work today. But these are really just two of many. The Internet Protocol suite is a large, complex, suite of protocols that inter-link and work in concert to provide the rich fabric of the Internet as we know it today. So, let us briefly mention a few more protocols and services:

- **Network Time Protocol (NTP)**

  This service is provided by special *Time Servers* and allows devices within a network to synchronize their dates and times. This is a UDP based service that allows servers to broadcast time synchronization information, and allows devices to request date and time information - normally after a reset.

- **Line Printer Daemon (LPD)**

  The LPD service is one of the most popular methods of printing within an IP internet. Stations spool print jobs to print servers which then can either print directly, or forward the print job to other networked hosts. Printer sharing, a requirement within most networks, is achieved with this simple service.

- **Packet Internet Groper (Ping)**

  Ping is not really a service, but is instead the colloquial name given to what has become a generic and widely accepted application. The Packet Internet Groper relies on the ICMP Echo Request/Reply service, and is used extensively by network management applications when testing for reachability. In short, an ICMP Echo Request packet is directed to a host, which is then required to respond with an ICMP Echo Reply. If the reply is received by the originating host, the remote device must then be reachable.

- **System Log (Syslog)**

  Many devices produce detailed logging information that may relate to such things as connections that have been established, etc. This information, in turn, can then be used for anything from simple internal usage statistics to client billing. Of course, large networks will require centralized information gathering, and this is where our Syslog service is key. Syslog allows devices to send logging information to a central server which will then deal with it in an implementation specific manner. Obvious uses are for network access devices such as Remote Access Servers (RAS), where we may wish to log both legitimate user access and security breaches.

- **Network File System (NFS)**

  Today, more than ever, data volumes are rising at an incredible rate. Distributed data, while still widely implemented, is giving way to large, centralized, data depositories and with this, the need for centralized data stores. The Network File System allows stations to *map* drives to themselves as if they were installed locally, and provides for the seamless sharing of the data that is the very lifeblood of industry today. The concepts of NFS are employed, and copied, within the more modern network operating systems, yet NFS itself remains the standard by which all others are judged.

31.1.5 Standardization

Before leaving the general subject of IP, we should firstly consider the standardization process that these protocols go through. IP has never achieved formal *International Standard* status, although it is true to say that it is most certainly the *de facto* standard for most networks today. There is no IEEE or ISO document that tells us how IP and its associated protocols work, but instead we rely on documents called *Request For Comments*, or RFCs.

RFCs themselves are more than just vehicles to document protocols. Although RFCs are mostly used to document protocols and their operation, they are also used to document *all* activities of the ruling body of the Internet Protocol Suite, the aptly named *Internet Architecture Board* (IAB). Having said this, an RFC can be written by anyone that feels that they have something to add. Once written, the document can be passed to the RFC Editor for publication and, as its name suggests, comments. This can of course lead to confusion since no RFC number is ever re-issued. Instead, as a protocol evolves and matures into something that can be implemented in a standard fashion, new RFCs are written, and the *State* of it can change. Those wishing to track a protocol then, must keep a close eye on RFCs as they are released. Table 31-1 outlines the various states that a protocol can be in at any time, and shows how a protocol traverses from a *Proposed* standard, through *Draft*, and *Standard*, onward to *Historic*. One interesting point though, is that in order for a protocol to be promoted from *Proposed Standard*, to *Draft Standard*, it takes a minimum of six months, and requires a minimum of two independent implementations. Equally, before a protocol can become a *Standard Protocol*, it must serve its time as a *Draft Protocol* for a minimum of four months.

Table 31-1: Internet Protocol Suite States

Protocol State	*Description*
Informational	Typically a protocol developed by another standards organization, or independent vendor. These have no direct application in the Internet and are published via RFC for general convenience only.
Experimental	Generally developed as part of an ongoing project or research, or protocols that are not intended for operational use.
Proposed Standard	These are protocols that may be considered for future standardization. Typically, there still remains a considerable amount of work to be performed in this area before promotion to the *Draft Standard* state.

Table 31-1: Internet Protocol Suite States

Protocol State	Description
Draft Standard	Protocols in this state are under current consideration for promotion to *Standard* state. At this stage, the protocol must be extensively tested, and requires as much feedback as possible.
Standard	This is an established protocol and has been assigned a *standard number* (STD). These form two major groups, namely the IP protocols that apply to the whole Internet, and the *Network Specific* protocols that are implemented only for specific network types.
Historic	These protocols are either superseded, or interest has merely died. These protocols are unlikely to become Standards.

Table 31-2, shows the RFCs related to many of the most common protocols. Those listed show the most recent at time of writing, although as previously stated, these can be superseded by later revisions.

Table 31-2: Sample RFC Index

RFC	Protocol	RFC	Protocol
768	UDP	904	EGP
791	IP	959	FTP
792	ICMP	1058	RIP (version 1)
793	TCP	1583	OSPF
821	SMTP	1723	RIP (version 2)
854,855	Telnet	1771,1772	BGP

31.2 Other Protocols

As we have said, TCP/IP is by no means the only protocol suite in use. Novell has championed the cause of the Internetwork Packet Exchange (IPX) protocol that we will discuss in chapter 36, but historically there are many, many more. Some of these were too proprietary and did not have the installed base to survive. For example, Wang's Wangnet relied on a *Broadband* physical layer that utilized CATV technologies, and then used totally proprietary protocols over this. Digital Equipment Corporation (DEC), on the other hand, utilized existing physical and Data Link layers, and is still in use around the world in many installations.

In a similar fashion, the Apple Corporation's *AppleTalk* protocol runs over Ethernet, and Token Ring. Building on the Network Access layers from existing standards, has once again ensured acceptance globally. Finally, it is worth mentioning IBM's System Network Architecture (SNA) that is still used extensively within the mainframe world. Although proprietary, the protocol has stood the test of time, and in many cases remains the only protocol that these machines can use. Figure 31-3 shows the architectures of the major protocol suites and contrasts these with both the OSI seven layer model, and the architecture of the Internet Protocol suite (TCP/IP).

OSI	DECnet	SNA	Internet (TCP/IP)
Application	User	User	Application
	Network Application	Transaction Services	
Presentation		Presentation Services	
Session	Session Control	Data Flow Control	
Transport	End Communications	Transmission Control	Transport or Service
Network	Routing	Path Control	Network or Routing
Data Link	Data Link	Data Link	Network Access or Physical
Physical	Physical	Physical Control	

Figure 31-3: Comparison of Major Protocol Suites

31.2.1 Non-Routable Protocols

The real purpose of this entire section is to introduce the concepts of routing. That said, we must remember that not all protocols are routable. For example, SNA that we met above cannot be routed, so many vendors allow the encapsulation of SNA packets within TCP/IP packets. SNA can then be *tunneled* through internets and decapsulated at the destination network. IBM's NetBios suffers a similar fate, and is generally encapsulated in TCP/IP packets where it must be routed. Finally, DEC's *Local Area Transport* (LAT) is non-routable, runs only within Ethernet environments, and in this case no vendor even provides an encapsulation method.

Do not believe that this fact in any way decreases their usefulness, nor that it reduces their following. Many of these protocols are indeed *legacy* protocols and the vendors are moving to IP. That said, with a large installed base such migration takes time, and these protocols will therefore be with us for many years to come.

31.3 Summary

In this chapter we have introduced what lies beyond the Data Link layer, and talked of some of those protocols. These need to remain independent of the underlying network infrastructure, and indeed add a further level of complexity in the process. Today, the most common layer three protocol is IP, and it is this that we shall discuss in greatest depth in the coming chapters. The Internet Protocol suite or colloquially, TCP/IP, brings a huge number of application protocols that we take for granted today. Where would commerce be without email, or the *WorldWide Web* for instance? Life today seems to revolve around the vast repository of information that is contained globally. Our thirst for knowledge is supplemented by our requirement to obtain that information fast. Thus, we need the ability to download our data at faster and faster rates, over resilient network links, and with certain guarantees regarding the successful delivery of the data itself.

Certainly protocols within the Internet Protocol suite will provide the guarantees referred to above. IP is ideally suited to the creation of multiple, heterogeneous networks that together can be linked to form an *internet*. The process by which data is passed between networks is called routing, and the protocols making this process dynamic are *routing protocols*. All of these will be introduced in later chapters. IP is of course not the only player. IPX remains a firm favorite within Novell installations, and we shall discuss this in chapter 36. Equally, when discussing routing, we must be aware that latencies exist due to the fact that these devices are predominantly software based. Advances in technology mean that we can now perform much of this functionality in hardware though, and the Layer 3 switch is therefore born. We shall discuss this major enhancement to routing technology in chapter 37, and from there we can contrast the networks of yesterday to those of tomorrow.

IP Addressing

At the very heart of the Internet Protocol suite is the Internet Protocol (IP) itself, and at the very heart of IP, is the addressing scheme that it uses. But why do we need another addressing scheme here when we have a perfectly adequate scheme at the Data Link Layer? The answer is simply independence.

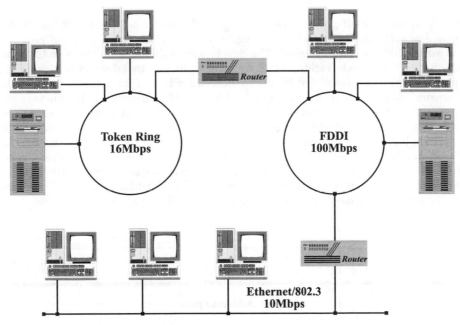

Figure 32-1: Example of *Routed* internet

We are fortunate, to an extent, in that Ethernet/802.3, Token Ring, and FDDI networks all use a similar addressing scheme. The address itself is 6 octets in length, and in all cases is structured with an *Organizationally Unique Identifier* (OUI), and a vendor specific section. True, there is a difference between the presentation of Ethernet/802.3 addresses and their ring topology counterparts in that Ethernet/802.3 addresses use a non-canonical form, whereas the others are canonical. Broadly however they are the same. But what of other systems, even those that are yet to be developed? Can we guarantee that the same scheme will be followed? And indeed even moving data between say Ethernet and Token Ring, our addressing needs to change. We must have a scheme that is both independent of the underlying network architecture, and provides a hierarchical structure that will allow us to group stations together. This system should also be flexible, and have sufficient granularity to be able to identify individual hosts within an internet. Consider figure 32-1 where we have stations connected to a number of different network technologies. Certainly we could bridge or switch between them using *translational bridging*, but this would not necessarily provide us with the segregation that we require. Our only solution where we require segregation, is to route between the networks themselves.

Of course, the technology does not need to be different for us to require routing. The object of any Network Layer addressing scheme is simply to be able to uniquely identify any network within an internet, and indeed to be able to uniquely identify any host on any one of those networks.

32.1 IP Address Structure

The IP Address itself provides us with a globally unique addressing structure that provides sufficient granularity to identify a host within any network, and any network within an internetwork. The developers of this scheme chose to base this around a 32 bit (4 octet) address that was then split into two distinct sections. The first section, that represented by the highest order bits of the address, defines the *Network Identifier*, and the lowest order bits, the *Host Identifier*. In this way our first criteria, that of being able to identify any host within any network is met. This does not, however, achieve our goal totally, since this would mean that we would require a high degree of administration, and much wastage of address space overall. For example, consider figure 32-2 that shows the simple 32 bit address space available. Here, without further information, we would have no way with which to determine which bits constituted the *Network Id*, and which constituted the *Host Id*. What we really need then, is a slightly more flexible approach.

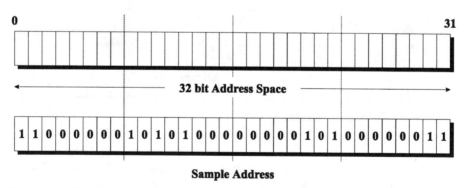

Figure 32-2: IP Address Space

The flexibility that we need comes as multiple Addresses *Classes*, where we have clearly defined Network and Host Id field lengths, and with them, corresponding address ranges. In all, there are five such defined classes known as classes A through E. Of these, three are used for normal *User* networks, and two are reserved for *special* purposes. Now, we would have additional flexibility in our network and host addressing, a hierarchical structure, and sufficient room for future expansion - at least that is what the developers thought. What we have introduced in fact, is the addressing scheme used for IP version 4 (IPv4), and although this is severely over-committed at this time, we shall ignore the developments that are taking place[1] until later in this chapter.

32.1.1   Dotted Decimal Notation

Before examining the actual makeup of IP addresses, we should first introduce the manner in which they are represented. Being human, we find it incredibly difficult to remember long strings of numbers (32 in a row), especially when they are all ones and zeroes. Representing an IP address in this way is therefore not to be recommended since the possibility of introducing errors is far too high. Instead, we need to find a better way, and this is known as *Dotted Decimal Notation*.

Here the address is divided into its four individual octets, and then each of these is expressed as a decimal value. The four decimal numbers are then separated by periods (or dots) - hence the name. For example, figure 32-3 expands on the sample address shown in figure 32-2. In figure 32-3 we have added the decimal weights of each bit position, and from this we can see that the address is actually **192.168.5.3**.

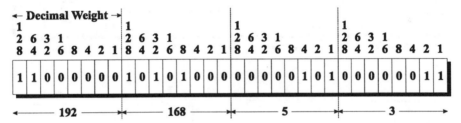

Figure 32-3: Example IP Address Using Dotted Decimal Notation

Although *Dotted Decimal Notation* is by far the most popular representation of IP Addresses, it is not alone. Two other methods can be used, albeit rarely, and are known as *Dotted Binary Notation*, and *Dotted Hexadecimal Notation*. With Dotted Binary Notation, we merely break the address into its four individual octets, and then separate these with periods. Our address would then simply be written as **11000000.10101000.00000101.00000011**. In the case of Dotted Hexadecimal Notation, we break the address into its four individual octets, convert these to their hexadecimal equivalents, and then separate each octet with a period. Our address would now be written as **C0.A8.05.03**.

---

[1] As many readers will be aware, there is a move to introduce a larger address space (128 bits) under what is known as IP version 6 (IPv6). Although much work remains to be completed in this area, the new addressing scheme will be introduced later in this chapter.

32.1.2 User Address Classes

One of the primary motivations for creating various *Classes* of address was to be able to make best use of the available address space itself. If within the address we had a fixed number of bits that represented the *Network Id*, and a fixed length of *Host Id*, then we would have a very inflexible scheme throughout. For example, if we had say 16 bits for the Network Id, and 16 bits for the Host Id, then we would be able to represent 65536 (since this number is 2^{16}) hosts on each of 65536 networks. Now this would be fine for huge networks, but very few actually require this number of hosts to be uniquely addressed. Remember, the IP Addressing scheme is designed to be *global*, and address many different scenarios. The answer then lies in using a number of classes where each allows a different number of Network, and corresponding Host, Ids as figure 32-4 shows.

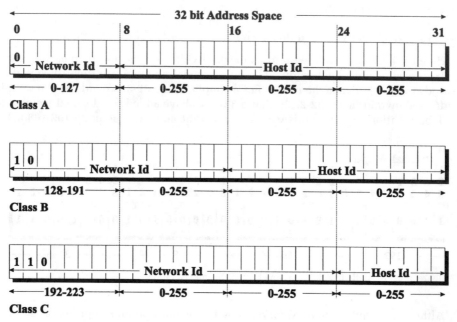

Figure 32-4: IP Address Classes

Class A addresses always have the highest order bit of the highest order octet set to zero. These addresses then use 8 bits for the Network Id, and 24 bits for the Host Id. The highest order octet will then have a possible value in the range of 0 to 127 although in reality, a Network Id of zero is illegal, and the Network Id 127 is reserved. Class A Network Ids will therefore always be in the range of 1 through 126. The Host Id for Class A addresses is always 24 bits long. Hence, in theory, the Host Id portion of the address could have a possible value in the range of 0.0.0, through 255.255.255. In fact, hosts may never be assigned an Id of all zeroes for two reasons. Firstly, old implementations of IP use a Host Id of all zeroes as the *All Zeroes Broadcast* address and use this to broadcast to all hosts on the network. Secondly, a Host Id of all zeroes today is used as a colloquialism that means *This*

Network. Thus, an all zeroes Host Id is illegal and may not be assigned to a station or any other device. Equally, hosts may not be assigned a Host Id of 255.255.255 since this is referred to as the *All Ones Broadcast* and is used by modern implementations to broadcast to all hosts on a network. Class A hosts then will have Host Ids assigned in the range of 0.0.1, through 255.255.254. The addresses 10.5.1.3 and 104.244.3.62 are both examples of Class A addresses.

Class B Addresses split the address space evenly between networks and hosts, using 16 bits for each. The highest order octet of the address always has the highest order bits set to **10**, and there are no reserved network addresses within this class. Thus, the highest order octet will always be in the range 128 through 191, and Network Ids will be between 128.0 and 191.255. As with Class A addresses, the use of an *all zeroes* or *all ones* Host Id is prohibited. Hence, the hosts will have Host Ids in the range of 0.1 through 255.254. 178.16.216.48 is an example of a Class B address.

Class C Addresses use a 24 bit Network Id and use the bit pattern **110** as the highest order bits in the highest order octet. Again, there are no reserved Network Ids, so our highest order octet will now be in the range of 192 to 223. Network Ids will then be in the range of 192.0.0 to 223.255.255. Since we are still required to reserve 0 and 255 as Host Ids, the Host Id assigned to any host will be from 1 to 254. From our previous example, we can say that the address of 192.168.5.3 is a Class C address. In addition, if this were to be assigned to a host, the host would be 3, on network 192.168.5. Table 32-1 summarizes the different address classes discussed here.

Table 32-1: Summary of IP Address Classes

	Address Class		
	A	*B*	*C*
Max. Number of Nets	126	16,384	2,097,152
Network Range	1 to 126	128.0 to 191.255	192.0.0 to 223.255.255
Max. Number of Hosts	16,777,214	65,534	254
Host Range	0.0.1 to 255.255.254	0.1 to 255.254	1 to 254
Address Range	1.0.0.1 to 126.255.255.254	128.0.0.1 to 191.255.255.254	192.0.0.1 to 223.255.255.254

Obviously, if we are to connect to a public service (such as the Internet), our Network Id *must* be unique. Network Ids are normally assigned through the relevant local addressing authority, or by our Internet Service Provider (ISP) who would have assigned our address from the pool that they hold. In any event, once we have a Network Id allocated, we can then apply our Host Ids in any way that seems appropriate to us. If we are allocated an entire Network (for example 192.168.5.0), then there are no demands made as to how hosts are added.

Of course this is only relevant where we have a large number of hosts to accommodate. If we were to have a single PC and wish to connect this to the Internet through an ISP, then it is quite possible that our provider would allocate the address that we would use for that session, at the time we log in. This then means that we are not holding an address permanently when we maybe only login in for just 30 minutes a day to pick up email. IP addresses are becoming a rare commodity, and the wastage and excesses of the past are now catching up with us. Until we have a larger address space available, such as that which IP version 6 promises, we shall need to conserve those addresses that we have left.

32.1.3 "Special" Address Classes

As we said previously, there are in fact five classes of address, yet we have so far examined only the three that are assigned as *User* classes. Of the two other classes, Class D is reserved for *Multicasting*, and Class E is reserved for *Experimental* use only. Figure 32-5 shows the makeup of these addresses, and as you will see they lack the structure of the other three in terms of Network and Host Ids.

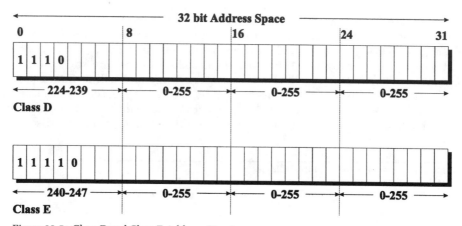

Figure 32-5: Class D and Class E Address Structure

Certainly as far as experimentation is concerned, we cannot define a structure since this could change on an as-needed basis. Equally, only those people that are directly involved in an experiment itself would use the addressing scheme, and it is forbidden to use any address from this range on a *public* network without first seeking approval from the relevant Internet Assigned Numbers Authority (IANA).[2] In real terms, it is extremely unlikely that any Class E address will ever be deployed outside laboratories, thus their use is extremely limited and is mentioned here purely for completeness.

Class D addresses allow the use of *Multicasts* at the IP layer. Today, the Internet protocols are moving away from the *Broadcast* methods of exchanging data that was so popular previously, and Multicasting is certainly here to stay. The *Open Shortest Path First* (OSPF) routing protocol for example, uses the addresses

---

[2] The Internet Assigned Numbers Authority (IANA) is ultimately responsible for overseeing the allocation of all IP Network Addresses. While local authorities have been set up to assist in the administration and address allocation, the IANA is the overall governing body.

224.0.0.5, and 224.0.0.6 so that routers can exchange routing information. Also, the *Router Discovery Protocol* (RDP) uses an address of 224.0.0.1 to communicate with *all* multicast capable devices. Needless to say, this address is also known as the *All Hosts Multicast* address. Table 32-2 lists several common Multicast addresses.

As we mentioned before, neither Class D, nor Class E addresses have a defined structure. We have explained the reasons for Class E, but what of Class D? In fact there is no concept of networks or hosts when Multicasting, and for Class D addresses the low 23 bits of the IP address are mapped over the low 23 bits of the MAC address. The IANA has a reserved block of MAC addresses specifically for Multicasting usage, with an Organizationally Unique Identifier (OUI) of 00-00-5E. This means that when used for Multicasting, the MAC address used will always be in the range **01-00-5E-00-00-00** through **01-00-5E-7F-FF-FF**. Since there are 28 significant bits in an IP multicast address however, this means that more than one IP host group can map to the same MAC address.

Table 32-2: Registered IP Multicast Addresses

Address	Description of Service Type
224.0.0.0	Reserved
224.0.0.1	All Systems on This Subnet
224.0.0.2	All Routers on This Subnet
224.0.0.3	Unassigned
224.0.0.4	Distance Vector Multicast Routing Protocol (DVMRP)
224.0.0.5	All OSPF Routers
224.0.0.6	All OSPF Designated Routers
224.0.0.7	ST Routers
224.0.0.8	ST Hosts
224.0.0.9	RIP II Routers
224.0.0.10-224.0.0.255	Unassigned
224.0.1.0	Versatile Message Transaction Protocol (VMTP)
224.0.1.1	Network Time Protocol (NTP)
224.0.1.2	SGI Dogfight
224.0.1.3	RWhod
224.0.1.4	VNP
224.0.1.5	Artificial Horizons - Aviator
224.0.1.6	Name Service Server (NSS)
224.0.1.7	Audio News Service
224.0.1.8	SUN NIS+ Information Service
224.0.1.9	Multicast Transport Protocol (MTP)
224.0.1.10-224.0.1.255	Unassigned
224.0.2.1	Unofficial "rwho" Group - BSD
224.0.2.2	SUN RPC PMAPPROC_CALLIT
224.0.3.0-224.0.3.255	RFE Generic Service
224.0.4.0-224.0.4.255	RFE Individual Conferences
224.1.0.0-224.1.255.255	ST Multicast Groups
224.2.0.0-224.2.255.255	Multimedia Conference Calls
232.x.x.x	Versatile Message Transaction Protocol (VMTP)

32.2 Subnetting

So far we have considered the situation whereby we have a single network, and we have described the addressing scheme that would be used in terms of three *Classes*. In fact, few organizations have infrastructures that are this simple, since most have divided their systems into many networks. To accommodate this, these organizations would now have to be allocated potentially large numbers of *Network Ids* so that each network would be unique. As we have said, Network Ids are becoming scarce, so we must find a method that makes use of the address space that can otherwise potentially be wasted. For instance, consider what would happen if we had, say, 98 stations to connect on one network, and 64 on another. From the previous section we would need a minimum of two Class C networks. Equally, if we wanted to connect 276 stations on one network, 200 on another, and 150 on a further network, we would need one Class B and two Class C networks. To say that we would be wasting addresses now is an understatement! The answer lies in what has become known as *Subnetting* - the ability to *trade* Host Id bits, for Network Id bits.

Essentially by talking of address *Classes*, we have introduced a two tiered addressing scheme that allows us a two level hierarchy. We can talk of devices (Hosts) that reside on Networks. With subnetting however, we extend this principle such that hosts group together on *Subnets*, which in turn are grouped into *Networks* - a three level hierarchy. Consider figure 32-6.

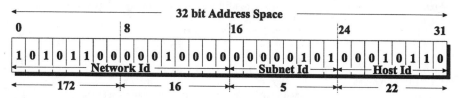

Figure 32-6: Example Subnet Address

In the figure we see that we have a *Class B* address (172.16.0.0) but we have taken the third octet and re-defined this as being a *Subnet Id*. This address would now represent Host 22, on Subnet 5, of Network 172.16.0.0. The only question that arises now, is how do we communicate that this no longer represents an address of Host 5.22 on Network 172.16.0.0? The answer to this lies in what is called the *Subnet Mask* - a 32 bit binary mask that identifies which bits in the IP Address define the Network Id, and which define the Host Id. Essentially we, as humans, can say that our example represents Host 22 on Subnet 5, of Network 172.16. In actual fact, networking devices would perceive this simply as Host 22, on Network 172.16.5.0. They would see it as if we had created a Class C address from a Class B Network. Subnets have only local significance, so that is why we can say that our networking device would *perceive* the network to be 172.16.5.0 based on its own subnet mask. Indeed, when we begin talking about subnetted addresses, the whole concept of address classes can become meaningless. The reason for this lies in the mechanics of the Subnet Mask which we discuss next, and routing itself which will be discussed in chapter 34.

32.2.1 Subnet Mask Operation

The Subnet Mask is the key to subnetting an IP Address since, as we said above, it is this that defines which bits represent the Network Id, and which represent the Host Id. The mask is 32 bits long, having one bit position for each bit position in the IP Address itself. The IP Address, together with its subnet mask, now become inter-linked in defining the address of the device. The actual operation of the Subnet Mask is glamorous in its simplicity and can be easily understood by applying the following rules:

- If the bit in the subnet mask is a one, then the corresponding bit in the IP Address should be considered to be part of the Network Id.

- If the bit in the subnet mask is a zero, then the corresponding bit in the IP Address should be considered to be part of the Host Id.

- The mask should contain at least as many bits set to one (and in the relevant bit positions) as the originally assigned Network Id. This is known as the *Natural Subnet Mask*. For example:

  - A mask used with a Class A address must have the most significant 8 bits set to ones.

  - A mask used with a Class B address must have the most significant 16 bits set to ones.

  - A mask used with a Class C address must have the most significant 24 bits set to ones.

- The *all ones* and *all zeroes* Subnet Ids should be used with caution. In the early days, use of these were both prohibited, however restrictions relating to the *all zeroes* subnet Id were later relaxed. Many vendors do now support the use of both the *all zeroes*, and *all ones* subnets although to maintain compatibility care must be taken. From our example, if network 172.16.0.0 had been subnetted as shown in figure 32-6, we would therefore only be able to guarantee the use of 254 of the possible 256 subnets.

Subnet masks themselves are generally specified in the same way that IP Addresses are, i.e., in *Dotted Decimal Notation*. A *Natural* Subnet Mask for a Class A address would therefore be **255.0.0.0**, for a Class B address it would be **255.255.0.0**, and for a Class C address it would be **255.255.255.0**. In order to understand this better though, let us consider figure 32-7, which shows the Class B address that we used previously (172.16.5.22), together with its *Natural* Subnet mask.

From our rules above, we can see that wherever a bit is set to a *one* in the Subnet Mask, the corresponding bit in the IP Address is in fact part of the *Network Id*. Where the bit is set to a *zero*, the corresponding bit is part of the *Host Id*. Stations calculate on which Network they and other devices reside, by performing a bit-wise, "*Logical AND*" between the IP Address and their Subnet Mask. This then has the effect of *masking off* the Host ID itself, and leaves the Network ID intact. As we can see from the figure, our address of **172.16.5.22**, when used with a mask of **255.255.0.0**, yields a Network Address of **172.16.0.0**.

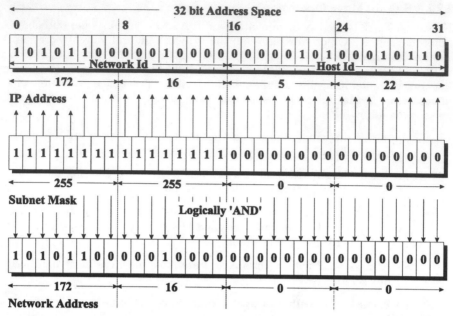

Figure 32-7: Example IP Address with "Natural" Subnet Mask

Expanding on this, figure 32-8 shows our example of figure 32-6, complete with Subnet Mask. Clearly, if we are to operate in the same manner as network devices, we no longer need to talk in terms of Address *Classes* since these no longer have any meaning. In this example, we see that we have a *Host Id* of **22**, on *Network* **172.16.5**, (although it would be more normal to represent this as **172.16.5.0**). That said, if we wish, we can still say that this would be *Host Id* 22, on *Subnet* 5, of *Network* 172.16.0.0. Each method of presentation is correct, provided that we specify *exactly* what we mean.

Obviously, we are not restricted to merely subnetting only Class B Addresses. The concept of the Subnet Mask works equally well with *any* address, and provided that the rules that we have already mentioned are adhered to, the mask can be of almost any length. Consider the example where we have a host with an IP Address of 215.85.33.37, and a Subnet Mask of 255.255.255.240:

IP Address:	192.168.5.37 Class C Address
Subnet Mask:	255.255.255.240 Non-Natural Subnet Mask
IP Address in binary becomes:	**1100 0000 1010 1000 0000 0101 0010 0101**
Subnet Mask in binary becomes:	**1111 1111 1111 1111 1111 1111 1111 0000**
Logically AND together to get:	*1100 0000 1010 1000 0000 0101 0010 0000*
Or, in Dotted Decimal Notation:	**192** . **168** . **5** . **2**
In other words:	Host **5**, on Subnet **2**, of Network **192.168.5.0**
Or:	Host **5**, on Network **192.168.5.2**

Once again, notice that we *speak* the address in two ways to avoid confusion. In truth though, it does not matter which we choose provided that we are consistent.

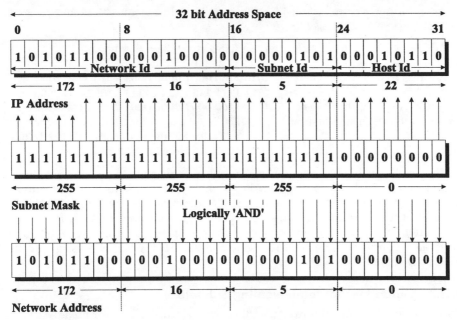

Figure 32-8: Example Class B Network with Non-Natural Subnet Mask

Taking this one stage further, we can now say that the address itself would provide for 15 possible subnets,[3] and each of which could accommodate 14 possible hosts. Table 32-3 provides the address ranges for hosts for each of the subnets.

Table 32-3: Host Address Ranges for Network 192.168.5.0 with Subnet Mask 255.255.255.240

Subnet Number	Host Address Ranges	
	Low Host Address	*High Host Address*
Subnet 0	192.168.5.1	192.168.5.14
Subnet 1	192.168.5.17	192.168.5.30
Subnet 2	192.168.5.33	192.168.5.46
Subnet 3	192.168.5.49	192.168.5.62
Subnet 4	192.168.5.65	192.168.5.78
Subnet 5	192.168.5.81	192.168.5.94
Subnet 6	192.168.5.97	192.168.5.110
Subnet 7	192.168.5.113	192.168.5.126
Subnet 8	192.168.5.129	192.168.5.142
Subnet 9	192.168.5.145	192.168.5.158
Subnet 10	192.168.5.161	192.168.5.174
Subnet 11	192.168.5.177	192.168.5.190
Subnet 12	192.168.5.193	192.168.5.206
Subnet 13	192.168.5.209	192.168.5.222
Subnet 14	192.168.5.225	192.168.5.238

[3] The use of 15 possible subnets assumes that subnet 0 (all zeroes) subnet is valid, and that subnet 15 (all ones) subnet is not. As we have already said, these subnets should be used with caution.

As a further example, consider the host IP Address of 172.16.26.231, and a Subnet Mask of 255.255.252.0:

IP Address:	172.16.26.231	Class B Address
Subnet Mask:	255.255.252.0	Non-Natural Subnet Mask
IP Address in binary becomes:	**1010 1100 0001 0000 0001 1010 1110 0111**	
Subnet Mask in binary becomes:	**1111 1111 1111 1111 1111 1100 0000 0000**	
Logically AND together to get:	*1010 1100 0001 0000 0001 1000 0000 0000*	
Or, in Dotted Decimal Notation:	**172 . 16 . 24 . 0**	
In other words:	Host **2.231**, on Subnet **6**, of Network **172.16.0.0**	
Or:	Host **2.231**, on Network **172.16.24.0**	

This is obviously more complex since we have chosen to use 6 bits to define the subnet. Thus, we now have a 10 bit Host Id that will provide us with 1022 possible hosts (i.e., 2^{10}-2), on each of 63 subnets.[4] We calculate that this address resides on subnet 6, because octet 3 has the value **0001 1010**, and the mask for this octet is **1111 1100**. Thus, when calculating the subnet number, only the high 6 bits of the octet are significant (i.e., 000110) which means that when we assign decimal weights we obtain the result of 6.

32.2.2 Guidelines for Implementing Subnets

As we have seen from the examples that we have used, we can broadly use any mask against any address. It is normal, wherever possible, to try to assign either 4 or 8 bit masks, and to implement these on octet boundaries. In principle, *any* bits can be used for a mask provided that it contains at least as many bits set to one (and in the relevant bit positions) as the originally assigned Network Id. As we have said previously, a mask assigned to a Class A address cannot be less than 255.0.0.0, and cannot be less than 255.255.0.0, or 255.255.255.0 for Class B and Class C addresses, respectively. Indeed although it would be extremely foolish to do, a mask of 255.255.198.192 *could* be assigned to the Host address of 172.16.181.162. This would be legal, but breaking it down as before would reveal that its interpretation would be anything but straightforward.

Of course, we are still only using 6 bits as the Subnet Id, but the address now becomes almost impossible for humans to interpret. The fundamental rule in subnetting then, has to be to keep the structure both as simple and logical as possible. Apart from this, common sense should prevail.

32.3 Routing Fundamentals

In order for devices to *directly* communicate, they *must* reside on the same *Network*,[5] (or *Subnet*) - a process known as *Direct Routing*. For example, if we consider figure 32-9, we see that we have a number of devices that share a common

---

[4] The use of 63 subnets assumes that we shall allow the use of subnet 0 (all zeroes), and prohibit the use of subnet 63 (all ones). In other words, this number is calculated from the value 2^6-1.

[5] Here, when we talk about a Network, we are referring to that defined by a Layer 3 addressing scheme, and not the physical connectivity. Effectively then, we are talking about a group of devices linked by a common, logical, Network.

LAN. *Each*, in theory, should be able to communicate with *any* other. In practice however, this would not be the case.

Certainly, provided that there is a concept of network addressing, each device may be able to communicate with any other using an alternative protocol. As far as IP is concerned though, they would not be able to do so. What would be possible, is for Stations A and B to communicate with each other, and to exchange data with Servers 1 and 2. Equally, Stations C and D would be able to communicate, and they would be able to talk to Server 3. A and B would not be able to communicate with C or D however, and they would not be able to use Server 3. Likewise, C and D would be unable to use Servers 1 or 2, and could not talk to A or B. The reason? Simply that although we have a single, common LAN, we have multiple *Networks*.

When a Host wishes to communicate with another device, it must be in possession of three fundamental pieces of information. Its own IP Address, its Subnet Mask, and the IP Address of the device with which it would like to

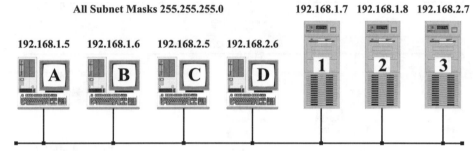

Figure 32-9: Sample Routed Network

communicate. The *Source* station will then logically *AND* its own IP Address with its Subnet Mask to mask-off the Host Id. It next *AND*s the *Destination* IP Address with its own Subnet Mask. Finally, it compares the results of the two *AND* operations. Where they are the same, the station knows the Destination host is on the same Network (or Subnet) as itself, and it can therefore communicate directly. Where they are different, then it must use a router to forward the data on its behalf. This process is known as *Indirect Routing* and is shown in figure 32-10.

Stations that reside on the logical networks 192.168.1.0 and 192.168.2.0 can exchange data with stations on network 192.168.3.0 (and vice versa) through the router. Basically, when a device wishes to communicate outside of its own subnet, it passes the data to a router, which then *routes* this to its final destination. As you will see, the ports of the router also have IP Addresses assigned. Thus Station A, for example, can communicate directly with the router interface (*Direct Routing*) which will then forward the data onwards (*Indirect Routing*).

Notice also that the *upper* port of the router has two IP Addresses assigned in this particular case. This is so that hosts on network 192.168.1.0 can communicate with those on network 192.168.2.0. In this case, if Station A wished to send data to Server 3, it would send the data to the router, which would then send it back out of the same port to the server. Although, on the face of it, this may seem illogical, it is in fact quite useful where security is an issue and all devices are on a single LAN. Routers can normally be configured with filters that allow an administrator to restrict certain stations from accessing sensitive data. It is also perfectly legal for any host to be configured with multiple IP Addresses, in which case it is said to be *Multi-Homed*.

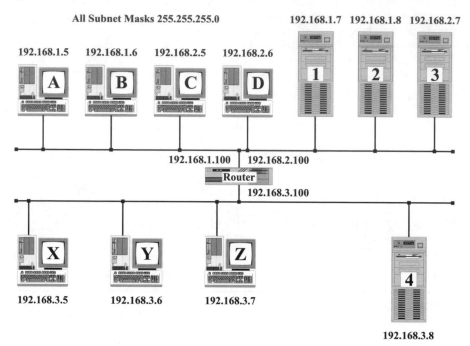

Figure 32-10: Example of Indirect Routing

Equally, if we were to remove the lower network (192.168.3.0) in the previous example, and configure the router such that it had just one network connection, this would also be legal. We would still be able to route between networks 192.168.1.0 and 192.168.2.0 if the port was configured with IP Addresses that related to each network. In this case the router could be said to be *Multi-Homed*, although routers configured in such a way are more often referred to as being *one-arm routers*.

32.4 Address Resolution

We have said that once a host has determined that it resides on the same Subnet (Network) as a Destination, it can perform *Direct Routing*, and communicate directly. But is this really true? IP Addresses operate at Layer 3, and allow packets to be routed throughout an internet. The delivery of frames however takes place at Layer 2, and hosts use MAC addresses for communication. Consider figure 32-11.

From the addressing scheme that we have employed, it is clear that all stations *should* be able to communicate with each other. What we need now, is an automatic method by which hosts can discover the MAC addresses of the stations that they wish to communicate with. This functionality is provided by the *Address Resolution Protocol* (ARP) which is a simple, Link Layer, protocol designed to obtain the MAC address of a host, given only its IP Address. The protocol itself plays a vital role in IP internets, produces very little overhead, and is used by all devices in an IP environment, regardless of type.

All Subnet Masks 255.255.255.0

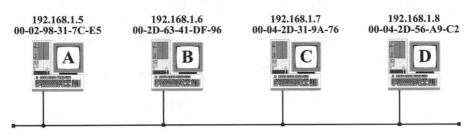

Figure 32-11: Example Address Resolution

32.4.1 Address Resolution Protocol (ARP)

ARP is relatively simple in operation, relying on the broadcast nature of LANs. To understand exactly how the protocol works though, it is best to take the example presented in figure 32-11.

Assume from here, that Station A wishes to communicate with Station D. It will have already ascertained that both reside on the same subnet by *AND*ing the IP Addresses with its Subnet Mask, and comparing the results. Station A will now generate a frame (an *ARP Request*), the format of which complies with the underlying LAN architecture, and contains among other things, its own IP Address, its own MAC Address, and the IP Address of Station D (the *target*). This frame will then be broadcast, and will be received by all attached stations.

Since the frame is a broadcast, all stations must act on it. Each station, with the exception of Station D however, will discard the frame as irrelevant since the *target* IP Address will not match theirs. Station D on the other hand, will record the IP and MAC Addresses of Station A[6] in its *ARP Cache*, insert its MAC address into the frame, and then transmit it back to Station A as a unicast. This *ARP Response* will be received only by Station A, which will now record the IP and MAC Addresses of Station D in its ARP Cache. The two stations can now exchange data without further delay.

32.4.2 ARP Frame Format

As we have said, ARP is a relatively simple protocol. It is designed to be generic, and a variation is actually used by other protocol suites such as AppleTalk - the

---

[6] In actual fact, any station can record the IP and MAC Addresses of a station originating an ARP Request and thereby reduce the amount of broadcast traffic on the LAN. The operation of ARP in this promiscuous mode is not mandatory however.

AppleTalk Address Resolution Protocol (AARP). When used in an Ethernet/802.3, IP environment, ARP will generally use Ethernet (as opposed to 802.3), and uses an EtherType of 0806. Figure 32-12 shows the complete protocol format encapsulated within an Ethernet frame, and we then discuss the various fields below:

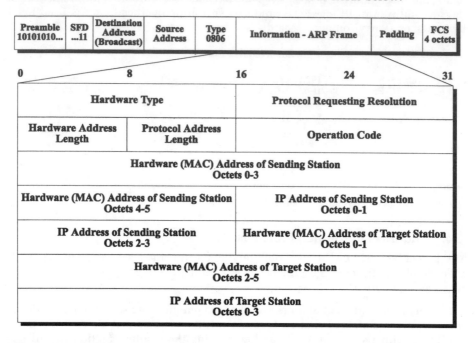

Figure 32-12:   ARP Frame Format

The 16 bit *Hardware Type* field identifies the hardware technology of the underlying LAN. Obviously, this will be identical for both Requests and Responses, and will assume a value according to the hardware type shown in table 32-4.

The 16 bit *Protocol Requesting Resolution* field identifies the Layer 3 protocol (IP in this case), and uses standard EtherTypes. Hence for IP, this will assume the value 0800. The next two 8 bit fields (the *Hardware* and *Protocol Address Lengths*) are broadly redundant since we already know the Hardware and Protocol types. Nevertheless, these fields will contain the values 6 and 4, respectively, for IP in an Ethernet environment.

The 16 bit *Operation Code* is used to define the type of ARP frame this is. This field will take the value 1 for an ARP Request, and 2 for an ARP Response. Two other possible values (3, and 4) are used to indicate that ARPs sister protocol, the *Reverse Address Resolution Protocol* (RARP)[7] is being used. In this case 3 is used for a RARP Request, and 4 is used for a RARP Response.

---

[7] In actual fact, any station can record the IP and MAC Addresses of a station originating an ARP Request and thereby reduce the amount of broadcast traffic on the LAN. The operation of ARP in this promiscuous mode is not mandatory however.

The remaining fields within the frame are relatively self-explanatory. ARP Requests are transmitted with all fields completed with the exception of the Hardware (MAC) Address of Target Station. Responses are then transmitted with this field also completed. The trace in figure 32-13 demonstrates this point by showing a complete ARP exchange between two stations.

Table 32-4: ARP Hardware Type Codes

Code (Hex.)	Code (Dec.)	Description
0001	1	Ethernet
0003	3	Amateur Radio AX.25
0004	4	Proteon ProNET Token Ring
0005	5	Chaos
0006	6	IEEE 802.x type Networks
0007	7	ARCNET
000B	11	LocalTalk
000C	12	LocalNet (IBM PCNet, or SYTEK LocalNET)
000D	13	Ultra link
000E	14	SMDS
000F	15	Frame Relay
0010	16	Asynchronous Transfer Mode (ATM)

```
μSCOPE              PACKET TRACE DECODE REPORT          (c) T.Kenyon 1995
---------------------------------------------------------------------------
==========================μscope=========================================
Frame   : 2                 Len    : 82          Error   : None
T Elapsed: 19:04:01:241     T Delta : 00:00:19:894
----------------------------[mac]----------------------------------------
Dest Mac : ffffffffffff     Sourc Mac: 0000e80f04af     Type   : ARP
----------------------------[arp]----------------------------------------
HW Type  : 10Mb Ethernet    Protocol : IP          Opcode  : ARP REQuest
HW AddLen: 6   Bytes        PR AddLen: 4   Bytes

SrHW Addr: 0000e80f04af  ◄
SrPR Addr: 192 168 12 36

DeHW Addr: 000000000000
DePR Addr: 192 168 12 99
=========================[data:  40]=====================================
002A  AB DC EA AD 33 34 32 38 34 32 33 31 31 33 34 37    ....342842311347
003A  39 33 43 33 00 00 00 00 00 00 00 00 00 00 00 00    93C3............
004A  00 00 00 00 AC 62 DB 2D                             .....b.-
==========================μscope=========================================
Frame   : 3                 Len    : 64          Error   : None
T Elapsed: 19:04:01:241     T Delta : 00:00:00:000
----------------------------[mac]----------------------------------------
Dest Mac : 0000e80f04af     Sourc Mac: Xyplex064892      Type   : ARP
----------------------------[arp]----------------------------------------
HW Type  : 10Mb Ethernet    Protocol : IP          Opcode  : ARP RESPonse
HW AddLen: 6   Bytes        PR AddLen: 4   Bytes

SrHW Addr: 080087064892  ◄
SrPR Addr: 192 168 12 99

DeHW Addr: 0000e80f04af
DePR Addr: 192 168 12 36
=========================[data:  22]=====================================
002A  AB DC EA AD 33 34 32 38 34 32 33 31 31 33 34 37    ....342842311347
003A  39 33 82 8C E3 27                                   93...'
```

Station 192.168.12.36 sends an ARP Request looking for the MAC Address of station 192.168.12.99

Station 192.168.12.99 responds with it's MAC Address in an ARP Response

Figure 32-13: Trace of ARP Exchange

32.4.3 The Reverse Address Resolution Protocol (RARP)

Before leaving the subject of Address Resolution, we should say a few words about the Reverse Address Resolution Protocol (RARP) that we briefly mentioned earlier. RARP is normally referred to as a sister protocol to ARP, although in truth the frame format is identical, with only the *Operation Code* changing to reflect RARP operations.

RARP is used by devices, typically at *boot-up*, when they need to determine which IP address they should use. At this time, the device may not be in possession of its operating system, and may need to download this from a TFTP server for example. To do this, it will need to have an IP Address yet it may know only its MAC address and have little other knowledge. RARP can then be used to send a request to a RARP server that will search a database to match the MAC Address to an IP Address. The server then returns the IP address to the device in question, so that it can commence the download of its operating system, and participate in normal IP operations.

Like ARP Requests, RARP Requests are sent as broadcast frames, although for a RARP Request, apart from the Hardware and Protocol Types, etc., the frame contains only the Source Stations MAC Address, and uses an EtherType of 8035. RARP Responses are sent as Unicast frames, and contain the MAC and IP Addresses of the requesting station, and the MAC and IP Addresses of the responding RARP server.

RARP is popular among developers of internetworking devices such as routers and switches, and other devices that need to download operating systems or parameter files. RARP is compact, the code is readily available, it is easy to implement, and most importantly the code can be easily stored in Read Only Memory (ROM). This makes it the perfect choice for any device that requires an IP Address to be assigned at startup.

32.5 The Dynamic Host Configuration Protocol (DHCP)

Today, more than ever before, we are facing network management problems as our networks grow, and demands for services increase. One of our biggest problems is that of Address Allocation, in a world where IP Addresses are fast becoming a scarce resource. This problem is, at least in part, due to the phenomenal growth in the popularity of the Internet Protocol suite, and the equally explosive growth in the numbers of inexpensive PCs that are connected to our networks. Companies are now fast running out of IP Addresses, and must make better use of those that they have. The Dynamic Host Configuration Protocol (DHCP) does this, and more, by offering the following key benefits:

- **IP Address Leasing**
  IP Addresses are *leased* or shared by multiple users. When a device boots up, it requests an IP Address from a DHCP Server in much the same way that it would if using RARP. The main difference to RARP however, is that DHCP allows the Network Administrator to either configure a static address mapping between MAC and IP Addresses, or to allocate an address from a common, *Address pool*. If configured from a pool, the address will be *leased* for a configurable period of time. When that time expires, the client can either renew the lease, or the address can be returned to the pool so that it can be allocated to another host. Where we have a large number of clients that only communicate with other devices infrequently, we can therefore substantially reduce the pressure on IP Address space allocation.

- **Centralized Configuration Management**

  By allocating addresses centrally, we automatically simplify the tracking of addresses, and have central control over configurations generally. Unlike RARP which allocates only an IP Address based upon a static mapping to a MAC Address, DHCP also allows the station to be provided with other key information. This includes the address of the *Default Gateway*,[8] the address of *Domain Name Service* (DNS)[9] servers, and NetBIOS information, etc. In general, with DHCP we merely need to modify centrally held configuration files, and changes will be automatically propagated to client stations.

- **Mobile Computing Support**

  One of the biggest administrative headaches that face administrators today, is that staff are more mobile than ever before. Today, an employee with his laptop may be allocated a specific network point that will reside on a particular IP Subnet. During the day, that same employee may move around the building, and need to login to the network from various locations, and from various subnets. Previously, this would have required the laptop to be manually re-configured for each subnet as our user roves, but with DHCP this is no longer necessary. Instead, the DHCP server can be configured so that it allocates IP Addresses from specific ranges, and of course other information that relates to that subnet as well.

DHCP is built upon the Internet Protocol suite's Bootstrap Protocol (BootP). It is based on a client-server architecture, and as with ARP/RARP, relies upon the broadcasting of initial information. DHCP is a relatively new protocol and was introduced by Microsoft with their Windows '95 and NT operating systems. Certainly, DHCP provides a number of advantages over previous methods of address allocation, and its use is now an integral part of many large networks.

32.6 IP Version 6 Addressing

Before leaving the subject of IP Addressing, we must briefly mention the presence of IP version 6. The current version of IP (version 4) is badly strained with too little address space available to keep up with the constant demand. IPv4 has served us well, but we have to say that it is a victim of its own success. Certainly the originators of IP, all those years ago, could not have foreseen the demand for communications on the global scale that the Internet has brought. Companies rely upon facilities such as email and e-commerce, and the rate at which people are joining the Internet continues to rise. Clearly we need more addresses if we are to survive, yet this will also require a radical change to the way that IP actually works.

IP Version 6 (IPv6) increases the length of the address from 32 bits to 128 bits, therefore providing us with those extra addresses that we so badly need. In

---

[8] The Default Gateway is the common name given to the default router within a network. Each station should be configured with the address of a router, so that if it cannot directly deliver the packet itself, it will know where to send it. This concept is discussed further in chapter 34.
[9] The Domain Name Service (DNS) is the service that is used to map machine names, mail names, etc., to IP Addresses. Further discussion of this crucial service is beyond the scope of this volume however.

addition, it also provides us with more hierarchical levels than just *Network Id*, possible *Subnet Id*, and *Host Id*. In short, it is better structured, and allows us far greater flexibility overall. Without going into all of the different address structures possible in version 6, it is worth noting just a few of the most important.

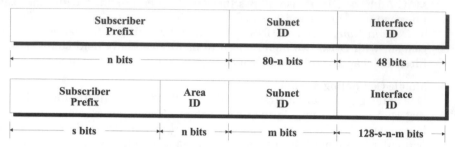

Figure 32-14: IPv6 Unicast Address Structure

Figure 32-14 shows us the basic structure of IPv6 unicast addresses. In the first example, the 48 bit *Interface Id.* would be the IEEE 802.x MAC Address. This allows us to ensure global uniqueness, and also removes the requirement for address resolution. Alternatively, the second example can be used where we might require further hierarchical structure. In this case, we can use part of the space occupied by the *Interface Id.* to allow for these other levels of addressing.

Of course, things will not change overnight, and we will doubtless be faced with many years of transition as we migrate to IPv6-only internets. Figure 32-15 shows how IPv4 hosts can co-exist in an IPv6 environment. In the first example, we see the format for where we wish to *tunnel* an IPv6 packet over an IPv4 network, and in the second example, how an IPv4-only host can send data over an IPv6 network.

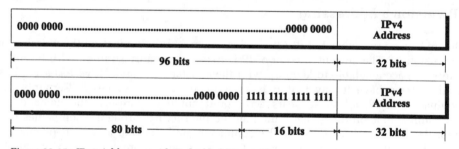

Figure 32-15: IPv6 Addresses with Embedded IPv4 Addresses

Finally, before leaving the subject of IPv6 Addressing, it is interesting to note that the traditional *types* of address are changing. To date, we have used and understood the concepts of the *Unicast*, *Multicast*, and *Broadcast*. In IPv6 though, things are slightly different.

Gone is the Broadcast Address. This is far too hungry of CPU cycles, and therefore wasteful overall. Instead, more and more protocols that once used broadcasts to transmit information, will now use *Multicasts* instead. Also, a new address type is added - the *Anycast* address. An Anycast address, is in fact the same as a Unicast, except that it is assigned to multiple interfaces. Obviously the interfaces must be configured in such a way that they know that they are part of an Anycast, but apart from this, they are identical. When a packet is sent to an Anycast, it is then merely delivered to the interface that is closest rather than to all interfaces that have that address.

32.7 Summary

In this chapter we have introduced the concepts of IP Addressing, and we have touched on the subject of routing. The actual IP Address itself is crucial to the operation of IP internets, in just the same way that the MAC Address is crucial to the eventual delivery of data. IP Addresses lend themselves to the creation of hierarchical internets, and indeed the very structure of the address is biased this way. But addressing at Layer 3 is anything but the end of the story. Devices need to communicate at the Network Layer (Layer 3), but they must be able to communicate across the physical medium of the LAN. Address Resolution, using the Address Resolution Protocol, is therefore required, and forms an integral element of IP.

At the simplest level, the IP Address provides us with a method to identify Networks and Hosts, and for routing this is all that we really need. The problems however are many-fold, due in part to the runaway success of IP itself. Our 32 bit address that has served us so well for so many years is now woefully inadequate to take us through the 21st century. DHCP can assist in the short term, but a long term fix requires a much larger address space. IPv6 is our life saver with its 128 bit address space, and new address types, but with this comes its own issues. Migration to the new version will not happen overnight, and integration of version 4 and version 6 is bound to cause problems no matter how much care we take during implementation. In short, networks will have to conform, but we shall need to plan and implement piece-by-piece if we are to avoid the potential major problems ahead.

The Internet Protocol

If we are to understand routing in an IP environment, then it is essential that we have at least a basic understanding of the Internet Protocol (IP) itself. This chapter is not designed to be an exhaustive study of the protocol and its operation, but since there are mechanisms on which routers rely, these at least need to be introduced.

The Internet Protocol itself provides us with an *unreliable* Datagram delivery service. Without trying to cast too dark a picture though, it is termed unreliable because it is *connectionless*, and datagram delivery relies upon *best efforts*, i.e., there is no handshaking that takes place between end systems at this layer. That said, it is the very cornerstone on which all protocols within the Internet Protocol suite are built, it allows for the prioritization of packets, and it provides for the *fragmentation* of data where necessary. IP does not have in-built facilities to report errors, yet this is obviously a requirement if we are to build any reliability on top of IP. This error reporting mechanism comes in the form of a further protocol, the Internet Control Message Protocol (ICMP), which today is generally considered to be integral to IP itself. Since ICMP is key to the operation of IP, this will be discussed later in the chapter.

33.1 IP Datagram Encapsulation

The Datagram is the name given to the unit of data (the *Protocol Data Unit* (PDU)) at Network or Routing layer. IP Datagrams are encapsulated directly within MAC frames as shown in figure 33-1, and they in turn carry data from the upper layers. The figure actually shows *Telnet* data being carried, but of course this could just as easily be Data from any Application Layer protocol. Also, the figure shows that the Datagram is carried in an Ethernet frame, using the EtherType 0800. IP however, is not restricted to Ethernet only environments, and can be carried over any standards compliant LAN or WAN technology and can also use 802.2 (LLC), and/or the Sub Network Access Protocol[1] (SNAP).

Notice also that we have to re-align our terminology slightly when talking about the Internet Protocol suite. The Protocol Data Unit for Transmission Control Protocol (TCP) packets is called a *Segment*, yet coincidentally, the PDU for packets

---

[1] See section E for a full description of LLC and SNAP.

using the User Datagram Protocol[2] (UDP) are referred to as Datagrams since they add little to that of IP.

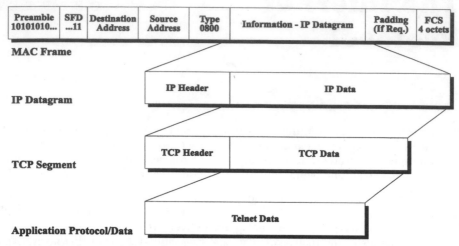

Figure 33-1: IP Datagram Encapsulation

33.2 The IP Datagram Header

The format of the IP Datagram Header is shown in figure 33-2. Here we see the Datagram as would be seen where the framing at the Data Link Layer was Ethernet, with an EtherType of 0800. For the purpose of clarity, we have ignored the upper layers that would be carried as the IP payload such as TCP, or UDP, and we have also ignored any application data. The header itself comprises some 12 fields which are all mandatory, and then may also carry options. Of those 12 mandatory fields, one has a fixed value, and one is only used in extremely rare circumstances. These fields can then be described as follows:

The first octet comprises two, four bit, fields namely the *Version* number, and the *Internet Header Length*. In the case of the version number, this is fixed and always assumes the value 4 (IPv4). Although IPv6 is now undergoing ratification, the header format is totally different and therefore is totally incompatible. No negotiation over versions ever takes place, and datagrams that are received with an unrecognizable version will be dropped without warning the sending station. The *Internet Header Length* field is used to indicate the length of the IP Header, and therefore where the IP data would start within the *Information* field of the frame. This field is always specified in terms of 32 bit (four octet) words, and since it is rare to use the *Options* field within the header, this field will normally take the value of 5 (i.e., 20 octets).

[2] As we saw in chapter 31 there are two Transport Layer protocols that can be employed. These are known as the Transmission Control Protocol (TCP) and the User Datagram Protocol (UDP).

The *Type-of-Service* field of one octet can be used to define how the Datagram and its fragments (if applicable) should be handled. Generally this field is not used by devices, although this facility obviously does exist. Certainly, the major use of the field was perceived as being when Datagrams pass through routers. In this way, a router could select the appropriate route based upon some pre-defined criteria as shown in table 33-1. From the table, we see that the three *Precedence* bits allow the definition of general types of Datagram. The remaining four, defined, bits then specify that the Datagram should be routed with *Minimum Delay* (D), *Highest Throughput* (T), *Highest Reliability* (R), or over a path that represents the *Least Monetary Cost* (M). Sadly, although this field was defined through the IP Protocol, only the *Open Shortest Path First* (OSPF) protocol supports its usage, and even this is now being withdrawn because too few vendors have implemented it.

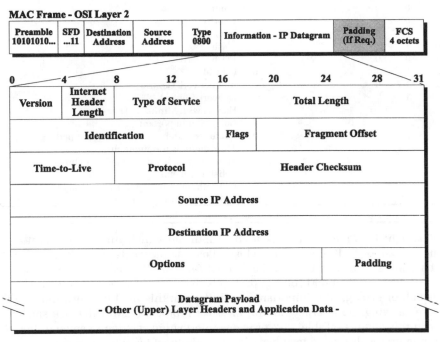

Figure 33-2: IP Datagram Header Format

The two octet *Total Length* field is used to define the total overall length of the Datagram, in octets, and includes both the header and data areas. The two octet *Identification* field is a unique number that is used to identify this Datagram, and indeed all fragments of it (where applicable). This field is used in two ways. In the first instance, it can be used to detect where a Datagram has been duplicated and, where this does occur, the duplicate can be ignored. Secondly, when used in conjunction with the *Flags* and *Fragment Offset* fields, the *Identification* field is used to identify all fragments of the Datagram. The *Flags*, and *Fragment Offset* fields are used to control the process of fragmentation, which can be extremely important when we talk about routing. Fragmentation itself is discussed later, and with it the operation of these two fields. The eight bit *Time-to-Live* field is also used by routers only, and is implemented to ensure that Datagrams do not circulate endlessly in the event that a routing loop occurs. In theory, a station that transmits a Datagram will set a value in this field that *should* represent the number of seconds that the Datagram is allowed to live on the network. In practice, this value is used as a simple *Hop count*, and is decremented by one each time that the Datagram passes through a router. When the field is decremented to zero, the Datagram is discarded by the router, and an ICMP error message is sent to the source station.

Table 33-1: IP Datagram Header Type of Service Field

0	1	2	3	4	5	6	7	
Precedence			D	T	R	M	r	Description
0	0	0					0	Routine
0	0	1					0	Priority
0	1	0					0	Immediate
0	1	1					0	Flash
1	0	0					0	Flash Override
1	0	1					0	Critical
1	1	0					0	Internetwork Control
1	1	1					0	Network Control
			1				0	Handle with Minimum Delay
			0				0	Delay is unimportant
				1			0	Route through highest Throughput path
				0			0	Throughput is unimportant
					1		0	Route over path with highest Reliability
					0		0	Reliability is unimportant
						1	0	Use path representing Least Monetary Cost
						0	0	Monetary Cost is unimportant

Note: Bit 7 is Reserved and is always set to zero.

The eight bit *Protocol* field is used to indicate which upper layer protocol is being carried as the IP Datagram payload. Possible protocols are TCP and UDP that we have already mentioned, and the *Exterior Gateway Protocol* (EGP), and the *Open Shortest Path First* (OSPF) routing protocols that we will meet in the next chapter. Of equal, or even greater importance to IP though, this field can also indicate that we are carrying the *Internet Control Message Protocol* (ICMP) that we shall meet later in this chapter. Table 33-2 provides information relating to some of the most common protocols carried together with their *Protocol Ids*.

Table 33-2: IP Protocol Ids

Protocol Id.			
Dec.	Hex	Keyword	Description
1	01	ICMP	The Internet Control Message Protocol
2	02	IGMP	The Internet Group Management Protocol
3	03	GGP	The Gateway-to-Gateway Protocol
6	06	TCP	The Transmission Control Protocol
8	08	EGP	The Exterior Gateway Protocol
9	09	IGP	Any *Private* Interior Gateway Protocol
17	11	UDP	The User Datagram Protocol
89	59	OSPFIGP	The Open Shortest Path First (OSPF) Protocol

The two octet *Header Checksum* is used to ensure that the IP Datagram Header has been received intact. Only the header itself is checked, and where the checksum fails, the Datagram is discarded immediately. Since the *Time-to-Live* field is decremented by routers as they handle Datagrams though, it follows that the *Checksum* must be re-calculated at each router that the Datagram visits. Thus, routers make changes, albeit subtly, to all Datagrams that they handle.

The four octet *Source* and *Destination IP Address* fields identify the sender and intended recipient(s). Finally, the variable length *Options* are rarely used (but for the sake of completeness are discussed in the next section), and the variable length *Data* carries the payload of the IP Datagram itself. The actual data may contain upper layer headers such as TCP or UDP where appropriate, the Application protocol, and the application data.

33.2.1 IP Datagram Options

IP Datagram *options* are rarely set. Where they are set however, each option can be of a variable length, and therefore we may not necessarily end on a four octet boundary as dictated by the *Internet Header Length* field within the header. Where this is the case, a variable length (one to three octets) *Padding* field is added to re-align the header onto a 32 bit word boundary.

Each option comprises a single octet header, where the bits are designated as follows: The highest order bit is used as a *Copy* flag, such that when set to binary one this option should be copied to all fragments of the Datagram, should the need to fragment arise. Where this bit is set to binary zero, then the option should not be copied to fragments of this Datagram. The next two bits specify the *Option Class* that defines the *type* of option, and the final five bits specify the *option number*, which defines the option itself. Obviously, the option itself will then contain further octets as required. Table 33-3 shows the values of particular bit patterns for the option *Class*, and option *Number*.

Table 33-3: IP Datagram Options

Class		Number					Description
1	2	3	4	5	6	7	
0	0						Control - Datagram or Network
0	1						Reserved - Not used
1	0						Debugging and Measurement
1	1						Reserved - Not used
		0	0	0	0	0	End of Option List
		0	0	0	0	1	No Operation (NO-OP)
		0	0	0	1	0	Security/Handling Restrictions
		0	0	0	1	1	Loose Source Routing
		0	0	1	0	0	Internet Timestamp
		0	0	1	1	1	Record Route
		0	1	0	0	0	Stream Identifier
		0	1	0	0	1	Strict Source Routing

Where options are used, the list will always be delimited by the End-of-Options List option. Both *Loose* and *Strict Source Routing* allow the source station to identify a list of networks that must be traversed en route to the destination, and the order in which they must be visited. In the case of *Loose Source Routing*, other networks may also be crossed, but with *Strict Source Routing*, no network apart from the specified list may be used. The *Record Route* and *Internet Timestamp* options require that intervening routers should enter their addresses into the Datagram as it passes. In the case of the *Timestamp* option, the current time is also added to this information. Finally, the remaining options, *Stream Identifier* and *Security/Handling Restrictions*, allow the sending station to identify a particular data *stream*, or specify security options respectively.

33.2.2 Datagram Fragmentation

Fragmentation is potentially an important part of routing, since a Datagram generated on one network may not be able to traverse another if it is too big. For example, in figure 33-3 we may have two Token Ring stations on different LANs that must communicate via an Ethernet LAN.

The so called *Maximum Transmission Unit* (MTU) of a network defines the maximum data payload that may be carried. In this case, since Token Ring LANs can carry significantly larger frames than Ethernet LANs, we potentially have a problem. Two solutions are possible: Firstly, we could limit the size of the frames that are generated by Token Ring stations. This would make inefficient use of the Token Ring LAN though, especially for those frames that do not need to leave it. Alternatively, we could to break the frame up into smaller *fragments* for transmission over the Ethernet, and that is exactly what IP routers allow us to do.

To describe this functionality, we need to also revisit the IP Datagram Header, and in particular the *Identification*, *Flags*, and *Fragment Offset* fields. You will recall that the *Identification* field carries a unique value for each Datagram. Where a Datagram is fragmented, this *Id.* is then also copied to each fragment so that they can be identified as being part of the same Datagram. The *Flags* field of the header is just three bits wide. The highest order bit is reserved and is always set to zero. The next bit is referred to as the *Do Not Fragment* bit, and when set to one instructs routers that they must not fragment the Datagram under any circumstances. Frames with this bit set, arriving at a router that would normally need to fragment them in order to allow them to pass, will now be discarded. When a frame is discarded in this way, an ICMP[3] message is then passed back to the source station informing it that an error of this kind has occurred. The final bit is referred to as the *More Fragments Follow* bit, and indicates that more fragments of *this* Datagram are yet to be received. Finally, in terms of fragmentation control, the final 13 bits of this two octet field are used to define the offset of *this* fragment within the overall Datagram. Specified in 8 octet blocks (known as *Fragment Blocks*), this then gives the relative position of this fragment within the original Datagram. In this way, the Datagram can eventually be re-assembled by the destination station.

Returning to figure 33-3, Datagrams that arrive at either router and are larger than the maximum Ethernet/802.3 frames size, will be fragmented if they must traverse

---

[3] The Internet Control Message Protocol (ICMP) is used to report errors on behalf of IP and is discussed later.

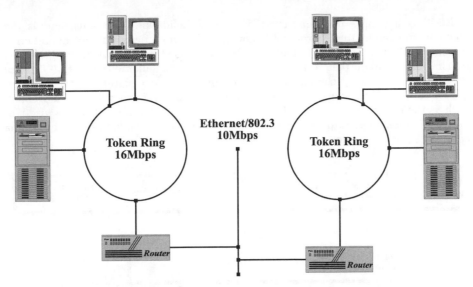

Figure 33-3: Fragmentation Example

the Ethernet/802.3 LAN. This is regardless of whether they are destined for the opposite Token Ring, or simply an Ethernet/802.3 station. The mechanics are such that the Datagram will be split such that no fragment exceeds the MTU of the network that must be traversed. The first fragment will then have the *More Fragments Follow* flag set to one, and the *Offset* field set to all zeroes. Second and subsequent fragments up to and including the penultimate fragment will have the *More Fragments Follow* flag set to one, and the *Offset* field set to indicate the position of this fragment within the Datagram. The final fragment will have all flags set to zero, and the *Offset* field set to indicate the position of this fragment within the Datagram. Thus, by using a simple *Flag* and *Offset* mechanism such as this, we are able to indicate fragmentation efficiently, and rebuild the Datagram at the destination. Lastly, before leaving the operation of fragmentation, it should be pointed out that *all* routers are capable of performing fragmentation. However, once a Datagram has been fragmented, it will only be re-assembled by the destination station(s), and never by an intermediate node such as another router - a fragment can however be further fragmented if required. So, if a station on the left hand Token Ring were to transmit a Datagram to a station on the right, the router on the left of the figure would have to fragment it. The router on the right would not re-assemble the Datagram though, this would be done at the final destination station on the right hand Token Ring.

33.3 The Internet Control Message Protocol (ICMP)

The Internet Control Message Protocol (ICMP) is generally considered to be an integral part of IP. In fact, it is specified completely independently, and although it is not used outside of the IP world, it certainly could be.

ICMP is a simple protocol which is carried inside IP Datagrams, and is the mechanism used by the IP protocol to communicate both network control and error messages. As we mentioned above, ICMP can be used by a router to indicate to a transmitting station that a Datagram needs to be fragmented, yet the *Do Not Fragment* flag is set. It can also be used to inform a source station that a Datagram has been discarded because the *Time-to-Live* has expired, or that there is a problem with a Datagram, or for a number of other reasons. Equally, ICMP is used in *network management* to test for *Network* or device *Reachability* through the common *Ping* application.

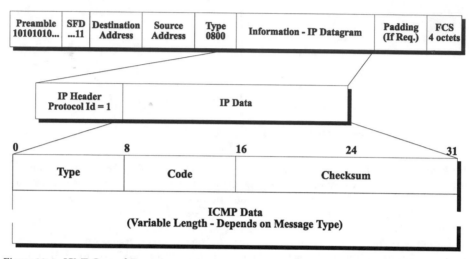

Figure 33-4: ICMP General Format

Within ICMP, there are only rudimentary checks in the form of a *Checksum*, which means that ICMP adds no real reliability to the little that is provided by IP itself. Obviously then, ICMP messages are equally unreliable. Indeed if an error occurs that results in an error message being sent, should that error message not be delivered for any reason, then that is just unfortunate. In short, we never send error messages about error messages, thereby adhering to the overall philosophy of IP where we aim for compact efficiency. Figure 33-4 shows the structure of ICMP messages, and their relation to the IP Datagram. In this case, we are also using an Ethernet frame.

ICMP messages all have a four octet header, which is then followed by a variable length data field. The exact format and length of the Datagram will depend on the type of ICMP message, which is identified by the 8 bit *Type* field. The *Code* field is then used to further define the message, and the *Data* field will carry data where required. Table 33-4 shows each of the Types of ICMP message and, where applicable, their associated Code values (both expressed in decimal). The messages themselves are then described separately below.

The Internet Protocol

Table 33-4: ICMP Message Types

Type	Code	Description
00	00	Echo Reply
03	00	Destination Unreachable - Network Unreachable
03	01	Destination Unreachable - Host Unreachable
03	02	Destination Unreachable - Protocol Unreachable
03	03	Destination Unreachable - Port Unreachable
03	04	Destination Unreachable - Fragmentation Req. (*Do Not* Flag set)
03	05	Destination Unreachable - Source Route Failed - IP Option set
03	06	Destination Unreachable - Network Unknown
03	07	Destination Unreachable - Host Unknown
03	08	Destination Unreachable - Source Host Isolated
03	09	Destination Unreachable - Dest. Net Administratively Disabled
03	10	Destination Unreachable - Dest. Host Administratively Disabled
03	11	Destination Unreachable - Net Unreachable for Type-of-Service
03	12	Destination Unreachable - Host Unreachable for Type-of-Service
04	00	Source Quench
05	00	Redirect - Redirect Datagram to Network
05	01	Redirect - Redirect Datagram for Host
05	02	Redirect - Redirect Datagrams for Type-of-Service and Network
05	03	Redirect - Redirect Datagrams for Type-of-Service and Host
08	00	Echo Request
09	00	Router Advertisement
10	00	Router Solicitation
11	00	Time Exceeded - Time-to-Live Expired
11	01	Time Exceeded - Fragment Re-assembly Time Expired
12	00	Parameter Problem
13	00	Timestamp Request
14	00	Timestamp Reply
15	00	Information Request
16	00	Information Reply
17	00	Address Mask Request
18	00	Address Mask Reply

33.3.1 Echo Request/Reply

The ICMP Echo Request and Reply messages (Types 0 and 8) are used primarily to test network reachability. Incorporated into the *Packet Internet Groper* (PING) application, hosts that receive an ICMP Echo Request must return an ICMP Echo Reply to the sender with all data intact.

After the 4 octet header, Echo Request/Reply messages contain a 16 bit *Identifier* and a 16 bit *Sequence Number*, that can be used to identify this message and match requests to replies. Following this, the message contains a variable length *Data* field that contains optional data that must be returned intact.

33.3.2 Destination Unreachable

The *Destination Unreachable* ICMP message is used by both routers and hosts to indicate to source hosts that an IP Datagram could not be delivered. The *Code* field then specifies the exact reason why Datagram delivery failed.

The message itself contains a 4 octet *pad* of all zeroes that immediately follows the header. This, in turn, is then followed by the header of the failing Datagram, and the first 64 bits (8 octets) of the original IP data. In this way, the source station should be able to determine which Datagram(s) has not been delivered, and also take action where appropriate.

33.3.3 Source Quench

Although rarely used, Source Quench can provide an elementary form of *Flow Control*. Broadly, where Datagrams arrive at a host or router faster than they can be processed, the Datagram is discarded, and a Source Quench message is sent to the source host. On receipt of this message type, the source host then leaves bigger gaps between Datagrams, thereby allowing the receiving device chance to catch up. There is no opposite to Source Quench. Instead, after a short period of time the transmitter will start to leave smaller gaps again, until it receives more Source Quench messages. In this way, the transmitter and receiver eventually reach an equilibrium.

Source Quench messages contain a 4 octet *pad* of all zeroes that immediately follows the header. This in turn is followed by the header of the discarded Datagram, and the first 64 bits (8 octets) of the original IP data. In this way, the source station is able to determine which Datagram(s) was discarded, and of course, re-send it.

33.3.4 Redirect

It is only ever routers that send redirection ICMP messages, and then only to source hosts. Stations on a network must be configured with what is known as a *Default Gateway*,[4] which is the address of the router to which they should direct all Datagrams that they cannot directly deliver themselves. Routers however typically have better routing information than stations, and this can mean that a station might actually be better to direct its datagrams via an alternative route.

Consider the scenario of figure 33-5 where we have two routes from the top network to the bottom. Obviously, the route offered by the router on the right (Router 3) is superior to that offered by the routers on the left (Routers 1 and 2). If Station A is configured to use Router 1 as its *Default Gateway* though, it will send all Datagrams destined for the bottom network to Router 1 regardless. Router 1 will route the Datagram on behalf of the station but, assuming that it knows about Router 3 and the routes that it offers, it will also send an ICMP Redirect back to the source station (Station A). Thus, providing that Station A takes notice of these messages, it will now know that an alternative route exists and use it next time. Sadly, although routers will generally send redirects out, few stations actually take any notice of them.

Besides the 4 octet header, the Redirect message contains the 4 octet IP Address of the router that is suggested as the better route, the header of the Datagram that was affected, and the first 64 bits (8 octets) of IP data. In being presented with the header, the station receiving the Redirect will now be able to determine the

---

[4] The Default Gateway will be discussed in chapter 34.

destination address that was being used and amend its own internal tables accordingly.

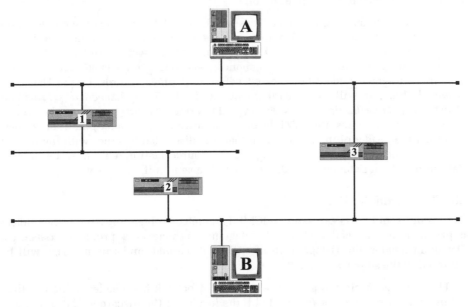

Figure 33-5: ICMP Redirect

33.3.5 Router Advertisement and Solicitation

The ICMP Router Advertisement and Solicitation messages allow routers to advertise their presence, and also allow stations to query a network looking for routers that are attached. Typically, stations might send a *Router Solicitation* when they boot-up, via either a broadcast (using the *Limited Broadcast* address of 255.255.255.255) or a multicast (using the *All-Routers Multicast* address of 224.0.0.2). Capable routers would then respond with a *Router Advertisement*.

Router Solicitations comprise the 4 octet ICMP header, followed by 4 octets that are reserved, and normally set to all zeroes. Advertisements have the ICMP header, which is followed by a single octet that carries a *Number of Addresses* field, a single octet that carries the *Size of each Address*, and a two octet *Lifetime* field that dictates how long the information may be considered valid. This information is then followed by a number of *Router Addresses* (as dictated by the *Number of Addresses* field), and a four octet *Preference Level* for each router address. As with solicitations, Advertisements can either be multicast (to the *All-Systems Multicast* address of 224.0.0.1), or broadcast (using the *Limited Broadcast* address of 255.255.255.255).

33.3.6 Time Exceeded

As we have already said, when Datagrams are passed from router to router en-route to their final destination, the *Time-to-Live* field in the Datagram header is decremented. If this field is ever decremented to zero, then the Datagram is discarded, and an ICMP *Time Exceeded - Time to Live Exceeded* message (Type 11, Code 0) is returned to the source station.

When a Datagram is fragmented, it is possible that the various fragments could pass through the internet using different routes, and indeed some could even become lost or discarded. To avoid destination stations waiting indefinitely for all fragments to arrive, once the first fragment is received a timer is started. Now, all remaining fragments *must* be received before that timer expires, or the Datagram received thus far will be discarded and an ICMP *Time Exceeded - Fragment Reassembly Time Expired* message (Type 11, Code 01) is returned to the source station. For both cases, the ICMP header is followed by a 4 octet *pad* of all zeroes, and then the header of the IP Datagram that was discarded together with the first 64 bits (8 octets) of IP data. Once again, the source station will now be able to determine which Datagram was discarded and re-send it if necessary.

33.3.7 Parameter Problem

Both routers and hosts can send an ICMP Parameter Problem message if they detect a problem in the header of an IP Datagram. Whenever a problem exists in a Datagram header, the Datagram itself will be discarded, and this message will be returned to the source station.

The message itself comprises the standard 4 octet ICMP header, which is then followed by a single octet *Pointer* field, the header of the discarded Datagram, and the first 64 bits (8 octets) of IP data. The Pointer is then used to identify the octet within the original Datagram header that is believed to be the start of the error.

33.3.8 Timestamp Request/Reply

The ICMP Timestamp messages are useful where we wish to determine the round-trip delays associated with certain network paths. The *Timestamp Request* message is sent from a device containing the ICMP header, a two octet *Identifier* field, a two octet *Sequence Number* field, and then three, four octet *Timestamp* fields. The first of the timestamps is known as the *Originate Timestamp*, and is filled in by the source device as the message is transmitted. The second timestamp, known as the *Receive Timestamp*, is entered by the receiving device as soon as the message is received. Finally, the third timestamp is the *Transmit Timestamp*, and this is completed as the message is returned to the originating station as a *Timestamp Reply*. All times are in milliseconds since midnight, Greenwich Mean Time (GMT). That said, there is no requirement that network devices have real time clocks that are set, and there is no real way of ensuring that all clocks are synchronized anyway. Hence, although we have a method for determining round-trip times, these may be less than accurate.

33.3.9 Information Request/Reply

This ICMP message has been broadly replaced by BootP/DHCP and RARP, but was originally designed so that a device could request its address. A station, typically at power-up, would send an *Information Request* that contained a header, a two octet *Identifier*, and a two octet *Sequence Number*. This would be sent as a broadcast with the IP Header *Source* and *Destination* addresses set to zeroes. The response would then be sent back with these fields fully and correctly specified.

33.3.10 Address Mask Request/Reply

Like the *Information Request* and *Reply*, the *Address Mask Request* and *Reply* was used by stations that wished to obtain more information - in this case, the *Subnet Mask* that they should use. A Station would broadcast an *Address Mask Request*, that contained the ICMP Header, a two octet *Identifier*, a two octet *Sequence Number*, and a four octet *Subnet Mask* field set to zeroes. An *authoritative* host would then, on receipt of this request, fill in the *Subnet Mask* field with the mask that should be used, and then send the message back as a unicast *Address Mask Reply*.

33.4 Summary

We have now taken a brief look at the operation of possibly the single most important protocol today - the Internet Protocol, or IP. It is significant because the vast majority of networks today are IP based, and even those companies that still use *legacy* systems will use IP if they need to connect to the Internet.

In the last chapter we discussed the addressing scheme that IP uses, and we know that this address space is under extreme pressure. IP itself however, works well and provides us with most of the functionality that is asked of it today. Things will change of course, and the advent of IP version 6 is a reminder that we live in an ever evolving world. Version 6 brings with it a number of improvements over version 4, but that is not to say that the entire fabric of networking will change overnight. IP version 4 will be with us for many years to come, and must continue to provide us with the delivery mechanism for our data.

The Internet Control Message Protocol (ICMP) is an integral part of IP itself, and provides the feedback that IP lacks. In fact, ICMP is very *general purpose* in the way that it works, and it includes a number of features that are extremely useful. For example, we all take the simple *Ping* application for granted, yet it is built on ICMP. Network Management takes this facility and builds on it. It is compact, and allows us to quickly determine the operational status of any IP ready network device, and its reachability. ICMP allows routers to advertise their existence, and inform stations that better routes exist. We can gauge the round-trip delays associated with links through the *Timestamp* functions, and we can also flow control devices. In short, ICMP is not just an error reporting mechanism, although that is an important role that ICMP plays.

Routing Principles

When we examined the operation of Subnetting and IP Addresses generally, we could not help but to stumble into the realms of routing. Indeed the whole idea of the IP Address was to enable a routed environment, and it is therefore difficult to divorce the two completely.

You will recall we said that devices must exist on the same Network (and therefore share a common Network Id) if they are to be able to directly exchange data - something that we referred to as *Direct Routing*. Equally, we said that where source and destination hosts reside on different networks, then this required the use of a *Router*, and we referred to this as *Indirect Routing*. But what exactly is routing anyway? Essentially, routing can be defined as the task of finding the *best* path from a sender to a desired destination. To understand how this is achieved, we shall need to take the principles that we have considered thus far, and enlarge upon them. To do this we must re-examine the mechanics of routing itself, and look at the protocols that allow the entire routing process to be dynamic. Routing itself is based on reasonably simple principles. That said, we shall see that the creation of large internets which are comprised of disparate systems and routing protocols, can become extremely complex.

34.1 Routers

Routers are at the very heart of internetworks, so before discussing the principles of routing in great detail, it is worthwhile taking a few moments to compare and contrast routers with other internetworking devices. When we considered the LAN technologies in the previous sections of this volume, we met devices such as Repeaters and Bridges. These devices each perform a valuable function in the networking world, but each is also very specific in what it does. Routers are again quite different in the way that they handle data, although modern day routers do have functionality that overlaps other devices. Figure 34-1 demonstrates the functionality of each device when compared to each other, and when compared to the OSI Reference Model.

- **Repeaters/Hubs**
  Repeaters or Hubs, as we have already seen, as known as Physical Layer devices. They are used to connect LAN segments together, and as their name suggests, repeat data from one port to all other ports. Essentially, these devices have little intelligence, provide no resilience, and no traffic separation at all.

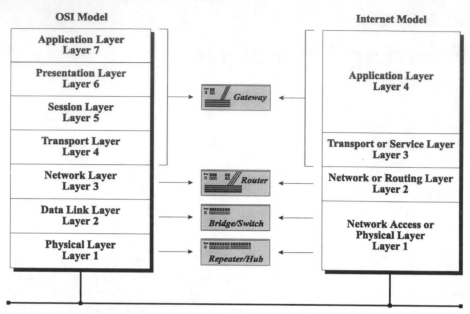

Figure 34-1: Internetworking Devices

- **Bridges and Switches**

  Bridges and Switches, like Repeaters, can link LAN segments, although these devices operate at the Data Link rather than the Physical Layer. This means that unlike their Repeater counterparts, these devices make forwarding decisions based upon an addressing scheme (the MAC Address), and rely on knowledge of end node location. In short, Bridges and Switches forward data frames from one port to another, only when that frame is required on the destination segment. In addition, these devices therefore provide a measure of data segmentation, and this means that the bandwidth required to link these LANs is potentially lower. In turn, this then opens up the possibility of linking geographically distant LANs together over lower speed WAN links. Finally, Bridges and Switches can also be used to create resilient networks using what is called the *Spanning Tree Protocol*. With this, multiple paths can exist between source and destination nodes such that if a device or link should fail, an alternative path can be used.

- **Routers**

  The router is a device that operates at the OSI Network Layer (Layer 3) and is totally protocol dependent. Protocols that may be routed, such as IP, AppleTalk, DECnet, etc., are then termed *Routable Protocols*. Routers are interested in Networks, as opposed to end nodes (or hosts), and therefore maintain tables of Networks that they believe to be reachable, and of course how to get there. Routers run a number of protocols that enable them to exchange reachability information, and these are generally termed *Routing Protocols* - a number of which are discussed in the next chapter. This means that these devices must understand Network Layer addressing (i.e., IP

Addressing), and must of course also be able to use the Data Link Layer addressing scheme. Typically, these devices also have Layer 2 functionality and can also act as Bridges. This has led to the name *Brouter*, being applied to these devices in the past, although today this is seldom used. Routers are, in the Internet world, also referred to as *Gateways*, although a Gateway is really a totally different device. For our discussions, we shall always use the name router to describe these devices, so as not to create unnecessary confusion.

- **Gateways**

  A Gateway, in its truest sense, is a device that allows two (or more) dissimilar systems to communicate. In short, this device links systems using disparate protocol stacks, and the functionality is typically implemented in software. As an example, we may have a host that is directly connected to an X.25 network (a *native* X.25 device) that needs to communicate with an IP host. The device that performs the protocol conversion then, is a *Gateway*.

34.1.1 Router Specifications

Routers are often specified in a number of ways. Obviously, when selecting the device, the type(s) of connection required will be important. Consider figure 34-2, where we wish to interconnect a number of different LAN and WAN types. Our choices will now be limited to vendors that support those various interfaces, and in the concentration that our topology dictates. This however is not the only criteria that we should use, since there is one that is far more fundamental - performance.

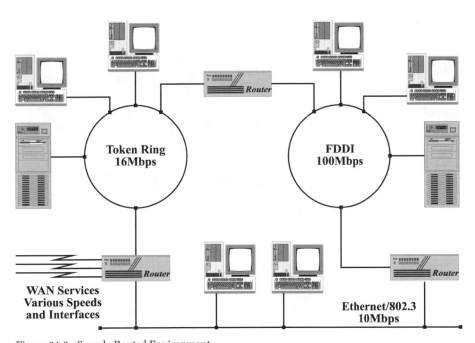

Figure 34-2: Sample Routed Environment

The majority of routers available today are based upon software. Thus, although faster hardware platforms and more efficient software coding mean that our overall speeds will increase, latency remains the single biggest issue with these devices. The rate at which the router can forward will therefore ultimately determine its applicability within any particular design. Aggregate LAN-to-LAN forwarding rates greater than 100,000 packets per second (PPS) are not uncommon. Similarly, aggregate LAN-to-WAN/WAN-to-LAN rates of 20,000 packets per second are fairly normal although this will of course depend heavily on the speed of WAN service.

34.1.2 Basic Router Operation

Before embarking on an in-depth discussion on the operation of routers, we need to understand a few basic facts. Routers will only handle frames that are explicitly addressed to them. Of course, acting as network hosts as they do, they will take note and act on broadcast and multicast frames as they arrive, but they will only forward these where they have been explicitly configured to do so. In this way, unlike bridges and switches, these devices will effectively block broadcast storms. In addition, once a frame has been accepted by the router, it will always be handled in a specific way. Consider figure 34-3.

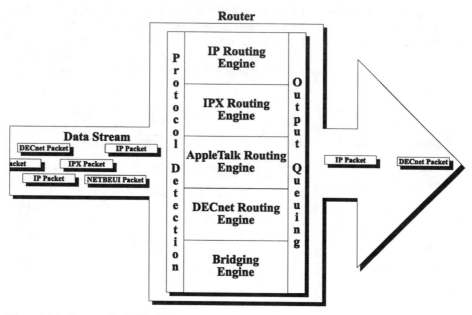

Figure 34-3: Router - Basic Block Diagram

The router will determine the protocol by examining the frame. If the frame is an Ethernet frame, then it will look at the *Type* field. If it is an IEEE 802.x frame such as an 802.3, or 802.5 frame, then it may well have an 802.2 (LLC) header[1] that will indicate the protocol through the *DSAP* field. Equally, frames may use the Sub

---

[1] IEEE 802.2 (LLC) is discussed in section E along with the Sub-Network Access Protocol (SNAP).

Network Access Protocol[1] (SNAP) which will identify the protocol. Alternatively, there is one specific Novell IPX frame that uses 802.3 with no protocol identifier. Known as *Raw 802.3*, the first two octets of data (part of the IPX Header) are always FFFF, thus the protocol can be identified through this. In any event, the protocol must be established before further processing can take place.

It is imperative that we know the *type* of data we are dealing with, since routers are protocol dependent devices, and they rely on the Network Addresses that will be buried within the headers. Once we have this information, the router can then direct the packet data (i.e. the Network Layer information including the header) to the relevant protocol engine. This assumes that the router is both capable of forwarding packets of this protocol type, and that it has been configured to do so of course. Frames that arrive and which are carrying a protocol that the router does not know will be bridged if the router is configured to do this. If not, they are simply discarded.

Once the packet has arrived at the relevant protocol engine, the decision whether to forward the frame or discard it is made. Essentially, if the packet is destined for a remote network for which the router has no information, it will be discarded. If the router has sufficient information to forward the packet, it will be placed in the relevant output queue ready for transmission onwards towards its destination.

34.2 The Routing Table

At the very heart of the Router's Protocol Engine, is the routing table. The routing table, like the bridge/switch filter table, defines how packets should be handled, and therefore contains certain vital pieces of information. At the very minimum, this will include a list of reachable networks, and the next hop that should be used to forward packets en-route to that destination. The *Next Hop*, in this particular case is then defined as being the address of the *inbound* port of the next router in the forwarding process. For example, let us consider figure 34-4.

IP Routers, as part of their initial configuration, must be configured with an IP Address for each of their interfaces[2] . Thus, when they build their routing tables they will have some initial information. For example, table 34-1 shows the initial routing table for router 1 in figure 34-4. As we see, this contains networks 192.168.1.0, and 192.168.2.0, and requires no *Next Hop* information since these are locally attached

Table 34-1: Routing Table - Router 1

Network	Next Hop
192.168.1.0	None - Direct Connect
192.168.2.0	None - Direct Connect

networks and router 1 can access them directly. Equally, the initial routing table for router 2 would indicate networks 192.168.2.0, and 192.168.3.0, and would again require no *Next Hop* information since it is directly connected to these two networks.

[2] In actual fact, Point-to-Point WAN links do not actually need to be configured with IP Addresses. These Addressless Links (or un-numbered links), as they are known, are legal when used with certain Routing Protocols such as OSPF. This is discussed in greater detail later.

Having now described how our routing tables look at start-up, we can now consider what they will look like after the routers are each in possession of full routing information. Obviously, each router will need to obtain, or be configured with, reachability information for *all* networks. How the routers obtain this information will be discussed later, but for now let us consider how the routing tables of each router will look once they have all the information. This can be seen in table 34-2.

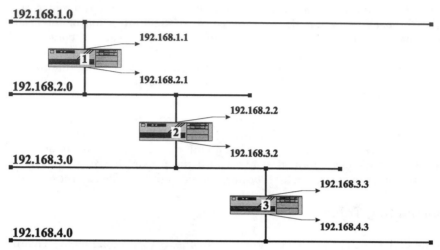

Figure 34-4: Simple Routed Network

Table 34-2: Full Routing Table Example

Router 1		Router 2		Router 3	
Network	Next Hop	Network	Next Hop	Network	Next Hop
192.168.1.0	None	192.168.2.0	None	192.168.3.0	None
192.168.2.0	None	192.168.3.0	None	192.168.4.0	None
192.168.3.0	192.168.2.2	192.168.1.0	192.168.2.1	192.168.1.0	192.168.3.2
192.168.4.0	192.168.2.2	192.168.4.0	192.168.3.3	192.168.2.0	192.168.3.2

So from our example, we can see that any packet that arrives at router 2 across network 192.168.2.0, and is destined for network 192.168.4.0, will be forwarded to router 3 on interface 192.168.3.3. Equally, packets arriving at router 3 across network 192.168.4.0, that are destined for networks 192.168.1.0, or 192.168.2.0, will be forwarded to router 2 through interface 192.168.3.2.

34.2.1 Route Quality

Our routers now have a means through which they can make decisions about how packets can be handled and onward forwarded. Of course, this is not the full story though, since the whole premise of routing is built on the ability to determine the *best* route to any particular destination. Certainly our examples so far have been relatively simple, and there has been only one route from which to choose - but this

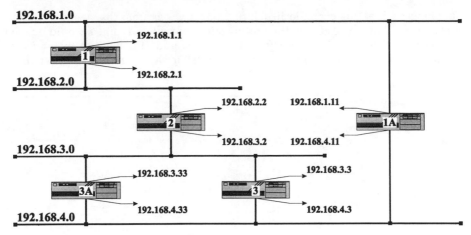

Figure 34-5: Multiple Routes Example

is not always the case. Unlike bridges, in a routed environment we can have multiple paths to destinations, and use all these paths simultaneously. Remember routers will only ever handle frames that are addressed to them at the Data Link Layer, and therefore we have no loops. Consider the example of figure 34-5.

Now, we have two routers that can service Network 192.168.4.0 from network 192.168.3.0, and we also have a *one hop* route from network 192.168.1.0, to network 192.168.4.0. Clearly, if we are to decide the *best* route to take, we must have some measure of goodness (the *cost*) and this comes in what is known as a *Metric*. There are no fixed rules governing how this is calculated, but typically, it will be based upon one of the following:

- **A Hop Count**
  This is the simplest form of metric, and is based on the number of networks that a packet has to traverse (*Hop*) en-route to its destination. This is used by routing protocols such as the Routing Information Protocol (RIP) and calculations based upon this are said to use a *Distance Vector*, or *Bellman-Ford Algorithm*.

- **Interface Speed**
  Using Interface speed is a far better method of calculating just how good a route is. For example, we may have two routes between a source and destination network, yet uses several 2Mbps WANs, and the other uses a single low speed WAN. A simple Hop Count would indicate that using the single link was best, yet multiple high speed hops could actually be far better. Protocols that use this method of determining the metric include the Open Shortest Path First (OSPF) protocol, and refer to this as being a *Link State* Protocol since it bases its decisions on the status of the link itself. Finally, protocols such as OSPF also incorporate a feature known as *Equal Cost - Multi-Path* that allows a router to *load share* over multiple, equal cost paths where they exist.

Looking back at our example in figure 34-5, if we assume that we are using a simple Hop Count as the metric, the routing tables of routers 1, and 2 would now be as shown in table 34-3. Obviously each router would still have to maintain its routing table, but for the purposes of this discussion we shall only consider these two routers.

Table 34-3: Routing Tables - Routers 1 and 2

| | Router 1 | | | Router 2 | |
Network	Next Hop	Metric	Network	Next Hop	Metric
192.168.1.0	None	1	192.168.2.0	None	1
192.168.2.0	None	1	192.168.3.0	None	1
192.168.3.0	192.168.2.2	2	192.168.1.0	192.168.2.1	2
192.168.4.0	192.168.2.2	3	192.168.4.0	192.168.3.3	2
	192.168.1.11	2		192.168.3.33	2

34.2.2 Other Routing Table Information

We have now expanded on our original ideas of the routing table and added the metric to the information that it contains. But is this all? Certainly there is no other *real* information that must be used when making routing decisions, so in essence we do not need anything else. In practice though, vendors generally put information into the table to aid in general router administration. This information might include the following:

- **Metric Type**
  Metrics are divided into two types namely Type 1 and Type 2. The reasons for this are that as our internetworks expand and we cross Autonomous Systems (AS), the metrics can become huge. Thus, a Type 1 metric is the sum of all internal paths within the AS, and the sum of the paths that are external to the AS. In other words, a Type 1 metric is the *total* cost of all paths between the source and destination. A Type 2 metric on the other hand is the cost of only those paths that are external to the AS. In this case, we assume that the cost of crossing the AS itself is insignificant in relation to the whole cost.

- **Routing Protocol**
  Routers are not limited to running only a single routing protocol. Indeed, many routers will not only run multiple routing protocols, but will also run multiple protocols on a single interface. Thus, since administrators may favor the routes learned through one protocol over another, they often publish how the routes were learned in the routing table. For example, we might learn routes to a destination network through both OSPF and RIP. Now we know that OSPF uses a *Link State* algorithm whereas RIP uses a *Distance Vector*, so we may prefer the OSPF route rather than the RIP route.

- **Preference**
  Just as we may prefer to use routes learned through a particular protocol, we may also decide that where multiple routes do exist, we would prefer to use one over all others due to its reliability or true monetary cost. For example,

we may have two routes to a single destination where both are of the same speed, but one is a leased line connection and the other is through a dial-up ISDN connection. Equally, we may have learned of the leased line through RIP, and the ISDN connection through OSPF. Now, if we favor OSPF routes, we will constantly dial the ISDN link and that will cost us more money. The solution to this is to override this, and make the leased line our *preferred* route.

34.3 Packet Processing

In order to fully understand how our router will forward a packet, and the changes that take place at the Data Link and Network Layers, we shall consider the simple example presented in figure 34-6. Here, Station A wishes to communicate with Station B. Since these two stations are on different networks though, Station A must *Indirectly* route the packet via Router 1, which in turn, must pass it onto Router 2 for final delivery.

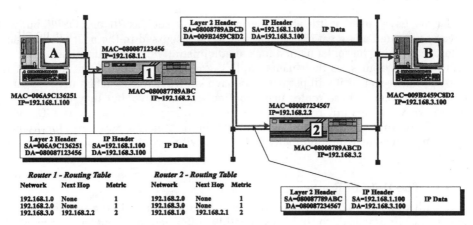

Figure 34-6: Packet Processing Example

Examining the entire process in detail, we see that Station A generates the IP Datagram with the source and destination IP Addresses set as those for Station A and Station B, respectively. At this time, the Time-to-Live (TTL) field in the datagram header will be set, and the Header Checksum will be calculated. At the Data Link Layer, the Source MAC Address will be the MAC Address of Station A, and the Destination MAC Address will be the interface of Router 1. If the station has the router's MAC Address cached in its ARP cache then it uses it directly, if not it will send an ARP Request to obtain the information. Once it has the MAC Address, the frame is then constructed, and transmitted over network 192.168.1.0.

When the frame is received by router 1, it is processed by first removing the Data Link Layer information, and then passing the remaining packet to the IP Protocol engine. The Destination IP Address is now examined, and Router 1 consults its Routing Table to ascertain whether it is holding routing information about the target network. In this case it is, and it determines that it must send the Datagram to

Router 2 to onward route the packet. To do this, it decrements the Time-to-Live field, and recalculates the Header Checksum. It now passes this to the Data Link Layer at the output interface, where it is re-framed using its own MAC address as the source address, and the MAC address of Router 2 as the Destination. As before, if the router does not have the MAC Address information cached, it will use ARP to obtain it. One we have the MAC Address information, the frame will be constructed, and then transmitted over network 192.168.2.0.

On arrival at Router 2, the router will perform exactly the same operations as those performed by Router 1. When it examines the Destination IP Address, it will consult its routing table and ascertain that it is directly connected to that network and can therefore deliver the packet directly. Again, it will generate the Data Link Layer frame based upon its own MAC Address as the Source, and this time, the MAC Address of the destination station as the Destination. If Station B's MAC Address is not cached, it will ARP for that information.

34.4 Static Routes

So far, we have talked a little about routing protocols such as RIP and OSPF, but we have not applied any great detail. These will be discussed in the next chapter, but before explaining these, let us first look at administratively defined routes, or *Static* routes. Static routes, as their name implies, are ones that have been programmed into the router so that it will permanently have knowledge of a distant network, and how to get there. These routes make routing less adaptive, but they are common where we wish to limit routing update traffic over networks such as ISDN etc. Using Static routes, we will not need to dial the link just to pass a routing update between routers, as would normally be the case with a routing protocol such as RIP or OSPF.

34.4.1 The Default Route

A Default route is a *special* Static route that is programmed into a router where it would be impractical to hold reachability information about every possible network. For example, if we attach to the Internet via an Internet Service Provider (ISP), it would be impractical to assume that our router would hold reachability information about every available network. Instead, we would program our router with a default route that points at our ISP, and packets to all destinations for which we do not have an explicit route would be forwarded this way. The Default Route is typically referenced as being network 0.0.0.0, and of course the Next Hop would be the IP Address of the router that we connect to at the ISP.

34.5 Broadcast and Multicast Forwarding

Before leaving the subject of routing principles, we should mention one special case, at least in passing. We said earlier in this chapter that routers will not forward multicast and broadcast packets. Sometimes however, we really do need these packets to be forwarded. For example, if we have a reasonably large internetwork and we have hosts that are all part of a multicast group spread across it, then we must have a means of delivering multicast packets to all group members. If we were to flood all networks with the packets, it would certainly be counterproductive, and we could say that it was really no better than broadcasting. Also, sometimes we would want to forward broadcasts so that a device can, say, load its operating system or other parameters. For example, let us briefly consider figure 34-7.

In the figure, we shall firstly assume that we have three distinct multicast groups (A, B, and C). From this, we can say that packets destined for Group A need to be propagated to networks 192.168.1.0, and 192.168.2.0. They do not however need to appear on networks 192.168.3.0, or 192.168.4.0. Equally, Group B's packets need to arrive on networks 192.168.1.0, and 192.168.4.0, and packets for Group C need to arrive on networks 192.168.2.0, and 192.168.3.0. Our routers must therefore be aware of where group members exist, and then forward multicast packets for those hosts accordingly. Several protocols are used. First, hosts use the *Internet Group Management Protocol* (IGMP)[5] to allow them to *register* their group memberships with routers and other hosts. Secondly, the routers will exchange group membership information with each other, typically using either the *Distance Vector Multicast Routing Protocol* (DVMRP),[6] or *Multicast OSPF* (MOSPF).

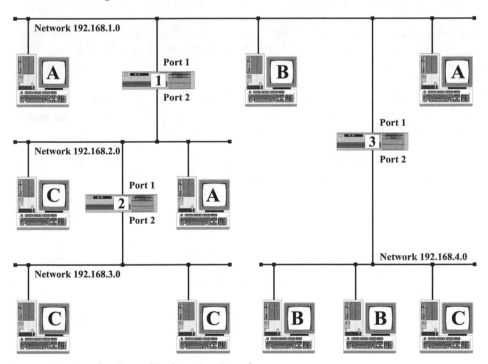

Figure 34-7: Broadcasting and Multicasting Example

[5] Further discussion of IGMP is beyond the scope of this book. However, further information can be found in the book entitled TCP/IP Explained, also by Philip Miller.
[6] Further discussion of DVMRP and MOSPF is beyond the scope of this book. However, further information can be found in the book entitled TCP/IP Explained, also by Philip Miller.

Turning our attentions to broadcasting, we may well have a host (say one of the hosts on network 192.168.3.0) that needs to download its operating system from one of the hosts on network 192.168.1.0. In this case, we shall assume that the host requesting its operating system will firstly need to obtain its IP Address and information about its operating system files from a *BootP*[7] server, also on network 192.168.1.0. Now, since the host does not know its own IP Address or the address of the server, it will need to send a broadcast packet asking a BootP server to provide it with that information. In this case, we would configure Routers 1 and 2 so that they would forward broadcasts destined for, and generated by, this protocol only. Such a facility is variously called a *BootP Helper*, *BootP Relay*, or *UDP Broadcast Forwarding* by different vendors. The point is however, routers do not normally forward broadcasts of *any* kind, and must be explicitly configured if they are to do so.

34.6 Summary

In this chapter we have looked at the very rudiments of routing with no particular regard for the protocols that make the whole process both automatic, and adaptive. As you will now appreciate, the principles and processes involved in routing itself are relatively straightforward and simple, although large, complex internets can appear daunting at first sight. Certainly routers are more complex than other devices that are found within the average network, and they perform a most valuable role.

In the next chapter we shall complete the story of routing in an IP environment when we discuss routing protocols such as RIP and OSPF. These are complex in their own right, but typically they are easy to enable and configure. Of course, they bring with them a certain mystique, but the golden rule of routing is that you should always break the problem down to its lowest level. Only then can you fully appreciate the mechanics of what is happening in the internetwork itself.

---

[7] As with other protocols, further discussion on BootP is beyond the scope of this book. Again, further information can be found in the book entitled TCP/IP Explained, also by Philip Miller.

IP Routing Protocols CHAPTER 35

Few internetworks are totally static. New sites are added to companies, and with them comes the need to add new networks. Even beyond this, links will fail from time-to-time, causing chaos if we are not careful. In order that our internetworks can adapt to these alterations as they occur, we need to ensure that our routers detect changes to active routes and act accordingly. Our routers need to react speedily so that they can route our data over the best possible paths, whatever they may be. The way that we do this, is to have our routers exchange information through *Routing Protocols*.

Routing Protocols fall into two distinct groups, namely *Interior Gateway Protocols* (IGPs), and *Exterior Gateway Protocols* (EGPs). These can be categorized as follows:

- **Interior Gateway Protocols (IGPs)**

  Interior Gateway Protocols, as we described in chapter 31, are used within what is known as an *Autonomous System* (AS). An AS can be defined as being a group of networks (an internetwork) that has a common administrative policy. For example, within any particular AS, we would find only one routing protocol running (in this case, the routing policy). We must be careful in our definition however, since the word policy can mean different things to different people. The *classic* definition of an AS tells us that an AS is *"an internetwork controlled by a single administrative or technical authority."* This was fine when we had just one IGP to choose from - the AS definition was then purely based on people. Today, this is not the case. Today then, we base our definition more upon the protocols in use. Examples of standardized IGPs include the *Routing Information Protocol* (RIP), the *Open Shortest Path First* (OSPF) protocol, both of which are discussed in this chapter. In addition, there are several proprietary IGPs such as Cisco's *Interior Gateway Routing Protocol* (IGRP), and their *Enhanced Interior Gateway Routing Protocol* (EIGRP).

- **Exterior Gateway Protocols (EGPs)**

  In chapter 31 we said that EGPs were implemented where we wished to join Autonomous Systems together. While this is true, we now also find that the distinction between IGPs and EGPs is becoming blurred in that the latest EGPs can be used intra-IGP. Examples of standardized EGPs include the *Exterior Gateway Protocol* (EGP) itself, and also the newer *Border Gateway Protocol* (BGP). Indeed it is BGP that can operate as in two modes (*Internal*

BGP and *External BGP*) so that it is capable of operating in both inter and intra AS modes.

For the purposes of this chapter we shall spend the majority of our time discussing IGPs, since it is these that are implemented within most networks. Of course, EGPs have their place, but since it is typically only extremely large internetworks, and large service providers that require their use, their implementation is naturally limited.

35.1 Routing Information Protocol (RIP)

Any discussion of routing protocols must start at the beginning, and RIP is indeed where dynamic routing really began. RIP, as we know it today, is based on the original Berkeley Software Distribution[1] 4.3 *routed* (or route daemon) program. There are today, two versions, with version II enhancing RIP operation within subnetted environments, and providing the ability to multicast updates. Certainly, even with the improvements that RIP II brings, RIP has a number of shortcomings that mean that its use within larger internets is limited. That said, it is reasonably compact, easy to understand, and very easy to implement. In this section, we shall deal first with RIP version I, and then compare this to version II.

35.1.1 RIP Metrics

RIP uses a simple *Distance Vector Algorithm* to calculate the quality of a route. This means that we rely on a simple network *Hop Count*, or the number of networks that must be traversed to the destination. While, on the face of it, this may seem perfectly adequate in many cases, it is not necessarily the best definition of route quality within relatively complex internets. For example, consider figure 35-1.

Within a RIP environment, and based purely on the number of networks to be traversed, the preferred route between the *Source*, and *Target* networks would be via Routers 1 and 2. In reality the *best* route, based on interface speed, would be via Routers 5, 6, 7, and 8 although this would never be chosen. Router 1 would see the metric to the *Target* network as 2, Router 5 would see this metric as 4, and Router 3 would see the metric as 5. To RIP, there is no competition, the route to the left is best!

As we can see then, RIP will not always provide us with the best routing information when based on hops, but this need not be a major issue. Most vendors allow metrics to be administratively altered so that the we have some means of controlling the chosen route. For example, we could set the metric of the link between Routers 1, and 2 to say 10. Now, RIP would choose the right-most path that we have already decided is the best. In this way, we retain control over our internetwork and routing, yet we also have the resilience and ability to adapt to

---

[1] The Berkley Software Distribution (BSD) version 4.3 UNIX is significant since it was this version that fully implemented TCP/IP. Berkley, being the main supplier of operating systems to educational establishments at that time, then became the vehicle for the distribution of the Internet Protocol suite. At least in part then, Berkley must take some credit for the phenomenal success of IP today.

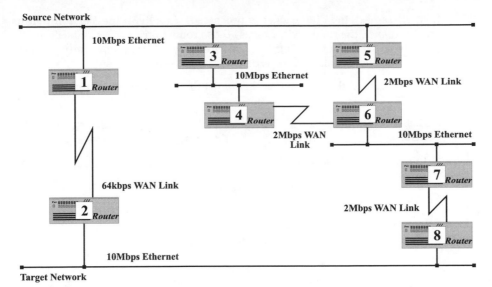

Figure 35-1: RIP Example

path changes. If our favored route should fail, then we will use the left-hand route because it is there and available. The price that we pay, is that we have now increased the administrative overhead on the network - something that we would possibly not be prepared to do for larger internets.

35.1.2 Protocol Format

RIP uses the *User Datagram Protocol* (UDP) to transport it over an IP network. The messages themselves can be up to 512 octets in length and contain information regarding networks that the router believes to be reachable, and the metric associated with reaching them. The format is shown in figure 35-2, which shows that the packet starts with a 4 octet header. This header contains the following:

- A single octet *Operation* code, that will contain a 1 for a *Request*, and a 2 for a *Response*. Where the operation is a Request, it means that receiving routers should send all or part of their routing tables. Response messages then contain all (or part) of the sending router's routing table.

  RIP is, at least in theory, a *Request/Response* protocol, where we can request information about a specific route, or ask for a complete update. In most implementations though, RIP routers merely send the entire contents of their routing tables at regular intervals using *Response* operation codes.

- A single octet *Version* number that contains the version number of the current implementation. Typically this will be 1 or 2, to indicate RIP I and RIP II, respectively, although this field is interpreted as follows:

  If the Version is zero, then the packet is discarded without further processing. If the Version is one, then the packet is discarded if any of the fields labeled *Reserved - Must be Zero* are non-zero. If these fields are correctly specified (i.e., all zeroes), then the packet is processed. Finally, if the Version field is greater than 1, the router will process those route entries that can be correctly processed, and ignore all others. In this way, RIP automatically remains backwards compatible with regards to any future enhancements.

- A two octet field that is Reserved and must therefore always be zero.

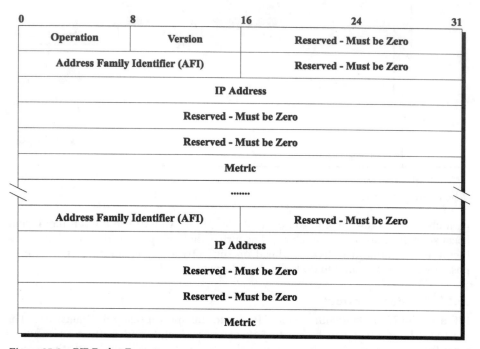

Figure 35-2: RIP Packet Format

Following the RIP header, the RIP message contains information about a variable number of routes, up to the maximum message length of 512 octets. Information about each route takes 20 octets, and comprises a two octet *Address Family Identifier* (AFI), a four octet *IP Address*, a four octet *Metric*, and 10 octets that are *Reserved*. The Address Family Identifier is used to identify the *type* of routing information that is being carried. RIP is a general purpose routing protocol and is used outside of the Internet Protocol suite. As a result, when carrying IP routes, the AFI field will carry the value 2. The IP Address field will of course only ever require 4 octets for IP networks, and will contain the network address of the network being advertised. Finally, the *Metric* field contains the distance that the advertised route is from this router in terms of a *hop count*.

RIP updates require 20 octets per advertised route. Thus, with a 4 octet header, the maximum number of routes that we can advertise per packet is just 25. This means that for large internetworks we may well require more than one packet per update, and therefore we may consume a large amount of bandwidth.

35.1.3 Protocol Operation

RIP updates are typically sent every 30 seconds by routers broadcasting their entire routing tables across their interfaces. In using broadcasts, we will inevitably waste precious CPU cycles of other network devices that have no interest in RIP, but it does provide an effective method of propagating routing information. For example, we will consider figure 35-3 and see how each of the routers learns about all the routes that are available - a process known as *convergence*. In the figure, we see a simple internetwork comprising three routers and four networks. In addition, we have simplified the routing tables so that each shows just the reachable networks, the next hops, and the applicable metric. We then show how these would look at start-up.

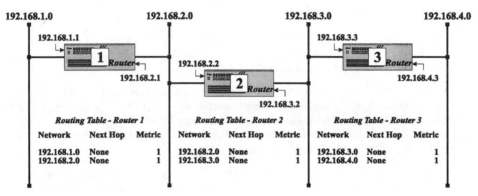

Figure 35-3: Routing Tables at Start-Up

Looking from the perspective of Router 1, after some period of time it will transmit its routing table across network 192.168.2.0.[2] That update will be sent as a RIP *Response*, and will contain information that relates to network 192.168.1.0 only. There is after all no point in transmitting information about 192.168.2.0 since reachability is implied if we are sending the update across it. Router 2 will receive the update from Router 1, and will update its own routing table by first checking to see whether or not it is already holding information about the network(s) being advertised. If it is already holding information then it will see whether this new information represents a better route. If it does it will use it, if not it will discard it. In the case that it chooses to use this information, it increments the metric that is being advertised by one, and then adds this route information to its routing table. At this point, Router 2's routing table would contain the information shown in the figure, and also Network 192.168.1.0, Next Hop 192.168.2.1, Metric 2.

Router 2 will eventually send out its own routing update over both interfaces (192.168.2.2, and 192.168.3.2). In each case, the network over which the update is sent will be omitted from the update. Router 1 will receive the update across network 192.168.2.0, which will contain information about network 192.168.3.0. Router 1 will now examine its own routing table and decide that since it has no

---

[2] We have assumed here that RIP is not enabled on Router 1's interface connected to network 192.168.1.0. Of course if RIP was enabled, then an update would also be sent over this interface.

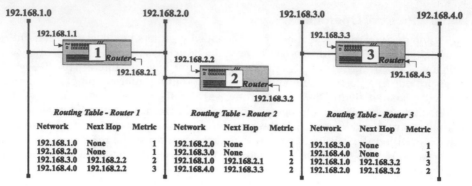

Figure 35-4: RIP Example - After Convergence

information about network 192.168.3.0, it will use the information from router 2 with a metric of 2. The routing table of Router 1 will now include the entry; Network 192.168.3.0, Next Hop 192.168.2.2, Metric 2.

Router 3 will have also received an update across network 192.168.3.0. This update will include information about networks 192.168.1.0 and 192.168.2.0. Router 3 will ascertain that it has no better information on these networks and will use it adding the entries; Network 192.168.1.0, Next Hop 192.168.3.2, Metric 3, and Network 192.168.2.0, Next Hop 192.168.3.2, Metric 2.

Continuing on, we would see that Router 3 would send an update informing Router 2 about Network 192.168.4.0, which would be propagated to Router 1, and so on. As we can see, each router tells its neighbors about reachable networks until they all have information about all destinations as shown in figure 35-4.

35.1.4 RIP Updates and Timers

Most RIP implementations send updates as specified through a configurable update timer, typically configured at 30 seconds. Also, most implementations use a *Discard* timer of around 180 seconds, although again this is generally configurable. What this means is that unsolicited routing updates that comprise the entire routing table are sent each update time. If a router does not receive an update to a previously learned route within the Discard timer, that route is purged from the routing table. This however has two drawbacks.

In the first case, we typically would have to wait six update times (i.e., 180 seconds divided by 30 seconds) before we realize that a previously advertised route is no longer available. Secondly, we may receive an update from a neighbor that contains fresh information about a route, yet we have just sent an update ourselves. This would then delay our information being propagated by up to 30 seconds if we must wait for the *update timer* to expire (which may be up to 30 seconds away).

The answer to the first dilemma is that we can send an update that tells our neighbors that routes are no longer available. Obviously we cannot do this if the router fails, but if it is shut down gracefully, then it can send updates making all of its routes unavailable. Secondly, we can send what are known as *Triggered*

Updates. In other words an update at any time, if we are in possession of new information. So, if we receive an update from a neighbor that tells us that a route to a particular destination no longer exists, we can propagate that immediately without waiting for the next update.

35.1.5 Split Horizon, Poison Reverse, and Infinity

Since RIP advertisements are normally the entire routing table of the router, from our discussions so far, what we would actually see are our metrics gradually increasing as updates take place. For example, let us a closer look at the update procedure from the perspective of Router 2.

- Router 1 advertises a route to network 192.168.1.0. This is placed in Router 2's routing table with a metric of 2.

- Router 2 advertises this route (along with its others) to Router 3 across network 192.168.3.0. Router 3 now knows of a route to network 192.168.1.0 via Router 2 and with a metric of 3.

- Router 3 advertises a route to this same network (network 192.168.1.0) along with the other routes that it is holding in its routing table, back across network 192.168.3.0. This time though, the metric is 4 since we take the metric in the routing table and increment it by 1.

- Now, Router 2 will not use this route because it has a better one using Router 1. But what happens if router 1 should fail? While we are waiting for the routes to network 192.168.1.0 to time-out, Router 2 will believe that it has a route to network 192.168.1.0 via Router 3! Router 2 would also advertise this back to Router 3, which would advertise it back to Router 2, and so on - incrementing the metric each time.

- Ignoring this increasing metric for a moment, what happens if a packet, destined for network 192.168.1.0, arrives at Router 2 through interface 192.168.3.2? Router 2 will forward it to Router 3, which will forward it to Router 2........ Etc. What we now have is a routing loop, and our packet will bounce backwards and forwards between Routers 2 and 3 until the *Time-to-Live* in the IP Datagram Header expires.

What we actually have here are two problems. In the first case, we have two (or more) routers that are exchanging routing information based on deception. Each claims to have a route to Network 192.168.1.0, yet neither actually does in the absence of Router 1. In order to break this metric counting, we actually place a limit on the distance away (number of hops), a destination network can be. That limit is 15. Any more than 15 hops is rounded back to 16 which we refer to as *Infinity*, and this signifies that the network is unreachable. This means of course that RIP learned routes cannot be more than 15 hops away, and that naturally limits the *diameter* of RIP internetworks.

In order to stop this *count to infinity* completely, we can actually use one of two features that are standard in RIP. The first, known as *Split Horizon*, simply ensures that no route is advertised through the interface on which it was learned. Thus, if we return to our previous example, Router 3 would never advertise a route to network 192.168.1.0 over network 192.168.3.0 since it learned it through that interface. The second method is called *Poison Reverse*, and means that we do advertise routes through the interfaces on which they were learned, only this time we *Poison* them by advertising a metric of 16 (infinity). In this case, again returning to our example, Router 3 would advertise a route to network 192.168.1.0 across network 192.168.3.0, but it would advertise it with a metric of 16 - unreachable.

35.1.6 RIP Version II

RIP version II is the latest version of RIP. It addresses several of the shortcomings of version I, and brings with it several enhancements. As you will have noticed, RIP version I fails to accommodate subnet masks of any description. Thus, when using RIP version I, we can only use the natural mask of any address class. Equally, RIP version I provides no authentication, nor does it allow for updates to be multicast (rather than broadcast). All of these are addressed by version II.

Overall, version II is an improvement, and it is even more so when we consider that backwards compatibility is maintained by simply using many of the previously *Reserved* fields. Figure 35-5 shows the general format of RIP II packets.

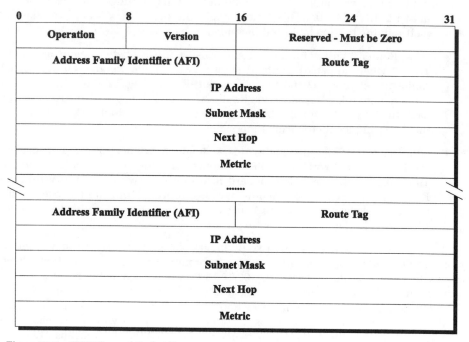

Figure 35-5: RIP II General Packet Format

As with version I, we retain the same four octet header, although the *Version* field will now have a value of 2, to reflect version II of the protocol. The new *Route Tag* field is designed to allow the embedding of information that is carried from another *Autonomous System*. For example, if we are importing a route from say

EGP or BGP, we can use this field to carry the Autonomous System Number (ASN) of the Autonomous System in which that network resides. The *Subnet Mask* field contains the four octet subnet mask that relates to the IP Network Address that is advertised in the *IP Address* field. Finally, the newly introduced *Next Hop* field contains the IP Address of the next router en route to the destination. Where the advertising router is providing the optimal route, then this field is set to 0.0.0.0. If, however, there is a better route via a different router, then the address of that router would be inserted here.

Version II does not address all of the problems associated with RIP version I. For instance, it does not increase the network diameter above 15 *Hops*, since the need to limit *counting to infinity* is a function of *Distance Vector Algorithms* generally. Similarly, version II does not improve convergence times, and it still relies upon updates that comprise entire routing tables. These in turn of course, still consume a large amount of network bandwidth. Version II does support the use of multicasts (assigned address 224.0.0.9) to exchange information, and this is a major leap forward. Of course even with this, its use is still limited to smaller enterprises.

35.2 Open Shortest Path First (OSPF)

The Open Shortest Path First (OSPF) protocol is also an Interior Gateway Protocol (IGP). OSPF however, represents a radical re-think over many of the concepts that were presented for the Routing Information Protocol (RIP), and indeed OSPF is the protocol of choice for many vendors, and end-users. Certainly OSPF is the protocol most used within large *open* enterprises, due to its scaleability, resilience, and lower overhead with respect to routing updates.

OSPF is vastly more complex as a protocol than RIP, but this complexity is mostly hidden within vendor supplied graphical and command line interfaces. For example, with RIP, a router will learn of distant networks, but in terms of knowing how to get there will know only of the *Next Hop* en route. With OSPF, the router will certainly know the Next Hop to reach the destination, but it will also know the topology of the entire internetwork. As a result of this, it can make far better routing decisions than RIP ever could. Now, add several other facts. Firstly, OSPF uses a *Link State Algorithm* and thus bases metrics on true interface speeds. Secondly, after initial convergence, OSPF sends updates only when the topology has changed. This means that the bandwidth consumed by routing updates is reduced. Thirdly, re-convergence following a topology change is far faster than RIP. We support the use of *Areas* to group networks together, to localize routing update traffic, and to speed re-convergence when failures do occur. Finally, OSPF supports *Type-of-Service* routing which means that we can route our traffic based on the information carried in the IP Datagram Header's Type-of-Service field. All-in-all then, what we have with OSPF, is a routing protocol that is absolutely superior in most all cases.

35.2.1 OSPF Metrics

As we said above, OSPF uses the *true* interface speed in determining the metric. Thus, metrics with OSPF tend to be quoted as being a great deal larger than those of say RIP. For example, as we shall see later, a router will advertise the metric associated with a particular link[3] in a 16 bit field. This means that in theory, the metric could be as high as 65,536 for just one router link. This then becomes cumulative as we create a path to a destination, and allows for a 24 bit metric to be defined.

If we were to return to our RIP example presented in figure 35-1, OSPF would choose the route, Router 5, 6, 7, 8 as a path between the source and target networks. This of course represents the *best* route given the link costs, although it carries a higher hop count.

35.2.2 Type-of-Service Routing

The Type-of-Service field in the IP Datagram header can be used to request that datagrams are routed over specific paths based upon the *quality of service* that they offer. Figure 35-6 shows an example where we have two paths between networks, each offering different service levels.

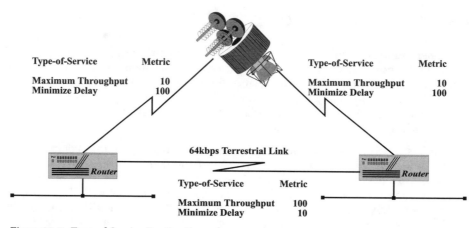

Figure 35-6: Type-of-Service Routing Example

The path over the satellite would provide superb throughput, but with potentially excessive delays. Thus, the *metrics* associated with the satellite link for *Maximum Throughput* are lower than those associated with the *Minimize Delay* Type-of-Service for the same link. The terrestrial link at just 64kbps would provide very little delay, yet is less than ideal for the transmission of bulk data. Thus, if we have say an FTP session and a Telnet session, we would want our FTP data to travel via the satellite, and the Telnet data via the terrestrial link. Once again, we can see that the *metrics* associated with the terrestrial link and the *Minimize Delay* Type-of-Service are lower than those associated with *Maximum Throughput* Type-of-Service on the terrestrial link.

---

[3] OSPF refers to the physical interface as a Link. When comparing OSPF to other protocols, this must be borne in mind since the terms Link and Interface potentially have different meanings outside of the context of those protocols being compared.

Obviously, we would have to rely on the application(s) to request the Type-of-Service that we require, and sadly too few applications will do this. In a similar vein, it is not mandatory to support multiple Types-of-Service. Indeed, routers must support the basic Type-of-Service zero (simply called TOS-0) that requests no special handling and means that all TOS bits in the IP Datagram Header are zeroed. Beyond this however, they do not have to support any other service type at all. As a result of this, the Internet Engineering Task Force (IETF) that oversees the development of Internet protocols is now also considering the removal of TOS routing from OSPF.

35.2.3 Equal Cost Multi-Path Routing

One of the major features of OSPF is its ability to use multiple paths to a destination where they exist. OSPF routers learn the topology of the entire internetwork of which they are a part, so they will therefore be able to identify where two (or more) paths exist to the same destination, and with the same metric. If this is the case, then the router can choose to pass packets over each path as it wishes. Most other Interior Gateway Protocols (IGPs) will not do this, but would instead use the path that was learned first. This then sets OSPF apart from most other standardized IGPs.

OSPF does not dictate how multiple paths are stored internally at the router, nor does it place any minimum or maximum limits as to the number of paths that may be held. Instead, the OSPF RFC simply states that this facility is possible, and leaves its final implementation totally up to the vendor.

35.2.4 Areas

There are two problems that face administrators of large enterprises. The first is the overall reliability and stability of individual devices and links, and the re-convergence time when failures occur. The second is the amount of routing update traffic that flows around the internetwork, and the *bursty* nature of these regular updates. OSPF addresses both of these concerns by allowing large internetworks to be divided into *Areas*, or groups of networks.

We said before, OSPF routers maintain a complete picture of the topology of the internetwork of which they are part. In actual fact though, this is not strictly true, since it would be more correct to say that they maintain a complete *topological database* of the *Area* in which they reside. Furthermore, this database is also identical for *all* routers within that Area. In short, by dividing our network into Areas, we will see faster re-convergence following a topology change, since each router is maintaining detailed information about fewer other routers. In addition, this also provides us with a reduction in routing update traffic and that has advantages all of its own. In order to see how this basically works though, we should consider an example such as figure 35-7, in which we have four areas.

Firstly, Areas are specified by 32 bit (4 octet) numbers, and are always written in dotted decimal notation. Each router within an area will contain enough detailed information to allow all *intra-Area* routing to take place since it will have it's own copy of an identical topological database. Those routers at the edge of an Area will contain multiple databases - one for each Area to which they attach. These *Area Border Routers* (ABRs) as they are known, then exchange *summary* information across the area border itself. There is nothing special about an ABR except that it maintains multiple copies of the topological databases. In essence, any router can become an ABR, it is just a case of configuring it correctly

Area 0.0.0.0 is referred to as the *Backbone Area* and must exist in all OSPF internetworks. Where the internetwork has not been divided into areas, then Area 0.0.0.0 will be the only area defined, and this is normally an automatic default. All other areas *must* attach to the Backbone Area, and all *inter-Area* traffic must flow through the Backbone itself. Where it is not possible to directly link an area to the backbone, through geography or other topological constraints, special *Virtual Links* are created that allow *inter-Area* traffic to transit through another area.

Finally, although not shown in our figure, there is another type of router that we should talk about, the so called *Autonomous System Border Router* or ASBR. As with the ABR, there is nothing very special about an ASBR. Most routers can become an ASBR when required, and they simply run multiple routing protocols. These routers then occupy a position at the edge of the Autonomous System (AS) and exchange information between this AS and another, through what are known as AS External Routes.

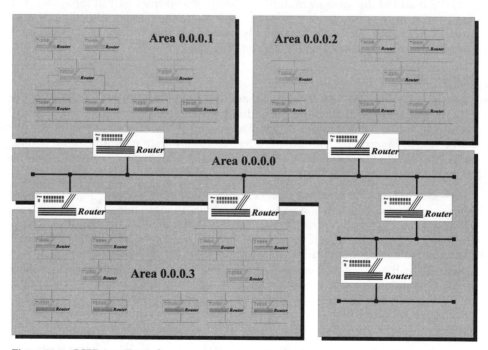

Figure 35-7: OSPF Area Example

In terms of how many routers we must have before we can create separate areas, there is no hard and fast rule. Obviously each area must contain at least one router, but beyond that common sense should prevail. The idea of creating areas is, as much as anything else, to bring added manageability to the network. As you can see from the figure, there are also no rules that relate to how many routers can act as entry/exit points to an area. For example, connecting to Area 0.0.0.3 we have two, yet we have just one to areas 0.0.0.1, and 0.0.0.2. There are different *types* of Area and Network however, and these are discussed below:

- **Stub and Transit Networks**
  A Stub Network is one where there is only one OSPF router attached. A Transit network is one where there are two or more OSPF routers attached, and can therefore not only handle locally generated traffic, but can also handle traffic that is in transit.

- **Stub Areas and Not So Stubby Stub Areas (NSSAs)**
  A Stub Area is configured where there is only a single point of exit from the area. A Not so Stubby Stub Area (NSSA) is also where we have an area with just a single entry/exit point, but the difference lies in how the area handles AS External Routes as generated by ASBRs. In the case of the Stub Area, AS External Routes are not flooded throughout the area itself, and therefore ASBRs cannot be placed in them. The advantage is that our topological databases remain smaller, and therefore routers in Stub Areas use less memory overall. In the case of NSSAs, these are Stub Areas that will flood AS External Routes, so therefore ASBRs can be placed in them.

35.2.5 OSPF Operation and Protocol Format

Before we can begin to even slightly understand the complexities of the protocol itself, we must first talk in more general terms about OSPF's basic operation. OSPF, as we have said before, is really quite complex. So, although what we present here is an overview of the protocol operation, we can only ever achieve full understanding once we completely understand each message type that OSPF uses.

OSPF routers do not exchange routing updates with *all* other routers on a network. Instead, they exchange routing information with only a maximum of two other routers known as the *Designated Router* (DR), and the *Backup Designated Router* (BDR). In Figure 35-8 we see an example where we have a common network with a number of routers, one acting as the DR, and another acting as the BDR. All other routers would then exchange information with these two routers, synchronize their databases, and eventually become *adjacent* as described below.

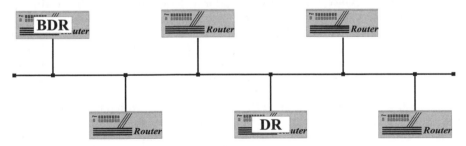

Figure 35-8: DR and BDR in an OSPF Network

The first router that goes live on the network will become the *Designated Router* automatically, and the second router will become the *Backup Designated Router*. The reason for this is that OSPF routers use a compact, *Hello* protocol that informs partner routers of their existence, and passes certain other pieces of information. Any router can become a DR or BDR, and it is really only timing that chooses which router it will be. Figure 35-9 shows the format of the Hello Packet.

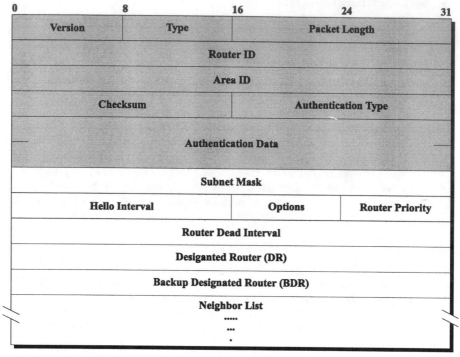

Figure 35-9: OSPF Hello Protocol

Unlike RIP, OSPF does not have just one single packet format. Instead, OSPF uses a standard Header (shown shaded in the figure) that is applicable to all of the various message types, and then the actual message follows. The *Version* field identifies the version number of the protocol which is currently 2. The *Type* field identifies the message type and will be a 1 for a Hello message. Other valid types are: 2 for a *Database Description*, 3 for a *Link State Request*, 4 for a *Link State Update*, and 5 for a *Link State Acknowledgment*. Each of these other message types will be described later however. The *Packet Length* field informs as to how long the actual packet is (in octets). The *Router ID* is a unique identifier for *this* router within the internetwork. It will normally assume the value of the highest assigned IP Address of any interface, although this need not be the case and it may be administratively assigned. The *Area ID* is the Area within which this router resides, and the *Checksum* is used to ensure that the data has arrived intact. The *Authentication Type* and *Authentication Data* fields allow the router to optionally authenticate neighbor routers prior to exchanging routing information with them. In this way, we can ensure that we will only exchange data with trusted neighboring devices, and therefore ensure a basic level of security.

Moving to the Hello message itself, this contains the *Subnet Mask* for the network, and then a number of OSPF specific fields. The *Hello Interval* indicates the frequency at which *this* router will send *Hello* packets (in seconds). The *Options* field conveys certain optional OSPF information, such as the Multicast capabilities of the router, and whether or not the router supports multiple *Types-of-Service* among other things. The *Router Priority* field can be administratively defined, and is used to determine which router will become the DR (and/or BDR) in the event that two or more routers come on-line at exactly the same time, or when a re-election is required following a failure. The *Router Dead Interval* is how long (in seconds) that we will wait to receive an update from a router before declaring it dead. The *Designated Router*, and *Backup Designated Router* fields define which routers *this* router believes to be the DR and BDR, respectively. Finally, the variable length *Neighbor List* lists all routers that we have received Hello packets from within the last *Router Dead Interval*.

So, the first router that becomes active on a network will transmit Hello packets typically every 10 seconds, via a multicast, and if it is the only router on-line will receive no Hellos from other routers. It will therefore declare itself to be the DR and convey this in the next (and subsequent) Hello packets. The next router to come on-line on that network will commence the sending of Hellos, and will of course receive Hellos from the DR. These Hello packets will include each other in the *Neighbor List* and therefore each will know of the other's existence. Since there is currently no BDR, the second router will become the BDR by default. Further routers, as they come on-line, will send their Hellos and will learn who the DR and BDR are from the Hello packets of established routers.

Once a new router has seen itself mentioned in the *Neighbor List* of a Hello packet from the DR, it can now assume that *bi-directional communications* are possible, and that it can begin the synchronization of topological databases. To do this, the new router and the DR will exchange *Database Description* packets, which contain *basic* information about the routing information that they are holding. Based on this information received, each router then formulates and exchanges a series of *Link State Requests* that request further information about a single database element. On receipt of these requests, the routers then exchange *Link State Updates*, each of which contain full database information, and are acknowledged. At this point, the new router and the DR have synchronized their databases, and can now use the new routing information. Updates occur on a per-network basis, so the DR will now update all other routers that share that network with the information that the *new* router provided. In this way, all routers will then be synchronized.

Link State Updates contain what are known as *Link State Advertisements* (LSAs), of which there are a number of different types, each conveying a specific database element. The types themselves are briefly described below[4] :

---

[4] The actual makeup of LSAs is beyond the scope of this volume. For further information, please refer to TCP/IP Explained also by Philip Miller.

- **Router Links Advertisements**

  The Router Links Advertisement is used by the router to advertise the state and associated cost of each of the router's links to the area. This includes the different metrics associated with each *Type-of-Service* where multiple *Type-of-Service* routing is supported.

- **Network Links Advertisements**

  The Network Links Advertisement is only ever originated by the Designated Router (DR), and simply contains the Subnet Mask for the network for which this is the DR, and a list of other routers that are attached to the network. In this way, all routers are advertised through a single packet.

- **Summary Links Advertisements**

  These are originated by Area Border Routers (ABRs) to advertise destinations that belong to the Autonomous System but which are outside of the Area.

- **AS External Link Advertisements**

  AS External Link Advertisements are generated by Autonomous System Border Routers and are used to advertise routes to networks that are outside of the Autonomous System (AS).

35.2.6 Creating the Routing Table

Once the databases of the router and DR are synchronized, the router can create a routing table based on that information. What actually happens now, is that the router will create what is known as a *Shortest Path Tree* in which it places itself at the top (root), and then calculates the true path cost to all reachable networks. Where *Type-of-Service* routing is supported, the router will calculate a new routing table for each Type-of-Service, although as we have previously stated, TOS routing is not mandatory and is rarely implemented (if ever).

35.2.7 Maintaining Adjacency

Once all of the routers within an Area have the same information, adjacency is maintained on a network-by-network basis through the use of Hello and Link State Update packets. If a router which was sending Hellos on a regular basis suddenly ceases, then it will be dropped from the *Neighbor List* of other routers after the *Router Dead Interval* has expired. This will cause the DR to delete those Link States (and subsequently the routes) that the failed router *was* advertising, and cause re-convergence through *Link State Updates*.

In all then, the simple Hello protocol holds the key to OSPF operation. Certainly, outside of the Hello protocol, OSPF is much more complex than other *interior* routing protocols such as RIP. That said, it does bring with it a number of advantages such as the speed of convergence, and the ability to split our network into areas that also greatly assist the convergence process.

35.3 Exterior Gateway Protocols

Exterior Gateway Protocols are used to link Autonomous Systems (ASs) together. In part, much of their use has been superseded by the likes of OSPF that can happily exchange information with other IGPs. The power of EGPs however, lies in the fact that the administrative authorities that control the ASs themselves need to be able to decide on exactly what information should be propagated. This is particularly true when we wish to link multiple organizations with their own internetworks, yet maintain a high level of control. Two protocols exist in this arena, and we shall look briefly at each. True they are less commonly implemented than IGPs, so we shall not dwell on their operation, but their existence is significant and we must mention them if only for the sake of completeness.

35.3.1 Exterior Gateway Protocol (EGP)

The Exterior Gateway Protocol (EGP) is the original EGP, and is simply used to link our ASs together. Figure 35-10 shows an example where each AS runs its own IGP, and then these are linked via EGP. The IGPs that are used in each AS could be the same, as may be the case where we wish to link two organizations. Alternatively, they may be different as we have shown in the figure.

The top router in AS 1 will run both OSPF and EGP. As a result, this would be an ASBR as far as OSPF is concerned, and would provide summary information into the OSPF Area in which it resides. It would then exchange routing information with the router in AS 2, that is running both EGP and RIP. In operation, EGP has three distinct sections to its operation as follows:

- EGP relies on *Neighbors* (peers) with which to exchange routing information. At start-up then, routers running EGP will attempt to *acquire* one or more neighbors with whom to exchange routing information. In this state, the router will periodically transmit *Request* commands until it receives a *Confirm* response. Once this response has been received, the routers will negotiate certain information, such as the intervals at which they exchange routing information, and how often they confirm neighbor reachability. Now, they will transition to the next phase - *Neighbor Reachability* itself.

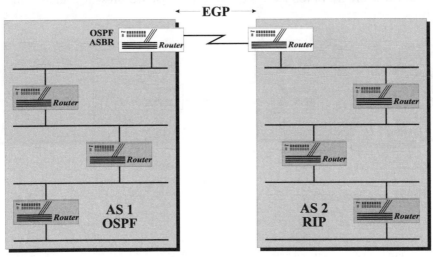

Figure 35-10: Simple Internetwork Employing EGP

- In the *Neighbor Reachability* phase, the routers will test the reachability to each other through a simple *Hello* protocol, the interval of which was negotiated in the *Neighbor Acquisition* phase. In this way, our routers will know that their neighbor is alive, and that the routing information that they have received from them remains valid.

- Finally, our routers will exchange network reachability information based on the local policies that would be administratively set within the router. This reachability information comprises a list of networks that can be reached within the AS, together with their associated metrics. The metrics themselves are based on the number of *Network hops* as in RIP, and are specified by a single octet. Thus, the maximum allowable metric using EGP would be 254, since 255 is deemed to mean network unreachable.

As we can see, EGP is a simple protocol based broadly on the same principles as RIP. Certainly, we have to increase the metric of routes since RIP allows us a maximum hop count of just 15. That said, RIP and EGP have both been around for a long time and served us extremely well. Now replaced by the newer BGP that we shall introduce next, EGP is not widely implemented, but remains significant in the development of routing protocols generally.

35.3.2 Border Gateway Protocol (BGP)

BGP is the latest Exterior Gateway Protocol, and is also starting to gain some popularity as an IGP as well. The reason is that BGP introduces what are known as *Internal* and *External* neighbors as shown in figure 35-11.

By having these internal and external neighbors, this now allows external information to be carried across an Autonomous System. As with EGP, few internetworks will require the use of BGP at all - and particularly *Exterior BGP*. We will however briefly introduce it here in order that we present a more complete picture.

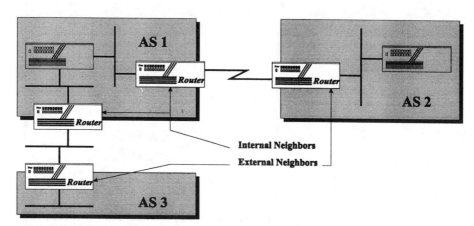

Figure 35-11: BGP Internal and External Neighbors

- Routers that wish to exchange BGP information, firstly open a TCP connection, and then commence the *Open* phase in which they send *Open* packets to open BGP communications. The response to an *Open* packet is a *KeepAlive* packet, which will be exchanged on a regular basis in much the same way as the *Hello* packet in EGP.

- Once the BGP connection is open, and *KeepAlives* have been exchanged, the routers next exchange routing information through *Update* packets. When new routes become available, these are advertised through an *Update*. Equally, when routes become unavailable and need to be withdrawn, the *Update* packet is again used.

- Finally, the BGP connection can be closed through either a normal, *graceful*, shutdown of a router, or through an error condition being detected. In this case, the router that wishes to initiate the closure sends a *Notification* packet that indicates the reason why the connection should be closed.

Although the basic operation of BGP is simple, the protocol itself is reasonably complex and it uses a number of different message formats. BGP brings with it a number of enhancements over EGP which include authentication, and route aggregation that we will discuss next. However, it really is only the very largest of internetworks that require the use of this protocol, and it will therefore never achieve the same levels of popularity that the IGPs enjoy.

35.4 Route Aggregation

Route Aggregation is defined as being the process of combining the characteristics of several routes in such a way that a single route can be advertised. In essence, what we try to achieve is an overall reduction in the amount of information that routers must exchange, and also a corresponding reduction in the size of the routing tables that these devices must maintain.

For example, let us consider the case where a local Internet Service Provider (ISP) has an allocation of IP Addresses that include the entire Class C address range of 192.168.0.0, through 192.168.255.0.[5] It would then allocate them to its customers, and would have to advertise routes to them to the next tier up towards the Internet core. By applying aggregation, the ISP now need only advertise a route to 192.168.0.0, provided that everyone agrees that this actually means *all* networks in the Class C address range that begins 192.168. The ISP advertises just one route, and the next tier merely has to store that one route rather than 256 separate routes.

Today, BGP is the protocol of choice for most ISPs, and much of its success is due to route aggregation. Let us not be fooled that BGP is the only choice where aggregation is required though, since OSPF can also aggregate routes if required. Obviously, the protocol that we choose would be related to the number of routes that we initially have, and the environment in which we wish to implement it.

---

[5] In actual fact, no ISP or indeed other organization would be allocated these addresses since the entire range of addresses that start 192.168 are reserved as private addresses, and may be used by anyone. Also, ISPs will not forward traffic either to or from these addresses.

35.5 Summary

In this chapter we have discussed the most significant routing protocols of the Internet Protocol suite. Are they the only ones - no. If we were to cover *all* applicable protocols, then we would need to discuss many more that are standardized, and an equal number of proprietary protocols too.

Routing is a large subject, and we could spend a lifetime delving into the complexities of each protocol. This chapter has, we hope, introduced the basic mechanics of the major players, and indicated the strengths and weaknesses of them. Certainly, RIP is simple and very easy to implement. It has its drawbacks in that it does not provide an accurate picture of true *least cost*. OSPF is far more complex, but does provide us with a fairer routing model. It chooses routes based on interface cost rather than hop count, and since each router maintains a complete topological database, each router has intimate knowledge of the area in which it resides.

Moving to Exterior Gateway Protocols, we typically have the choice of two that are standardized. The older protocol, known simply as the Exterior Gateway Protocol, is very much like RIP in the way that it works. It lacks the finesse of the later protocols such as the Border Gateway Protocol (BGP), but again has been with us for many years. Finally we have BGP itself. Favored by the ISPs today, BGP runs over our reliable TCP transport, and gives us aggregation among other things. Certainly the latest in exterior gateway protocol thinking, and moving into the realms of the Interior Gateway Protocols as well, BGP is poised to take over within the largest internetworks.

IPX

The Internetwork Packet eXchange (IPX) protocol is a Novell proprietary protocol derived from Xerox Network Systems (XNS). As with the Internet Protocol suite, IPX does not stand-alone but is rather a whole suite of protocols named after one of the major elements. IPX is the Network layer (Layer 3) protocol that defines a connectionless, *best effort*, datagram delivery service along with an addressing scheme. In essence, the actual IPX protocol is to the Novell IPX suite, what IP is to the Internet Protocol suite. It is these areas, together with a discussion of IPX routing, that we shall discuss here.

36.1 IPX Architecture

Figure 36-1 shows the relationship of IPX to the OSI model, and also shows the other major protocols that comprise the IPX suite.

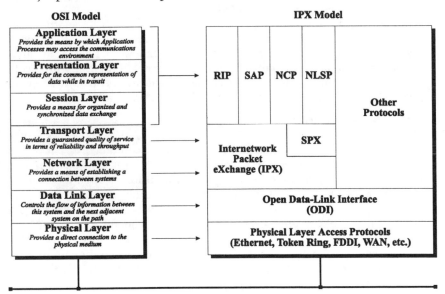

Figure 36-1: IPX Architecture

As shown in the figure, IPX uses several other protocols and services to deliver functionality to the users' desktop. Specifically, these include the following:

- **Routing Information Protocol (RIP)**

  This allows servers and routers to exchange routing information and operates in a similar fashion to that described for RIP in an IP environment - indeed, RIP for IPX even uses the same basic protocol format. You will note that here we have made no distinction between servers or routers. This is because in a Novell environment, servers can route between multiple installed interfaces and between different physical encapsulations. Thus, both servers and routers use this protocol to propagate routing information.

- **Service Advertisement Protocol (SAP)**

  This is a proprietary protocol that enables network related services such as file and print services to be advertised. The SAP is an important element of IPX networks since it is through SAP exchanges that devices can determine what services are available on the network.

- **Sequenced Packet eXchange (SPX)**

  SPX is the Layer 4 protocol, used where connection-oriented services are required. This protocol can be likened to the Transmission Control Protocol (TCP) from the Internet Protocol suite although, in direct contrast to the IP world, few IPX applications use connection-oriented communication.

- **NetWare Core Protocols (NCP)**

  The NetWare Core Protocols are at the very center of Novell's functionality. It is these that provide client-to-server connectivity, file transfer, etc., and are critical to the provision of all services.

- **NetWare Link Services Protocol (NLSP)**

  In addition to the Routing Information Protocol (RIP), another routing protocol known as the NetWare Link Services Protocol (NLSP) is available within later versions of Novell software. NLSP is a Link State protocol operating in a similar manner to IP's OSPF. Since Link State protocols are more efficient than their Distance Vector counterparts, it is ultimately hoped that NLSP will replace the traditional RIP/SAP environments.

- **Underlying Network Technologies**

  In the same way that IP does not introduce new LAN/WAN access protocols, IPX relies on all existing standardized media access protocols. These include our established Ethernet/802.3, Token Ring, and FDDI LAN access methods, and all major WAN protocols as well. In addition, IPX supports multiple logical networks on a single IPX interface, each with its own specific encapsulation type. For example, where we have an Ethernet/802.3 environment, IPX supports the use of Ethernet version II, IEEE 802.3 with 802.2 LLC, 802.3 with 802.2 and SNAP, and also a proprietary *Raw* 802.3. In the latter case, this means that the IPX protocol is carried directly in an 802.3 frame with no LLC, and therefore no protocol identification.

36.2 IPX Addressing

IPX uses an 80 bit address, made up of a 32 bit Network Id, and a 48 bit Node Id. The Network Id is expressed in hexadecimal, and can be any valid hexadecimal string - it has no specific structure, cannot be subnetted (as with IP addresses), and is always locally assigned by the network administrator. Node Ids are then the MAC address assigned to the network interface cards (NICs) for LANs, and are normally borrowed from the first or lowest LAN MAC address for WAN ports. For example, consider figure 36-2.

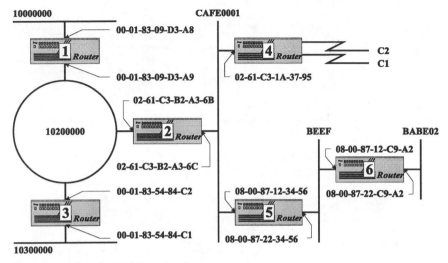

Figure 36-2: Sample IPX Internetwork

Our figure then shows several routers, each with a number of interfaces. We can now see that the IPX addresses assigned to say router 1 would be **10000000.00018309D3A8**, and **10200000.00018309D3A9**. Equally, on Router 4, the LAN interface would have the IPX address of **CAFE0001.0261C31A3795**. The WAN interfaces would then be **C1.0261C31A3795**, and **C2.0261C31A3795**, respectively, assuming that we can ignore all leading zeroes in the Network ID portion of the address.

Finally, before leaving the subject of addressing, let us look into the concepts of assigning multiple IPX network addresses to a single interface. Moreover, we need to examine the reasons why we may wish to configure a router, or indeed a server in this way. For this, we need to look back a short way into the history of Novell, and the way in which workstations communicate with servers. For example, most IP stations in an Ethernet/802.3 environment use Ethernet version II framing. That is not to say that this is the only option available, just that most implementations are configured in this way. In an IPX environment, as we said in the previous section, this is not necessarily so, and indeed it may well depend on the age of the Novell software. For example, let us consider figure 36-3.

We have stations and servers that are using two different frame types over an Ethernet/802.3 LAN. Stations 1, 2, and 4 are using a *Raw* 802.3 frame type, as is Server A. Stations 3 and 5 are using 802.3 with 802.2 LLC, as are Servers B and C. This means that those stations using the Raw 802.3 frame type will have access to Server A on Network B9036716. Those stations that are using the 802.3/802.2

framing will be able to access Servers B and C on Network B9036799. If any station needs to access a server using a different frame type, then they would need to send the packet to the *one armed* router. This router will have both network Ids configured, by using two different frame types. In general, Novell versions up to and including 3.11 used the *Raw* 802.3 frame type by default. Versions after this then defaulted to using 802.3 with 802.2 LLC.

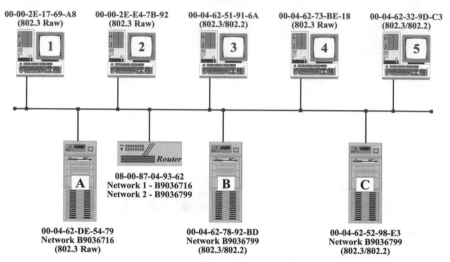

Figure 36-3: IPX Network - Multiple Network Addresses

36.3 IPX Datagram Format

The IPX datagram format is based upon Xerox's Xerox Network System (XNS) format. It is reasonably simple in structure, and is shown in figure 36-4. In the figure, we see that the first field is the two octet *Checksum* field which is not used and is set to the hexadecimal value FFFF. As a result of this, Novell is able to use the *Raw 802.3* frame format since the protocol is identifiable by the FFFF pattern being the first two octets of MAC payload data.

The two octet *Packet Length* field is used to indicate the total length of the IPX packet, including the header and data. The minimum packet size will always be 30 octets. The single octet *Transport Control* field is similar, yet opposite, to the *Time-to-Live* field in an IP environment. You will recall that in the case of IP, the *Time-to-Live* is set by the sending station, and then decremented each time the packet passes through a router. In the case of IPX, the *Transport Control* field is set to zero by the sending station, and then incremented by each router. When the value of this field reaches 16, the packet is then discarded as its lifetime is deemed to have expired.

The one octet *Packet Type* field describes the type of packet that this is, and works in a similar fashion to the *Protocol* field of the IP Header. Table 36-1 provides the common packet types for an IPX environment.

The four octet *Destination Network* field, together with the six octet *Destination Node* field provide the IPX address of the destination station. The two octet *Destination Socket* field defines the *socket number* of the Application process to which the data should be directed. A Socket is the name given to addressing at this level, and table 36-2 lists some *well known*, or reserved, sockets.

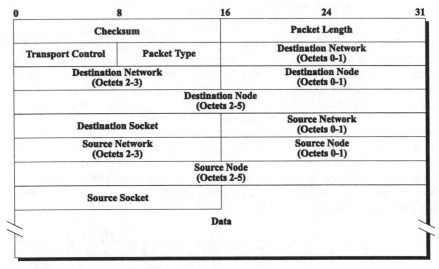

Figure 36-4: IPX Datagram Header Format

Table 36-1: Common IPX Packet Types

Packet Type	Description
1	Routing Information Protocol (RIP) packet
4	Service Advertisement Protocol (SAP) packet
5	Sequenced Packet Exchange (SPX) packet
17	NetWare Control Protocol (NCP) packet
20	NetBIOS packet

The *Source Network* (4 octets), *Source Node* (6 octets), and *Source Socket* (2 octets) provide the IPX address of the source station, and the socket number of the process. In this way, the station that receives the datagram will know to whom any response should be directed. The remainder of the datagram is then taken up with the actual *payload*, or IPX data which will be of variable length.

Table 36-2: Well Known IPX Socket Numbers

Socket Number	Description
451	NetWare Core Protocols
452	Service Advertisement Protocol (SAP)
453	Routing Information Protocol (RIP)
455	NetBIOS
456	Diagnostic use only
4000-6000	Dynamically assigned for use with and by File Servers

36.4 Routing Information Protocol (RIP)

The IPX Routing Information Protocol (IPX-RIP) is, for many networks, the only choice of routing protocol available. Certainly, NLSP that we shall briefly describe below is now available in the latest versions of Novell, but there remain a large number of legacy Novell installations at this time.

IPX-RIP is similar in operation to IP-RIP that we discussed before, and is based upon the simple *distance-vector* algorithm, whereby we count hops to a destination. The IPX-RIP protocol format is shown in figure 36-5. From this, we can see the standard IPX Header (shaded), which is then followed by the two octet *Operation* field. Where this field is a 1, it defines this packet as being a RIP *Request*, and would be sent by either a workstation or a server. The Request format can be used where we wish to obtain information about either specific, or *all* networks that are available. Where we wish to obtain information about *all* reachable networks (a general request), the requesting router would send the packet with at least one *Network Number* field set to the hexadecimal value FFFFFFFF. If we require information about one or more specific networks, then the *Network Number* fields reflect the network Ids which we are interested in. In both cases, the *Metric* and *Ticks* fields are irrelevant.

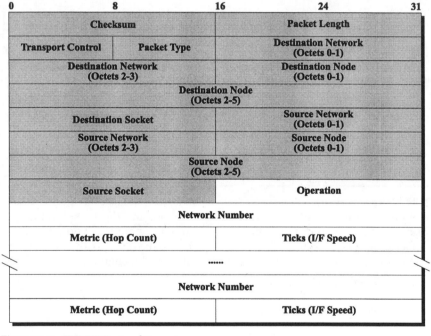

Figure 36-5: IPX-RIP Protocol Format

If the *Operation* field is a 2, then this indicates that the packet is a RIP *Response*. The response could be a reply to a specific or general request, or a periodic update (normally once every minute). In the case of the *Response* message, the *Network*

Number fields reflect the Network Ids of networks that the router believes to be reachable. The two octet *Metric* fields provide information that relates to how many *hops* the distant network is away. Finally, the two octet *Ticks* fields are used as a tie-break when two or more paths exist to the same destination and these paths each have the same Metric. The *Tick* count itself is a measure of delay associated with an interface. Thus, if multiple paths exist, the best path can potentially be chosen. In actual fact, many vendors ignore the *Tick Count*. Indeed, even where they do not it can be of little value. For example, in figure 36-6 we would choose the route to the left (Routers 1 & 2) since the *Hop Count* is less - although it is the worst route.

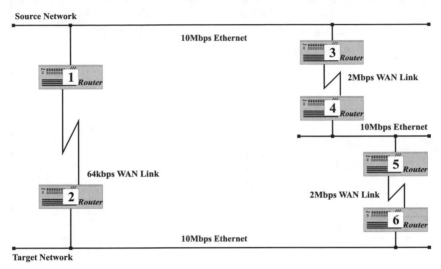

Figure 36-6: IPX-RIP Example of Multiple Paths

36.5 Service Advertisement Protocol (SAP)

Novell NetWare is based on File and Print Services that allow multiple users to share these resources. Nodes that provide these services then need to advertise their availability, which they do through the Service Advertisement Protocol (SAP).

SAP packets, the format of which is shown in figure 36-7, are periodically broadcast (typically every 60 seconds) by the nodes that are providing the service. These SAP broadcasts are then received by other stations, servers, and routers so that all *local* devices are aware of which services are available. We say *local*, since IPX routers, like their IP counterparts, will not forward broadcast packets. Instead, IPX routers will assemble tables of SAPs that have been received, and then broadcast these over their directly connected networks. In this way, all available services are eventually propagated throughout the IPX internetwork in a similar fashion to the way that reachable networks are propagated via RIP.

The SAP packet itself comprises a two octet *Operation* field that can assume any value between 1 and 4. Where the operation is a 1, this implies that the packet contains a *Request*, which can be either *general* or *specific*. In the case of a general request, the four octet *Service Type* field will contain the hexadecimal value FFFFFFFF and is asking for the location of all servers on a network. The specific request will use a specific *Service Type*, and requests the location of servers offering that particular service.

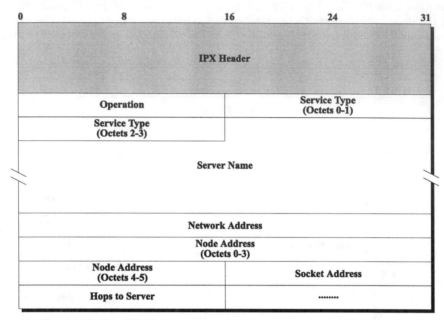

Figure 36-7: IPX SAP Packet Format

If the operation is a 2, then this indicates that the packet is a *Response*. In this case, the packet can contain up to a maximum of eight SAP entries. An operation code of 3 is known as a *Get Nearest Server Request*, and allows a station to request the location of the nearest file server. Conversely, an operation code of 4 is a *Get Nearest Server Response*, and allows the server(s) to respond.

The four octet *Service Type* field allows the identification of the type of service being advertised. These values are strictly controlled by Novell, but examples are a value of 4 for a File Server, 7 for a Print Server, and so on. The *Server Name* is 48 octets in length and provides a unique name for the server within the IPX internetwork. The four octet *Network Address*, six octet *Node Address*, and two octet *Socket Address* are the standard IPX addresses and are used to identify the server or station that originated the packet. Finally, the two octet *Hops to Server* field provides a measure of the distance back to the service itself. As the service is advertised by successive servers, this field is incremented. As with routes however, a maximum of 16 hops is allowed.

36.6 NetWare Link Services Protocol (NLSP)

Although the NetWare Link Services Protocol (NLSP) is not widely implemented today, this does represent the very latest thinking for IPX networks. IP-RIP has many shortcomings, and IP routing is generally thought to be improved by the introduction of OSPF. IPX networks will, in much the same way, also be much improved with the eventual acceptance of NLSP.

NLSP itself is based upon the ISO *Intermediate System-to-Intermediate System* (IS-IS) protocol, and uses a Link State Algorithm in much the same way as OSPF. This means that better routing decisions are now taken, and due to the nature of the protocol, it also works far better over WAN architectures. For example, one of the biggest drawbacks of IPX networks in WAN environments is the amount of bandwidth consumed by the continual updates caused by RIPs and SAPs. Apply this to *demand* networks such as ISDN, and we see that the protocols must be *spoofed*[1] to stop the link from being permanently dialed. NLSP strives to remove much of this wastage, although it requires later versions of the Novell operating system, and also full implementation by router vendors - the latter still lacking in many circles.

36.7 NetWare Core Protocol (NCP)

Although not part of any discussion relating to internetworking, the NetWare Core Protocol (NCP) is arguably at the very heart of Novell's operation, and therefore worthy of mention in passing. NCP provides the ability for client-server interaction such as the establishment and destruction of service connections, and also the opening and closing of files. NCP runs over IPX, but is totally proprietary, and Novell have never fully released the specifications of it. Running over IPX as it does, NCP can be routed, but relies upon the service and route advertisements that we have discussed above.

36.8 Summary

We have now discussed the IPX protocol that has for many years dominated LANs. At its heart, IPX itself is a good protocol, and has certainly served to drive the client-server market. True, it does have its enemies - the die hard IP network architect, and almost anyone that has a large WAN infrastructure. This is even recognized by Novell, and they are moving towards IP transports themselves. The bottom line however, is that Novell drove the *downsizing* movement of the eighties and nineties, and with it fueled the explosion of the LAN.

True, IPX is unsophisticated in many areas. One could argue that since the IPX protocol itself was born from the Xerox XNS protocol, it brought with it few enhancements. IPX is exceedingly wasteful of bandwidth for example, and we need only look to the Service Advertisement Protocol here. One SAP packet can carry just eight advertisements, so in large networks we must transmit multiple packets per advertisement interval - and that is normally 60 seconds. Equally, RIP brings all

---

[1] Spoofing is the name applied to a feature whereby a router or other device will *pretend* that an update has been sent. For example, a router might only send a RIP and/or SAP update over an ISDN connection when the link has been established so that legitimate user data can be sent. The router at the other end of the link would then complete this illusion and ignore the fact that it has not received an update to refresh its information.

of the shortcomings that are inherent in the IP version of the protocol, and NLSP has not achieved universal acceptance by any means. IPX does however have a sound network addressing scheme, and uses the *MAC Address* to address individual Nodes. Even IP has learnt something from this, since in IPv6 that is exactly what is proposed as the *Host Id* in a unicast address.

Layer 3 Switching

Having looked at the principles of both switching (an OSI Layer 2 operation), and routing (an OSI Layer 3 operation), we also need to take a brief look at devices that incorporate elements of both techniques. Such devices are known variously as *Layer 3 Switches*, *IP Switches*, *Multi-Layer Switches* or *Routing Switches*, and are one of today's hottest "*hot topics*" in networking. Our review of this type of device will be brief, chiefly because the technology is still very much in its infancy - at least as far as any kind of standardization is concerned. Understandably, many users are hesitant to implement a layer-3 switching solution until the standards coalesce, and products which conform to a recognized standard start to become available.

So why is this such a hot issue? The answer lies in the way technologies have developed, especially in terms of LAN speeds, and *interconnection* devices such as bridges, switches, and routers. As we have already seen in earlier sections, LAN speeds - particularly in the Ethernet world - have increased dramatically in the last few years, from 10 to 100 to 1000 megabits per second. We have also seen a dramatic increase in the proliferation of devices to interconnect segments of these high-speed networks, principally in the shape of switches (i.e., devices operating at OSI Layer 2). The development of *Application Specific Integrated Circuit* (ASIC) technology has enabled many manufacturers to build very high throughput switches, since their forwarding decisions are made in hardware rather than software. This in turn is possible because the format of the frame - or at least the portion of the frame which contains the information used in the decision process (i.e., the Destination and Source MAC addresses) - is consistent for any given LAN technology. This is regardless of the protocols carried in the frame, or the method used to convey LLC information.[1] In other words, the DA and the SA are always the first 12 bytes in the frame header - excluding any preamble and SFD. The use of switches to interconnect network segments has one potential drawback though. The topology of the network is essentially compressed into a flat address scheme (i.e., one based on layer-2 or MAC addressing). In other words, all hosts are connected to the same network (albeit to different segments).

One of the main reasons for implementing routing (i.e., creating an internetwork) is to take advantage of the traffic control and separation potential of working at the Network Layer of addressing (i.e., OSI Layer 3). Here, the concept of networks as separately addressable entities comes into play. Using Layer-3 addressing avoids

---

[1] See also section B (Ethernet/IEEE 802.3) for different frame formats.

problems such as broadcast storms (which are inherent to bridged/switched networks), allows a more controllable approach to traffic separation, and simplifies security controls. Doing this, we utilize a bipartite address scheme in which the network address is used for primary traffic routing decisions, rather than the end-station address. The device at the heart of this internetworking topology has always been the router - a device which relies heavily on software, rather than hardware, to make its decisions. The reason for this is not hard to discover, when we take into account the task we expect the router to perform. While the switch (or bridge) can easily predict where its decision-process information is located, a router has to be able to cope with different formats of information, at both layer 2 and layer 3.

To find out what layer-3 protocol is being carried within the frame, the router must be able to distinguish between 4 different layer-2 LLC structures (for Ethernet/802.3 networks), and be able to understand both 2-byte (*EtherType*) and 1-byte (802.2) protocol identifier codes. Once the layer-3 protocol has been ascertained, the router must then extract the network (and possibly host) address information from the packet level structure, in order to make its forwarding decision. Furthermore, it will typically have to be able to do this for several higher-level protocols (e.g., IP, IPX, AppleTalk, DECnet, and OSI).

Once the forwarding decision has been made, the packet will then have to be re-encapsulated at the frame level, in a form appropriate to the technology of the forwarding network (even if it is the same as the network from which it was received). The task of the router is thus much more complex than that of the switch, and up to now has been a task which has only been considered as suitable for a software-based solution.

In the face of ever-increasing *wire-speeds*, the traditional router is increasingly being regarded as a bandwidth bottleneck, primarily because of its reliance on software forwarding techniques. Increasing the speed of the physical router ports (e.g., providing 100BaseX or Gigabit ports instead of 10BaseX ports) does not solve the throughput problem, and in fact may even make it worse. The problem actually lies in the speed at which forwarding decisions and re-encapsulation take place, not with the speed at which frames enter and leave the router.

Speeding up the routing process - or at least the throughput of routed traffic - is thus the major challenge currently facing network equipment manufacturers. Several approaches have been adopted, some of which are proprietary and therefore present interoperability issues in multi-vendor environments. The following is therefore a brief summary of some of the ways in which manufacturers are seeking to solve the routing bandwidth conundrum.

In very broad terms, most techniques use a *route once - switch many* approach to speeding up the routing process, by analyzing the correlation between layer 2 and layer 3 addresses. Once the correlation between two end-points has been established, the traffic between them can then be simply switched at layer 2, instead of having to be processed at layer 3 every time. This approach allows the continued use of established routing protocols such as RIP, OSPF, and BGP to be used to maintain the routing information (and so re-converge an internetwork in case of link failures, etc.), while taking advantage of the high frame/packet throughputs of hardware-based switches. This is also the basic strategy of *router-accelerator* products, which use an existing router to converge and maintain the internetwork, and then interrogate the router's forwarding table to determine topology information.

37.1 Classical IP Over ATM (IPOA) and Multi-Protocol Over ATM (MPOA)

These techniques are one way of combining the intelligence (or power) of routing with the speed and efficiency of ATM cell-switching. In IPOA (and MPOA), ATM end-stations are grouped into Logical IP Subnets (LIS), which are interconnected via routers. ATM to IP address translation is provided by ATMARP. By using the Next Hop Resolution Protocol (NHRP), routers can establish an *exit point* from the ATM *cloud* which is nearest to the destination subnet. This takes advantage of one of the fundamental differences between IP and ATM in that IP is *connectionless*, while ATM is *connection-oriented*. Using ATM as the *cloud* via which routers are interconnected allows a logical connection (a Virtual Circuit, or VC) to be established between routers to carry packets between subnets. This then obviates the need to process packets on a *hop-by-hop* basis, as is normally required in traditional IP routed internets.

37.2 IP Switching

This is a proprietary technique, developed by Ipsilon Networks Inc. (now Nokia IPRG). This takes the *IP over ATM* approach, but does not implement the virtual-circuit connections between routers in the underlying ATM *cloud*. Instead, this uses classical IP routing methods.

This takes advantage of the robustness of IP (i.e., connectionless) routing, while at the same time providing the advantages of ATM's speed, capacity, and scaleability. In essence, an IP Switch device takes standard ATM switch hardware, and replaces the control software layer(s) above the ATM Adaptation Layer 5 (AAL-5) with the routers standard IP routing software. Routing decisions made by the router element may be cached in the switch hardware, depending on the decision of a *flow classifier*. In this context, a *flow* is a sequence of packets sent from source to destination, based on information in the IP and UDP/TCP headers (e.g., source and destination addresses and port numbers). Once a flow has been recognized by the flow classifier, subsequent packets of that flow can be switched rather than routed. The flow classifier can also make *policy* type decisions, based on criteria such as whether flows are (or are likely to be) short-term or long-term in nature. IP Switching also provides improved support for Quality of Service (QoS), and Multicast routing compared with classical (i.e., purely software-based) IP routing engines.

37.3 Tag Switching

This technique was developed by Cisco Systems Inc., and uses a modification of the label switch technology, operating on a *tag* carried within the frame to control forwarding. The *tag* may be carried as an interlayer *shim* between the layer-2 and layer-3 headers, or may be incorporated directly into either a (modified) layer-2 or layer-3 header. Tag forwarding information is held by a *tag-switch* in the form of a database known as the *Tag Information Base* (TIB), in which each entry carries details of the outbound tag, the outbound interface, and the outbound link level information. The tag in the inbound frame is used as a lookup key into the TIB, and is then replaced by an outbound tag before being forwarded through the outbound interface/port. As the tag-matching process operates on fixed-length information, it can be implemented fairly easily in hardware rather than software, thus speeding throughput considerably. The tag itself is essentially independent of the Network Layer, and can thus be associated or bound to a single route, an aggregate route, or a multicast function. Tag Switching, like IP Switching, also provides enhanced QoS and Multicast support, and additionally provides better load-balancing capabilities over classical routers.

37.4 Cell-Switched Router (CSR)

This technique is being developed by the Toshiba Corporation (Japan), and is an extension of the IPOA/MPOA approach. Routers of this type combine the functionality of an IP router (at Layer 3) with that of an ATM switch (at Layer 2). The ATM VCs may be of two types - Default and Dedicated. Default VCs are used for datagrams (packets) which must be assembled or disassembled at the CSRs themselves, while Dedicated VCs are used to carry traffic which flows between defined end-points. For *through traffic*, VCs may be concatenated to form a *Bypass Pipe*, thus speeding the overall forwarding process (provided that all en-route devices are CSRs). The *ingress* CSR (i.e., the point at which a packet first enters the CSR *cloud*, and therefore typically an end-station's default router) also performs flow classification, and decides whether a packet should be forwarded via a dedicated or default VC. Unlike IPOA/MPOA, CSRs use IP routing for inter-subnet forwarding, and ATM routing for intra-subnet forwarding. Both QoS and Multicast traffic are supported through CSR.

37.5 Aggregate-Route Based IP Switching (ARIS)

This technique was introduced by IBM, and aims to improve packet forwarding throughput by switching packets (datagrams) at wire speed. The device at the heart of ARIS is the ISR (Integrated Switched Router), which combines an IP router with a *classic* LAN switch device (i.e., one which uses *classic* technologies such as Ethernet/802.3, rather than being based on an ATM switch at Layer 2).

ARIS uses an inter-router message protocol to establish switched paths between *well-known* ingress and egress points in the internetwork. The existence of the networks/subnets themselves is derived from standard IP routing protocols such as OSPF and BGP. ISRs maintain three databases in order to establish and manage the switched paths over which packets may be forwarded: The *Routing Information Base* (RIB) which broadly equates to the routing table in a classical router; the *Forwarding Information Base* (FIB) which provides the *label* information for the forwarding process itself, such as destination prefix/outbound interface or port/next-hop IP address/and exit point; and the *Virtual Circuit Information Base* (VCIB) which contains the mapping between exit point Ids and the labels.

37.6 Multi-Protocol Label Switching (MPLS)

This technique is being developed by the Internet Engineering Task Force (IETF) MPLS Group, with the aim of providing a standards-based mechanism to integrate layer-2 switching and layer-3 routing. This will improve forwarding performance, flexibility, and scaleability. Although developed by the IETF, MPLS is not intended solely for the IP environment, but can be used to enhance performance of other network-layer protocols (e.g., IPX). MPLS uses standard routing protocols (such as OSPF and BGP in an IP environment) to establish and maintain network and route availability. The information gathered through the routing protocols is then used to generate and distribute the labels used to enhance packet forwarding. Using existing protocols for both switches and routers in this way is intended to allow co-existence of MPLS and non-MPLS devices within the same routing domain. The principal element in MPLS is the *binding* of labels to network-layer routes. When an *inbound* packet is received by a router in an MPLS domain, it is allocated a label which will control the way in which it is forwarded (a process known as *label-swapping*). When the labeled packet is received by another label-switch, the label carried by the packet is used as a lookup into the *Label Information Base* (LIB), which contains information such as encapsulation type and the outbound interface or Port Id, plus the outbound label. MPLS is still in the early stages of development, and issues such as scaleability and loop control are still under discussion.

37.7 Summary

This chapter has introduced some of the elements of the Layer 3 Switch. The device itself is still very much in its infancy, and there remains much debate over the real way forward. Each vendor seems to have their own idea, but one cannot feel that the whole issue surrounding the Layer 3 Switch debate is really all over nothing. Technology is moving on, and with it we will see faster routers. Vendors are claiming now that they have the first *hardware based* units that bring routing at wire speeds. Do we still need the Layer 3 switch with its proprietary methods if we can have a hardware based router? The answer is certainly no. So, the Layer 3 switch could become a stop-gap until we have faster technologies, or it could be further developed into a real standards based device. Without the backing of bona-fide standards, the device has no future, and even then it will only have real life expectancy if the price is competitive.

Section G

Cabling
Infrastructure

Original LAN Cabling Implementations

An important aspect of any LAN implementation is the cabling infrastructure over which it will run. Over the years, many changes have occurred as to the best practices of the time. Original implementations of technologies, such as Ethernet and Token Ring, were very much based on specific cable types with design rules that reflected the transmission properties of that medium. These days, many organizations are installing more generic cabling systems known as Structured Cabling Systems, which have become supported as the technologies mature. The purpose of this section is to investigate the cabling infrastructures supported by the LAN technologies discussed in this book. This starts with a discussion of original implementations (still very much supported, if not widely implemented), in this chapter, and followed by a more detailed discussion of Structured Cabling Systems in chapter 39.

38.1 Ethernet 10Base5

Ethernet/802.3 can run over several different cable types. Although originally developed using a common coaxial cable to which all computers were attached, developments fueled by user demands, now enable this technology to use different cable types depending upon local office requirements. In this section we shall examine Ethernet's cabling roots, coaxial cable, which although not used much in new implementations, is still widely installed in many existing installations.

38.1.1 Ethernet 10Base5 Cable

The original IEEE 802.3 specification described 10Base5 as the medium of choice for CSMA/CD (Ethernet) networks. Colloquially known as *Thick Ethernet*, this medium is based on RG8 (Beldon 9880) cable which is either 10.28mm (0.405 inches) or 9.53mm (0.375 inches) in diameter. The cable, shown in figure 38-1, consists of a single solid copper conductor shrouded in a dielectric to provide the best possible transmission characteristics. The dielectric is then encased within shielding which consists of two alternate layers of foil and braided metal to provide the maximum protection from external interference, such as EMI (Electromagnetic Interference). To complete the construction, the cable has a heavy duty PVC jacket which is either yellow or orange in color. This jacket is typically marked at 2.5m intervals with a black band, more on this later. From this high quality construction comes excellent transmission properties, as demonstrated by the velocity or propagation which is 0.77c, where c is equal to the speed of light in a vacuum

(300,000,000 m/s). The final cable characteristic of note is the impedance level. Impedance is in essence, the cable resistance to an AC signal and is set at 50Ω, a figure worth remembering, as all components of the network must match this impedance level so as not to cause an impedance mismatch.

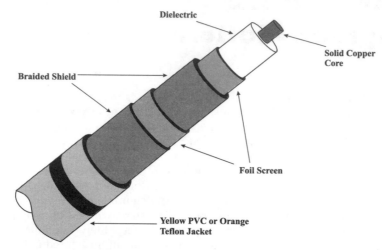

Figure 38-1:   10Base5 Cable Construction

The issue of impedance matching is one that will re-occur throughout this section, so is best explained at this early stage. It is not the intention of the author to delve in to electronics theory, merely to describe the effects this theory has on practical implementations. Impedance matching within the physical infrastructure of a local area network is one such example. The definition of impedance given in the previous paragraph is a very simplistic view, and no excuse is offered for this, save to say that from the perspective of implementing a cabling infrastructure, it is the matching of this impedance that is important, not the impedance itself. Ethernet provides an easy to demonstrate example of the importance of impedance matching. Ethernet is based on the ability to broadcast data over the network medium and recognize when collisions have occurred so as to re-send data if required. From the discussions on Ethernet in section B of this text, you will recall that a collision is detected by an increased DC element on the medium while transmission is still occurring. This DC element is caused by two signals colliding on the cable. So what has all this got to do with impedance matching? The answer is fairly straightforward. If a component is added to the signal path with a different characteristic impedance to cable, then part of the signal will be reflected back in the direction from which the signal originated. This will have the same net result as two data signals colliding on the cable and raise the DC element on the cable. There is, therefore a possibility that this event could be detected as a collision by the transmitting station, thus causing it to try to re-send the data. Unfortunately, this problem would continue to cause "phantom collisions" for every attempted transmission, effectively rendering the network inoperable. Although collisions do not occur in all technologies, the importance of impedance matching remains as signal reflections can "interfere" with the data signal thus corrupting the received

Original LAN Cabling Implementations

input. For this reason it is important that all components within a signal path, whether they be cable, connectors, patching equipment, etc., all have the same characteristic impedance. For 10Base5 networks this is set at 50Ω and should be adhered to for all products.

Another characteristic common to all cable types is Attenuation. A simple definition describes attenuation as signal loss over distance, that is, the further a signal has to travel, the weaker it gets. Attenuation is also affected by frequency, so the higher the signal frequency, the greater the attenuation, therefore a lesser distance can be achieved over a given cable type. For Ethernet networks, the maximum signaling frequency is known, as is the attenuation rate of 10Base5 cable plant. This means that it is possible to prescribe a maximum distance over which a signal can travel without degrading beyond the sensitivity range of a device's receiver. This distance is then set as the maximum allowable length of a single segment of 10Base5 cable, and is equal to 500m (1641.67 ft). If distances beyond this range need to be encompassed within the network design, then either an alternative media, such as fiber, or repeaters must be employed to regenerate the signal.

Installing 500m segments of 10Base5 cable is at best impractical, and would typically be achieved by installing shorter lengths and then joining them together.

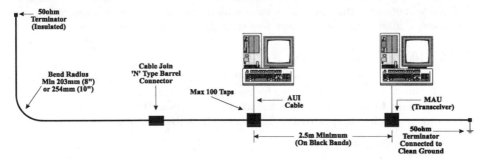

Figure 38-2:   Thick Ethernet (10Base5) Installation

This is likely because of the heavy and bulky nature of the cable itself. Installers must try to minimize the number of joins and bends, since these can create signal *reflections* that can disrupt network traffic. This is due to the fact that a small impedance mismatch is inevitable, even with careful product selection. It is therefore recommended that smaller segments are installed using what are known as *lambda* (λ) lengths of 23.4m (76.83 ft), or odd multiples thereof e.g., 70.2m, 117m, etc., and joints are made using in-line "N" Type barrel connectors[1] . Since the velocity of propagation in this type of cable is approximately 0.77c, 23.4m broadly equates to a single wavelength at 10MHz given the formula:

λ=(speed of light/Frequency in Hertz)*Velocity of propagation

or

λ=(300000000/10000000)*0.77=23.1m

[1] "N" Type Connectors are described later in this section.

The primary reason for matching the signal wavelength, or odd multiples of it, is that it is very important that any signal reflection that occurs at the joint, does not add in-phase with the data transmission signal. Too many occurrences of in-phase signal reflections can increase the DC element of the signal to a level where it may be confused with a collision, thus resulting in collision resolution. By following the installation guidelines for joining cables at the distances quoted, most signal reflections that do occur will be out of phase with the transmission signal, and an element of self cancellation will ensure that the problem outlined above do not occur.

As with most cabling infrastructures, there are a series of handling and installation guidelines that must be followed to ensure ideal transmission characteristics. The first of these is that it is recommended that straight cable runs are installed, but where there is no alternative but to bend the cable, it is recommended that a minimum bend radius of 203mm (8 inches) or preferably 254mm (10 inches) is used. In addition, it is recommended that to reduce the effects of Electromagnetic Interference (EMI), the cable is not installed within 1m of fluorescent lighting, or parallel to power cables. Another important factor is the termination of the cable. Both ends of the 10Base5 segment must be terminated with 50Ω terminating resistors, of which one should be connected to a clean ground. It is important not to connect both to ground as there may be a potential difference between the ground levels which could induce a current on the screening, which in turn would interfere with the data signal on the core.

38.1.2   10Base5 Connectivity

Two methods of connectivity exist for 10Base5 cable. The first is the "N" type, or Barrel connector which is intrusive by nature, as it requires the cable to be cut for an installation to be made. The second option is the "Bee Sting" or "Vampire" connector[2] , which is non-intrusive, as it can be installed on a live network.

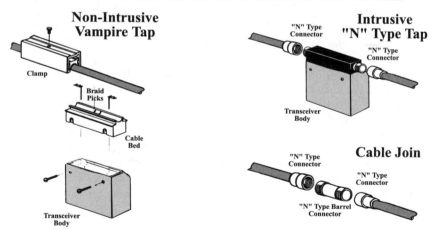

Figure 38-3:   10Base5 Connectivity Options

---

[2] Connections to 10Base5 cable are also called Taps, as they allow you to tap into the data cable.

The N-type connector, as we have said, requires the cable to be cut to be installed, but once in place provides a very robust connection that is ideal for both jointing cable and adding taps (transceivers) to the network. The connector is fitted by either soldering or crimping the connector components in place and then assembling the various components to form a screw on connector. Once in place, this can be joined to either a jointing connector, as shown in figure 38-3, or the MDI (Media Dependant Interface) of a Transceiver.

Bee Sting (or Vampire) taps are so called because of the method of installation and the fact that they do not require the cable to be cut to be installed. The primary components, also shown in figure 38-3, are the cable bed with clamp section, the center probe, and the braid picks. Installation is achieved by drilling a hole in the cable with a special drill bit that stops just short of reaching the core of the cable. Once drilled, the cable bed and clamp section are place around the cable and clamped up tight such that the braid picks push through the outer jacket and make contact with the shielding within the cable. The final part is to screw in the center probe which pushes through the remaining dielectric to make contact with the core of the cable. The whole assembly is then mounted on a transceiver to complete the tap. It is possible to install this kind of tap on a live network, however, care should be taken to ensure all metallic swarf is removed after drilling is completed to ensure that an electrical short does not occur when the probe is fitted. These type of connections are common, but are not as robust as the N-type. They also do not provide a mechanism for jointing cable, merely for tapping it.

Simply tapping a 10Base5 cable does not complete the requirements for connecting a station to the network. The tap is no more than the MDI of a Transceiver. The transceiver body itself must then be attached, and this in turn, connected to the station. The connectivity between the transceiver and the station is achieved via an Attachment Unit Interface (AUI) cable, more simply known as the *Drop* Cable. The connection of this cable is via a 15 pin "D" Type connector,

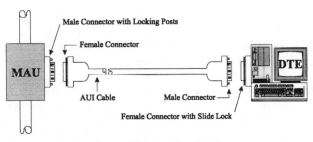

Figure 38-4: Attachment Unit Interface (AUI)

normally fitted with a slide lock to prevent the cable from becoming disconnected. The cable itself, is a multi-pair cable with each pair twisted and shielded to provide maximum protection from Electro-Magnetic Interference (EMI). AUI cable is available in two forms, one which is known as Standard AUI, which is approximately 10.5mm in diameter, and another, known as Office AUI which is approximately 6mm in diameter. The difference between the two is the quality of transmission characteristics, and therefore the maximum link distance that can be achieved. For Standard AUI this is up to 50m, while Office AUI is more typically limited to 15-20m.

Table 38-1, shows the pin assignments for the AUI D-type connectors, together with their individual usage. Signaling on the AUI is based on differential circuits, and each cable pair is individually screened. Hence, as the table indicates, each circuit has three individual pins assigned to adhere to this requirement. Two pins for the differential circuit connection, and one for the screen or *shield*.

Table 38-1: AUI Cable Contact Assignments

Contact	Circuit	Usage
1	CI-S	Control In Shield
2	CI-A	Control In Circuit A
3	DO-A	Data Out Circuit A
4	DI-S	Data In Shield
5	DI-A	Data In Circuit A
6	VC	Voltage Common
7	CO-A	Control Out Circuit A
8	CO-S	Control Out Shield
9	CI-B	Control In Circuit B
10	DO-B	Data Out Circuit B
11	DO-S	Data Out Shield
12	DI-B	Data In Circuit B
13	VP	Voltage Plus
14	VS	Voltage Shield
15	CO-B	Control Out Circuit B
Shell	PG	Protective Ground (Conductive Shell of Connector)

Note: In common with other circuits, the Voltage Plus and Voltage Common use a single pair within the sheath. Also, the "A" element of a circuit is always positive relative to the "B" element for a *HI* signal, and negative for a *LO*.

For a more detailed discussion of the purpose of these circuits, please refer to chapter 5, earlier in this text.

Attenuation and Impedance are not the only factors that have a bearing on installation and connectivity to 10Base5 cable. Another characteristic of equal importance is that of Jitter, that is timing irregularities that occur due to the electrical characteristics of connections on the cable length. To minimize the effects of jitter so that signal degradation does not exceed acceptable limits, a restriction is placed on the allowable number of taps placed on the segment. This limit is set at 100, which must be spaced at a minimum of 2.5m apart, hence the black bands on the cable jacket at 2.5m separation. That is not to say that all taps must be placed on a black band, simply that they are there as guidelines, and good practice dictates that they should be used for tap positioning. This is especially true where cable runs are it inaccessible places and it is not easy to determine where existing taps are located. If all installed taps are located on a band, then the 2.5m separation rule is unlikely to be compromised.

38.1.3 10Base5 Design Summary

In modern networks, the use of 10Base5 is pretty much limited to legacy implementations, but is still widespread and performing well. For those wishing to add to existing installations, the main features of any 10Base5 installation are shown in table 38-2.

Table 38-2: 10Base5 Design Guidelines

Design Aspect	Recommended Guidelines
Maximum Segment Length	500m
Maximum Number of Taps	100
Minimum Tap Separation	2.5m
Tap Positioning	On marked black bands
Termination	50Ω Terminating Resistors - Ground at one end.
Installation Lengths	23.4m and odd multiples thereof.
Minimum Bend Radius	8-10 inches (203-254mm)
AUI Cable Length	50m for Standard AUI or 15-20m for Office AUI

38.2 Ethernet 10Base2

10Base2 is another type of coaxial media which again, is rarely installed today. To most people this media type is more commonly known as either *Thin Ethernet*, *Thin-wire Ethernet*, or *Cheapernet*. 10Base2 makes use of a thinner (4.6mm), less expensive RG58 cable which, due to its lower velocity of propagation (0.65c minimum), and higher attenuation rate, has a maximum segment length of 185m (607.42 ft), and a maximum station count of 30 stations per segment. Beyond this, the cable has a minimum bond radius of 50.8mm (2 inches), and a minimum station separation is 0.5m (19.7 inches).

This was a popular choice for small LANs in the earlier days of Ethernet/802.3 since it was easy to install, and most importantly, cheap. Most specifically, and certainly one of the overriding factors, was that new stations could simply be daisy-chained from existing cables. Also, many station network interface cards (NICs) incorporated an *on-board* transceiver, which allowed stations to be directly connected to the media, which of course further reduced installation costs. Figure 38-5 shows an example of the cable construction, which when compared with

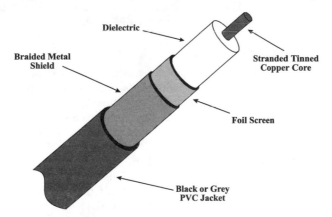

Figure 38-5:   10Base2 Cable Construction

10Base5 (discussed in the previous section), is smaller, and less well constructed, leading to a significant drop in transmission characteristics, hence the tighter restrictions regarding segment length and station count.

The thinner, more flexible construction makes 10Base2 ideal for the office environment. It can easily be run around office trunking, or even tacked directly to the skirtings, as its minimum bend radius of just 50mm (2 inches) allows it to be placed around corners with ease. The rules regarding fluorescent lighting and power cables are the same for this cable type as previously quoted for 10Base5, being 1m separation from the lighting and never run in parallel with power cables. Also like its heavier counterpart, 10Base2 cable must be terminated at either end with 50Ω terminating resistors, again matching the impedance level of the cable. One small but significant difference is that the ISO 8802-3 standard makes no direct reference to ground the terminators, therefore grounding is to be avoided.

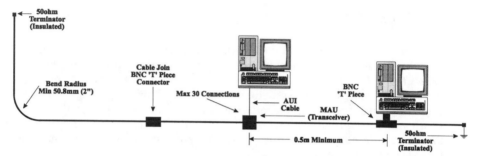

Figure 38-6:   10Base2 Installation and Configuration Rules

Figure 38-6 shows a typical 10Base2 installation with many of the design rules highlighted. It is important to note that like 10Base5, the medium must be unbroken from end to end to ensure a broadcast type environment can be maintained. Should a terminator become disconnected, or a cable joint come apart, or even should the cable break, then successful transmission will be impossible as all data will be reflected back from the point of disconnection, emulating continuous collisions. This would mean that no successful data transmission could take place, and the network would be rendered as unusable.

38.2.1   10Base2 Connectivity

Connectivity to a 10Base2 segment is made via a Media Dependant Interface attached to a transceiver, in much the same way as 10Base5. With 10Base2, the MDI is a Bayonet Neill Concelman (BNC) connector, shown in figure 38-7. The BNC connector is attached via solder or crimp-fit components to the cable in an intrusive fashion requiring the cable to be cut. There is no non-intrusive option for this cable type. Most NIC's come with the transceiver built on the card, thus eliminating the need for an external AUI in the same way as 10Base5. This eases installation as the station can connect via the use of a simple 'T' piece, directly on to the NIC. Where the transceiver is not "built in", an external transceiver unit must be used, and attached to the station via an AUI as before.

Original LAN Cabling Implementations

The most common method of installation for 10Base2, is to permanently install the majority of the cable, daisy chaining between wall plates, each with two BNC connectors. That is to connect the first BNC connector back to the previous wall plate, and the second on to the next wall plate. This then allows the user to connect a 10Base2 "flylead" consisting of two lengths of cable joined by a "T" piece, directly to the back of their station. Indeed, many stations can be daisy chained together, as long as the first and last connect back to the wall plate. It is this ease of use that made 10Base2 attractive to many users, but also led to its lack of popularity among network managers as it becomes difficult to keep track of station counts when users can easily add stations simply by this daisy chaining approach. Many network managers have found that their networks have been out of specification due to user additions outside their knowledge.

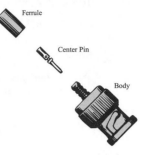

Figure 38-7:   BNC Connector

One important point to note is that both 10Base5 and 10Base2, operate on the basis of providing broadcast bus to the stations attached. This requires that the medium be unbroken from end to end, between two 50Ω terminating resistors. While this may seem obvious, it is probably the single most common fault on a 10Base2 segment when users can so easily disconnect, or reconfigure the cabling connections. It also requires that when cabling between wall sockets is installed, any of these sockets that remain unused must have a simple cable loop attached to ensure the cable run is continuous.

38.3   Token Ring

Much of the development of Token Ring has been influenced by IBM and the supported cabling infrastructure is no different. For many years, the only media type supported was Shielded Twisted Pair (STP) cabling, as defined by IBM. The primary reason for this was that traditionally, most of the installations based on Token Ring were so because of the ease of which it was possible to integrate larger computer devices from IBM, such as mainframe and mini computers. In addition many organizations were tempted by the fault tolerant nature of the technology and its more deterministic approach, when compared to Ethernet. Therefore, when considering Token Ring technology, a detailed discussion of the IBM Cabling System, based on STP media is required because of the widespread implementation in the market place.

38.3.1   IBM Cabling System (ICS)

The IBM Cabling System was borne out of a need to provide a universal communications cabling infrastructure to address two main requirements. Firstly, there was an opportunity to take advantage of the de-regulation of the telecommunications industry, which had previously required that telcos be responsible for in-house telephony infrastructures. Secondly, most if not all computer systems at the time made use of proprietary cabling systems, which meant that network managers were forced to replace cabling when replacing computer systems, or even just making moves and changes. There was therefore, an obvious gap in cabling technology to allow a single cabling infrastructure to support lots of different communications technologies over a single media type.

The IBM Cabling System is based on two pair STP that was based on state of the art cabling technology at the time. It was designed to fulfill the following requirements:

- A generic media type that could be used to support multiple applications.

- Based on two twisted pair cable, with one pair for transmission and one for reception. Twisted pair was chosen as it fulfilled the requirement.

- Excellent transmission characteristics such as very low signal attenuation, plus high immunity the crosstalk[3] between transmit and receive pairs.

- High quality Electro-Magnetic Interference (EMI) attributes e.g., immunity to external noise sources and low radiation of electrical energy from the cabling.

The two main applications were, of course, data and telephony. Most data applications were based on a form of coaxial cabling, while telephony was based on low cost twisted pair. It made sense to adapt data applications to a twisted pair environment rather than the other way round due to the difficulty of providing any form of duplex operation over coax. When selecting the type of twisted pair cabling on which to base the system, telephony cable of that time was of inferior quality and not suitable for the high frequency signalling required in a data environment. It

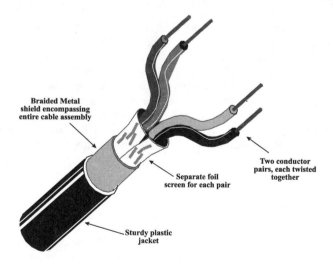

Braided Metal shield encompassing entire cable assembly

Two conductor pairs, each twisted together

Separate foil screen for each pair

Sturdy plastic jacket

Figure 38-8:   Shielded Twisted Pair (STP) Cable

[3] Crosstalk is discussed in more detail in section 39.4.2.

Original LAN Cabling Implementations

was therefore decided to adopt STP as the media for ICS. To achieve the low levels of attenuation required, 150Ω cable was chosen above the more standard 100Ω twisted pair used in telephone installations. To further aid the transmission qualities, it was also decided that a conductor diameter of 22AWG (0.6mm) would be used, with solid core conductors for all building cabling, and stranded conductors for patch (fly) leads. The larger conductor diameter, and its solid nature, both assisted in providing very low signal attenuation rates. The qualities of the cable are further enhanced by thick insulation on each conductor and shielding that is then applied. The shielding consists of a foil screen surrounding each pair, and an overall braided metal shield. It is this shielding that provides the excellent EMI immunity characteristics of the cable, and the low crosstalk between adjacent pairs. Shielded Twisted Pair cable to this specification has the capacity to propagate signals with a frequency of up to 350 MHz (Mega Hertz), which, as you will see later in this text, is significantly faster than has been standardized for Unshielded Twisted Pair (UTP).

Figure 38-8 shows the construction of Shielded Twisted Pair cable, where it should be noted that the foil screening is applied to each pair separately.

IBM Type 1A

IBM Type 1A (formerly Type 1) is a two pair STP cable with 22AWG solid core conductors. This cable is capable of supporting a maximum signalling rate of 350MHz and has a characteristic impedance of 150Ω. This cable is the premium cable of the IBM cabling system and is used primarily for distribution cabling from the wiring closet out to the wall socket. Due to its size (the cable is fairly bulky), and the solid nature of its conductors, Type 1A is not recommended for patch leads or work area fly leads.

IBM Type 2A

Type 2A is a hybrid cable that is of the same construction as Type 1A, with the addition of 4 pairs of 24AWG (0.5mm) UTP inserted between the braided shield and the outer jacket. The purpose of this cable is to allow data to be propagated on the STP core and voice signals on the UTP. Take up of this type of cable is, on the whole, regional as some countries (the UK for instance) do not encourage voice and data transfer on the same physical cable.

IBM Type 3

IBM Type 3 is a UTP cable, consisting of 4 pairs of 24AWG UTP with solid core conductors. Designed primarily to support voice applications, Type 3 can also support low speed data up to a signalling rate of 10MHz. The characteristic impedance also varies from other IBM cable types, being 100Ω inline with other UTP cables.

IBM Type 5

Type 5 cable is a fiber cable consisting of 2 pairs of 100/140μm[4] fiber for backbone or campus cabling. A fiber repeater would be required to convert electrical to optical signals.

---

[4] Fiber cable specifications are discussed in detail in the Structured Cabling Section.

IBM Type 6A

Type 6A consists of two pair STP construction with each pair being of 26AWG (0.4mm) stranded copper core. This makes the cable lighter and far more flexible than Type 1A, although the same signalling rate is supported. Type 6A is ideal for patch cables or work area fly leads where the flexibility of the cable is appreciated. Due to the stranded nature of the cable and the smaller conductor diameter, cable distances are reduced from those that can be expected with Type 1A.

IBM Type 9A

Type 9A is very similar to Type 1A but makes use of 26AWG solid core conductors instead of the larger 22AWG found in Type 1A. Because of this difference, the attenuation rate of the cable is higher and therefore one can only expect to achieve about two thirds of the distance.

It can be seen from the preceding text that the IBM Cabling System includes a range of cables suitable for high speed data transfer, while also allowing for voice applications. It is acknowledged that the description of ICS within this text is not exhaustive, nor is it designed to be so. It is merely an overview of the primary cable types included because of their significance within the Token Ring environment.

38.3.2 STP Connectivity

In conjunction with the development of the ICS cabling media, a new connector was designed to provide the high reliability required at high signalling rates. The designers of the connector had to meet the following criteria:

- The connector must be very reliable, providing high quality connection, even after a large number of connections and disconnections.

- High quality transmission characteristics, including low crosstalk between pairs and low signal loss at the point of connection.

- Automatic wrapping capability such that the transmit pair connect to the receive pair when the connector is disconnected. This is an unusual feature for a connector, but of paramount importance in a Token Ring environment.

- A single connector that could mate with another identical connector to form a connection. This again is unusual but eliminates the requirement for a "plug and socket" type arrangement. This type of connector is known as a hermaphrodite connector, meaning without gender.

The resulting connector designed specifically for STP and Token Ring is the Media Interface Connector (MIC), often known as the IBM MIC connector as it is the single most identifiable aspect of any IBM cabling installation. The MIC, shown in figure 38-9, offers all of the prerequisites mentioned above in a single high quality, if bulky connector. The connector contains two shorting bars, shown in figure 38-10, to enable the wrapping of transmit to receive pairs when disconnected, an inherent part of the Token Ring wrap facility.

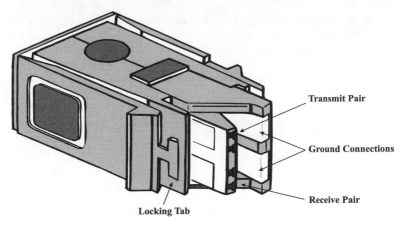

Figure 38-9:   Media Interface Connector (MIC)

To further aid the flexibility of the MIC connector, it is designed so that cable entry may be from three different angles. Figure 38-10 shows the rear cable entry point, however 45° and 90° cable entry is also supported to provide neater cable management if required. It should also be noted that where Type 6A or Type 9A cable is used, strain relief will be required to provide the necessary support.

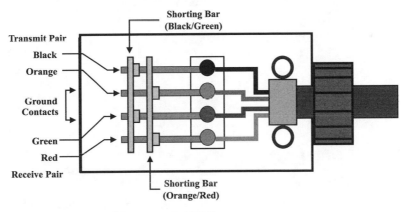

Figure 38-10:   Internal Structure of a MIC Connector

38.4 Summary

In this section we have discussed the original media specifications for both Ethernet and Token Ring technologies. In the Ethernet environment, the original specification dictated the use of 10Base5 coaxial cable, an extremely high quality media type with excellent transmission characteristics. In 1988 this was supplemented with the addition of 10Base2 coaxial cable, a smaller, more flexible alternative with reduced transmission capability. While both media types are supported in an Ethernet environment, they are little different from most other data cabling of their generation in that they are designed to support just a single application. In the Token Ring world, the IBM Cabling System was dominant and also had the advantage that it could support multiple applications such a voice (through additional cables) or other IBM applications such as 3270 or 5250 terminal applications through the use of adapters. This was the first multi-application cabling system on the market and was a revolution in the world of cabling where network managers were becoming increasingly frustrated with the need to change cable types whenever they changed applications.

Structured Cabling Systems

Cabling infrastructures have developed from very humble origins, to what we are familiar with today. When computers were first developed, communications between the Central Processing Unit (CPU) and Input/Output (I/O) devices, i.e., "dumb" terminals, teletypes, etc. was a modest 300 - 9600 bps. A typical cabling environment would be based on multi-pair cable wired in a point to point fashion between host and its peripherals. Should a new connection ever be required, then a cable would be run for the host out to the new location. In the years that followed silicon, the raw material for all CPUs, reduced in price and made the concept of moving some of the processing power out to the terminals more attractive. This concept, known as distributed processing, required advances in cabling technology by a fair order of magnitude. These so called "smart" terminals needed to transfer data at rates significantly higher than before, simply so that the terminal could "feed" its own local processor. Early cable implementations based on multi-pair cable and running some form of serial type communications was quite obviously not up to the task. Many manufacturers were looking to run their systems at speeds between 1 and 4.27 Mbps and therefore deployed proprietary cabling systems, typically based on some form of coaxial cable. This, too, was typically deployed in a star topology, with point to point links back to the central host computer, again under the basis that if a new location was required, then a new cable needed to be laid to accommodate it.

The introduction of the PC in 1980, and the development of the Local Area Network (LAN), required yet another advance in cable technology, with data rates and distances between devices increasing yet again. As we discussed in the previous chapter, Ethernet and Token Ring were both developed utilizing their own specific media type and topology, each with clearly defined rules regarding its deployment. Consider for a moment the "applications" available to an organization at this point (early 1980s). Most large computer systems were based on proprietary cabling and topology (e.g., IBM, ICL, Bull, Wang, Digital, etc.), LANs had arrived with much being made of their standardized approach in an attempt to move away from the proprietary nature of central computer systems, but also using proprietary media options. The telephone system was yet another application in most office buildings, with yet another cable type to accommodate. All of these applications shared one feature, should any moves or changes be required, then the only solution was typically to pull in new cable. It was obvious to most that some form of generic cabling system capable of running any application was needed to provide not only respite from the problems inherent with proprietary cabling, but also a way forward to support the applications of the future, while maintaining support for those already available. The need established, the next stage was to develop the cabling system, now known as the Structured Cabling System (SCS).

39.1 Basic Principles

Back in the early 1980s, two manufacturers took up the challenge of developing a generic cabling system. IBM adopted an approach that would see its results based on the cabling infrastructure being developed for Token Ring, with the inclusion of options to support telephony. AT&T on the other hand was a telephony company, already providing telephony solutions to millions of customers. Their approach was very much based on taking the telephony media solution and enhancing it to support data. In either case however, the main principles were very much based on a cabling topology that telecoms companies had been using for years. As early as 1970, telephony companies had begun to move away from a dedicated line per phone approach, across to a new idea known as "block wiring". This approach was very much based on 'flooding' the building with telephony sockets, typically in some form a grid pattern, such that a socket would exist in every conceivable location it might be needed at some point in the future. Each socket would be wired back to a centralized distribution point conveniently located on each floor, with these distribution points then linked back to a Main Distribution Frame (MDF) in the telecoms room, typically adjacent to the PABX. Service to a telephony outlet could then be provided by "patching" between the PABX and the MDF, and then again between the riser link cable and the distribution cable at the floor distribution point.

For this block wiring scheme to be successful, low cost media had to be used to ensure the overall costs of "flooding" the building with distribution cables was not prohibitive. For telephony, this was not a problem as the low speed signalling rates employed with analogue voice did not demand a high specification cable. As both IBM and AT&T found out, the same was not so easily accomplished for data cabling signalling at rates of many millions of bits per second. However, both organizations managed to overcome any early problems to release the first two structured cabling systems on the market, IBM in 1984 and AT&T in 1985. The IBM system was based on STP cable with the MIC connector being used for termination. AT&T on the other hand achieved a successful upgrading of its UTP telephony cable and based their solution on this new higher rated UTP, with the RJ45 8 pin connector as the termination of choice. Since these early heady days in the structured cabling market, many other manufacturers have joined in with alternate solutions based on similar media types or alternatively a third option of FTP (Foil Screened Twisted Pair).

39.1.1 SCS Objectives

All Structured Cabling Systems, no matter what vendor they be from all aim to fulfill the same key objectives. The first and perhaps most important, being the use of a single common cable type capable of supporting all applications desired to run across it. For this to remain cost effective it is also essential that the minimum of additional equipment is required to achieve functional connectivity. In addition to a common media type, SCS are also based on a flood wiring approach to minimize the impact of moves, additions, and changes (often called MAC). The idea being based on the philosophy that if there is potential for a user to occupy a given area, then there should be a cabling point terminated in that area in advance. By adopting this approach, another objective, that of minimizing the ongoing cost of ownership, can be achieved.

Two further objectives were also critical to the future success of SCS. Firstly, the ability to adopt the topology of the system to match that of any given application. This is essential if a single generic cabling system is to be able to support the many differing applications available. Secondly, and also key is the reliability of the system. Network managers are not likely to deploy a system that makes their task of supporting applications that much harder.

39.1.2 Topology

Structured Cabling Systems are essentially based on a "star" topology, organized in the form of a hierarchical or 'tree' like fashion, as shown in figure 39-1.

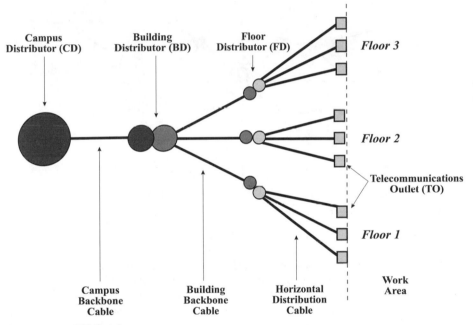

Figure 39-1:   SCS Topology

The hierarchy is separated into four levels, combining campus distribution, building distribution, floor distribution, and work area cabling. At the intersection of each area is a distribution point which provides the administration (patching) points for the system. Through careful application of patch cables at these administration points, an end-to-end signalling path can be achieved from any outlet, to any other part of the system. The various elements of the system, shown in the diagram, are often known by differing names. Those shown are taken from the International cabling standard ISO/IEC 11801. Table 39-1 shows a comparison in element names between the International standards and those used by the US standards organization ANSI (American National Standards Institute).

Any SCS implemented, requires only those levels from the standard topology necessary to support the office, building, or campus in question. As a minimum requirement, all systems must comprise at least the horizontal distribution level, terminated at one end at the Telecommunications Outlets (TO), and at the other end, the Floor Distributor. For many smaller buildings, this may be all that is required. However, if the building spans several floors, or the system spans several buildings, then either the building distribution level or both building and campus distribution levels will be required. Figure 39-2 shows a campus wide system, encompassing four separate buildings, each with three floors.

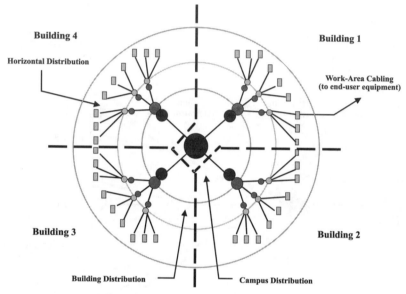

Figure 39-2: Campus Topology

At each point of administration, i.e., the distribution points, provision is made for the presentation of application specific equipment such as computer systems, repeaters, switches, etc., so that they can be patched into the system for user connectivity. This has been omitted from the diagram for the sake of clarity, as has another option, satellite floor distribution points. These are additional distribution points per floor used where cabling distance limitations or user density dictates a single distributor as impractical. When implemented, these are "tied" back to the main floor distributor via an extension to the backbone cabling known as tie-cables.

No specification is given at this stage as to the media employed or the termination systems (patch panels) at the distribution points. This is due to the fact that multiple options are available for either, and in many cases the chosen specification is due to many site specific issues, rather than application specific. An example of this may be where an implementation in an engineering works, or power plant, may prefer the use of fiber cable rather than copper, due to the

Structured Cabling Systems

immunity to electromagnetic interference (EMI), or safety reasons. It is important to understand the principle behind SCS is the approach, not just the media chosen. This is based on the "flood wiring" of all areas within the building with horizontal distribution cables, terminated at the TO. All of these are then brought back to a single (or multiple) distribution point on each floor. Further, all floors are then inter-connected, as are all buildings, such that any point within the system can connect to any other if so desired.

39.1.3 SCS Components

Many components go to make up a structured cabling system, however, some more than others are core components used in every system. These include the cable, connectors, patch panels and application specific adapters. The last of these, the adapters, may not always be first on the shopping list, but they are key to the operation of the system as a whole. Its one thing having a generic cabling system, over which you may wish to run any given application. It is something else entirely, getting that application to work. Remember, most applications (e.g., Ethernet, Token Ring, Voice, Video, IBM 3270, etc.) were designed to operate over a specific media. For an SCS to function seamlessly, the application must either be modified to support the change in media type (as in the case of Ethernet), or the application must be "fooled" into thinking it is still operating over its media of choice. Hence the need for application specific adapters.

The Balun

It will become apparent, if not already, that the generic media utilized in structured cabling systems, is twisted pair cable. For many applications, such as IBM 3270, this poses a potential problem. That is the signalling characteristics of the application itself. All applications designed to run over coaxial type media, use an un-balanced signalling method where the data signal is measured in reference to a

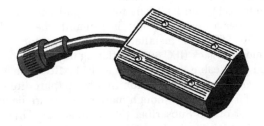

Figure 39-3:   A Typical Balun

ground signal. Therefore the finite value of the data signal is of significance. Signalling on twisted pair cable is based on a balanced method, where two conductors are used for signal transmission, one carrying a mirror image of the other. In this instance it is not the value of the signal that is of importance, more the differential between the two, with no reference to ground.

In order to run "un-balanced" applications over a balanced media infrastructure, it is therefore necessary to provide some form of conversion at both the user end, and the host end of the cabling system, such that the application is "unaware" of the twisted pair media in the middle. Such a converter is known as a BALUN, taken from the terms BALanced-to-UNbalanced converter. In addition to signal conversion, the balun also overcomes problems of impedance mismatch (i.e., RG-62 coaxial cable as used in IBM 3270 applications, has an imedance level of 93Ω, whereas UTP has an impedance level of 100Ω).

Baluns have been available for many years, but their use within data cabling systems has been a significant contribution in allowing many terminal based applications to operate over structured cabling systems on twisted pair cabling.

The Cable

As already mentioned, the generic cable specified for structured cabling systems if twisted pair cable. This, however, is not the whole story, as twisted pair cable comes in many different guises, offering different performance characteristics. There is Unshielded or Shielded Twisted Pair (UTP and STP, respectively), as well as Foil screened Twisted Pair (FTP or S-UTP). If this choice is not enough, then there are various categories of UTP (and FTP), each capable of different levels of performance. Then to further confuse matters, it is also totally viable to implement fiber cable instead of twisted pair copper.

One key point that should be made is that although the media options do offer some choice, typically, once this choice is made the same media type is installed across the entire system. This provides the ability to achieve commonality across the entire site, with all basic components being of the same type. This makes supporting MAC work far easier than previous proprietary cable installations. Later in this chapter we will discuss each of the media types in more depth and evaluate the options and limitations they offer.

The Connector

The connector used to terminate the cabling is, of course, dependant on the media chosen with which to implement the system. The choice however, essentially boils down to three, one for UTP and FTP, one for STP and one for Fiber (an additional connector type for fiber is available but is generally being phased out of new implementations). For UTP/FTP installations, the connector specified is the RJ-45 which is an 8 pin modular jack (IEC 603-7) offering the ability to terminate all cores of a 4 pair twisted pair cable. For STP the IBM MIC connector (IEC 807-8) is utilized offering 2 pair (4 core) termination in a hermaphrodite (ungendered) form. Fiber installations offer a choice, although market trends are beginning to eliminate other offerings in favor of the Subscriber (SC) connector. This is a square shaped connector capable of providing high quality termination with highly reproducible results. Older connectors such as the Straight Tip (ST) are still found in legacy installations, but are rarely installed in green field sites today. As with the cabling, the connectors are discussed in more detail later in this chapter.

39.2 Structured Cabling Standards

The whole concept of structured wiring is basically a simple one that provides marked benefits over both dedicated and proprietary systems. It is, however, beneficial that the design and implementation of such "open" systems be laid down in internationally agreed standards beyond the control of either a single manufacturer, or tied to a specific application. The provides the advantage to the consumer, who is not therefore tied into vendor-specific implementations. The vendors themselves, are simply provided with a predefined set of performance criteria to which their components must adhere. Once these criteria are met, the consumer should, in theory, be able to source product from any vendor and implement it in their system with assurances with regard to minimum performance specification.

39.2.1 U.S. Standards

Early structured cabling systems, like those initially developed by AT&T and IBM, were not governed by any such standards, and the risk of a proprietary implementation was high. However, this was initially addressed by two industry associations in the US, namely the Electronics Industry Association (EIA) and the Telecommunications Industry Association (TIA), who joined forces to produce a document entitled "Commercial Building Telecommunications Wiring Standard" which was published in 1990 as EIA/TIA Standard 568. This document, which although fundamentally flawed by today's standards, not only became the fore-father of structured cabling design standards, but defined many of the principles inherent in modern structured cabling systems. These included the basic topology of the system, and the wiring areas within it, as described earlier in the chapter.

In addition to defining the basic topology of a structured cabling system, EIA/TIA-568 also published performance criteria for both copper and fiber-optic cable, and details on cabling system administration. The first edition of this document, published in 1991, also made allowances for cable plant installed to support the main data application of the day, Ethernet. This meant that a structured cabling system could include the use of both 10Base2 and 10Base5 media. This inclusion of coaxial media was only one area where the document was essentially flawed. It is worth remembering at this point that one of the main concepts behind SCS is the use of a generic media type, which 10Base2 and 10Base5 are not. To add to this, the first edition of EIA/TIA 568 did not include performance criteria for different grades of UTP cable. The only criteria included was roughly the equivalent of what we know call Category 3 UTP. This meant that systems could not be designed, in accordance with the standard, for higher speed applications.

39.2.2 Technical Service Bulletins (TSBs)

In an attempt to correct some of the shortcomings of the EIA/TIA 568 standard, Technical Service Bulletins were released to provide addendums to the specification. TSB-36 entitled "Additional Cable Specifications for Unshielded Twisted-Pair Cables" included performance criteria for cables to support applications with signalling rates up to 100MHz, and introduced for the first time a classification of performance called the "Category" system, in which cables are categorized by their performance capability.

Unfortunately, TSB-36 only lays down criteria for the specification of cables and ignores the connecting hardware at either end of the cable. To correct this, TSB-40 was released entitled "Additional Transmission Specifications for Unshielded Twisted-Pair Connecting Hardware". This document was subsequently superseded by TSB-40A which added such information as connector pin layouts and color coding schemes, guidelines on cable installation practices, and test specifications for the verification of the performance criteria of the connecting hardware. It should be noted that these test criteria are based on laboratory testing and not field testing of installed equipment, which is still a contentious issue.

The specifications within TSB-36 and TSB-40A, along with a lot of new material from organizations such as the EIA/TIA, International Standards Organization (ISO), and other development bodies, have been incorporated into a revised edition of EIA/TIA 568 and has been accredited with "real" standard status by the American National Standards Institute (ANSI). This revised edition is known as ANSI/EIA/TIA 568-A. This latest standard provides an ideal design platform on which a structured cabling system can be built.

39.2.3   Additional US Standards

Although ANSI/EIA/TIA 568-A is perhaps the most significant structured cabling document from the US, others exist that do have great importance is the overall design of building cabling systems. These standards are summarized in the text below:

ANSI/EIA/TIA 569 -   Commercial Building Standard for Telecommunication Pathways and Spaces

This document focuses on the correct design of those elements within a building's infrastructure that are relevant to the telecommunications systems within those premises. This includes recommendations for the physical spaces and cabling pathways used by modern cabling systems and telecommunications equipment. These recommendations are essentially based on the following areas.

- Telecommunications Spaces - which include work areas, telecommunications closets, equipment rooms and entrance facilities. This includes sizing, loading, and environmental considerations.

- Telecommunications Pathways - which include horizontal and backbone cable distribution systems (conduits, cable trays, etc.) and pathway grounding requirements. This includes information on the number of pathways to install, acceptable types, and installation procedures.

An in depth description of the contents of this document is beyond the scope of this text, and the reader is urged, if considering a structured cabling system of their own, to obtain a copy of all standards mentioned in this book.

ANSI/EIA/TIA 570 -   Residential and Light Commercial Telecommunications Wiring Standard

This document focuses on recommendations for the installation of cabling systems to be used within both residential and light commercial premises. This is based on a recognition that residential premises often have computer equipment similar to that found within commercial buildings. It also recognizes the needs of individuals that require remote access through teleworking. It suggests the preparation of telecommunications cabling systems within residential premises for LANs and access to remote networks.

ANSI/EIA/TIA 606 - Administration Standard for the Telecommunications Infrastructure of Commercial Buildings

The main objective of this document is the provision of a series of recommendations for the documentation and ongoing administration of the premises telecommunications infrastructure. This is achieved via the promotion of the use of an administration scheme that remains independent of any application using the system. The recommendations for documentation include:

- Assign a unique identifier to each element within the cabling system

- Create an individual record for each of the identified elements

- Provide a link between all related records.

The standard does not distinguish between electronic or manual recording systems.

System administration is known to be one of the most important aspects of any structured cabling system and it is important to keep records up to date. Remember, if changes are made to the system and these are not recorded in the system administration records, then it is the same as not documenting the system in the first instance. Good system administration also allows for easier tracking of individual components and facilitates easier troubleshooting.

ANSI/EIA/TIA 607 - Grounding & Bonding Requirements for Telecommunications in Commercial Buildings

This document provides recommendations for grounding and bonding issues within a telecommunications cabling system. It is not expected to supersede any requirements laid down in national or local electrical codes/safety regulations, merely provide guidelines to allow telecommunications infrastructure to meet stated performance criteria.

39.2.4 International Standards

In addition to the work done by ANSI and the EIA/TIA committees, the International Standards Organization (ISO) has also done a lot of work on structured cabling systems standards, particularly in conjunction with its sister organization the International Electrotechnical Committee (IEC). These organizations have worked to enhance the recommendations of the original EIA/TIA 568 and TSBs and produced a truly International standard known as ISO/IEC 11801, which is entitled "Information Technology - Generic Cabling for Customer Premises Cabling". This document encompasses all design aspects of a structured cabling system and allows for the system to be designed from a performance perspective much more simply than was previously possible. This document was ratified by ISO/IEC as a standard in 1995 and has been adopted in most countries in the world.

Due to the nature of cabling systems, it is impossible for an International standard to be specific on every aspect as some aspects remain country specific, e.g., grounding and bonding. Therefore ISO/IEC 11801 is a very generic document, with country specific variations existing. ANSI/EIA/TIA 568A is an example of this, as is EN50173 within Europe. The discussion on structured cabling systems within this text however, is consistent throughout all three of these documents in the main part, with any notable variations highlighted wherever possible.

One area that is very different between ANSI and ISO standards is the terminology used to describe different components within the system. Table 39-1 shows the differences that exist between the two standards in this regard. This is not uncommon, and it must be remembered that as the topology has emerged primarily from a telecoms background, other terminology is also prevalent within the industry, especially with those from a similar telecoms background.

Table 39-1: Comparison of ISO/IEC & ANSI Terminology

ISO/IEC 11801	ANSI 568A
Telecommunications Outlet	Telecommunications Outlet
Horizontal Cable	Horizontal Wiring
Floor Distributor	Telecommunications (Wiring) Closet
Building Backbone	Intra-Building (Riser) Backbone
Building Distributor	Intermediate Cross-Connect
Campus Backbone	Inter-Building Backbone
Campus Distributor	Main Cross-Connect

39.3 Areas within an SCS System

The topology of a structured cabling system, as shown in figure 39-1, is further defined in figure 39-4, with the various sub-systems described below.

Structured cabling systems comprise three cabling subsystems; the campus backbone subsystem, the building backbone subsystem, and the horizontal cabling

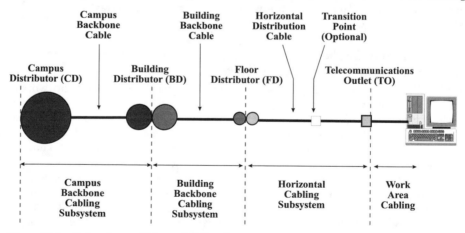

Figure 39-4: Subsystems within an SCS Topology

subsystem. In addition to this there is also the work area cabling, which is necessary but considered outside the scope of the SCS standards due to it being application specific. Each of the cabling subsystems is bounded by a distribution point which provides the mechanism for inter-connecting the subsystems and for linking in application specific equipment i.e., PABX, Bridges, Repeaters, etc.

The horizontal cabling subsystem extends from the floor distributor to the telecommunications outlet, and encompasses the horizontal distribution cables, the connecting hardware at either end, and the cross-connect patching at the floor distributor. The standard recommends that if it is at all possible, all horizontal distribution cables should be continuous, however a single transition point[1] can be included between the floor distributor and the telecommunications outlet.

Several media options exist for the horizontal cabling subsystem, with some differences between the ISO/IEC 11801 and ANSI/EIA/TIA standards. Table 39-2 summarizes these options as well as the differences between standards.

Table 39-2: Horizontal Cabling Media Options

ISO/IEC 11801	*ANSI/EIA/TIA 568A*

2n pairs 100Ω Balanced pair cable
          Category 3, 4, or 5
	4 pair 100Ω UTP/FTP cable
	          Category 3, 4, or 5

n quad elements 120Ω star quad cable Category 4+, or 5+	
2 pair 150Ω STP cable	2 pair 150Ω STP cable
62.5/125 µm optical fiber	62.5/125 µm optical fiber

Two minor differences exist between the ISO and ANSI standards at this level. These are the inclusion of 120Ω star quad cable in the ISO standard, due to some use in Europe, and the fact that that the ISO document talks about balanced pair cables and does not draw a distinction between construction methods. However, in the main part, the two documents agree on important areas such as performance characteristics and cable categorization.

The building backbone subsystem includes the building backbone cable and its termination hardware at either end within the building and floor distributors. In addition, it also includes the cross-connect patching at the building distributor. As with the horizontal cabling, the building backbone has multiple media options, as shown in table 39-3, however, if a copper backbone is installed, the standards expressly forbid any form of splice or jointing within the backbone. This means that transition points are not allowed in this part of the cabling system.

The campus backbone cabling subsystem extends from the building distributor through to the campus distributor and incorporates the campus backbone cable. Also included is the mechanical termination of the backbone cable at either end and the cross-connect patching within the campus distributor. Although the campus backbone subsystem has the same media options available as the building backbone, the use of copper cables in the campus backbone is relatively rare due to

---

[1] Transition Points are discussed in section 39.3.1.

the increased cable distances involved and the need to provide electrical isolation between buildings. For these reasons, it is far more common to see the campus backbone cabled using fiber optic cable and of course, the fiber terminating hardware at either end.

It should be noted that the standards do not encourage, nor discourage, the use of mixed media for any of the cabling subsystems and therefore this is left to the discretion of the designer and the requirements of the particular installation. It is not uncommon to find both fiber and copper in the backbone, especially the building backbone, with the fiber being allocated for data service distribution and the copper for voice services. Where this is the case, some thought must be given to the application specific equipment required to provide copper to fiber signal conversion, if necessary, at the point of inter-connection.

Table 39-3: Backbone Cabling Media Options

ISO/IEC 11801	ANSI/EIA/TIA 568A
2n pairs 100Ω Balanced pair cable Category 3, 4, or 5	4+ pairs 100Ω UTP/FTP cable Category 3, 4 or 5
n quad elements 120Ω star quad cable Category 4+, or 5+	
2 pair 150Ω STP cable	2 pair 150Ω STP cable
62.5/125 μm optical fiber	62.5/125 μm optical fiber
8/125 μm optical fiber	8/125 μm optical fiber

39.3.1 Transition Points

The name Transition Point indicates its function, to transition between one type of cabling to another. This could be from one cable type to another, or from permanent to temporary cabling, or from fixed cabling to a trailing, more movable cable. Some manufacturers provide 25 pair cables, which in theory, could be used for horizontal distribution cables to a fixed point out on the floor, the transition point. At this point they would be terminated, and four pair cables would be used to connect the transition point to the telecommunications outlet. This is useful where pre-wired furniture, or "service posts" are implemented in the office.

Although transition points can aid in the flexibility of the horizontal distribution system, their use should be carefully considered before widespread installation. As with any other point of interconnection, a transition point is a source of increased crosstalk on the cabling link and can have an adverse affect on attenuation. Therefore, as the standards state, all horizontal distribution should be kept continuous wherever possible. In addition, cabling system vendors, especially those offering extensive warranties, may impose restrictions on the use of transition points based on all or any of the following:

- Where, within the cable run, a TP may be placed
- The maximum length of the cable run
- The cable or connectors used

- The maximum transmission speed supported
- The use of TPs at all

39.3.2 Distance Limits

The structured cabling standards set distinct limitations on the maximum length of cable runs for each of the cabling subsystems within the system as a whole. These limits, shown in figure 39-5, are designed as maximum figures and can be reduced for any given design.

The horizontal distribution cables are limited to a maximum of 90m from the floor distributor to the telecommunications outlet. This distance should not be breached, even if transition points are used. It should also be noted that this 90m limit is imposed for all media types, including fiber. In addition to the 90m distribution limit, there is also a limit of 5m imposed for patch cords and work area fly leads. This equates to a maximum transmission distance between application specific equipment placed at the floor distributor, and end user equipment in the work area of 100m, which is equal to the maximum transmission distance for most high speed data applications over twisted pair media.

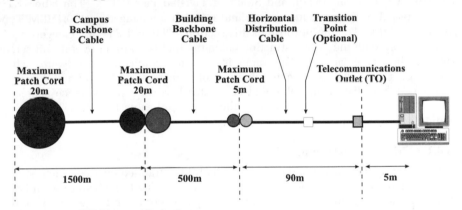

Figure 39-5:   SCS Distance Limitations

For the building backbone, the permitted maximum distance of the cable run should not exceed 500m, again irrespective of media type. This distance is measured from the terminating hardware at either end of the backbone cable, and does not include the patch cords. For the building distributor, like the campus distributor, the maximum patch cord length is set at 20m. The campus backbone has a limit of 1500m, which when added to the building backbone equates to an overall backbone length of 2km. This equates to the maximum supported distance for most high speed data applications over multimode fiber optic cable.

Care should be taken when designing a structured cabling system to take into consideration the applications that are intended to run over the system. This is because the maximum distance limits set for the various cabling subsystems can often exceed the maximum supported transmission distances of many common applications. An example of this is Ethernet, which has a maximum transmission limit of 100m over UTP cable. It is perfectly legitimate to design a structured cabling system with a UTP backbone of up to 500m, but Ethernet will not run over it unless the backbone is reduced to 100m, or changed to fiber. This scenario is true for many applications, therefore application standards, or manufacturers guidelines, should be sought and understood before any system is designed.

39.4 Twisted Pair Media Options

As discussed thus far, there are different media options available for structured cabling systems, and some explanation of these media types is probably warranted at this stage. For copper based cabling, the choice is essentially based on whether to implement a shielded or unshielded variety of twisted pair cable, or whether to depart from copper and implement fiber. In this section we will discuss twisted pair media in more depth to understand the options and allow an informed choice to be made, while fiber is discussed in section 39.5.

When considering twisted pair cable (balanced pair in ISO terminology), there are basically three types to consider. There is Unshielded Twisted Pair (UTP), Foil-Screened Twisted Pair (FTP), and Shielded Twisted Pair (STP). The latter, STP, was discussed in the previous chapter and remains unchanged as 150Ω IBM Type 1A, 6A, and 9A. For the purpose of this section, UTP and FTP are categorized in the same way with the only distinction being the inclusion of an overall foil screen beneath the cable jacket. The same is true for connecting hardware, where screening is provided for the termination of screened cable and not for UTP. Therefore when discussing cable and connector hardware performance characteristics, the reader should be aware that these are applicable to both UTP and FTP media.

39.4.1 Cable Construction

Both UTP and FTP are available with either solid or stranded core conductors, with the solid core version designed for distribution cables due to its better transmission characteristics, and the stranded version for patch cords or fly leads. In either instance, the most common form of the media is a four pair variety with each of the

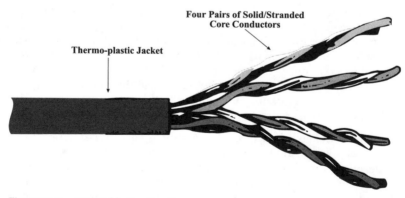

Figure 39-6:   UTP Cable Construction

four pairs twisted together to enhance the signalling characteristics of the cable. This construction technique is shown in figure 39-6 below. As already mentioned, FTP differs from UTP only by the inclusion of a foil screening that surrounds the four pairs beneath the jacket. Theoretically, this screening helps to minimize the susceptibility of the cable to outside Electro-Magnetic Interference (EMI), and reduce the levels radiating from the cable itself. This is only true if the cable is installed correctly with all the grounding and bonding guidelines issued by the manufacturer followed. Failure to do so will actually cause the screening to act as a large aerial, attracting all the unwanted interference from the surrounding atmosphere, and causing potentially disastrous consequences to the signals being transmitted. It should also be mentioned that modern cable technology means that it is not specifically a requirement to install screened cable, even though many countries are tightening their regulations with regard to EMI. Most vendors of UTP cabling systems can demonstrate compliance with these regulations for their systems, even though they are based on UTP.

UTP and FTP cables are constructed with the twists in them to provide better transmission characteristics. There are no specific guidelines as to the rate of twist for cables, this is seen as a matter for the manufacturer, merely that the cable performs to stated performance criteria.

39.4.2 Transmission Characteristics

Generally, when considering twisted pair cables, the most important criteria is what is the maximum rate of signalling that can be transmitted over the cable, and over what distance. These may sound like simple enough criteria, but a complex set of parameters need to be considered to determine either. For this reason, the EIA/TIA committee responsible for TSB-36 decided, on the back of work done by the industry, to formalize the categorization of UTP cables such that users and designers would have a simplified choice for their cabling system. This led to the development of the "Category" system we know today in which five categories of UTP/FTP exist. For the purposes of structured cabling, categories 1 and 2 are not good enough to support the majority of applications and are therefore not considered by either this text or the standards themselves. Therefore only Category 3, 4, and 5 cable will be discussed, as will the differences between them. Before this though, it is necessary to have a basic understanding of some of the main transmission characteristics that affect UTP cable, and how their effects can be minimized (elimination is not possible).

Mutual Capacitance

Mutual Capacitance is an effect that occurs when wires are arranged in close proximity to each other, as in the case of UTP cables. In this arrangement, they will exhibit a "capacitive coupling" effect between the pairs such that a coupling of AC signals between the pairs will occur. The net result of this is that "crosstalk" will occur between pairs with the signal on one pair interfering with the signal on another. The only way to minimize the capacitive coupling effect is to reduce the mutual capacitance of the cable to as low as possible. This is achieved via the construction of the cable, using high quality materials and introducing twisting to the pairs. Because the capacitance of the cable is largely due to the construction, it is imperative that installation guidelines are followed to ensure the internal structure of the cable remains intact.

Characteristic Impedance

Characteristic impedance is the reactance of a cable to an AC signal and is pre-defined for a specific cable type. UTP has an impedance level of 100Ω +/- 15%, which is largely determined by the construction of the cable. Factors such as how many twists per foot are made in each pair, the diameters of the conductors, and the thickness of the insulation are all important in determining the characteristic impedance for the cable. Again, installation such that it damages the cable structure can adversely affect the impedance, causing unwanted signal reflections.

Attenuation

Attenuation is something that affects all signals in all media types and is best described as the gradual reduction of the signal power in relation to distance travelled. Therefore a signal will become "weaker" the greater the distance it must travel. In copper cables, attenuation increases with frequency such that the higher the frequency (Hz), the greater the attenuation, the shorter the distance it can travel. Attenuation is expressed as a ratio of the losses compared with the original signal power, and uses a logarithmic scale known as deciBels (dB). Typically, as it is losses being considered, the attenuation rate is normally expressed as a negative value i.e., -ndB. As attenuation is directly linked to distance, it is a primary factor in determining cable lengths for any given signalling rate.

In order to calculate the level of losses occurring, table 39-4 shows a general guide to equating dB losses to percentage signal losses. It demonstrates that an increase of 3dB effectively doubles the amount of losses, or put another way, each 3dB loss will halve the signal power still left.

Factors that affect attenuation are the quality of the materials used and the method of construction. It is impossible to eliminate, but the effects can be reduced. Evidence of this can be seen in table 39-5 where Category 5 UTP suffers much lower attenuation than Category 3 at the same signalling rates. In fact, Category 3 UTP suffers to such an extent at higher signalling rates, the maximum supported rate has to be limited so as not to compromise the 100m distance limit assigned to the horizontal cabling subsystem.

Table 39-4: deciBel Losses Vs Percentage Losses

deciBels	Ratio	Percentage Power Loss
0dB	1:1	0%
-3dB	1:2	50%
-6dB	1:4	75%
-9dB	1:8	87.5%
-10dB	1:10	90%
-20dB	1:100	99%
-30dB	1:1000	99.9%

Near End CrossTalk (NEXT)

Near End CrossTalk (NEXT) is the unwanted coupling of signals between pairs within a cable, and is directly related to the mutual capacitive coupling effect described earlier. It is so called because it is always measured at the near end, where the power of a transmission signal is at it strongest. If the signal power is at its greatest then the crosstalk effect is going to be at its worst. Like attenuation, NEXT also varies with frequency, worsening as the signalling rate increases. The other factor NEXT shares with attenuation is the measurement is also made as a ratio in deciBels (dB). In this instance the ratio is between the power of the unwanted crosstalk signal, as measured on an adjacent pair, compared to the power of the original transmission signal. As the comparison is a power ratio, the greater the ratio is, the less the crosstalk is between pairs. This means that unlike attenuation, where low dB values are better, with NEXT, the higher the value, the better the performance. Again, as with attenuation, the ratio values are as shown in the center column of table 39-4.

NEXT causes manufacturers big problems when designing cables, and more specifically connecting hardware as the capacitive coupling effect is at its worst at the point of termination. Within the cable techniques such as varying the number of twists per foot between pairs, and better materials help reduce the effect. For connecting hardware, it is imperative that manufacturers guidelines are followed to ensure NEXT does not exceed acceptable limits.

Signalling Rate

The last characteristic we will consider is the Signalling Rate. The signalling rate is determined by the application making use of the cable infrastructure and varies from one application to another. With digital signals, the signalling rate can be described as the rate of change of the state of the signal, and is measured in Hertz (Hz). For most data applications, this rate of change is in the millions per second range, or MegaHertz (MHz). We have already discussed how this rate of state change in the signal can directly affect the attenuation and the NEXT for any given cable. It is therefore extremely important that it is taken into consideration when selecting cable type for a particular installation. As cable technology enhances, the maximum signalling rate supported will increase, however application developers are also assisting in allowing faster applications to run over existing cable plant by developing fancy encoding schemes that allow the signalling rate to reduce, while the data transfer rate increases. This approach is being used to allow technologies such as 1000BaseT to be developed to run over existing cabling systems.

39.4.3   UTP Categories

As you can imagine, given the number of parameters involved, it is possible to manufacture cable to many different specifications, each with different performance characteristics. This could easily lead to confusion in the market place with users not being aware of the performance capability of their installed systems. To overcome this issue, the EIA/TIA, off the back of work undertaken previously by the industry itself, decided to formalize the specification of UTP cables such that users would be able to easily determine the minimum performance capability of the cable they purchase.

Although five cable categories exist, only categories three through five are considered suitable for structured cabling systems due to the need to support data, as well as voice applications. The difference between the cables in each category is how they perform in relation to the parameters specified in the previous section. Therefore a cable which is less susceptible to attenuation and NEXT is likely to be in a higher category than one with higher attenuation and more crosstalk. Frequency is also a key factor in cable performance, with both attenuation and crosstalk varying with frequency changes. Table 39-5 demonstrates the difference between the three categories of cable in relation to the maximum allowable attenuation and NEXT for each cable category at a range of different frequencies. It should be noted that although only spot frequencies are quoted in the table, the standards do actually dictate that the attenuation and NEXT values for each category should not be exceeded at any frequency between 0MHz and the maximum supported frequency for that category. That is 16MHz for Category 3 UTP, 20MHz for Category 4 UTP and 100MHz for Category 5 UTP.

Based on the specifications stated, the EIA/TIA specified in TSB-36 that Category 3 UTP cables would support a maximum signalling rate of 16MHz. Likewise Category 4 would support applications with a signalling rate up to 20MHz and Category 5 up to 100MHz. This enables designers and customers to know the expected performance of any given installation based on the cables used, or does it?

Table 39-5: Cable Attenuation and NEXT Maximum Values for each Category

| Frequency (MHz) | ISO/IEC 11801 | | | | | | ANSI/EIA/TIA 568A | | | | | |
| | Cat 3 (dB) | | Cat 4 (dB) | | Cat 5 (dB) | | Cat 3 (dB) | | Cat 4 (dB) | | Cat 5 (dB) | |
	Att	XT	Att	XT	Att	XT	Att	XT	Att	XT	Att	XT
1	2.6	41	2.1	56	2.1	62	2.6	41	2.1	56	2.1	62
4	5.6	32	4.3	47	4.3	53	5.6	32	4.3	47	4.3	53
10	9.8	26	7.2	41	6.6	47	9.8	26	7.2	41	6.6	47
16	13.1	23	8.9	38	8.2	44	13.1	23	8.9	38	8.2	44
20	N/S	N/S	10.2	36	9.2	42	N/S	N/S	10.2	36	9.2	42
31.25	N/S	N/S	N/S	N/S	11.8	39	N/S	N/S	N/S	N/S	11.8	39
62.5	N/S	N/S	N/S	N/S	17.1	35	N/S	N/S	N/S	N/S	17.1	35
100	N/S	N/S	N/S	N/S	22.0	32	N/S	N/S	N/S	N/S	22.0	32

N/S = Not Supported   Att = Attenuation   XT = Near End CrossTalk

In fact there is more to it than just the cables. The connecting hardware plays an equal importance in determining the performance capacity of any link, and therefore has been categorized in the same fashion. It is possible to purchase Category 3, Category 4, or Category 5 connectors and patch panels, as well as other connecting hardware arrangements. When implementing a structured cabling system, if a specific performance capability is required then all components, cable and hardware, must conform to the required specifications. The performance of a link is ultimately determined by the lowest category component in that link, i.e., Category 3 connectors will nullify the benefits of a Category 5 cable.

It should also be remembered that cable and connecting hardware is only 50% of what it takes to gain maximum performance from any cabling system. Installation is equally important and it is imperative that manufacturers guidelines are followed to ensure the best return on the investment.

Table 2-6: Connecting Hardware Attenuation and NEXT Maximum Values for each Category

Frequency (MHz)	ISO/IEC 11801 Cat 3 (dB)		Cat 4 (dB)		Cat 5 (dB)		ANSI/EIA/TIA 568A Cat 3 (dB)		Cat 4 (dB)		Cat 5 (dB)	
	Att	XT	Att	XT	Att	XT	Att	XT	Att	XT	Att	XT
1	0.4	58	0.1	>65	0.1	>65	0.4	58	0.1	>65	0.1	>65
4	0.4	46	0.1	58	0.1	>65	0.4	46	0.1	58	0.1	>65
10	0.4	38	0.1	50	0.1	60	0.4	38	0.1	50	0.1	60
16	0.4	34	0.2	46	0.2	56	0.4	34	0.2	46	0.2	56
20	N/S	N/S	0.2	44	0.2	54	N/S	N/S	0.2	44	0.2	54
31.25	N/S	N/S	N/S	N/S	0.2	50	N/S	N/S	N/S	N/S	0.2	50
62.5	N/S	N/S	N/S	N/S	0.3	44	N/S	N/S	N/S	N/S	0.3	44
100	N/S	N/S	N/S	N/S	0.4	40	N/S	N/S	N/S	N/S	0.4	40

N/S = Not Supported   Att = Attenuation   XT = Near End CrossTalk

The standards also dictate color coding for 4-pair UTP/FTP cables to distinguish between pairs. In addition, 25-pair UTP cables are also available for backbone implementations, in which case a supplementary code is required for the secondary color. For 4-Pair Cables, the first 4 "pair" colors - Blue/Orange/Green/Brown - are each paired with a White conductor. The conductors may have either solid color insulation, or the main color may have a "trace" band or stripe of the paired color - i.e., the first pair may be solid White + solid Blue, or may be White with a Blue tracer + Blue with a White tracer. This latter arrangement makes it easier to keep track of which White belongs with which color.

Table 39-7: UTP/FTP Color Coding

Pair Colors	Group Colors - 25 Pair cables
Blue	White (4 & 25 Pair cables)
Orange	Red
Green	Blue
Brown	Yellow
Slate (25 Pair cables only)	Violet

For 25-Pair Cables, five groups of five colors are used. The groups are identified using the colors White/Red/Black/Yellow/Violet, with each group containing pairs using the identifiers Blue/Orange/Green/Brown/Slate. The first group will thus have pairs of White+Blue/White+Orange/White+Green/White+Brown and White + Slate, the second group will have pairs of Red+Blue/Red+Orange/Red+Green/etc., and so on.

39.4.4   UTP Connector

The standard connector for UTP and FTP cables is the eight way modular jack, often referred to as an RJ-45 connector. This connector, shown in figure 39-7 and specified in ISO/IEC 603-7, is available in screened and unscreened varieties for FTP and UTP, respectively. It is based on Insulation Displacement Contacts (IDC) which are crimped onto the individual conductors to ensure continuity from the cable through the connecting hardware.

The RJ-45 is available in jack and socket configuration, which is keyed to ensure correct orientation is maintained. Once the jack is inserted, it is secured in place via a retaining lug on the back, which must be depressed while the jack is removed.

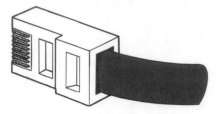

Figure 39-7:   UTP RJ-45 Connector

Both ISO and ANSI standards include pin-pair/color layouts for terminating four pair cable in the RJ-45 jack and socket. Two different schemes are included, neither offering any advantage over the other, and both shown in table 39-8. These termination layouts are known as TIA 568A and TIA 568B. The most important factor in implementing a termination layout for connecting hardware is not which you choose, but that the same code is maintained throughout the entire system.

Although it is not strictly necessary to maintain the same code on the patch leads, it is highly recommended to avoid possible confusion. Because it is possible to have systems terminated to TIA 568A or TIA 568B, the standards also include an alternative color code layout for patch leads only. This alternative is also shown in table 39-8. This allows installers to maintain a stock of patch leads and not worry which scheme they are implementing.

Table 39-8: RJ-45 Wiring Codes

Pin No.	TIA 568A	TIA 568B	Patch Leads
1	White/Green	White/Orange	Blue
2	Green/White	Orange/White	Orange
3	White/Orange	White/Green	Black
4	Blue/White	Blue/White	Green
5	White/Blue	White/Blue	Red
6	Orange/White	Green/White	Yellow
7	White/Brown	White/Brown	Brown
8	Brown/White	Brown/White	Slate

Due to the increased handling of patch leads, these should be made from stranded conductor cable, while distribution cables should have a solid conductor for increased performance capability. Which termination scheme is adopted is unimportant, with some manufacturers favoring one over another, while others provide products for both.

39.5 Fiber Optic Media

The use of fiber optic cabling in office cabling systems and LAN applications has been growing steadily over the last ten years, largely due to increased distance capability and falling costs. These days fiber is the most common media for structured cabling backbone media, especially for data applications. Apart from greater distances, fiber also provides the distinct advantage of electrical isolation between buildings, or locations within a building. This meets the requirements of electrical regulations in many countries around the world.

Two main types of fiber optic cable exist, multimode and singlemode fiber. The difference between the two is the way light is accepted into the cable and then travels along it. To understand this process it is necessary to have a basic understanding of how the cable is constructed.

39.5.1 Fiber Optic Cable Construction

There area two basic elements to optical fiber, the "Core" and the "Cladding" which are shown in figure 39-8. Both of these elements are made from glass during a manufacturing process that makes them inseparable. Although both of these elements are made from glass, they are made from slightly different chemical formulations which impart slightly different optical properties to each element.

The first stage of fiber manufacture is based on a "bait tube" of Cladding glass material which is internally coated with a layer of Core glass. This is achieved by heating the tube while at the same time, introducing an air-borne stream of chemicals which will form the Core glass. As the stream passes over the heat source, it forms a "soot" deposit on the inner surface of the bait tube. This "soot" becomes a layer of sintered glass, which is built up as the heat source gradually traverses the length of the tube. The tube is continuously rotated during the process, to ensure that the coating is formed to a uniform thickness. The core layer does not completely fill the inner diameter of the tube, which is left slightly hollow.

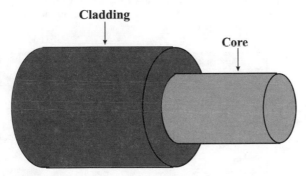

Figure 39-8:   Fiber Core/Cladding Construction

The next stage in the manufacturing process is to heat the bait tube to the point at which it softens enough to collapse in on itself, creating a solid billet instead of a hollow tube. This solid billet is known as a "preform", and is essentially a large version of the finished article, with the correct ratio of Core to Cladding diameters. The final stage of manufacture of "raw" fiber (i.e., before it is made up into cable), involves heating the preform billet in a vertical furnace, to the point where it softens sufficiently enough to be drawn out into a thin, flexible fiber. As the fiber is drawn, the ratio of core to cladding diameter remains unchanged, and the finished diameters are reached.

The drawn fiber is then coated with a thin protective layer of polymer material, known as the "primary buffer" before being wound onto a drum. All fiber receives this coating, regardless of the type of cable construction in which it will ultimately be used.

39.5.2 Principles of Fiber Optic Transmission

As previously mentioned, the basis of light transmission through fiber cable is based on the difference in Refractive Indices between the core and the cladding. The Refractive Index is essentially a way of expressing the speed of light through the medium, when compared to that through a vacuum. By giving the Core and Cladding elements slightly different Refractive Indices, light can be made to "bounce" within the Core, and thus provide a light guide function. It is not the value of the Refractive Index which causes the light to "bend" within the Core, but the fact that the Indices of the Core and Cladding are different. As an illustration of this, consider the way in which a straw placed at an angle in a glass of water appears to be "bent" where it enters the water. This phenomenon is caused by the fact that a change of Refractive Index takes place, in this case between the water in the glass and the surrounding air. In the case of water and air, the difference in RI's is quite large, and generally the larger the difference, the greater the refraction (or "bend") in the light path. The difference in RI between the Core and Cladding in optical fiber is more subtle, and amounts to a change of only a few percent.

In truth, the light does not actually bend, but is totally internally reflected when the light rays meet the boundary between core and cladding. To ensure total internal reflection occurs, the light rays must be made to travel at a shallow enough angle so as to allow reflection, or they will penetrate the cladding and be lost. This principle is shown in figure 39-9.

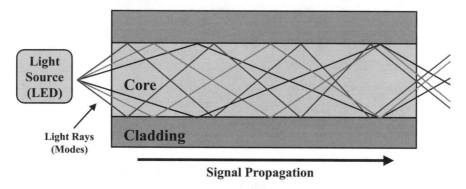

Figure 39-9: Principle of Total Internal Reflection

The method illustrated is known as Multimode - Step Index Fiber, which was the first type developed. The fiber is so named because the light source is omni-directional (typically a Light Emitting Diode - LED) which emits light consisting of many rays, or modes travelling in slightly different directions. The Step Index refers to a stepped change in the Refractive Index between core and cladding. It can be seen that the various modes enter the fiber at one end and travel on a straight path until they reach the boundary between the core and the cladding. Because of the stepped RI change between the two, if the angle of "attack" is shallow enough, then total internal reflection will "bounce" the light mode back into the core. This will continue down the length of the fiber until the modes of light reach the far end and emanate from the fiber.

While this method of light propagation works reasonably well, it does have limitations which restrict the rate at which successive signal pulses may be sent, and the distance over which they may be transmitted. Light rays travel in more or less straight lines and at the same speed. Therefore those modes that travel further will arrive after those that have a shorter distance to cover. In the example shown, it can be seen that the mode travelling down the center of the core travels a shorter distance than others that "bounce" around. The net result is that the modes arrive spread rather than all at the same time. This effect is known as Modal Dispersion and is a direct cause of signal degradation, and furthermore increases as the signalling rate, or distance covered, increases. To overcome these limitations a new form of Multimode fiber was developed known as Multimode Graded Index fiber.

Graded Index is a clever solution to the problem of Modal Dispersion. It is based on constantly changing Refractive Index from the center to the edge of the core, plus the standard RI change at the boundary with the cladding. This is achieved during the manufacturing process, whereby the chemical formulation is varied as layers of soot are built up inside the bait tube. The net result of the gradual change in RI means that modes will be refracted in many small steps, rather than one large one at the boundary. This has the effect of causing the light to take a curved path through the core. In addition, because the properties of the core glass change the closer to

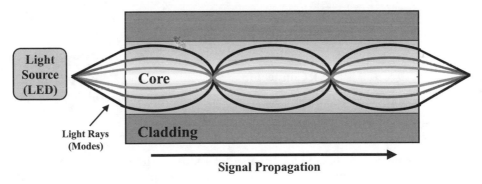

Figure 39-10: MultiMode Graded Index Fiber

the cladding it gets, there is a change in the velocity of propagation of the light mode. This results in the light nearer the cladding "speeding up", while the light travelling straight down the center travels slightly slower. The overall effect of this is that more of the light modes arrive at the far end at the same time, producing a clearer signal, thus allowing faster signalling rates and longer distances. MMGI fiber, is now the standard fiber used for most LAN implementations with distance limitations of up to 2km. The principle of Multimode Graded Index fiber transmission is demonstrated in figure 39-10.

While MMGI fiber remains the most commonly installed type of fiber for structured cabling systems and LAN applications, to achieve the maximum data rates and longest distance, a more specialized version of fiber is required. This "specialized" type of fiber is known as SingleMode (or MonoMode), and is based on Step-Index construction, although the core diameter is typically less than one tenth the diameter of that used in MultiMode fiber. To utilize this form of fiber, a special light source must be used to produce a very narrow, coherent beam of uni-direction light rays, which effectively "floods" the Core with a parallel bundle of modes. In practice, this can only be achieved by a Laser type device, typically in the form of an Edge-Emitting LED (E-LED). These are considerably more expensive than standard high-intensity LED devices, and are normally found only in specialized, long-haul systems i.e., where distances exceed 5 - 10 km.

39.5.3 Fiber Optic Connectors

There are a few different types of connector available for terminating fiber cable, the most popular of which are the Sub-Miniature Assembly (SMA), the Straight Tip (ST), and the Subscriber Connector (SC), all shown in figure 39-11. Of these, the SMA connector is only found in legacy installations and no longer installed in green-field sites. The remaining two, the ST and the SC are both commonplace in the market today. However, the SC, the latest version available, produces much lower losses over a fiber coupling than any of its rivals, and accordingly is the preferred connector in the eyes of the structured cabling standards. It is likely that all over versions will begin to dwindle in popularity as time passes because of this.

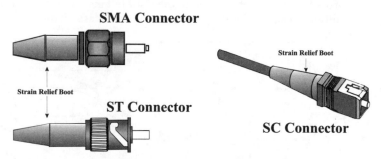

Figure 39-11:   Fiber Optic Connectors

The ST connector is based on a bayonet type fitting, while the SC is a push-pull mechanism. Both provide reasonable performance characteristics, with perhaps the SC being more reproducible. The additional advantage of the SC connector is that by being square in shape, connector density on a patch panel, or end-user equipment, is greatly increased over the ST or the SMA connectors.

39.5.4 Fiber Optic Performance Criteria

There are two main performance criteria that need to considered for fiber cable installations, which are Attenuation and Bandwidth. Unlike copper cables, where crosstalk was a problem, fiber cables are immune from outside interference as the signal carried is based on light and not an electrical current.

Attenuation

Fiber, like copper cable, suffers from a gradual loss of signal power in relation to distance travelled. These losses are exacerbated by factors such as impurities in the fiber, bending losses, mismatch between coupled fibers, and coupling losses due to connectors and splices, all of which must be taken into consideration when calculating the losses of any given fiber link. One big difference between attenuation in copper and fiber, is that fiber attenuation is not linked to signalling frequency, in fact it remains constant across all frequencies.

What is far more important for fiber attenuation is the wavelength of the light source generating the signal. You will therefore find fiber cable attenuation specified not just as dB losses per kilometer, but the wavelength will also be quoted. A particular fiber is also likely to have multiple attenuation figures quoted, one for each wavelength of light source supported by the fiber, i.e., 3.6 dB/km @ 850 nm, and 1.8 dB/km @ 1300 nm. The reason for this is best shown in figure 39-12 which depicts a spectral response curve for a fiber cable, with the different attenuation rates per wavelength change. You will notice that three "windows" are marked at 850nm, 1300nm, and 1550nm, where the attenuation rate is either low or diminishing. Light sources are therefore set to operate at one of these wavelengths to guarantee best performance from the fiber cable. The fibers themselves are optimized to operate at single or dual window operation, again to maximize potential. Multimode fiber is available for 850nm, or 850/1300nm dual window, while singlemode fiber can be found for 1300nm, or 1300/1550 dual window.

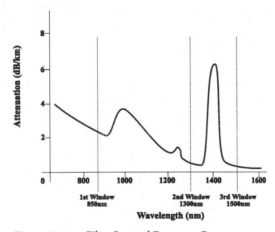

Figure 39-12:   Fiber Spectral Response Curve

It is important that the wavelength for operation is known for two reasons. The first is wavelength matching between transmitter and receiver. Failure to match the light source wavelength to the receiver will result in signal failure between devices. The second reason is based on implementation testing, where the installation should be tested for attenuation at the wavelength at which it is intended to be used. Failure to do this may result in results being obtained which bear no resemblance to the losses being experienced by the system.

Bandwidth

Bandwidth is the term used to describe the fiber's "data carrying" capacity and is always expressed in terms of the maximum signalling rate that can be supported in relation to distance. It is important when discussing any type of cable to understand that signalling rate, expressed in Hertz (Hz) is not the same as data rate, expressed in bits per second (bps). The signalling rate is the rate at which the signal is modulated which may, or may not, be the same as the data rate, depending on the data encoding mechanism employed.

For multimode fiber, bandwidth has a linear relationship with distance and is expressed in terms of MHz/km at a specific wavelength. Again, fiber may have two figures quoted if it supports dual window light sources. The linear relationship between bandwidth and distance allows some trade-off if increased distance, or increased bandwidth is required, i.e., if a fiber has a bandwidth of 250 MHz/km @ 1300 nm, a signalling rate of 250 MHz may be used over 1 km, or the signalling rate may be dropped to 125 MHz to support a distance of 2 km, or the signalling rate may be increased to 500 MHz, provided the distance is reduced to 500 meters.

Calculating the bandwidth availability for singlemode fiber is a far more complex subject, due in part to the method of propagation used. In addition to distance, it is also necessary to consider the spectral width of the laser utilized in the light source. A parameter known as the "Chromatic Dispersion Coefficient" is used to describe the fact that even a laser light source cannot generate light modes at exactly the right frequency all the time, and it is this variation in frequency that must be considered. Bandwidth for singlemode fiber is therefore extremely difficult to measure and is quoted in ps/km/nm (picosecond/kilometer/nanometer).

39.6 Application Classes

ISO/IEC 11801 introduced a concept of classification for applications that allowed designers to take a more logical, performance-based approach to structured cabling system design. The application class system is designed to group together different applications based on their signalling rate requirements, in classes that directly correlate to cable categories. This provides the designer with a distinct advantage as it removes the necessity to understand the various encoding methods employed that distinguish application data transfer rates from their signalling rates. Table 39-9 shows the application classes currently defined in ISO/IEC 11801, as well as some examples of applications in each class.

Table 39-9: Application Classes

Class	Maximum Rate	Signalling	Example
Class A	< 100 KHz		Voice, RS-232
Class B	< 1 MHz		ISDN
Class C	< 16 MHz		10BaseT, 4Mbps Token Ring
Class D	< 100 MHz		100BaseTX, 16Mbps Token Ring (Passive)
Optical Class			FDDI (SMF & MMF), ATM 622Mbps

With performance classes defined for applications, and also for cable categories, it becomes possible to map application classes against cable category performance, to define maximum support transmission distances for each application class. Table 39-10 defines the media required to support each distance defined, for each application class. It should be remembered that although it may be feasible to run an application over a given distance, cross reference with the application standards should be made to maintain application compliance.

Table 39-10: Application Class Vs Cable Category Vs Distance

Application Class	Cable Length		
	0 - 90m (Horizontal/Backbone)	90 - 160m (Backbone)	160 - 500m (Backbone)
Class A	Cat 3 - 5	Cat 3 - 5	Cat 3 - 5
Class B	Cat 3 - 5	Cat 3 - 5	Cat 3 - 5
Class C	Cat 3 - 5	Cat 5	Optical Fiber
Class D	Cat 5	Optical Fiber	Optical Fiber

39.7 SCS Patching Options

Having discussed media options, back to structured cabling design and the implementation of end-user equipment into the system. Provision is made at all of the subsystem boundaries to integrate this type of equipment to provide application services. Many applications, especially high speed data applications, often require equipment at each level of distribution to provide signal regeneration and maintain conformance with application standards cabling limitations. Therefore, it is not uncommon to find application specific transmission equipment at each of the distributors with the cabling system. From these locations, connections can be made into the floor distribution and/or backbone cabling as desired. In addition to deciding where application specific equipment should be placed, a decision must be made as to how to present it to the cabling system. Two methods exist, one offering a direct connection, the other an indirect connection. These are discussed in the sections that follow.

39.7.1 Inter-Connect Patching

The Inter-Connect or direct patching method, shown in figure 39-13, utilizes direct patched connections from the ports of the application equipment, to the horizontal and/or backbone patch panels. This is the simplest method of connectivity and is especially convenient when the port presentation is the same on both equipment and patch panel i.e., RJ-45.

With two methods of patching available it is inevitable that each has its advantage, and disadvantage over the other. With Inter-Connect patching the advantage is based on performance. You will notice from the diagram that the number of connections made to complete the link between user equipment in the work area and application equipment in the distributor is kept to a minimum. This aids in minimizing the amount of crosstalk on the link. As crosstalk is worst at points of interconnection, the fewer that exist, the better the results. The downside to the Inter-Connect method is presentation. Where large amounts of equipment, or high port densities exist, there is no doubt that the large number of patch cables can easily become a tangled mess with cables going in all directions.

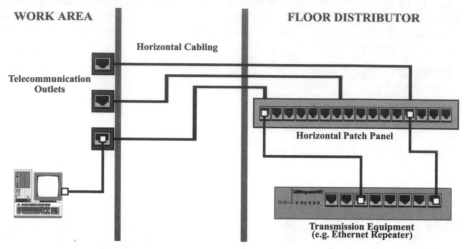

Figure 39-13: Inter-Connect Patching

39.7.2 Cross-Connect Patching

Cross-Connect or indirect patching involves the addition of extra patch panels on which the connections to the application equipment are permanently terminated. In order to make a connection between user port on the cabling system, and application port on the equipment, a patched link between the two patch panels is required, as shown in figure 39-14.

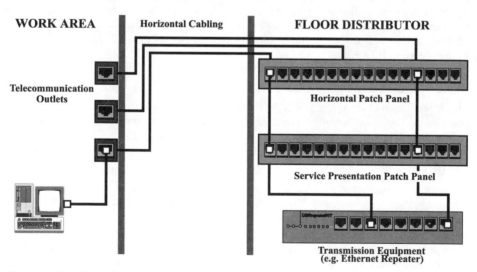

Figure 39-14: Cross-Connect Patching

The main advantage of this method is much neater and tidier cable presentation within the distributor. In addition, if the application equipment comes with a different port presentation than the patching system, then the need for different types of patch lead can be eliminated by terminating the equipment on patch panels. Unfortunately, this does come with a performance penalty, with more crosstalk on the link. However, this is only likely to be significant if the full bandwidth of the cabling is being being pushed to its limits over the maximum 90m distribution distance. Good installation practices can assist in keeping crosstalk to a minimum, and should be adhered to at all times.

39.8 SCS and LAN Applications

Having a structured cabling system is only half the battle, being able to effectively configure the application to run over the infrastructure is just as important. There are many applications that can run over structured cabling, from data applications to voice and video, most of which are beyond the scope of this text. However, in this section we will discuss some of the main points required to achieve effective operation of the three key LAN applications discussed in this book, Ethernet, Token Ring, and FDDI. Many manufacturers provide excellent reference material regarding the mapping of different applications to their cabling systems which are recommended reading if different applications are being considered.

39.8.1 Mapping Ethernet onto SCS

Ethernet, particularly 10/100/1000 BaseT is probably one of the easiest of all applications to map onto a structured cabling system, as the standards were specifically written for twisted pair media and there is no requirement for any special adapters. A typical installation, shown in figure 39-15, requires active equipment to be placed in the floor distributor for user connectivity. This equipment can be a hub/repeater, a bridge/switch, or even a router, depending on

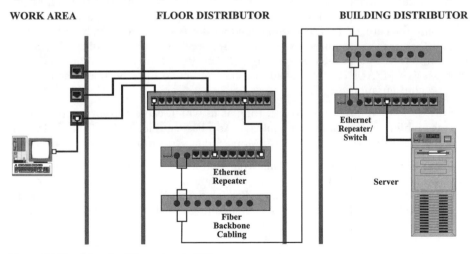

Figure 39-15: Mapping Ethernet on to SCS

the network design being implemented. Invariably today, it is most likely to be a switch of some form providing dedicated bandwidth to the desktop. All of the Ethernet twisted pair media standards indicate a maximum link distance of 100m, matching the maximum distance from floor distributor to user equipment (including patch leads). The active equipment can then be patched to the backbone cabling (fiber or twisted pair) to additional equipment located at the building distributor (typically in the computer room or close to it).

Patch leads are typically available in two forms, straight through or cross-over. The straight through version matches pins at both ends of the cable, while cross-over cables will cross transmit to receive pairs within the cable. With Ethernet using pairs 2 and 3, i.e., the orange and green pairs, this involves swapping pins 1 and 2 with 3 and 6 at one end. Whether to use a straight through cable or a cross-over is determined by the connection that is being made. For example, if the connection is between an end-user PC and a hub port, then straight through patch cables can be used at either end of the distribution cabling. On the other hand, if the connection is from one switch port to another, then a cross-over cable must be used at one end of the connection. For each connection, it is worth checking the type of port being connected. If connecting MDI to MDI[2] , or MDI-X to MDI-X then a cross over is required. If the connection is MDI to MDI-X then a straight through cable can be used.

39.8.2 Mapping Token Ring onto SCS

As a technology, Token Ring has always operated over a star topology cabling system, and therefore maps onto a structured cabling system quite easily. However, Token Ring was developed for 150Ω STP cabling and therefore requires a media filter to be added if the SCS is based on 100Ω UTP. Whether this media filter is an external adapter to the end-user PC or not depends on the type of network interface card (NIC) employed. Older NICs were very much based on STP and would provide DB9 presentation for fly lead attachment. In this instance, an external media filter provides conversion from DB9 to RJ-45 as well as cable type conversion. Newer NICs are available with RJ-45 presentation and a media filter built onto the card. In this scenario, a media filter is still necessary, but comes built in and therefore not required externally. Figure 39-16 shows a typical Token Ring installation, in this case based on active Token Ring MSAUs. It should be noted that passive MSAUs can be transposed for the active ones without changing the cabling configuration.

Care should be taken with Token Ring as to which cable category is required to support which version of the technology. As a basic guide, 4Mbps Token Ring will operate over category 3 UTP, while 16Mbps and above requires category 5 or better.

Patch leads in Token Ring are somewhat simpler than Ethernet in that there is no cross-over cable required for connectivity of end devices. All connections can be made via straight through patch leads. For reference, Token Ring transmits on pins 3 and 6, and receives on pins 4 and 5. Depending on which wiring code (T568A or

---

[2] MDI and MDI-X ports are described in the Ethernet chapters of this text.

T568B) is employed means that transmission takes place on the green (or orange) pair, and reception is on the blue pair.

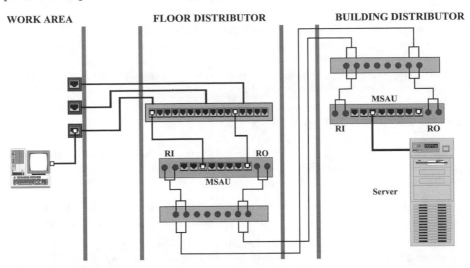

Figure 39-16:   Mapping Token Ring on to SCS

39.8.3 Mapping FDDI onto SCS

FDDI, like Token Ring, can be designed around a star topology, but also has the ability to be connected in a dual ring configuration. For structured cabling systems, FDDI implementation is normally based on a star/tree topology providing single attachment to end-user devices.   Where dual attachment is required, this is normally confined to the backbone, and not extended over the horizontal

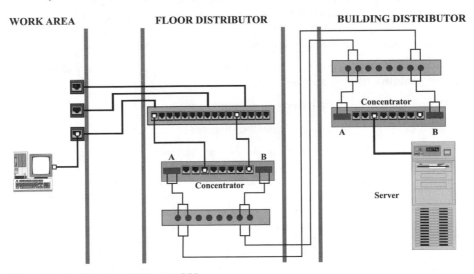

Figure 39-17:   Mapping FDDI on to SCS

distribution cabling. This means that FDDI concentrators would need to be placed at the floor distributor, which could be singularly, or dual attached, to the backbone cabling.

It is normal for FDDI to operate over a fiber backbone with either fiber, or twisted pair, for the horizontal distribution. Figure 39-17 shows a typical UTP installation, but it should be noted that fiber distribution cabling could just as easily replace the UTP shown. Where copper cabling is implemented, category 5 UTP is a minimum requirement, over a maximum link distance of 100m.

39.9 Electro-Magnetic Compatibility

In many countries around the world, regulations are being introduced to more strictly control Electro-Magnetic Compatibility (EMC). So what is EMC? The simple answer can be found in the following statement;

"levels of electromagnetic disturbance and intrinsic immunity shall be such that the equipment in question plus all other equipment shall operate as intended"

This statement taken from the EC directive on EMC, tells us that equipment both generates an electro-magnetic disturbance, and can be susceptible to an electro-magnetic disturbance generated by something else. It also states that compliance is achieved through not disturbing anything else, nor being disturbed by some other equipment. Although this compliance is only necessary in EC countries, similar regulations exist in the US, and other areas. So how does this affect cabling systems? The answer to this is somewhat more complex and is attempted in the text that follows.

The regulations typically apply to active equipment, while a cabling system is passive. However, when an application runs over the system it becomes active and regulations apply. So once the system is commissioned it will need to be compliant with local EMC regulations regarding electro-magnetic emissions and immunity from externally generated interference, in short EMC regulations. This raises some questions, the answers to which are still in the process of being defined.

- How do you test a newly installed system to guarantee future compliance with compatibility regulations?

- Whose responsibility is it to ensure compliance?

- What happens in the event of non-compliance?

This situation has led to some misunderstanding and misinformation regarding the suitability of different cable types for building cabling purposes. This has been most notable in the debate about whether or not structured cabling systems need to be installed using screened cables and components. On one side of the debate, the proponents of screened systems will insist that only screened systems will be able to meet the EMC regulations, while vendors of unshielded systems, will insist exactly the opposite. Based on the latest independent research, it is clear that UTP systems are perfectly capable of meeting the requirements of the regulations provided that they are designed and installed according to the proper practices.

What is also clear is that the use of screened systems does not automatically guarantee compliance with the regulations, and indeed if not properly installed a screened system may actually make the EMC situation worse.

One method being developed to allow installers to pre-test a new system in an attempt to ensure future compliance is to test for *balance.* Perfectly balanced cables will have very low emissions and high immunity to electro-magnetic interference EMI. The quest on how to test for balance has led to the development of a test known as Longitudinal to Differential Conversion Loss, or LDCL for short. LDCL is essentially a measure of how much of the power from an interfering signal (the "transverse" element) converts into a signal which affects the signal carried by the cable (the "longitudinal" element). The higher the conversion loss, the more immune the cabling is to external sources of interference (and by implication, the less likely the cable is to radiate interference to other nearby cables and/or equipment).

In addition to new complex testing, installation practices can have a tremendous effect on future EMC compliance. These practices can (and do) affect the performance of cables in respect of interference. The elements most in the control of the installer are:

- Maximum untwisted length of pairs at the termination point (13mm for Category 5 and 25mm for Category 3/4).

- Minimum bend radius (8x cable diameter during cable laying and 4x cable diameter installed in backbox)

One area where application developers can assist in ensuring compliance is with the signalling rate used by their applications. As with NEXT, the emissions from a system, and its susceptibility to EMI, is affected more as the signalling rate rises on the cable. Many developers are designing applications today that utilize complex encoding mechanisms designed to keep the signalling rate down, but the data transfer rate up. FDDI is an early example of this where although the data transfer rate is 100Mbps, the signalling rate on the cable is kept to a maximum of 31.25MHz via the use of MLT-3 encoding. Other applications are following suit to allow faster applications (such as Gigabit technology) to utilize the installed base of structured cabling systems.

Although screened cables are not mandatory for compliance to EMC regulations, nor are they likely to be in the near future, there are some important guidelines worth considering should you decide upon a screened solution. To be fully effective the screening/shielding must be continuous end-to-end within a cabling link and must fully enclose all relevant components. These include connectors, patch panels and cable, and must provide 360° coverage around the component. This continuity is based on end-to-almost-end as equipment to equipment screening should be avoided so as not to introduce earth loops. In practice, most installations maintain continuity throughout the link and stop short at the final connector that attaches to the end user equipment. In addition to the above considerations, it should also be borne in mind that local power and grounding regulations will also apply, in that the screening of the data cabling may be providing a grounding path between areas of a building (or between different buildings), where different ground potentials exist. In such cases, even small potential differences i.e. 1 Volt, may be enough to create a path that carries several Amps of ground loop current. This is well beyond the capability of the very small cross-sectional area of the screening foil and drain wire and will inevitably lead to problems.

39.10 Design Guidelines

Implementing a structured cabling system requires careful planning plus the following of some standards based design guidelines. This section attempts to cover as many of the issues as possible, with options wherever appropriate.

39.10.1 The Design Process

The basis of a sensible approach to the design of a structured cabling system is to start from the edge and work back to the center. This means the place to start is the work area. Things that must be considered along the way include:

- Work Areas - sizing, TO density, fly leads, adapters, etc.
- Horizontal Cabling - media type, transition points, resilience, etc.
- Floor Distributor - location, layout, resilience, security, etc.
- Backbone Cabling - media types, routes, capacity, resilience, etc.
- Building and Campus Distributors - location, layout, security, etc.
- Cabling Pathways - types, routes, etc.
- Power and Earth Bonding
- System Administration

In addition to the basic cabling system, consideration must be given to matters such as power at the distributors, cabling pathways from the distributors and for distribution cabling, the demarcation between the SCS and other cabling systems and, of course, system administration. To maximize the potential of the cabling system, system administration is paramount and begins at the planning stage. There is no point in adding it as an after thought, it never works as well. The system needs to be designed with the ongoing administration in mind. This includes factors such as outlet identification, numbering/naming schemes, color coding, to name but a few.

39.10.2 The Work Area

The work area, horizontal distribution, and floor distributor location may seem like a straight forward element to design, flood wiring each floor to every location, but there are in fact many elements that can be considered in a good design. For example, in theory, a single floor distributor is capable of supporting up to 25,000 square meters of floor space on a single floor, and even more if it is used to support multiple floors. This however, would inevitably lead to an unmanageable system as the floor distributor would be too large and complex. In addition, it is unlikely that all patch leads would be maintained at the limit of 5m. For these reasons the standards suggest a limit of 1000 square meters of floor space as the maximum area to be supported from a single floor distributor. The main advantage of implementing this in the standards, is that it virtually guarantees distributors are kept relatively simple, an important point when one considers the idea behind structured cabling is that it is supposed to be straight forward, and make MAC (Moves, Additions, and Changes) work easy.

One of the first things to consider in the design of the cabling system is the size of the work area. The standards suggest work area sizing of between $2m^2$ and $10m^2$, but in truth, the size of the work area is going to depend on the use the area is put to, and the likely user density in the future. An example may be a ground floor reception area, where a work area sizing of even $10m^2$ is likely to be too small. On the other hand, a dealer trading floor may require a work area sizing of $2m^2$ or less. This is then a very site specific decision, taken once the use of the areas and the density of the users is well understood.

The number of Telecommunication Outlets (TO) per work area is also something that needs consideration at this early stage. The standards provide some guidelines, but once again flexibility is allowed for the designer. Only a minimum requirement is stated, that of at least 2 TOs per work area, with at least one being fed by balanced pair copper. The second and/or subsequent TOs can be either balanced pair copper or fiber. This is to accommodate the typical user requirement of one data and one voice outlet at the desk. However, there are many occasions where more might be considered. The dealer trading floor is again a good example, this time of where many more than 2 TOs per work area would be required.

Ideally the work areas should be designed to form logical "zones", which can then be arranged to take advantage of one or more of the possible methods of resilience that may be employed. A number of attempts of planning and some calculation may be required to get the right balance of zoning, while always ensuring wherever possible to minimize the floor distributor complexity and administration. Some careful and detailed work at the planning stage will be of great benefit once the system is installed. Some buildings, mainly due to their size, may require multiple floor distributors to service all locations on a floor. This is typically because of the 90m distribution limit, or the overall floor area exceeds 1000 square meters. This can however, prove to be beneficial as it can be utilized to add resilience to the overall design.

The basic design for horizontal distribution cabling provides for no resilience, but there are several options available. Some consideration, however, is required as to the additional expense, and the effectiveness of the resilient solutions. For example, additional TOs could be provided at the work area, but how much benefit is achieved. Should a TO fail, due to breakage or some other factor, who is affected, just a single user and does this justify the expense of the 50-100% increase in materials and labor? On the other hand, who is affected should an entire floor distributor fail? This could be again due to damage, or fire, etc., and would affect the entire floor. In this instance, multiple floor distributors would seem like a good idea, but only if fed by multiple backbones. Figure 39-18 shows some of the options available.

Overlaying, or interleaving, the cabling such that multiple pathways are used can provide a high degree of resilience in the event of a single pathway being damaged.

It does however come at a price, in that installation and material cost are likely to be much higher. The third example, which uses multiple floor distributors and interleaving the cabling is the most resilient design, but extreme care must be taken to ensure ongoing administration is not made too complex in the quest to achieve resilience.

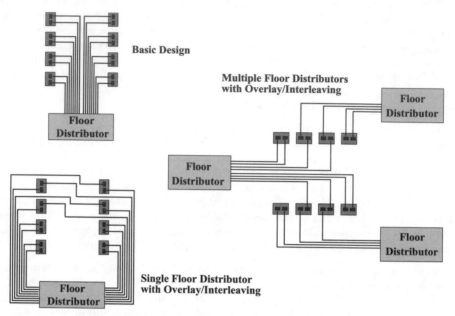

Figure 39-18: Horizontal Cabling Resilience Options

39.10.3 Distributor Layout

The floor distributor requires careful planning as it is perhaps the most important area within the cabling system, it is certainly the place most accessed for moves and changes.

A typical floor distributor contains:

- termination of all horizontal distribution cabling on to patch panels

- termination of building backbone cabling, also on to patch panels

- transmission equipment for inter-connect or cross-connect patching

There are many things to consider when planning the floor distributor including, type of patch panel to be employed, floor distributor housing (cabinet, rack, wall mounting, etc.), sizing, location, and security, to name just some. One of the most important tasks is to determine the size of the floor distributor and its layout. For sizing, care must be taken to include the presentation area for cable termination panels, additional space for patch cable management, space for transmission equipment and power distribution. If cabinets are to be used, the calculations are normally made in a unit known as a "U". Cabinets, patch panels, cable management and power distribution panels are nearly always quoted as a number of U, where 1U is equal to 1¾ inches or 43mm. Do not underestimate the amount of space required for cable management. Inadequate provision at this stage can lead to a "rats nest" of patch cables later. As a rough guide, 1U of cable management should be included for every 1-2U of patching.

Where multiple cabinets are required for a floor distributor, there are two options as to the layout of each cabinet. The first is based on a functional approach whereby different elements of the system are allocated to different cabinets, i.e., all horizontal distribution cabling in one and all transmission equipment in the other. An alternative to this is a more modular approach whereby each cabinet contains a proportion of all elements, some horizontal distribution cabling, some transmission equipment, etc. The advantage of the second approach is that should a cabinet be lost, i.e., due to a power failure, then a proportion of users would be totally unaffected and able to continue without disruption.

39.10.4 The Backbone

Designing the backbone cabling is not without its difficulties either. For example, which media do you choose? And how much of it do you install? There is no doubt that for higher speed applications, fiber offers the best performance characteristics and distance. However, distributing voice services over fiber in the backbone can be a costly business. So, is two backbones a solution? The answer is possibly.

There are three main considerations when designing a backbone to the cabling system, media type(s), capacity, and resilience. Each of these are discussed below.

Two main options exist for possible media types within the backbone. There is twisted pair or fiber. For LAN applications, fiber is the preferred choice due to its extended distance support at high data rates. However, if the maximum backbone distance is within 100m, or the maximum data rate low/medium, then copper twisted pair remains a viable option. Whichever is chosen, care must be taken to ensure that any active transmission equipment has the necessary interfaces to match the cabling selected. For voice service distribution in the backbone, copper still remains the media of choice, although some manufacturers provide distributed PBXs that can be interlinked via fiber. With this in mind it is still very common to find two distinct backbones installed, a fiber version for data applications, and a low specification twisted pair backbone for voice. This allows low cost twisted pair, typically in high density bundles, to be implemented as a voice backbone, direct from the main distribution frame (MDF) direct to each floor distributor.

$$R = \sum_{1}^{A} f_i\, n_i / g_i$$

Figure 39-19: Backbone Capacity Formula

Capacity planning for the backbone can be extremely hazardous, especially on a green field site where little is known about the applications to be used. Even in an occupied building, estimating the backbone capacity requirements can be very difficult. Experience is one solution, which can often provide an answer that is more or less accurate. For others, a more scientific approach is required. The formula shown in figure 39-19, and explained below is one answer to this problem.

In the formula, the following key applies:

- **R** is the resultant multiplier to be used to find the backbone capacity.

- **f** is the ratio of lines for a single application to the total number of lines.

- A line is equal to a unit of cabling, i.e., a four pair UTP[3] or a pair of optical fibers.

- **n** is a constant, either 1 if the application shares a common backbone, or 0 if it uses a dedicated backbone.

- **g** is equal to the grouping factor, i.e., the number of users sharing a piece of transmission equipment, such as 24 if a 24 port repeater is being used.

- **A** is the number of applications using the horizontal cabling system.

Although the formula appears quite complex, it is in fact very simple. To calculate R, simply repeat the calculation fn/g for each application, and then sum the results. The following example shows how the formula can be used.

In this example there are 1000 users on a floor of a building, each requiring a telephone and LAN connectivity. For the purposes of this example, all voice services are provided by a dedicated backbone. In addition, of the 1000, 800 are connected via Ethernet using 24 port repeaters, and 200 by Token Ring using 24 port MSAUs. From this we can determine that A is equal to 3 as there are 3 applications, voice, Ethernet, and Token Ring. In addition, the total number of lines is 2000, and the grouping factor for both Ethernet and Token Ring is 24.

With this in mind, the calculation fn/g can be made for each application in turn:

Voice	f = 1000/2000 = 0.5	n=0	g=1
	fn/g=0.5 × 0/1 = **0**		
Ethernet	f = 800/2000 = 0.4	n=1	g=24
	fn/g=0.4 × 1/24 = **0.0167**		
Token Ring	f = 200/2000 = 0.1	n=1	g=24
	fn/g=0.1 × 1/24 = **0.0042**		

R is therefore equal to 0 + 0.0167 + 0.0042 = 0.0209

---

[3] With Token Ring employing full Ring In/Ring Out connectivity, 2 lines will be needed per rack of equipment. This can be accommodated by halving the grouping factor.

Structured Cabling Systems

The final part of the calculation is to take the resultant (R) and multiply it by the total number of lines required (2000).

$$2000 \times 0.0209 = 41.8$$

Therefore 42 lines must be provided in the backbone to support all applications that will share a common backbone. This equates to 42 times 4 pair UTP, or 84 fibers (remember, it takes two fibers to form a link). In addition to the 42 lines required, an additional 10-20% should be added for expansion and a further 10-20% for resilience. To complete the above example, assuming 2 pair voice circuits, 2000 pairs of voice grade UTP would also be required, which could be implemented using 10 × 200 pair cables.

The last element for backbone design is resilience. This is extremely important as the loss of a backbone could be enough to put a whole floor, or even a whole building out of action. The simplest and most effective method is to implement multiple backbones, preferably via multiple risers. Where this is utilized, obviously the capacity should be split across all backbones, and it could be implemented with multiple floor distributors to enhance the resilience of the system. Where multiple risers/backbones are employed, it may be worth considering additional capacity in each backbone, such that should one backbone ever be unavailable, the remaining backbones have the additional capacity to provide its services.

One last note about backbone design. Care should always be taken when designing a system backbone, that the desired applications will support the distances involved. Many applications have specific distance limitations for each media type, which do not always match the cabling standards distance limits for backbone cabling.

39.11 Testing and Certification

The main issues surrounding testing is to ensure that the "designed" performance criteria are being met, and verifying that performance margins are satisfied such that current applications will operate correctly, and that there is sufficient performance "headroom" for future applications. The current design standards ANSI/EIA/TIA 568A and ISO/IEC 11801 do not provide detailed information on the testing and certification of installed cabling systems. For some years this left a void whereby it was impossible to "certify" a system, because there was no standard to "certify" it against. This situation is now, in part, no longer so much of a problem due to a publication from the EIA/TIA known as TSB 67 which is entitled "Transmission Performance Specifications for Field Testing of Unshielded Twisted-Pair Cabling Systems". This document has become the de facto standard for testing installed cabling systems since its release in October 1995 and specifies performance criteria for categories 3, 4, and 5 UTP cabling systems.

39.11.1 TSB 67

This document is specifically designed to address the needs for testing installed structured cabling systems and provide a benchmark against which performance can be "signed off". The testing specified is designed to operate using simple to use, and relatively inexpensive, hand-held test equipment, the calibration of which is also included within the document. In addition to performance criteria the document also specifies two different cable configurations for test purposes. These are defined as a Link and a Channel, and both are explained below:

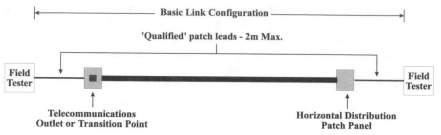

Figure 39-20: Basic Link Configuration

The Link configuration is defined as the cable from the Telecommunications outlet, or Transition Point (if it exists), back to the patch panel at the floor distributor, with the addition of a 2m test lead at either end. This results in the maximum length of a link configuration being 94m. The main idea behind the link configuration is to test the permanently installed cabling, as patch leads and equipment cables can easily be changed, while permanent cabling cannot.

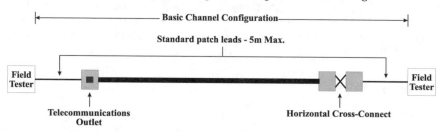

Figure 39-21: Basic Channel Configuration

The Channel configuration, on the other hand, represents the overall data path from application equipment in the floor distributor, to end-user equipment in the work area, and therefore a maximum distance of 100m. Included in the channel configuration are patch leads and equipment cables, in an attempt to correlate channel test results with application standards performance requirements.

For performance criteria such as attenuation and NEXT, TSB 67 specifies different pass and fail criteria for both channel and link configurations. It is therefore important that the correct configuration is selected on the test equipment to match the cable configuration under test. Failure to do so could lead to inaccurate test results that pass a system that if tested correctly would fail.

TSB 67 is fairly limited in its scope, and only specifies four parameters for testing purposes. The parameters included are a rudimentary Wire Map test,

Length testing, Attenuation, and NEXT testing. Additional parameters, required to ensure support of applications such as 1000BaseT, like Return Loss, Far-End CrossTalk (FEXT), Delay, and Delay Skew are all expected to be included in TSB 95 when it is published towards the end of 1999. The text that follows discusses each of the included parameters and the pass/fail criteria specified in the document.

Wire Map

The primary aim of the wire map test is the verification of correct termination and wire placement within the connectors at either end. For each of the conductors, the wire map test should display the following:

- Continuity

- Short Circuits between two or more conductors

- Crossed pairs

- Reversed pairs

- Split pairs

- Any other mis-wiring

Figure 39-22 shows how some of these faults may be displayed on the test equipment screen.

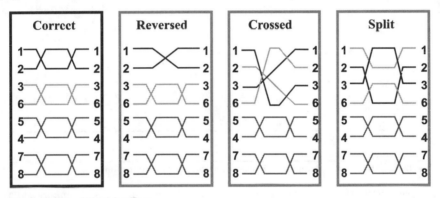

Figure 39-22:   Wire Map Test

Length Testing

Length testing is conducted to ensure the installed cabling does not exceed standards based design guidelines. For a Link to pass a length test, it must not exceed 94m in length between test equipment. Likewise, for a Channel configuration to pass then the limit is 100m.

To guarantee accurate length measurements, the test equipment must be aware of the Nominal Velocity of Propagation (NVP) for the specific cable type being tested. The NVP is the speed at which an electrical signal can propagate down the cable, and varies from one cable type to another. This means that a category 5 UTP cable from one vendor, may well have a different NVP than that from another. A cable tester uses a simple equation based on speed and time to establish the distance travelled, and therefore the length of the cable. It stands to reason then that for this measurement to be accurate, the tester must know the speed (or NVP) in advance. Most popular cable test equipment will be pre-programmed with the NVP of many common cable types. However, if your cable type is not included, then you must program the NVP yourself. This can be done via a simple test on a pre-determined length of cable (at least 50m for accuracy). Set the test equipment to "Get NVP" mode and the test equipment will ask for the test cable length. It will then measure the time taken for a signal to travel the complete length of the cable. By using the formula of Speed = Distance/Time the NVP can be determined.

Attenuation

TSB 67 specifies attenuation as the loss of power of the signal envelope within a link or channel. Because of the difference between a link and a channel, two different sets of pass/fail criteria have been defined, one for each. The figures quoted in tables 39-11 and 39-12, show the maximum allowable attenuation rates for link and channel configurations respectively. Although the figures quoted are shown for a range of "spot" frequencies, the test equipment should be capable of testing the entire sweep of frequencies from 0-100MHz.

Table 39-11: Maximum Attenuation Figures for a Link Configuration

Frequency (MHz)	Category 3 (dB)	Category 4 (dB)	Category 5 (dB)
1.0	3.2	2.2	2.1
4.0	6.1	4.3	4.0
8.0	8.8	6.0	5.7
10.0	10.0	6.8	6.3
16.0	13.2	8.8	8.2
20.0	n/a	9.9	9.2
25.0	n/a	n/a	10.3
31.25	n/a	n/a	11.5
62.5	n/a	n/a	16.7
100.0	n/a	n/a	21.6

Table 39-12: Maximum Attenuation Figures for a Channel Configuration

Frequency (MHz)	Category 3 (dB)	Category 4 (dB)	Category 5 (dB)
1.0	4.2	2.6	2.5
4.0	7.3	4.8	4.5
8.0	10.2	6.7	6.3
10.0	11.5	7.5	7.0
16.0	14.9	9.9	9.2
20.0	n/a	11.0	10.3
25.0	n/a	n/a	11.4
31.25	n/a	n/a	12.8
62.5	n/a	n/a	18.5
100.0	n/a	n/a	24.0

All the figures quoted in tables 39-11 and 39-12 are based on measurement at 20° Celsius. It should be noted that attenuation rises with temperature on twisted pair cabling and therefore, a factor of 1.5% per degree Celsius for Category 3 cable, and

0.4% per degree for Category 5 cable, can be used to estimate results at temperatures other than 20° Celsius. When comparing the published figures for link and channel attenuation, it is noticeable that on the whole the maximum attenuation rates for a link configuration are approximately 10% lower than those for channel configuration. The reason for this is not only the extended distance of a channel configuration, 100m compared with 94m, but the use of up to 10m of stranded patch cords which have higher attenuation rates than solid core cables.

Near End CrossTalk (NEXT)

As we have seen, NEXT is a measure of how much signal power is coupled to adjacent pairs, thereby leading to distortion of a signal on those pairs. As with attenuation, NEXT increases with frequency, and therefore needs to be tested across a range of different frequencies. The test is performed with a handheld cable tester, which applies a balanced signal to a single pair and measures the coupling effect on the other three pairs.

Table 39-13: Minimum NEXT Figures for a Link Configuration

Frequency (MHz)	Category 3 (dB)	Category 4 (dB)	Category 5 (dB)
1.0	40.1	54.7	60.0
4.0	30.7	45.1	51.8
8.0	25.9	40.2	47.1
10.0	24.3	38.6	45.5
16.0	21.0	35.3	42.3
20.0	n/a	33.7	40.7
25.0	n/a	n/a	39.1
31.25	n/a	n/a	37.6
62.5	n/a	n/a	32.7
100.0	n/a	n/a	29.3

This test is repeated for all pair combinations at a complete sweep of frequencies ranging from 0.15MHz up to the set limit for the cable category (100MHz for Category 5). Tests are performed at 0.15MHz intervals from 0-31.25MHz, and 0.25MHz intervals thereafter. In all tests, the worst case pair must pass the minimum requirements laid out in the document, and summarized in tables 39-13 and 39-14.

Table 39-14: Minimum NEXT Figures for a Channel Configuration

Frequency (MHz)	Category 3 (dB)	Category 4 (dB)	Category 5 (dB)
1.0	39.1	53.3	60.0
4.0	29.3	43.3	50.6
8.0	24.3	38.2	45.6
10.0	22.7	36.6	44.0
16.0	19.3	33.1	40.6
20.0	n/a	31.4	39.0
25.0	n/a	n/a	37.4
31.25	n/a	n/a	35.7
62.5	n/a	n/a	30.6
100.0	n/a	n/a	27.1

It is worth noting that as NEXT is a measure of the ratio between the power of the original transmission signal and the power of the coupled signal on an adjacent pair, the higher the ratio, the less the effect of crosstalk. For this reason, high values for NEXT (expressed in dB) represent better results than a lower value. It also explains why the values in the tables decrease as the frequency increases. This is in direct contrast to attenuation, where lower values were preferable.

For all tests, the test equipment should indicate a Pass or Fail, based on the allowable limits for the cable under test. Should the result be closer to the test limit than the accuracy of the test equipment, then the result should be marked Pass* or Fail*, with the asterisk indicating this to be extremely close to the limit.

Another point of note is that testing should be carried out at both ends of the cable link. The primary reason for this is the NEXT test that only measures the Near End, and thus has to be repeated at the other end. Many modern cable testers have the ability to test both ends simultaneously, primarily because they incorporate a slave tester at one end while the master controls things from the other. This obviously simplifies the testing process, as each cable run only requires a single visit.

There are occasions when short links (less than 15m) may consistently fail NEXT tests for no apparent reason. This is because it is possible for short links to demonstrate additional NEXT due to resonance effects linked to Return Loss and/or Balance of the link. This phenomenon is still under investigation and if encountered the following guidelines should be followed.

- Ensure that the correct components and installation practices have been used.

- Ensure that only "qualified" test leads are used for testing (Link configurations).

- Verify that the NEXT failures are only present in short links less than 15m.

- Verify that the failures are from both directions.

If all these criteria are met, then there is little that can be done apart from running a longer cable. If any of the above criteria is not met, then it is likely that there is another cause to the NEXT failure.

39.11.2 TSB 95

TSB 95, entitled "Additional Transmission Performance Guidelines for 100 Ohm 4-Pair Category 5 Cabling", is designed to address additional test parameters, not included in TSB 67, but now deemed to be important. This is mainly due to new transmission methods employed by high speed technologies such as 1000BaseT. In addition to the parameters already defined within TSB 67, TSB 95 will detail performance specifications for parameters such as Return Loss, ELFEXT, Delay, and Delay Skew. Each of these is explained below:

Return Loss

Return Loss is basically a measure of the ratio between the signal power of a transmitted signal in relation to the power that is reflected. A simple way to think of this is to compare it to an echo created by impedance variations along the length of a link. At each variation in impedance, some signal power is reflected towards the source; it is the ratio of this compared to the original power that is measured. As with many other parameters, it varies with frequency and must therefore be tested across a sweep of frequencies.

ELFEXT

Far End CrossTalk (FEXT) is similar to NEXT except that the signal is generated at the near end and the crosstalk is measured at the far end. ELFEXT (Equal Level FEXT) is a calculated, rather than measured parameter, which is designed to normalize the results with respect to length. It is calculated by subtracting the attenuation of the disturbing pair from the FEXT this pair has induced in an adjacent pair. The example below demonstrates the calculation and also shows how this normalizes the results with respect to length.

Two links are considered, both made from the same materials and with the same level of workmanship. One link is 60m in length, the other is 90m.

	Attenuation	FEXT	ELFEXT
Link 1	-11dB	-45dB	-45 - (-11) = -34dB
Link 2	-20dB	-54dB	-54 - (-20) = -34dB

Propagation Delay

Propagation Delay is a measure of the time it takes for a signal to propagate from one end of a link to the other. For Category 5 UTP, a typical delay is approximately 5ns per meter. A maximum delay of 570ns is allowable for horizontal cabling in most of the structured cabling standards. This parameter is important because it is the principle reason for length limitation in LAN cabling. Technologies such as Ethernet impose strict delay limitations when implemented over twisted pair cabling.

Propagation Delay Skew

Propagation Delay Skew (or Skew) is a measure of the difference in the propagation delay of the fastest and the slowest pairs in a UTP cable. Although the NVP for all pairs is the same, each pair is a different overall length due to the different twist rates. This means that the signal will have further to travel on the tightest twisted pair compared to the slackest pair. When travelling at the same speed, the signal will reach the far end on the shortest pair first.

Skew is important because some technologies (such as Gigabit Ethernet) make use of all four pairs in the cable. If the skew is significant then signals sent at the same time from one end, may arrive at significantly different times at the far end. If this delay is significant enough, the receiver will be unable to compensate for it and transmission problems may occur.

Current expectations are that although existing category 5 cable systems will need to be re-tested to provide compliance with TSB 95, most are not expected to fail. TSB 95 is currently under ballot and is expected to be released shortly.

39.12 Future Trends

So what does the future hold for structured cabling systems; a new version of EIA/TIA 568, a 2nd edition of ISO/IEC 11801, category 6 and 7 UTP, ... Many things are in the pipeline, those mentioned are just the short term future, as all are expected by early in the year 2000. Work is well under way on a new release of EIA/TIA 568 which will be known as EIA/TIA 568-B "Commercial Building Telecommunications Wiring Standard". This is a major new release of the standard and will incorporate, or replace, EIA/TIA 568-A, EIA/TIA 568-A addendums 1, 2, 3, 4, and 5, TSB 67, and TSB 95. The main additions will be the inclusion of Category 5E performance levels, 50/125 µm fiber, and the allowance of an alternate fiber connector other than the SC.

A 2nd edition of ISO/IEC 11801 is expected in early 2000 and will include specifications for Category 6 and Category 7 cabling as well as Class E and F applications. This will represent a major step forward in the transmission capabilities of twisted pair cabling. Category 6/Class E will support applications with signalling rates up to 250MHz, while Category 7/Class F will support up to 600MHz. It is likely that Category 6 implementations will be available in either UTP or FTP, while Category 7 systems will probably be based on STP cabling. In the last month or so, the ISO/IEC committee has finally agreed on the connector to be used for Category 7 systems. Two have been chosen, an RJ like solution and a non-RJ like solution. With these in place, there is no reason to assume this standard will be delayed for too long.

So what is next? A good question, that one could guess at and still be way off mark. Will developers push twisted pair cabling beyond the GHz barrier, or will the world finally adopt widespread fiber to the desktop. One thing is for sure, the advances in cabling technology will only increase, as they have to, to stay one step ahead of the application developers.

39.13 Summary

In this chapter we have discussed many aspects of structured cabling from its basic topology, to testing the installed system. With SCS being based on a flood wired approach, using low cost twisted pair cables, the intention is to be able to satisfy any application/user requirements with a single system rather than the complexity of multiple proprietary cabling solutions. SCS has essentially one aim, that is to make MAC work easy for the network manager. This reduces the overall cost of ownership, and facilitates an easier life.

Much of the chapter concentrated on the structured cabling standards for both design and installation testing. These standards are important if the generic nature of SCS is to be maintained, and any proprietary aspect repelled. The design standards concentrate on the layout of the system, including the topology and the various subsystems within it. On the other hand, the installations testing requirements are all based on performance. These days the design is accepted, and only performance seems to be an issue. Tomorrow's standards will concentrate on increasing this while the design is unlikely to change for many years to come.

Appendices

Vendor Identification and Addressing

Ethernet, Token Ring, and FDDI hardware addresses are 48 bits (6 octets), expressed as 12 hexadecimal digits. These 12 hex digits consist of the first, *leftmost* 6 digits that match the vendor of the interface within the station, and the last, *rightmost* 6 digits which specify the interface serial number for that interface vendor. These addresses can be written in a number of ways. For example, the addresses might be written unhyphenated (e.g., 123456789ABC), with one hyphen (e.g., 123456-789ABC), with colons between each octet (e.g., 12:34:56:78:9A:BC). Most people however write addresses hyphenated by octets (e.g., 12-34-56-78-9A-BC), and this has now become the accepted form.

A.1 Vendor Identification

The information contained in this section relates to physical station addresses, not multicast nor broadcast - hence, the second hex digit (reading from the left) will always be even, and never odd. Represented here, are the *Organizationally Unique Identifiers* (OUIs) of known vendors as taken from RFC 1700 (Assigned Numbers).

Table A-1: Vendor Information

OUI	Vendor
00-00-0C	Cisco
00-00-0E	Fujitsu
00-00-0F	NeXT
00-00-10	Sytek
00-00-1D	Cabletron Systems
00-00-20	DIAB (Data Industrier AB)
00-00-22	Visual Technology
00-00-2A	TRW
00-00-32	GPT Limited (reassigned from DEC Computers Ltd)
00-00-5A	S & Koch
00-00-5E	IANA
00-00-65	Network General
00-00-6B	MIPS
00-00-77	MIPS
00-00-7A	Ardent
00-00-89	Cayman Systems Gatorbox
00-00-93	Proteon
00-00-9F	Ameristar Technology

Table A-1: Vendor Information (Continued)

OUI	Vendor
00-00-A2	Wellfleet
00-00-A3	Network Application Technology
00-00-A6	Network General (internal assignment, not for products)
00-00-A7	NCD (X-terminals)
00-00-A9	Network Systems
00-00-AA	Xerox (Xerox machines)
00-00-B3	CIMLinc
00-00-B7	Dove (Fastnet)
00-00-BC	Allen-Bradley
00-00-C0	Western Digital
00-00-C5	Farallon phone net card
00-00-C6	HP Intelligent Networks Operation (formerly Eon Systems)
00-00-C8	Altos
00-00-C9	Emulex (Terminal Servers)
00-00-D7	Dartmouth College (NED Router)
00-00-DD	Gould
00-00-DE	Unigraph
00-00-E2	Acer Counterpoint
00-00-EF	Alantec
00-00-FD	High Level Hardvare (Orion, UK)
00-01-02	BBN (BBN internal usage (not registered))
00-17-00	Kabel
00-80-64	Wyse Technology/Link Technologies
00-80-2D	Xylogics, Inc. Annex terminal servers
00-80-8C	Frontier Software Development
00-80-C2	IEEE 802.1 Committee
00-80-D3	Shiva
00-AA-00	Intel
00-DD-00	Ungermann-Bass
00-DD-01	Ungermann-Bass
02-07-01	Racal InterLan
02-04-06	BBN - BBN internal usage (not registered)
02-60-86	Satelcom MegaPac (UK)
02-60-8C	3Com (IBM PC; Imagen; Valid; Cisco)
02-CF-1F	CMC (Masscomp; Silicon Graphics; Prime EXL)
08-00-02	3Com (Formerly Bridge)
08-00-03	ACC (Advanced Computer Communications)
08-00-05	Symbolics (Symbolics LISP machines)
08-00-08	BBN
08-00-09	Hewlett-Packard
08-00-0A	Nestar Systems
08-00-0B	Unisys
08-00-11	Tektronix, Inc.
08-00-14	Excelan (BBN Butterfly, Masscomp, Silicon Graphics)
08-00-17	NSC
08-00-1A	Data General
08-00-1B	Data General
08-00-1E	Apollo
08-00-20	Sun (Sun machines)
08-00-22	NBI
08-00-25	CDC

Vendor Identification and Addressing

OUI	Vendor
08-00-26	Norsk Data (Nord)
08-00-27	PCS Computer Systems GmbH
08-00-28	TI (Explorer)
08-00-2B	DEC
08-00-2E	Metaphor
08-00-2F	Prime Computer Prime 50-Series LHC300
08-00-36	Intergraph (CAE stations)
08-00-37	Fujitsu-Xerox
08-00-38	Bull
08-00-39	Spider Systems
08-00-41	DCA Digital Comm. Assoc.
08-00-46	Sony
08-00-47	Sequent
08-00-49	Univation
08-00-4C	Encore
08-00-4E	BICC
08-00-56	Stanford University
08-00-5A	IBM
08-00-67	Comdesign
08-00-68	Ridge
08-00-69	Silicon Graphics
08-00-6E	Concurrent (Masscomp)
08-00-75	DDE (Danish Data Elektronik A/S)
08-00-7C	Vitalink (TransLAN III)
08-00-80	XIOS
08-00-86	Imagen/QMS
08-00-87	Xyplex Networks
08-00-89	Kinetics (AppleTalk-Ethernet interface)
08-00-8B	Pyramid
08-00-8D	XyVision (XyVision machines)
08-00-90	Retix Inc (Bridges)
80-00-10	AT&T
AA-00-00	DEC - obsolete
AA-00-01	DEC - obsolete
AA-00-02	DEC - obsolete
AA-00-03	DEC (Global physical address for some DEC machines)
AA-00-04	DEC (Local logical address for systems running DECNET)

A.2   Multicast Addresses

Multicast addresses consist of the multicast bit, the 23-bit vendor component (OUI), and the 24-bit group identifier assigned by the vendor. For example, the IEEE 802.1 Committee is assigned the vendor component 00-80-C2, so multicast addresses assigned by them have the first 24-bits 01-80-C2 as seen in the 802.1D Spanning Tree Protocol. Table A-2, taken from RFC 1700, shows many common Multicast Addresses

Table A-2: Multicast Addresses

Multicast Address	Ethernet Type	Description
01-00-5E-00-00-00 to 01-00-5E-7F-FF-FF	0800	Internet Multicast
01-00-5E-80-00-00 to 01-00-5E-FF-FF-FF	Multiple	Internet reserved by IANA
01-80-C2-00-00-00	802.3/802.2	Spanning tree (for bridges)
01-80-C2-00-00-01 to 01-80-C2-00-00-0F	Multiple	Reserved by IEEE 802.1 Committee
09-00-02-04-00-01	8080	Vitalink printer
09-00-02-04-00-02	8080	Vitalink management
09-00-09-00-00-01	8005	HP Probe
09-00-09-00-00-01	802.3/802.2	HP Probe
09-00-09-00-00-04	8005	HP DTC
09-00-1E-00-00-00	8019	Apollo DOMAIN
09-00-2B-00-00-00	6009	DEC MUMPS
09-00-2B-00-00-01	8039	DEC DSM/DTP
09-00-2B-00-00-02	803B	DEC VAXELN
09-00-2B-00-00-03	8038	DEC Lanbridge Traffic Monitor (LTM)
09-00-2B-00-00-04	Multiple	DEC MAP End System Hello
09-00-2B-00-00-05	Multiple	DEC MAP Intermediate System Hello
09-00-2B-00-00-06	803D	DEC CSMA/CD Encryption
09-00-2B-00-00-07	8040	DEC NetBios Emulator
09-00-2B-00-00-0F	6004	DEC Local Area Transport (LAT)
09-00-2B-00-00-1x	Multiple	DEC Experimental
09-00-2B-01-00-00	8038	DEC LanBridge Copy packets (All bridges)
09-00-2B-01-00-01	8038	DEC LanBridge Hello packets (All local bridges) 1 packet per second, sent by the designated LanBridge
09-00-2B-02-00-00	Multiple	DEC DNA Lev. 2 Routing Layer routers
09-00-2B-02-01-00	803C	DEC DNA Naming Service Advertisement
09-00-2B-02-01-01	803C	DEC DNA Naming Service Solicitation
09-00-2B-02-01-02	803E	DEC DNA Time Service
09-00-2B-03-xx-xx	Multiple	DEC default filtering by bridges
09-00-2B-04-00-00	8041	DEC Local Area Sys. Transport (LAST)
09-00-2B-23-00-00	803A	DEC Argonaut Console
09-00-4E-00-00-02	8137	Novell IPX
09-00-56-00-00-00 to 09-00-56-FF-FF-FF	Multiple	Stanford reserved
09-00-56-FF-00-00 to 09-00-56-FF-FF-FF	805C	Stanford V Kernel, version 6.0
09-00-77-00-00-01	Multiple	Retix spanning tree bridges
09-00-7C-02-00-05	8080	Vitalink diagnostics
09-00-7C-05-00-01	8080	Vitalink gateway
0D-1E-15-BA-DD-06	Multiple	HP
AB-00-00-01-00-00	6001	DEC Maintenance Operation Protocol (MOP) Dump/Load Assistance

Multicast Address	Ethernet Type	Description
AB-00-00-02-00-00	6002	DEC Maintenance Operation Protocol (MOP) Remote Console 1 System ID packet every 8-10 minutes, by every: DEC LanBridge DEC DEUNA interface DEC DELUA interface DEC DEQNA interface (certain mode)
AB-00-00-03-00-00	6003	DECNET Phase IV end node Hello packets 1 packet every 15 seconds, sent by each DECNET host
AB-00-00-04-00-00	6003	DECNET Phase IV Router Hello packets 1 packet every 15 seconds, sent by the DECNET router
AB-00-00-05-00-00 to AB-00-03-FF-FF-FF	Multiple	Reserved DEC
AB-00-03-00-00-00	6004	DEC Local Area Transport (LAT) - old
AB-00-04-00-xx-xx	Multiple	Reserved DEC customer private use
AB-00-04-01-xx-yy	6007	DEC Local Area VAX Cluster groups Sys. Communication Architecture (SCA)
CF-00-00-00-00-00	9000	Ethernet Configuration Test protocol (Loopback)

A.3 Broadcast Addresses

Broadcast addresses have all 48 bits set to 1 (the 24-bit vendor component, and the 24-bit group identifier assigned by the vendor). Table A-3, again taken from RFC 1700, shows many common Broadcast Addresses although of primary interest here are the Ethernet Type codes (EtherTypes) with which they are used, rather than the addresses themselves.

Table A-3: Broadcast Addresses

Broadcast Address	Ethernet Type	Description
FF-FF-FF-FF-FF-FF	0600	XNS packets, Hello or gateway search. Six packets every 15 seconds, per XNS station
FF-FF-FF-FF-FF-FF	0800	IP (e.g., RWHOD via UDP) as needed
FF-FF-FF-FF-FF-FF	0804	CHAOS
FF-FF-FF-FF-FF-FF	0806	ARP (for IP and CHAOS) as needed
FF-FF-FF-FF-FF-FF	0BAD	Banyan
FF-FF-FF-FF-FF-FF	1600	VALID packets, Hello or gateway search. One packet every 30 seconds, per VALID station
FF-FF-FF-FF-FF-FF	8035	Reverse ARP
FF-FF-FF-FF-FF-FF	807C	Merit Internodal (INP)
FF-FF-FF-FF-FF-FF	809B	EtherTalk

Ethernet Type Codes

As we have seen throughout, it is important that we are able to identify the protocol that is being carried across our internetwork. There are various methods by which this may be achieved, from the proprietary *Raw 802.3* framing of Novell, to the use of *Service Access Points* (SAPs) with IEEE 802.2. Alternatively there is the *EtherType* used by Ethernet, and the *Sub-Network Access Protocol* (SNAP). This appendix lists most common EtherType codes together with the protocol and/or vendor to which the code is registered. Once again, this information is available in RFC 1700 (Assigned Numbers).

Table B-1: Ethernet Type Codes

Dec.	Hex.	Description
0-1500	0000-05DC	IEEE 802.3 Length Field
257-511	0101-01FF	Experimental
512	0200	Xerox PUP
513	0201	PUP Address Translation
1024	0400	Nixdorf
1536	0600	Xerox NS IDP
1632	0660	DLOG
1633	0661	DLOG
2048	0800	Internet Protocol (IP)
2049	0801	X.75 Internet
2050	0802	NBS Internet
2051	0803	ECMA Internet
2052	0804	Chaosnet
2053	0805	X.25 Level 3
2054	0806	Address Resolution Protocol (ARP)
2055	0807	XNS Compatibility
2076	081C	Symbolics Private
2184-2186	0888-088A	Xyplex
2304	0900	Ungermann-Bass Network Debugger
2560	0A00	Xerox IEEE 802.3 PUP
2561	0A01	PUP Address Translation
2989	0BAD	Banyan Systems
4096	1000	Berkley Trailer Negotiation
4097-4111	1001-100F	Berkley Trailer (Encapsulated in IP)
5632	1600	Valid Systems
16962	4242	PCS Basic Block Protocol
21000	5208	BBN Simnet
24576	6000	DEC Unassigned (Experimental)
24577	6001	DEC MOP Dump/Load

Dec.	Hex.	Description
24578	6002	DEC MOP Remote Console
24579	6003	DEC DECNet Phase IV Route
24580	6004	DEC Local Area Transport (LAT)
24581	6005	DEC Diagnostic Protocol
24582	6006	DEC Customer Protocol
24583	6007	DEC LAVC, SCA
24584-24585	6008-6009	DEC Unassigned
24592-24596	6010-6014	3Com Corporation
28672	7000	Ungermann-Bass Download
28674	7002	Ungermann-Bass Diagnostic/Loopback
28704-28713	7020-7029	LRT
28720	7030	Proteon
28724	7034	Cabletron
32771	8003	Cronus VLN
32772	8004	Cronus Direct
32773	8005	HP Probe
32774	8006	Nestar
32776	8008	AT&T
32784	8010	Excelan
32787	8013	SGI Diagnostics
32788	8014	SGI Network Games
32789	8015	SGI Reserved
32790	8016	SGI Bounce Server
32793	8019	Apollo Computers
32815	802E	Tymshare
32816	802F	Tigan Inc.
32821	8035	Reverse Address Resolution Protocol (RARP)
32822	8036	Aeonic Systems
32824	8038	DEC LANBridge
32825-32828	8039-803C	DEC Unassigned
32829	803D	DEC Ethernet Encryption
32830	803E	DEC Unassigned
32831	803F	DEC LAN Traffic Monitor
32832-32834	8040-8042	DEC Unassigned
32836	8044	Planning Research Corporation
32838-32839	8046-8047	AT&T
32841	8049	ExperData
32859	805B	Stanford V Kernel - Experimental
32860	805C	Stanford V Kernel - Production
32861	805D	Evans & Sutherland
32864	8060	Little Machines
32866	8062	Counterpoint Computers
32869-32870	8065-8066	University of Mass. @ Amherst
32871	8067	Veeco Integrated Auto
32872	8068	General Dynamics
32873	8069	AT&T
32874	806A	Autophon
32876	806C	ComDesign
32877	806D	Computgraphic Corporation
32878-32887	806E-8077	Landmark Graphics Corporation
32890	807A	Matra
32891	807B	Dansk Data Elektronik

Dec.	Hex.	Description
32892	807C	Merit Internodal
32893-32895	807D-807F	Vitalink Communications
32896	8080	Vitalink TransLAN III
32897-32899	8081-8083	Counterpoint Computers
32923	809B	AppleTalk
32924-32926	809C-809E	Datability
32927	809F	Spider Systems Ltd.
32931	80A3	Nixdorf Computers
32932-32947	80A4-80B3	Siemens Gammasonics Inc.
32960-32963	80C0-80C3	DCA Data Exchange Cluster
32964-32965	80C4-80C5	Banyan Systems
32966	80C6	Pacer Software
32967	80C7	Applitek Corporation
32968-32972	80C8-80CC	Intergraph Corporation
32973-32974	80CD-80CE	Harris Corporation
32975-32978	80CF-80D2	Taylor Instrument
32979-32980	80D3-80D4	Rosemount Corporation
32981	80D5	IBM SNA Service on Ethernet
32989	80DD	Varian Associates
32990-32991	80DE-80DF	Integrated Solutions TRFS
32992-32995	80E0-80E3	Allen -Bradley
32996-33008	80E4-80F0	Datability
33010	80F2	Retix
33011	80F3	AppleTalk Address Resolution Protocol (AARP)
33012-33013	80F4-80F5	Kinetics
33015	80F7	Apollo Computer
33023-33027	80FF-8103	Wellfleet Communications (Bay/NorTel)
33031-33033	8107-8109	Symbolics Private
33072	8130	Hayes Microcomputers
33073	8131	VG Laboratory Systems
33074-33078	8132-8136	Bridge Communications (3Com Corporation)
33079-33080	8137-8138	Novell Inc.
33081-33085	8139-813D	KTI
33096	8148	Logicraft
33097	8149	Network Computing Devices
33098	814A	Alpha Micro
33100	814C	SNMP
33101-33102	814D-814E	BIIN
33103	814F	Technically Elite Concept
33104	8150	Rational Corporation
33105-33107	8151-8153	Qualcomm
33116-33118	815C-815E	Computer Protocol Pty Ltd.
33124-33126	8164-8166	Charles River Data Systems
33149-33164	817D-818C	Protocol Engines
33165	818D	Motorola Computer
33178-33187	819A-81A3	Qualcomm
33188	81A4	ARAI Bunkichi
33189-33198	81A5-81AE	RAD Network Devices
33207-33209	81B7-81B9	Xyplex
33228-33237	81CC-81D5	Apricot Computers
33238-33245	81D6-81DD	Artisoft
33254-33263	81E6-81EF	Polygon

Table B-1: Ethernet Type Codes (Continued)

Dec.	Hex.	Description
33264-33266	81F0-81F2	Comsat Labs
33267-33269	81F3-81F5	SAIC
33270-33272	81F6-81F8	VG Analytical
33283-33285	8203-8205	Quantum Software
33313-33314	8221-8222	Ascom Banking Systems
33342-33344	823E-8240	Advanced Encryption Systems
33379-33386	8263-826A	Charles River Data Systems
33407-33410	827F-8282	Athena Programming
33434-33435	829A-829B	Inst Ind Info Tech
33436-33451	829C-82AB	Taurus Controls
33452-34451	82AC-8693	Walker Richer & Quinn
34452-34461	8694-869D	Idea Courier
34462-34465	869E-86A1	Computer Network Technology
37767-34476	86A3-86AC	Gateway Communications
34523	86DB	SECTRA
34526	86DE	Delta Controls
34527	86DF	ATOMIC
34528-34543	86E0-86EF	Landis & Gyr Powers
34560-34576	8700-8710	Motorola
35478-35479	8A96-8A97	Invisible Software
36864	9000	Loopback
36865	9001	3Com (Bridge) XNS System Management
36866	9002	3Com (Bridge) TCP-IP System
36867	9003	3Com (Bridge) Loop Detect
65280	FF00	BBN VITAL-LanBridge Cache
65280-65295	FF00-FF0F	ISC Bunker Ramo

A Glossary of Networking Terms

This appendix attempts to list most common Networking terms. It is broadly taken from the glossary that appears in TCP/IP Explained, also by Philip Miller, which in turn was inspired by RFC 1392. The reader should reference this latter document for further information about any term listed, or indeed possibly for any term that is not mentioned here. While it is our desire, to provide a volume that is as complete as possible, one could spend the rest of ones life on an Appendix such as this alone.

C.1 Networking Terms

1Base5	An early variant of the IEEE specification that defines a 1Mbps system based on CSMA/CD.
10Base2	Defined by IEEE 802.3B, this standard allows the Carrier Sense Multiple Access with Collision Detect (CSMA/CD) network access method to be used over 50Ω (RG58) coaxial cable. Sometimes referred to as *Thin Ethernet*.
10Base5	The original specification for the CSMA/CD network access method (IEEE 802.3) defining 50Ω co-axial cable as the medium. Sometimes referred to as *Thick Ethernet*.
10BaseF	Defined by IEEE 802.3J, this standard builds on the original specification of CSMA/CD to include fiber optic medium. Three separate definitions exist namely 10BaseFB (synchronous inter-repeater links), 10BaseFP (a passive star topology), and 10BaseFL (a standardization of the Fiber Optic Inter-Repeater Link (FOIRL) specification).
10BaseT	A standard for the use of twisted pair medium in 802.3 environments. Defined in IEEE 802.3I, this is often called *"UTP"* or *"Twisted Pair Ethernet"*.
100Base-Fx	A standard defining the use of *fiber optic* medium in 100Mbps 802.3 environments. Defined by IEEE 802.3U, this is also referred to as *fast Ethernet*.

100Base-T2	A standard that provides 100Mbps data transfer over Category 3 (or better) cable plant. 100Base-T2 is defined by IEEE 802.3y.
100Base-T4	Defined within IEEE 802.3U, this specification is for a 100Mbps system that utilizes 4 pairs of voice grade twisted pair cable.
100BaseTx	A standard defining the use of, Category 5, *twisted pair* medium in 100Mbps 802.3 environments. Defined by IEEE 802.3U, this is also referred to as *fast Ethernet*.
100VG-AnyLAN	Defined through IEEE 802.12, this standard provides for a 100Mbps, prioritized, data transfer system. In a similar fashion to the IEEE 802.3 specifications, this uses twisted pair cable plant.
1000Base-CX	Known typically as *Short Haul Copper*, this specification for a 1000Mbps (Gigabit) Ethernet system was introduced in IEEE 802.3z. Distance is restricted to just 25m and *shielded* twisted pair cable must be used.
1000Base-LX	This is a specification for the transmission of data at 1000Mbps (Gigabit) using the CSMA/CD access method. Specifically, this provides for transmission over what is termed *Long Wavelength Fiber* and provides for greater distance.
1000Base-SX	This is a specification for the transmission of data at 1000Mbps (Gigabit) using the CSMA/CD access method. Specifically, this provides for transmission over what is termed *Short Wavelength Fiber* and provides for shorter distances.
1000Base-T	1000Base-T is specified in IEEE 802.3ab and is for a Gigabit Ethernet system that will run over *twisted pair* cable plant.
10Broad36	10Broad36 provides a *broadband* (as opposed to *baseband*) specification for the transmission of IEEE 802.3 data. Rarely implemented today, this is one of the original 802.3 specifications.
802.x	A set of standards developed by the IEEE. Several such standards now exist including 802.1, 802.2, 802.3, 802.4, 802.5, etc.
822 Header	*See RFC 822 Header.*

ABR	*See Area Border Router.*
Abstract Syntax Notation One	Commonly referred to as ASN.1, this is a formal language used in an OSI environment, and also to encode SNMP packets.
ACK	*See Acknowledgment.*
Acknowledgment	An indication that data has arrived at its intended recipient. Typically thought of as a Positive Acknowledgment where reliability is required, this indicates that the data has arrived without error. See also Negative Acknowledgment.
Active Monitor	A station on a token ring network responsible for overall ring timing and protocol error recovery.
Address	A method of uniquely identifying a host (or person) within an internet. Several address types exist within an IP environment namely the Domain Name, IP Address, MAC Address, and when referring to a person, an email Address.
Address Mask	*See Subnet Mask.*
Address Resolution Protocol	A general purpose Layer 2 protocol designed to allow the mapping of Internet (or other protocol) Addresses to MAC Addresses.
Adjusted Ring Length	A term used to describe the maximum transmission distance on a token ring network in a wrapped condition.
Agent	A (typically) small piece of code (software) that is used to exchange information with some other device. For example in an SNMP environment, the Network Management Station may request information from a managed device through its agent.
American National Standards Institution	An American standards making body responsible for the creation, and approval, of many standards in the USA. One such standard is X3T9.5, the standard describing FDDI.
American Standard Code for Information Interchange	A standard encoding scheme that is commonly used within the computer industry. ASCII (as it is commonly known) is based on a 7 bit scheme.
Anonymous FTP	Available on many FTP servers, anonymous FTP allows a user to gain access to public areas of the host without the need for a formal userID and password.

ANSI	*See American National Standards Institution.*
AppleTalk	Developed by Apple Computer Inc., this describes a protocol suite that allows Apple computers to exchange data. Several implementations exist including LocalTalk (a low speed proprietary system), EtherTalk (a 10Mbps system that runs over Ethernet), and TokenTalk (to run over Token Ring networks).
Application Layer	The uppermost layer (Layer 7) of the OSI Model, this layer provides access to the network environment. Application protocols such as FTAM reside at this layer.
A Port	The first of two Ports that are used to connect a dual attached device to both the primary and secondary rings on an FDDI network.
ARCHIE	An Internet utility that gathers and indexes information on Internet resources.
Area Border Router	A router that spans two or more routing Areas and exchanges routing information between them. This router then assumes a special role and maintains multiple topological databases.
ARL	*See Adjusted Ring Length.*
ARP	*See Address Resolution Protocol.*
AS	*See Autonomous System.*
ASBR	*See Autonomous System Border Router.*
ASCII	*See American Standard Code for Information Interchange.*
ASN.1	*See Abstract Syntax Notation One.*
Authentication	A method by which a person (or process) can identify itself. Several protocols within the Internet suite (such as PPP, RIP II, and OSPF) incorporate authentication methods.
Auto-Negotiation	An automated negotiation facility whereby IEEE 802.3 devices can negotiate the best possible connection. For example, in multiple technology device ports such as those found on typical 10/100 Ethernet Switches can support 10Mbps, or 100Mbps, at either Full, or Half Duplex. By using Auto-Negotiation, the device and port exchange information so that the best connection is established.

Autonomous System	A collection of networks under a single administration and employing a common routing policy. For example an Autonomous System may run an Interior Gateway Protocol such as OSPF.
Autonomous System Border Router	A router that joins different Autonomous Systems together. By its definition then, such a router will run multiple routing protocols.
Bandwidth	Generally, this is taken to mean the amount of data that can be passed over a particular communications channel within a given time.
Baseband Signaling	A communication method whereby only one signal may be present on the medium at any time. Ethernet's 10Base-X specifications are examples of such a system.
Beaconing	A process used in ring technologies to aid in recovery from physical ring errors.
BGP	*See Border Gateway Protocol.*
Binary	A method of arithmetic using the base 2, which limits the digits that can be used to 0 and 1. Normally, a binary number is written using the subscript 2 at the end to avoid confusion.
Bootstrap Protocol	A protocol that uses UDP and IP to allow network devices to determine (normally) start-up infor-mation. Typically a diskless device may inquire its IP Address, the address of the server that has its image file, the address of the router that should be used, and the name of the file that should be used.
BootP	*See Bootstrap Protocol.*
Border Gateway Protocol	A protocol generally defined as being an Exterior Gateway Protocol, and used to join Autonomous Systems together. Later implementations also define *Interior BGP*, that allows the protocol to be used within an Autonomous System.
B Port	The second of two Ports used to connect a dual attached device to both the primary and secondary rings on an FDDI network.
Bridge	A Store and Forward device, operating at Layer 2 of the OSI Model (the Data-Link Layer), and used to segment traffic between LANs. *See also Switch.*

British Standards Institute	The standards making body responsible for approving standards applicable to the United Kingdom.
Broadband	A transmission method where multiple signals may co-exist on the network medium at the same time. Frequency Division Multiplexing is normally employed in this case, and the IEEE 802.3 10Broad36 specification is an example.
Broadcast	A packet or frame destined for all devices on a network segment or internetwork a.k.a. a broadcast address.
Brouter	A combination device that is capable of routing specific frame types and bridging all others.
BSI	*See British Standards Institute.*
Byte	A basic unit of data transmission where each byte can be used to identify a single character. Normally bytes are 8 (binary) data bits in length however since some systems use bytes that are longer than 8 bits, the term octet is generally used when referring to networking. *See also Octet.*
CCITT	*See Intn'l Telegraph & Telephone Consultative Committee.*
Checksum	A value that is calculated, based upon the contents of a packet or frame, and then transmitted with it. A receiving station then performs the same calculation and compares its result with that received to ensure that the data has arrived intact.
Circuit Switching	A communication method that requires that a dedicated path be set up between two communicating hosts for the duration of the connection.
Claim Token	A process used on Token Passing Technologies such as Token Ring or FDDI to elect the end device responsible for releasing the first Token onto the Ring.
Client	A system that requests the services of another. For example a device requesting a file using the File Transfer Protocol is a client of the host on which the file resides.

Congestion	A situation that arises in networking terms when data arrives at a rate faster than it can be processed.
Connectionless	A data communication method that does not require stations to agree to exchange data and therefore has no inherent acknowledgment or *hand-shaking* capability. The Internet Protocol (IP) uses this method of communication. However, where data is to be transmitted with positive acknowledgments, the Transmission Control Protocol (TCP) can be used create a connection oriented environment.
CRC	*See Cyclic Redundancy Check.*
CSMA/CD	*See Carrier Sense Multiple Access with Collision Detect.*
Cyclic Redundancy Check	Used in Checksum calculations, the CRC provides the formula that is applied to the data as it is transmitted. Normally a polynomial function, the CRC is generated on transmission and checked on reception. *See also Checksum.*
Datagram	The basic unit of transmission in an IP environment. IP packets are called datagrams and contain sufficient information to allow them to be routed between source and destination host making them independent of each other.
DECnet	A proprietary networking protocol developed by the Digital Equipment Corporation (DEC) to link their machines together. Currently two implementations exist namely Phase IV which is totally proprietary, and Phase V which is based on OSI protocols, and is therefore open.
Default Route	A routing table entry that is used to route packets to networks that are not otherwise explicitly mentioned. The route (normally shown as 0.0.0.0) indicates to hosts and other devices that, in the absence of any other routing information, they should direct packets to the device advertising the default route for onward delivery.
Dial-up	A method of communicating with a remote device over the Public Switched Telephone Network (PSTN). Such connections are therefore considered transitory rather than dedicated.

Dijkstra's Algorithm	An algorithm used to determine the best cost path between any two networks. Dijkstra's algorithm is used in OSPF.
Disk Operating System	An operating system employed on many Internet hosts. The most commonly implemented Disk Operating System is Microsoft's MSDOS that was used on Personal Computers (PCs) before the advent of the Windows operating environment. Arguably, DOS is a generic term applied to *any* Disk Operating System, and it is only since the advent of the PC that it has become synonymous with Microsoft.
Distance Vector Algorithm	Otherwise known as the Bellman-Ford routing algorithm, this is a widely used method of gauging route quality. With this method, the quality of the route is based on the number of networks that the packet must traverse. Protocols such as the Routing Information Protocol (RIP) use this method.
Distance Vector Multicast Routing Protocol	Although not widely implemented, this protocol allows host group information derived from the Internet Group Message Protocol (IGMP) to be propagated throughout an internet.
DIX Ethernet	*See Ethernet.*
DNS	*See Domain Name System.*
Domain	There are many types of *Domain* such as a routing domain, named domain, and mail domain. In general, a domain can be considered as a group of entities sharing a common purpose.
Domain Name System	A host naming convention and protocol allowing the mapping of host names to IP Addresses. The Domain Name System also allows other information to be stored about hosts and networks such as the location of Mail Servers, etc.
DOS	*See Disk Operating System.*
Dotted Decimal Notation	A method of representing a binary number in decimal. The most common implementation is the representation of IP Addresses where each octet of the 32 bit (4 octet) address is represented as its decimal equivalent separated from its neighbor by a dot.

Dual Attached Station	An FDDI station attached to both primary and secondary rings.
Dual Homing	A mechanism on an FDDI network to allow Dual Attached devices to be connected to a single ring to provide resilience.
DVMRP	*See Distance Vector Multicast Routing Protocol.*
E1	Used to describe a digital line within a PTO environment in Europe operating at 2.048Mbps.
E3	A multiplexed circuit that combines 16 E1 circuits, and has an aggregate bandwidth of 34.368Mbps.
Early Token Release	An extension to the standard token ring token passing protocol that improves bandwidth utilization by appending the token to the end of the data frame.
EBCDIC	*See Extended Binary Coded Decimal Interchange Code.*
EGP	A generic name given to a group of routing protocols used between Autonomous Systems. In addition, it is also the name given to one such protocol - the *Exterior Gateway Protocol.*
EIA	*See Electrical Industries Association.*
Electrical Industries Association	A standards making body in the USA responsible for the introduction of many data communications standards. The most common EIA standard is possibly EIA RS-232.
Electronic Mail	The colloquial name for a system that allows network users to exchange messages. email is one of the most common network applications.
email	*See Electronic Mail.*
email Address	The address of an electronic mail user. Normally specified as a fully qualified Domain Name, this uniquely identifies a user anywhere within an internet.
Encapsulation	A method by which data from one logical layer (or protocol) can be carried within another. For example, TCP uses the services of IP and is therefore transported as IP data. As such, a TCP segment is said to be encapsulated within an IP datagram and the IP datagram is encapsulated within the physical frame, e.g., Ethernet.

Encryption	This is a technique that allows the octets within a packet to be modified in such a way as to ensure that any device eavesdropping will not be able to read the information. Data is encrypted by the transmitter and then decrypted by the receiver.
Ethernet	The original medium access system (developed by Digital, Intel, and Xerox) employing the CSMA/CD system. Ethernet defines a 10Mbps Baseband signaling system, originally developed for use with coaxial cable. This has since been enhanced by the IEEE and now uses multiple media types including Twisted Pair and Fiber Optic cables. *See also 10Base5, 10Base2, 10BaseT, and 10BaseF, etc.*
Extended Binary Coded Decimal Interchange Code	Standard method of encoding characters to codes, using 8 bit encoding. This scheme was developed, and is primarily used, by IBM.
Exterior Gateway Protocol	This term has dual meanings. Firstly it describes a suite of routing protocols used to link Autonomous Systems together. Two such protocols exist namely EGP and BGP. Secondly it is the name given to the original protocol for this purpose called the Exterior Gateway Protocol.
External Data Representation	A standard protocol developed by Sun Microsystems for representation of data in a machine independent format.
FCS	*See Frame Check Sequence.*
FDDI	*See Fiber Distributed Data Interface.*
Fiber Distributed Data Interface	Developed by the American National Standards Institute (ANSI) as standard X3T9.5. This defines a 100Mbps ring topology that was originally developed for use over Fiber Optic cabling only. Today several variants exist that define other media namely SMF-PMD (Single Mode fiber), MMF-PMD (Multi-Mode fiber), and TP-PMD (Twisted Pair).
File Transfer Protocol	A protocol that allows users on one machine to transfer files to/from another.
FINGER	A management protocol that allows one host machine to interrogate another network device to obtain information about valid or current users.

Fragment	A part of an IP datagram. When a router forwards a packet, it must know the maximum payload (data) allowed on the network over which the packet must pass - also known as the Maximum Transmission Unit (MTU) of the network. When the maximum amount of data allowed is less than the packet size, it must be broken into smaller pieces in an orderly fashion so that it may be re-built by the receiving host. Each smaller part is then called a fragment.
Fragmentation	The process by which packets are broken into smaller pieces in order to adhere to the constraints imposed by the network technology over which the data must pass.
Frame	The unit of data transfer at the Data-Link (Network Access) layer. The frame then contains header and addressing information as defined by the data-link layer protocol.
Frame Check Sequence	Used by receiving stations to ensure that a frame has been received intact. Provides basic error checking.
FTP	*See File Transfer Protocol.*
Functional Address	Used by end stations to denote a functional entity such as the active monitor on Token Ring Networks.
Full Duplex	A mode of transmission whereby both ends of the link can simultaneously transmit and receive.
Gateway	Within the context of the Internet Protocol Suite, a gateway is a router. In a more pure sense, a gateway normally translates application or other protocols. For example, TCP/IP to LAT allows a user running a Telnet session to attach to a LAT based host and viceversa.
Gigabit Medium Independent Interface	The Gigabit Medium Independent Interface is the interface between the *Reconciliation*, and *Physical Coding* sublayers. This is found only in Gigabit (IEEE 802.3z) interfaces.
GMII	*See Gigabit Medium Independent Interface.*
GOPHER	A simple protocol (and application by the same name) that allows a client host to access hierarchical information stored on a server.

Half Duplex	A method of transmission where each end of a link may transmit, but with only one end transmitting at any one time. *See also, Full Duplex,* and *Simplex.*
HDLC	*See High-Level Data Link Control.*
Header	This is the portion of a packet or frame that immediately precedes the data area. Typically, this will contain addressing and/or other control information.
Heterogeneous Network	A network that runs multiple network layer protocols such as IP, IPX, DECnet, etc. This is in direct contrast to a homogenous network where only a single protocol is employed.
Hierarchical Routing	An attempt to simplify the problems associated with routing in large networks by breaking the network into multiple levels. OSPF attempts to achieve this by introducing the concept of Areas.
High-Level Data Link Control	A general purpose Data-Link control protocol that is in wide use over WAN links.
Homogenous Network	A network that runs only a single network layer protocol (such as IP). This is in direct contrast to a Heterogeneous Network where multiple protocols may be employed.
Hop	Within the context of routing, this term describes the quality of a route between a source and destination network (the *metric*). In this case the path between stations is described as a series of hops (either router or network) that the data must traverse.
Host	A device (normally a user device) that resides on a network.
Host Address	The unique address assigned to a device on a network. Several addresses can be applied to a device namely a MAC Address (at layer 2), an IP Address (at layer 3), or a name.
Host Name	A name given to a device that uniquely identifies it. Names within an IP environment are generally referred to as Domain Names.
HTML	*See Hypertext Mark-up Language.*
HTTP	*See Hypertext Transfer Protocol.*

Hub	A device that allows multiple network devices to inter-communicate. This may be a *repeater* (for Ethernet/802.3 devices), a *Multi-station Access Unit* (for Token Ring), or a *Concentrator* (for FDDI). Alternatively, this may be a chassis that can comprise multiple LAN technologies.
Hypertext Mark-up Language	A language used to create pages of information used on the World Wide Web.
Hypertext Transfer Protocol	The protocol used to manipulate (upload and download) World Wide Web pages.
IAB	*See Internet Architecture Board.*
IANA	*See Internet Assigned Numbers Authority.*
ICMP	*See Internet Control Message Protocol.*
IEEE	*See Institute of Electrical and Electronic Engineers.*
IESG	*See Internet Engineering Steering Group.*
IETF	*See Internet Engineering Task Force.*
IGP	*See Interior Gateway Protocol.*
IGMP	*See Internet Group Management Protocol.*
In-Band	The term used to describe the transmission of information (normally management information) along with normal user data. This is in contrast to *out-of-band*, where such control or management data is passed over a different channel.
Institute of Electrical & Electronic Engineers	An American standards body that responsible for the introduction and standardization of many, now commonly used, network access methods.
Integrated Services Digital Network	A Wide Area technology used to transport Voice, Data, Video, and other information over a single cable. This is normally a dialed, circuit-switched service, and with its introduction, ISDN is now emerging as the successor to many traditional leased circuits. That said, some countries (most notably Germany) can provide it as a leased service in preference to traditional *leased lines*.
Interior Gateway Protocol	The collective term given to a suite of protocols that allow routers within an Autonomous System to exchange network reachability information. In addition, it is also the name given to one such protocol, namely the *Interior Gateway Protocol*.

Intermediate System	An OSI term that is used to describe a device responsible for the forwarding of Network Layer data. This is analogous to a router.
Intermediate System to Intermediate System	The standard Interior Gateway protocol used in an OSI environment.
International Standards Organization	An international organization responsible for the introduction of many standards including those that are computer and communications related.
International Telecommunications Union	Formerly the CCITT, this standards making body works mainly in the telecommunications sector developing and introducing new standards. Many new and emerging technologies such as ISDN owe much to the work of this organization.
Intn'l Telegraph & Telephone Consultative Committee	Part of International Telecommunications Union (ITU), the CCITT (as it was referred to) is responsible for making recommendations regarding data communications.
Internet	The world wide network to which many businesses, educational establishments, government departments, and individuals now subscribe. The Internet (denoted by the capital I) is a collection of networks interconnected for the common goal of global communications.
internet	An internet (denoted by a small i), is a collection of networks interconnected with routers and run primarily for private use. Also referred to as an *internetwork*.
Internet Address	*See Host Address.*
Internet Architecture Board	The technical body that oversees the development of the Internet.
Internet Assigned Numbers Authority	A central registry of all numbers associated with Internet protocols (Port Numbers, Protocol IDs etc.). Those numbers assigned are published at regular intervals through RFCs titled Internet Assigned Numbers documents, an example of this document is RFC 1700.
Internet Control Message Protocol	A protocol that is considered as an integral part of IP used to report errors, and other information, and for rudimentary testing.
Internet Engineering Steering Group	A group providing first level technical review of all Internet standards and is responsible for the day-to-day management of the IETF.

Internet Engineering Task Force	A large group of individuals, vendors, and researchers who are responsible for the evolution of the Internet protocols.
Inter Frame Gap	Used in most LAN Technologies to enforce a quiet period between data frames.
Internet Group Management Protocol	An integral extension to the Internet Protocol (IP) that allows host groups to be formed. This protocol then allows routers capable of multicast forwarding to determine where host group members reside and forward relevant multicasts to them.
Internet Protocol	The network layer protocol of the Internet Protocol Suite. The Internet Protocol is a connectionless, best efforts protocol that relies on upper layer protocols to provide reliability where required.
Internet Relay Chat	A protocol that allows Internet users to converse (in *data* terms) in real-time.
Internet Research Steering Group	The body that oversees the operations of the Internet Research Task Force. *See also Internet Research Task Force.*
Internet Research Task Force	The body that considers long term Internet issues from a theoretical standpoint.
Internet Society	A society that provides the forum for discussion of the operation and use of the Internet.
Internetwork Packet Exchange	A protocol loosely based upon Xerox's Internetwork Datagram Protocol (IDP) and developed by Novell. IPX is the Network Layer protocol used within Novell's NetWare architecture.
Inter-operability	The term used to describe the ability of software and/or hardware from multiple vendors to communicate seamlessly.
IP	*See Internet Protocol.*
IP Address	A form of Host Address applicable to the Internet Protocol Suite. In this address form, a 32 bit number (normally expressed in Dotted Decimal Notation) is used to uniquely identify each host within the internet. *See also Dotted Decimal Notation.*
IPX	*See Internetwork Packet Exchange.*

IRC	*See Internet Relay Chat.*
IRSG	*See Internet Research Steering Group.*
IRTF	*See Internet Research Task Force.*
IS	*See Intermediate System.*
ISOC	*See Internet Society.*
IS-IS	*See Intermediate System to Intermediate System.*
ISDN	*See Integrated Services Digital Network.*
ISO	*See International Standards Organization.*
ITU	*See International Telecommunications Union.*
KERBEROS	A security system developed by the Massachusetts Institute of Technology (MIT) used to validate user access and using a system that encrypts data.
Kermit	A File Transfer Protocol (not FTP) that can be used to easily transfer files between hosts.
LAN	*See Local Area Network.*
LAT	*See Local Area Transport.*
Layer	Communications methods are described by functional models (architectures) to break the process into tasks that perform specific functions. These functions are then thought of as layers of the architecture which are, in turn, implemented as protocols.
Leased Line	A dedicated data circuit over which data may be passed. Leased lines are point-to-point Wide Area links (WANs).
Line-Printer Protocol	A general purpose protocol used to share printer resources over an internet. Used mainly in UNIX environments, the Line Printer Protocol allows client hosts to access other hosts known as *Print Servers.*
Link Quality Monitoring	A method of determining Link Quality by passing frames over a link. Mainly used in a WAN environment, one host sends diagnostic packets that contain the number of packets and octets sent. The receiving end then compares these figures with the number of packets and octets received, and from this determines how much data has been lost.

Link State Advertisement	Used in OSPF, this packet type is used to advertise information about reachable networks, the state of router interfaces, and the metrics associated with these interfaces.
Link State Algorithm	The algorithm used by protocols such as OSPF to determine the quality of a received route. This is in contrast to the Distance Vector Algorithm used by protocols such as RIP.
Link State Update	A packet type used by OSPF to advertise routing information. Link State Updates contain Link State Advertisements.
LLC	*See Logical Link Control.*
Local Area Network	A network that is designed to span no more than a few kilometers. Typically these networks would be Ethernet, Token Ring, or FDDI networks and have data transmission speeds of up to 100Mbps (*fast Ethernet*), or 1000Mbps (*Gigabit Ethernet*).
Local Area Transport	Developed by the Digital Equipment Corporation (DEC), this proprietary protocol is designed to allow users to connect to DEC hosts. It is extremely efficient in the way that it operates by allowing data from multiple sessions to be carried in a single packet. However, it operates at the MAC layer and it is therefore not routable.
Logical Link Control	This is the upper sub-layer of the OSI Data-Link layer and is defined by IEEE 802.2. Its purpose is simply to provide a uniform interface to the Network Layer regardless of the underlying network technology.
LP	*See Line-Printer Protocol.*
LQM	*See Link Quality Monitoring.*
LSA	*See Link State Algorithm and/or Link State Advertisement.*
LSU	*See Link State Update.*
MAC	*See Media Access Control.*
MAC Address	The hardware address of a device. Each device connected to a network technology such as Ethernet, Token Ring, or FDDI will have such an address that uniquely identifies it.

MAC Frames	A special type of frame used in technologies such as Token Ring and FDDI to aid in the overall management of the ring.
Mail Exchange Record	A Domain Name System Resource Record that defines which device can handle mail for a particular domain.
Mail Exploder	Part of the mail delivery system that allows a single mail message to be delivered to multiple hosts.
Mail Gateway	A host that connects two or more electronic mail systems. These systems may be either similar or dissimilar.
Mail Server	A host that distributes electronic mail items in response to requests from the electronic mail system.
MII	See Medium Independent Interface.
MAN	See Metropolitan Area Network.
Management Information Base	A set of parameters that can be manipulated to obtain information or configure network devices.
Manchester Encoding	A method of signal encoding that combines data encoding and timing information.
Maximum Receive Unit	The maximum amount of data that can be received by a host. This figure, particularly when applied to protocols such as the Point-to-Point Protocol (PPP), can be negotiated by each host connected to the link.
Maximum Transmission Unit	The maximum amount of data (payload) that can be carried by a particular network type. For example, Ethernet has a Maximum Transmission Unit of 1500 octets.
MDI	See Medium Dependent Interface.
Media Access Control	The lower sub-layer of the Data-Link layer of the OSI Model. The term MAC Address is applied to the address at this layer, for example, the hardware address of the host.
Media Filter	A device used to attenuate a signal on a standard token ring network to minimize the effects of an impedance mismatch. Also provides STP to UTP conversion.

Medium Dependent Interface	The Medium Dependent Interface (MDI) is that part of the network interface that makes the connection to the Physical medium itself. Hence, this interface is naturally dependent upon the media type used and will use connectors such as the BNC, RJ45, SC, etc.
Medium Independent Interface	This is the interface between the *Reconciliation*, sub-layer, and the *PHY* for 802.3 systems. In the case of 10Mbps, this will be between the *Reconciliation* sub-layer and the *Physical Layer Signaling* sub-layer. In the case of 100Mbps systems, this connects the *Reconciliation* sub-layer, to the *Physical Coding Sublayer*.
Metropolitan Area Network	The term applied to networks designed to span campuses or other medium sized areas. Obviously larger that LANs (yet smaller geographically than WANs) this describes an internet that covers a medium sized area.
MIB	*See Management Information Base.*
MIME	*See Multipurpose Internet Mail Extensions.*
MLT-3 Encoding	A mechanism used in FDDI which is based on Tri Polar Encoding to reduce the signaling rate to 31.25 MHZ for transmission over twisted pair cabling.
M Port	A Port on an FDDI concentrator that provides connectivity to slave devices such as other concentrators or N Stations.
MRU	*See Maximum Receive Unit.*
MSAU	*See Multi-Station Access Unit.*
MTU	*See Maximum Transmission Unit.*
Multicast	The term used to describe a packet or frame destined for multiple (but not all) addresses on a network or internet.
Multi-Homed Host	A host that has more than one connection to a network.
Multi-Link Protocol	A protocol used to allow efficient load sharing over multiple Point-to-Point WAN links.
Multipurpose Internet Mail Extensions	An extension to the Internet Mail service allowing non-text items such as graphical, audio, and fax data to be carried.

Multi-Station Access Unit	A device utilized in token ring networks to provide station connectivity to the ring.
MX Record	*See Mail Exchange Record.*
NAK	*See Negative Acknowledgment.*
Namespace	A (typically) hierarchical naming system in which each name, at a given level within the hierarchy is unique. A typical example can be found in the Domain Name System (DNS).
NCP	*See NetWare Core Protocols.*
Negative Acknowledgment	An acknowledgment sent in response to a corrupted packet. Such negative acknowledgements normally require the transmitting station to re-transmit the data.
NetWare Core Protocol	A set of protocols used to support the Novell NetWare operating system. These protocols are at the very heart of NetWare operation and require the implementation of Novell's Internetwork Packet Exchange protocol (IPX). *See Also Internetwork Packet Exchange (IPX).*
Network	A data communications system used to interconnect computer systems either locally or remotely. *See also Local Area Network (LAN), Metropolitan Area Network (MAN), and Wide Area Network (WAN).*
Network Address	*See Host Address and IP Address.*
Network File System	Developed by Sun Microsystems to allow computers to access files over a network as if they were to reside on local disks. The Network File System is therefore independent of machine hardware or architecture.
Network Information Center	A central administration that provides assistance and support to Internet users.
Network Interface Card	A hardware device that is used to provide the physical connection between the host (or other network device) and the actual network medium. Typically, these devices will be installed within the network device itself.
NetWare Link Services Protocol	Developed by Novell, this protocol attempts to provide OSPF style functionality (Link State Algorithm support) to Novell NetWare.

Network Management Station	A station that implements a network management protocol, such as SNMP and through *In-Band* management, manages devices in the network.
Network News Transfer Protocol	A protocol used for the posting and distribution of news articles.
Network Time Protocol	A protocol used to ensure accurate time services are available within an internet.
NFS	*See Network File System.*
NIC	*See Network Information Center, and/or Network Interface Card.*
NLSP	*See NetWare Link Services Protocol.*
NMS	*See Network Management Station.*
NNTP	*See Network News Transfer Protocol.*
Node	Another name for an addressable device connected to a network.
NRZI	The encoding mechanism used in FDDI for transmission over fiber optic cabling.
NTP	*See Network Time Protocol.*
Object Identifier	A means of identifying a particular Management Information Base (MIB) Variable. This is always specified as a variable length string of numbers separated by dots.
Octet	Eight bits of data are used to define an octet which can then be used to represent a single character, or other type of information. The term byte may sometimes be used, however, since some machines define a byte as being longer than 8 bits, the term octet is generally used in networking. *See also Byte.*
OID	*See Object Identifier.*
Open Shortest Path First	One of the family of Interior Gateway Protocols (IGPs) that are designed to allow the exchange of routing information within an Autonomous System (AS). OSPF uses a Link State, rather than Distance Vector, Algorithm.
Open Systems Interconnection	A suite of protocols designed by the International Standards Organization (ISO).

Optical Bypass Relay	A device used on a dual ring FDDI topology to provide resilience and allow N Stations to be removed without wrapping the ring.
Organizationally Unique Identifier	A three octet field at the start of MAC Addresses (802.3/802.5/FDDI) that identifies the vendor of the equipment.
OSI	*See Open Systems Interconnection.*
OSI Reference Model	A seven layer architecture used to describe the way in which computers can communicate. In addition, the model also defines the interfaces required between each layer so that multi-vendor networks can be created.
OSPF	*See Open Shortest Path First.*
OUI	*See Organizationally Unique Identifier.*
Out-of-Band	A management technique where management data is sent outside of the normal data stream.
Packet	The basic unit of data transmitted across a network is a *Frame*. The term packet can be used to describe the data at the *Network* layer of the protocol stack, and the term *Protocol Data Unit* (PDU) can define data at any level. *See also Frame and Protocol Data Unit.*
Packet Internet Groper	A simple application that is used to test the reachability of network devices. Based on the Internet Control Message Protocol (ICMP), this uses Echo Request and Reply codes.
Packet Switching	A communications method that requires packets to be individually routed between hosts.
PDU	*See Protocol Data Unit.*
Phantom Current	A DC current applied by a station on a token ring network to open the relay at the MSAU to allow station insertion to the ring.
Physical Layer Signaling	The Physical Layer Signaling (PLS) sub-layer, together with the *Attachment Unit Interface* (AUI) define the electrical and mechanical characteristics of the interface between the *Data Terminal Equipment* (DTE) and the *Medium Attachment Unit* (MAU) in Ethernet/802.3 environments. In short, the PLS sub-layer provides for the encoding/decoding of data and the interface to the AUI itself.

Physical Medium Attachment	The Physical Medium Attachment (PMA), together with the *Medium Dependent Interface* (MDI) provides the functionality associated with the *Medium Attachment Unit* (MAU) in an Ethernet/802.3 environment. This includes electrical/optical conversion, analogue/digital conversion, and any other conversions required.
Physical Medium Dependent	The Physical Medium Dependent (PMD) sub-layer of the *PHY* within Ethernet/802.3 100Mbps environments provides for the electrical/optical conversion, analogue/digital conversion and any other conversions required.
PING	*See Packet Internet Groper.*
PLS	*See Physical Layer Signaling.*
PMA	*See Physical Medium Attachment.*
PMD	*See Physical Medium Dependent.*
Point of Presence	A site that contains a collection of telecommunications equipment (normally modems) and allows users to gain access to other, larger networks. This term is most commonly used by Internet service providers.
Point-to-Point Protocol	A protocol used over serial Point-to-Point links to allow the transmission of multiple protocols.
POP	*See Post Office Protocol.*
PoP	*See Point of Presence.*
Port	This has two meanings. Firstly, some may refer to the physical connectors of a device as ports. Within a TCP/IP environment however, the term is used to describe a de-multiplexing value so that data destined for a particular application can be uniquely identified. Both TCP and UDP use the concept of ports for this purpose.
Post Office Protocol	A Mail delivery protocol.
Postal Telegraph and Telephone	A telecommunications service provider. This is sometimes referred to as a PTT.
Postmaster	The person responsible for electronic mail at a particular site.
PPP	*See Point-to-Point Protocol.*

Preamble	A constantly alternating signal transmitted prior to a data frame to allow line synchronization between devices on a network.
Protocol	A description of the rules and formats associated with the transfer of data.
Protocol Converter	A program that is used to convert between different protocols that serve the same purpose.
Protocol Data Unit	The more formal name for a packet. Each layer within an architecture will create Protocol Data Units (PDUs) which are passed to the layer below for transmission. Equally, each layer accepts PDUs from the layer below for processing.
Protocol Stack	A layered set of protocols that inter-operate to provide a network function.
Proxy ARP	Sometimes referred to as promiscuous ARP, this is a technique that allows one device (typically a router) to answer Address Resolution Protocol (ARP) requests generated by other devices. Most commonly used where a network has been subnetted, with more modern implementations, the reliance on this is now diminished.
PSTN	*See Public Switched Telephone Network.*
PTO	*See Public Telecommunications Operator.*
PTT	*See Postal Telegraph and Telephone.*
Public Switched Telephone Network	The normal telephone service provided by PTTs. A user accessing a network from a remote location may do so using a dial-up modem using the Public Switched Telephone Network.
Public Telecommunications Operator	The name more commonly applied to PTTs since de-regulation.
Queue	A backup of packets that are awaiting transmission or processing.
RARP	*See Reverse Address Resolution Protocol.*
RCP	*See Remote Copy Protocol.*
RDP	*See Router Discovery Protocol.*
Reassembly	The process by which a previously fragmented packet can be re-assembled. Within TCP/IP, fragmentation takes place at the IP layer. Thus, reassembly also takes place at this layer for received data that was fragmented.

Reconciliation Sub-layer	Used in 100Mbps, and 1000Mbps Ethernet/802.3 environments, the Reconciliation sub-layer provides a standard interface between the *Medium Access Control* (MAC) sub-layer and the *PHY*.
Remote Copy Protocol	A protocol (and normally a program by the same name) that allows a file to be copied from one machine to another.
Remote Procedure Call	A protocol used for implementing a distributed client-server model of computing.
Repeater	A networking device that transparently propagates data from one segment to another. Repeaters are normally used to either increase network length or to increase the number of device connections.
Request for Comments	The vehicle by which Internet protocols are described and general information about proposed standards, experiments, and meeting notes are disseminated to the Internet community.
Reverse Address Resolution Protocol	A protocol, similar to ARP, allowing the resolution of IP Addresses where only the MAC Address is known.
RFC	*See Request for Comments.*
RFC 822 Header	The standard format for electronic mail message headers.
RIF	*See Routing Information Field.*
RIP	*See Routing Information Protocol.*
RIP II	*See Routing Information Protocol.*
Rlogin	A virtual terminal application similar to Telnet except than in this variant we rely on trusted hosts. The user must therefore be known on the host to which access is desired.
Round Trip Delay Time	A measurement of the delays involved in sending data across a network.
Route	The path taken by data as it travels from one network to another.
routed	A program implemented on many UNIX hosts to propagate routing information - short for Router daemon.

Router	A Store-and-Forward device used to forward data from one network to another based on network layer information.
Router Discovery Protocol	An extension to the Internet Control Message Protocol (ICMP) used to allow host systems to discover their local router(s).
Routing	The process of selecting the best path over which to send data destined for a distant network.
Routing Domain	A group of routers that exchange routing information within an Autonomous System.
Routing Information Field	Used by devices in a Source Route bridged network to specify a path to the destination device.
Routing Information Protocol	A Distance Vector based routing protocol. This protocol was the original routing protocol used with TCP/IP and has served the internet community well. Today two versions exist namely RIP and RIP II.
RPC	*See Remote Procedure Call.*
Segment	The TCP unit of data transfer. TCP PDUs are therefore more correctly referred to as being segments.
Sequenced Packet Exchange	A reliable transport layer protocol used by Novell NetWare. This protocol (more commonly referred to as SPX) uses the services of IPX to transport it.
Serial Line IP	A simple protocol used to carry IP datagrams over serial lines.
Server	The name typically given to a machine that is used to provide resources to another host. These services may be File services, Print Services, or Naming services as found in the Domain Name System.
Simple Mail Transfer Protocol	A TCP based protocol used to transmit and receive electronic mail messages.
Simple Network Management Protocol	A protocol for managing network devices that was originally developed for the management of IP hosts. SNMP can now also be used to manage IPX devices.

Simplex	A transmission system where only one end of a link ever transmits. *See also Half Duplex and Full Duplex.*
Single Attached Station	An FDDI station attached to the primary ring only.
SLIP	*See Serial Line IP.*
Small Office/Home Office	A term introduced by Microsoft to describe the emerging market introduced by small businesses and home users.
SMDS	*See Switched Multi-megabit Data Service.*
SMI	*See Structure of Management Information.*
SMTP	*See Simple Mail Transfer Protocol.*
SNA	*See Systems Network Architecture.*
SNMP	*See Simple Network Management Protocol.*
SOHO	*See Small Office/Home Office.*
Source Routing	This term can have two meanings. Firstly it can be used to describe a bridging protocol used primarily in Token Ring environments. Secondly within IP, a host can predetermine the route that a datagram will take by loading a list of routers that it must visit into the options field of the IP Datagram header. Two types of Source Routing exist when applied to an IP environment namely Loose Source Routing and Strict Source Routing.
S Port	The Port on a single attached device used to connect that device to the M Port of a concentrator.
Spanning Tree Protocol	A simple protocol used in bridged networks to ensure a loop free topology.
Spoofing	The term used to fool a device into thinking that a response has been received. This is predominately used in IPX environments.
SPX	*See Sequenced Packet Exchange.*
Std	A group of RFCs that define Internet standards.
Structure of Management Information	Rules governing objects accessible via network management. *See also Management Information Base and Simple Network Management Protocol.*

Stub Network	A Stub Network is one where there is only a single entry/exit point for traffic.
Subnet	A portion of a network that shares the same network address as other portions. These subnets are then distinguished through a Subnet Mask.
Subnet Address	The part of an IP Address that identifies the subnet on which the device resides.
Subnet Mask	A 32 bit mask which, when logically ANDed with an IP Address masks off the Host portion of the Address.
Switched Multi-megabit Data Service	A frame/cell switched, high speed public data network service.
Systems Network Architecture	A proprietary architecture developed by IBM to allow their machines to be networked.
T1	A US standard communications facility used to carry data at 1.544Mbps.
T3	A US standard communications facility used to carry data at 44.746Mbps.
Talk	A simple protocol that allows users at different machines to communicate in real time.
TCP	*See Transmission Control Protocol.*
TCP/IP	The colloquial name given to the Internet Protocol Suite, derived from the two major protocols namely TCP and IP.
Telecommunications Industries Association	A US standards making body, now incorporating the Electrical Industries Association (EIA).
Telnet	The Internet suite Network Virtual Terminal (NVT) Protocol allowing a workstation to access network hosts as if it were connected locally.
Terminal Server	A simple device used to take a raw *serial* bit stream from a dumb terminal or other device, and packetize it for use on a LAN.
TFTP	*See Trivial File Transfer Protocol.*
TIA	*See Telecommunications Industries Association.*
Time-to-Live	A field within the IP datagram header that ensures the timely removal of packets that would otherwise endlessly circulate on networks. Such situations might occur due to router failure and the subsequent creation of routing loops.

TN3270	A variant of the Telnet protocol used to access IBM hosts.
TN5250	A variant of the Telnet protocol used to access IBM hosts.
Token	A special sequence of octets used in Token Passing Technologies such as Token Ring or FDDI which are used by stations to gain access to transmit data.
Token Ring	A Local Area Networking system originally developed by IBM and standardized by the IEEE as IEEE 802.5. Also, and more correctly, referred to as a *Token Passing Ring*.
Topology	This term is used to describe the *geography* of an internet. Through routing protocols, routers and hosts can then learn the topology of the internet.
TOS	*See Type of Service.*
Transceiver	A simple OSI layer one Ethernet (IEEE 802.3) device that allows a device to be connected to a network.
Transit Network	A transit network is one that can pass data between networks. Thus, a transit network is one that has more than one attached router.
Translational Bridging	A bridge type that translates between one network type and another.
Transmission Control Protocol	One of the major protocols within the *Internet Protocol Suite*. TCP, as it is generally known, provides a reliable, connection-oriented environment over which applications such as Telnet and FTP run.
Transport Control Protocol	Used as a generic Layer 4 (OSI Model) protocol providing a reliable, connection oriented, communications environment.
Trap	Within an SNMP environment, a Trap PDU is sent from a managed device to a management station when it wishes to provide unsolicited information.
Trivial File Transfer Protocol	A UDP based protocol used to transfer files between devices. Although this is a general purpose file transfer protocol, it is typically used where simplicity is required such as the loading of operating systems to diskless hosts.

TTL	*See Time to Live.*
Tunneling	The process of encapsulating a foreign protocol within say an IP datagram so that it can be passed over an IP network.
Twisted Pair	A type of media referring to a *balanced* transmission line that comprises Twisted Pair cabling (either shielded or un-shielded). *See also 10BaseT, 100BaseTx, 1000BaseCx, 1000BaseTx,* etc.
Type of Service	A field within the IP datagram header used to define the way in which the datagram should be handled. Once set, this field can then be interrogated by routers and specific routes can be chosen based on its contents.
UDP	*See User Datagram Protocol.*
Unicast	A packet or frame destined for just one device on a network or internet. For example, a Unicast Address is used to address a single host system.
UNIX	A host operating system originally developed by AT&T.
User Datagram Protocol	A connectionless transport protocol used within the Internet Protocol Suite. The protocol adds little to the basic services offered by IP with the exception of a de-multiplexing function.
VINES IP	The Network layer protocol used by the Vines network operating system from Banyan.
Virtual Circuit	A network service that provides a connection oriented service regardless of the underlying network technology.
WAIS	*See Wide Area Information Service.*
WAN	*See Wide Area Network.*
WHOIS	A program that allows a user to query database(s) of information regarding users, domain names, and networks.
Wide Area Information Service	A distributed information service.
Wide Area Network	A network created to span large geographic areas normally over serial lines, and commonly via PTO circuits.

World Wide Web	A hyper-text based distributed information system based on a client-server model. With the explosive growth of the Internet, there are now countless servers offering information on just about any subject imaginable.
WWW	*See World Wide Web.*
X	This is the generic name given to a UNIX windows system.
X.25	Developed by the CCITT, this specification describes how data can be passed over a public switched data network (by *Packet Switching* techniques).
X3T9.5	*See Fiber Distributed Data Interface (FDDI).*
X.400	An ISO standard for Electronic Mail.
X.500	The ISO standard for electronic directory services.
XDR	*See External Data Representation.*
Xerox Network System	A suite of Network protocols developed by the Xerox Corporation, and on which Novell's IPX protocol was based.
XNS	*See Xerox Network System.*
Yellow Pages	Originally this was the name for the Domain Name System implemented by Sun. Today, although many people still refer to this system as Yellow Pages, the more correct name should be the Network Information Service (NIS).
YP	*See Yellow Pages.*
Zone	A logical grouping of devices. This term is of particular importance to protocols such as AppleTalk where Apple machines are grouped into more user-friendly, named, zones.

Bibliography Appendix   D

Most of this book has been prepared directly from the relevant standards. These
have included the ISO standards, IEEE standards, and in the case of IP related
protocols, *Request for Comments* documents. In addition, a great quantity of other
information has been checked and cross-referenced to many worthy authors. These
latter works are then listed at the end of this section. Finally, we must mention the
ever-present *World Wide Web*, the source of so much information.

D.1   ISO/IEC, and ANSI/IEEE Standards

ISO/IEC 10038: 1993(E), ANSI/IEEE Std 802.1D, 1993 Edition. Information
Technology - Telecommunications and information exchange between systems -
Local area networks - Media access control (MAC) bridges.

Draft Standard P802.1Q/D11, 1998. IEEE Standards for Local and Metropolitan
Area Networks: Virtual Bridged Local Area Networks.

ISO/IEC 8802-2: 1994(E), ANSI/IEEE Std 802.2, 1994 Edition. Information
Technology - Telecommunications and information exchange between systems -
Local and metropolitan area networks - Specific requirements Part2: Logical Link
Control.

ISO/IEC 8802-2: 1994/Amd.3:1995(E), IEEE P 802.2c. Information Technology -
Telecommunications and information exchange between systems - Local and
metropolitan area networks - Specific requirements Part2: Logical Link Control.
Amendment 3: Conformance Requirements.

ISO/IEC 8802-3: 1996(E), ANSI/IEEE Std 802.3, 1996 Edition. Information
Technology - Telecommunications and information exchange between systems -
Local and metropolitan area networks - Specific requirements Part3: Carrier sense
multiple access with collision detection (CSMA/CD) access method and physical
layer specifications.

IEEE Std 802.3u - 1995 (Supplement to ISO/IEC 8802-3:1993, ANSI/IEEE Std 802.3,
1993 Edition). Media Access Control (MAC) Parameters, Physical Layer, Medium
Attachment Units, and Repeater for 100Mb/s Operation Type 100Base-T (Clauses
21-30).

IEEE Std 802.3x - 1997, and IEEE Std 802.3y - 1997 (Supplement to ISO/IEC 8802-3: 1996, ANSI/IEEE Std 802.3, 1996 Edition). Specification for 802.3 Full Duplex Operation, and Physical Layer Specification for 100Mb/s Operation on Two Pairs of Category 3 or Better Balanced Twisted Pair Cable (100Base-T2).

IEEE *Draft* P802.3z/D4.2 Supplement to Carrier Sense Multiple Access with Collision Detection (CSMA/CD) Access Method & Physical Layer Specifications: Media Access Control (MAC) Parameters, Physical Layer, Repeater and Management Parameters for 1000Mb/s Operation.

IEEE *Draft* P802.3ac/D2.0 Supplement to Carrier Sense Multiple Access with Collision Detection (CSMA/CD) Access Method & Physical Layer Specifications: Frame Extensions for Virtual Bridged Local Area Networks (VLAN) Tagging on 802.3 Networks.

ISO/IEC 8802-5: 1998, ANSI/IEEE Std 802.5, 1998 Third Edition. Information Technology - Telecommunications and information exchange between systems - Local and metropolitan area networks - Specific requirements Part5: Token Ring Access Method and physical layer specifications.

ISO/IEC 8802-5: 1998, ANSI/IEEE Std 802.5, 1998 Third Edition, Amendment 1. Information Technology - Telecommunications and information exchange between systems - Local and metropolitan area networks - Specific requirements Part5: Token Ring Access Method and physical layer specifications. AMENDMENT 1: Dedicated Token Ring Operation and Fiber Optic Media.

D.2 RFCs

768   J. Postel, "User Datagram Protocol", 08/28/1980.

791   J. Postel, "Internet Protocol", 09/01/1981.

792   J. Postel, "Internet Control Message Protocol", 09/01/1981.

793   J. Postel, "Transmission Control Protocol", 09/01/1981.

826   D. Plummer, "Ethernet Address Resolution Protocol: Or converting network protocol addresses to 48.bit Ethernet address for transmission on Ethernet hardware", 11/01/1982.

903   R. Finlayson, T. Mann, J. Mogul, M. Theimer, "Reverse Address Resolution Protocol", 06/01/1984.

904   International Telegraph and Telephone Co, D. Mills, "Exterior Gateway Protocol formal specification", 04/01/1984.

917   J. Mogul, "Internet subnets", 10/01/1984.

919   J. Mogul, "Broadcasting Internet datagrams", 10/01/1984.

950   J. Mogul, J. Postel, "Internet standard subnetting procedure", 08/01/1985.

1000   J. Postel, J. Reynolds, "Request For Comments reference guide", 08/01/1987.

1058   C. Hedrick, "Routing Information Protocol", 06/01/1988.

1112   S. Deering, "Host extensions for IP multicasting", 08/01/1989.

1122	R. Braden, "Requirements for Internet hosts - communication layers", 10/01/1989.
1160	V. Cerf, "The Internet Activities Board", 05/25/1990.
1256	S. Deering, "ICMP Router Discovery Messages", 09/05/1991.
1358	L. Chapin, "Charter of the Internet Architecture Board (IAB)", 08/07/1992.
1392	G. Malkin, T. Parker, "Internet Users' Glossary", 01/12/1993.
1515	D. McMaster, K. McCloghrie, S. Roberts, "Definitions of Managed Objects for IEEE 802.3 Medium Attachment Units (MAUs)", 09/10/1993.
1516	D. McMaster, K. McCloghrie, "Definitions of Managed Objects for IEEE 802.3 Repeater Devices", 09/10/1993.
1583	J. Moy, "OSPF Version 2", 03/23/1994.
1584	J. Moy, "Multicast Extensions to OSPF", 03/24/1994.
1587	R. Coltun, V. Fuller, "The OSPF NSSA Option", 03/24/1994.
1597	Y. Rekhter, T. J. Watson, B. Moskowitz, D. Karrenberg, G. De Groot, "Address Allocation for Private Internets", 03/1994.
1623	F. Kastenholz, "Definitions of Managed Objects for the Ethernet-like Interface Types", 05/24/1994.
1700	J. Reynolds, J. Postel, "ASSIGNED NUMBERS", 10/20/1994.
1723	G. Malkin, "RIP Version 2 Carrying Additional Information", 11/15/1994.
1771	Y. Rekhter, T. Li, "A Border Gateway Protocol 4 (BGP-4)", 03/21/1995.
1772	Y. Rekhter, P. Gross, "Application of the Border Gateway Protocol in the Internet", 03/21/1995.
1800	J. Postel, "INTERNET OFFICIAL PROTOCOL STANDARDS", 07/11/1995.
1883	S. Deering, R. Hinden, "Internet Protocol Version 6", 12/1995.
1884	S. Deering, R. Hinden, "IP Version 6 Addressing Architecture", 12/1995.
1885	A. Conta, S. Deering, "Internet Control Message Protocol (ICMPv6 for the Internet Protocol Version (IPv6) Specification", 12/1995.

D.3 Other References

Miller P., TCP/IP Explained (Digital Press, 1997).

McNamara J., Local Area Networks; An introduction to the Technology, Second Edition (Digital Press, 1996).

Hancock B., Advanced Ethernet/802.3 Management and Performance, Second Edition (Digital Press, 1995).

Gallo M. A. and Hancock W. M., Networking Explained (Digital Press, 1999).

Naugle M., Network Protocol Handbook (McGraw-Hill, 1994).

Spurgeon C. E., Practical Networking with Ethernet (Thomson Computer Press, 1997).

Saunders S., Gigabit Ethernet Handbook (McGraw-Hill, 1998).

Comer D. E., Internetworking with TCP/IP Volume 1; Principles, Protocols, and Architecture, Second Edition (Prentice-Hall International Editions, 1991).

Comer D. E. and D. L. Stevens, Internetworking with TCP/IP Volume 2; Design, Implementation, and Internals, Second Edition (Prentice Hall International Editions, 1991).

Dickie M., Routing in Today's Internetworks: The Routing Protocols of IP, DECnet, NetWare, and AppleTalk, (Van Nostrand Reinhold, 1994).

Feit S., TCP/IP Architecture, Protocols, and Implementation, (McGraw-Hill, 1993).

Halsall F., Data Communications, Computer Networks and Open Systems, Third Edition, (Addison-Wesley, 1992).

Marsden B. W., Communication Network Protocols: OSI Explained, Third Edition (Chartwell-Bratt, 1991).

Spragins J. D. with J. L. Hammond, and K. Pawlikowski, Telecommunications Protocols and Design (Addison Wesley, 1991).

Tanenbaum A. S., Computer Networks, Second Edition, (Prentice-Hall International Editions, 1989).

Carlo T., Love R., Siegel M., and Wilson T., Understanding Token Ring Protocols and Standards (Artech House, 1998).

Albert B. and Jayasumana A., FDDI and FDDI II Architecture, Protocols and Performance (Artech House, 1994).

Index

1

1000Base-CX..150, 700
1000Base-Lx 37, 80, 150, 700
1000Base-Sx 37, 80, 150, 700
1000Base-T 150, 700
1000Base-X 93
100Base-Fx 37, 80, 93, 125, 699
100Base-T2 ....184, 209, 700
100Base-T4 ....125, 184, 214, 700
100Base-Tx 28, 35, 125, 184, 700
100Base-X 125
100VG-Anylan.............................201, 219, 700
10Base2...79, 82, 633, 699
10Base5............................32, 78, 81, 627, 699
10Base-F 80, 83, 93, 699
10Base-FB 37, 80, 93, 97
10Base-FL 37, 80, 93, 95
10Base-FP 37, 80, 93
10Base-T 28, 35, 79, 82, 699
10Broad36 ....9, 34, 206, 700
1Base5...201, 699

4

4B/5B Encoding..136, 442

5

5B6B Encoding...231

8

802 15
802.1 15
802.10 16
802.11 16
802.12 16
802.14 17
802.1B 15
802.1D 15
802.1E 15
802.1k 15
802.2 15
802.3 15
802.3U 125
802.3z 149
802.4 15
802.5 15
802.6 16
802.7 16
802.9 16
802.X...700

A

822 Header..700

A Port...435, 702
Able Identification 191
Abort Sequence 316
ABR..600, 701
Abstract Syntax Notation One 701
Access Control..314
Access Control (AC) Field............................401
Access List 119
Access Priority..349
ACK..701
Acknowledgment 701
Active Line State 445
Active Monitor 286, 293, 313, 338, 356, 701
Active Retiming MAU.............................300, 305
Adaptive Switch...266
Address...701
Address Family Identifier 592
Address Mask 701
Address Mask Request 575
Address Resolution Protocol....................555, 701
Addressing...46
Adjusted Ring Length.....................306, 310, 701
Advanced Research Projects Agency
    Network 530
Agent...701
Aggregate-Route Based IP Switching...............622
Alignment Errors 54
All Routes Explorer.........................272, 368, 371
All Routes Explorer Frames 516
Alliance For Strategic Token Ring
    Advancement And Leadership (ASTRAL)..380
Aloha...22
American National Standards Institution 701
American Standard Code For Information
    Interchange.......................................701
Anonymous FTP..701
ANSI..11, 702
ANSI X3.263 135
ANSI/EIA/TIA 569 648
ANSI/EIA/TIA 570 648
ANSI/EIA/TIA 606 649
ANSI/EIA/TIA 607 649
Anycast..561
Appletalk 241, 537, 578, 702
Application Layer..14, 702
Application Programming Interface 523

ARCHIE 702
Arcnet 7
ARE .... *See* All Routes Explorer
Area Border Router 702
Area Border Routers 600
Areas 599
ARIS 622
ARL .... *See* Adjusted Ring Length
ARP 555, 702
ARPANET 530
AS 702
AS External Link Advertisement 604
ASBR 600, 702
ASCII 702
ASN.1 702
Asynchronous Service 457
Asynchronous Transfer Mode 6, 31
ATM 6
ATM Adaptation Layer 621
Attachment Unit Interface 42, 65
Attenuation 102, 306, 656, 665, 682
AUI 42, 65
Authentication 602, 702
Automatic Beacon Resolution 363
Auto-Negotiation 131, 702
Autonomous System 534, 703
Autonomous System Border Router 600, 703
Auto-Partitioning 110

B

B Port 436, 703
Backbone Area 600
Backbone Cabling 677
Backup Designated Router 601
Balanced Differential Signaling 82
Balun 646
Bandwidth 703
Bandwidth On Demand 248
Base Page 187
Baseband 284
Baseband Signaling 703
Bayonet Neill Concelman 34, 79
Beacon Process 360, 463
Beaconing 703
Bee-Sting 33
Beesting Connection 78
Bellman-Ford Algorithm 583
BFOC/2.5 80
BGP 534, 589, 703
Binary 703
Blocking 258
BNC Connector 34, 79, 634
Bootp 533, 703
Bootstrap Protocol 533, 703
Border Gateway Protocol 534, 589, 703
Bridge 39, 703

Bridge ID 370
Bridge Priority 261
Bridge Transit Delay 256
Bridges 577
British Standards Institute 704
Broadband 205, 704
Broadband Signaling 9
Broadcast 322, 544, 704
Broadcast Address 49
Broadcast Storms 279
Brouter 704
BSI 704
Burst Errors 295
Burst Limit 153
Bus Topology 7, 40
Bypass State 390
Byte 704

C

Cable Tap 206
Carrier Extension 151
Carrier_Extend 170
CARRIER_STATUS 75
Category 5 UTP 658
CCITT 704
CD0 71
CD1 70
Channel Attenuation 172
Characteristic Impedance 297, 656
Cheapernet 34
Checksum 704
Circuit Switching 704
Claim Token 313, 347, 357, 448, 461, 704
Class I Repeaters 143
Class II Repeaters 143
Classic Token Ring 381
Client 704
Clocked Data One 70
Clocked Data Zero 71
Collision 7, 84
Collision Detection 111
Collision Domain 40
Collision Domains 249
Collision Enforcement 208
Collision Fragments 59
Collision Presence 204
Collision Window 64
Collision-To-Jam 109
Concentrators 421
Configuration BPDU 260
Configuration Control Elements 479
Configuration Element Management 438
Configuration Management 476
Configuration Report Server 364, 406
Congestion 705
Connection Management 476

Connectionless 705
Contention Resolution 46
Control Signal 1.. 71
Control Signal Zero 71
Convergence 593
Count To Infinity.. 595
C-Port... 381
CRC 53, 705
Cross-Connect... 668
CS0... 71
CS1... 71
CSMA/CD 7, 15, 22, 54, 194, 503, 705
Cut Through 242, 266
Cyclic Redundancy Check......................... 53, 705

D

DAC .... *See* Dual Attached Concentrator
DARPA 530
DAS.............................*See* Dual Attached Station
Data Framing.. 46
Data Link Layer 12
Data Link Library 43
Data Scrambling 120
Data Terminal Equipment............................... 65
Data Transfer Unit (DTU)............................... 380
Data_Indication 47
Data_Request 46
Database Description.. 602
Datagram... 705
Decnet... 241, 578, 705
Dedicated Token Ring............. 288, 379, 401, 411
Default Gateway 559, 572
Default Route... 586, 705
Defense Advanced Research Projects Agency 530
Demand Priority 220
Demand Priority Access Method...................... 16
Designated Bridge 262
Designated Router 601
Destination Address..................................... 47, 318
Destination Service Access Point 489
Destination Unreachable.................................. 571
DHCP 533
Dial-Up 705
Differential Manchester Encoding........... 292, 336
Dijkstra's Algorithm 706
Direct Routing 552, 577
Directed Beacon Frames 464
Discard Timer.. 252, 594
Disconnect (DISC) 512
Disconnect Mode (DM) 512
Disk Operating System.................................... 706
Distance Vector Algorithm 583, 706
Distance Vector Multicast Routing Protocol587, 706
Distributed Processing 4
DIX Ethernet 23, 706
DLL 43

DNS...533, 706
Domain...706
Domain Name Service....................................533, 535
Domain Name System 706
DOS...706
Dotted Binary Notation 543
Dotted Decimal Notation............................543, 706
Dotted Hexadecimal Notation............................543
Downstream Neighbor...9
DSAP..505, 580
DTE...65
DTR Concentrator...382
DTR Registration 390
DTR Timers...384
Dual Attached Concentrator...............................433
Dual Attached Station 433, 707
Dual Homing...438, 707
Dual Ring 420
Dual Ring Of Trees 420
Dual-Duplex..210
Duplex Mode 131
Duplicate Address Check (DAC).......................394
Duplicate Address Detection 480
Duplicate Address Test 348
DVMRP 587, 707
Dynamic Host Configuration Protocol.....533, 558

E

E1 707
E3 707
Early Token Release 283, 287, 334, 707
Eavesdrop Protection 120
EBCDIC 707
Echo Protocol...474
Echo Reply..571
Echo Request 571
EGP...534, 589, 707
EIA 707
EIA/TIA-568 647
EIGRP...589
Elasticity Buffer 291, 294, 445
Electrical Industries Association 707
Electrical Installers Association........................11
Electro-Magnetic Compatibility 672
Electromagnetic Interference 82, 296, 627
Electronic Mail 707
Electronics Industry Association 647
Email 707
Email Address 707
Embedded Routing Information Field 271
Empty...275
Encapsulation 707
Encapsulation Bridging....................................484
Encryption 708
End Frame Delimiter 133
End Node 220

End Of Frame Sequence (EFS)..........................334
Ending Delimiter...315
End-Of-Stream Delimiter 211
Enhanced Interior Gateway Routing Protocol.589
Entity Co-Ordination Management 476
Equal Cost Multi-Path 599
Error Counters 355
Error Detection 46
Ethernet 5, 708
Ethernet II..519
Ethertype 51, 564
ETR ....*See* Early Token Release
Exchange Identification (XID) Frames 508
Extend Field 160
Extended Binary Coded Decimal Interchange
    Code 708
Extended Capability..132
Extended Frame Service 475
Extension Bits 152
Exterior Gateway Protocol 534, 589, 708
External BGP 590
External Data Representation 708

F

Fan-Out Unit 89
Far End Crosstalk 685
Fast Link Pulse...186
FCS 53, 708
FCS Errors 54
FDDI........... . *See* Fiber Distributed Data Interface
FDDI Topology 420
Fiber Backbone...97
Fiber Distributed Data Interface 5, 31, 417, 708
Fiber Media Interface Connector (FMIC) 308
Fiber Optic Cable 299
Fiber Optic Inter-Repeater Link........................95
Fiber Optic Station Attachment 308
File Transfer Protocol 532, 708
Filter Table 245, 250
FINGER...708
Fixed Latency Buffer...293
Fixed Shroud Duplex Connector......................429
Floor Distributor...676
Flow Control 183
Foil Screened Twisted Pair 295, 298, 654
FOIRL 36, 80, 93, 95
Forward Delay Time 262
Forwarding 259
Fragment...709
Fragment Extension 110
Fragment Free Switch.......................................266
Fragmentation 568, 709
Fragments 109
Frame...709
Frame Bursting...151
Frame Check Sequence...... 53, 319, 403, 505, 709

Frame Control Field 324, 402
Frame Reject (FRMR) 512
Frame Relay 531
Frame Status Field 320
Frequency Division Multiplexed 10
Frequency Errors 295
FTP...532, 709
Full Duplex........................29, 131, 183, 193, 709
Functional Address 322, 709

G

GARP..274
GARP Multicast Registration Protocol............276
GARP VLAN Registration Protocol....................277
Gateway 709
Gateways..579
Generic Attribute Registration Protocol 274
Get Nearest Server..616
Giant Frames...54
Gigabit Ethernet...149
Gigabit Media Independent Interface 150
Gigabit Medium Independent Interface..........709
GMII 150, 185, 709
GMRP..276
GOPHER...709
Graded Index Fiber..663
Group Attribute 277
GVRP..277

H

Half Duplex.............................184, 195, 200, 710
Halt Line State 444
Hard Errors 354
HDLC...710
Headend...10, 207
Header...710
Header Hub..203
Heartbeat...86
Hello Packet..602
Hello Time 262
Heterogeneous Network 710
Hierarchical Routing 710
High Speed Token Ring 288, 410
High-Level Data Link Control 503, 710
Homogenous Network..710
Hop...710
Horizontal Cabling 651
Host 710
Host Address 710
Host Identifier...542
Host Name 710
HTML...710
HTTP...533, 710
Hub...6, 39, 711
Hypertext Mark-Up Language..........................711

Hypertext Transfer Protocol 711
Hyper-Text Transfer Protocol 533

I

IAB 711
IANA 711
IBM Cabling System 295, 635
ICMP 532, 569, 711
ICMP Redirect 572
IDL 71
Idle 71
Idle Line State 444
IEEE 10, 711
IEEE 802.1D/8802-1D 523
IEEE 802.2 29
IEEE 802.3 5
IEEE 802.4 7
IEEE 802.5 .... 5, 287
IEEE 802.5 AMD 1 379
IESG 711
IETF 711
IFG 57
IGMP 276, 587, 711
IGP 534, 711
IGRP 589
In-Band 711
Indirect Routing 553, 577
Infinity 595
Information 52
Information Transfer Frames 510
Input 73
Input_Idle 73
INPUT_UNIT 75
Institute Of Electrical & Electronic Engineers . 711
Integrated Services Digital Network 711
Inter-Connect 667
Inter-Frame Gap 57, 133, 320
Inter-Frame Gap Shrinkage 111, 115
Interior Gateway Protocol 534, 711
Interior Gateway Protocols 589
Interior Gateway Routing Protocol 589
Intermediate Hub 203
Intermediate System 712
Intermediate System To Intermediate System 712
Internal BGP 590
Internal Clock 291
International Standards Organization 10, 418, 712
International Telecommunications Union 712
Internet 712
Internet Address 712
Internet Architecture Board 536, 712
Internet Assigned Numbers Authority 712
Internet Control Message Protocol .. 532, 569, 712
Internet Engineering Steering Group 712
Internet Engineering Task Force 713
Internet Group Management Protocol 587, 713

Internet Protocol 528, 563, 713
Internet Relay Chat 713
Internet Research Steering Group 713
Internet Research Task Force 713
Internet Society 713
Internetwork Packet Exchange 528, 537, 713
Internetworking 527
Inter-Operability 713
Interoperable LAN/MAN Security 16
Intn'l Telegraph & Telephone Consultative
    Committee 712
Intrusion Protection 119
IP 528, 563, 713
IP Address 713
IP Switch 619
IP Version 6 559
IPOA 621
IPX 241, 528, 581, 713
IRC 714
IRSG 714
IRTF 714
ISDN 714
IS-IS 714
ISO 10, 714
ISO/IEC 11801 .... 299, 643, 649, 666
ISO/IEC 603-7 659
ISOC 714
Isolate 72
ITU 714

J

Jabber 98, 110
Jabber Detect 132
Jabber Protection 85
Jabbering 78
Jitter 102, 289
Joinempty 274
Joinin 275

K

Keepalive 607
KERBEROS 714
Kermit 714

L

Lambda Length 32
LAN 714
LAN Topology 7
LAT 538, 714
Late Count 458
Latency Buffer 291
Layer 714
Layer 3 Switch 619
Learning 258
Leased Line 714

Leaveall 275
Leaveempty 275
Leavein 275
Light Emitting Diode................................. 662
Line Printer Daemon................................. 535
Line States 444
Line-Printer Protocol................................. 714
Link Budget 28
Link Code Word 187
Link Pulse 87, 186
Link Quality Monitoring............................. 714
Link Segment Delay 146
Link Segment Delay Value........................ 179
Link Segments 111
Link State Acknowledgment 602
Link State Advertisement 715
Link State Algorithm.......................... 534, 715
Link State Request 602
Link State Update 602, 715
Link Status 132
Link Training 227
Listening 258
LLC 13, 29, 43, 580, 715
LLC PDU 504
Lobe Media Test (LMT)............................. 393
Lobe Test 346
Local Area Network 3, 715
Local Area Transport 538, 715
Logical Link Control 13, 15, 43, 503, 715
Long Haul Fiber Optics................................. 4
Long Wavelength Fiber 171
Longitudinal To Differential Conversion Loss 673
Loose Source Routing 568
LP 715
LQM 715
LSA 715
LSU 715

M

M Port 436, 717
MAC............................ See Media Access Control
MAC Address 715
MAC Address VLAN................................... 268
MAC Control 197
MAC Frames...................................... 324, 403, 716
MAC Receiver 333, 453
MAC Transmitter 454
Mail Exchange Record 716
Mail Exploder.. 716
Mail Gateway 716
Mail Server 716
MAN 4, 31, 716
Management Information Base.................. 91, 716
Management Routing Interface (MRI) 406
Manchester Encoding........................ 69, 204, 716
Master Line State 444

MAU...................................... 33, 42, 65, 77
Mau_Available... 74
Mau_Not_Available...................................... 74
Mau_Request 73
Maximum Age Time.................................... 262
Maximum Drive Distance 306
Maximum Receive Unit 716
Maximum Transmission Unit 568, 716
MDI 42, 77, 185, 716
MDI-X... 79
Media Access Control 42, 313, 418, 447, 716
Media Dependant Interface........................ 631
Media Filter 299, 716
Media Independent Interface...................... 126
Media Interface Connector.................... 301, 638
Medium Allocation 46
Medium Attachment Unit...................... 42, 65
Medium Dependent Interface 42, 77, 717
Medium Independent Interface 717
Message Code 190
Metric... 583
Metropolitan Area Network 4, 31, 717
MIB... 91, 122, 717
MIC.................. See Media Interface Connector
MII.................................... 126, 185, 716
MIME 717
Mixing Segments 111
MLT3.. 141
MLT-3... 431
MLT-3 Encoding.. 717
Modal Dispersion 663
Monitor Mode....................................... 66, 78
MOSPF.. 276, 587
MPOA 621
MRU 717
MSAU 717
MTU... 568, 717
Multi Level Transmission - 3 Level 141
Multicast 321, 546, 717
Multicast Address 49
Multicast OSPF................................... 276, 587
Multi-Homed 554
Multi-Homed Host 717
Multi-Layer Switch 619
Multi-Link PPP 248
Multi-Link Protocol 717
Multimode Fiber PMD 428
Multi-Port Transceiver 89
Multi-Protocol Label Switching.................. 623
Multipurpose Internet Mail Extensions........... 717
Multi-Station Access Unit.................... 300, 718
Mutual Capacitance................................... 655
MX Record.. 718

N

NAC.................... See Null Attached Concentrator

NAK 718
Namespace 718
Natural Subnet Mask....................................... 549
NCP 610, 617, 718
NDIS 43
Near End Crosstalk.................................. 656, 683
Nearest Active Upstream Neighbor
    Notification 348
Negative Acknowledgment.............................. 718
Neighbor 605
Neighbor Acquisition 606
Neighbor Notification 391
Neighbor Notification Protocol........................ 470
Neighbor Reachability..................................... 605
Netbios... 29, 522
Netware Core Protocol 617, 718
Netware Core Protocols.................................. 610
Netware Link Services Protocol 610, 718
Network 718
Network Address.. 718
Network Diameter 115
Network Driver Interface 43
Network File System.............................. 536, 718
Network Identifier... 542
Network Information Center......................... 718
Network Interface Card...................... 33, 42, 718
Network Layer... 13
Network Links Advertisement......................... 604
Network Management Station 719
Network News Transfer Protocol 719
Network Time Protocol............................ 535, 719
NEXT .... See Near End Crosstalk
Next Hop Resolution Protocol 621
Next Page Function....................................... 187
NFS 536, 719
NHRP 621
NIC... 33, 42, 719
NLSP.. 610, 719
NMS 719
NNTP 719
Node 719
Noise Line State 445
Non-Canonical.. 313
Non-Restricted Token 461
Non-Return To Zero................................. 208, 233
Non-Return To Zero Inverting 139, 442, 719
Non-Source Routed Frames (NSR) 516
Normal 72
Normal Link Pulse 186
Normal Mode.. 66, 78
Not So Stubby Stub Area 601
Novell Netware... 521
NRZI .... See Non Return To Zero Inverting
NSSA 601
NTP 719
Null Attached Concentrator............................. 434

O
Object Identifier..719
OBR............................... See Optical Bypass Relay
Octet..719
ODI...43
OID..719
Open Datalink Interface 43
Open Shortest Path First 532, 534, 589, 719
Open Systems Interconnection........................719
Optical Bypass Relay......................439, 477, 720
Optical Transmit Data......................................96
Organizationally Unique Identifier..132, 519, 720
OSI..720
OSI Model..530
OSI Reference Model...........................10, 11, 720
OSPF 532, 534, 589, 720
OUI...50, 720
Out-Of-Band 720
Out-Of-Window Collision 64
Output_Idle..72
OUTPUT_STATUS...75
OUTPUT_UNIT...74
Overlapping VLAN...268

P
Packet..720
Packet Internet Groper 535, 571, 720
Packet Switching 720
Pad Field..53
Parallel Detection 189
Parameter Management Protocol 473
Parameter Problem 574
Partition...106
Passive MAU 300, 305
Path Cost..261
Path Delay Value 115, 146, 179
Path Variability Value 116
Pause Function 199
PDU 563, 720
PDV 115, 146
Phantom Current 302, 346, 720
Phantom Signal 298
PHY .... See Physical Layer Protocol
PHY Address 161
PHY Identifier..132
PHY Receiver/Transmitter 289
Physical Connection Management....................476
Physical Layer 12
Physical Layer Entities.....................................126
Physical Layer Protocol............126, 185, 418, 441
Physical Layer Signaling................42, 65, 78, 720
Physical Media Components............................289
Physical Medium Attachment 721
Physical Medium Dependent..........418, 427, 721
Physical Signalling Components 289
Ping...117, 535, 571, 721

PLS..................................... 42, 65, 77, 78, 721
PMA..721
PMD................ *See* Physical Medium Dependent
Point Of Presence...721
Point-To-Point Protocol 531, 721
Poison Reverse 596
POP 721
Port 721
Port Mode 381
Port Priority...262
Port Trunking...278
Port-Based VLAN 268
Post Office Protocol......................................721
Postal Telegraph And Telephone...................721
Postmaster 721
Power Down 131
PPP..531, 721
Preamble.. 48, 107, 722
Presentation Layer 13
Prioritization 254
Promiscuous Mode..228
Propagation Delay 685
Propagation Delay Skew 685
Protocol 722
Protocol Based VLAN 268
Protocol Converter 722
Protocol Data Unit........................... 447, 563, 722
Protocol Identifier 504
Protocol Stack 722
Proxy ARP 722
PSTN...722
PTO 722
PTT 722
Public Switched Telephone Network 722
Public Telecommunications Operator 722
PVV 116

Q

Quality Of Service................................... 46, 598
Quartet Channeling.......................................231
Queue 722
Quiet Line State 444

R

RARP 556, 722
RCP 722
RDP 722
Reassembly...722
Receive Not Ready (RNR) 511
Receive Ready (RR) 511
Receive Threshold 102
Reconciliation Sublayer............................126, 723
Redundant Link 117
Refractive Index 662
Reject (REJ)..511

Remote Copy Protocol...................................723
Remote Fault..98, 188
Remote Login 532
Remote Procedure Call 723
Repeater 39, 577, 723
Request For Comments 536, 723
Request Initialization 348
Reserved Addresses......................................252
Resource Allocation Protocol........................474
Restricted Token..460
Return Loss 684
Reverse Address Resolution Protocol......556, 723
RFC...536, 723
RFC 822 Header...723
RG58... 28
RG8..32
RIF 723
Ring Error Monitor 315, 364, 406
Ring In/Out Ports...300
Ring Latency..293
Ring Management...480
Ring Number..370
Ring Parameter Server.............................364, 406
Ring Purge...315, 356
Ring Scheduling Algorithm 422, 458
Ring Topology 8
Ring Wrap..304
RIP.....................................534, 589, 610, 723
RIP II 596, 723
RIP Response 593
RJ45 Connector..79, 432
Rlogin...532, 723
RMT .... *See* Ring Management
Root Bridge 261
Root Hub 225
Root Path Cost 260
Root Port 261
Round Robin Polling 224
Round Trip Collision Delay 114, 144
Round Trip Delay Time 723
Round Trip Propagation................................144
Round-Robin.. 4
Round-Trip Collision Delay...........................179
Routable Protocols..578
Route 723
Route Aggregation 607
Route Designators...367
Route Tag...596
Route_Query_Command 517
Route_Query_Response...................................517
Route_Selected 517
Routed..590, 723
Router..39, 577, 724
Router Advertisement 573
Router Discovery Protocol.......................547, 724
Router ID..602

Router Links Advertisement 604
Router Solicitation 573
Router-Accelerator 621
Routing 724
Routing Control Field 367
Routing Domain 724
Routing Information Field 319, 367, 504, 724
Routing Information Protocol 534, 589, 724
Routing Protocols 578
Routing Switch 619
Routing Table 581
RPC 724
RS 126
RS-232 11
Running Disparity 163
Runt Frames 54

S

S Port 436, 725
SAC .... *See* Single Attached Concentrator
SAP 610, 615
SAS .... *See* Single Attached Station
SC 36, 80
SC Connector 299, 429, 664
Scrub Function 479
SDV 115
Segment 563, 724
Segment Delay Value 115
Segment Variability Value 116
Selector Field 187
Sequenced Packet Exchange 610, 724
Serial Line IP 724
Server 724
Service Access Points 505
Service Advertisement Protocol 610, 615
Service Data Unit 447
Service Requirement 277
Session Layer 13
Set Asynchronous Balanced Mode Extended
    (SABME) 512
Shielded Twisted Pair 637, 654
Shielded Twisted Pair (STP) 295
Short Haul Copper 171
Short Wavelength Fiber 171
Shortest Path Tree 604
SIDL 98
Signal Quality Error 67
Signal_Quality_Error 73
Signal_Quality_Error Message Test 74
SIGNAL_STATUS 75
Signalling Rate 657
Silver Satins 35
Simple Mail Transfer Protocol 533, 535, 724
Simple Network Management Protocol . 121, 724
Simplex 725
Single Attached Concentrator 434

Single Attached Station 433, 725
Singlemode Fiber (SMF) PMD 429
SLIP 725
Slot Time 60
SMA 36, 80
Small Office/Home Office 725
SMDS 725
SMI 725
SMT .... *See* Station Management
SMTP 533, 725
SNA 537, 725
SNAP 63, 241, 581
SNMP 91, 105, 119, 121, 533, 725
Soft Errors 354
SOHO 725
Source Address 50, 318
Source Quench 572
Source Route Bridging 288, 365
Source Route Transparent Bridge 377
Source Routing 241, 725
Source Service Access Point 489
Spanning Tree Algorithm 252, 375
Spanning Tree Explorer 272
Spanning Tree Explorer Frames 516
Spanning Tree Protocol 578, 725
Specifically Routed Frame 273, 373, 516
Speed Selection 131
Split Horizon 595
Spoofing 725
SPX 610, 725
SQE(T) 67, 81, 86
SSAP 505
ST Connector 36, 299, 429, 664
Stacking Station 350
Standby Monitor 286, 358, 363
Star Topology 40
Start Delimiter 401
Start Frame Delimiter 48
Starting Delimiter 314
Start-Of-Stream Delimiter 139, 211
Static Route 586
Station Counters 337
Station Emulation 381
Station Flags 338
Station Management 419, 467
Station Timers 343
Status Information Protocol 472
Status Report Protocol 471
Std 725
Step Index Fiber 662
Store And Forward 242
Store-And-Forward Switch 265
Stored Upstream Address (SUA) 390
Straight Tip Connector 80
Strict Source Routing 567
Structure Of Management Information 725

Structured Cabling 11
Structured Cabling System 642
Stub Network 601, 726
Stuck Beacon Recovery.................................... 480
Sub Miniature Assembly 80
Sub Network Access Protocol.................. 519, 581
Sub-Layer Management 506
Sub-Miniature Assembly 36
Subnet.. 548, 726
Subnet Address 726
Subnet Mask 549, 726
Subnetting 548
Sub-Network Access Protocol 489
Subscriber Connector............................... 36, 80
Summary Links Advertisement....................... 604
Supervisory Frames 510
SVV.. 116
Switch... 39
Switched Multi-Megabit Data Service............ 726
Symbol Decoder/Encoder 290
Symbol Types... 443
Synchronous Idle 98
Synchronous Service 457
Syslog 535
System Load Protocol 15
System Network Architecture 537
Systems Network Architecture....................... 726

T

T1... 726
T3... 726
Tag Information Base 622
Tag Switching 621
Tagged Frames 269
Talk... 726
Tap.. 32, 78
Target Token Rotation Time............................ 458
TCP 726
TCP/IP 29, 241, 726
Technology Ability 187
Telecommunication Outlets 675
Telecommunications Industry Association 647
Telnet.. 105, 119, 532, 726
Terminal Server 726
Test Frames 509
TFTP 533, 726
The Medium Attachment Unit 77
Thick Ethernet.. 28
Thin Ethernet 28, 34
TIA 11, 726
TIA 568A 660
TIA 568B 660
Time Exceeded... 574
Timestamp... 574
Time-To-Live.. 726
TKP Protocol 382

TMS 380... 283
TN3270 727
TN5250 727
Token 8, 313, 727
Token Holding Time 316
Token Holding Timer....................................... 422
Token Passing Bus... 7, 15
Token Passing Protocol 380
Token Passing Ring 15
Token Ring................... 5, 125, 283, 313, 503, 727
Token Rotation Timer 458
Topological Database 599
Topology 643, 727
Topology Change Flag...................................... 260
Topology Change Notification BPDU 260
TOS 727
TP-PMD...........................See Twisted Pair PMD
Trace Function 464
Training Frames 227
Transceiver.. 33, 77, 727
Transit Network.. 727
Transition Point... 652
Translational Bridging 484, 486, 727
Transmission Control Protocol 528, 532, 727
Transmission Path.. 113
Transmit Immediate....................................... 397
Transparent Bridging 365
Transparent Frame 272
Transport Control 612
Transport Control Protocol 727
Transport Layer 13
Trap... 727
Tree Topology... 41
Triggered Updates 595
Trivial File Transfer Protocol.................. 533, 727
Truncated Binary Exponential Back-Off 60
Trunk Coupling Units 300
Trunk Port.. 269
TSB 67... 679
TSB 95... 684
TSB-36 647
TSB-40A... 648
TTL... 728
Tunneling 728
Turn Around 161
Twisted Pair... 728
Twisted Pair (TP) PMD 430
TXI Heart Beat 398
TXI Protocol.. 383, 390
Type 1 296
Type 1 Metric 584
Type 1A 296
Type 2 Metric 584
Type 2A 296
Type 6A 297
Type 9A 297

Type Of Service 565, 728

U

UDP 532, 728
Unicast 728
Unicast Address 48, 321
UNIX 43, 728
Unnumbered Acknowledgement (UA) 512
Unnumbered Frames 511
Unnumbered Information Frames 508
Unshielded Twisted Pair 295, 654
Update Timer 594
User Datagram Protocol 532, 728
UTP .... *See* Unshielded Twisted Pair

V

Vampire Connection 78
Vampire Tap 33
Velocity Of Propagation 629, 681
VINES IP 728
Virtual Circuit 728
Virtual LAN 242, 267
Virtual Links 600
VLAN 242
VLAN Identifier 270

W

WAIS 728
WAN .... 728. *See* Wide Area Network

Wave Division Multiplexing 27
WDM .... *See* Wave Division Multiplexing
WHOIS 728
Wide Area Information Service 728
Wide Area Network 5, 31, 728
Wire Speed 241
Wireless LAN Medium Access Control 16
World Wide Web 729
Wrap Mode 424
WWW 729

X

X 729
X.25 729
X.400 729
X.500 729
X3T9.5 .... 11, 729
XDR 729
Xerox Network System 612, 729
XNS 612, 729

Y

Yellow Pages 729
YP 729

Z

Zone 729